STUDY GUIDE

Richard O. Straub

University of Michigan, Dearborn

to accompany

Kathleen Stassen Berger

The Developing Person Through the Life Span

Sixth Edition

WORTH PUBLISHERS

Study Guide
by Richard O. Straub
to accompany
Berger: **The Developing Person Through the Life Span**, Sixth Edition

ISBN: 0-7167-0315-7 (EAN: 9780716703150)

First Printing 2004

Cover art: *Beachside Generations* by Christian Pierre

Worth Publishers
41 Madison Avenue
New York, New York 10010
www.worthpublishers.com

Contents

Preface   v

How to Manage Your Time Efficiently, Study More Effectively, and Think Critically   vii

CHAPTER 1   Introduction   1

CHAPTER 2   Theories of Development   17

CHAPTER 3   Heredity and Environment   35

CHAPTER 4   Prenatal Development and Birth   53

CHAPTER 5   The First Two Years: Biosocial Development   69

CHAPTER 6   The First Two Years: Cognitive Development   83

CHAPTER 7   The First Two Years: Psychosocial Development   99

CHAPTER 8   The Play Years: Biosocial Development   113

CHAPTER 9   The Play Years: Cognitive Development   127

CHAPTER 10   The Play Years: Psychosocial Development   141

CHAPTER 11   The School Years: Biosocial Development   157

CHAPTER 12   The School Years: Cognitive Development   171

CHAPTER 13   The School Years: Psychosocial Development   187

CHAPTER 14   Adolescence: Biosocial Development   201

CHAPTER 15   Adolescence: Cognitive Development   217

CHAPTER 16   Adolescence: Psychosocial Development   229

CHAPTER 17   Early Adulthood: Biosocial Development   245

CHAPTER 18   Early Adulthood: Cognitive Development   261

CHAPTER 19   Early Adulthood: Psychosocial Development   273

CHAPTER 20   Middle Adulthood: Biosocial Development   289

CHAPTER 21   Middle Adulthood: Cognitive Development   303

CHAPTER 22   Middle Adulthood: Psychosocial Development   317

CHAPTER 23   Late Adulthood: Biosocial Development   333

CHAPTER 24   Late Adulthood: Cognitive Development   349

CHAPTER 25   Late Adulthood: Psychosocial Development   365

EPILOGUE   Death and Dying   381

APPENDIX B   More About Research Methods   391

Preface

This Study Guide is designed for use with *The Developing Person Through the Life Span*, Sixth Edition, by Kathleen Stassen Berger. It is intended to help you to evaluate your understanding of that material, and then to review any problem areas. "How to Manage Your Time Efficiently, Study More Effectively, and Think Critically" provides detailed instructions on how to use the textbook and this Study Guide for maximum benefit. It also offers additional study suggestions based on principles of time management, effective note-taking, evaluation of exam performance, and an effective program for improving your comprehension while studying from textbooks.

Each chapter of the Study Guide includes a Chapter Overview, a set of Guided Study questions to pace your reading of the text chapter, a Chapter Review section to be completed after you have read the text chapter, and three review tests. One chapter in each section of the text includes a crossword puzzle that provides an alternative way of testing your understanding of the terms and concepts. The review tests are of two types: Progress Tests that consist of questions focusing on facts and definitions and a Thinking Critically Test that evaluates your understanding of the text chapter's broader conceptual material and its application to real-world situations. For all three review tests, the correct answers are given, followed by textbook page references (so you can easily go back and reread the material), and complete explanations not only of why the answer is correct but also of why the other choices are incorrect.

I would like to thank Betty and Don Probert of The Special Projects Group for their exceptional work in all phases of this project. My thanks also to Danielle Pucci and Stacey Alexander for their skillful assistance in the preparation of this Study Guide. We hope that our work will help you to achieve your highest level of academic performance in this course and to acquire a keen appreciation of human development.

Richard O. Straub
March 2004

How to Manage Your Time Efficiently, Study More Effectively, and Think Critically

How effectively do you study? Good study habits make the job of being a college student much easier. Many students, who *could* succeed in college, fail or drop out because they have never learned to manage their time efficiently. Even the best students can usually benefit from an in-depth evaluation of their current study habits.

There are many ways to achieve academic success, of course, but your approach may not be the most effective or efficient. Are you sacrificing your social life or your physical or mental health in order to get A's on your exams? Good study habits result in better grades *and* more time for other activities.

Evaluate Your Current Study Habits

To improve your study habits, you must first have an accurate picture of how you currently spend your time. Begin by putting together a profile of your present living and studying habits. Answer the following questions by writing *yes* or *no* on each line.

_____ 1. Do you usually set up a schedule to budget your time for studying, recreation, and other activities?

_____ 2. Do you often put off studying until time pressures force you to cram?

_____ 3. Do other students seem to study less than you do, but get better grades?

_____ 4. Do you usually spend hours at a time studying one subject, rather than dividing that time between several subjects?

_____ 5. Do you often have trouble remembering what you have just read in a textbook?

_____ 6. Before reading a chapter in a textbook, do you skim through it and read the section headings?

_____ 7. Do you try to predict exam questions from your lecture notes and reading?

_____ 8. Do you usually attempt to paraphrase or summarize what you have just finished reading?

_____ 9. Do you find it difficult to concentrate very long when you study?

_____ 10. Do you often feel that you studied the wrong material for an exam?

Thousands of college students have participated in similar surveys. Students who are fully realizing their academic potential usually respond as follows: (1) yes, (2) no, (3) no, (4) no, (5) no, (6) yes, (7) yes, (8) yes, (9) no, (10) no.

Compare your responses to those of successful students. The greater the discrepancy, the more you could benefit from a program to improve your study habits. The questions are designed to identify areas of weakness. Once you have identified your weaknesses, you will be able to set specific goals for improvement and implement a program for reaching them.

Manage Your Time

Do you often feel frustrated because there isn't enough time to do all the things you must and want to do? Take heart. Even the most productive and successful people feel this way at times. But they establish priorities for their activities and they learn to budget time for each of them. There's much in the saying "If you want something done, ask a busy person to do it." A busy person knows how to get things done.

If you don't now have a system for budgeting your time, develop one. Not only will your academic accomplishments increase, but you will actually find more time in your schedule for other activities. And you won't have to feel guilty about "taking time off," because all your obligations will be covered.

Establish a Baseline

As a first step in preparing to budget your time, keep a diary for a few days to establish a summary, or baseline, of the time you spend in studying, socializing, working, and so on. If you are like many students, much of your "study" time is nonproductive; you may sit at your desk and leaf through a book, but the time is actually wasted. Or you may procrastinate. You are always getting ready to study, but you rarely do.

Besides revealing where you waste time, your diary will give you a realistic picture of how much time you need to allot for meals, commuting, and other fixed activities. In addition, careful records should indicate the times of the day when you are consistently most productive. A sample time-management diary is shown in Table 1.

Plan the Term

Having established and evaluated your baseline, you are ready to devise a more efficient schedule. Buy a calendar that covers the entire school term and has ample space for each day. Using the course outlines provided by your instructors, enter the dates of all exams, term paper deadlines, and other important academic obligations. If you have any long-range personal plans (concerts, weekend trips, etc.), enter the dates on the calendar as well. Keep your calendar up to date and refer to it often. I recommend carrying it with you at all times.

Develop a Weekly Calendar

Now that you have a general picture of the school term, develop a weekly schedule that includes all of your activities. Aim for a schedule that you can live with for the entire school term. A sample weekly schedule, incorporating the following guidelines, is shown in Table 2.

1. Enter your class times, work hours, and any other fixed obligations first. *Be thorough.* Using information from your time-management diary, allow plenty of time for such things as commuting, meals, laundry, and the like.

Table 1   Sample Time-Management Diary

Activity	Monday Time Completed	Duration Hours: Minutes
Sleep	7:00	7:30
Dressing	7:25	:25
Breakfast	7:45	:20
Commute	8:20	:35
Coffee	9:00	:40
French	10:00	1:00
Socialize	10:15	:15
Videogame	10:35	:20
Coffee	11:00	:25
Psychology	12:00	1:00
Lunch	12:25	:25
Study Lab	1:00	:35
Psych. Lab	4:00	3:00
Work	5:30	1:30
Commute	6:10	:40
Dinner	6:45	:35
TV	7:30	:45
Study Psych.	10:00	2:30
Socialize	11:30	1:30
Sleep		

Prepare a similar chart for each day of the week. When you finish an activity, note it on the chart and write down the time it was completed. Then determine its duration by subtracting the time the previous activity was finished from the newly entered time.

2. Set up a study schedule for each of your courses. The study habits survey and your time-management diary will direct you. The following guidelines should also be useful.

(a) Establish regular study times for each course. The 4 hours needed to study one subject, for example, are most profitable when divided into shorter periods spaced over several days. If you cram your studying into one 4-hour block, what you attempt to learn in the third or fourth hour will interfere with what you studied in the first 2 hours. Newly acquired knowledge is like wet cement. It needs some time to "harden" to become memory.

(b) Alternate subjects. The type of interference just mentioned is greatest between similar topics. Set up a schedule in which you spend time on several *different* courses during each study session. Besides reducing the potential for interference, alternating subjects will help to prevent mental fatigue with one topic.

(c) Set weekly goals to determine the amount of study time you need to do well in each course. This will

Table 2   Sample Weekly Schedule

Time	Mon.	Tues.	Wed.	Thurs.	Fri.	Sat.
7–8	Dress Eat	Dress Eat	Dress Eat	Dress Eat	Dress Eat	
8–9	Psych.	Study Psych.	Psych.	Study Psych.	Psych.	Dress Eat
9–10	Eng.	Study Eng.	Eng.	Study Eng.	Eng.	Study Eng.
10–11	Study French	Free	Study French	Open Study	Study French	Study Stats.
11–12	French	Study Psych. Lab	French	Open Study	French	Study Stats.
12–1	Lunch	Lunch	Lunch	Lunch	Lunch	Lunch
1–2	Stats.	Psych. Lab	Stats.	Study or Free	Stats.	Free
2–3	Bio.	Psych. Lab	Bio.	Free	Bio.	Free
3–4	Free	Psych.	Free	Free	Free	Free
4–5	Job	Job	Job	Job	Job	Free
5–6	Job	Job	Job	Job	Job	Free
6–7	Dinner	Dinner	Dinner	Dinner	Dinner	Dinner
7–8	Study Bio.	Study Bio.	Study Bio.	Study Bio.	Free	Free
8–9	Study Eng.	Study Stats.	Study Psych.	Open Study	Open Study	Free
9–10	Open Study	Open Study	Open Study	Open Study	Free	Free

This is a sample schedule for a student with a 16-credit load and a 10-hour-per-week part-time job. Using this chart as an illustration, make up a weekly schedule, following the guidelines outlined here.

depend on, among other things, the difficulty of your courses and the effectiveness of your methods. Many professors recommend studying at least 1 to 2 hours for each hour in class. If your time-management diary indicates that you presently study less time than that, do not plan to jump immediately to a much higher level. Increase study time from your baseline by setting weekly goals [see (4)] that will gradually bring you up to the desired level. As an initial schedule, for example, you might set aside an amount of study time for each course that matches class time.

(d) Schedule for maximum effectiveness. Tailor your schedule to meet the demands of each course. For the course that emphasizes lecture notes, schedule time for a daily review soon after the class. This will give you a chance to revise your notes and clean up any hard-to-decipher shorthand while the material is still fresh in your mind. If you are evaluated for class participation (for example, in a language course), allow time for a review just before the class meets. Schedule study time for your most difficult (or least motivat-

ing) courses during hours when you are the most alert and distractions are fewest.

(e) Schedule open study time. Emergencies, additional obligations, and the like could throw off your schedule. And you may simply need some extra time periodically for a project or for review in one of your courses. Schedule several hours each week for such purposes.

3. After you have budgeted time for studying, fill in slots for recreation, hobbies, relaxation, household errands, and the like.

4. Set specific goals. Before each study session, make a list of specific goals. The simple note "7–8 PM: study psychology" is too broad to ensure the most effective use of the time. Formulate your daily goals according to what you know you must accomplish during the term. If you have course outlines with advance assignments, set systematic daily goals that will allow you, for example, to cover fifteen chapters before the exam. And be realistic: Can you actually

expect to cover a 78-page chapter in one session? Divide large tasks into smaller units; stop at the most logical resting points. When you complete a specific goal, take a 5- or 10-minute break before tackling the next goal.

5. Evaluate how successful or unsuccessful your studying has been on a daily or weekly basis. Did you reach most of your goals? If so, reward yourself immediately. You might even make a list of five to ten rewards to choose from. If you have trouble studying regularly, you may be able to motivate yourself by making such rewards contingent on completing specific goals.

6. Finally, until you have lived with your schedule for several weeks, don't hesitate to revise it. You may need to allow more time for chemistry, for example, and less for some other course. If you are trying to study regularly for the first time and are feeling burned out, you probably have set your initial goals too high. Don't let failure cause you to despair and abandon the program. Accept your limitations and revise your schedule so that you are studying only 15 to 20 minutes more each evening than you are used to. The point is to identify a regular schedule with which you can achieve some success. Time management, like any skill, must be practiced to become effective.

Techniques for Effective Study

Knowing how to put study time to best use is, of course, as important as finding a place for it in your schedule. Here are some suggestions that should enable you to increase your reading comprehension and improve your note-taking. A few study tips are included as well.

Using SQ3R to Increase Reading Comprehension

How do you study from a textbook? If you are like many students, you simply read and reread in a *passive* manner. Studies have shown, however, that most students who simply read a textbook cannot remember more than half the material ten minutes after they have finished. Often, what is retained is the unessential material rather than the important points upon which exam questions will be based.

This *Study Guide* employs a program known as SQ3R (*Survey, Question, Read, Recite,* and *Review*) to facilitate, and allow you to assess, your comprehension of the important facts and concepts in *The Developing Person Through the Life Span*, Sixth Edition, by Kathleen Stassen Berger.

Research has shown that students using SQ3R achieve significantly greater comprehension of textbooks than students reading in the more traditional passive manner. Once you have learned this program, you can improve your comprehension of any textbook.

Survey Before reading a chapter, determine whether the text or the study guide has an outline or list of objectives. Read this material and the summary at the end of the chapter. Next, read the textbook chapter fairly quickly, paying special attention to the major headings and subheadings. This survey will give you an idea of the chapter's contents and organization. You will then be able to divide the chapter into logical sections in order to formulate specific goals for a more careful reading of the chapter.

In this Study Guide, the *Chapter Overview* summarizes the major topics of the textbook chapter. This section also provides a few suggestions for approaching topics you may find difficult.

Question You will retain material longer when you have a use for it. If you look up a word's definition in order to solve a crossword puzzle, for example, you will remember it longer than if you merely fill in the letters as a result of putting other words in. Surveying the chapter will allow you to generate important questions that the chapter will proceed to answer. These question correspond to "mental files" into which knowledge will be sorted for easy access.

As you survey, jot down several questions for each chapter section. One simple technique is to generate questions by rephrasing a section heading. For example, the "Preoperational Thought" head could be turned into "What is preoperational thought?" Good questions will allow you to focus on the important points in the text. Examples of good questions are those that begin as follows: "List two examples of . . .." "What is the function of . . .?" "What is the significance of . . .?" Such questions give a purpose to your reading. Similarly, you can formulate questions based on the chapter outline.

The *Guided Study* section of this Study Guide provides the types of questions you might formulate while surveying each chapter. This section is a detailed set of objectives covering the points made in the text.

Read When you have established "files" for each section of the chapter, review your first question, begin reading, and continue until you have discovered its answer. If you come to material that seems to answer an important question you don't have a file for, stop and write down the question.

Using this Study Guide, read the chapter one section at a time. First, preview the section by skimming it, noting headings and boldface items. Next, study the appropriate section objectives in the *Guided Study*. Then, as you read the chapter section, search for the answer to each objective.

Be sure to read everything. Don't skip photo or art captions, graphs, marginal notes. In some cases, what may seem vague in reading will be made clear by a simple graph. Keep in mind that test questions are sometimes drawn from illustrations and charts.

Recite When you have found the answer to a question, close your eyes and mentally recite the question and its answer. Then *write* the answer next to the question. It is important that you recite an answer in your own words rather than the author's. Don't rely on your short-term memory to repeat the author's words verbatim.

In responding to the objectives, pay close attention to what is called for. If you are asked to identify or list, do just that. If asked to compare, contrast, or do both, you should focus on the similarities (compare) and differences (contrast) between the concepts or theories. Answering the objectives carefully will not only help you to focus your attention on the important concepts of the text, but it will also provide excellent practice for essay exams.

Recitation is an extremely effective study technique, recommended by many learning experts. In addition to increasing reading comprehension, it is useful for review. Trying to explain something in your own words clarifies your knowledge, often by revealing aspects of your answer that are vague or incomplete. If you repeatedly rely upon "I know" in recitation, you really may not know.

Recitation has the additional advantage of simulating an exam, especially an essay exam; the same skills are required in both cases. Too often students study without ever putting the book and notes aside, which makes it easy for them to develop false confidence in their knowledge. When the material is in front of you, you may be able to recognize an answer, but will you be able to recall it later, when you take an exam that does not provide these retrieval cues?

After you have recited and written your answer, continue with your next question. Read, recite, and so on.

Review When you have answered the last question on the material you have designated as a study goal, go back and review. Read over each question and your written answer to it. Your review might also include a brief written summary that integrates all of your questions and answers. This review need not

take longer than a few minutes, but it is important. It will help you retain the material longer and will greatly facilitate a final review of each chapter before the exam.

In this Study Guide, the *Chapter Review* section contains fill-in and one- or two-sentence essay questions for you to complete after you have finished reading the text and have written answers to the objectives. The correct answers are given at the end of the chapter. Generally, your answer to a fill-in question should match exactly (as in the case of important terms, theories, or people). In some cases, the answer is not a term or name, so a word close in meaning will suffice. You should go through the Chapter Review several times before taking an exam, so it is a good idea to mentally fill in the answers until you are ready for a final pretest review. Textbook page references are provided with each section title, in case you need to reread any of the material.

Also provided to facilitate your review are two *Progress Tests* that include multiple-choice questions and, where appropriate, matching or true–false questions. These tests are not to be taken until you have read the chapter, written answers to the objectives, and completed the *Chapter Review*. Correct answers, along with explanations of why each alternative is correct or incorrect, are provided at the end of the chapter. The relevant text page numbers for each question are also given. If you miss a question, read these explanations and, if necessary, review the text pages to further understand why. The *Progress Tests* do not test every aspect of a concept, so you should treat an incorrect answer as an indication that you need to review the concept.

Following the two Progress Tests is a *Thinking Critically Test*, which should be taken just prior to an exam. It includes questions that test your ability to analyze, integrate, and apply the concepts in the chapter. As with the *Progress Tests*, answers for the *Thinking Critically Test* are provided at the end of each chapter, along with relevant page numbers.

The chapter concludes with *Key Terms*, either in list form only or also in a crossword puzzle. In either form, as with the *Guided Study* objectives, it is important that the answers be written from memory, and in list form, in your own words. The *Answers* section at the end of the chapter gives a definition of each term, sometimes along with an example of its usage and/or a tip to help you remember its meaning.

One final suggestion: Incorporate SQ3R into your time-management calendar. Set specific goals for completing SQ3R with each assigned chapter. Keep a record of chapters completed, and reward yourself for being conscientious. Initially, it takes more time and effort to "read" using SQ3R, but with practice, the steps will become automatic. More importantly, you will comprehend significantly more material and retain what you have learned longer than passive readers do.

Taking Lecture Notes

Are your class notes as useful as they might be? One way to determine their worth is to compare them with those taken by other good students. Are yours as thorough? Do they provide you with a comprehensible outline of each lecture? If not, then the following suggestions might increase the effectiveness of your note-taking.

1. Keep a separate notebook for each course. Use 8 $1/2$ × 11-inch pages. Consider using a ring binder, which would allow you to revise and insert notes while still preserving lecture order.

2. Take notes in the format of a lecture outline. Use roman numerals for major points, letters for supporting arguments, and so on. Some instructors will make this easy by delivering organized lectures and, in some cases, by outlining their lectures on the board. If a lecture is disorganized, you will probably want to reorganize your notes soon after the class.

3. As you take notes in class, leave a wide margin on one side of each page. After the lecture, expand or clarify any shorthand notes while the material is fresh in your mind. Use this time to write important questions in the margin next to notes that answer them. This will facilitate later review and will allow you to anticipate similar exam questions.

Evaluate Your Exam Performance

How often have you received a grade on an exam that did not do justice to the effort you spent preparing for the exam? This is a common experience that can leave one feeling bewildered and abused. "What do I have to do to get an A?" "The test was unfair!" "I studied the wrong material!"

The chances of this happening are greatly reduced if you have an effective time-management schedule and use the study techniques described here. But it can happen to the best-prepared student and is most likely to occur on your first exam with a new professor.

Remember that there are two main reasons for studying. One is to learn for your own general academic development. Many people believe that such knowledge is all that really matters. Of course, it is possible, though unlikely, to be an expert on a topic without achieving commensurate grades, just as one can, occasionally, earn an excellent grade without truly mastering the course material. During a job interview or in the workplace, however, your A in Cobol won't mean much if you can't actually program a computer.

In order to keep career options open after you graduate, you must know the material and maintain competitive grades. In the short run, this means performing well on exams, which is the second main objective in studying.

Probably the single best piece of advice to keep in mind when studying for exams is to *try to predict exam questions.* This means ignoring the trivia and focusing on the important questions and their answers (with your instructor's emphasis in mind).

A second point is obvious. How well you do on exams is determined by your mastery of both lecture and textbook material. Many students (partly because of poor time management) concentrate too much on one at the expense of the other.

To evaluate how well you are learning lecture and textbook material, analyze the questions you missed on the first exam. If your instructor does not review exams during class, you can easily do it yourself. Divide the questions into two categories: those drawn primarily from lectures and those drawn primarily from the textbook. Determine the percentage of questions you missed in each category. If your errors are evenly distributed and you are satisfied with your grade, you have no problem. If you are weaker in one area, you will need to set future goals for increasing and/or improving your study of that area.

Similarly, note the percentage of test questions drawn from each category. Although exams in most courses cover both lecture notes and the textbook, the relative emphasis of each may vary from instructor to instructor. While your instructors may not be entirely consistent in making up future exams, you may be able to tailor your studying for each course by placing additional emphasis on the appropriate area.

Exam evaluation will also point out the types of questions your instructor prefers. Does the exam consist primarily of multiple-choice, true–false, or essay questions? You may also discover that an instructor is fond of wording questions in certain ways. For example, an instructor may rely heavily on questions that require you to draw an analogy between a theory or concept and a real-world example. Evaluate both your instructor's style and how well you do with each format. Use this information to guide your future exam preparation.

Important aids, not only in studying for exams but also in determining how well prepared you are, are the Progress and Thinking Critically Tests provided in this Study Guide. If these tests don't include all of the types of questions your instructor typically writes, make up your own practice exam questions. Spend extra time testing yourself with question formats that are most difficult for you. There is no better way to evaluate your preparation for an upcoming exam than by testing yourself under the conditions most likely to be in effect during the actual test.

A Few Practical Tips

Even the best intentions for studying sometimes fail. Some of these failures occur because students attempt to work under conditions that are simply not conducive to concentrated study. To help ensure the success of your time-management program, here are a few suggestions that should assist you in reducing the possibility of procrastination or distraction.

1. If you have set up a schedule for studying, make your roommate, family, and friends aware of this commitment, and ask them to honor your quiet study time. Close your door and post a "Do Not Disturb" sign.

2. Set up a place to study that minimizes potential distractions. Use a desk or table, not your bed or an extremely comfortable chair. Keep your desk and the walls around it free from clutter. If you need a place other than your room, find one that meets as many of the above requirements as possible—for example, in the library stacks.

3. Do nothing but study in this place. It should become associated with studying so that it "triggers" this activity, just as a mouth-watering aroma elicits an appetite.

4. Never study with the television on or with other distracting noises present. If you must have music in the background in order to mask outside noise, for example, play soft instrumental music. Don't pick vocal selections; your mind will be drawn to the lyrics.

5. Study by yourself. Other students can be distracting or can break the pace at which your learning is most efficient. In addition, there is always the possibility that group studying will become a social gathering. Reserve that for its own place in your schedule.

If you continue to have difficulty concentrating for very long, try the following suggestions.

6. Study your most difficult or most challenging subjects first, when you are most alert.

7. Start with relatively short periods of concentrated study, with breaks in between. If your attention starts to wander, get up immediately and take a break. It is better to study effectively for 15 minutes and then take a break than to fritter away 45 minutes out of an hour. Gradually increase the length of study periods, using your attention span as an indicator of successful pacing.

Critical Thinking

Having discussed a number of specific techniques for managing your time efficiently and studying effectively, let us now turn to a much broader topic: What exactly should you expect to learn as a student of developmental psychology?

Most developmental psychology courses have two major goals: (1) to help you acquire a basic understanding of the discipline's knowledge base, and (2) to help you learn to think like a psychologist. Many students devote all of their efforts to the first of these goals, concentrating on memorizing as much of the course's material as possible.

The second goal—learning to think like a psychologist—has to do with critical thinking. Critical thinking has many meanings. On one level, it refers to an attitude of healthy skepticism that should guide your study of psychology. As a critical thinker, you learn not to accept any explanation or conclusion about behavior as true until you have evaluated the evidence. On another level, critical thinking refers to a systematic process for examining the conclusions and arguments presented by others. In this regard, many of the features of the SQ3R technique for improving reading comprehension can be incorporated into an effective critical thinking system.

To learn to think critically, you must first recognize that psychological information is transmitted through the construction of persuasive arguments. An argument consists of three parts: an assertion, evidence, and an explanation (Mayer and Goodchild, 1990).

An assertion is a statement of relationship between some aspect of behavior, such as intelligence, and another factor, such as age. Learn to identify and evaluate the assertions about behavior and mental processes that you encounter as you read your textbook, listen to lectures, and engage in discussions with classmates. A good test of your understanding of an assertion is to try to restate it in your own words. As you do so, pay close attention to how important terms and concepts are defined. When a researcher asserts that "intelligence declines with age," for example, what does he or she mean by "intelligence"? Assertions such as this one may be true when a critical term ("intelligence") is defined one way (for example, "speed of thinking"), but not when defined in another way (for example, "general knowledge"). One of the strengths of psychology is the use of *operational* definitions that specify how key terms and concepts are measured, thus eliminating any ambiguity about their meaning. "Intelligence," for example, is often operationally defined as performance on a test measuring various cognitive skills. Whenever you encounter an assertion that is ambiguous, be skeptical of its accuracy.

When you have a clear understanding of an argument's assertion, evaluate its supporting evidence, the second component of an argument. Is it *empirical*? Does it, in fact, support the assertion? Psychologists accept only *empirical (observable) evidence* that is based on direct measurement of behavior. Hearsay, intuition, and personal experiences are not acceptable evidence. Chapter 1 discusses the various research methods used by developmental psychologists to gather empirical evidence. Some examples include surveys, observations of behavior in natural settings, and experiments.

As you study developmental psychology, you will become aware of another important issue in evaluating evidence—determining whether or not the research on which it is based is faulty. Research can be faulty for many reasons, including the use of an unrepresentative sample of subjects, experimenter bias, and inadequate control of unanticipated factors that might influence results. Evidence based on faulty research should be discounted.

The third component of an argument is the explanation provided for an assertion, which is based on the evidence that has been presented. While the argument's assertion merely *describes* how two things (such as intelligence and age) are related, the explanation tells *why*, often by proposing some theoretical mechanism that causes the relationship. Empirical evidence that thinking speed slows with age (the assertion), for example, may be explained as being caused by age-related changes in the activity of brain cells (a physiological explanation).

Be cautious in accepting explanations. In order to think critically about an argument's explanation, ask yourself three questions: (1) Can I restate the explanation in my own words?; (2) Does the explanation make sense based on the stated evidence?; and (3) Are there alternative explanations that adequately

explain the assertion? Consider this last point in relation to our sample assertion: It is possible that the slower thinking speed of older adults is due to their having less recent experience than younger people with tasks that require quick thinking (a disuse explanation).

Because psychology is a relatively young science, its theoretical explanations are still emerging, and often change. For this reason, not all psychological arguments will offer explanations. Many arguments will only raise additional questions for further research to address.

Some Suggestions for Becoming a Critical Thinker

1. Adopt an attitude of healthy skepticism in evaluating psychological arguments.

2. Insist on unambiguous operational definitions of an argument's important concepts and terms.

3. Be cautious in accepting supporting evidence for an argument's assertion.

4. Refuse to accept evidence for an argument if it is based on faulty research.

5. Ask yourself if the theoretical explanation provided for an argument "makes sense" based on the empirical evidence.

6. Determine whether there are alternative explanations that adequately explain an assertion.

7. Use critical thinking to construct your own effective arguments when writing term papers, answering essay questions, and speaking.

8. Polish your critical-thinking skills by applying them to each of your college courses, and to other areas of life as well. Learn to think critically about advertising, political speeches, and the material presented in popular periodicals.

Some Closing Thoughts

I hope that these suggestions help make you more successful academically, and that they enhance the quality of your college life in general. Having the necessary skills makes any job a lot easier and more pleasant. Let me repeat my warning not to attempt to make too drastic a change in your life-style immediately. Good habits require time and self-discipline to develop. Once established they can last a lifetime.

Chapter One

Chapter Overview

The first chapter introduces the study of human development. The first section defines development, introduces the life-span perspective, identifies five characteristics of the scientific study of human development, and explains different aspects of the overlapping contexts in which people develop. The story of David illustrates the effects of these contexts.

The next two sections discuss the strategies developmentalists use in their research, beginning with the scientific method and including scientific observation, correlational research, experiments, surveys, and case studies. To study people over time, developmentalists have created several research designs: cross-sectional, longitudinal, and cross-sequential. The ecological-systems approach—Bronfenbrenner's description of how the individual is affected by, and affects, many other individuals, groups of individuals, and larger systems in the environment—can be used with any research strategy.

The final section discusses the ethics of research with humans. In addition to ensuring confidentiality and safety, developmentalists who study children are especially concerned that the benefits of research outweigh the risks.

NOTE: Answer guidelines for all Chapter 1 questions begin on page 10.

Guided Study

The text chapter should be studied one section at a time. Before you read, preview each section by skimming it, noting headings and boldface items. Then read the appropriate section objectives from the following outline. Keep these objectives in mind and, as you read the chapter section, search for the information that will enable you to meet each objective. Once you have finished a section, write out answers for its objectives.

Studying the Life Span: Five Characteristics (pp. 3–18)

1. Identify five characteristics of development identified by the life-span perspective.

2. Discuss the three broad, overlapping contexts that affect development throughout the life span, noting the threee domains into which development is divided.

3. Discuss the relationship between race and ethnicity.

Developmental Study as a Science (pp. 18–23)

4. List and describe the basic steps of the scientific method.

5. Describe scientific observation and correlation as research strategies, noting at least one advantage (or strength) and one disadvantage (or weakness) of each.

6. Describe the components of an experiment, and discuss the main advantage and some of the limitations of this research method.

7. Describe surveys and case studies, noting at least one advantage (or strength) and one disadvantage (or weakness) of each.

Studying Changes Over Time (pp. 23–28)

8. Describe three basic research designs used by developmental psychologists.

9. Describe the ecological systems approach to the study of human development, and explain how this approach leads to an understanding of the overlapping contexts in which people develop.

Ethics and Science (pp. 29–30)

10. Briefly summarize some of the ethical issues involved in conducting research with human subjects.

Chapter Review

When you have finished reading the chapter, work through the material that follows to review it. Complete the sentences and answer the questions. As you proceed, evaluate your performance for each section by consulting the answers beginning on page 10. Do not continue with the next section until you understand each answer. If you need to, review or reread the appropriate section in the textbook before continuing.

Studying the Life Span: Five Characteristics (pp. 3–18)

1. The scientific study of human development can be defined as the science that seeks to understand

   _____

   _____ .

2. Central to the study of development is the

   _____-_____

   _____ , which recognizes the

   sources of continuity and discontinuity from the

   beginning of life to the end.

   The five developmental characteristics embodied within the life-span perspective are that development is

   a. _____

   b. _____

   c. _____

   d. _____

   e. _____

3. Three important insights of this perspective are

   the concepts of _____ _____ ,

which refers to the continual change that occurs within each person and each social group; the _____ _____ , in which even a tiny change in one system can have a profound effect on the other systems of development; and the power of _____ , in which even large changes seemingly have no effect.

4. A group of people born within a few years of each other is called a _____ . These people tend to be affected by history in _____ (the same way/different ways).

5. A widely shared idea that is built more on shared perceptions than on objective reality is a _____ _____ . An important point about such ideas is that they _____ (often change/are very stable) over time.

6. A contextual influence that is determined by a person's income, education, place of residence, and occupation is called _____ _____ , which is often abbreviated _____ . Although poverty is a useful signal for severe problems throughout life, other variables, such as the presence of _____ _____ within a family, play a crucial role in determining individual development. Another variable is _____ _____ , which refers to the degree to which neighbors create a functioning, informal network of people who show concern for each other.

7. The values, assumptions, and customs as well as the physical objects that a group of people have adopted as a design for living constitute a _____ .

8. The impact of cultural variations in _____ _____ can be seen in the fact that children who _____ (sleep alone/sleep with parents) are taught to be independent of their families, while those who _____ (sleep alone/sleep with parents) are taught to depend on them for warmth and protection. A _____ is a kind of farming commune developed in _____ , whose members share _____ .

9. A collection of people who share certain attributes, such as ancestry, national origin, religion, and language and, as a result, tend to have similar beliefs, values, and cultural experiences is called a(n) _____ _____ . Biological traits used to differentiate people whose ancestors come from different regions is the definition of _____ .

10. The study of human development can be divided into three domains: _____ , _____ , and _____ .

11. One of the most encouraging aspects of the life-span perspective is that development is characterized by _____ , or the capability of change.

12. (In Person) Because his mother contracted the disease _____ during her pregnancy, David was born with a heart defect and cataracts over both eyes. Thus, his immediate problems centered on _____ problems. However, because he was born at a particular time, he was already influenced by the larger _____ context. Particularly in the church community, the _____-_____ context benefitted him. David's continuing development of his skills is a testimony for _____ .

Developmental Study as a Science (pp. 18–23)

13. In order, the basic steps of the scientific method are

   a. _____

   b. _____

   c. _____

   d. _____

   e. _____

14. A specific, testable prediction that forms the basis of a research project is called a _____ .

15. To repeat an experimental test procedure and obtain the same results is to _____ the test of the hypothesis.

16. In designing research studies, scientists are concerned with four issues: _____ , or whether a study measures what it purports to measure; _____ , or whether its measurements are correct; _____ , or whether the study applies to other populations and situations; and _____ , or whether it solves real-life problems.

17. When researchers observe and record, in a systematic and unbiased manner, what research subjects do, they are using _____ _____ .

18. People may be observed in a _____ setting or in a _____ .

19. A chief limitation of observation is that it does not indicate the _____ of the behavior being observed.

20. A number that indicates the degree of relationship between two variables is a _____ . To say that two variables are related in this way _____ (does/ does not) necessarily imply that one caused the other.

21. The method that allows a scientist to determine cause and effect is the _____ . In this method, researchers manipulate a(n) _____ variable to determine its effect on a(n) _____ variable.

22. In an experiment, the subjects who receive a particular treatment constitute the _____ _____ ; the subjects who do not receive the treatment constitute the _____ _____ .

23. To determine whether a difference between two groups occurred purely by coincidence, or chance, researchers apply a mathematical test of statistical _____ .

24. Experiments are sometimes criticized for studying behavior in a situation that is _____ .

25. Another limitation is that participants in this research technique (except very young children) who know they are research subjects may attempt to _____ _____ . The most accurate and ethical way to conduct developmental research on children is the _____ _____ .

26. In a(n) _____ , scientists collect information from a large group of people by personal interview, written questionnaire, or some other means.

27. Potential problems with this research method are that the questions may be _____ and respondents may give answers they think the researcher _____ .

28. An intensive study of one individual is called a(n) _____ _____ . An advantage of this method is that it provides a rich _____ description of development, rather than relying only on _____ data. Another important use is that it provides a good _____ _____ for other research.

Studying Changes Over Time (pp. 23–28)

29. Research that involves the comparison of people of different ages is called a _____ - _____ research design.

30. With cross-sectional research it is very difficult to ensure that the various groups differ only in their _____ . In addition, every cross-sectional study will, to some degree, reflect _____ _____ .

31. Research that follows the same people over a relatively long period of time is called a _____ research design.

State three drawbacks of this type of research design.

32. The research method that combines the longitudinal and cross-sectional methods is the

_____-_____

research method.

33. The approach that emphasizes the influence of the systems that support the developing person is called the _____-_____

approach. This approach was emphasized by

_____ .

34. According to this model, the family, the peer group, and other aspects of the immediate social setting constitute the _____ .

35. Systems that link one microsystem to another constitute the _____ .

36. Community institutions such as school and church make up the _____ .

37. Cultural values, political philosophies, economic patterns, and social systems make up the

_____ .

38. The final system in this model is the

_____ , which emphasizes the

importance of historical time on development.

Ethics and Science (pp. 29–30)

39. Developmental researchers work from a set of moral principles that constitute their

_____ _____

_____ . Researchers who study

humans must obtain _____

_____ , which refers to written permission, ensure that their subjects are not

_____ and that they are allowed to

stop at any time.

40. A research study that is a compilation of data from many other sources is called a

_____-_____ .

Progress Test 1

Multiple-Choice Questions

Circle your answers to the following questions and check them against the answers beginning on page 11. If your answer is incorrect, read the explanation for why it is incorrect and then consult the appropriate pages of the text (in parentheses following the correct answer).

1. The scientific study of human development is defined as the study of:
   a. how and why people change or remain the same over time.
   b. psychosocial influences on aging.
   c. individual differences in learning over the life span.
   d. all of the above.

2. The research method that involves a compilation of data from many other sources is the:
   a. case study.
   b. meta-analysis.
   c. cross-sectional study.
   d. scientific observation.

3. Which of the following is *not* one of the three important aspects of the social context discussed in the text?
   a. historical
   b. socioeconomic
   c. cultural
   d. racial

4. Which of the following describes a neighborhood in which people pitch in to keep children safe, keep trash off the streets, and generally show concern for one another?
   a. cohort effect
   b. collective efficacy
   c. meta-analysis
   d. butterfly effect

5. The ecological-systems approach to developmental psychology focuses on the:
   a. biochemistry of the body systems.
   b. macrosystems only.
   c. internal thinking processes.
   d. overall environment of development.

6. Researchers who take a life-span perspective on development focus on:
   a. the sources of continuity from the beginning of life to the end.
   b. the sources of discontinuity throughout life.
   c. the "nonlinear" character of human development.
   d. all of the above.

7. That fluctuations in body weight are affected by genes, appetite, caregiving, culture, and food supply indicates that body weight:
   a. is characterized by linear change.
   b. is a dynamic system.
   c. often has a butterfly effect.
   d. is characterized by all of the above.

8. A hypothesis is a:
   a. conclusion.
   b. prediction to be tested.
   c. statistical test.
   d. correlation.

9. A developmentalist who is interested in studying the influences of a person's immediate environment on his or her behavior is focusing on which system?
   a. mesosystem   c. microsystem
   b. macrosystem   d. exosystem

10. Socioeconomic status is determined by a combination of variables, including:
    a. age, education, and income.
    b. income, ethnicity, and occupation.
    c. income, education, and occupation.
    d. age, ethnicity, and occupation.

11. A disadvantage of experiments is that:
    a. people may behave differently in the artificial environment of the laboratory.
    b. control groups are too large to be accommodated in most laboratories.
    c. they are the method most vulnerable to bias on the part of the researcher.
    d. proponents of the ecological approach overuse them.

12. In an experiment testing the effects of group size on individual effort in a tug-of-war task, the number of people in each group is the:
    a. hypothesis.
    b. independent variable.
    c. dependent variable.
    d. level of significance.

13. Which research method would be most appropriate for investigating the relationship between parents' religious beliefs and their attitudes toward middle-school sex education?
    a. experimentation
    b. longitudinal research
    c. naturalistic observation
    d. the survey

14. A kibbutz is most accurately described as a(n):
    a. farming commune whose members share work, income, and child care.
    b. group of people born in the same region, social class, and historical era.
    c. research method often used by developmental psychologists.
    d. idea that is built more on shared perceptions than on objective reality

15. Developmentalists who carefully observe the behavior of schoolchildren during recess are using a research method known as:
    a. the case study.
    b. cross-sectional research.
    c. scientific observation.
    d. cross-sequential research.

True or False Items

Write T (*true*) or F (*false*) on the line in front of each statement.

_____ 1. Scientists rarely repeat an experiment.
_____ 2. (In Person) The case study of David clearly demonstrates that for some children only nature (or heredity) is important.
_____ 3. Observation usually indicates a clear relationship between cause and effect.
_____ 4. Each social context influences development independently.
_____ 5. Cohort differences are an example of the impact of the social context on development.
_____ 6. Every trait of an individual can be altered at any point in the life span.
_____ 7. Socioeconomic status is rarely measured solely by family income.
_____ 8. The influences between and within Bronfenbrenner's systems are unidirectional and independent.
_____ 9. People of different ethnic groups can all share one culture.
_____ 10. Longitudinal research is particularly useful in studying development over a long age span.

_____ **11.** Children who sleep with their parents are taught to depend on their parents for protection and typically become bold and independent as adults.

Progress Test 2

Progress Test 2 should be completed during a final chapter review. Answer the following questions after you thoroughly understand the correct answers for the Chapter Review and Progress Test 1.

Multiple-Choice Questions

1. An individual's personal sphere of development refers to his or her:
   a. microsystem and mesosystem.
   b. exosystem.
   c. macrosystem.
   d. microsystem, mesosystem, exosystem, macrosystem, and chronosystem.

2. Developmental psychologists explore three areas of development:
   a. physical, cognitive, psychosocial.
   b. physical, biosocial, cognitive.
   c. biosocial, cognitive, psychosocial.
   d. biosocial, cognitive, emotional.

3. The most important principle of the developmental research code of ethics is:
   a. never physically or psychologically harm those who are involved in research.
   b. maintain confidentiality at all costs.
   c. obtain informed consent from all participants.
   d. ensure that participants do not understand the true purpose of their research study.

4. When developmentalists speak of the "butterfly effect," they are most directly referring to the idea that:
   a. a small event may have a powerful impact on development.
   b. development is fundamentally a nonlinear event.
   c. each context of development is a dynamic system.
   d. each context of development interacts with the others.

5. According to the ecological-systems approach, the macrosystem would include:
   a. the peer group.   c. cultural values.
   b. the community.   d. the family.

6. When developmentalists speak of the "power of continuity," they are referring to the insight that:
   a. a change in one developmental system often affects many other things.
   b. a small change can become huge.
   c. a large change may have no perceptible effect.
   d. all of the above occur.

7. Professor Cohen predicts that because "baby boomers" grew up in an era that promoted independence and assertiveness, people in their 40s and 50s will respond differently to a political survey than will people in their 20s and 30s. The professor's prediction regarding political attitudes is an example of a(n):
   a. meta-analysis.
   b. hypothesis.
   c. independent variable.
   d. dependent variable.

8. A cohort is defined as a group of people:
   a. of similar national origin.
   b. who share a common language.
   c. born within a few years of each other.
   d. who share the same religion.

9. In a test of the effects of noise, groups of students performed a proofreading task in a noisy or a quiet room. To what group were students in the noisy room assigned?
   a. experimental   c. randomly assigned
   b. comparison   d. dependent

10. In differentiating ethnicity and culture, we note that:
   a. ethnicity is an exclusively biological phenomenon.
   b. an ethnic group is a group of people who were born within a few years of each other.
   c. people of many ethnic groups can share one culture, yet maintain their ethnic identities.
   d. racial identity is always an element of culture.

11. If developmentalists discovered that poor people are happier than wealthy people are, this would indicate that wealth and happiness are:
   a. unrelated.
   b. correlated.
   c. examples of nature and nurture, respectively.
   d. causally related.

12. The plasticity of development refers to the fact that:
    a. development is not always linear.
    b. each human life must be understood as imbedded in many contexts.
    c. there are many reciprocal connections between childhood and adulthood.
    d. human characteristics can be molded into different forms and shapes.

13. In an experiment testing the effects of noise level on mood, mood is the:
    a. hypothesis.
    b. independent variable.
    c. dependent variable.
    d. scientific observation.

14. An important factor in the impact of living in poverty on development is:
    a. family size.
    b. the presence of supportive relationships within the family.
    c. the child's gender.
    d. the family's nationality.

15. Which of the following statements concerning ethnicity and culture is not true?
    a. Ethnicity is determined genetically.
    b. Race is a social construction.
    c. Racial identity is an element of ethnicity.
    d. Ethnic identity provides people with shared values and beliefs.

Matching Items

Match each definition or description with its corresponding term.

Terms

_____ 1. independent variable
_____ 2. dependent variable
_____ 3. culture
_____ 4. replicate
_____ 5. chronosystem
_____ 6. exosystem
_____ 7. mesosystem
_____ 8. socioeconomic status
_____ 9. cohort
_____ 10. ethnic group
_____ 11. cross-sectional research
_____ 12. longitudinal research

Definitions or Descriptions

a. group of people born within a few years of each other
b. determined by a person's income, education, and occupation
c. research study comparing people of different ages at the same time
d. the historical conditions that affect development
e. collection of people who share certain attributes, such as national origin
f. shared values, attitudes, and customs maintained by people in a specific setting
g. local institutions such as schools
h. the variable manipulated in an experiment
i. connections between microsystems
j. to repeat a study and obtain the same findings
k. the variable measured in an experiment
l. research study retesting one group of people at several different times

Thinking Critically About Chapter 1

Answer these questions the day before an exam as a final check on your understanding of the chapter's terms and concepts.

1. Dr. Ahmed is conducting research that takes into consideration the relationship between the individual and the environment. Evidently, Dr. Ahmed is using the:
   a. ecological-systems approach.
   b. longitudinal method.
   c. cross-sectional method.
   d. case study method.

2. In order to study the effects of temperature on mood, Dr. Sanchez had students fill out questionnaires in very warm or very cool rooms. In this study, the independent variable consisted of:
   a. the number of students assigned to each group.
   b. the students' responses to the questionnaire.
   c. the room temperature.
   d. the subject matter of the questions.

3. Jahmal is writing a paper on the role of the social context in development. He would do well to consult the writings of:
   a. Piaget.   c. Bronfenbrenner.
   b. Freud.   d. Skinner.

4. Summarizing her presentation on race and biology, Trisha notes that:
   a. a racial group is a collection of people who share ancestral heritage.
   b. race is a biological construction defined by the genetic traits of a group of people.
   c. social scientists recognize that all racial categories are imprecise.
   d. all of the above are true.

5. Esteban believes that high doses of caffeine slow a person's reaction time. In order to test his belief, he has five friends each drink three 8-ounce cups of coffee and then measures their reaction time on a learning task. What is wrong with Esteban's research strategy?
   a. No independent variable is specified.
   b. No dependent variable is specified.
   c. There is no comparison condition.
   d. There is no provision for replication of the findings.

6. When researchers find that the results of a study are statistically significant, this means that:
   a. they may have been caused purely by chance.
   b. it is unlikely they could be replicated.
   c. it is unlikely they could have occurred by chance.
   d. the sample population was representative of the general population.

7. When we say that the idea of old age as we know it is a "social construction," we are saying that:
   a. the idea is built on the shared perceptions of members of society.
   b. old age has only recently been regarded as a distinct period of life.
   c. old age cannot be defined.
   d. the idea is based on a well-tested hypothesis.

8. Professor Jorgenson believes development is plastic. By this she means that:
   a. change in development occurs in every direction, not always in a straight line.
   b. human lives are embedded in many different contexts.
   c. there are many cultures that influence development.
   d. every individual, and every trait within each individual, can be altered at any point in the life span.

9. Karen's mother is puzzled by the numerous discrepancies between the developmental psychology textbook she used in 1976 and her daughter's contemporary text. Karen explains that the differences are the result of:
   a. the lack of regard by earlier researchers for the scientific method.
   b. changing social conditions and cohort effects.
   c. the widespread use of cross-sectional research today.
   d. the widespread use of longitudinal research today.

10. If height and body weight are correlated, which of the following is true?
    a. There is a cause-and-effect relationship between height and weight.
    b. Knowing a person's height, one can predict his or her weight.
    c. Both A and B are true.
    d. Neither is true.

11. An example of longitudinal research would be when an investigator compares the performance of:
    a. several different age groups on a memory test.
    b. the same group of people, at different ages, on a test of memory.
    c. an experimental group and a comparison group on a test of memory.
    d. several different age groups on a test of memory as each group is tested repeatedly over a period of years.

12. For her developmental psychology research project, Lakia decides she wants to focus primarily on qualitative data. You advise her to conduct:
    a. a survey.
    b. an experiment.
    c. a cross-sectional study.
    d. a case study.

13. Professor Johnson warns her students to be skeptical of the results of a controversial study because it has not been replicated. By this she means that:
    a. there was no experimental group.
    b. there was no comparison group.
    c. the study has not yet been repeated by other researchers in order to verify the original findings.
    d. the results are statistically insignificant.

14. Dr. Weston is comparing research findings for a group of 30-year-olds with findings for the same individuals at age 20, as well as with findings for groups who were 30 in 1990. Which research method is she using?
    a. longitudinal research
    b. cross-sectional research
    c. case study
    d. cross-sequential research

15. To find out whether people's attitudes regarding an issue vary with their ages, Karen distributes the same survey to groups of people in their 20s, 30s, 40s, 50s, and 60s. Karen is evidently conducting:
    a. longitudinal research.
    b. cross-sectional research.
    c. cross-sequential research.
    d. a case study.

Key Terms

Using your own words, write a brief definition or explanation of each of the following terms on a separate piece of paper.

1. scientific study of human development
2. life-span perspective
3. multidirectional
4. multicontextual
5. multicultural
6. multidisciplinary
7. plastic
8. dynamic systems
9. butterfly effect
10. cohort
11. social construction
12. socioeconomic status (SES)
13. culture
14. ethnic group
15. race
16. scientific method
17. hypothesis
18. replicate
19. scientific observation
20. correlation
21. experiment
22. independent variable
23. dependent variable
24. experimental group
25. comparison group
26. survey
27. case study
28. cross-sectional research
29. longitudinal research
30. cross-sequential research
31. ecological-systems approach
32. code of ethics

ANSWERS

CHAPTER REVIEW

1. how and why people change, and how they do not change, from conception until death
2. life-span perspective

  a. multidirectional
  b. multicontextual
  c. multicultural
  d. multidisciplinary
  e. plastic

3. dynamic systems; butterfly effect; continuity

4. cohort; the same way

5. social construction; often change

6. socioeconomic status; SES; supportive relationships; collective efficacy

7. culture

8. sleeping places; sleep alone; sleep with parents; kibbutz; Israel; work, meals, income, and child care

9. ethnic group; race

10. biosocial; cognitive; psychosocial

11. plasticity

12. rubella; physical; historical; cultural-ethnic; plasticity

13. **a.** formulate a research question;
    b. develop a hypothesis;
    c. test the hypothesis;
    d. draw conclusions;
    e. make the findings available.

14. hypothesis

15. replicate

16. validity; accuracy; generalizability; usefulness

17. scientific observation

18. naturalistic; laboratory

19. cause

20. correlation; does not

21. experiment; independent; dependent

22. experimental group; comparison group

23. significance

24. artificial

25. produce the results they believe the experimenter is looking for; natural experiment

26. survey

27. biased; expects (wants)

28. case study; qualitative; quantitative; starting point

29. cross-sectional

30. ages; cohort differences

31. longitudinal

Over time, some subjects may leave the study. Some people may change simply because they are part of the study. Longitudinal studies are time-consuming

and expensive.

32. cross-sequential

33. ecological-systems; Urie Bronfenbrenner

34. microsystem

35. mesosystem

36. exosystem

37. macrosystem

38. chronosystem

39. code of ethics; informed consent; harmed

40. meta-analysis

PROGRESS TEST 1

Multiple-Choice Questions

1. **a.** is the answer. (p. 3)

    b. & c. The study of development is concerned with a broader range of phenomena, including physical aspects of development, than these answers specify.

2. **b.** is the answer. (p. 29)

    a. In this research method, one individual is studied intensively.

    c. In this research method, groups of people who differ in age are compared.

    d. In this research method, people are unobtrusively watched and their behavior is recorded.

3. **d.** is the answer. (p. 6)

4. **b.** is the answer. (p. 9)

5. **d.** is the answer. This approach sees development as occurring within five interacting levels, or environments. (p. 27)

6. **d.** is the answer. (p. 4)

7. **b.** is the answer. (p. 5)

    a. Body weight does not always increase in a linear fashion.

    c. Although it is possible that a small change in a person's body weight could set off a series of changes that culminate in a major event, the question is concerned with the interconnectedness of body weight, nutrition, and other dynamic developmental systems.

8. **b.** is the answer. (p. 19)

9. **c.** is the answer. (p. 27)

    a. This refers to systems that link one microsystem to another.

    b. This refers to cultural values, political philosophies, economic patterns, and social conditions.

d. This includes the community structures that affect the functioning of smaller systems.

10. c. is the answer. (p. 9)

11. a. is the answer. (p. 22)

12. b. is the answer. (p. 20)

a. A possible hypothesis for this experiment would be that the larger the group, the less hard a given individual will pull.

c. The dependent variable is the measure of individual effort.

d. Significance level refers to the numerical value specifying the possibility that the results of an experiment could have occurred by chance.

13. d. is the answer. (p. 22)

a. Experimentation is appropriate when one is seeking to uncover cause-and-effect relationships; in this example the researcher is only interested in determining whether the parents' beliefs *predict* their attitudes.

b. Longitudinal research would be appropriate if the researcher sought to examine the development of these attitudes over a long period of time.

c. Mere observation would not allow the researcher to determine the attitudes of the participants.

14. a. is the answer. (p. 12)

b. This describes a cohort.

c. A kibbutz is a group of people, not a research method.

d. This is a social construction.

15. c. is the answer. (p. 19)

a. In this method, *one* subject is studied over a period of time.

b. & d. In these research methods, two or more *groups* of subjects are studied and compared.

True or False Items

1. F   Just the opposite. Scientists always try to replicate their or other people's work. (p. 19)

2. F   The case study of David shows that both nature and nurture are important in affecting outcome. (pp. 16–17)

3. F   A disadvantage of observation is that the variables are numerous and uncontrolled, and therefore cause-and-effect relationships are difficult to pinpoint. (p. 19)

4. F   Each social context affects the way a person develops, and each is affected by the other contexts. (p. 6)

5. T (p. 7)

6. T (p. 15)

7. F   In government statistics it often is. (p. 9)

8. F   Quite the reverse is true. (p. 27)

9. T (p. 13)

10. T (p. 25)

11. F   This is true of children who sleep alone. (p. 11)

PROGRESS TEST 2

Multiple-Choice Questions

1. d. is the answer. (p. 27)

2. c. is the answer. (p. 3)

3. a. is the answer. (p. 29)

b. & c. Although these are important aspects of the code of ethics, protecting participants from harm is the most important.

4. a. is the answer. (p. 6)

b., c., & d. Although these are true, they are not the butterfly effect.

5. c. is the answer. (p. 27)

a. & d. These are part of the microsystem.

b. This is part of the exosystem.

6. c. is the answer. (p. 6)

a. This is the insight of interacting systems.

b. This insight is the butterfly effect.

7. b. is the answer. (p. 19)

a. In a meta-analysis, the results of a number of separate research studies are combined.

c. & d. Variables are treatments (independent) or behaviors (dependent) in *experiments*, which this situation clearly is not.

8. c. is the answer. (p. 7)

a., b., & d. These are attributes of an ethnic group.

9. a. is the answer. The experimental group is the one in which the variable or treatment—in this case, nose—is present. (p. 21)

b. Students in the quiet room would be in the comparison condition.

c. Presumably, all students in both groups were randomly assigned to their groups.

d. The word *dependent* refers to a kind of variable in experiments; groups are either experimental or control.

10. c. is the answer. (p. 13)

a. & d. Ethnicity refers to shared attributes, such as ancestry, national origin, religion, and language.

b. This describes a cohort.

11. **b.** is the answer. (p. 20)

   a. Wealth and happiness clearly *are* related.

   c. For one thing, poverty is clearly an example of nurture, not nature.

   d. Correlation does not imply causation.

12. **d.** is the answer. (p. 4)

13. **c.** is the answer. (p. 20)

   a. Hypotheses make *specific,* testable predictions.

   b. Noise level is the independent variable.

   d. Scientific observation is a research method in which participants are watched, while their behavior is recorded unobtrusively.

14. **b.** is the answer. (p. 10)

   a., c., & d. The text does not suggest that these variables affect poverty's influence on development.

15. **a.** is the answer. Ethnic identity is a product of the social environment and the individual's consciousness. (p. 13)

Matching Items

1. h (p. 20)	5. d (p. 27)	9. a (p. 7)
2. k (p. 20)	6. g (p. 27)	10. e (p. 13)
3. f (p. 10)	7. i (p. 27)	11. c (p. 23)
4. j (p. 19)	8. b (p. 9)	12. l (p. 25)

THINKING CRITICALLY ABOUT CHAPTER 1

1. **a.** is the answer. (p. 27)

2. **c.** is the answer. Room temperature is the variable being manipulated. (p. 20)

   a. & d. These answers are incorrect because they involve aspects of the experiment other than the variables.

   b. This answer is the dependent, not the independent, variable.

3. **c.** is the answer. (p. 27)

   a. Piaget is notable in the area of cognitive development.

   b. Freud was a pioneer of psychoanalysis.

   d. Skinner is notable in the history of learning theory.

4. **c.** is the answer. (p. 14)

   a., c., & d. These are the three domains of development.

5. **c.** is the answer. In order to determine the effects of caffeine on reaction time, Esteban needs to measure reaction time in a comparison group that does not receive caffeine. (p. 21)

   a. Caffeine is the independent variable.

   b. Reaction time is the dependent variable.

   d. Whether or not Esteban's experiment can be replicated is determined by the precision with which he reports his procedures, which is not an aspect of research strategy.

6. **c.** is the answer. (p. 21)

7. **a.** is the answer. (p. 7)

8. **d.** is the answer. (p. 15)

   a. This describes the multidirectional nature of development.

   b. This describes the multicontextual nature of development.

   c. This describes the multicultural nature of development.

9. **b.** is the answer. (pp. 6–7)

   a. Earlier developmentalists had no less regard for the scientific method.

   c. & d. Both cross-sectional and longitudinal research were widely used in the 1970s.

10. **b.** is the answer. (p. 20)

   a. Correlation does not imply causation.

11. **b.** is the answer. (p. 25)

   a. This is an example of cross-sectional research.

   c. This is an example of an experiment.

   d. This type of study is not described in the text.

12. **d.** is the answer. (p. 22)

   a., b., & c. These research methods generally yield *quantitative,* rather than qualitative, data.

13. **c.** is the answer. (p. 19)

   a., b., & c. Although any of these may be true, none has anything to do with replication.

14. **d.** is the answer. (p. 27)

   a. & c. In these research methods, only one group of people is studied.

   b. Dr. Weston's design includes comparison of groups of people of different ages *over time.*

15. **b.** is the answer. (p. 23)

   a. In longitudinal research, the same individuals are studied over a long period of time.

   c. In cross-sequential research, groups of people of different ages are followed over a long period of time.

d. In a case study, one person is studied intensively.

KEY TERMS

1. The **scientific study of human development** is the science that seeks to understand how and why people change, and how and why they remain the same, as they grow older. (p. 3)

2. The **life-span perspective** on human development recognizes that human growth is lifelong and characterized by both continuity (as in temperament) and discontinuity (as in health habits). (p. 4)

3. To say that development is **multidirectional** is to say that it progresses in a nonlinear sequence of predictable and unexpected changes. (p. 4)

4. To say that development is **multicontextual** means that it takes place within multiple contexts—cultural, historical, and socioeconomic. (p. 4)

5. The **multicultural** nature of human development indicates that it takes place within many cultural settings worldwide and reflects a variety of values, traditions, and tools for living. (p. 4)

6. The **multidisciplinary** nature of development means that many different academic fields contribute to our understanding of change. (p. 4)

7. **Plastic** is the capability of any human characteristics to be molded or reshaped by time and circumstances. (p. 4)

8. **Dynamic systems** refer to a process of continual change within a person or group and in which each change is connected systematically to every other development in each individual and every society. (p. 5)

9. The **butterfly effect** is the insight that even small events (such as the breeze created by the flap of a butterfly's wings) may set off a series of changes that culminate in a major event. (p. 6)

10. A **cohort** is a group of people who, because they were born within a few years of each other, experience many of the same historical changes. (p. 7)

11. A **social construction** is an idea that is built more on the shared perceptions of social order than on objective reality. (p. 7)

12. An individual's **socioeconomic status (SES)** is determined by his or her income, education, place of residence, occupation, and other variables. (p. 9)

13. **Culture** refers to the set of shared values, assumptions, customs, and physical objects that a group of people have developed over the years as a design for living to structure their life together. (p. 10)

14. An **ethnic group** is a collection of people who share certain attributes, such as national origin, religion, ancestry, and/or language and who, as a result, tend to identify with each other and have similar daily encounters with the social world. (p. 13)

15. **Race** is a misleading social construction that was originally based on biological differences between people whose ancestors came from different regions of the world. (p. 14)

16. The **scientific method** is a general procedural model that helps researchers remain objective as they study behavior. The five basic steps of the scientific method are (1) formulate a research question; (2) develop a hypothesis; (3) test the hypothesis; (4) draw conclusions; and (5) make the findings available. (p. 18)

17. In the scientific method, a **hypothesis** is a specific, testable prediction. (p. 19)

18. To use **replication** is to repeat a test of a research hypothesis and try to obtain the same results using a different but related group of participants or procedures in order to test its validity. (p. 19)

19. **Scientific observation** is the unobtrusive watching and recording of participants' behavior in a situation that is being studied, either in the laboratory or in a natural setting. (p. 19)

20. **Correlation** is a number that indicates the degree of relationship between two variables such that one is likely (or unlikely) to occur when the other occurs or one is likely to increase (or decrease) when the other increases (or decreases). (p. 20)

21. The **experiment** is the research method designed to untangle cause from effect by manipulating one variable to see the effect on another variable. (p. 20)

22. The **independent variable** is the variable that is manipulated in an experiment. (p. 20)

23. The **dependent variable** is the variable that is being studied in an experiment. (p. 20)

Example: In the study of the effects of a new drug on memory, the participants' memory is the dependent variable.

24. The **experimental group** of an experiment is one in which participants are exposed to the independent variable being studied. (p. 21)

25. The **comparison group** of an experiment is one in which the treatment of interest, or independent variable, is withheld so that comparison to the experimental group can be made. (p. 21)

26. The **survey** is the research method in which information is collected from a large number of people, either through written questionnaires or through interviews. (p. 22)

27. The **case study** is the research method involving the intensive study of one person. (p. 22)

28. In **cross-sectional research,** groups of people who differ in age but share other important characteristics are compared with regard to the variable under investigation. (p. 23)

29. In **longitudinal research,** the same group of individuals is studied over a period of time to measure both change and stability as they age. (p. 25)

30. **Cross-sequential research** follows a group of people of different ages over time, thus combining the strengths of the cross-sectional and longitudinal methods. (p. 27)

31. The **ecological-systems approach** to developmental research takes into consideration the relationship between the individual and the environment. (p. 29)

32. Developmental psychologists and other scientists work from a **code of ethics,** which is a set of moral principles that guide their research. (p. 29)

Chapter Two

Theories of Development

Chapter Overview

Developmental theories are systematic statements of principles and generalizations that provide a coherent framework for studying and explaining development. Many such theories have influenced our understanding of human development. This chapter describes and evaluates five broad theories—psychoanalytic theory, behaviorism, cognitive theory, sociocultural theory, and epigenetic theory—that will be used throughout the book to present information and to provide a framework for interpreting events and issues in human development. Each of the theories has developed a unique vocabulary with which to describe and explain events as well as to organize ideas into a cohesive system of thought.

Three of the theories presented—psychoanalytic theory, behaviorism, and cognitive theory—are "grand theories" that are comprehensive in scope but inadequate in the face of recent research findings. Two of the theories—sociocultural and epigenetic—are considered "emergent theories" because they may become the comprehensive theories of the future. Rather than adopt any one theory exclusively, most developmentalists take an eclectic perspective and use many or all of the theories.

As you study this part of the chapter, consider what each of the theories has to say about your own development, as well as that of friends and relatives in other age groups. It is also a good idea to keep the following questions in mind as you study each theory: Which of the theory's principles are generally accepted by contemporary developmentalists? How has the theory been criticized? In what ways does this theory agree with the other theories? In what ways does it disagree?

NOTE: Answer guidelines for all Chapter 2 questions begin on page 29.

Guided Study

The text chapter should be studied one section at a time. Before you read, preview each section by skimming it, noting headings and boldface items. Then read the appropriate section objectives from the following outline. Keep these objectives in mind and, as you read the chapter section, search for the information that will enable you to meet each objective. Once you have finished a section, write out answers for its objectives.

What Theories Do (pp. 33–34)

1. Define developmental theory, and describe how developmental theories help explain human behavior and development. In your answer, be sure to differentiate grand theories, minitheories, and emergent theories.

Grand Theories (pp. 34–45)

2. Discuss the major focus of psychoanalytic theories, and describe the conflicts that could occur during Freud's stages of psychosexual development.

3. Describe the crises of Erikson's theory of psychosocial development, and contrast them with Freud's stages.

4. Discuss the major focus of behaviorism, and explain the basic principles of classical and operant conditioning.

5. (Thinking Like a Scientist) Discuss Harlow's research with infant monkeys, and explain how it contributed to revisions of psychoanalytic theories and behaviorism.

6. Discuss social learning theory as an application of behaviorism.

7. Identify the primary focus of cognitive theory, and briefly describe Piaget's stages of cognitive development.

8. Discuss the process that, according to Piaget, guides cognitive development.

Emergent Theories (pp. 45–52)

9. Discuss the basic ideas of Vygotsky and the sociocultural theory of development.

10. Discuss the basic ideas of epigenetic theory.

11. (In Person) Discuss the ethology of infant social instincts and adult caregiving impulses.

What Theories Can Contribute (pp. 52–56)

12. Summarize the contributions and criticisms of the major developmental theories, and describe the eclectic perspective of contemporary developmentalists.

13. Explain the nature–nurture controversy as it pertains to hyperactivity and sexual orientation.

Chapter Review

When you have finished reading the chapter, work through the material that follows to review it. Complete the sentences and answer the questions. As you proceed, evaluate your performance for each section by consulting the answers beginning on page 29. Do not continue with the next section until you understand each answer. If you need to, review or reread the appropriate section in the textbook before continuing.

What Theories Do (pp. 33–34)

1. A systematic set of principles and generalizations that provides a coherent framework for studying and explaining development is called a(n)

_____ _____ .

2. Developmental theories form the basis for educated guesses, or _____ , about behavior; they generate _____ , and they offer insight and guidance for everyday concerns by providing a _____ view of human development.

3. Developmental theories fall into three categories: _____ theories, which traditionally offer a comprehensive view of development; _____ theories, which explain a specific area of development; and _____ theories, which may be the comprehensive theories of the future.

Grand Theories (pp. 34–45)

4. Psychoanalytic theories interpret human development in terms of intrinsic _____ and _____ , many of which are _____ (conscious/unconscious) and _____ .

5. According to Freud's _____ theory, children experience sexual pleasures and desires during the first six years as they pass through three _____ _____ . From infancy to early childhood to the preschool years, these stages are the _____ stage, the _____ stage, and the _____ stage. One of Freud's most influential ideas was that each stage includes its own potential _____ between child and parent.

Specify the focus of sexual pleasure and the major developmental need associated with each of Freud's stages.

oral _____

_____

anal _____

_____

phallic _____

_____

genital _____

_____

6. Erik Erikson's theory of development, which focuses on social and cultural influences, is called a(n) _____ theory. In this theory, there are _____ (number) developmental stages, each characterized by a particular developmental _____ related to the person's relationship to the social environment. Unlike Freud, Erikson proposed stages of development that _____ (span/do not span) a person's lifetime.

Complete the following chart regarding Erikson's stages of psychosocial development.

Age Period	Stage
Birth to 1 yr.	trust vs. _____
1–3 yrs.	autonomy vs. _____
3–6 yrs.	initiative vs. _____
7–11 yrs.	_____ vs. inferiority
Adolescence	identity vs. _____
Young adulthood	_____ vs. isolation
Middle adulthood	_____ vs. stagnation
Older adulthood	_____ vs. despair

7. A major theory in American psychology, which directly opposed psychoanalytic theory, was _____ . This theory, which emerged early in the twentieth century under the influence of _____ , is also called _____ theory because of its emphasis on how we learn specific behaviors.

8. Behaviorists have formulated laws of behavior that are believed to apply _____ (only at certain ages/at all ages). The learning process, which is called _____ , takes two forms: _____ _____ and _____ _____ .

9. In classical conditioning, which was discovered by the Russian scientist _____ and is also called _____ conditioning, a person or an animal learns to associate a(n) _____ stimulus with a meaningful one.

10. According to _____ , the learning of more complex responses is the result of _____ conditioning, in which a person learns that a particular behavior produces a particular _____ , such as a reward. This type of learning is also called _____ conditioning.

11. The process of repeating a consequence to make it more likely that the behavior in question will recur is called _____ . The consequence that increases the likelihood that a behavior will be repeated is called the _____ .

12. (Thinking Like a Scientist) The behavior of infant monkeys separated from their mothers led researcher _____ to investigate the origins of _____ in infant monkeys. These studies, which demonstrated that infant monkeys clung more often to "surrogate" mothers that provided _____ (food/contact comfort), disproved _____ theory's idea that infants seek to satisfy oral needs and _____ view that reinforcement directs behavior.

13. The application of behaviorism that emphasizes the ways that people learn new behaviors by observing others is called _____ _____ . The process whereby a child patterns his or her behavior after a parent or teacher, for example, is called _____ .

14. This process is most likely to occur when an observer is _____ or _____ and when the model is _____ . This type of learning is also affected by the individual's _____ . Human social learning is related to _____ , _____ , _____ , and feelings of _____ .

15. The structure and development of the individual's thought processes and the way those thought processes affect the person's understanding of the world are the focus of _____ theory. A major pioneer of this theory is _____ .

16. In Piaget's first stage of development, the _____ stage, children experience the world through their senses and motor abilities. This stage occurs between birth and age _____ .

17. According to Piaget, during the preschool years (up to age _____), children are in the _____ stage. A hallmark of this stage is that children begin to think _____ . Another hallmark is that sometimes the child's thinking is _____ , or focused on seeing the world solely from his or her own perspective.

18. Piaget believed that children begin to think logically in a consistent way at about _____ years of age. At this time, they enter the _____ _____ stage.

19. In Piaget's final stage, the _____ _____ stage, reasoning expands from the purely concrete to encompass _____ thinking. Piaget believed most children enter this stage by age _____ .

20. According to Piaget, cognitive development is guided by the need to maintain a state of mental balance, called _____ _____ .

21. When new experiences challenge existing understanding, creating a kind of imbalance, the individual experiences _____ _____ , which eventually leads to mental growth.

22. According to Piaget, people adapt to new experiences either by reinterpreting them to fit into, or _____ with, old ideas. Some new experiences force people to revamp old ideas so that they can _____ new experiences.

Emergent Theories (pp. 45–52)

23. In contrast to the grand theories, the two emerging theories draw from the findings of _____ (one/many) discipline(s).

24. Sociocultural theory sees human development as the result of _____ _____ between developing persons and their surrounding society and _____ .

25. A major pioneer of this perspective was _____ , who was primarily interested in the development of _____ competencies.

26. Vygotsky believed that these competencies result from the interaction between _____ and more mature members of the society, acting as _____ , in a process that has been called an _____ _____ _____ .

27. In Vygotsky's view, the best way to accomplish the goals of apprenticeship is through _____ _____ , in which the tutor engages the learner in joint activities.

28. According to Vygotsky, a mentor draws a child into the _____ _____ _____ _____ , which is defined as the range of skills that a person can exercise and master with _____ but cannot perform independently.

Cite a contribution and a criticism of sociocultural theory.

29. The newest of the emergent theories,
_____ theory, emphasizes the interaction between
_____ and the _____ .
This idea contrasts sharply with the idea of
_____ , according to which everything is set in advance by genes.

30. In using the word *genetic*, this theory emphasizes
that we have powerful _____
and abilities that arise from our
_____ heritage.

31. The prefix "epi" refers to the various
_____ factors that affect the expression of _____
_____ . These include _____
factors such as injury, temperature, and crowding. Others are _____ factors such
as nourishing food and freedom to play.

32. Some epigenetic factors are the result of the evolutionary process called _____
_____ , in which, over generations,
genes for useful traits that promote survival of
the species become more prevalent.

33. "Everything that seems to be genetic is actually
epigenetic." This statement highlights the fact
that _____ (some/most/all) genetic
instructions are affected by the environment.

34. (In Person) The study of animal behavior as it is
related to the evolution and survival of a species
is called _____ . Newborn animals
and human infants are genetically programmed
for _____ _____ as a
means of survival. Similarly, adult animals and
humans are genetically programmed for
_____ _____ .

What Theories Can Contribute (pp. 52–56)

35. Which major theory of development emphasizes:

   a. the importance of culture in fostering development? _____

   b. the ways in which thought processes affect
   actions? _____

   c. environmental influences? _____

   d. the impact of "hidden dramas" on development? _____
   _____

   e. the interaction of genes and environment? ____
   _____

36. Which major theory of development has been
criticized for:

   a. being too mechanistic?
   _____

   b. undervaluing genetic differences?
   _____

   c. being too subjective?
   _____

   d. neglecting society?
   _____

   e. neglecting individuals?
   _____

37. Because no one theory can encompass all of
human behavior, most developmentalists have
a(n) _____ perspective, which capi-
talizes on the strengths of all the theories.

38. The debate over the relative influence of heredity
and environment in shaping personal traits and
characteristics is called the
_____–_____ contro-
versy. Traits inherited at the moment of conception give evidence of the influence of
_____ ; those that emerge in
response to learning and environmental influences give evidence of the effect of
_____ .

39. Developmentalists agree that, at every point, the
_____ between nature and nurture
is the crucial influence on any particular aspect of
development.

40. Children who are especially impulsive, restless,
and unable to attend to anything for more than a
moment may be suffering from
_____ . This disorder is more common in _____ (girls/boys).

State several pieces of evidence that genetic inheritance is responsible for AD/HD

41. All the grand theories tended to explain homosexuality in terms of _____ (nature/nurture). However, new research suggests that it is at least partly due to _____ (nature/nurture).

Progress Test 1

Multiple-Choice Questions

Circle your answers to the following questions and check them with the answers on page 30. If your answer is incorrect, read the explanation for why it is incorrect and then consult the appropriate pages of the text (in parentheses following the correct answer).

1. The purpose of a developmental theory is to:
   a. provide a broad and coherent view of the complex influences on human development.
   b. offer guidance for practical issues encountered by parents, teachers, and therapists.
   c. generate testable hypotheses about development.
   d. do all of the above.

2. Which developmental theory emphasizes the influence of unconscious drives and motives on behavior?
   a. psychoanalytic   c. cognitive
   b. behaviorism   d. sociocultural

3. Which of the following is the correct order of the psychosexual stages proposed by Freud?
   a. oral stage; anal stage; phallic stage; latency; genital stage
   b. anal stage; oral stage; phallic stage; latency; genital stage
   c. oral stage; anal stage; genital stage; latency; phallic stage
   d. anal stage; oral stage; genital stage; latency; phallic stage

4. Erikson's psychosocial theory of human development describes:
   a. eight crises all people are thought to face.
   b. four psychosocial stages and a latency period.
   c. the same number of stages as Freud's, but with different names.
   d. a stage theory that is not psychoanalytic.

5. Which of the following theories does *not* belong with the others?
   a. psychoanalytic   c. sociocultural
   b. behaviorism   d. cognitive

6. An American psychologist who explained complex human behaviors in terms of operant conditioning was:
   a. Lev Vygotsky.   c. B. F. Skinner.
   b. Ivan Pavlov.   d. Jean Piaget.

7. Pavlov's dogs learned to salivate at the sound of a bell because they associated the bell with food. Pavlov's experiment with dogs was an early demonstration of:
   a. classical conditioning.
   b. operant conditioning.
   c. positive reinforcement.
   d. social learning.

8. The nature–nurture controversy considers the degree to which traits, characteristics, and behaviors are the result of:
   a. early or lifelong learning.
   b. genes or heredity.
   c. heredity or experience.
   d. different historical concepts of childhood.

9. Modeling, an integral part of social learning theory, is so called because it:
   a. follows the scientific model of learning.
   b. molds character.
   c. follows the immediate reinforcement model developed by Bandura.
   d. involves people's patterning their behavior after that of others.

10. Which developmental theory suggests that each person is born with genetic possibilities that must be nurtured in order to grow?
    a. sociocultural   c. behaviorism
    b. cognitive   d. epigenetic

11. Vygotsky's theory has been criticized for neglecting:
    a. the role of genes in guiding development.
    b. developmental processes that are not primarily biological.
    c. the importance of language in development.
    d. social factors in development.

12. Which is the correct sequence of stages in Piaget's theory of cognitive development?
    a. sensorimotor, preoperational, concrete operational, formal operational
    b. sensorimotor, preoperational, formal operational, concrete operational
    c. preoperational, sensorimotor, concrete operational, formal operational
    d. preoperational, sensorimotor, formal operational, concrete operational

13. When an individual's existing understanding no longer fits his or her present experiences, the result is called:
    a. a psychosocial crisis.
    b. equilibrium.
    c. disequilibrium.
    d. negative reinforcement.

14. In explaining the origins of homosexuality, the grand theories have traditionally emphasized:
    a. nature over nurture.
    b. nurture over nature.
    c. a warped mother–son or father–daughter relationship.
    d. the individual's voluntary choice.

15. The zone of proximal development refers to:
    a. a stage during which the child exhibits preoperational thinking.
    b. the influence of a pleasurable stimulus on behavior.
    c. the range of skills a child can exercise with assistance but cannot perform independently.
    d. the tendency of a child to model an admired adult's behavior.

True or False Items

Write T (*true*) or F (*false*) on the line in front of each statement.

_____ 1. Behaviorists study what people actually do, not what they might be thinking.

_____ 2. Erikson's eight developmental stages are centered not on a body part but on each person's relationship to the social environment.

_____ 3. Most developmentalists agree that the nature–nurture controversy has been laid to rest.

_____ 4. Few developmental theorists today believe that humans have instincts or abilities that arise from our species' biological heritage.

_____ 5. Of the major developmental theories, cognitive theory gives the most emphasis to the interaction of genes and experience in shaping development.

_____ 6. New research suggests that homosexuality is at least partly genetic.

_____ 7. According to Piaget, a state of cognitive equilibrium must be attained before cognitive growth can occur.

_____ 8. In part, cognitive theory examines how an individual's understandings and expectations affect his or her behavior.

_____ 9. According to Piaget, children begin to think only when they reach preschool age.

_____ 10. Most contemporary researchers have adopted an eclectic perspective on development.

Progress Test 2

Progress Test 2 should be completed during a final chapter review. Answer the following questions after you thoroughly understand the correct answers for the Chapter Review and Progress Test 1.

Multiple-Choice Questions

1. Which developmental theorist has been criticized for suggesting that every child, in every culture, in every nation, passes through certain fixed stages?
    a. Freud   c. Piaget
    b. Erikson   d. all of the above.

2. Of the following terms, the one that does *not* describe a stage of Freud's theory of childhood sexuality is:
    a. phallic.
    b. oral.
    c. anal.
    d. sensorimotor.

3. We are more likely to imitate the behavior of others if we particularly admire and identify with them. This belief finds expression in:
   a. stage theory.
   b. sociocultural theory.
   c. social learning theory.
   d. Pavlov's experiments.

4. How do minitheories differ from grand theories of development?
   a. Unlike the more comprehensive grand theories, minitheories explain only a part of development.
   b. Unlike grand theories, which usually reflect the thinking of many researchers, minitheories tend to stem from one person.
   c. Only the recency of the research on which they are based keeps minitheories from having the sweeping influence of grand theories.
   d. They differ in all the above ways.

5. According to Erikson, an adult who has difficulty establishing a secure, mutual relationship with a life partner might never have resolved the crisis of:
   a. initiative versus guilt.
   b. autonomy versus shame and doubt.
   c. intimacy versus isolation.
   d. identity versus role confusion.

6. Who would be most likely to agree with the statement, "anything can be learned"?
   a. Jean Piaget   c. John Watson
   b. Lev Vygotsky   d. Erik Erikson

7. Classical conditioning is to _____ as operant conditioning is to _____ .
   a. Skinner; Pavlov   c. Pavlov; Skinner
   b. Watson; Vygotsky   d. Vygotsky; Watson

8. Behaviorists have found that they can often solve a person's seemingly complex psychological problem by:
   a. analyzing the patient.
   b. admitting the existence of the unconscious.
   c. altering the environment.
   d. administering well-designed punishments.

9. According to Piaget, an infant first comes to know the world through:
   a. sucking and grasping.
   b. naming and counting.
   c. preoperational thought.
   d. instruction from parents.

10. According to Piaget, the stage of cognitive development that generally characterizes preschool children (2 to 6 years old) is the:
    a. preoperational stage.   c. oral stage.
    b. sensorimotor stage.   d. psychosocial stage.

11. In Piaget's theory, cognitive equilibrium refers to:
    a. a state of mental balance.
    b. a kind of imbalance that leads to cognitive growth.
    c. the ultimate stage of cognitive development.
    d. the first stage in the processing of information.

12. You teach your dog to "speak" by giving her a treat each time she does so. This is an example of:
    a. classical conditioning.   c. reinforcement.
    b. respondent conditioning.   d. modeling.

13. A child who must modify an old idea in order to incorporate a new experience is using the process of:
    a. assimilation.
    b. accommodation.
    c. cognitive equilibrium.
    d. guided participation.

14. Which of the following is a common criticism of sociocultural theory?
    a. It places too great an emphasis on unconscious motives and childhood sexuality.
    b. Its mechanistic approach fails to explain many complex human behaviors.
    c. Development is more gradual than its stages imply.
    d. It neglects developmental processes that are not primarily social.

15. A major pioneer of the sociocultural perspective was:
    a. Jean Piaget.   c. Lev Vygotsky.
    b. Albert Bandura.   d. Ivan Pavlov.

Matching Items

Match each theory or term with its corresponding description or definition.

Theories or Terms

_____ **1.** psychoanalytic theory
_____ **2.** nature
_____ **3.** behaviorism
_____ **4.** social learning theory
_____ **5.** cognitive theory
_____ **6.** nurture
_____ **7.** sociocultural theory
_____ **8.** conditioning
_____ **9.** emergent theories
_____ **10.** modeling
_____ **11.** epigenetic theory

Descriptions or Definitions

a. emphasizes the impact of the immediate environment on behavior
b. relatively new, comprehensive theories
c. emphasizes that people learn by observing others
d. environmental influences that affect development
e. a process of learning, as described by Pavlov or Skinner
f. emphasizes the "hidden dramas" that influence behavior
g. emphasizes the cultural context in development
h. emphasizes how our thoughts shape our actions
i. the process whereby a person learns by imitating someone else's behavior
j. emphasizes the interaction of genes and environmental forces
k. traits that are inherited

Thinking Critically About Chapter 2

Answer these questions the day before an exam as a final check on your understanding of the chapter's terms and concepts.

1. Many songbirds inherit a genetically programmed species song that enhances their ability to mate and establish a territory. The evolution of such a trait is an example of:
   a. selective adaptation.
   b. epigenetic development.
   c. accommodation.
   d. assimilation.

2. When a pigeon is rewarded for producing a particular response, and so learns to produce that response to obtain rewards, psychologists describe this chain of events as:
   a. operant conditioning.   **c.** modeling.
   b. classical conditioning.   **d.** reflexive actions.

3. Professor Swenson, who believes that a considerable amount of development involves the developing person coming to associate neutral stimuli with meaningful stimuli, would most likely agree with the writings of:
   a. Freud.
   b. Erikson.
   c. Vygotsky.
   d. Pavlov.

4. Dr. Ivey's research focuses on the biological forces that shape each child's characteristic way of reacting to environmental experiences. Evidently, Dr. Ivey is working from a(n) _____ perspective.
   a. psychoanalytic   **c.** sociocultural
   b. cognitive   **d.** epigenetic

5. Which of the following is the best example of guided participation?
   a. After watching her mother change her baby sister's diaper, 4-year-old Brandy changes her doll's diaper.
   b. To help her son learn to pour liquids, Sandra engages him in a bathtub game involving pouring water from cups of different sizes.
   c. Seeing his father shaving, 3-year-old Kyle pretends to shave by rubbing whipped cream on his face.
   d. After reading a recipe in a magazine, Jack gathers ingredients from the cupboard.

6. A child who calls all furry animals "doggie" will experience cognitive _____ when she encounters a hairless breed for the first time. This may cause her to revamp her concept of "dog" in order to _____ the new experience.
   a. disequilibrium; accommodate
   b. disequilibrium; assimilate
   c. equilibrium; accommodate
   d. equilibrium; assimilate

7. A confirmed neo-Freudian, Dr. Thomas strongly endorses the views of Erik Erikson. She would be most likely to disagree with Freud regarding the importance of:
   a. unconscious forces in development.
   b. irrational forces in personality formation.
   c. early childhood experiences.
   d. sexual urges in development.

8. After watching several older children climbing around a new junglegym, 5-year-old Jennie decides to try it herself. Which of the following best accounts for her behavior?
   a. classical conditioning
   b. modeling
   c. guided participation
   d. reinforcement

9. I am 8 years old, and although I understand some logical principles, I have trouble thinking about hypothetical concepts. According to Piaget, I am in the _____ stage of development.
   a. sensorimotor
   b. preoperational
   c. concrete operational
   d. formal operational

10. Two-year-old Jamail has a simple understanding for "dad," and so each time he encounters a man with a child, he calls him "dad." When he learns that these other men are not "dad," Jamail experiences:
    a. conservation.   c. equilibrium.
    b. cognition.   d. disequilibrium.

11. (In Person) Most adults become physiologically aroused by the sound of an infant's laughter. These interactive reactions, in which caregivers and babies elicit responses in each other:
    a. help ensure the survival of the next generation.
    b. do not occur in all human cultures.
    c. are the result of conditioning very early in life.
    d. are more often found in females than in males.

12. The school psychologist believes that each child's developmental needs can be understood only by taking into consideration the child's broader social and cultural background. Evidently, the school psychologist is working within the _____ perspective.
    a. psychoanalytic   c. social learning
    b. epigenetic   d. sociocultural

13. Four-year-old Bjorn takes great pride in successfully undertaking new activities. Erikson would probably say that Bjorn is capably meeting the psychosocial challenge of:
    a. trust vs. mistrust.
    b. initiative vs. guilt.
    c. industry vs. inferiority.
    d. identity vs. role confusion.

14. Dr. Cleaver's developmental research draws upon insights from several theoretical perspectives. Evidently, Dr. Cleaver is working from a(n) _____ perspective.
    a. cognitive
    b. behaviorist
    c. eclectic
    d. sociocultural

15. Dr. Bazzi believes that development is a lifelong process of gradual and continuous growth. Based on this information, with which of the following theories would Dr. Bazzi most likely agree?
    a. Piaget's cognitive theory
    b. Erikson's psychosocial theory
    c. Freud's psychoanalytic theory
    d. behaviorism

Key Terms

Writing Definitions

Using your own words, write a brief definition or explanation of each of the following terms on a separate piece of paper.

1. developmental theory
2. grand theories
3. minitheories
4. emergent theories
5. psychoanalytic theory
6. behaviorism
7. conditioning
8. classical conditioning
9. operant conditioning
10. reinforcement
11. social learning theory
12. modeling
13. self-efficacy
14. cognitive theory
15. cognitive equilibrium

16. sociocultural theory

17. apprenticeship in thinking

18. guided participation

19. zone of proximal development

20. epigenetic theory

21. preformism

22. selective adaptation

23. ethology

24. eclectic perspective

25. nature

26. nurture

Cross-Check

After you have written the definitions of the key terms in this chapter, you should complete the crossword puzzle to ensure that you can reverse the process—recognize the term, given the definition.

ACROSS

2. Behaviorism focuses on the sequences and processes involved in the _____ of behavior.

8. An instinctive or learned behavior that is elicited by a specific stimulus.

11. All the genetic influences on development.

12. Developmental perspective that accepts elements from several theories.

14. Influential theorist who developed a stage theory of cognitive development.

17. All the environmental (nongenetic) influences on development.

19. Type of theory that brings together information from many disciplines into a comprehensive model of development.

DOWN

1. Theory that focuses on some specific area of development.

3. Theory that emphasizes the interaction of genetic and environmental factors in development.

4. The process by which the consequences of a behavior make the behavior more likely to occur.

5. Comprehensive theory of development that has proven to be inadequate in explaining the full range of human development.

6. Theory of personality and development that emphasizes unconscious forces.

7. Learning process that occurs through the association of two stimuli or through the use of reinforcement.

9. Influential theorist who outlined the principles of operant conditioning.

10. The study of behavior as it relates to the evolution and survival of a species.

13. An early and especially strong proponent of learning theory in America.

14. Russian scientist who outlined the principles of classical conditioning.

15. The developer of psychoanalytic theory.

16. The process of learning by imitating another person's behavior.

18. Psychoanalytic theorist who viewed development as a series of psychosocial crises.

ANSWERS

CHAPTER REVIEW

1. developmental theory

2. hypotheses; discoveries; coherent

3. grand; mini; emergent

4. motives; drives; unconscious; irrational

5. psychoanalytic; psychosexual stages; oral; anal; phallic; conflicts

Oral stage: The mouth is the focus of pleasurable sensations as the baby becomes emotionally attached to the person who provides the oral gratifications derived from sucking.

Anal stage: Pleasures related to control and self-control, initially in connection with defecation and toilet training, are paramount.

Phallic stage: Pleasure is derived from genital stimulation.

Genital stage: Mature sexual interests that last throughout adulthood emerge.

6. psychosocial; eight; crisis (challenge); span

Age Period	Stage
Birth to 1 yr.	trust vs. **mistrust**
1–3 yrs.	autonomy vs. **shame and doubt**
3–6 yrs.	initiative vs. **guilt**
7–11 yrs.	**industry** vs. inferiority
Adolescence	identity vs. **role confusion**
Young adulthood	**intimacy** vs. isolation
Middle adulthood	**generativity** vs. stagnation
Older adulthood	**integrity** vs. despair

7. behaviorism; John B. Watson; learning

8. at all ages; conditioning; classical conditioning; operant conditioning

9. Ivan Pavlov; respondent; neutral

10. B. F. Skinner; operant; consequence; instrumental

11. reinforcement; reinforcer

12. Harry Harlow; attachment; contact comfort; psychoanalytic; behaviorism's

13. social learning; modeling

14. uncertain; inexperienced; admirable and powerful, nurturing, or similar to the observer; self-understanding; self-confidence; social reflection; self-efficacy

15. cognitive; Jean Piaget

16. sensorimotor; 2

17. 6; preoperational; symbolically; egocentric

18. 7; concrete operational

19. formal operational; abstract (hypothetical); 12

20. cognitive equilibrium

21. cognitive disequilibrium

22. assimilate; accommodate

23. many

24. dynamic interaction; culture

25. Lev Vygotsky; cognitive

26. novices; mentors (or tutors); apprenticeship in thinking

27. guided participation

28. zone of proximal development; assistance

Sociocultural theory has emphasized the need to study development in the specific cultural context in which it occurs. The theory has been criticized for neglecting the importance of developmental processes that are not primarily social, such as the role of biological maturation in development.

29. epigenetic; genes; environment; preformism

30. instincts; biological

31. environmental; genetic instructions; stress; facilitating

32. selective adaptation

33. all

34. ethology; social contact; infant caregiving

35. a. sociocultural
    b. cognitive
    c. behaviorism
    d. psychoanalytic
    e. epigenetic

36. a. behaviorism
    b. cognitive
    c. psychoanalytic
    d. epigenetic
    e. sociocultural

37. eclectic

38. nature–nurture; genes (nature); nurture

39. interaction

40. attention-deficit/hyperactivity disorder (AD/HD); boys

    AD/HD children:

    - often have close male relatives with the same problem

    - are overactive in every context

    - calm down when they take stimulants

41. nurture; nature

PROGRESS TEST 1

Multiple-Choice Questions

1. **d.** is the answer (pp. 33–34)

2. **a.** is the answer. (p. 34)

   b. Behaviorism emphasizes the influence of the immediate environment on behavior.

   c. Cognitive theory emphasizes the impact of *conscious* thought processes on behavior.

   d. Sociocultural theory emphasizes the influence on development of social interaction in a specific cultural context.

3. **a.** is the answer. (pp. 35, 37)

4. **a.** is the answer. (p. 36)

   b. & c. Whereas Freud identified four stages of psychosexual development, Erikson proposed eight psychosocial stages.

   d. Although his theory places greater emphasis on social and cultural forces than Freud's did, Erikson's theory is nevertheless classified as a psychoanalytic theory.

5. **c.** is the answer. Sociocultural theory is an emergent theory. (p. 34)

   a., b., & d. Each of these is an example of a grand theory.

6. **c.** is the answer. (p. 38)

7. **a.** is the answer. In classical conditioning, a neutral stimulus—in this case, the bell—is associated with a meaningful stimulus—in this case, food. (p. 38)

   b. In operant conditioning, the consequences of a voluntary response determine the likelihood of its being repeated. Salivation is an involuntary response.

   c. & d. Positive reinforcement and social learning pertain to voluntary, or operant, responses.

8. **c.** is the answer. (p. 53)

   a. These are both examples of nurture.

   b. Both of these refer to nature.

   d. The impact of changing historical concepts of childhood on development is an example of how environmental forces (nurture) shape development.

9. **d.** is the answer. (p. 42)

   a. & c. These can be true in all types of learning.

   b. This was not discussed as an aspect of developmental theory.

10. **d.** is the answer. (pp. 48–49)

a. & c. Sociocultural theory and behaviorism focus almost entirely on environmental factors (nurture) in development.

b. Cognitive theory emphasizes the developing person's own mental activity but ignores genetic differences in individuals.

11. **a.** is the answer. (p. 48)

    b. Vygotsky's theory does not emphasize biological processes.

    c. & d. Vygotsky's theory places considerable emphasis on language and social factors.

12. **a.** is the answer. (pp. 43, 44)

13. **c.** is the answer. (p. 43)

    a. This refers to the core of Erikson's psychosocial stages, which deals with people's interactions with the environment.

    b. Equilibrium occurs when existing schemes *do* fit a person's current experiences.

    d. Negative reinforcement is the removal of a stimulus as a consequence of a desired behavior.

14. **b.** is the answer. (pp. 54–55)

    c. This is only true of psychoanalytic theory.

    d. Although the grand theories have emphasized nurture over nature in this matter, no theory suggests that sexual orientation is voluntarily chosen.

15. **c.** is the answer. (p. 47)

    a. This is a stage of Piaget's cognitive theory.

    b. This describes positive reinforcement.

    d. This is an aspect of social learning theory.

True or False Items

1. T (p. 38)

2. T (p. 36)

3. F   Although most developmentalists believe that nature and nurture interact in shaping development, the practical implications of whether nature or nurture plays a greater role in certain abilities keep the controversy alive. (p. 54)

4. F   This assumption lies at the heart of epigenetic theory. (p. 48)

5. F   Epigenetic theory emphasizes the interaction of genes and experience. (p. 48)

6. T (p. 55)

7. F   On the contrary, *dis*equilibrium often fosters greater growth. (p. 43)

8. T (p. 43)

9. F   The hallmark of Piaget's theory is that, at every age, individuals think about the world in unique ways. (p. 43)

10. T (p. 53)

PROGRESS TEST 2

Multiple-Choice Questions

1. **d.** is the answer. (pp. 35, 36, 43)

2. **d.** is the answer. This is one of Piaget's stages of cognitive development. (pp. 35, 43)

3. **c.** is the answer. (p. 42)

4. **a.** is the answer. (p. 34)

   b. *Grand* theories, rather than minitheories, usually stem from one person.

   c. This describes emergent theories.

5. **d.** is the answer. (p. 36)

6. **c.** is the answer. (p. 37)

   a. Piaget formulated a cognitive theory of development.

   b. Vygotsky formulated a sociocultural theory of development.

   d. Erikson formulated a psychoanalytic theory of development.

7. **c.** is the answer. (p. 38)

8. **c.** is the answer. (p. 38)

   a. & b. These are psychoanalytic approaches to treating psychological problems.

   d. Behaviorists generally do not recommend the use of punishment.

9. **a.** is the answer. These behaviors are typical of infants in the sensorimotor stage. (p. 43)

   b., c., & d. These are typical of older children.

10. **a.** is the answer. (pp. 43, 44)

    b. The sensorimotor stage describes development from birth until 2 years of age.

    c. This is a psychoanalytic stage described by Freud.

    d. This is not the name of a stage; "psychosocial" refers to Erikson's stage theory.

11. **a.** is the answer. (p. 43)

    b. This describes *dis*equilibrium.

    c. This is formal operational thinking.

    d. Piaget's theory does not propose stages of information processing.

12. **c.** is the answer. (p. 39)

a. & b. Teaching your dog in this way is an example of operant, rather than classical (respondent), conditioning.

d. Modeling involves learning by imitating others.

13. **b.** is the answer. (pp. 43–44)

    a. Assimilation occurs when new experiences do *not* clash with existing ideas.

    c. Cognitive equilibrium is mental balance, which occurs when ideas and experiences do *not* clash.

    d. This is Vygotsky's term for the process by which a mentor engages a child in shared learning activities.

14. **d.** is the answer. (p. 48)

    a. This is a common criticism of psychoanalytic theory.

    b. This is a common criticism of behaviorism.

    c. This is a common criticism of psychoanalytic and cognitive theories that describe development as occurring in a sequence of stages.

15. **c.** is the answer. (p. 46)

Matching Items

1. f (p. 34)	**5.** h (p. 43)	**9.** b (p. 34)
2. k (p. 53)	**6.** d (p. 53)	**10.** i (p. 42)
3. a (p. 38)	**7.** g (p. 45)	**11.** j (p. 48)
4. c (p. 42)	**8.** e (p. 38)	

THINKING CRITICALLY ABOUT CHAPTER 2

1. **a.** is the answer. (p. 50)

   b. This term was not used to describe development.

   c. & d. These terms describe the processes by which cognitive concepts incorporate (assimilate) new experiences or are revamped (accommodated) by them.

2. **a.** is the answer. This is an example of operant conditioning because a response recurs due to its consequences. (p. 38)

   b. & d. In classical conditioning, the individual learns to associate a neutral stimulus with a meaningful stimulus.

   c. In modeling, learning occurs through the observation of others, rather than through direct exposure to reinforcing consequences, as in this example.

3. **d.** is the answer. In classical conditioning, an organism comes to associate a neutral stimulus

with a meaningful one and then responds to the former stimulus as if it were the latter. (p. 38)

4. **d.** is the answer. (p. 49)

a. Psychoanalytic theorists focus on the role of unconscious forces in development.

b. Cognitive theorists emphasize how the developing person actively seeks to understand experiences.

c. Sociocultural theorists focus on the social context, as expressed through people, language, and customs.

5. **b.** is the answer. (p. 46)

a. & c. These are both examples of modeling.

d. Guided participation involves the coaching of a mentor. In this example, Jack is simply following written directions.

6. **a.** is the answer. (pp. 43, 45)

b. Because the dog is not furry, the child's concept of dog cannot incorporate (assimilate) the discrepant experience without being revamped.

c. & d. Equilibrium exists when ideas (such as what a dog is) and experiences (such as seeing a hairless dog) do *not* clash.

7. **d.** is the answer. (p. 36)

8. **b.** is the answer. Evidently, Jennie has learned by observing the other children at play. (p. 42)

a. Classical conditioning is concerned with the association of stimuli, not with complex responses, as in this example.

c. Guided participation involves the interaction of a mentor and a child.

d. Reinforcement is a process for getting a response to recur.

9. **c.** is the answer. (p. 44)

10. **d.** is the answer. When Jamail experiences something that conflicts with his existing understanding, he experiences disequilibrium. (p. 43)

a. Conservation is the ability to recognize that objects do not change when their appearances change.

b. Cognition refers to all mental activities associated with thinking.

c. If Jamail's thinking were in equilibrium, all men would be "dad"!

11. **a.** is the answer. (p. 51)

b. & c. Infant social reflexes and adult caregiving impulses occur in all cultures (b), which indicates that they are the product of nature rather than nurture (c).

d. The text does not address the issue of gender differences in infant reflexes or caregiving impulses.

12. **d.** is the answer. (p. 45)

13. **b.** is the answer. (p. 37)

a. According to Erikson, this crisis concerns younger children.

c. & d. In Erikson's theory, these crises concern older children.

14. **c.** is the answer. (p. 53)

a., b., & d. These are three of the many theoretical perspectives upon which someone working from an eclectic perspective might draw.

15. **d.** is the answer. (p. 38)

a., b., & c. Each of these theories emphasizes that development is a discontinuous process that occurs in stages.

KEY TERMS

Writing Definitions

1. A **developmental theory** is a systematic statement of principles and generalizations that provides a coherent framework for studying and explaining development. (p. 33)

2. **Grand theories** are comprehensive theories of human development that have proven to be inadequate in the face of research evidence that development is more diverse than the theories proposed. Examples of grand theories are psychoanalytic and cognitive theories and behaviorism. (p. 34)

3. **Minitheories** are less general and comprehensive than grand theories, focusing instead on some specific area of development. (p. 34)

4. **Emergent theories,** such as sociocultural theory and epigenetic theory, are newer comprehensive theories that bring together information from many disciplines but are not yet a systematic and comprehensive whole. (p. 34)

5. **Psychoanalytic theory,** a grand theory, interprets human development in terms of intrinsic drives and motives, many of which are irrational and unconscious. (p. 34)

6. **Behaviorism,** a grand theory, emphasizes the sequences and processes by which behavior is learned. (p. 38)

7. **Conditioning** is the learning process that occurs either through the association of two stimuli (classical conditioning) or through the use of positive or negative reinforcement or punishment (operant conditioning). (p. 38)

8. **Classical conditioning** is the process by which a neutral stimulus becomes associated with a meaningful one so that both are responded to in the same way. (p. 38)

9. **Operant conditioning** is the process by which a response is gradually learned through reinforcement or punishment. (p. 38)

10. **Reinforcement** is the process by which the consequences of a particular behavior strengthen the behavior, making it more likely that the behavior will be repeated. (p. 39)

11. An application of behaviorism, **social learning theory** emphasizes that people often learn new behaviors through observation and imitation of other people. (p. 42)

12. **Modeling** refers to the process by which we observe other people's behavior and then pattern our own after it. (p. 42)

13. In social learning theory, **self-efficacy** is the belief that one is effective. (p. 42)

14. **Cognitive theory,** a grand theory, emphasizes that the way people think and understand the world shapes their attitudes, beliefs, and behaviors. (p. 43)

15. In Piaget's theory, **cognitive equilibrium** is a state of mental balance, in which a person's thoughts about the world seem not to clash with each other or with his or her experiences. (p. 43)

16. **Sociocultural theory,** an emergent theory, seeks to explain development as the result of a dynamic interaction between developing persons and the surrounding social and cultural forces. (p. 45)

17. In sociocultural theory, an **apprenticeship in thinking** is the process by which novices learn by interacting with more skilled parents, teachers, or other mentors. (p. 46)

18. In sociocultural theory, **guided participation** is a learning process in which the learner is tutored, or mentored, through social interaction with a skilled teacher. (p. 46)

19. According to Vygotsky, developmental growth occurs when mentors draw children into the **zone of proximal development,** which is the range of skills the child can exercise and master with assistance but cannot perform independently. (p. 47)

20. **Epigenetic theory** emphasizes the genetic origins of behavior but also stresses that genes, over time, are directly and systematically affected by environmental forces. (p. 48)

21. **Preformism** is the idea that every aspect of development is set in advance by genes and then gradually emerges through maturation. (p. 48)

22. **Selective adaptation** is the evolutionary process through which useful genes that enhance survival become more frequent within individuals. (p. 50)

23. **Ethology** is the study of patterns of animal behavior as it relates to the evolution and survival of a species. (p. 51)

24. Developmentalists who work from an **eclectic perspective** accept elements from several theories, instead of adhering to only a single perspective. (p. 53)

25. **Nature** refers to all the traits, capacities, and limitations that a person inherits from his or her parents at the moment of conception. (p. 53)

26. **Nurture** refers to all the environmental influences that affect a person's development following the moment of conception. (p. 53)

Cross-Check

ACROSS	DOWN
2. learning	1. minitheory
8. response	3. epigenetic
11. nature	4. reinforcement
12. eclectic	5. grand
14. Piaget	6. psychoanalytic
17. nurture	7. conditioning
19. emergent	9. Skinner
10. ethology	13. Watson
	14. Pavlov
	15. Freud
	16. modeling
	18. Erikson

Chapter Three

Heredity and Environment

Chapter Overview

Conception occurs when the male and female reproductive cells—the sperm and ovum, respectively—come together to create a new, one-celled zygote with its own unique combination of genetic material. The genetic material furnishes the instructions for development—not only for obvious physical characteristics, such as sex, coloring, and body shape but also for certain psychological characteristics, such as bashfulness, moodiness, and vocational aptitude.

Every year scientists make new discoveries and reach new understandings about genes and their effects on the development of individuals. This chapter presents some of their findings, including that most human characteristics are polygenic and multifactorial, the result of the interaction of many genetic and environmental influences. Perhaps the most important findings have come from research into the causes of genetic and chromosomal abnormalities. The chapter discusses the most common of these abnormalities and concludes with a section on genetic counseling. Genetic testing before and after conception can help predict whether a couple will have a child with a genetic problem.

Many students find the technical material in this chapter difficult to master, but it *can* be done with a great deal of rehearsal. Working through the Chapter Review several times and mentally reciting terms are both useful techniques for rehearsing this type of material.

NOTE: Answer guidelines for all Chapter 3 questions begin on page 46.

Guided Study

The text chapter should be studied one section at a time. Before you read, preview each section by skimming it, noting headings and boldface items. Then read the appropriate section objectives from the following outline. Keep these objectives in mind and, as you read the chapter section, search for the information that will enable you to meet each objective. Once you have finished a section, write out answers for its objectives.

The Genetic Code (pp. 59–70)

1. Identify the mechanisms of heredity, and describe the process of conception and the first hours of development of the zygote.

2. Explain how sex is determined.

3. Distinguish between monozygotic and dizygotic twins, and describe the processes of duplication, division, and differentiation.

4. Explain the polygenic and multifactorial nature of human traits, and explain the additive and non-additive patterns of genetic interaction, giving examples of the traits that result from each type of interaction.

From Genotype to Phenotype (pp. 70–75)

8. Differentiate genotype from phenotype.

9. Discuss the interaction of genes and environment in the development of Alzheimer's disease, alcoholism, and schizophrenia.

5. Discuss *X*-linked genes in terms of genotype and phenotype, and explain the concept of parental imprinting or tagging.

Chromosomal and Genetic Abnormalities (pp. 75–88)

10. Describe the most common chromosomal abnormalities, including abnormalities involving the sex chromosomes.

6. Discuss the benefits of genetic diversity.

7. (Thinking Like a Scientist) Describe the Human Genome Project.

11. Identify two common genetic disorders, and discuss reasons for their relatively low incidence of occurrence.

12. Describe four situations in which couples should seek genetic testing and counseling.

13. Describe genetic testing methods, and discuss decision options for couples who might have a child with a serious disorder.

Chapter Review

When you have finished reading the chapter, work through the material that follows to review it. Complete the sentences and answer the questions. As you proceed, evaluate your performance for each section by consulting the answers beginning on page 46. Do not continue with the next section until you understand each answer. If you need to, review or reread the appropriate section in the textbook before continuing.

The Genetic Code (pp. 59-70)

1. The work of body cells is done by _____ , under the direction of instructions stored in molecules of _____ , each of which is called a _____ . The sum total of these genetic instructions for a given species is called its _____ .

2. Each normal person inherits _____ chromosomes, _____ from each parent. The genetic instructions in chromosomes are organized into units called _____ , each of which contains instructions for a specific _____ , which in turn is composed of chemical building blocks called _____ _____ .

3. Genetic instructions are "written" in a chemical code, made up of four pairs of bases:

    _____ , _____ , _____ , and _____ .

    These pairs are arranged in groups of _____ (how many?), which are called _____ .

4. The human reproductive cells, which are called _____ , include the male's _____ and the female's _____ .

5. When the gametes' nuclei fuse, a living cell called a _____ is formed.

6. This new cells receives _____ chromosomes from the father and _____ from the mother.

7. The sum total of all the genes a person inherits is called the _____ .

8. The chromosomes in a pair are generally identical or similar. Some genes come in several slight, normal variations called _____ .

9. The developing person's sex is determined by the _____ pair of chromosomes. In the female, this pair is composed of two _____ -shaped chromosomes and is designated _____ . In the male, this pair includes one _____ and one _____ chromosome and is therefore designated _____ .

10. The critical factor in the determination of a zygote's sex is which _____ (sperm/ovum) reaches the other gamete first. In a stressful pregnancy, _____ (XX/XY) embryos are more likely to be expelled in a miscarriage, or _____ .

11. (text and Changing Policy) At birth, the overall sex ratio has always _____ (favored males/favored females/been roughly equal). In countries such as China, prenatal tests that show the sex of the child have been used to

    _____ .

12. Identical twins, which develop from one
_____ (are/are not) genetically
identical.

13. Twins who begin life as two separate zygotes created by the fertilization of two ova are called
_____ twins. Such twins have
approximately _____ percent of
their genes in common.

14. Dizygotic births occur naturally about once in
every _____ births. Women in their
_____ (what age?) are three times as
likely to have dizygotic twins than women in
their _____ .

15. Within hours after conception, the zygote begins
to grow through the process of
_____ . At about the eight-cell stage,
the cells start to _____ , with vari-
ous cells beginning to specialize and reproduce at
different rates. Genes affect this process through
_____-_____
_____ mechanisms that code for
specific proteins.

16. The sum total of all the genetic traits that are
actually expressed is called the
_____ .

17. Most human characteristics are affected by many
genes, and so they are _____ ; and
by many factors, and so they are
_____ .

18. A phenotype that reflects the sum of the contributions of all the genes involved in its determination illustrates the _____ pattern of
genetic interaction. Examples include genes that
affect _____ and
_____ _____ .

19. Less often, genes interact in a _____
fashion. In one example of this pattern, some
genes are more influential than others; this is
called the _____-_____
pattern. In this pattern, the more influential gene
is called _____ , and the weaker
gene is called _____ .

20. In one variation of this pattern, the phenotype is
influenced primarily, but not exclusively, by the
dominant gene; this is the _____
pattern.

21. Some recessive genes are located only on the X
chromosome and so are called
_____-_____ .
Examples of such genes are the ones that determine _____ . Because they have
only one X chromosome, _____
(females/males) are more likely to have these
characteristics in their phenotype.

22. Complicating inheritance further is the fact that
dominant genes sometimes do not completely
_____ the phenotype. This may be
caused by _____ ,
_____ , or other factors.

23. Whether a gene is inherited from the mother or
the father _____ (does/does not)
influence its behavior. This tendency of genes is
called _____ , or tagging.

24. When the twenty three chromosome pairs divide
up during the formation of gametes, which of the
two pairs will end up in a particular gamete is
determined by _____ .

25. Genetic variability is also affected by the
_____-_____ of genes,
and by the interaction of genetic instructions in
ways unique to the individual. Another mechanism of genetic diversity is _____ ,
which refers to the alteration of genetic information caused by _____ factors.

26. Genetic diversity helps safeguard
_____ .

27. (Thinking Like a Scientist) The international
effort to map the complete human genetic code is
referred to as the _____
_____ _____ . In 2000,
they published two drafts, revealing, most importantly, that all living creatures _____
(have different/share) genes.

From Genotype to Phenotype (pp. 70–75)

28. A person who has a gene in his or her genotype that is not expressed in the phenotype but that can be passed on to the person's offspring is said to be a _____ of that gene.

29. The complexity of genetic interaction is particularly apparent in _____ , which is the study of the genetic origins of _____ characteristics. These include traits such as _____ ; psychological disorders such as _____ ; and _____ traits such as _____ .

30. Most behavioral traits are affected by the _____ of large numbers of _____ with _____ factors. Traits that are plastic early in life _____ (always/do not always) remain plastic thereafter.

31. The most-feared form of senility is _____ disease, which occurs when the protein _____ accumulates in the brain and kills cells. When this disease occurs before age _____ , which is referred to as _____-_____ ," the cause is entirely _____ . More common is the _____- _____ form of the disease, which is more prevalent in people over 80 who inherited a particular allele of the _____ gene. Although the gene increases the risk of the disease, other health indicators are also factors, including _____ .

32. Psychopathologies such as _____ are genetically based traits that are also subject to _____ influence.

33. Environmental influences _____ (do/do not) play an important role in the appearance of schizophrenia. One predisposing factor is birth during _____ , probably because a certain _____ is more prevalent at this time of year.

34. Alcoholism _____ (is/is not) partly genetic; furthermore, its expression _____ (is/is not) affected by the environment. Certain temperamental traits correlate with abusive drinking, including _____ .

35. On a practical level, genes and environment affect _____ (most/ every/few) human characteristic(s).

Chromosomal and Genetic Abnormalities (pp. 75–88)

Researchers study genetic and chromosomal abnormalities for three major reasons. State them.

36. Chromosomal abnormalities occur during the formation of the _____ , producing a sperm or ovum that does not have the normal complement of chromosomes.

37. The variable that most often correlates with chromosomal abnormalities is _____ _____ . When cells in a zygote end up with more or fewer than 46 chromosomes the result is a person who is _____ .

38. Most fetuses with chromosomal abnormalities are _____ _____ . Nevertheless, about 1 in every _____ newborns has one chromosome too few or one too many, leading to a cluster of characteristics called a _____ .

39. The most common extra-chromosome syndrome is _____ , which is also called _____-_____ . People with this syndrome age _____ (faster/more slowly) than other adults. By middle age, people with Down syndrome almost invariably develop _____ , which severely impairs their already limited _____ skills.

List several of the physical and psychological characteristics associated with Down syndrome.

40. About 1 in every 500 infants is either missing a _____ chromosome or has two or more such chromosomes. One resulting syndrome is _____ , in which a boy inherits the _____ chromosome pattern.

41. Most of the known genetic disorders are _____ (dominant/recessive). Genetic disorders usually _____ (are/are not) seriously disabling. It is much _____ (more/less) likely that a person is a carrier of one or more harmful genes than that he or she has abnormal chromosomes.

42. Two exceptions are the central nervous system disease called _____ and the disorder that causes its victims to exhibit uncontrollable tics and explosive outbursts, called _____ .

43. In some individuals, part of the X chromosome is attached by such a thin string of molecules that it seems about to break off; this abnormality is called _____ _____ syndrome.

44. Genetic disorders that are _____ and _____ claim more victims than dominant ones. Three common recessive disorders are _____ , _____ , and_____ -_____ .

45. Through _____ _____ , couples today can learn more about their genes and about their chances of conceiving a child with chromosomal or other genetic abnormalities.

46. List four situations in which genetic counseling is strongly recommended.

a. _____

b. _____

c. _____

d. _____

47. Among the many reproductive alternatives available to those who are carriers of a serious condition or at high risk because of their age or family history are _____

_____ .

The innovative new prenatal therapy called _____ _____ involves the altering of an organism's genetic instructions.

Progress Test 1

Circle your answers to the following questions and check them against the answers beginning on page 47. If your answer is incorrect, read the explanation for why it is incorrect and then consult the appropriate pages of the text (in parentheses following the correct answer).

Multiple-Choice Questions

1. When a sperm and an ovum merge, a one-celled _____ is formed.
   a. zygote   c. gamete
   b. reproductive cell   d. monozygote

2. Genes are discrete segments that provide the biochemical instructions that each cell needs to become:
   a. a zygote.
   b. a chromosome.
   c. a specific part of a functioning human body.
   d. deoxyribonucleic acid.

3. In the male, the 23rd pair of chromosomes is designated _____ ; in the female, this pair is designated _____ .
   a. XX; XY   c. XO; XXY
   b. XY; XX   d. XXY; XO

4. Since the 23rd pair of chromosomes in females is XX, each ovum carries an:
   a. XX zygote.   c. XY zygote.
   b. X zygote.   d. X chromosome.

5. When a zygote splits, the two identical, independent clusters that develop become:
   a. dizygotic twins.   c. fraternal twins.
   b. monozygotic twins.   d. trizygotic twins.

6. Which of the following is a predisposing factor
for schizophrenia?
   a. birth during late winter
   b. having a close relative with the illness
   c. inadequate oxygen at birth
   d. Each of the above is a predisposing factor.

7. Most of the known genetic disorders are:
   a. dominant.   c. seriously disabling.
   b. recessive.   d. sex-linked.

8. When we say that a characteristic is multifactorial, we mean that:
   a. many genes are involved.
   b. many environmental factors are involved.
   c. many genetic and environmental factors are
      involved.
   d. the characteristic is polygenic.

9. Genes are segments of molecules of:
   a. genotype.
   b. deoxyribonucleic acid (DNA).
   c. karyotype.
   d. phenotype.

10. The potential for genetic diversity in humans is
so great because:
    a. there are approximately 8 million possible
       combinations of chromosomes.
    b. when the sperm and ovum unite, genetic com-
       binations not present in either parent can be
       formed.
    c. just before a chromosome pair divides during
       the formation of gametes, genes cross over,
       producing recombinations.
    d. of all the above reasons.

11. A chromosomal abnormality that affects males
only involves a(n):
    a. XO chromosomal pattern.
    b. XXX chromosomal pattern.
    c. YY chromosomal pattern.
    d. XXY chromosomal pattern.

12. Polygenic complexity is most apparent in
_____ characteristics.
    a. physical   c. recessive gene
    b. psychological   d. dominant gene

13. Babies born with trisomy-21 (Down syndrome)
are often:
    a. born to older parents.
    b. unusually aggressive.
    c. abnormally tall by adolescence.
    d. blind.

14. To say that a trait is polygenic means that:
    a. many genes make it more likely that the indi-
       vidual will inherit the trait.
    b. several genes must be present in order for the
       individual to inherit the trait.
    c. the trait is multifactorial.
    d. most people carry genes for the trait.

15. Some genetic diseases are recessive, so the child
cannot inherit the condition unless both parents:
    a. have Kleinfelter syndrome.
    b. carry the same recessive gene.
    c. have XO chromosomes.
    d. have the disease.

Matching Items

Match each term with its corresponding description or definition.

Terms

_____ **1.** gametes
_____ **2.** chromosome
_____ **3.** genotype
_____ **4.** phenotype
_____ **5.** monozygotic
_____ **6.** dizygotic
_____ **7.** additive
_____ **8.** fragile *X* syndrome
_____ **9.** carrier
_____ **10.** zygote
_____ **11.** alleles
_____ **12.** XX
_____ **13.** XY

Descriptions or Definitions

a. chromosome pair inherited by genetic females
b. identical twins
c. sperm and ovum
d. the first cell of the developing person
e. a person who has a recessive gene in his or her genotype that is not expressed in the phenotype
f. fraternal twins
g. a pattern in which each gene in question makes an active contribution to the final outcome
h. a DNA molecule
i. the behavioral or physical expression of genetic potential
j. a chromosomal abnormality
k. alternate versions of a gene
l. chromosome pair inherited by genetic males
m. a person's entire genetic inheritance

Progress Test 2

Progress Test 2 should be completed during a final chapter review. Answer the following questions after you thoroughly understand the correct answers for the Chapter Review and Progress Test 1.

1. Which of the following provides the best broad description of the relationship between heredity and environment in determining height?
   a. Heredity is the primary influence, with environment affecting development only in severe situations.
   b. Heredity and environment contribute equally to development.
   c. Environment is the major influence on physical characteristics.
   d. Heredity directs the individual's potential and environment determines whether and to what degree the individual reaches that potential.

2. "Late-onset" Alzheimer's disease:
   a. is less common than the "early-onset" form of the illness.
   b. is entirely genetic.
   c. is multifactorial and associated with abnormal genes as well as hypertension and other health indicators.
   d. is associated with an abnormal gene found more often in African-Americans than in European-Americans

3. Males with fragile *X* syndrome are:
   a. feminine in appearance.
   b. less severely affected than females.
   c. frequently retarded intellectually.
   d. likely to have fatty deposits around the breasts.

4. Disorders that are _____ are most likely to pass undetected from generation to generation.
   a. dominant
   b. dominant and polygenic
   c. recessive
   d. recessive and multifactorial

5. The effect of a gene on a particular physical characteristic depends on whether the gene comes from the mother or the father. This is called:
   a. the dominant–recessive pattern.
   b. imprinting.
   c. the additive pattern.
   d. molecular genetics.

6. Dizygotic twins result when:
   a. a single egg is fertilized by a sperm and then splits.
   b. a single egg is fertilized by two different sperm.
   c. two eggs are fertilized by two different sperm.
   d. either a single egg is fertilized by one sperm or two eggs are fertilized by two different sperm.

7. Molecules of DNA that in humans are organized into 23 complementary pairs are called:
   a. zygotes.   c. chromosomes.
   b. genes.   d. ova.

8. Shortly after the zygote is formed, it begins the processes of duplication and division. Each resulting new cell has:
   a. the same number of chromosomes as was contained in the zygote.
   b. half the number of chromosomes as was contained in the zygote.
   c. twice, then four times, then eight times the number of chromosomes as was contained in the zygote.
   d. all the chromosomes except those that determine sex.

9. If an ovum is fertilized by a sperm bearing a Y chromosome:
   a. a female will develop.
   b. cell division will result.
   c. a male will develop.
   d. spontaneous abortion will occur.

10. When the male cells in the testes and the female cells in the ovaries divide to produce gametes, the process differs from that in the production of all other cells. As a result of the different process, the gametes have:
    a. one rather than both members of each chromosome pair.
    b. 23 chromosome pairs.
    c. X but not Y chromosomes.
    d. chromosomes from both parents.

11. Most human traits are:
    a. polygenic.
    b. multifactorial.
    c. determined by dominant–recessive patterns.
    d. both a. and b.

12. Genotype is to phenotype as _____ is to _____ .
    a. genetic potential; physical expression
    b. physical expression; genetic potential
    c. sperm; ovum
    d. gamete; zygote

13. The genes that influence height and skin color interact according to the _____ pattern.
    a. dominant–recessive   c. additive
    b. X-linked   d. nonadditive

14. X-linked recessive genes explain why some traits seem to be passed from:
    a. father to son.
    b. father to daughter.
    c. mother to daughter.
    d. mother to son.

15. A 35-year-old woman who is pregnant is most likely to undergo which type of test for the detection of prenatal chromosomal or genetic abnormalities?
    a. pre-implantation testing
    b. ultrasound
    c. amniocentesis
    d. alpha-fetoprotein assay

True or False Items

Write T (*true*) or F (*false*) on the line in front of each statement.

_____ 1. Most human characteristics are multifactorial, caused by the interaction of genetic and environmental factors.

_____ 2. Chromosomal abnormalities can occur only for genetic reasons.

_____ 3. Research suggests that susceptibility to alcoholism is at least partly the result of genetic inheritance.

_____ 4. The human reproductive cells (ova and sperm) are called gametes.

_____ 5. Only a very few human traits are polygenic.

_____ 6. The zygote contains all the biologically inherited information—the genes and chromosomes—that a person will have during his or her life.

_____ 7. A couple should probably seek genetic counseling if several earlier pregnancies ended in spontaneous abortion.

_____ 8. Many genetic conditions are recessive; thus, a child will have the condition even if only the mother carries the gene.

_____ 9. Two people who have the same phenotype may have a different genotype for a trait such as eye color.

_____ 10. When cells divide to produce reproductive cells (gametes), each sperm or ovum receives only 23 chromosomes, half as many as the original cell.

_____ 11. Most genes have only one function.

_____ 12. Psychopathologies such as depression and phobias are caused by environmental factors.

Thinking Critically About Chapter 3

Answer these questions the day before an exam as a final check on your understanding of the chapter's terms and concepts.

1. Randy's son was born with an XXY chromosomal pattern. It is likely that his son's condition will:
   a. go undetected until puberty.
   b. benefit from hormone supplements.
   c. develop some female sex characteristics at puberty.
   d. be characterized by all of the above.

2. Dr. Jansen, who studies the genetic origins of psychological characteristics, would probably describe herself as a:
   a. genetic engineer.
   b. molecular geneticist.
   c. behavior geneticist.
   d. developmental biologist.

3. Which of the following is an inherited abnormality that quite possibly could develop into a recognizable syndrome?
   a. Just before dividing to form a sperm or ovum, corresponding gene segments of a chromosome pair break off and are exchanged.
   b. Just before conception, a chromosome pair splits imprecisely, resulting in a mixture of cells.
   c. A person inherits an X chromosome in which part of the chromosome is attached to the rest of it by a very slim string of molecules.
   d. A person inherits a recessive gene on his Y chromosome.

4. Some men are color-blind because they inherit a particular recessive gene from their mother. That recessive gene is carried on the:
   a. X chromosome.
   b. XX chromosome pair.
   c. Y chromosome.
   d. X or Y chromosome.

5. If your mother is much taller than your father, it is most likely that your height will be:
   a. about the same as your mother's, because the X chromosome determines height.
   b. about the same as your father's, because the Y chromosome determines height.
   c. somewhere between your mother's and father's heights because of parental imprinting.
   d. greater than both your mother's and father's because of your grandfather's dominant gene.

6. If a dizygotic twin develops schizophrenia, the likelihood of the other twin experiencing serious mental illness is much lower than is the case with monozygotic twins. This suggests that:
   a. schizophrenia is caused by genes.
   b. schizophrenia is influenced by genes.
   c. environment is unimportant in the development of schizophrenia.
   d. monozygotic twins are especially vulnerable to schizophrenia.

7. A person's skin turns yellow-orange as a result of a carrot-juice diet regimen. This is an example of:
   a. an environmental influence.
   b. an alteration in genotype.
   c. polygenic inheritance.
   d. incomplete dominance.

8. Jason has an inherited, dominant disorder that causes him to exhibit uncontrollable tics and explosive outbursts. Jason most likely would be diagnosed with:
   a. Klinefelter syndrome.
   b. Huntington's disease.
   c. Fragile X syndrome.
   d. Tourette syndrome.

9. If a man carries the recessive gene for cystic fibrosis and his wife does not, the chances of their having a child with cystic fibrosis is:
   a. one in four.
   b. fifty-fifty.
   c. zero.
   d. dependent upon the wife's ethnic background.

10. Forty-eight-year-old Clayton has an accumulation of amyloid B in his brain that is causing some cognitive dysfunction. Clayton would probably be diagnosed with:
   a. trisomy-21.
   b. early onset Alzheimer's disease.
   c. Down syndrome.
   d. schizophrenia.

11. Schizophrenia is most accurately described as a(n):
    a. genetic psychopathology.
    b. environmental psychopathology.
    c. multifactorial psychopathology
    d. psychopathology of unknown cause.

12. Laurie and Brad, who both have a history of alcoholism in their families, are concerned that the child they hope to have will inherit a genetic predisposition to alcoholism. Based on information presented in the text, what advice should you offer them?
    a. "Stop worrying, alcoholism is only weakly genetic."
    b. "It is almost certain that your child will become alcoholic."
    c. "Social influences, such as the family and peer environment, play a critical role in determining whether alcoholism is expressed."
    d. "Wait to have children until you are both middle aged, in order to see if the two of you become alcoholic."

13. Sixteen-year-old Joey experiences some mental slowness and hearing and heart problems, yet he is able to care for himself and is unusually sweet-tempered. Joey probably:
    a. is mentally retarded.
    b. has Alzheimer's disease.
    c. has Kleinfelter syndrome.
    d. has Down syndrome.

14. Genetically, Claude's potential height is 6'0. Because he did not receive a balanced diet, however, he grew to only 5'9". Claude's actual height is an example of a:
    a. recessive gene.
    b. dominant gene.
    c. genotype.
    d. phenotype.

15. Winona inherited a gene from her mother that, regardless of her father's contribution to her genotype, will be expressed in her phenotype. Evidently, the gene Winona received from her mother is a(n) _____ gene.
    a. polygenic   c. dominant
    b. recessive   d. X-linked

Key Terms

Writing Definitions

Using your own words, write on a separate piece of paper a brief definition or explanation of each of the following terms.

1. DNA
2. chromosome
3. genome
4. gene
5. gamete
6. zygote
7. genotype
8. allele
9. 23rd pair
10. XX
11. XY
12. spontaneous abortion
13. monozygotic twins
14. dizygotic twins
15. on–off switching mechanisms
16. phenotype
17. multifactorial
18. polygenic
19. additive gene
20. dominant–-recessive pattern
21. dominant gene
22. recessive gene
23. X-linked
24. Human Genome Project
25. carrier
26. behavior genetics
27. mosaic
28. fragile X syndrome
29. genetic counseling

Cross-Check

After you have written the definitions of the key terms in this chapter, you should complete the crossword puzzle to ensure that you can reverse the process—recognize the term, given the definition.

ACROSS

2. Cluster of distinct characteristics that tend to occur together in a given disorder.
7. A person who has a gene in his or her genotype that is not evident in his or her phenotype.
8. The sum total of all the genes a person inherits.
10. The single cell formed from the fusing of an ovum and a sperm.
13. The stronger gene in an interacting pair of genes.
14. All of the genetic traits that are expressed in a person.
16. Genes that are on the X chromosome.
17. The sequence of chemical bases held within DNA molecules that directs development.
18. One of 46 in each normal human cell.
19. A genetic disease that nearly always develops in people with a particular allele of a particular gene.
20. The genes that affect height, hair curliness, and skin color are of this type.

DOWN

1. A genetic disorder in which part of the X chromosome is attached to the rest of it by a very slim string of molecules.
3. Fraternal twins.
4. All the nongenetic factors that can affect development.
5. The growth process in which cells begin to specialize, taking different forms and dividing at different rates.
6. The basic unit of genetic instruction.
7. The genetic process that during the formation of gametes adds greatly to genetic diversity.
9. A spontaneous abortion.
11. The international project that aims to map the complete human genetic code.
12. Type of trait produced by the interaction of many genes (rather than by a single gene).
13. The most common extra-chromosome syndrome (also called trisomy-21).
15. The weaker gene in an interacting pair of genes.

ANSWERS

CHAPTER REVIEW

1. proteins; DNA; chromosome; genome
2. 46; 23; genes; protein; amino acids
3. adenine; guanine; cytosine; thymine; three; triplets
4. gametes; sperm; ova
5. zygote
6. 23; 23
7. genotype
8. alleles
9. 23rd; X; XX; X; Y; XY
10. sperm; XY; spontaneous abortion
11. been roughly equal; abort female fetuses
12. zygote; are
13. dizygotic; 50
14. 60; late 30s; early 20s
15. duplication; differentiate; on–off switching
16. phenotype
17. polygenic; multifactorial

18. additive; height; skin color (or hair curliness)

19. nonadditive; dominant–recessive; dominant; recessive;

20. incomplete dominance

21. X-linked; color blindness, many allergies, several diseases, and some learning disabilities; males

22. penetrate; temperature; stress

23. does; parental imprinting

24. chance

25. crossing-over; mutation; environmental

26. health

27. Human Genome Project; share

28. carrier

29. behavior genetics; psychological; personality; sociability, assertiveness, moodiness, and fearfulness; schizophrenia, depression, and attention-deficit/hyperactivity disorder; cognitive; memory for numbers, spatial perception, and fluency of expression

30. interaction; genes; environmental; do not always

31. Alzheimer's; amyloid B; 50; early-onset; genetic; late-onset; ApoE; hypertension, diabetes, and high cholesterol

32. depression, antisocial behavior, phobias, and compulsions, environmental

33. do; late winter; virus

34. is; is; a quick temper, a willingness to take risks, and a high level of anxiety

35. every

They provide insight into the complexities of genetic interactions, knowledge about their origins suggests how to limit their harmful consequences, and misinformation and prejudice compound the problems of people who are affected by such abnormalities.

36. gametes

37. maternal age; mosaic

38. spontaneously aborted; 200; syndrome

39. Down Syndrome; trisomy-21; faster; Alzheimer's disease; communication

Most people with Down syndrome have certain facial characteristics—a thick tongue, round face, slanted eyes—as well as distinctive hands, feet, and fingerprints. Many also have hearing problems, heart abnormalities, muscle weakness, and short stature. Almost all experience some mental slowness.

40. sex; Klinefelter syndrome; XXY

41. dominant; are not; more

42. Huntington's disease; Tourette syndrome

43. fragile X

44. recessive; multifactorial; cystic fibrosis, thalassemia, sickle-cell anemia

45. prenatal genetic counseling

46. Genetic counseling is recommended for (a) those who have a parent, sibling, or child with a serious genetic condition; (b) those who have a history of spontaneous abortions, stillbirths, or infertility; (c) couples who are from the same ethnic group or subgroup; and (d) women over age 35 and men age 40 or older.

47. avoid pregnancy, plan to adopt or use artificial insemination or in vitro fertilization; genetic engineering

PROGRESS TEST 1

Multiple-Choice Questions

1. **a.** is the answer. (p. 61)

   b. & c. The reproductive cells (sperm and ova), which are also called gametes, are individual entities.

   d. *Monozygote* refers to one member of a pair of identical twins.

2. **c.** is the answer. (p. 60)

   a. The zygote is the first cell of the developing person.

   b. Chromosomes are molecules of DNA that *carry* genes.

   d. DNA molecules contain genetic information.

3. **b.** is the answer. (p. 62)

4. **d.** is the answer. When the gametes are formed, one member of each chromosome pair splits off; because in females both are X chromosomes, each ovum must carry an X chromosome. (p. 62)

   a., b., & c. The zygote refers to the merged sperm and ovum that is the first new cell of the developing individual.

5. **b.** is the answer. *Mono* means "one." Thus, monozygotic twins develop from one zygote. (p. 64)

   a. & c. Dizygotic, or fraternal, twins develop from two (*di*) zygotes.

   d. A trizygotic birth would result in triplets (*tri*), rather than twins.

6. **d.** is the answer. (p. 73)

7. **a.** is the answer. (p. 77)

   c. & d. Most dominant disorders are neither seriously disabling nor sex-linked.

8. **c.** is the answer. (p. 65)

a., b., & d. *Polygenic* means "many genes"; *multifactorial* means "many factors," which are not limited to either genetic or environmental factors.

9. **b.** is the answer. (p. 60)

    a. Genotype is a person's genetic potential.

    c. A karyotype is a picture of a person's chromosomes.

    d. Phenotype is the actual expression of a genotype.

10. **d.** is the answer. (p. 68)

11. **d.** is the answer. (p. 77)

    a. & b. These chromosomal abnormalities affect females.

    c. There is no such abnormality.

12. **b.** is the answer. (p. 71)

    c. & d. The text does not equate polygenic complexity with either recessive or dominant genes.

13. **a.** is the answer. (p. 76)

14. **b.** is the answer. (p. 65)

15. **b.** is the answer. (p. 77)

    a. & c. These abnormalities involve the sex chromosomes, not genes.

    d. In order for an offspring to inherit a recessive condition, the parents need only be carriers of the recessive gene in their genotypes; they need not actually have the disease.

Matching Items

1. c (p. 61)	**5.** b (p. 64)	**9.** e (p. 70)
2. h (p. 59)	**6.** f (p. 64)	**10.** d (p. 61)
3. m (p. 61)	**7.** g (p. 65)	**11.** k (p. 62)
4. i (p. 65)	**8.** j (p. 80)	**12.** a (p. 62)
		13. l (p. 62)

PROGRESS TEST 2

Multiple-Choice Questions

1. **d.** is the answer. (p. 75)

2. **c.** is the answer. (pp. 71–72)

    a. In fact, it is more common than the early-onset form of the illness.

    d. The abnormal gene is found more often in European-Americans than in African-Americans.

3. **c.** is the answer. (p. 80)

    a. Physical appearance is usually normal in this syndrome.

b. Males are more frequently and more severely affected.

d. This is true of the *XXY* chromosomal abnormality, but not the fragile *X* syndrome.

4. **d.** is the answer. (p. 80)

5. **b.** is the answer. (p. 68)

    a. & c. These patterns are based on the interaction of both parents' genes.

    d. Molecular genetics is the study of the chemical codes that make up a particular molecule of DNA.

6. **c.** is the answer. (p. 64)

    a. This would result in monozygotic twins.

    b. Only one sperm can fertilize an ovum.

    d. A single egg fertilized by one sperm would produce a single offspring or monozygotic twins.

7. **c.** is the answer. (p. 59)

    a. Zygotes are fertilized ova.

    b. Genes are the smaller units of heredity that are organized into sequences on chromosomes.

    d. Ova are female reproductive cells.

8. **a.** is the answer. (p. 65)

9. **c.** is the answer. The ovum will contain an *X* chromosome; with the sperm's *Y* chromosome, it will produce the male *XY* pattern. (p. 62)

    a. Only if the ovum is fertilized by an *X* chromosome from the sperm will a female develop.

    b. Cell division will occur regardless of whether the sperm contributes an *X* or a *Y* chromosome.

    d. Spontaneous abortions are likely to occur when there are chromosomal or genetic abnormalities; the situation described is perfectly normal.

10. **a.** is the answer. (p. 62)

    b. & d. These are true of all body cells *except* the gametes.

    c. Gametes have either *X* or *Y* chromosomes.

11. **d.** is the answer. (p. 65)

12. **a.** is the answer. Genotype refers to the sum total of all the genes a person inherits; phenotype refers to the actual expression of the individual's characteristics. (pp. 61, 65)

13. **c.** is the answer. (pp. 65–66)

14. **d.** is the answer. *X*-linked genes are located only on the *X* chromosome. Because males inherit only one *X* chromosome, they are more likely than

females to have these characteristics in their phenotype. (p. 66)

15. **c.** is the answer. (p. 83)

   a. Pre-implantation testing is conducted on zygotes grown in vitro.

   b. Ultrasound is used to detect visible signs of abnormality.

   d. Alpha-fetoprotein assay is used to detect the presences of AFP, an indicator of neural-tube defects.

True or False Items

1. T (p. 65)
2. F Chromosomal abnormalities may be environmentally caused, as with parents' exposure to excessive radiation . (p. 75)
3. T (p. 73)
4. T (p. 61)
5. F Most traits are polygenic. (p. 65)
6. T (p. 61)
7. T (p. 82)
8. F A trait from a recessive gene will be part of the phenotype only when the person has two recessive genes for that trait. (p. 80)
9. T (pp. 65)
10. T (p. 62)
11. F Most genes have several functions. (p. 65)
12. F These psychopathologies are partly genetic in origin. (p. 73)

THINKING CRITICALLY ABOUT CHAPTER 3

1. **d.** is the answer. (p. 77)
2. **c.** is the answer. (p. 71)

   a. Genetic engineering is the altering of an organism's genetic instructions by inserting additional genetic material.

   b. Molecular genetics, which was not discussed in this chapter, is the study of genes at the molecular, rather than behavioral, level.

   d. There is no such profession.
3. **c.** is the answer. This describes the fragile X syndrome. (p. 80)

   a. This phenomenon, which is called *crossing over*, merely contributes to genetic diversity.

   b. This is merely an example of a particular non-additive gene interaction pattern.

   d. For a recessive gene to be expressed, both parents must pass it on to the child.

4. **a.** is the answer. (p. 66)

   b. The male genotype is *XY*, not *XX*.

   c. & d. The mother contributes only an *X* chromosome.
5. **c.** is the answer. (p. 68)

   a., b., & d. It is unlikely that these factors account for height differences from one generation to the next.
6. **b.** is the answer. Since monozygotic twins are genetically identical, while dizygotic twins share only 50 percent of their genes, greater similarity of traits between monozygotic twins suggests that genes are an important influence. (p. 73)

   a. & c. Even though schizophrenia has a strong genetic component, it is not the case that if one twin has schizophrenia the other also automatically does. Therefore, the environment, too, is an important influence.

   d. This does not necessarily follow.
7. **a.** is the answer. (p. 75)

   b. Genotype is a person's genetic potential, established at conception.

   c. Polygenic inheritance refers to the influence of many genes on a particular trait.

   d. Incomplete dominance refers to the phenotype being influenced primarily, but not exclusively, by the dominant gene.
8. **d.** is the answer. (p. 80)
9. **c.** is the answer. Cystic fibrosis is a recessive gene disorder; therefore, in order for a child to inherit this disease, he or she must receive the recessive gene from both parents. (p. 78)
10. **b.** is the answer. (p. 71)
11. **c.** is the answer. (p. 73)
12. **c.** is the answer. (pp. 73–74)

   a. Some people's inherited biochemistry makes them highly susceptible to alcoholism.

   b. Despite a strong genetic influence on alcoholism, the environment also plays a critical role.

   d. Not only is this advice unreasonable, but it might increase the likelihood of chromosomal abnormalities in the parents' sperm and ova.
13. **d.** is the answer. (p. 76)
14. **d.** is the answer. (p. 65)

   a. & b. Genes are discrete units of a chromosome.

   c. Genotype refers to genetic potential.
15. **c.** is the answer. (p. 66)

   a. There is no such thing as a "polygenic gene." *Polygenic* means "many genes."

b. A recessive gene paired with a dominant gene will not be expressed in the phenotype.

d. *X*-linked genes may be dominant or recessive.

KEY TERMS

Writing Definitions

1. **DNA (deoxyribonucleic acid)** is the molecular basis of heredity. (p. 59)

2. **Chromosomes** are molecules of DNA that contain the genes organized in precise sequences. (p. 59)

3. A **genome** is the full set of chromosomes and genes that make up the genetic material of an organism. (p. 60)

4. **Genes** are segments of a chromosome, which is a DNA molecule; they are the basic units for the transmission of hereditary instructions. (p. 60)

5. **Gametes** are the human reproductive cells. (p. 61)

6. The **zygote** is the one-celled organism formed during conception by the union of sperm and ovum. (p. 61)

7. The total of all the genes a person inherits—his or her genetic potential—is called the **genotype.** (p. 61)

8. An **allele** is one of the normal versions of a gene that has several possible sequences of base pairs. (p. 62)

9. The **23rd pair** of chromosomes determines the individual's sex. (p. 62)

10. **XX** is the twenty-third chromosome pair that, in humans, determines that the developing fetus will be female. (p. 62)

11. **XY** is the twenty-third chromosome pair that, in humans, determines that the developing fetus will be male. (p. 62)

12. Also known as a miscarriage, a **spontaneous abortion** is the natural termination of a pregnancy before the fetus is fully developed. (p. 62)

13. **Monozygotic,** or identical, **twins** develop from one zygote that splits in two, producing two genetically identical zygotes. (p. 64)

    Memory aid: Mono means "one"; **monozygotic twins** develop from one fertilized ovum.

14. **Dizygotic,** or fraternal, **twins** develop from two separate ova fertilized by different sperm at roughly the same time, and therefore are no more genetically similar than ordinary siblings. (p. 64)

    Memory aid: A fraternity is a group of two (*di*) or more nonidentical individuals.

15. **On–off switching mechanisms** are genetic processes in which the proteins of certain genes switch various genes on or off in order to control their protein production. (p. 65)

16. The actual physical or behavioral expression of a genotype, the result of the interaction of the genes with each other and with the environment, is called the **phenotype.** (p. 65)

17. Most human traits are also **multifactorial** traits—that is, influenced by many factors, including genetic and environmental factors. (p. 65)

    Memory aid: The roots of the words polygenic and multifactorial give their meaning: *poly* means "many" and genic means "of the genes"; *multi* means "several" and factorial obviously refers to factors.

18. Most human traits, especially psychological traits, are **polygenic traits**; that is, they are affected by many genes. (p. 65)

19. When a trait is determined by **additive genes,** the phenotype reflects the sum of the contributions of all the genes involved. The genes affecting height, for example, interact in this fashion. (p. 65)

20. The **dominant–recessive** pattern is the interaction of a gene's alleles in such a way that one, the dominant gene, has a stronger influence than the other, recessive gene. (p. 66)

21. A **dominant gene** is the stronger, controlling member of an interacting pair of genes. (p. 66)

22. A **recessive gene** is the weaker member of an interacting pair of genes. (p. 66)

23. **X-linked** genes are genes that are located only on the X chromosome. Since males have only one X chromosome, they are more likely to have the characteristics determined by these genes in their phenotype than are females. (p. 66)

24. The **Human Genome Project** is an international effort to map the complete human genetic code. (p. 68)

25. A person who has a recessive gene that is not expressed in his or her genotype but that can be passed on to the person's offspring is called a **carrier** of that gene. (p. 70)

26. **Behavior genetics** is the study of the genetic origins of personality, psychological disorders, intellectual abilities, and other psychological characteristics. (p. 71)

27. **Mosaic** refers to the condition in which a person has a mixture of cells, some normal and some with too few or too many chromosomes. (p. 75)

28. The **fragile X syndrome** is a single-gene disorder in which part of the X chromosome is attached by such a thin string of molecules that it seems about to break off. Although the characteristics associated with this syndrome are quite varied, some mental deficiency is relatively common. (p. 75)

29. **Genetic counseling** involves a variety of tests through which couples can learn more about their genes, and can thus make informed decisions about their childbearing and child-rearing future. (p. 82)

Cross-Check

ACROSS

2. syndrome
7. carrier
8. genotype
10. zygote
13. dominant
14. phenotype
16. X-linked
17. genetic code
18. chromosome
19. Alzheimer's
20. additive

DOWN

1. fragile X
3. dizygotic
4. environment
5. differentiation
6. gene
7. crossing-over
9. miscarriage
11. Human Genome
12. polygenic
13. Down syndrome
15. recessive

Chapter Four

Prenatal Development and Birth

Chapter Overview

Prenatal development is complex and startlingly rapid—more rapid than any other period of the life span. During prenatal development, the individual changes from a one-celled zygote to a complex human baby. This development is outlined in Chapter 4, along with some of the problems that can occur—among them prenatal exposure to disease, drugs, and other hazards—and the factors that moderate the risks of teratogenic exposure.

For the developing person, birth marks the most radical transition of the entire life span. No longer sheltered from the outside world, the fetus becomes a separate human being who begins life almost completely dependent upon his or her caregivers. Chapter 4 also examines the birth process and its possible variations and problems.

The chapter concludes with a discussion of the significance of the parent–infant bond, including factors that affect its development.

NOTE: Answer guidelines for all Chapter 4 questions begin on page 64.

Guided Study

The text chapter should be studied one section at a time. Before you read, preview each section by skimming it, noting headings and boldface items. Then read the appropriate section objectives from the following outline. Keep these objectives in mind and, as you read the chapter section, search for the information that will enable you to meet each objective. Once you have finished a section, write out answers for its objectives.

From Zygote to Newborn (pp. 91–97)

1. Describe the significant developments of the germinal period.

2. Describe the significant developments of the embryonic period.

3. Describe the significant developments of the fetal period, noting the importance of the age of viability.

Risk Reduction (pp. 97–107)

4. Explain the main goal of teratology, and discuss several factors that determine whether a specific teratogen will be harmful.

5. (Table 4.4) Identify at least five teratogens, and describe their possible effects on the developing embryo or fetus.

6. (Changing Policy) Discuss AIDS and alcohol as teratogens, and describe the protective steps that may be taken to prevent their damaging effects.

7. Distinguish among low-birthweight (LBW), preterm, and small-for-gestational-age (SGA) infants, and identify the causes of low birthweight.

The Birth Process (pp. 107–116)

8. Describe the birth process.

9. Describe the test used to assess the neonate's condition at birth.

10. Explain the causes of cerebral palsy, and discuss the special needs of high-risk infants.

11. Discuss the importance of a strong parental alliance and parent–infant bonding to a healthy start for the baby.

Chapter Review

When you have finished reading the chapter, work through the material that follows to review it. Complete the sentences and answer the questions. As you proceed, evaluate your performance for each section by consulting the answers on page 64. Do not continue with the next section until you understand each answer. If you need to, review or reread the appropriate section in the textbook before continuing.

From Zygote to Newborn (pp. 91–97)

1. Prenatal development is divided into _____ main periods. The first two weeks of development are called the _____ period; from the _____ week through the _____ week is known as the _____ period; and from this point until birth is the _____ period. Some developmentalists prefer to divide pregnancy into 3-month periods called _____ .

2. At about the _____-celled stage, clusters of cells begin to take on distinct traits. The first clear sign of this process, called _____ , occurs about _____ week(s) after conception, when the multiplying cells separate into outer cells that will become the _____ and inner cells that will become the _____ .

3. The next significant event is the burrowing of the outer cells of the organism into the lining of the uterus, a process called _____ . This process _____ (is/is not) automatic.

4. At the beginning of the period of the embryo, a thin line down the middle of the developing individual forms a structure that will become the _____ _____ , which will develop into the _____ _____ _____ .

Briefly describe the major features of development during the second month.

5. Eight weeks after conception, the embryo weighs about _____ and is about _____ in length. The organism now becomes known as the _____ .

6. The genital organs are fully formed by week _____ . If the fetus has a(n) _____ chromosome, the SRY gene on this chromosome sends a signal that triggers development of the _____ (male/female) sex organs. Without that gene, no signal is sent and the fetus begins to develop _____ (male/female) sex organs.

7. By the end of the _____ month, the fetus is fully formed, weighs approximately _____ , and is about _____ long. These figures _____ (vary/do not vary) from fetus to fetus.

8. During the fourth, fifth, and sixth months the brain increases in size by a factor of _____ . This neurological maturation is essential to the regulation of such basic body functions as _____ and _____ . The brain develops new neurons in a process called _____ and new connections between them in a process called _____ . These developments occur during the _____ trimester.

9. By full term, brain growth is so extensive that the brain's advanced outer areas, called the _____ , must _____ _____ in order to fit into the skull.

10. The age at which a fetus has at least some chance of surviving outside the uterus is called the _____ _____ _____ , which occurs _____ weeks after conception.

11. At about _____ weeks after concep-
    tion, brain-wave patterns begin to resemble the
    _____ – _____
    cycles of a newborn.

12. A 28-week-old fetus typically weighs about
    _____ and has more than a
    _____ percent chance of survival.

13. Two crucial aspects of development in the last
    months of prenatal life are maturation of the
    _____ and _____
    systems.

14. Beginning at _____ (what week?),
    the fetus hears many sounds, as evidenced by
    increased fetal _____ and
    _____ _____ in
    response to loud noises.

15. (text and Table 4.3) The average newborn weighs
    _____ .

Risk Reduction (pp. 97–107)

16. The scientific study of birth defects is called
    _____ . Harmful agents that can
    cause birth defects, called _____ ,
    include _____
    _____ .

17. Substances that impair the child's action and
    intellect by harming the brain are called
    _____ _____ .
    Approximately _____ percent of all
    fetuses are born with major structural anomalies,
    and _____ percent with behavioral
    difficulties related to prenatal damage.

18. Teratology is a science of _____
    _____ , which attempts to evaluate
    the factors that can make prenatal harm more or
    less likely to occur.

19. Three crucial factors that determine whether a
    specific teratogen will cause harm, and of what
    nature, are the _____ of exposure,

the _____ of exposure, and the
developing organism's _____
_____ to damage from the
substance.

20. The time when a particular part of the body is
    most susceptible to teratogenic damage is called
    its _____ _____ . For
    physical structure and form, this is the entire
    period of the _____ . However, for
    _____ teratogens, the entire
    prenatal period is critical.

21. Some teratogens have a _____
    effect—that is, the substances are harmless until
    exposure reaches a certain frequency or amount.
    However, the _____ of some terato-
    gens when taken together may make them more
    harmful at lower dosage levels than when taken
    separately.

22. Genetic susceptibilities to the prenatal effects of
    alcohol and to certain birth disorders, such as
    cleft palate, may involve defective
    _____ .

23. When the mother-to-be's diet is deficient in
    _____ _____ ,
    neural-tube defects such as
    _____ _____
    or _____ may result.

24. Genetic vulnerability is also related to the sex of
    the developing organism. Generally,
    _____ (male/female) embryos and
    fetuses are more vulnerable to teratogens. This
    sex not only has a higher rate of teratogenic birth
    defects and later behavioral problems, but also a
    higher rate of _____
    _____ , and older members of this
    sex have more _____
    _____ .

25. (Changing Policy) It was once believed that a pregnant woman's _____ prevented all harmful substances from reaching the fetus. This belief was proven wrong when an epidemic of _____ led to an increase in babies who were born _____ , and an increase in newborns with deformed _____ was traced to maternal use of the drug _____ .

26. (Changing Policy) The most devastating viral teratogen is the _____ _____ _____ , which gradually overwhelms the body's _____ _____ and leads to _____ . Babies who are infected with this virus usually die by age _____ .

27. (Changing Policy) Pregnant women who are HIV-positive can reduce the risk of transmitting the virus to their newborns by giving birth by _____ _____ , by not _____-_____ , and by taking _____ _____ .

State three reasons why almost a million HIV-positive children continue to be born each year.

28. (Changing Policy) The most common teratogen in developed nations is _____ . High doses of this teratogen cause _____ _____ _____ , and less intense doses cause _____ _____ _____ . The damage is increased when alcohol is combined with other _____ _____ .

29. Newborns who weigh less than _____ are classified as _____-_____ babies. Below 3 pounds, they are called _____-_____-_____ babies; at less than 2 pounds they are _____-_____-_____ babies. Worldwide, rates of this condition _____ (vary/do not vary) from nation to nation.

30. Babies who are born 3 or more weeks early are called _____ .

31. Infants who weigh substantially less than they should, given how much time has passed since conception, are called _____ _____ _____ .

32. About 25 percent of all low-birthweight (LBW) births in the United States are linked to maternal use of _____ .

33. Two other common reasons for low birthweight are maternal _____ and _____ .

The Birth Process (pp. 107–116)

34. At about the 266th day, the fetal brain signals the release of certain _____ into the mother's bloodstream, which trigger her _____ _____ to contract and relax. The normal birth process begins when these contractions become regular. The average length of labor is _____ hours for first births and _____ hours for subsequent births.

35. The newborn is usually rated on the _____ _____ , which assigns a score of 0, 1, or 2 to each of the following five characteristics: _____ _____ . A score below _____ indicates that the newborn is in critical condition and requires

immediate attention; if the score is

_____ or better, all is well. This rat-

ing is made twice, at _____

minute(s) after birth and again at

_____ minutes.

36. The birth experience is influenced by several

factors, including _____

_____ .

37. In about 22 percent of U.S. births, a surgical

procedure called a _____

_____ is performed.

38. An increasing number of hospital deliveries occur

in the _____ _____ .

An even more family-oriented environment is the

_____ _____ . In addi-

tion, many North American mothers today use a

professional birth coach, or _____ , to

assist them.

39. The disorder _____

_____ , which affects motor centers

in the brain, often results from

_____ vulnerability, worsened by

exposure to _____ and episodes of

_____ , a temporary lack of

_____ during birth.

40. Another complication is an infection called

_____ _____

_____ , which is often fatal to

newborns if not quickly treated with

_____ .

41. Because they are often confined to intensive-care

nurseries or hooked up to medical machinery,

low-birthweight infants may be deprived of nor-

mal kinds of stimulation such as

_____ .

42. Providing extra soothing stimulation to vulnera-

ble infants in the hospital _____

(does/does not) aid weight gain and

_____ (does/does not) increase

overall alertness. One example of this is

_____ _____ , in

which mothers of low-birthweight infants spend

extra time holding their infants.

43. Among the minor developmental problems that

accompany preterm birth are being late to

_____ .

High-risk infants are often more

_____ , less _____ ,

and slower to _____ .

44. The deficits related to low birthweight usually

_____ (can/cannot) be

overcome.

The Beginning of Bonding (pp. 128–130)

45. The rate of LBW births among women born in

Mexico and now living in the United states is

_____ (higher/lower) than those of

other Americans. This difference has been attrib-

uted to _____ , or the strong

_____ _____ that such

women experience. Especially important is the

role played by a supportive _____ ,

who can help _____

_____ .

46. A crucial factor in the birth experience is the for-

mation of a strong _____

_____ between the prospective

parents.

47. Some new mothers experience a profound feeling

of sadness called _____

_____ .

48. The term used to describe the close relationship

that begins within the first hours after birth is the

_____–_____

_____ .

Progress Test 1

Multiple-Choice Questions

Circle your answers to the following questions and check them with the answers on page 64. If your answer is incorrect, read the explanation for why it is incorrect and then consult the appropriate pages of the text (in parentheses following the correct answer).

1. The third through the eighth week after conception is called the:
   a. embryonic period.
   b. ovum period.
   c. fetal period.
   d. germinal period.

2. The neural tube develops into the:
   a. respiratory system.
   b. umbilical cord.
   c. brain and spinal column.
   d. circulatory system.

3. To say that a teratogen has a "threshold effect" means that it is:
   a. virtually harmless until exposure reaches a certain level.
   b. harmful only to low-birthweight infants.
   c. harmful to certain developing organs during periods when these organs are developing most rapidly.
   d. harmful only if the pregnant woman's weight does not increase by a certain minimum amount during her pregnancy.

4. By the eighth week after conception, the embryo has almost all the basic organs except the:
   a. skeleton.   c. sex organs.
   b. elbows and knees.   d. fingers and toes.

5. The most critical factor in attaining the age of viability is development of the:
   a. placenta.   c. brain.
   b. eyes.   d. skeleton.

6. An important nutrient that many women do not get in adequate amounts from the typical diet is:
   a. vitamin A.   c. guanine.
   b. zinc.   d. folic acid.

7. An embryo begins to develop male sex organs if _____ , and female sex organs if _____ .
   a. genes on the Y chromosome send a signal; no signal is sent from an X chromosome
   b. genes on the Y chromosome send a signal; genes on the X chromosome send a signal
   c. genes on the X chromosome send a signal; no signal is sent from an X chromosome
   d. genes on the X chromosome send a signal; genes on the Y chromosome send a signal

8. A teratogen:
   a. cannot cross the placenta during the period of the embryo.
   b. is usually inherited from the mother.
   c. can be counteracted by good nutrition most of the time.
   d. may be a virus, a drug, a chemical, radiation, or environmental pollutants.

9. (Changing Policy) Among the characteristics of babies born with fetal alcohol syndrome are:
   a. slowed physical growth and behavior problems.
   b. addiction to alcohol and methadone.
   c. deformed arms and legs.
   d. blindness.

10. The birth process begins:
    a. when the fetus moves into the right position.
    b. when the uterus begins to contract at regular intervals to push the fetus out.
    c. about eight hours (in the case of firstborns) after the uterus begins to contract at regular intervals.
    d. when the baby's head appears at the opening of the vagina.

11. The Apgar scale is administered:
    a. only if the newborn is in obvious distress.
    b. once, just after birth.
    c. twice, one minute and five minutes after birth.
    d. repeatedly during the newborn's first hours.

12. Most newborns weigh about:
    a. 5 pounds.   c. $7^1/_2$ pounds.
    b. 6 pounds.   d. $8^1/_2$ pounds.

13. Low-birthweight babies born near the due date but weighing substantially less than they should:
    a. are classified as preterm.
    b. are called small for gestational age.
    c. usually have no sex organs.
    d. show many signs of immaturity.

14. Approximately one out of every four low-birth-weight births in the United States is caused by maternal use of:

    a. alcohol.

    b. tobacco.

    c. crack cocaine.

    d. household chemicals.

Matching Items

Match each definition or description with its corresponding term.

Terms

    _____   **1.** embryonic period

    _____   **2.** fetal period

    _____   **3.** placenta

    _____   **4.** preterm

    _____   **5.** teratogens

    _____   **6.** anoxia

    _____   **7.** HIV

    _____   **8.** critical period

    _____   **9.** neural tube

    _____   **10.** fetal alcohol syndrome

    _____   **11.** germinal period

15. The idea of a parent–infant bond in humans arose from:

    a. observations in the delivery room.

    b. data on adopted infants.

    c. animal studies.

    d. studies of disturbed mother–infant pairs.

Definitions or Descriptions

    a. term for the period during which a developing baby's body parts are most susceptible to damage

    b. external agents and conditions that can damage the developing organism

    c. the age when viability is attained

    d. the precursor of the central nervous system

    e. lack of oxygen, which, if prolonged during the birth process, may lead to brain damage.

    f. characterized by abnormal facial characteristics, slowed growth, behavior problems, and mental retardation

    g. a virus that gradually overwhelms the body's immune responses

    h. the life-giving organ that nourishes the embryo and fetus

    i. when implantation occurs

    j. the prenatal period when all major body structures begin to form

    k. a baby born 3 or more weeks early

Progress Test 2

Progress Test 2 should be completed during a final chapter review. Answer the following questions after you thoroughly understand the correct answers for the Chapter Review and Progress Test 1.

Multiple-Choice Questions

  1. Which of the following causes of infant mortality in the United States has been increasing in recent years?

    a. congenital abnormalities

    b. respiratory distress

    c. low birthweight

    d. all of the above

  2. In order, the correct sequence of prenatal stages of development is:

    a. embryo; germinal; fetus

    b. germinal; fetus; embryo

    c. germinal; embryo; fetus

    d. ovum; fetus; embryo

  3. Monika is preparing for the birth of her first child. If all proceeds normally, she can expect that her labor will last about:

    a. three hours.   **c.** ten hours.

    b. eight hours.   **d.** twelve hours.

4. (Table 4.4) Tetracycline and retinoic acid:
   a. can be harmful to the human fetus.
   b. have been proven safe for pregnant women after the embryonic period.
   c. will prevent spontaneous abortions.
   d. are safe when used before the fetal period.

5. (Table 4.4) The teratogen that, if not prevented by immunization, could cause deafness, blindness, and brain damage in the fetus is:
   a. rubella (German measles).
   b. anoxia.
   c. acquired immune deficiency syndrome (AIDS).
   d. neural-tube defect.

6. Kangaroo care refers to:
   a. the rigid attachment formed between mothers and offspring in the animal kingdom
   b. the fragmented care that the children of single parents often receive.
   c. a program of increased involvement by mothers of low-birthweight infants.
   d. none of the above.

7. Among the characteristics rated on the Apgar scale are:
   a. shape of the newborn's head and nose.
   b. presence of body hair.
   c. interactive behaviors.
   d. muscle tone and color.

8. A newborn is classified as low birthweight if he or she weighs less than:
   a. 7 pounds.
   b. 6 pounds.
   c. 5½ pounds.
   d. 4 pounds.

9. The most critical problem for preterm babies is:
   a. the immaturity of the sex organs—for example, undescended testicles.
   b. spitting up or hiccupping.
   c. infection from intravenous feeding.
   d. breathing difficulties.

10. (Changing Policy) The most common teratogen in developed nations is:
    a. nicotine.
    b. alcohol.
    c. pesticide exposure.
    d. caffeine.

11. Neurogenesis refers to the process by which:
    a. the fetal brain develops new neurons.
    b. new connections between neurons develop.
    c. the neural tube forms during the middle trimester.
    d. the cortex folds into layers in order to fit into the skull.

12. Which Apgar score indicates that a newborn is in normal health?
    a. 4   c. 6
    b. 5   d. 7

13. Synaptogenesis refers to the process by which:
    a. the fetal brain develops new neurons.
    b. new connections between neurons develop.
    c. the neural tube forms during the middle trimester.
    d. the cortex folds into layers in order to fit into the skull.

14. When there is a strong parental alliance:
    a. mother and father cooperate because of their mutual commitment to their children.
    b. the parents agree to support each other in their shared parental roles.
    c. children are likely to thrive.
    d. all of the above are true.

15. The critical period for preventing physical defects appears to be the:
    a. zygote period.
    b. embryonic period.
    c. fetal period.
    d. entire pregnancy.

True or False Items

Write T (*true*) or F (*false*) on the line in front of each statement.

_____ 1. Newborns can recognize some of what they heard while in the womb.

_____ 2. Eight weeks after conception, the embryo has formed almost all the basic organs.

_____ 3. Only 1 percent of births in the United States take place in the home.

_____ 4. In general, behavioral teratogens have the greatest effect during the embryonic period.

_____ 5. The effects of cigarette smoking during pregnancy remain highly controversial.

_____ 6. The Apgar scale is used to measure vital signs such as heart rate, breathing, and reflexes.

_____   7. Newborns usually cry on their own, moments after birth.

_____   8. Research has shown that immediate mother–infant contact at birth is necessary for the normal emotional development of the child.

_____   9. Low birthweight is often correlated with maternal malnutrition.

_____   10. Cesarean sections are rarely performed in the United States today because of the resulting danger to the fetus.

Thinking Critically About Chapter 4

Answer these questions the day before an exam as a final check on your understanding of the chapter's terms and concepts.

1. (Table 4.4 and Changing Policy) Babies born to mothers who are powerfully addicted to a psychoactive drug are *most* likely to suffer from:
   a. structural problems.
   b. behavioral problems.
   c. both a. and b.
   d. neither a. nor b.

2. I am about 1 inch long and 1 gram in weight. I have all of the basic organs (except sex organs) and features of a human being. What am I?
   a. a zygote   c. a fetus
   b. an embryo   d. ovum

3. Karen and Brad report to their neighbors that, 5 weeks after conception, a sonogram of their child-to-be revealed female sex organs. The neighbors are skeptical of their statement because:
   a. sonograms are never administered before the ninth week.
   b. sonograms only reveal the presence or absence of male sex organs.
   c. the fetus does not begin to develop female sex organs until about the eighth week.
   d. it is impossible to determine that a woman is pregnant until six weeks after conception.

4. Five-year-old Benjamin can't sit quietly and concentrate on a task for more than a minute at a time. Dr. Simmons, who is a teratologist, suspects that Benjamin may have been exposed to _____ during prenatal development.
   a. human immunodeficiency virus
   b. a behavioral teratogen
   c. rubella
   d. lead

5. Sylvia and Stan, who are of British descent, are hoping to have a child. Doctor Caruthers asks for a complete nutritional history and is particularly concerned when she discovers that Sylvia may have a deficiency of folic acid in her diet. Doctor Caruthers is probably worried about the risk of _____ in the couple's offspring.
   a. FAS   c. neural-tube defects
   b. brain damage   d. FAE

6. Three-year-old Kenny was born underweight and premature. Today, he is small for his age. His doctor suspects that:
   a. Kenny is a victim of fetal alcohol syndrome.
   b. Kenny suffers from fetal alcohol effects.
   c. Kenny's mother smoked heavily during her pregnancy.
   d. Kenny's mother used cocaine during her pregnancy.

7. Which of the following is an example of an interaction effect?
   a. Some teratogens are virtually harmless until exposure reaches a certain level.
   b. Maternal use of alcohol and tobacco together does more harm to the developing fetus than either teratogen would do alone.
   c. Some teratogens cause damage only on specific days during prenatal development.
   d. All of the above are examples of interaction effects.

8. Fetal alcohol syndrome is common in newborns whose mothers were heavy drinkers during pregnancy, whereas newborns whose mothers were moderate drinkers may suffer fetal alcohol effects. This finding shows that to assess and understand risk we must know:
   a. the kind of alcoholic beverage (for example, beer, wine, or whiskey).
   b. the level of exposure to the teratogen.
   c. whether the substance really is teratogenic.
   d. the timing of exposure to the teratogen.

9. Your sister and brother-in-law, who are about to adopt a 1-year-old, are worried that the child will never bond with them. What advice should you offer?
   a. Tell them that, unfortunately, this is true; they would be better off waiting for a younger child who has not yet bonded.
   b. Tell them that, although the first year is a biologically determined critical period for attachment, there is a fifty-fifty chance that the child will bond with them.

c. Tell them that bonding is a long-term process between parent and child that is determined by the nature of interaction throughout infancy, childhood, and beyond.

d. Tell them that if the child is female, there is a good chance that she will bond with them, even at this late stage.

10. Which of the following newborns would be most likely to have problems in body structure and functioning?

a. Anton, whose Apgar score is 6
b. Debora, whose Apgar score is 7
c. Sheila, whose Apgar score is 3
d. Simon, whose Apgar score is 5

11. At birth, Clarence was classified as small for gestational age. It is likely that Clarence:

a. was born in a rural hospital.
b. suffered several months of prenatal malnutrition.
c. was born in a large city hospital.
d. comes from a family with a history of such births.

12. Of the following, who is *most* likely to give birth to a low-birthweight child?

a. 21-year-old Janice, who was herself a low-birthweight baby.
b. 25-year-old May Ling, who gained 25 pounds during her pregnancy.
c. 16-year-old Donna, who diets frequently despite being underweight.
d. 30-year-old Maria, who has already given birth to 4 children.

13. An infant born 266 days after conception, weighing 4 pounds, would be designated a _____ infant.

a. preterm
b. low-birthweight
c. small-for-gestational-age
d. b. & c.

14. An infant who was born at 35 weeks, weighing 6 pounds, would be called a _____ infant.

a. preterm
b. low-birthweight
c. small-for-gestational-age
d. premature

15. The five characteristics evaluated by the Apgar scale are:

a. heart rate, length, weight, muscle tone, and color.
b. orientation, muscle tone, reflexes, interaction, and responses to stress.
c. reflexes, breathing, muscle tone, heart rate, and color.
d. pupillary response, heart rate, reflex irritability, alertness, and breathing.

Key Terms

Using your own words, write a brief definition or explanation of each of the following terms on a separate piece of paper.

1. germinal period
2. embryonic period
3. fetal period
4. implantation
5. embryo
6. fetus
7. age of viability
8. teratogens
9. behavioral teratogens
10. risk analysis
11. critical period
12. threshold effect
13. interaction effect
14. human immunodeficiency virus (HIV)
15. fetal alcohol syndrome (FAS)
16. low birthweight (LBW)
17. preterm birth
18. small for gestational age (SGA)
19. Apgar scale
20. cesarean section
21. cerebral palsy
22. anoxia
23. kangaroo care
24. parental alliance
25. postpartum depression
26. parent–infant bond

ANSWERS
CHAPTER REVIEW

1. three; germinal; third; eighth; embryonic; fetal; trimesters

2. eight; differentiation; one; placenta; embryo

3. implantation; is not

4. neural tube; central nervous system

First, the upper arms, then the forearms, palms, and webbed fingers appear. Legs, feet, and webbed toes follow. At eight weeks, the embryo's head is more rounded, and the facial features are fully formed. The fingers and toes are separate.

5. $1/30$ ounce (1 gram); 1 inch (2.5 centimeters); fetus

6. 12; Y; male; female

7. third; 3 ounces (87 grams); 3 inches (7.5 centimeters); vary

8. six; breathing; sucking; neurogenesis; synaptogenesis; middle

9. cortex; fold into layers

10. age of viability; 22

11. 28; sleep–wake

12. 3 pounds (1,300 grams); 95

13. respiratory; cardiovascular

14. 28 weeks; heartbeat; body movements

15. $7^1/2$ pounds (3,400 grams)

16. teratology; teratogens; viruses, drugs, chemicals, pollutants, stressors, and malnutrition

17. behavioral teratogens; 3; 10 to 20

18. risk analysis

19. timing; amount; genetic vulnerability

20. critical period; embryo; behavioral

21. threshold; interaction

22. enzymes

23. folic acid; spina bifida; anencephaly

24. male; spontaneous abortions; learning disabilities

25. placenta; rubella; deaf; limbs; thalidomide

26. human immunodeficiency virus (HIV); immune system; AIDS; 5

27. cesarean section; breast-feeding; antiretroviral drugs

One reason is that the women and their medical providers may not be aware that they have the virus. Another reason is that the drugs for treating HIV infections are very expensive. A third reason is that the woman's sociocultural context prevents her from admitting she has the disease.

28. alcohol; fetal alcohol syndrome; fetal alcohol effects; psychoactive drugs

29. 2,500 grams ($5^1/2$ pounds); low-birthweight; very-low-birthweight; extremely-low-birthweight; vary

30. preterm

31. small for gestational age

32. tobacco

33. illness; malnutrition

34. hormones; uterine muscles; eight ; three

35. Apgar scale; heart rate, breathing, muscle tone, color, and reflexes; 4; 7; one; five

36. the parents' preparation for birth, the physical and emotional support provided by birth attendants, the position and size of the fetus, the practices of the mother's culture

37. cesarean section

38. labor room; birthing center; doula

39. cerebral palsy; genetic; teratogens; anoxia; oxygen

40. Group B streptococcus (GBS); antibiotics

41. rocking (or regular handling)

42. does; does; kangaroo care

43. smile, hold a bottle, and to communicate; distractible; obedient; talk

44. can

45. lower; familia; family support; father; reduce maternal stress and help ensure the future mother is healthy, well-nourished, and drug free

46. parental alliance

47. postpartum depression

48. parent–infant bond

PROGRESS TEST 1

Multiple-Choice Questions

1. **a.** is the answer. (p. 91)

   b. This term, which refers to the germinal period, is not used in the text.

c. The fetal period is from the ninth week until birth.

d. The germinal period covers the first two weeks.

2. **c.** is the answer. (p. 93)

3. **a.** is the answer. (p. 98)

    b., c., & d. Although low birthweight (b), critical periods of organ development (c), and maternal malnutrition (d) are all hazardous to the developing person during prenatal development, none is an example of a threshold effect.

4. **c.** is the answer. The sex organs do not begin to take shape until the fetal period. (p. 94)

5. **c.** is the answer. (p. 95)

6. **d.** is the answer. (p. 100)

7. **a.** is the answer. (p. 94)

8. **d.** is the answer. (p. 97)

    a. In general, teratogens can cross the placenta at any time.

    b. Teratogens are agents in the environment, not heritable genes (although *susceptibility* to individual teratogens has a genetic component).

    c. Although nutrition is an important factor in healthy prenatal development, the text does not suggest that nutrition alone can usually counteract the harmful effects of teratogens.

9. **a.** is the answer. (p. 103)

10. **b.** is the answer. (p. 107)

11. **c.** is the answer. (p. 108)

12. **c.** is the answer. (p. 96)

13. **b.** is the answer. (p. 106)

14. **b.** is the answer. (p. 106)

15. **c.** is the answer. (p. 115)

Matching Items

1. j (p. 91)	**5.** b (p. 97)	**9.** d (p. 93)
2. c (p. 91)	**6.** e (p. 111)	**10.** f (p. 103)
3. h (p. 92)	**7.** g (p. 102)	**11.** i (p. 91)
4. k (p. 106)	**8.** a (p. 98)	

PROGRESS TEST 2

Multiple-Choice Questions

1. **c.** is the answer. (p. 104)

a. & b. These causes of infant mortality have taken a marked downturn over the past 15 years.

2. **c.** is the answer. (p. 91)

3. **b.** is the answer. (p. 107)

    a. The average length of labor for subsequent births is three hours.

4. **a.** is the answer. (p. 101)

5. **a.** is the answer. (p. 100)

6. **c.** is the answer. (p. 112)

7. **d.** is the answer. (p. 108)

8. **c.** is the answer. (p. 104)

9. **d.** is the answer. (p. 96)

10. **b.** is the answer. (p. 103)

11. **a.** is the answer. (p. 94)

12. **d.** is the answer. (p. 108)

13. **b.** is the answer. (p. 94)

14. **d.** is the answer. (p. 114)

15. **b.** is the answer. (p. 98)

True or False Items

1. T (p. 97)

2. T (p. 94)

3. T (p. 110)

4. F   Behavioral teratogens can affect the fetus at any time during the prenatal period. (p. 98)

5. F   There is no controversy about the damaging effects of smoking during pregnancy. (p. 106)

6. T (p. 108)

7. T (p. 107)

8. F   Though highly desirable, mother–infant contact at birth is not necessary for the child's normal development or for a good parent–child relationship. Many opportunities for bonding occur throughout childhood. (p. 115)

9. T (p. 107)

10. F   About 22 percent of births in the United States are now cesarean. (p. 109)

THINKING CRITICALLY ABOUT CHAPTER 4

1. **c.** is the answer. (pp. 101, 103–104)

2. **b.** is the answer. (p. 93)

   a. The zygote is the fertilized ovum.

   c. The developing organism is designated a fetus starting at the ninth week.

   d. The ovum is the female egg that is fertilized by the sperm.

3. **c.** is the answer. (p. 94)

4. **b.** is the answer. (p. 97)

   a. This is the virus that causes AIDS.

   c. Rubella may cause blindness, deafness, and brain damage.

   d. The text does not discuss the effects of exposure to lead.

5. **c.** is the answer. (p. 100)

   a. FAS is caused in infants by the mother-to-be drinking high doses of alcohol during pregnancy.

   b. Brain damage is caused by the use of social drugs during pregnancy.

   d. FAE is caused in infants by less intense drinking by the mother-to-be.

6. **c.** is the answer. (p. 106)

7. **b.** is the answer. (p. 98)

8. **b.** is the answer. (p. 98)

9. **c.** is the answer. (p. 115)

   a. & b. Bonding in humans is not a biologically determined event limited to a critical period, as it is in many other animal species.

   d. There is no evidence of any gender differences in the formation of the parent–infant bond.

10. **c.** is the answer. If a neonate's Apgar score is below 4, the infant is in critical condition and needs immediate medical attention. (p. 108)

11. **b.** is the answer. (p. 107)

    a., c., & d. Prenatal malnutrition is the most common cause of a small-for-dates baby.

12. **c.** is the answer. Donna has two risk factors that are related to having an LBW baby, including being a teenager and underweight. (p. 107)

    a. & d. Neither of these has been linked to increased risk of having LBW babies.

    b. In fact, based only on her age and normal weight gain, May Ling's baby would *not* be expected to be LBW.

13. **d.** is the answer. (pp. 104, 106)

    a. & c. At 266 days, this infant is full term.

14. **a.** is the answer. (p. 106)

    b. Low birthweight is defined as weighing less than $5\frac{1}{2}$ pounds.

    c. Although an infant can be both preterm and small for gestational age, this baby's weight is within the normal range of healthy babies.

    d. This term is no longer used to describe early births.

15. **c.** is the answer. (p. 108)

KEY TERMS

1. The first two weeks of development after conception, characterized by rapid cell division and the beginning of cell differentiation, are called the **germinal period.** (p. 91)

   Memory aid: A *germ cell* is one from which a new organism can develop. The *germinal* **period** is the first stage in the development of the new organism.

2. The **embryonic period** is approximately the third through the eighth week of prenatal development, when the rudimentary forms of all body structures develop. (p. 91)

3. From the ninth week after conception until birth is the **fetal period,** when the organs grow in size and mature in functioning. (p. 91)

4. **Implantation** is the process by which the outer cells of the organism burrow into the uterine lining and rupture its blood vessels to obtain nourishment and trigger the bodily changes that signify the beginning of pregnancy. (p. 92)

5. **Embryo** is the name given to the developing organism from the third through the eighth week. (p. 93)

6. **Fetus** is the name for the developing organism from eight weeks after conception until birth. (p. 94)

7. About 22 weeks after conception, the fetus attains the **age of viability,** at which point it has at least some slight chance of survival outside the uterus if specialized medical care is available. (p. 95)

8. **Teratogens** are external agents and conditions, such as viruses, drugs, chemicals, stressors, and malnutrition, that can impair prenatal development and lead to birth defects and even death. (p. 97)

9. **Behavioral teratogens** tend to damage the brain, impairing the future child's intellectual and emotional functioning. (p. 97)

10. The science of teratology is a science of **risk analysis**, meaning that it attempts to evaluate what factors make prenatal harm more or less likely to occur. (p. 97)

11. In prenatal development, a **critical period** is the time when a particular organ or other body part is most susceptible to teratogenic damage. (p. 98)

12. A **threshold effect** is the harmful effect of a substance that occurs when exposure to it reaches a certain level. (p. 98)

13. An **interaction effect** occurs when one teratogen intensifies the harmful effects of another. (p. 98)

14. **Human immunodeficiency virus (HIV)** is the most devastating viral teratogen. HIV gradually overwhelms the body's immune system, making the individual vulnerable to the host of diseases and infections that constitute AIDS. (p. 102)

15. Prenatal alcohol exposure may cause **fetal alcohol syndrome (FAS)**, which includes abnormal facial characteristics, slow physical growth, behavior problems, and mental retardation. Likely victims are those who are genetically vulnerable and whose mothers drink three or more drinks daily during pregnancy. (p. 103)

16. A birthweight of less than 2,500 grams (5½ pounds) is called **low birthweight (LBW).** Low-birthweight infants are at risk for many immediate and long-term problems. (p. 104)

17. When an infant is born three or more weeks before the due date, it is said to be a **preterm birth.** (p. 106)

18. Infants who weigh substantially less than they should, given how much time has passed since conception, are called **small for gestational age (SGA),** or small-for-dates. (p. 106)

19. Newborns are rated at one and then at five minutes after birth according to the **Apgar scale.** This scale assigns a score of 0, 1, or 2 to each of five characteristics: heart rate, breathing, muscle tone, color, and reflexes. A score of 7 or better indicates that all is well. (p. 108)

20. In a **cesarean section**, the fetus is removed from the mother surgically. (p. 109)

21. **Cerebral palsy** is a muscular control disorder caused by damage to the brain's motor centers during or before birth. (p. 111)

22. **Anoxia** is a temporary lack of fetal oxygen during the birth process that, if prolonged, can cause brain damage or even death. (p. 111)

23. **Kangaroo care** occurs when the mother of a low-birthweight infant spends at least one hour a day holding her infant between her breasts. (p. 112)

24. **Parental alliance** refers to the cooperation and mutual support between mother and father because of their commitment to their children. (p. 114)

25. **Postpartum depression** is a profound feeling of sadness, inadequacy, and hopelessness sometimes experienced by new mothers. (p. 115)

26. The term **parent–infant bond** describes the strong feelings of attachment between parent and child in the early moments of their relationship together. (p. 115)

Chapter Five

Chapter Overview

Chapter 5 is the first of a three-chapter unit that describes the developing person from birth to age 2 in terms of biosocial, cognitive, and psychosocial development. Physical development is the first to be examined.

The chapter begins with observations on the overall growth and health of infants, including information on infant sleep patterns. Following is a discussion of brain growth and development and the importance of experience in brain development. The chapter then turns to a discussion of sensory, perceptual, and motor abilities and the ages at which the average infant acquires them. Preventive medicine, the importance of immunizations during the first two years, and the possible causes of sudden infant death syndrome (SIDS) are discussed next. The final section explains the importance of nutrition during the first two years and the consequences of severe malnutrition and undernutrition.

NOTE: Answer guidelines for all Chapter 5 questions begin on page 79.

Guided Study

The text chapter should be studied one section at a time. Before you read, preview each section by skimming it, noting headings and boldface items. Then read the appropriate section objectives from the following outline. Keep these objectives in mind and, as you read the chapter section, search for the information that will enable you to meet each objective. Once you have finished a section, write out answers for its objectives.

Body Changes (pp. 121–125)

1. Describe the size and proportions of an infant's body, including how they change during the first two years.

2. Describe the infant's changing sleep patterns.

Early Brain Development (pp. 125–130)

3. Describe the ways in which the brain changes or matures during infancy.

4. (text and Thinking Like a Scientist) Discuss the role of experience in brain development.

The Senses and Motor Skills (pp. 130–136)

5. Distinguish among sensation, perception, and cognition.

6. Describe the development of an infant's sensory and perceptual abilities in terms of the senses of hearing, vision, taste, touch, and smell.

7. Describe the basic reflexes of the newborn, and distinguish between gross motor skills and fine motor skills.

8. Describe the basic pattern of motor-skill development, and discuss variations in the timing of motor-skill acquisition.

Public Health Measures (pp. 136–143)

9. Identify key factors in the worldwide decline in childhood mortality over the past century, and discuss the importance of childhood immunizations.

10. Identify risk factors for sudden infant death syndrome, and discuss possible explanations for ethnic group variations in the incidence of this situation.

11. Describe the nutritional needs of infants.

12. Discuss the causes and effects of malnutrition, and explain ways of preventing it.

Chapter Review

When you have finished reading the chapter, work through the material that follows to review it. Complete the sentences and answer the questions. As you proceed, evaluate your performance for each section by consulting the answers on page 79. Do not continue with the next section until you understand each answer. If you need to, review or reread the appropriate section in the textbook before continuing.

Body Changes (pp. 121–125)

1. The average North American newborn measures _____ and weighs a little more than _____ .

2. The phenomenon in which inadequate nutrition causes the body to stop growing but not the brain is called _____-_____ .

3 A standard, or average, of physical development that is derived for a specific group or population is a _____ .

4. By age 2, the typical child weighs about
_____ and measures
_____ . The typical
2-year-old is almost _____ (what
proportion?) of his or her adult weight and
_____ (what proportion?) of his or
her adult height.

5. A _____ is a point on a ranking
scale of _____ (what number?) to
_____ (what number?).

6. Throughout childhood, regular and ample
_____ correlates with maturation of
the _____ , _____ ,
_____ regulation, and
_____ adjustment in school and
within the family. Approximately _____
percent of 1-year-olds sleep through the night.

7. Over the first months of life, the relative amount
of time spent in the different _____
of sleep changes. The stage of sleep characterized
by flickering eyes behind closed lids and
_____ is called _____
_____ . During this stage of sleep
brain waves are fairly
_____ (slow/rapid). This stage of
sleep _____ (increases/decreases)
over the first months, as does the dozing stage
called _____ _____ .
Slow-wave sleep, also called _____
_____ , increases markedly at about
_____ months of age.

Early Brain Development (pp. 125–130)

8. At birth, the brain has attained about
_____ percent of its adult weight;
by age 2 the brain is about _____
percent of its adult weight. In comparison, body
weight at age 2 is about _____ per-
cent of what it will be in adulthood.

9. The brain's communication system consists primarily of nerve cells called _____
connected by intricate networks of nerve fibers,
called _____ and
_____ . About _____

percent of these cells are in the brain's outer layer
called the _____ .

10. Each neuron has many _____ but
only a single _____ .

11. Neurons communicate with one another at intersections called _____ . After
travelling down the length of the
_____ , electrical impulses excite
chemicals called _____ that carry
information across the _____
_____ to the _____ of
a "receiving" neuron. Most of the nerve cells
_____ (are/are not) present at birth,
whereas the fiber networks _____
(are/are not) rudimentary.

12. During the first months of life, brain development is most noticeable in the _____ .

13. From birth until age 2, the density of dendrites in
the cortex _____ (increases/
decreases) by a factor of _____ . The
phenomenal increase in neural connections over
the first two years has been called

_____ _____ .

Following this growth process, neurons in some
areas of the brain wither in the process called
_____ because _____
does not activate those brain areas.

14. Brain functions that require basic common experiences in order to develop are called
_____-_____ brain
functions; those that depend on particular, and
variable, experiences in order to develop are
called _____-_____
brain functions.

15. (Thinking Like a Scientist) Neuroscientists once
believed that brains were entirely formed by
_____ and _____
_____ ; today, most believe in
_____ , which is the concept that
personality, intellect, habits, and emotions change
throughout life for _____ (one/a
combination of) reason(s). William Greenough
discovered that the brains of rats who were raised

in stimulating environments were better developed, with more _____ branching, than the brains of rats raised in barren environments. Orphaned Romanian children who were isolated and deprived of stimulation showed signs of _____ damage. Placed in healthier environments, these children _____ (improved/did not improve); years later, persistent deficits in these children _____ (were/were not) found.

The Senses and Motor Skills (pp. 130–136)

16. The process by which the visual, auditory, and other sensory systems detect stimuli is called _____ ; _____ occurs when the brain tries to make sense out of a stimulus so that the individual becomes aware of it. At birth, both of these processes _____ (are/are not) apparent. In the process called _____ , a person thinks about what he or she has perceived. This process _____ (can/cannot) occur without either sensation or perception.

17. Generally speaking, newborns' hearing _____ (is/is not) very acute at birth. Newborns _____ (can/cannot) perceive differences in voices, rhythms, and language.

18. The least mature of the senses at birth is _____ . Newborns' visual focusing is best for objects between _____ and _____ inches away.

19. Increasing maturation of the visual cortex accounts for improvements in other visual abilities, such as the infant's ability to _____ on an object and _____ to its critical areas. The ability to use both eyes in a coordinated manner to focus on one object, which is called _____ _____ , develops at about _____ of age.

20. Taste, smell, and touch _____ (function/do not function) at birth. The ability to be comforted by the human _____ is a skill tested in the _____ Neonatal Behavioral Assessment Scale.

21. The infant's early sensory abilities seem organized for two goals: _____ _____ and _____ .

22. The most visible and dramatic body changes of infancy involve _____ _____ .

23. An involuntary physical response to a stimulus is called a _____ .

24. The involuntary response that causes the newborn to take the first breath even before the umbilical cord is cut, is called the _____ _____ . Because breathing is irregular during the first few days, other reflexive behaviors, such as _____ , _____ , and _____ , are common.

25. Shivering, crying, and tucking the legs close to the body are examples of reflexes that help to maintain _____ _____ .

26. A third set of reflexes fosters _____ . One of these is the tendency of the newborn to suck anything that touches the lips; this is the _____ reflex. Another is the tendency of newborns to turn their heads and start to suck when something brushes against their cheek; this is the _____ reflex.

27. Large movements such as running and climbing are called _____ _____ skills.

28. Most infants are able to crawl on all fours (sometimes called creeping) between _____ and _____ months of age.

List the major hallmarks in children's mastery of walking.

29. Abilities that require more precise, small movements, such as picking up a coin, are called _____ _____ skills. By _____ of age, most babies can reach

for, grab, and hold onto almost any object of the right size. By _____ months, most infants can transfer objects from one hand to the other.

30. Although the _____ in which motor skills are mastered is the same in all healthy infants, the _____ of acquisition of skills varies greatly.

31. The average ages, or _____ , at which most infants master major motor skills are based on a large sample of infants drawn from _____ (a single/many) ethnic group(s).

32. Motor skill norms vary from one _____ group to another.

33. Motor skill acquisition in identical twins _____ (is/is not) more similar than in fraternal twins, suggesting that genes _____ (do/do not) play an important role. Another influential factor is the

_____ .

Public Health Measures (pp. 136–143)

34. In 1900, about 1 in _____ (how many?) children died before age 5. This childhood death rate _____ (varied from one nation to another/was the same throughout the world). Today, in the healthiest nations such as _____ , _____ , and _____ , about 1 in _____ (how many?) children who survive birth die before age 6.

35. A key factor in reducing the childhood death rate was the development of _____—a process that stimulates the body's _____ system to defend against contagious diseases.

36. Another reason for lower infant mortality worldwide is a decrease in _____

_____ _____

_____ , in which seemingly healthy infants die unexpectedly in their

_____ .

37. A key factor in SIDS is _____ background. In ethnically diverse nations, babies of _____ descent are more likely, and babies of _____ descent are less likely, to succumb to SIDS than are babies of _____ descent. In ethnic groups with a low incidence of SIDS, babies are put to sleep _____ (in what position?).

Identify several other practices that may explain why certain ethnic groups have a low incidence of SIDS.

38. The ideal infant food is _____ , beginning with the thick, high-calorie fluid called _____ . The only situations in which formula may be healthier for the infant than breast milk are when _____

_____ .

State several advantages of breast milk over cow's milk for the developing infant.

39. The most serious nutritional problem of infancy is _____-_____

_____ .

40. Chronically malnourished infants suffer in three ways: Their _____ may not develop normally; they may have no _____ _____ to protect them against disease, and they may develop the diseases _____ or _____ .

41. Severe protein-calorie deficiency in early infancy causes _____ . In toddlers, protein-calorie deficiency is more likely to cause the disease called _____ , which involves swelling or bloating of the face, legs, and abdomen.

Progress Test 1

Multiple-Choice Questions

Circle your answers to the following questions and check them with the answers on page 80. If your answer is incorrect, read the explanation for why it is incorrect and then consult the appropriate pages of the text (in parentheses following the correct answer).

1. The average North American newborn:
   a. weighs approximately 6 pounds.
   b. weighs approximately 7 pounds.
   c. is "overweight" because of the diet of the mother.
   d. weighs 10 percent less than what is desirable.

2. Compared to the first year, growth during the second year:
   a. proceeds at a slower rate.
   b. continues at about the same rate.
   c. includes more insulating fat.
   d. includes more bone and muscle.

3. The major motor skill most likely to be mastered by an infant before the age of 6 months is:
   a. rolling over.
   b. sitting without support.
   c. turning the head in search of a nipple.
   d. grabbing an object with thumb and forefinger.

4. Norms suggest that the earliest walkers in the world are infants from:
   a. Western Europe.   c. Uganda.
   b. the United States.   d. Denver.

5. Head-sparing is the phenomenon in which:
   a. the brain continues to grow even though the body stops growing as a result of malnutrition.
   b. the infant's body grows more rapidly during the second year.
   c. axons develop more rapidly than dendrites.
   d. dendrites develop more rapidly than axons.

6. Dreaming is characteristic of:
   a. slow-wave sleep.
   b. transitional sleep.
   c. REM sleep.
   d. quiet sleep.

7. For a pediatrician, the most important factor in assessing a child's healthy growth is:
   a. height in inches.
   b. weight in pounds.
   c. body fat percentage.
   d. the percentile rank of a child's height or weight.

8. Brain functions that depend on babies' having things to see and hear, and people to feed and carry them, are called:
   a. experience-dependent.
   b. experience-expectant.
   c. pruning functions.
   d. transient exuberance.

9. Compared with formula-fed infants, breast-fed infants tend to have:
   a. greater weight gain.
   b. fewer allergies and digestive upsets.
   c. less frequent feedings during the first few months.
   d. more social approval.

10. Marasmus and kwashiorkor are caused by:
    a. bloating.
    b. protein-calorie deficiency.
    c. living in a developing country.
    d. poor family food habits.

11. The infant's first motor skills are:
    a. fine motor skills.   c. reflexes.
    b. gross motor skills.   d. unpredictable.

12. Which of the following is said to have had the greatest impact on human mortality reduction and population growth?
    a. improvements in infant nutrition
    b. oral rehydration therapy
    c. medical advances in newborn care
    d. childhood immunization

13. Which of the following is true of motor-skill development in healthy infants?

    a. It follows the same basic sequence the world over.
    b. It occurs at different rates from individual to individual.
    c. It follows norms that vary from one ethnic group to another.
    d. All of the above are true.

14. All the nerve cells a human brain will ever need are present:

    a. at conception.
    b. about 1 month following conception.
    c. at birth.
    d. at age 5 or 6.

15. Chronically malnourished children suffer in which of the following ways?

    a. They have no body reserves to protect them.
    b. Their brains may not develop normally.
    c. They may die from marasmus.
    d. All of the above are true of malnourished children.

Matching Items

Match each definition or description with its corresponding term.

Terms

_____ 1. neurons
_____ 2. dendrites
_____ 3. kwashiorkor
_____ 4. marasmus
_____ 5. gross motor skill
_____ 6. fine motor skill
_____ 7. reflex
_____ 8. protein-calorie malnutrition
_____ 9. transient exuberance
_____ 10. neurotransmitter

Definitions or Descriptions

a. protein deficiency during the first year in which growth stops and body tissues waste away
b. picking up an object
c. the most common serious nutrition problem of infancy
d. protein deficiency during toddlerhood
e. communication networks among nerve cells
f. running or climbing
g. an involuntary response
h. the phenomenal increase in neural connections over the first 2 years
i. nerve cells
j. a brain chemical that carries information across the synaptic gap between two neurons

Progress Test 2

Progress Test 2 should be completed during a final chapter review. Answer the following questions after you thoroughly understand the correct answers for the Chapter Review and Progress Test 1.

Multiple-Choice Questions

1. Dendrite is to axon as neural _____ is to neural _____ .
   a. input; output
   c. myelin; synapse
   b. output; input
   d. synapse; myelin

2. A reflex is best defined as a(n):
   a. fine motor skill.
   b. motor ability mastered at a specific age.
   c. involuntary physical response to a given stimulus.
   d. gross motor skill.

3. A norm is:
   a. a standard, or average, that is derived for a specific group or population.
   b. a point on a ranking scale of 1 to 99.
   c. a milestone of development that all children reach at the same age.
   d. all of the above.

4. Most babies can reach for, grasp, and hold onto an object by about the _____ month.
   a. second
   c. ninth
   b. sixth
   d. fourteenth

5. Regarding the brain's cortex, which of the following is *not* true?
   a. The cortex houses about 70 percent of the brain's neurons.
   b. The cortex is the brain's outer layer.
   c. The cortex is the location of most thinking, feeling, and sensing.
   d. Only primates have a cortex.

6. During the first weeks of life, babies seem to focus reasonably well on:
   a. little in their environment.
   b. objects at a distance of 4 to 30 inches.
   c. objects at a distance of 1 to 3 inches.
   d. objects several feet away.

7. Which sleep stage increases markedly at about 3 or 4 months?
   a. REM
   b. transitional
   c. fast-wave
   d. slow-wave

8. An advantage of breast milk over formula is that it:
   a. is always sterile and at body temperature.
   b. contains traces of medications ingested by the mother.
   c. can be given without involving the father.
   d. contains more protein and vitamin D than does formula.

9. Synapses are:
   a. nerve fibers that receive electrical impulses from other neurons.
   b. nerve fibers that transmit electrical impulses to other neurons.
   c. intersections between the axon of one neuron and the dendrites of other neurons.
   d. chemical signals that transmit information from one neuron to another.

10. Transient exuberance and pruning demonstrate that:
    a. the pace of acquisition of motor skills varies markedly from child to child.
    b. Newborns sleep more than older children because their immature nervous systems cannot handle the higher, waking level of sensory stimulation.
    c. The specifics of brain structure and growth depend partly on the infant's experience.
    d. Good nutrition is essential to healthy biosocial development.

11. Climbing is to using a crayon as _____ is to _____ .
    a. fine motor skill; gross motor skill
    b. gross motor skill; fine motor skill
    c. reflex; fine motor skill
    d. reflex; gross motor skill

12. Some infant reflexes are critical for survival. Hiccups and sneezes help the infant maintain the _____ and leg tucking maintains _____ .
    a. feeding; oxygen supply
    b. feeding; a constant body temperature
    c. oxygen supply; feeding
    d. oxygen supply; a constant body temperature

13. (Thinking Like a Scientist) Compared to the brains of laboratory rats that were raised in barren cages, those of rats raised in stimulating, toy-filled cages:
    a. were better developed and had more dendritic branching.
    b. had fewer synaptic connections.
    c. showed less transient exuberance.
    d. displayed all of the above characteristics.

14. In determining a healthy child's growth, a pediatrician focuses on
    a. the child's past growth.
    b. the growth of the child's brothers and sisters.
    c. the stature of other children.
    d. all of the above.

15. Infant sensory and perceptual abilities appear to be especially organized for:
    a. obtaining adequate nutrition and comfort.
    b. comfort and social interaction.
    c. looking.
    d. touching and smelling.

True or False Items

Write T (*true*) or F (*false*) on the line in front of each statement.

_____ 1. Imaging studies have identified a specific area of the brain that specializes in recognizing faces.

_____ 2. Putting babies to sleep on their stomachs increases the risk of SIDS.

_____ 3. Reflexive hiccups, sneezes, and thrashing are signs that the infant's reflexes are not functioning properly.

_____ 4. Infants of all ethnic backgrounds develop the same motor skills at approximately the same age.

_____ 5. The typical 2-year-old is almost one-fifth its adult weight and one-half its adult height.

_____ 6. Vision is better developed than hearing in most newborns.

_____ 7. Today, most infants in developed nations are breast-fed.

_____ 8. Certain basic sensory experiences seem necessary to ensure full brain development in the human infant.

_____ 9. Dendrite growth is the major reason that brain weight increases so dramatically in the first two years.

_____ 10. The only motor skills apparent at birth are reflexes.

Thinking Critically About Chapter 5

Answer these questions the day before an exam as a final check on your understanding of the chapter's terms and concepts.

1. Newborns cry, shiver, and tuck their legs close to their bodies. This set of reflexes helps them:
   a. ensure proper muscle tone.
   b. learn how to signal distress.
   c. maintain constant body temperature.
   d. communicate serious hunger pangs.

2. I am a chemical that carries information between nerve cells in the brain. What am I?
   a. a synapse.
   b. a dendrite
   c. a neurotransmitter
   d. a neuron

3. (Thinking Like a Scientist) Research studies of the more than 100,000 Romanian children orphaned and severely deprived in infancy reported all of the following *except*:
   a. all of the children were overburdened with stress.
   b. after adoption, the children gained weight quickly.
   c. during early childhood, many still showed signs of emotional damage.
   d. most of the children placed in healthy adoptive homes eventually recovered.

4. The Farbers, who are first-time parents, are wondering whether they should be concerned because their 12-month-old daughter, who weighs 22 pounds and measures 30 inches, is not growing quite as fast as she did during her first year. You should tell them that:
   a. any slowdown in growth during the second year is a cause for immediate concern.
   b. their daughter's weight and height are well below average for her age.
   c. growth patterns for a first child are often erratic.
   d. physical growth is somewhat slower in the second year.

5. Regarding body size, a child generally is said to be average if he or she is:
   a. at the 25th percentile.
   b. between the 25th and 40th percentiles.
   c. at the 50th percentile.
   d. at the 75th percentile or greater.

6. Concluding her presentation on sleep, Lakshmi notes each of the following *except*:
   a. dreaming occurs during REM sleep.
   b. quiet sleep increases markedly at about 3 or 4 months.
   c. the dreaming brain is characterized by slow brain waves.
   d. regular and ample sleep is an important factor in a child's emotional regulation.

7. Michael can focus on objects between 4 and 30 inches from him and is able to discriminate subtle sound differences. Michael most likely:
   a. is a preterm infant.
   b. has brain damage in the visual processing areas of the cortex.
   c. is a newborn.
   d. is slow-to-mature.

8. A baby turns her head and starts to suck when her receiving blanket is brushed against her cheek. The baby is displaying the:
   a. sucking reflex.   c. thrashing reflex.
   b. rooting reflex.   d. tucking reflex.

9. The pediatrician notices that Freddy seems indifferent to everything. Knowing that Freddy was abused as an infant, she suspects that:
   a. because of pruning, his brain's neuronal reactions has lost the capacity to react normally to stress.
   b. Freddy has a learning disability.
   c. Freddy has developed a personality disorder.
   d. as a result of the early abuse, Freddy is now mentally retarded.

10. Sensation is to perception as _____ is to _____ .
    a. hearing; seeing
    b. detecting a stimulus; making sense of a stimulus
    c. making sense of a stimulus; detecting a stimulus
    d. tasting; smelling

11. Sharetta's pediatrician informs her parents that Sharetta's 1-year-old brain is exhibiting transient exuberance. In response to this news, Sharetta's parents:
    a. smile, because they know their daughter's brain is developing new neural connections.
    b. worry, because this may indicate increased vulnerability to a later learning disability.
    c. know that this process, in which axons become coated, is normal.
    d. are alarmed, since this news indicates that the frontal area of Sharetta's cortex is immature.

12. (Thinking Like a Scientist) To say that most developmentalists are multidisciplinary and believe in plasticity, means they believe personality, intellect, and emotions:
    a. change throughout life as a result of biological maturation.
    b. change throughout life for a combination of reasons.

    c. remain stable throughout life.
    d. More strongly reveal the impact of genes as people get older.

13. Like all newborns, Serena is able to:
    a. differentiate one sound from another.
    b. see objects more than 30 inches from her face quite clearly.
    c. use her mouth to recognize objects by taste and touch.
    d. do all of the above.

14. Three-week-old Nathan should have the *least* difficulty focusing on the sight of:
    a. stuffed animals on a bookshelf across the room from his crib.
    b. his mother's face as she holds him in her arms.
    c. the checkerboard pattern in the wallpaper covering the ceiling of his room.
    d. the family dog as it dashes into the nursery.

15. Trying to impress his professor, Erik notes that the reason humans have a critical period for learning certain skills might be due to the fact that the brain cannot form new synapses after age 13. Should the professor be impressed with Erik's knowledge of biosocial development?
    a. Yes, although each neuron may have already formed as many as 15,000 connections with other neurons.
    b. Yes, although the branching of dendrites and axons does continue through young adulthood.
    c. No. Although Erik is correct about neural development, the brain attains adult size by about age 7.
    d. No. Synapses form throughout life.

Key Terms

Using your own words, write a brief definition or explanation of each of the following terms on a separate piece of paper.

1. head-sparing
2. norm
3. percentile
4. REM sleep
5. neuron
6. cortex
7. axon
8. dendrite
9. synapse

10. transient exuberance

11. experience-expectant

12. experience-dependent

13. sensation

14. perception

15. binocular vision

16. reflex

17. gross motor skills

18. fine motor skills

19. immunization

20. sudden infant death syndrome (SIDS)

21. protein-calorie malnutrition

22. marasmus

23. kwashiorkor

ANSWERS

CHAPTER REVIEW

1. 20 inches (51 centimeters); 7 pounds (3.2 kilograms)

2. head-sparing

3. norm

4. 30 pounds (13 kilograms); between 32 and 36 inches inches (81–91 centimeters); one-fifth; half

5. percentile; 1; 99

6. sleep; brain; learning, emotional, psychological; 80

7. stages; dreaming; REM sleep; rapid; decreases; transitional sleep; quiet sleep; 3 or 4

8. 25; 75; 20

9. neurons; axons; dendrites; 70; cortex

10. dendrites; axon

11. synapses; axon; neurotransmitters; synaptic gap; dendrite; are; are

12. cortex

13. increases; five; transient exuberance; pruning; experience

14. experience-expectant; experience-dependent

15. genes; prenatal influences; plasticity; a combination; dendritic; emotional; improved; were

16. sensation; perception; are; cognition; can

17. is; can

18. vision; 4; 30

19. focus; scan; binocular vision; 14 weeks

20. function; touch; Brazelton

21. social interaction; comfort

22. motor skills

23. reflex

24. breathing reflex; hiccups, sneezes, thrashing

25. body temperature

26. feeding; sucking; rooting

27. gross motor

28. 8; 10

On average, a child can walk while holding a hand at 9 months, can stand alone momentarily at 10 months, and can walk well unassisted at 12 months.

29. fine motor; 6 months; 6 months

30. sequence; age

31. norms; many

32. ethnic

33. is; do; pattern of infant care

34. 3; was the same throughout the world; Japan; the Netherlands; France; 200

35. immunization; immune

36. sudden infant death syndrome (SIDS); sleep

37. ethnic; African; Asian; European; on their backs

Chinese parents tend to their babies periodically as they sleep, which makes them less likely to fall into a deep, nonbreathing sleep. Bangladeshi infants are usually surrounded by many family members in a rich sensory environment, making them less likely to sleep deeply for very long.

38. breast milk; colostrum; the mother is HIV-positive, using toxic drugs, or has some other serious condition that makes her milk unhealthy

Breast milk is always sterile and at body temperature; it contains more iron, vitamin C, and vitamin A; it contains antibodies that provide the infant some protection against disease; it is more digestible than any formula; and it decreases the frequency of almost every infant illness and allergy.

39. protein-calorie malnutrition

40. brains; body reserves; marasmus; kwashiorkor

41. marasmus; kwashiorkor

PROGRESS TEST 1

Multiple-Choice Questions

1. **b.** is the answer. (p. 121)
2. **a.** is the answer. (p. 122)
3. **a.** is the answer. (p. 134)

   b. The age norm for this skill is 7.8 months.

   c. This is a reflex, not an acquired motor skill.

   d. This skill is acquired between 9 and 14 months.
4. **c.** is the answer. (p. 135)
5. **a.** is the answer. (p. 122)
6. **c.** is the answer. (p. 123)
7. **d.** is the answer. (p. 122)
8. **b.** is the answer. (p. 128)

   a. Experience-dependent functions depend on particular, and variable, experiences in order to develop.

   c. Pruning refers to the process by which some neurons wither because experience does not activate them.

   d. This refers to the great increase in the number of neurons, dendrites, and synapses that occurs in an infant's brain over the first two years of life.
9. **b.** is the answer. This is because breast milk is more digestible than cow's milk or formula. (p. 141)

   a., c., & d. Breast- and bottle-fed babies do not differ in these attributes.
10. **b.** is the answer. (pp. 141–142)
11. **c.** is the answer. (p. 132)

    a. & b. These motor skills do not emerge until somewhat later; reflexes are present at birth.

    d. On the contrary, reflexes are quite predictable.
12. **d.** is the answer. (p. 137)
13. **d.** is the answer. (p. 134)
14. **c.** is the answer. (p. 127)
15. **d.** is the answer. (p. 142)

Matching Items

1. i (p. 123)
2. e (p. 126)
3. d (p. 143)
4. a (p. 142)
5. f (p. 133)
6. b (p. 134)
7. g (p. 132)
8. c (p. 142)
9. h (p. 127)
10. j (p. 127)

PROGRESS TEST 2

Multiple-Choice Questions

1. **a.** is the answer. (p. 126)
2. **c.** is the answer. (p. 132)

a., b., & d. Each of these refers to voluntary responses that are acquired only after a certain amount of practice; reflexes are involuntary responses that are present at birth and require no practice.

3. **a.** is the answer. (p. 122)

   b. This defines percentile.
4. **b.** is the answer. (p. 134)
5. **d.** is the answer. All mammals have a cortex. (p. 125)
6. **b.** is the answer. (p. 131)

   a. Although focusing ability seems to be limited to a certain range, babies do focus on many objects in this range.

   c. This is not within the range at which babies *can* focus.

   d. Babies have very poor distance vision.
7. **d.** is the answer. (p. 123)
8. **a.** is the answer. (p. 141)

   b. If anything, this is a potential *disadvantage* of breast milk over formula.

   c. So can formula.

   d. Breast milk contains more iron, vitamin C, and vitamin A than cow's milk; it does not contain more protein and vitamin D, however.
9. **c.** is the answer. (p. 126)

   a. These are dendrites.

   b. These are axons.

   d. These are neurotransmitters.
10. **c.** is the answer. (p. 127)
11. **b.** is the answer. (pp. 133, 134)

    c. & d. Reflexes are involuntary responses; climbing and using a crayon are both voluntary responses.
12. **d.** is the answer. (p. 132)
13. **a.** is the answer. (p. 129)
14. **d.** is the answer. (p. 122)
15. **b.** is the answer. (p. 132)

True or False Items

1. T (p. 126)
2. T (p. 140)
3. F Hiccups, sneezes, and thrashing are common during the first few days, and they are entirely normal reflexes. (p. 132)
4. F Although all healthy infants develop the same motor skills in the same sequence, the age at which these skills are acquired can vary greatly from infant to infant. (p. 134)

5. T (p. 122)

6. F   Vision is relatively poorly developed at birth, whereas hearing is well developed. (p. 131)

7. F   Only half of all babies are breast-fed, even for a month. (p. 142)

8. T (p. 128)

9. T (p. 127)

10. T (p. 132)

THINKING CRITICALLY ABOUT CHAPTER 5

1. c. is the answer. (p. 132)

2. c. is the answer. (p. 127)

a. A synapse is the intersection between the axon of one neuron and the dendrites of other neurons.

b. Dendrites are nerve fibers that receive electrical impulses transmitted from other neurons.

d. Neurons are nerve cells.

3. d. is the answer. Although all of the children improved, persistent deficits remained in many of them. (p. 129)

4. d. is the answer. (p. 122)

a. & b. Although slowdowns in growth during infancy are often a cause for concern, their daughter's weight and height are typical of 1-year-old babies.

c. Growth patterns are no more erratic for first children than for later children.

5. c. is the answer. (p. 122)

6. c. is the answer. The dreaming brain is characterized by rapid brain waves. (p. 123)

7. c. is the answer. (p. 131)

8. b. is the answer. (p. 132)

a. This is the reflexive sucking of newborns in response to anything that touches their *lips*.

c. This is the response that infants make when their feet are stroked.

d. This is part of the reflex when the infant is cold.

9. a. is the answer. (pp. 127–128)

b., c., & d. Freddy's indifference and history point to an abnormal capacity to react to stress, not a learning disability, personality disorder, or mental retardation.

10. b. is the answer. (p. 130)

a. & d. Sensation and perception operate in all of these sensory modalities.

11. a. is the answer. Transient exuberance results in a proliferation of neural connections during infancy, some of which will disappear because they are not used; that is, they are not needed to process information. (p. 127)

b. & d. Transient exuberance is a normal developmental process that occurs in all healthy infants.

c. This describes the coating of axons with myelin, which speeds neural transmission.

12. b. is the answer. (p. 129)

13. a. is the answer. (p. 131)

b. Objects at this distance are out of focus for newborns.

c. This ability does not emerge until about one month of age.

14. b. is the answer. This is true because, at birth, focusing is best for objects between 4 and 30 inches away. (p. 131)

a., c., & d. Newborns have very poor distance vision; each of these situations involves a distance greater than the optimal focus range.

15. d. is the answer. (pp. 127)

KEY TERMS

1. Head-sparing is the phenomenon by which the brain continues to grow even though the body stops growing in a malnourished child. (p. 122)

2. A **norm** is an average, or standard, developed for a specific population. (p. 122)

3. A **percentile** is any point on a ranking scale of 1 to 99; percentiles are often used to compare a child's development to group norms. (p. 122)

4. REM sleep, or rapid eye movement sleep, is a stage of sleep characterized by flickering eyes behind closed eyelids, dreaming, and rapid brain waves. (p. 123)

5. A **neuron,** or nerve cell, is the main component of the central nervous system. (p. 125)

6. The **cortex** is the outer layer of the brain that is involved in most thinking, feeling, and sensing. (p. 125)

Memory aid: Cortex in Latin means "bark." As bark covers a tree, the cortex is the "bark of the brain."

7. An **axon** is the nerve fiber that sends electrical impulses from one neuron to the dendrites of other neurons. (p. 126)

8. A **dendrite** is a nerve fiber that receives the electrical impulses transmitted from other neurons via their axons. (p. 126)

9. A **synapse** is the point at which the axon of a sending neuron meets the dendrites of a receiving neuron. (p. 126)

10. **Transient exuberance** is the dramatic increase in the number of dendrites that occurs in an infant's brain over the first two years of life. (p. 127)

11. **Experience-expectant** brain functions are those that require basic common experiences (such as having things to see and hear) in order to develop. (p. 128)

12. **Experience-dependent** brain functions are those that depend on particular, and variable, experiences (such as experiencing language) in order to develop. (p. 128)

13. **Sensation** is the process by which a sensory system detects a particular stimulus. (p. 130)

14. **Perception** is the process by which the brain tries to make sense of a stimulus such that the individual becomes aware of it. (p. 130)

15. **Binocular vision** is the ability to use both eyes in a coordinated fashion to focus on a single object. (p. 131)

    Memory aid: Bi- indicates "two"; ocular means something pertaining to the eye. Binocular vision is vision for "two eyes."

16. A **reflex** is an involuntary physical response to a specific stimulus. (p. 132)

17. **Gross motor skills** are physical abilities that demand large body movements, such as climbing, jumping, or running. (p. 133)

18. **Fine motor skills** are physical abilities that require precise, small movements, such as picking up a coin. (p. 134)

19. **Immunization** is the process through which the body's immune system is stimulated (as by a vaccine) to defend against attack by a particular contagious disease. (p. 137)

20. **Sudden infant death syndrome (SIDS)** is a set of circumstances in which a seemingly healthy infant dies unexpectedly in his or her sleep. (p. 139)

21 **Protein-calorie malnutrition** results when a person does not consume enough food to thrive. (p. 142)

22. **Marasmus** is a disease caused by severe protein-calorie deficiency during the first year of life. Growth stops, body tissues waste away, and the infant dies. (p. 142)

23. **Kwashiorkor** is a disease caused by protein-calorie deficiency during toddlerhood. The child's face, legs, and abdomen swell with water, sometimes making the child appear well fed; the child becomes more vulnerable to other diseases. Other body parts are degraded, including the hair, which becomes thin, brittle, and colorless. (p. 143)

Chapter Six

Chapter Overview

Chapter 6 explores the ways in which the infant comes to learn about, think about, and adapt to his or her surroundings. It focuses on the various ways in which infant intelligence is revealed: through sensorimotor intelligence, perception, memory, and language development. The chapter begins with a description of Jean Piaget's theory of sensorimotor intelligence, which maintains that infants think exclusively with their senses and motor skills. Piaget's six stages of sensorimotor intelligence are examined.

The second section discusses the information-processing theory, which compares cognition to the ways in which computers analyze data. Eleanor and James Gibson's influential theory is also described. Central to this theory is the idea that infants gain cognitive understanding of their world through the affordances of objects, that is, the activities they can do with them.

The text also discusses the key cognitive elements needed by the infant to structure the environment discovered through his or her newfound perceptual abilities. Using the habituation procedure, researchers have found that the speed with which infants recognize familiarity and seek something novel is related to later cognitive skill. It points out the importance of memory to cognitive development.

Finally, the chapter turns to the most remarkable cognitive achievement of the first two years, the acquisition of language. Beginning with a description of the infant's first attempts at language, the chapter follows the sequence of events that leads to the child's ability to utter two-word sentences. The chapter concludes with an examination of three classic theories of language acquisition and a fourth, hybrid theory that combines aspects of each.

NOTE: Answer guidelines for all Chapter 6 questions begin on page 93.

Guided Study

The text chapter should be studied one section at a time. Before you read, preview each section by skimming it, noting headings and boldface items. Then read the appropriate section objectives from the following outline. Keep these objectives in mind and, as you read the chapter section, search for the information that will enable you to meet each objective. Once you have finished a section, write out answers for its objectives.

Sensorimotor Intelligence (pp. 147–153)

1. Identify and describe Piaget's first two stages of sensorimotor intelligence.

2. Identify and describe stages 3 and 4 of Piaget's theory of sensorimotor intelligence.

3. (Thinking Like A Scientist) Explain what object permanence is, how it is tested in infancy, and what these tests reveal.

4. Identify and describe stages 5 and 6 of Piaget's theory of sensorimotor intelligence.

5. Describe some major advances in the scientific investigation of infant cognition.

Information Processing (pp. 154–158)

6. Explain the information-processing theory of cognition.

7. Discuss the Gibsons' contextual view of perception, focusing on the idea of affordances and giving examples of the affordances perceived by infants.

8. Discuss research findings on infant memory.

Language: What Develops in Two Years? (pp. 158–167)

9. Identify the main features of baby talk, and explain its importance.

10. Describe language development during infancy, and identify its major hallmarks.

11. Differentiate three theories of language learning, and explain current views on language learning.

Chapter Review

When you have finished reading the chapter, work through the material that follows to review it. Complete the sentences and answer the questions. As you proceed, evaluate your performance for each section by consulting the answers beginning on page 93. Do not continue with the next section until you understand each answer. If you need to, review or reread the appropriate section in the textbook before continuing.

Sensorimotor Intelligence (pp. 147–153)

1. Cognition involves _____

_____ .

The first major theorist to realize that infants are active learners was _____ .

2. At every stage, people _____ their thinking to their _____ . This is revealed in two ways: by _____ of new information into previously developed

mental categories, or _____ ; and by _____ of previous mental categories to incorporate new information.

3. When infants begin to explore the environment through sensory and motor skills, they are displaying what Piaget called _____ intelligence. In number, Piaget described _____ stages of development of this type of intelligence.

4. The first two stages of sensorimotor intelligence are examples of _____ _____ _____ . Stage one begins with newborns' reflexes, such as _____ , _____ , _____ , and _____ . It lasts from birth to _____ of age.

5. Stage two begins when newborns show signs of _____ of their _____ to the specifics of the environment.

Describe the development of the sucking reflex during stages one and two.

6. In stages three and four, development switches to _____ _____ _____ , involving the baby with an object or with another person. During stage three, which occurs between _____ and _____ months of age, infants repeat a specific action that has just elicited a pleasing response.

Describe a typical stage-three behavior.

7. In stage four, which lasts from _____ to _____ months of age, infants can better _____ events. At this stage, babies also engage in purposeful actions, or _____-_____ behavior.

8. (text and Thinking Like a Scientist) A major cognitive accomplishment of infancy is the ability to understand that objects exist even when they are _____ . This awareness is called _____ _____ . To test for this awareness, Piaget devised a procedure to observe whether an infant will _____ for a hidden object. Using this test, Piaget concluded that this awareness does not develop until about _____ of age.

9. During stage five, which lasts from _____ to _____ months, infants begin experimenting in thought and deed. They do so through _____ _____ _____ , which involve taking in experiences and trying to make sense of them.

Explain what Piaget meant when he described the stage-five infant as a little scientist.

10. Stage six, which lasts from _____ to _____ months, is the stage of achieving new means by using _____ _____ .

11. One sign that children have reached stage six is _____ _____ , which is their emerging ability to imitate behaviors they noticed earlier.

12. Two research tools that have become available since Piaget's time are _____ studies and _____ , which reveals brain activity by showing increases in _____ supply to various parts of the brain as cognition occurs.

Information Processing (pp. 154–158)

13. A perspective on human cognition that is modeled on how computers analyze data is the _____-_____ theory.

Two aspects of this theory as applied to human development are _____ , which concern perception and so are analogous to computer input, and _____ , which involves storage and retrieval of ideas, or output.

14. Much of the current research in perception and cognition has been inspired by the work of the Gibsons, who stress that perception is a(n) _____ (active/passive/automatic) cognitive phenomenon.

15. According to the Gibsons, any object in the environment offers diverse opportunities for interaction; this property of an object is called an _____ .

16. Which of these an individual perceives in an object depends on the individual's _____ _____ and _____ _____ , on his or her _____ _____ , and on his or her _____ _____ of what the object might be used for.

17. A firm surface that appears to drop off is called a _____ _____ . Although perception of this drop off was once linked to _____ maturity, later research found that infants as young as _____ are able to perceive the drop off, as evidenced by changes in their _____ _____ and their wide open eyes.

18. Perception that is primed to focus on movement and change is called _____ _____ .

19. Babies have great difficulty storing new memories in their first _____ (how long?).

20. Research has shown, however, that babies can show that they remember when three conditions are met:
    (a) _____
    (b) _____
    (c) _____

21. When these conditions are met, infants as young as _____ months "remembered" events from two weeks earlier if they experienced a _____ _____ prior to retesting.

22. After about _____ months, infants become capable of retaining information for longer periods of time, with less reminding.

23. Most researchers believe there _____ (is one type of memory/are many types of memory).

Language: What Develops in Two Years?
(pp. 158–167)

24. Children the world over _____ (follow/do not follow) the same sequence of early language development. The timing of this sequence _____ (varies/does not vary).

25. Newborns show a preference for hearing _____ over other sounds, including the high-pitched, simplified adult speech called _____ _____ , which is sometimes called _____ - _____ speech.

26. By 4 months of age, most babies' verbal repertoire consists of _____ _____ .

27. At _____ months of age, babies begin to repeat certain syllables, a phenomenon referred to as _____ .

28. Deaf babies begin oral babbling _____ (earlier/later) than hearing babies do. Deaf babies may also babble _____ , with this behavior emerging _____ (earlier than/at the same time as/later than) hearing infants begin oral babbling.

29. The average baby speaks a few words at about _____ of age. When vocabulary reaches approximately 50 words, it suddenly begins to build rapidly, at a rate of _____ or more words a

month. This language spurt is called the
_____ _____ , because
toddlers learn a disproportionate number of
_____ .

30. Language acquisition may be shaped by our
_____ , as revealed by the fact that
North American infants learn more
_____ than Chinese or Korean
infants, who learn more _____ .
Alternatively, the entire _____
_____ may determine language
acquisition.

31. Another characteristic is the use of the
_____ , in which a single word
expresses a complete thought.

32. Children begin to produce their first two-word
sentences at about _____ months,
showing a clearly emerging understanding of
_____ , which refers to all the methods that languages use to communicate meaning,
apart from the words themselves.

33. Reinforcement and other conditioning processes
account for language development, according to
the learning theory of _____ .
Support for this theory comes from the fact that
there are wide variations in language
_____ , especially when children
from different cultures are compared. One longitudinal study that followed mother–infant pairs
over time found that the frequency of early
_____ _____ predict-
ed the child's rate of language acquisition many
months later.

34. The theorist who stressed that language is too
complex to be mastered so early and easily
through conditioning is _____ . This
theorist maintained that all children are born
with a LAD, or _____
_____ _____ , that
enables children to quickly derive the rules of
grammar from the speech they hear.

35. Embedded in the LAD, the universal grammar
structure of language is _____-
_____ , meaning that words are
"expected" by the developing brain.

Summarize the research support for theory two.

36. A third, _____-_____
theory of language proposes that
_____ _____ foster
infant language.

37. A new hybrid theory based on a model called an
_____ _____ com-
bines aspects of several theories. A fundamental
aspect of this theory is that _____
_____ .

Progress Test 1

Multiple-Choice Questions

Circle your answers to the following questions and
check them with the answers beginning on page 94. If
your answer is incorrect, read the explanation for
why it is incorrect and then consult the appropriate
pages of the text (in parentheses following the correct
answer).

1. In general terms, the Gibsons' concept of affordances emphasizes the idea that the individual
perceives an object in terms of its:
   a. economic importance.
   b. physical qualities.
   c. function or use to the individual.
   d. role in the larger culture or environment.

2. According to Piaget, when a baby repeats an
action that has just triggered a pleasing response
from his or her caregiver, a stage _____ behavior
has occurred.
   a. one   c. three
   b. two   d. six

3. Sensorimotor intelligence begins with a baby's first:
   a. attempt to crawl.
   b. reflex actions.
   c. auditory perception.
   d. adaptation of a reflex.

4. Piaget and the Gibsons would most likely agree that:
   a. perception is largely automatic.
   b. language development is biologically predisposed in children.
   c. learning and perception are active cognitive processes.
   d. it is unwise to "push" children too hard academically.

5. By the end of the first year, infants usually learn how to:
   a. accomplish simple goals.
   b. manipulate various symbols.
   c. solve complex problems.
   d. pretend.

6. When an infant begins to understand that objects exist even when they are out of sight, she or he has begun to understand the concept of object:
   a. displacement.   c. permanence.
   b. importance.   d. location.

7. Today, most cognitive psychologists view language acquisition as:
   a. primarily the result of imitation of adult speech.
   b. a behavior that is determined primarily by biological maturation.
   c. a behavior determined entirely by learning.
   d. determined by both biological maturation and learning.

8. Despite cultural differences, children all over the world attain very similar language skills:
   a. according to ethnically specific timetables.
   b. in the same sequence according to a variable timetable.
   c. according to culturally specific timetables.
   d. according to timetables that vary from child to child.

9. The average baby speaks a few words at about:
   a. 6 months.   c. 12 months.
   b. 9 months.   d. 24 months.

10. A single word used by toddlers to express a complete thought is:
    a. a holophrase.   c. babbling.
    b. baby talk.   d. an affordance.

11. A distinctive form of language, with a particular pitch, structure, etc., that adults use in talking to infants is called:
    a. a holophrase.   c. baby talk.
    b. the LAD.   d. conversation.

12. Habituation studies reveal that most infants detect the difference between a pah sound and a bah sound at:
    a. birth.   c. 3 months.
    b. 1 month.   d. 6 months.

13. The imaging technique in which the brain's magnetic properties indicate activation in various parts of the brain is called a(n):
    a. PET scan.   c. fMRI.
    b. EEG.   d. CAT scan.

14. A toddler who taps on the computer's keyboard after observing her mother sending e-mail is demonstrating:
    a. assimilation.   c. deferred imitation.
    b. accommodation.   d. dynamic perception.

15. In Piaget's theory of sensorimotor intelligence, reflexes that involve the infant's own body are examples of:
    a. primary circular reactions
    b. secondary circular reactions.
    c. tertiary circular reactions.
    d. none of the above.

Matching Items

Match each definition or description with its corresponding term.

Terms

_____ **1.** mental combinations
_____ **2.** affordances
_____ **3.** object permanence
_____ **4.** Noam Chomsky
_____ **5.** B. F. Skinner
_____ **6.** sensorimotor intelligence
_____ **7.** babbling
_____ **8.** holophrase
_____ **9.** adaptation
_____ **10.** deferred imitation
_____ **11.** dynamic perception

Definitions or Descriptions

a. cognitive process by which new information is taken in and responded to
b. repetitive utterance of certain syllables
c. perception that focuses on movement and change
d. the ability to witness, remember, and later copy a behavior
e. the realization that something that is out of sight continues to exist
f. trying out actions mentally
g. opportunities for interaction that an object offers
h. theorist who believed that verbal behavior is conditioned
i. a single word used to express a complete thought
j. theorist who believed that language ability is innate
k. thinking through the senses and motor skills

Progress Test 2

Progress Test 2 should be completed during a final chapter review. Answer the following questions after you thoroughly understand the correct answers for the Chapter Review and Progress Test 1.

Multiple-Choice Questions

1. Stage five (12 to 18 months) of sensorimotor intelligence is best described as:
   a. first acquired adaptations.
   b. the period of the little scientist.
   c. procedures for making interesting sights last.
   d. new means through symbolization.

2. Which of the following is *not* evidence of dynamic perception during infancy?
   a. Babies prefer to look at things in motion.
   b. Babies form simple expectations of the path that a moving object will follow.
   c. Babies use movement cues to discern the boundaries of objects.
   d. Babies quickly grasp that even though objects look different when seen from different viewpoints, they are the same objects.

3. (text and Thinking Like a Scientist) Research suggests that the concept of object permanence:
   a. fades after a few months.
   b. is a skill some children never acquire.
   c. may occur earlier and more gradually than Piaget recognized.
   d. involves pretending as well as mental combinations.

4. Which of the following is an example of a secondary circular reaction?
   a. 1-month-old infant staring at a mobile suspended over her crib
   b. a 2-month-old infant sucking a pacifier
   c. realizing that rattles make noise, a 4-month-old infant laughs with delight when his mother puts a rattle in his hand
   d. a 12-month-old toddler licks a bar of soap to learn what it tastes like

5. Eighteen-month-old Colin puts a collar on his stuffed dog, then pretends to take it for a walk. Colin's behavior is an example of a:
   a. primary circular reaction.
   b. secondary circular reaction.
   c. tertiary circular reaction.
   d. first acquired adaptation.

6. According to Piaget, assimilation and accommodation are two ways in which:
   a. infants adapt their reflexes to the specifics of the environment.
   b. goal-directed behavior occurs.
   c. infants form mental combinations.
   d. language begins to emerge.

7. For Noam Chomsky, the language acquisition device refers to:
   a. the human predisposition to acquire language.
   b. the portion of the human brain that processes speech.
   c. the vocabulary of the language the child is exposed to.
   d. all of the above.

8. The first stage of sensorimotor intelligence lasts until:
   a. infants can anticipate events that will fulfill their needs.
   b. infants begin to adapt their reflexes to the environment.
   c. infants interact with objects to produce exciting experiences.
   d. infants are capable of thinking about past and future events.

9. Whether or not an infant perceives certain characteristics of objects, such as "suckability" or "graspability," seems to depend on:
   a. his or her prior experiences.
   b. his or her needs.
   c. his or her sensory awareness.
   d. all of the above.

10. (Thinking Like a Scientist) Piaget was *incorrect* in his belief that infants do not have:
    a. object permanence.
    b. intelligence.
    c. goal-directed behavior.
    d. all of the above.

11. The purposeful actions that begin to develop in sensorimotor stage four are called:
    a. reflexes.
    b. affordances.
    c. goal-directed behaviors.
    d. mental combinations.

12. What is the correct sequence of stages of language development?
    a. crying, babbling, cooing, first word
    b. crying, cooing, babbling, first word
    c. crying, babbling, first word, cooing
    d. crying, cooing, first word, babbling

13. Compared with hearing babies, deaf babies:
    a. are less likely to babble.
    b. are more likely to babble.
    c. begin to babble vocally at about the same age.
    d. begin to babble manually at about the same age as hearing babies begin to babble vocally.

14. According to Skinner, children acquire language:
    a. as a result of an inborn ability to use the basic structure of language.
    b. through reinforcement and other aspects of conditioning.
    c. mostly because of biological maturation.
    d. in a fixed sequence of predictable stages.

15. A fundamental idea of the emergentist coalition model of language acquisition is that:
    a. all humans are born with an innate language acquisition device.
    b. some aspects of language are best learned in one way at one age, others in another way at another age.
    c. language development occurs too rapidly and easily to be entirely the product of conditioning.
    d. imitation and reinforcement are crucial to the development of language.

Matching Items

Match each definition or description with its corresponding term.

Terms

_____   **1.** goal-directed behavior
_____   **2.** visual cliff
_____   **3.** primary circular reaction
_____   **4.** baby talk
_____   **5.** assimilation
_____   **6.** little scientist
_____   **7.** accommodation
_____   **8.** secondary circular reaction
_____   **9.** tertiary circular reaction
_____   **10.** LAD
_____   **11.** grammar

Definitions or Descriptions

a. a device for studying depth perception
b. incorporating new information into an existing schema
c. readjusting an existing schema to incorporate new information
d. a feedback loop involving the infant's own body
e. a feedback loop involving people and objects
f. a hypothetical device that facilitates language development
g. also called child-directed speech
h. Piaget's term for the stage-five toddler
i. purposeful actions
j. a feedback loop involving active exploration and experimentation
k. all the methods used by a language to communicate meaning

Thinking Critically About Chapter 6

Answer these questions the day before an exam as a final check on your understanding of the chapter's terms and concepts.

1. A 9-month-old repeatedly reaches for his sister's doll, even though he has been told "no" many times. This is an example of:
   a. primary circular reactions.
   b. habituation.
   c. delayed imitation.
   d. goal-directed behavior.

2. If a baby sucks harder on a nipple, evidences a change in heart rate, or stares longer at one image than at another when presented with a change of stimulus, the indication is that the baby:
   a. is annoyed by the change.
   b. is both hungry and angry.
   c. has become habituated to the new stimulus.
   d. perceives some differences between stimuli.

3. As an advocate of the social-pragmatic theory, Professor Robinson believes that:
   a. infants communicate in every way they can because they are social beings.
   b. biological maturation is a dominant force in language development.
   c. infants' language abilities mirror those of their primary caregivers.

   d. language develops in many ways for many reasons.

4. According to Skinner's theory, an infant who learns to delight his father by saying "da-da" is probably benefiting from:
   a. social reinforcers, such as smiles and hugs.
   b. modeling.
   c. learning by imitation.
   d. an innate ability to use language.

5. When eighteen-month-old Jessica sees a hairless dog, she does not know what to call it. After her mother says, "See Jessie, not all dogs have fur," Jessica proudly calls "doggie!" Jessica's manipulation of her doggie schema to incorporate this experience is an example of:
   a. assimilation.
   b. accommodation.
   c. adaptation.
   d. a primary circular reaction.

6. At about 21 months, the typical child will:
   a. have a vocabulary of between 250 and 350 words.
   b. begin to speak in holophrases.
   c. put words together to form rudimentary sentences.
   d. do all of the above.

7. A 20-month-old girl who is able to try out various actions mentally without having to actually perform them is learning to solve simple problems by using:
   a. dynamic perception.
   b. object permanence.
   c. affordances.
   d. mental combinations.

8. A baby who attempts to interact with a smiling parent is demonstrating an ability that typically occurs in which stage of sensorimotor development?
   a. one
   b. two
   c. three
   d. four

9. Piaget referred to the shift in an infant's behavior from reflexes to deliberate actions as the shift from:
   a. secondary circular reactions to primary circular reactions.
   b. first acquired adaptations to secondary circular reactions.
   c. primary circular reactions to tertiary circular reactions.
   d. stage one primary circular reactions to stage two primary circular reactions.

10. A baby who realizes that a rubber duck that has fallen out of the tub must be somewhere on the floor has achieved:
    a. object permanence.
    b. deferred imitation.
    c. mental combinations.
    d. goal-directed behavior.

11. As soon as her babysitter arrives, 21-month-old Christine holds on to her mother's legs and, in a questioning manner, says "bye-bye." Because Christine clearly is "asking" her mother not to leave, her utterance can be classified as:
    a. babbling.
    b. a noun.
    c. a holophrase.
    d. subject-predicate order.

12. The 6-month-old infant's continual repetition of sound combinations such as "ba-ba-ba" is called:
    a. cooing.
    b. babbling.
    c. a holophrase.
    d. baby talk.

13. Nine-month-old Akshay, who looks out of his crib for a toy that has fallen, is clearly demonstrating:
    a. object permanence.
    b. goal-directed behavior.
    c. a secondary circular reaction.
    d. all of the above.

14. Monica firmly believes that her infant daughter "taught" herself language because of the seemingly effortless manner in which she has mastered new words and phrases. Monica is evidently a proponent of the theory proposed by:
    a. B. F. Skinner.
    b. Noam Chomsky.
    c. social pragmatic theorists.
    d. the emergentist coalition.

15. Like most Korean toddlers, Noriko has acquired a greater number of _____ in her vocabulary than her North American counterparts, who tend to acquire more _____ .
    a. verbs; nouns
    b. nouns; verbs
    c. adjectives; verbs
    d. adjectives; nouns

Key Terms

Writing Definitions

Using your own words, write a brief definition or explanation of each of the following terms on a separate piece of paper.

1. adaptation
2. sensorimotor intelligence
3. primary circular reactions
4. secondary circular reactions
5. object permanence
6. tertiary circular reactions
7. little scientist
8. deferred imitation
9. habituation
10. fMRI
11. information-processing theory
12. affordance
13. visual cliff
14. dynamic perception

15. reminder session
16. baby talk
17. babbling
18. naming explosion

19. holophrase
20. grammar
21. language acquisition device (LAD)

Cross-Check
After you have written the definitions of the key terms in this chapter, you should complete the crossword puzzle to ensure that you can reverse the process—recognize the term, given the definition.

ACROSS

1. the methods used by languages to communicate meaning
7. a brain-imaging technique
8. a circular reaction involving the infant's own body
9. a circular reaction involving people and objects
10. a type of perception primed to focus on movement
12. the process of getting used to an object
13. child-directed speech
15. a sudden increase in an infant's vocabulary

DOWN

2. the cognitive process by which new information is taken in
3. a type of circular reaction that involves active exploration
4. a single word used to express a complete thought
5. Piaget's term for the stage-five toddler
6. an opportunity for perception
10. imitation of something that occurred earlier
11. extended repetition of syllables
14. Chomsky's term for a brain structure that enables language

ANSWERS
CHAPTER REVIEW

1. intelligence, learning, memory, and language; Piaget
2. adapt; experiences; assimilation; schemas; accommodation
3. sensorimotor; six
4. primary circular reactions; sucking; grasping; staring; listening; 1 month

5. adaptation; reflexes

Stage-one infants suck everything that touches their lips. At about 1 month, they start to adapt their sucking to specific objects. After several months, they have organized the world into objects to be sucked for nourishment, objects to be sucked for pleasure, and objects not to be sucked at all.

6. secondary circular reactions; 4; 8

A stage-three infant may squeeze a duck, hear a quack, and squeeze the duck again.

7. 8; 12; anticipate; goal-directed
8. no longer in sight; object permanence; search; 8 months
9. 12; 18; tertiary circular reactions

Having discovered some action or set of actions that is possible with a given object, stage-five little scientists seem to ask, "What else can I do with this?"

10. 18; 24; mental combinations

11. deferred imitation

12. habituation; fMRI; oxygen

13. information-processing; affordances; memory

14. active

15. affordance

16. past experiences; current development; immediate motivation; sensory awareness

17. visual cliff; visual; 3 months; heart rate

18. dynamic perception

19. year

20. (a) real-life situations are used; (b) motivation is high; (c) special measures aid memory retrieval

21. 3 months; reminder session

22. six

23. are many types of memory

24. follow; varies

25. speech; baby talk; child-directed

26. squeals, growls, gurgles, grunts, croons, and yells, as well as some speechlike sounds

27. 6 or 7; babbling

28. later; manually; at the same time as

29. 1 year; 50 to 100; naming explosion; nouns

30. culture; nouns; verbs; social context

31. holophrase

32. 21; grammar

33. B. F. Skinner; fluency; maternal responsiveness

34. Noam Chomsky; language acquisition device

35. experience-expectant

Support for this theory comes from the fact that all babies babble a mama and dada sound by 6 months. No reinforcement is needed. All they need is for dendrites to grow, mouth muscles to strengthen, synapses to connect, and speech to be overheard.

36. social-pragmatic; social impulses

37. emergentist coalition; some aspects of language are best learned in one way at one age, others in another way at another age

PROGRESS TEST 1

Multiple-Choice Questions

1. **c.** is the answer. (p. 154)

2. **c.** is the answer. (p. 149)

3. **b.** is the answer. This was Piaget's most basic contribution to the study of infant cognition—that intelligence is revealed in behavior at every age. (p. 148)

4. **c.** is the answer. (pp. 147, 154)

   b. This is Chomsky's position.

   d. This issue was not discussed in the text.

5. **a.** is the answer. (p. 149)

   b. & c. These abilities are not acquired until children are much older.

   d. Pretending is associated with stage six (18 to 24 months).

6. **c.** is the answer. (p. 150)

7. **d.** is the answer. (pp. 165–166)

8. **b.** is the answer. (p. 159)

   a., c., & d. Children the world over, and in every Piagetian stage, follow the same sequence, but the timing of their accomplishments may vary considerably.

9. **c.** is the answer. (p. 160)

10. **a.** is the answer. (p. 161)

    b. Baby talk is the speech adults use with infants.

    c. Babbling refers to the first syllables a baby utters.

    d. An affordance is an opportunity for perception and interaction.

11. **c.** is the answer. (p. 159)

    a. A holophrase is a single word uttered by a toddler to express a complete thought.

    b. According to Noam Chomsky, the LAD, or language acquisition device, is an innate ability in humans to acquire language.

    d. These characteristic differences in pitch and structure are precisely what distinguish baby talk from regular conversation.

12. **b.** is the answer. (p. 152)

13. **c.** is the answer. (p. 152)

14. **c.** is the answer (p. 152)

    a. & b. In Piaget's theory, these refer to processes by which mental concepts incorporate new experiences (assimilation) or are modified in response to new experiences (accommodation).

    d. Dynamic perception is perception that is primed to focus on movement and change.

15. **a.** is the answer. (p. 148)

    b. Secondary circular reactions involve the baby with an object or with another person.

c. Tertiary circular reactions involve active exploration and experimentation, rather than mere reflexive action.

Matching Items

1. f (p. 152)	**5.** h (p. 162)	**9.** a (p. 147)
2. g (p. 154)	**6.** k (p. 148)	**10.** d (pp. 152)
3. e (p. 150)	**7.** b (p. 160)	**11.** c (p. 156)
4. j (p. 163)	**8.** i (p. 161)	

PROGRESS TEST 2

Multiple-Choice Questions

1. **b.** is the answer. (p. 152)

   a. & c. These are stages two and three.

   d. This is not one of Piaget's stages of sensorimotor intelligence.

2. **d.** is the answer. This is an example of perceptual constancy. (p. 156)

3. **c.** is the answer. (pp. 150–151)

4. **c.** is the answer. (p. 149)

   a. & b. These are examples of primary circular reactions.

   d. This is an example of a tertiary circular reaction.

5. **c.** is the answer. (pp. 151–152)

6. **a.** is the answer. (p. 147)

   b. Assimilation and accommodation are cognitive processes, not behaviors.

   c. Mental combinations are sequences of actions that are carried out mentally.

   d. Assimilation and accommodation do not directly pertain to language use.

7. **a.** is the answer. Chomsky believed that this device is innate. (p. 164)

8. **b.** is the answer. (pp. 148–149)

   a. & c. Both of these occur later than stage one.

   d. This is a hallmark of stage six.

9. **d.** is the answer. (p. 154)

10. **a.** is the answer. (pp. 150–151)

11. **c.** is the answer. (p. 150)

    a. Reflexes are involuntary (and therefore unintentional) responses.

    b. Affordances are perceived opportunities for interaction with objects.

    d. Mental combinations are actions that are carried out mentally, rather than behaviorally. Moreover, mental combinations do not develop until a later age, during sensorimotor stage six.

12. **b.** is the answer. (pp. 159–160)

13. **d.** is the answer. (p. 160)

    a. & b. Hearing and deaf babies do not differ in the overall likelihood that they will babble.

    c. Deaf babies begin to babble vocally several months later than hearing babies do.

14. **b.** is the answer. (p. 162)

    a., c., & d. These views on language acquisition describe the theory offered by Noam Chomsky.

15. **b.** is the answer. (p. 165)

    a. & c. These ideas are consistent with Noam Chomsky's theory.

    d. This is the central idea of B. F. Skinner's theory.

Matching Items

1. i (p. 150)	**5.** b (p. 147)	**9.** j (p. 151)
2. a (p. 155)	**6.** h (p. 152)	**10.** f (p. 164)
3. d (p. 148)	**7.** c (p. 147)	**11.** k (p. 161)
4. g (p. 159)	**8.** e (p. 149)	

THINKING CRITICALLY ABOUT CHAPTER 6

1. **d.** is the answer. The baby is clearly behaving purposefully, the hallmark of goal-directed behavior. (p. 150)

   a. This is a stage-four behavior, not stages one or two.

   b. He is clearly not getting used to the stimulus.

   c. Delayed imitation is the ability to imitate actions seen in the past.

2. **d.** is the answer. (p. 152)

   a. & b. These changes in behavior indicate that the newborn has perceived an unfamiliar stimulus, not that he or she is hungry, annoyed, or angry.

   c. Habituation refers to a *decrease* in physiological responsiveness to a familiar stimulus.

3. **a.** is the answer. (p. 165)

   b. This idea is more consistent with Noam Chomsky's theory.

   c. This idea is more consistent with B. F. Skinner's theory.

   d. This expresses the emergentist coalition theory.

4. **a.** is the answer. The father's expression of delight is clearly a reinforcer in that it has increased the likelihood of the infant's vocalization. (p. 162)

b. & c. Modeling, or learning by imitation, would be implicated if the father attempted to increase the infant's vocalizations by repeatedly saying "da-da" himself, in the infant's presence.

d. This is Chomsky's viewpoint; Skinner maintained that language is acquired through learning.

5. **b.** is the answer. (p. 147)

a. This answer would have been correct had Jessica initially recognized the hairless animal as a dog.

c. This answer is too general. Adaptation occurs in two very different ways.

d. Primary circular reactions are behaviors that involve the infant's body.

6. **c.** is the answer. (p. 161)

a. At 21 months of age, most children have much smaller vocabularies.

b. Speaking in holophrases is typical of younger infants.

7. **d.** is the answer. (p. 152)

a. Dynamic perception is perception primed to focus on movement and change.

b. Object permanence is the awareness that objects do not cease to exist when they are out of sight.

c. Affordances are the opportunities for perception and interaction that an object or place offers to any individual.

8. **c.** is the answer. (p. 149)

9. **d.** is the answer. (p. 148)

10. **a.** is the answer. Before object permanence is attained, an object that disappears from sight ceases to exist for the infant. (p. 150)

b. Deferred imitation is the ability to witness, remember, and later copy a particular behavior.

c. Mental combinations are actions that are carried out mentally.

d. Goal-directed behavior refers to purposeful actions initiated by infants in anticipation of events that will fulfill their needs and wishes.

11. **c.** is the answer. (p. 161)

a. Because Christine is expressing a complete thought, her speech is much more than babbling.

b. "Bye-bye" is not a noun.

d. The ability to understand subject-predicate order emerges later, when children begin forming 2-word sentences.

12. **b.** is the answer. (p. 160)

a. Cooing is the pleasant-sounding utterances of the infant at about 2 months.

c. The holophrase occurs later and refers to the toddler's use of a single word to express a complete thought.

d. Baby talk is the adult's speech to infants.

13. **d.** is the answer.. (p. 150)

14. **b.** is the answer. (pp. 163–164)

15. **a.** is the answer. (pp. 160–161)

KEY TERMS

1. A key element of Piaget's theory, **adaptation** is the cognitive process by which information is taken in and responded to. (p. 147)

2. Piaget's stages of **sensorimotor intelligence** (from birth to about 2 years old) are based on his theory that infants think exclusively with their senses and motor skills. (p. 148)

3. In Piaget's theory, **primary circular reactions** are a type of feedback loop involving the infant's own body, in which infants take in experiences (such as sucking and grasping) and try to make sense of them. (p. 148)

4. **Secondary circular reactions** are a type of feedback loop involving the infant's responses to objects and other people. (p. 149)

5. **Object permanence** is the understanding that objects continue to exist even when they cannot be seen, touched, or heard. (p. 150)

6. In Piaget's theory, **tertiary circular reactions** are the most sophisticated type of infant feedback loop, involving active exploration and experimentation. (p. 151)

7. **Little scientist** is Piaget's term for the stage-five toddler who learns about the properties of objects in his or her world through active experimentation. (p. 152)

8. **Deferred imitation** is the ability to witness, remember, and later copy a behavior they noticed hours or days earlier. (p. 152)

9. **Habituation** is the process of becoming so familiar with a stimulus that it no longer triggers the responses it did when it was originally experienced. (p. 152)

10. **Functional magnetic resonance imaging (fMRI)** is an imaging technique in which the brain's magnetic properties are measured to reveal changes

in activity levels in various parts of the brain. (p. 152)

11. **Information-processing theory** is a theory of human cognition that compares thinking to the ways in which a computer analyzes data, through the processes of input, connections, stored memories, and output. (p. 154)

12. **Affordances** are perceived opportunities for interacting with people, objects, or places in the environment. Infants perceive sucking, grasping, noisemaking, and many other affordances of objects at an early age. (p. 154)

13. A **visual cliff** is an experimental apparatus that provides the illusion of a drop between one surface and another. (p. 155)

14. **Dynamic perception** is perception that is primed to focus on movement and change. (p. 156)

15. A **reminder session** any perceptual experience of some aspect of an event that triggers the entire memory of the event. (p. 157)

16. **Baby talk** is a form of speech used by adults when talking to infants. It is simplified, it has a higher pitch, and it is repetitive. (p. 159)

17. **Babbling,** which begins at 6 or 7 months, is characterized by the extended repetition of certain syllables (such as "ma-ma"). (p. 160)

18. The **naming explosion** refers to the dramatic increase in the infant's vocabulary that begins at about 18 months of age. (p. 160)

19. Another characteristic of infant speech is the use of the **holophrase,** in which a single word is used to convey a complete thought. (p. 161)

20. The **grammar** of a language includes rules of word order, verb forms, and all other methods used to communicate meaning apart from words themselves. (p. 161)

21. According to Chomsky, children possess an innate **language acquisition device (LAD)** that enables them to acquire language, including the basic aspects of grammar. (p. 164)

Cross-Check

ACROSS	DOWN
1. grammar	2. adaptation
7. fMRI	3. tertiary
8. primary	4. holophrase
9. secondary	5. little scientist
10. dynamic	6. affordance
12. habituation	10. deferred
13. baby talk	11. babbling
15. naming explosion	14. LAD

Chapter Seven

The First Two Years: Psychosocial Development

Chapter Overview

Chapter 7 describes the emotional and social life of the developing person during the first two years. It begins with a description of the psychoanalytic theories of Freud and Erikson along with behaviorist, cognitive, epigenetic systems, and sociocultural theories, which help us understand how the infant's emotional and behavioral responses begin to take on the various patterns that form personality. Temperament, which affects later personality and is primarily inborn, is influenced by the individual's interactions with the environment.

The second section explores the infant's emerging emotions and how they reflect mobility and social awareness. Two emotions, contentment and distress, are apparent at birth and are soon joined by anger and fear. As self-awareness develops, many new emotions emerge, including embarrassment, shame, guilt, and pride.

The third section explores the social context in which emotions develop. By referencing their caregivers' signals, infants learn when and how to express their emotions. Emotions and relationships are then examined from a different perspective—that of parent–infant interaction. Videotaped studies of parents and infants, combined with laboratory studies of attachment, have greatly expanded our understanding of psychosocial development. This section concludes by exploring the impact of day care on infants.

NOTE: Answer guidelines for all Chapter 7 questions begin on page 109.

Guided Study

The text chapter should be studied one section at a time. Before you read, preview each section by skimming it, noting headings and boldface items. Then read the appropriate section objectives from the following outline. Keep these objectives in mind and, as you read the chapter section, search for the information that will enable you to meet each objective. Once you have finished a section, write out answers for its objectives.

Theories About Early Psychosocial Development (pp. 172–177)

1. Describe Freud's psychosexual stages of infant development.

2. Describe Erikson's psychosocial stages of infant development.

3. Contrast the perspectives of behaviorism, cognitive theory, and sociocultural theory regarding psychosocial development in the first two years of life.

4. Discuss the epigenetic theory explanation of the origins, characteristics, and role of temperament in the child's psychosocial development.

9. Define attachment, explain how it is measured and how it is influenced by context, and discuss the long-term consequences of secure and insecure attachment.

Emotional Development (pp. 178–180)

5. Describe the basic emotions expressed by infants during the first days and months.

10. Discuss the concept of social referencing, noting the difference in how the infant interacts with mother and father.

6. Describe the main developments in the emotional life of the child between 6 months and 2 years.

11. Discuss the impact of nonrelative care on young children, and identify the factors that define high-quality day care.

7. Discuss the links between the infant's emerging self-awareness and his or her continuing emotional development.

Conclusions in Theory and Practice (pp. 189–191)

12. State several conclusions that can be drawn from research on early psychosocial development.

The Development of Social Bonds (pp. 180–189)

8. Describe the synchrony of parent–infant interaction during the first year, and discuss its significance for the developing person.

Chapter Review

When you have finished reading the chapter, work through the material that follows to review it. Complete the sentences and answer the questions. As you proceed, evaluate your performance for each section by consulting the answers on page 109. Do not continue with the next section until you understand each answer. If you need to, review or reread the appropriate section in the textbook before continuing.

Introduction and Theories About Early Psychosocial Development (pp. 172–177)

1. Psychosocial development includes
   _____ development and
   _____ development.

2. In Freud's theory, development begins with the
   _____ stage, so named because the
   _____ is the infant's prime source of
   gratification and pleasure.

3. According to Freud, in the second year the prime focus of gratification comes from stimulation and control of the bowels. Freud referred to this period as the _____ stage.

Describe Freud's ideas on the importance of early oral experiences to later personality development.

4. Research has shown that toilet training may take a year or more if it is started before _____ months.

5. The theorist who believed that development occurs through a series of psychosocial crises is _____ . According to his theory, the crisis of infancy is one of
   _____ ,
   whereas the crisis of toddlerhood is one of
   _____ .

6. According to the perspective of
   _____ , personality is molded
   through the processes of _____ and

   _____ of the child's spontaneous behaviors. A strong proponent of this position was _____ .

7. Later theorists incorporated the role of _____ learning, that is, infants' tendency to observe and _____ the personality traits of their parents.

8. According to cognitive theory, a person's
   _____ , _____ , and
   _____ determine his or her perspective on the world. More specifically, infants use their early relationships to build a
   _____ _____ that
   becomes a frame of reference for organizing perceptions and experiences.

9. According to _____ theory, each infant is born with a _____ predisposition to develop certain emotional traits. Among these are traits of _____ .

10. These traits are similar to _____ . Although these traits are not learned, their expression is influenced by the _____ .

11. The correlations found thus far between neurological measurements and childhood behavior are _____ (large/small). The most famous long-term study of children's temperament is the _____ , begun more than forty years ago. This study found that babies differ in nine characteristics: _____
    _____
    _____

12. The study found that by two to three months, infants can be clustered into one of three types:
    _____ , _____ , and
    _____ . Another study categorized infants on the basis of brain patterns and observable behavior. Most showed consistent patterns of behavior, identified as _____ ,
    _____ , or _____ .

13. An important factor in healthy psychosocial development is _____
    _____ _____ between
    the developing child and the caregiving context.

14. According to _____ theory, the entire _____ context can have a major impact on infant-caregiver relationships and the infant's development.

Emotional Development (pp. 178–180)

15. The first emotions that can be reliably discerned in infants are _____ and _____ . Other early infant emotions include _____ , _____ , and _____ .

16. Fully formed fear emerges at about _____ . One expression of this new emotion is _____ _____ , which becomes full-blown by _____ months; another is _____ _____ , or fear of abandonment, which is most obvious at _____ months. During the second year, anger and fear typically _____ (increase/decrease) and become more _____ toward specific things.

17. Toward the end of the second year, the new emotions of _____ , _____ , _____ , and _____ become apparent. These emotions require an awareness of _____ _____ .

18. An important foundation for emotional growth is _____ ; very young infants have no sense of _____ . This emerging sense of "me" and "mine" soon becomes linked with _____ . Important in this development is children's ability to form their own positive _____ .

Briefly describe the nature and findings of the classic rouge-and-mirror experiment on self-awareness in infants.

The Development of Social Bonds (pp. 180–189)

19. The coordinated interaction of response between infant and caregiver is called _____ . Partly through this interaction, infants learn to _____ _____ and to develop some of the basic skills of _____ _____ . Two key factors in this process are the _____ of the interaction and _____ . This process is most evident in _____ interactions.

20. The emotional bond that develops between slightly older infants and their caregivers is called _____ .

21. Approaching, following, and climbing onto the caregiver's lap are signs of _____ - _____ behaviors, while clinging and resisting being put down are signs of _____ - _____ behaviors.

22. An infant who derives comfort and confidence from the secure base provided by the caregiver is displaying _____ _____ (Type B). In this type of relationship, the caregiver acts as a secure _____ _____ _____ from which the child is willing to venture forth.

23. By contrast, _____ _____ is characterized by an infant's fear, anger, or seeming indifference to the caregiver. Two extremes of this type of relationship are _____ - _____ (Type A) and _____ - _____ / _____ (Type C).

(text and Table 7.2) Briefly describe three types of insecure attachment.

24. The procedure developed by Mary Ainsworth to measure attachment is called the

    _____ _____ .

    Approximately _____ (what proportion?) of all normal infants tested with this procedure demonstrate secure attachment. When infant–caregiver interactions are inconsistent, infants are classified as _____ .

25. Attachment status _____(determines/does not determine) future emotional development.

26. It is estimated that _____ percent of mothers of young infants are clinically depressed. This figure is higher for _____-_____ mothers. Attachment appears to be determined by the mother's

    _____ _____ to her

    infant's attempts at _____ and

    _____ .

27. The search for information about another person's feelings is called _____

    _____ . For infants, this phenomenon is particularly noticeable at _____ .

28. Although early research on psychosocial development focused on _____–

    _____ relationships, it is clear that other relatives and unrelated people are crucial to the child's development. Recent studies have shown that infants use their fathers for social referencing _____ (less than/as much as/more than) they do their moms.

29. Although fathers tend to provide less

    _____ _____ than do mothers, they tend to_____ more, which helps the children master _____ skills and develop _____ control. Fathers, single mothers, and grandparents are capable of providing all necessary _____ and _____ nurturing for a child's healthy psychosocial development. Generally speaking, a father's involvement in infant care also benefits the mother's _____ and the father's _____ strength.

30. Infant day care programs include

    _____ , when fewer than 6 children are cared for in someone's home, and

    _____ -, in which 15 or more children are cared for in a separate child care facility. More than _____ (what percentage?) of all 1-year-olds in the United States are in regularly scheduled nonmaternal care.

31. Regarding the impact of nonmaternal care on young children, recent research studies have generally found that _____

    _____ .

List several benefits of good preschool education.

32. (Table 7.4) Researchers have identified four factors that seem essential to high-quality day care:

    a. _____

    b. _____

    c. _____

    d. _____

33. Early day care may be detrimental when the mother is _____ and the infant spends more than _____ (how many?) hours each week in a poor-quality program.

Conclusions in Theory and Practice (pp. 189–191)

34. Regarding the major theories of development,

    _____ _____ theory stands out as the best interpretation. Although the first two years are important, early

    _____ and _____

    development is influenced by the _____

behavior, the support provided by the
_____ , the quality of
_____ _____ , patterns
within the child's _____ , and traits
that are _____ .

Progress Test 1

Multiple-Choice Questions

Circle your answers to the following questions and check them with the answers on page 110. If your answer is incorrect, read the explanation for why it is incorrect and then consult the appropriate pages of the text (in parentheses following the correct answer).

1. Newborns have two identifiable emotions:
   a. shame and distress.
   b. distress and contentment.
   c. anger and joy.
   d. pride and guilt.

2. Synchrony begins to appear at about what age?
   a. 6 weeks
   b. 2 months
   c. 3 months
   d. 4 months

3. An infant's fear of being left by the mother or other caregiver, called _____ , is most obvious at about _____ .
   a. separation anxiety; 2 to 4 months
   b. stranger wariness; 2 to 4 months
   c. separation anxiety; 9 to 14 months
   d. stranger wariness; 9 to 14 months

4. Social referencing refers to:
   a. parenting skills that change over time.
   b. changes in community values regarding, for example, the acceptability of using physical punishment with small children.
   c. the support network for new parents provided by extended family members.
   d. the infant response of looking to trusted adults for emotional cues in uncertain situations.

5. A key difference between temperament and personality is that:
   a. temperamental traits are learned.
   b. personality includes traits that are primarily learned.
   c. personality is more stable than temperament.
   d. personality does not begin to form until much later, when self-awareness emerges.

6. The concept of a working model is most consistent with:
   a. psychoanalytic theory.
   b. behaviorism.
   c. cognitive theory.
   d. sociocultural theory.

7. Freud's oral stage corresponds to Erikson's crisis of:
   a. orality versus anality.
   b. trust versus mistrust.
   c. autonomy versus shame and doubt.
   d. secure versus insecure attachment.

8. Erikson felt that the development of a sense of trust in early infancy depends on the quality of the:
   a. infant's food.
   b. child's genetic inheritance.
   c. maternal relationship.
   d. introduction of toilet training.

9. Keisha is concerned that her 15-month-old daughter, who no longer seems to enjoy face-to-face play, is showing signs of insecure attachment. You tell her:
   a. not to worry; face-to-face play almost disappears toward the end of the first year.
   b. she may be right to worry, because face-to-face play typically increases throughout infancy.
   c. not to worry; attachment behaviors are unreliable until toddlerhood.
   d. that her child is typical of children who spend more than 20 hours in day care each week.

10. "Easy," "slow to warm up," and "difficult" are descriptions of different:
    a. forms of attachment.
    b. types of temperament.
    c. types of parenting.
    d. toddler responses to the Strange Situation.

11. The more physical play of fathers probably helps the infant master motor skills and may contribute to the:
    a. infant's self-awareness.
    b. growth of the infant's social skills and emotional expression.
    c. tendency of the infant to become securely attached.
    d. infant's fear of strangers and separation anxiety.

12. *Synchrony* is a term that describes:
    a. the carefully coordinated interaction between parent and infant.
    b. a mismatch of the temperaments of parent and infant.
    c. a research technique involving videotapes.
    d. the concurrent evolution of different species.

13. The emotional tie that develops between an infant and his or her primary caregiver is called:
    a. self-awareness.   c. affiliation.
    b. synchrony.   d. attachment.

14. Secure attachment is directly correlated with the promotion of:
    a. self-awareness.   c. dependency.
    b. social skills.   d. all of the above.

15. Interest in people, as evidenced by the social smile, appears for the first time when an infant is _____ weeks old.
    a. 3   c. 9
    b. 6   d. 12

True or False Items

Write T (*true*) or F (*false*) on the line in front of each statement.

_____ 1. The major developmental theories all agree that maternal care is better for children than nonmaternal care.

_____ 2. Approximately 25 percent of infants display secure attachment.

_____ 3. A baby at 11 months is likely to display both stranger wariness and separation anxiety.

_____ 4. Emotional development is affected by maturation of conscious awareness.

_____ 5. A securely attached toddler is most likely to stay close to his or her mother even in a familiar environment.

_____ 6. Current research shows that the majority of infants in day care are slow to develop cognitive and social skills.

_____ 7. Infants use their fathers for social referencing as much as they use their mothers.

_____ 8. Temperament is genetically determined and is unaffected by environmental factors.

_____ 9. Self-awareness enables toddlers to feel pride as well as guilt.

_____ 10. Genetic tendencies in temperament are most vulnerable to nurture during the early years of life.

Progress Test 2

Progress Test 2 should be completed during a final chapter review. Answer the following questions after you thoroughly understand the correct answers for the Chapter Review and Progress Test 1.

Multiple-Choice Questions

1. Infant–caregiver interactions that are marked by inconsistency are usually classified as:
   a. disorganized.
   b. insecure-avoidant.
   c. insecure-resistant.
   d. insecure-ambivalent.

2. Freud's anal stage corresponds to Erikson's crisis of:
   a. autonomy versus shame and doubt.
   b. trust versus mistrust.
   c. orality versus anality.
   d. identity versus role confusion.

3. Not until the sense of self begins to emerge do babies realize that they are seeing their own faces in the mirror. This realization usually occurs:
   a. shortly before 3 months.
   b. at about 6 months.
   c. between 15 and 24 months.
   d. after 24 months.

4. When there is goodness of fit, the parents of a slow-to-warm-up boy will:
   a. give him extra time to adjust to new situations.
   b. encourage independence in their son by frequently leaving him for short periods of time.
   c. place their son in regular day care so that other children's temperaments will "rub off" on him.
   d. do all of the above.

5. Emotions such as shame, guilt, embarrassment, and pride emerge at the same time that:
   a. the social smile appears.
   b. aspects of the infant's temperament can first be discerned.
   c. self-awareness begins to emerge.
   d. parents initiate toilet training.

6. Research on the NYLS temperamental character-istics indicates that:
   a. temperament is probably innate.
   b. the interaction of parent and child determines later personality.
   c. parents pass their temperaments on to their children through modeling.
   d. self-awareness contributes to the development of temperament.

7. In the second six months, stranger wariness is a:
   a. result of insecure attachment.
   b. result of social isolation.
   c. normal emotional response.
   d. setback in emotional development.

8. The caregiving environment can affect a child's temperament through:
   a. the child's temperamental pattern and the demands of the home environment.
   b. parental expectations.
   c. both a. and b.
   d. neither a. nor b.

9. While observing mothers playing with their infants in a playroom, you notice one mother who often teases her son, ignores him when he falls down, and tells him to "hush" when he cries. Mothers who display these behaviors usually have infants who exhibit which type of attach-ment?
   a. secure
   b. insecure-avoidant
   c. insecure-resistant
   d. disorganized

10. The later consequences of secure attachment and insecure attachment for children are:
    a. balanced by the child's current rearing cir-cumstances.
    b. irreversible, regardless of the child's current rearing circumstances.
    c. more significant in girls than in boys.
    d. more significant in boys than in girls.

11. The attachment pattern marked by anxiety and uncertainty is:
    a. insecure-avoidant.
    b. insecure-resistant/ambivalent.
    c. disorganized.
    d. Type B.

12. Compared with mothers, fathers are more likely to:
    a. engage in noisier, more boisterous play.
    b. encourage intellectual development in their children.
    c. encourage social development in their chil-dren.
    d. read to their toddlers.

13. Like Freud, Erikson believed that:
    a. problems arising in early infancy last a life-time.
    b. inability to resolve a conflict in infancy may result in later fixation.
    c. human development can be viewed in terms of psychosexual stages.
    d. all of the above are true.

14. Which of the following most accurately summa-rizes the relationship between early attachment and later social relationships?
    a. Attachment in infancy determines whether a child will grow to be sociable.
    b. Attachment relationships are sometimes, though rarely, altered as children grow older.
    c. There is, at best, only a weak correlation between early attachment and later social rela-tionships.
    d. Early attachment does not inevitably deter-mine future emotional development.

15. Which of the following is *not* true regarding syn-chrony?
    a. There are wide variations in the frequency of synchrony from baby to baby.
    b. Synchrony appears to be uninfluenced by cul-tural differences.
    c. The frequency of mother–infant synchrony has varied over historical time.
    d. Parents and infants spend about one hour a day in face-to-face play.

Matching Items

Match each theorist, term, or concept with its corresponding description or definition.

Theorists, Terms, or Concepts

_____ **1.** temperament
_____ **2.** Erikson
_____ **3.** the Strange Situation
_____ **4.** synchrony
_____ **5.** trust versus mistrust
_____ **6.** Freud
_____ **7.** social referencing
_____ **8.** autonomy versus shame and doubt
_____ **9.** self-awareness
_____ **10.** Ainsworth
_____ **11.** proximity-seeking behaviors
_____ **12.** contact-maintaining behaviors

Descriptions or Definitions

a. looking to caregivers for emotional cues
b. the crisis of infancy
c. the crisis of toddlerhood
d. approaching, following, and climbing
e. theorist who described psychosexual stages of development
f. researcher who devised a laboratory procedure for studying attachment
g. laboratory procedure for studying attachment
h. the relatively consistent, basic dispositions inherent in a person
i. clinging and resisting being put down
j. coordinated interaction between parent and infant
k. theorist who described psychosocial stages of development
l. a person's sense of being distinct from others

Thinking Critically About Chapter 7

Answer these questions the day before an exam as a final check on your understanding of the chapter's terms and concepts.

1. In laboratory tests of attachment, when the mother returns to the playroom after a short absence, a securely attached infant is most likely to:
   a. cry and protest the mother's return.
   b. climb into the mother's arms, then leave to resume play.
   c. climb into the mother's arms and stay there.
   d. continue playing without acknowledging the mother.

2. After a scary fall, 18-month-old Miguel looks to his mother to see if he should cry or laugh. Miguel's behavior is an example of:
   a. proximity-seeking behavior.
   b. social referencing.
   c. insecure attachment.
   d. the crisis of trust versus mistrust.

3. Which of the following is a clear sign of an infant's attachment to a particular person?
   a. The infant turns to that person when distressed.

   b. The infant protests when that person leaves a room.
   c. The infant may cry when strangers appear.
   d. They are all signs of infant attachment.

4. If you had to predict a newborn baby's personality "type" solely on the basis of probability, which classification would be the most likely?
   a. easy
   b. slow-to-warm-up
   c. difficult
   d. There is not enough information to make a prediction.

5. Professor Kipketer believes that infants' emotions are molded as their parents reinforce or punish their behaviors. Professor Kipketer evidently is a proponent of:
   a. cognitive theory.   **c.** epigenetic theory.
   b. behaviorism.   **d.** sociocultural theory.

6. Monica, who recently read a newspaper headline stating that "low-income infants are more likely to be insecurely attached to their mothers," is concerned that her own state of poverty will adversely influence any children she might have. You wisely tell her that:
   a. attachment status is determined by a mother's overt responses to an infant's attempts at synchrony and attachment.
   b. the correlation between income and attachment is due to the fact that most low-income mothers are clinically depressed.
   c. insecure attachment has not been shown to adversely influence a child's later development.
   d. all of the above are true.

7. Concluding her report on the impact of day care on young children, Deborah notes that infants are likely to become insecurely attached if:
   a. their own mothers are insensitive caregivers.
   b. the quality of day care is poor.
   c. more than 20 hours per week are spent in day care.
   d. all of the above are true.

8. Mashiyat, who advocates epigenetic theory in explaining the origins of personality, points to research evidence that:
   a. infants are born with definite and distinct temperaments that can change.
   b. early temperamental traits almost never change.
   c. an infant's temperament does not begin to clearly emerge until 2 years of age.
   d. temperament appears to be almost completely unaffected by the social context.

9. Kalil's mother left him alone in the room for a few minutes. When she returned, Kalil seemed indifferent to her presence. According to Mary Ainsworth's research with children in the Strange Situation, Kalil is probably:
   a. a normal, independent infant.
   b. an abused child.
   c. insecurely attached.
   d. securely attached.

10. Connie and Lev, who are first-time parents, are concerned because their 1-month-old baby is difficult to care for and hard to soothe. They are worried that they are doing something wrong. You inform them that their child is probably that way because:
    a. they are reinforcing the child's tantrum behaviors.
    b. they are not meeting some biological need of the child's.
    c. of his or her inherited temperament.
    d. at 1 month of age all children are difficult to care for and hard to soothe.

11. Two-year-old Anita and her mother visit a day-care center. Seeing an interesting toy, Anita runs a few steps toward it, then stops and looks back to see if her mother is coming. Anita's behavior illustrates:
    a. the crisis of autonomy versus shame and doubt.
    b. synchrony.
    c. dyssynchrony.
    d. social referencing.

12. Felix has a biting, sarcastic manner. Freud would probably say that Felix is:
    a. anally expulsive.
    b. anally retentive.
    c. fixated in the oral stage.
    d. experiencing the crisis of trust versus mistrust.

13. A researcher at the child development center places a dot on an infant's nose and watches to see if the infant reacts to her image in a mirror by touching her nose. Evidently, the researcher is testing the child's:
    a. attachment.   c. self-awareness.
    b. temperament.   d. social referencing.

14. Four-month-old Carl and his 13-month-old sister Carla are left in the care of a babysitter. As their parents are leaving, it is to be expected that:
    a. Carl will become extremely upset, while Carla will calmly accept her parents' departure.
    b. Carla will become more upset over her parents' departure than will Carl.
    c. Carl and Carla will both become quite upset as their parents leave.
    d. Neither Carl nor Carla will become very upset as their parents leave.

15. Dr. Hidalgo believes that infants use their early relationships to develop a set of assumptions that become a frame of reference for later experiences. Dr. Hidalgo evidently is a proponent of:
    a. cognitive theory.
    b. behaviorism.
    c. epigenetic theory.
    d. sociocultural theory.

Key Terms

Using your own words, write a brief definition or explanation of each of the following terms on a separate piece of paper.

1. trust versus mistrust
2. autonomy versus shame and doubt
3. working model
4. temperament
5. goodness of fit
6. stranger wariness
7. separation anxiety
8. self-awareness
9. synchrony
10. attachment
11. secure attachment
12. base for exploration
13. insecure attachment
14. insecure-avoidant
15. insecure-resistant/ambivalent
16. Strange Situation
17. disorganized
18. social referencing
19. infant day care

ANSWERS

CHAPTER REVIEW

1. emotional; social
2. oral; mouth
3. anal

Freud believed that the oral and anal stages are fraught with potential conflict that can have long-term consequences for the infant. If nursing is a hurried or tense event, for example, the child may become fixated at the oral stage, excessively eating, drinking, chewing, biting, or talking in quest of oral satisfaction.

4. 27
5. Erikson; trust versus mistrust; autonomy versus shame and doubt
6. behaviorism; reinforcement; punishment; John Watson
7. social; imitate
8. thoughts; perceptions; memories; working model
9. epigenetic; genetic; temperament
10. personality; environment
11. small; New York Longitudinal Study (NYLS); activity level, rhythmicity, approach–withdrawal, adaptability, intensity of reaction, threshold of responsiveness, quality of mood, distractibility, attention span
12. easy; difficult; slow to warm up; positive; inhibited; negative
13. goodness of fit
14. sociocultural; social
15. distress; contentment; curiosity; pleasure; anger
16. 9 months; stranger wariness; 10 to 14; separation anxiety; 9 to 14; decrease; targeted
17. pride, shame, embarrassment, guilt; what other people might be thinking
18. self-awareness; self; self-concept; self-evaluations

In the classic self-awareness experiment, babies look in a mirror after a dot of rouge is put on their nose. If the babies react to the mirror image by touching their nose, it is clear they know they are seeing their own face. Most babies demonstrate this self-awareness between 15 and 24 months of age.

19. synchrony; read other people's emotions; social interaction; timing; imitation; play
20. attachment
21. proximity-seeking; contact-maintaining
22. secure attachment; base for exploration
23. insecure attachment; insecure-avoidant; insecure-resistant/ambivalent

Some infants are avoidant: They engage in little interaction with their mother before and after her departure. Others are anxious and resistant: They cling nervously to their mother, are unwilling to explore, cry loudly when she leaves, and refuse to be comforted when she returns. Others are disorganized: They show an inconsistent mixture of behavior toward the mother.

24. Strange Situation; two-thirds; disorganized

25. does not determine

26. 10; low-income; overt responses; synchrony; attachment

27. social referencing; mealtime

28. mother–infant; as much as

29. basic care; play; motor; muscle; emotional; cognitive; self-confidence; emotional

30. family day care; center care; 50

31. children are not harmed by, and sometimes benefit from, professional day care

Good preschool education helps children learn more language, think with more perspective, develop better social skills, and achieve more in the long term.

32. (a) adequate attention to each child; (b) encouragement of sensorimotor exploration and language development; (c) attention to health and safety; (d) well-trained and professional caregivers.

33. insensitive; 20

34. no single; emotional; social; mothers'; father; day care; culture; inborn

PROGRESS TEST 1

Multiple-Choice Questions

1. **b.** is the answer. (p. 178)

   a., c., & d. These emotions emerge later in infancy, at about the same time as self-awareness emerges.

2. **c.** is the answer. (p. 180)

3. **c.** is the answer. (p. 178)

4. **d.** is the answer. (p. 185)

5. **b.** is the answer. (p. 175)

6. **c.** is the answer. (p. 174)

7. **b.** is the answer. (p. 173)

   a. Orality and anality refer to personality traits that result from fixation in the oral and anal stages, respectively.

   c. According to Erikson, this is the crisis of toddlerhood, which corresponds to Freud's anal stage.

   d. This is not a developmental crisis in Erikson's theory.

8. **c.** is the answer. (p. 173)

9. **a.** is the answer. (p. 181)

   c. Attachment behaviors are reliably found during infancy.

   d. There is no indication that the child attends day care.

10. **b.** is the answer. (pp. 175–176)

    a. "Secure" and "insecure" are different forms of attachment.

    c. The chapter does not describe different types of parenting.

    d. The Strange Situation is a test of attachment rather than of temperament.

11. **b.** is the answer. (p. 187)

12. **a.** is the answer. (p. 180)

13. **d.** is the answer. (p. 181)

    a. Self-awareness refers to the infant's developing sense of "me and mine."

    b. Synchrony describes the coordinated interaction between infant and caregiver.

    c. Affiliation describes the tendency of people at any age to seek the companionship of others.

14. **b.** is the answer. (pp. 181–184)

    a. The text does not link self-awareness to secure attachment.

    c. On the contrary, secure attachment promotes *independence* in infants and children.

15. **b.** is the answer. (p. 178)

True or False Items

1. F Sociocultural theorists contend that the entire social context can have an impact on the infant's development. (p. 177)

2. F Approximately 50 percent of infants display secure attachment. (p. 183)

3. T (p. 178)

4. T (p. 178)

5. F A securely attached toddler is most likely to explore the environment, the mother's presence being enough to give him or her the courage to do so. (p. 182)

6. F Researchers believe that high-quality day care is not likely to harm the child. In fact, it is thought to be beneficial to the development of cognitive and social skills. (p. 188)

7. T (p. 187)

8. F   Temperament is a product of both nature and nurture. (p. 175)

9. T (p. 179)

10. T (p. 175)

PROGRESS TEST 2

Multiple-Choice Questions

1. **a.** is the answer. (p. 184)

2. **a.** is the answer. (p. 173)

3. **c.** is the answer. (p. 179)

4. **a.** is the answer. (p. 177)

5. **c.** is the answer. (p. 179)

   a. & b. The social smile, as well as temperamental characteristics, emerge well before the first signs of self-awareness.

   d. Contemporary developmentalists link these emotions to self-consciousness, rather than any specific environmental event such as toilet training.

6. **a.** is the answer. (p. 175)

   b. & c. Although environment, especially parents, affects temperamental tendencies, the study noted that temperament was established within two or three months of birth.

   d. Self-awareness is not a temperamental characteristic.

7. **c.** is the answer. (p. 178)

8. **c.** is the answer. (pp. 176–177)

9. **d.** is the answer. (p. 184)

10. **a.** is the answer. (pp. 184–185)

    c. & d. The text does not suggest that the consequences of secure and insecure attachment differ in boys and girls.

11. **b.** is the answer. (p. 182)

    a. Insecure-avoidant attachment is marked by behaviors that indicate an infant is uninterested in a caregiver's presence or departure.

    c. Disorganized attachment is marked only by the inconsistency of infant–caregiver behaviors.

    d. Type B, or secure attachment, is marked by behaviors that indicate an infant is using a caregiver as a secure base from which to explore the environment.

12. **a.** is the answer. (p. 187)

13. **a.** is the answer. (p. 174)

b. & c. Freud alone would have agreed with these statements.

14. **d.** is the answer. (p. 184)

15. **b.** is the answer. (p. 181)

Matching Items

1. h (p. 174)	5. b (p. 173)	9. l (p. 179)
2. k (p. 173)	6. e (p. 173)	10. f (p. 182)
3. g (p. 182)	7. a (p. 185)	11. d (p. 181)
4. j (p. 180)	8. c (p 173)	12. i (p. 181)

THINKING CRITICALLY ABOUT CHAPTER 7

1. **b.** is the answer. (pp. 183–184)

   a., c., & d. These responses are more typical of insecurely attached infants.

2. **b.** is the answer. (p. 185)

3. **d.** is the answer. (pp. 182–183)

4. **a.** is the answer. About 50 percent of young infants can be described as "easy." (p. 205)

   b. About 15 percent of infants are described as "slow to warm up."

   c. About 10 percent of infants are described as "difficult."

5. **b.** is the answer. (p. 174)

   a. Cognitive theorists focus on a person's thoughts and values.

   b. Epigenetic theory explores the relative effects of nature and nurture on behavior.

   d. Sociocultural theory explores the entire social context.

6. **a.** is the answer. (p. 184)

   b. Only about 20 percent of low-income mothers are clinically depressed.

   c. Insecure attachment is a warning sign that something is amiss.

7. **d.** is the answer. (p. 188)

8. **a.** is the answer. (p. 175)

   b. Although temperament is genetic in origin, early temperamental traits *can* change.

   c. Temperament is apparent shortly after birth.

   d. As the person develops, the social context exerts a strong effect on temperament.

9. **c.** is the answer. (pp. 183, 184)

   a. & d. When their mothers return following an absence, securely attached infants usually re-establish social contact (with a smile or by climbing into their laps) and then resume playing.

b. There is no evidence in this example that Kalil is an abused child.

10. **c.** is the answer. (pp. 175–176)

a. & b. There is no evidence in the question that the parents are reinforcing tantrum behavior or failing to meet some biological need of the child's.

d. On the contrary, about 50 percent of infants are "easy" in temperamental style.

11. **d.** is the answer. (p. 185)

a. According to Erikson, this is the crisis of toddlerhood.

b. This describes a moment of coordinated and mutually responsive interaction between a parent and an infant.

c. Dyssynchrony occurs when the coordinated pace and timing of a synchronous interaction are temporarily lost.

12. **c.** is the answer. (p. 173)

a. & b. In Freud's theory, a person who is fixated in the anal stage exhibits messiness and disorganization or compulsive neatness.

d. Erikson, rather than Freud, proposed crises of development.

13. **c.** is the answer. (p. 179)

14. **b.** is the answer. The fear of being left by a caregiver (separation anxiety) is most obvious at 9 to 14 months. For this reason, 4-month-old Carl can be expected to become less upset than his older sister. (p. 178)

15. **a.** is the answer. (p. 174)

KEY TERMS

1. In Erikson's theory, the crisis of infancy is one of **trust versus mistrust,** in which the infant learns whether the world is essentially a secure place in which basic needs will be met. (p. 173)

2. In Erikson's theory, the crisis of toddlerhood is one of **autonomy versus shame and doubt,** in which toddlers strive to rule their own actions and bodies. (p. 173)

3. According to cognitive theory, infants use social relationships to develop a set of assumptions called a **working model** that organizes their perceptions and experiences. (p. 174)

4. **Temperament** refers to the "constitutionally based individual differences" in emotions, activity, and self-control. (p. 174)

5. **Goodness of fit** is the pattern of smooth interaction between the individual and the social milieu. (p. 177)

6. A common early fear, **stranger wariness** (also called fear of strangers) is first noticeable at about 6 months. (p. 178)

7. **Separation anxiety**, which is the infant fear of being left by the mother or other caregiver, is usually strongest at 9 to 14 months. (p. 178)

8. **Self-awareness** refers to a person's sense of himself or herself as being distinct from other people that makes possible many new self-conscious emotions, including shame, guilt, embarrassment, and pride. (p. 179)

9. **Synchrony** refers to the coordinated interaction between caregiver and infant that helps infants learn to express and read emotions. (p. 180)

10. **Attachment** is the enduring emotional tie that a person or animal forms with another. (p. 181)

11. A **secure attachment** is one in which the infant derives comfort and confidence from the "secure base" provided by a caregiver. (p. 182)

12. Responsive caregivers promote secure attachment by providing a secure **base for exploration** from which their children feel confident in venturing forth. (p. 182)

13. **Insecure attachment** is characterized by the infant's fear, anger, or seeming indifference toward the caregiver. (p. 182)

14. **Insecure-avoidant** is the pattern of attachment in which the infant seems uninterested in the caregiver's presence or departure. (p. 182)

15. **Insecure-resistant/ambivalent** is the pattern of attachment in which an infant resists active exploration, becomes very upset when the caregiver leaves, and both resists and seeks contact when the caregiver returns. (p. 182)

16. The **Strange Situation** is a laboratory procedure developed by Mary Ainsworth for assessing attachment. Infants are observed in a playroom, in several successive episodes, while the caregiver (usually the mother) and a stranger move in and out of the room. (p. 182)

17. **Disorganized** is the pattern of attachment that is neither secure nor insecure and is marked by inconsistent infant–caregiver interactions. (p. 184)

18. When infants engage in **social referencing,** they are looking to trusted adults for emotional cues on how to interpret uncertain situations. (p. 185)

19. **Infant day care** is regular care provided for babies by trained and paid nonrelatives. (p. 188)

Chapter Eight

The Play Years: Biosocial Development

Chapter Overview

Chapter 8 introduces the developing person between the ages of 2 and 6. This period is called the play years, emphasizing the central importance of play to the biosocial, cognitive, and psychosocial development of preschoolers.

The chapter begins by outlining growth rates and the changes in shape that occur from ages 2 through 6. This is followed by a look at brain growth and development and its role in the development of physical and cognitive abilities. A description of the acquisition of gross and fine motor skills follows, noting that mastery of such skills develops steadily during the play years along with intellectual growth. The section concludes with a discussion of the important issues of injury control and accidents, the major cause of childhood death except in times of famine.

The last section is in-depth exploration of child maltreatment, including its prevalence, contributing factors, consequences for future development, treatment, and prevention.

NOTE: Answer guidelines for all Chapter 8 questions begin on page 123.

Guided Study

The text chapter should be studied one section at a time. Before you read, preview each section by skimming it, noting headings and boldface items. Then read the appropriate section objectives from the following outline. Keep these objectives in mind and, as you read the chapter section, search for the information that will enable you to meet each objective. Once you have finished a section, write out answers for its objectives.

Body and Brain (pp. 197–203)

1. Describe normal physical growth during the play years, and account for variations in height and weight.

2. Describe changes in eating habits during the preschool years.

3. Discuss the processes of myelination and lateralization and their effect on development during the play years.

4. Describe the development of the prefrontal cortex during the play years and its impact on the developing person.

Motor Skills and Avoidable Injuries (pp. 203–208)

5. Distinguish between gross and fine motor skills, and discuss the development of each during the play years.

6. Discuss the significance of artistic expression and drawing during the play years.

7. Identify several factors that contribute to variation in the risk of accidental injury among children.

8. Explain what is meant by *injury control*, and differentiate three levels of prevention that have significantly reduced accidental death rates for children.

Child Maltreatment (pp. 208–214)

9. Identify the various categories of child maltreatment, and discuss several factors that contribute to its occurrence.

10. Describe current efforts to treat child maltreatment.

11. Discuss the consequences of child maltreatment.

12. Discuss foster care, kinship care, and adoption as intervention options in cases of child maltreatment.

Chapter Review

When you have finished reading the chapter, work through the material that follows to review it. Complete the sentences and answer the questions. As you proceed, evaluate your performance for each section by consulting the answers on page 123. Do not continue with the next section until you understand each answer. If you need to, review or reread the appropriate section in the textbook before continuing.

Body and Brain (pp. 197–203)

1. During the preschool years, from age _____ to _____ , children add almost _____ in height and gain about _____ in weight per year. By age 6, the average child in a developed nation weighs about _____ and measures _____ in height. In numbers, _____ are more useful than _____ in monitoring growth.

2. The range of normal physical development is quite _____ (narrow/broad).

3. In multiethnic countries, children of _____ descent tend to be tallest, followed by _____ , then _____ , and then _____ . The impact of _____ patterns on physical development can be seen in families in South Asia and India, where _____ (which gender?) are better fed and cared for than the other sex.

4. Of the many factors that influence height and weight, the most influential are the child's _____ , _____ , and _____ .

5. The dramatic differences between physical development in developed and underdeveloped nations are largely due to differences in the average child's _____ .

6. During the preschool years, annual height and weight gain is much _____ (greater/less) than during infancy. This means that children need _____

(fewer/more) calories per pound during this period.

7. The most prevalent nutritional problem in early childhood is an insufficient intake of _____ , _____ , and _____ .

8. An additional problem for American children is that they consume too many _____ .

9. By age 2, most pruning of the brain's _____ has occurred and the brain weighs _____ percent of its adult weight. By age 5, the brain has attained about _____ percent of its adult weight; by age 7 it is almost _____ percent.

10. Part of the brain's increase in size during childhood is due to the continued proliferation of _____ pathways and the ongoing process of _____ . This process, which is influenced by _____ , is essential for communication that is _____ and _____ . During the play years, this process proceeds most rapidly in brain areas dedicated to _____ and _____ .

11. The band of nerve fibers that connects the right and left sides of the brain, called the _____ _____ , grows and _____ rapidly during the play years. This helps children better coordinate functions that involve _____ .

12. The two sides of the body and brain _____ (are/are not) identical. The specialization of the two sides of the body and brain, which begins before _____ , is called _____ . Throughout the world, societies are organized to favor _____-handedness. Training of one side of the body is easier _____ (before/after) the process of _____ is complete.

13. Damage to the left side of the brain, where most _____ functions are located, is more serious in _____ than in _____ .

14. The left hemisphere of the brain controls the _____ side of the body and contains areas dedicated to _____ , _____ , and _____ . The right hemisphere controls the _____ side of the body and contains brains areas dedicated to _____ and _____ impulses.

15. The corpus callosum _____ (is/is not) fully developed in young children, which partly explains why their behaviors sometimes are _____ .

16. The final part of the brain to reach maturity is the _____ _____ . Development of this brain area is not completed until _____ .

17. Two signs of an undeveloped prefrontal cortex are _____ and _____ , which is the tendency to stick to a thought or action even after it has become inappropriate.

18. Brain development _____ (is/is not) smooth and linear, and brain functions _____ (improve/do not improve) at the same age for every child.

19. During the school years, many deficiencies in _____ , _____ _____ , _____ _____ , and _____ . _____ are directly tied to inadequate lateralization and to _____ and _____ of the frontal cortex.

Motor Skills and Avoidable Injuries (pp. 203–208)

20. Large body movements such as running, climbing, jumping, and throwing are called _____ _____ skills. These skills, which improve dramatically during the preschool years, require guided _____ , as well as a certain level of _____ _____ .

21. Most children learn these skills from _____ (other children/parents).

22. Skills that involve small body movements, such as pouring liquids and cutting food, are called _____ _____ skills. Preschoolers have greater difficulty with these skills primarily because they have not developed the _____ control, patience, or _____ needed—in part because the _____ of the central nervous system is not complete.

23. Many developmentalists believe that _____ _____ is a form of play that enhances the child's sense of accomplishment. The pictures children draw often reveal their _____ and _____ .

24. Except in times of famine, the leading cause of childhood death is _____ . Injuries and accidental deaths are _____ (more/less) frequent among boys than girls.

25. Not until age _____ does any disease become a greater cause of mortality.

26. Instead of "accident prevention," many experts speak of _____ (or _____ _____), an approach based on the belief that most accidents _____ (are/are not) preventable.

27. Preventive community actions that reduce everyone's chance of injury are called _____ _____ . Preventive actions that avert harm in the immediate situation constitute _____ _____ . Actions aimed at minimizing the impact of an adverse event that has already occurred constitute _____ _____ .

28. One risk factor in accident rates is _____ , with children in the _____ countries being more likely

than other children to die from _____
or an _____ .

29. (Changing Policy) The accidental death rate for American children between the ages of 1 and 5 has _____ (increased/ decreased) over the past 20 years.

Child Maltreatment (pp. 208–214)

30. Until a few decades ago, the concept of child maltreatment was mostly limited to obvious _____ assault, which was thought to be the outburst of a mentally disturbed person. Today, it is known that most perpetrators of maltreatment _____ (are/are not) mentally ill.

31. Intentional harm to, or avoidable endangerment of, someone under age 18 defines child _____ . Actions that are deliberately harmful to a child's well-being are classified as _____ . A failure to act appropriately to meet a child's basic needs is classified as _____ .

32. One sign of maltreatment is called _____ _____ _____ , in which an infant or young child gains little or no _____ , despite apparently normal health. Another sign is _____ , in which an older child seems too nervous to concentrate on anything. These phenomena are symptoms of _____ _____ _____ _____ , which was first described in combat victims. Children can also suffer from _____ neglect or from _____ neglect.

33. Since 1993, the ratio of the number of cases of _____ _____ , in which authorities have been officially notified, to cases of _____ _____ , which have been reported and verified, has been about _____ (what ratio?).

34. Laws requiring teachers, social workers, and other professionals to report possible maltreatment _____ (have/have not) resulted in increased reporting.

35. Maltreated children have difficulty learning in part because they may develop abnormal _____ patterns that make learning difficult. The most serious of these is _____ _____ _____ , which can cause the child's neck to break and damage _____ _____ and _____ _____ in the brain.

36. Abnormal brain development in an abused child may result in impaired _____ and delayed _____ _____ . In children who are neglected because their mothers are clinically depressed, the _____ (right/left) side of the prefrontal cortex develops more than the other side.

Describe other deficits of children who have been maltreated.

37. Public policy measures and other efforts designed to prevent maltreatment from ever occurring are called _____ _____ . An approach that focuses on spotting and treating the first symptoms of maltreatment is called _____ _____ . Last-ditch measures such as removing a child from an abusive home, jailing the perpetrator, and so forth constitute _____ _____ .

38. Some children are officially removed from their parents and placed in a _____ _____ arrangement with another adult or family who is paid to nurture them.

39. The number of children needing foster placement has _____ (increased/decreased) over the past decade in the United States.

40. In another type of foster care, called _____ _____ , a relative of the maltreated child becomes the approved caregiver. A final option is _____ .

Progress Test 1

Multiple-Choice Questions

Circle your answers to the following questions and check them with the answers beginning on page 123. If your answer is incorrect, read the explanation for why it is incorrect and then consult the appropriate pages of the text (in parentheses following the correct answer).

1. During the preschool years, the most common nutritional problem in developed countries is:
   a. serious malnutrition.
   b. excessive intake of sweets.
   c. insufficient intake of iron, zinc, and calcium.
   d. excessive caloric intake.

2. The brain center for speech is usually located in the:
   a. right brain.
   b. left brain.
   c. corpus callosum.
   d. space just below the right ear.

3. Which of the following is an example of tertiary prevention of child maltreatment?
   a. removing a child from an abusive home
   b. home visitation of families with infants by a social worker
   c. new laws establishing stiff penalties for child maltreatment
   d. public policy measures aimed at creating stable neighborhoods

4. (Changing Policy) Which of the following is not true regarding injury control?
   a. Broad-based television announcements do not have a direct impact on children's risk taking.
   b. Unless parents become involved, classroom safety education has little effect on children's actual behavior.
   c. Safety laws that include penalties are more effective than educational measures.
   d. Accidental deaths of 1- to 5-year-olds have held steady in the United States over the past two decades.

5. Children tend to have too much _____ in their diet, which contributes to _____ .
   a. iron; anemia
   b. sugar; tooth decay
   c. fat; delayed development of fine motor skills
   d. carbohydrate; delayed development of gross motor skills

6. Skills that involve large body movements, such as running and jumping, are called:
   a. activity-level skills.
   b. fine motor skills.
   c. gross motor skills.
   d. left-brain skills.

7. The brain's ongoing myelination during childhood helps children:
   a. control their actions more precisely.
   b. react more quickly to stimuli.
   c. control their emotions.
   d. do all of the above.

8. The leading cause of death in childhood is:
   a. accidents.
   b. untreated diabetes.
   c. malnutrition.
   d. iron deficiency anemia.

9. Regarding lateralization, which of the following is not true?
   a. Some cognitive skills require only one side of the brain.
   b. Brain centers for generalized emotional impulses can be found in the right hemisphere.
   c. The left hemisphere contains brain areas dedicated to spatial reasoning.
   d. The right side of the brain controls the left side of the body.

10. Which of the following factors is most responsible for differences in height and weight between children in developed and developing countries?
    a. the child's genetic background
    b. health care
    c. nutrition
    d. age of weaning

11. The area of the brain that directs and controls the other areas is the:
    a. corpus callosum.
    b. myelin sheath.
    c. prefrontal cortex.
    d. temporal lobe.

12. The relationship between accident rate and income can be described as:
    a. a positive correlation.
    b. a negative correlation.
    c. curvilinear.
    d. no correlation.

13. Which of the following is true of the corpus callosum?
    a. It enables short-term memory.
    b. It connects the two halves of the brain.
    c. It must be fully myelinated before gross motor skills can be acquired.
    d. All of the above are correct.

14. The improvements in eye–hand coordination that allow preschoolers to catch and then throw a ball occur, in part, because:
    a. the brain areas associated with this ability become more fully myelinated.
    b. the corpus callosum begins to function.
    c. fine motor skills have matured by age 2.
    d. gross motor skills have matured by age 2.

15. During the school years, inadequate lateralization of the brain and immaturity of the prefrontal cortex may contribute to deficiencies in:
    a. cognition.
    b. peer relationships.
    c. emotional control.
    d. all of the above.

True or False Items

Write T (*true*) or F (*false*) on the line in front of each statement.

_____ 1. Growth between ages 2 and 6 results in body proportions more similar to those of an adult.

_____ 2. During childhood, the legs develop faster than any other part of the body.

_____ 3. For most people, the brain center for speech is located in the left hemisphere.

_____ 4. The health, genes, and nutrition of the preschool child are major influences on growth.

_____ 5. Brain development is not smooth and linear.

_____ 6. Fine motor skills are usually easier for preschoolers to master than are gross motor skills.

_____ 7. Most serious childhood injuries truly are "accidents."

_____ 8. Children often fare as well in kinship care as they do in conventional foster care.

_____ 9. Most child maltreatment does not involve serious physical abuse.

_____ 10. Myelination is essential for basic communication between neurons.

_____ 11. Brain lateralization begins before birth.

Progress Test 2

Progress Test 2 should be completed during a final chapter review. Answer the following questions after you thoroughly understand the correct answers for the Chapter Review and Progress Test 1.

Multiple-Choice Questions

1. Each year from ages 2 to 6, the average child gains and grows, respectively:
    a. 2 pounds and 1 inch.
    b. 3 pounds and 2 inches.
    c. $4^1/_2$ pounds and 3 inches.
    d. 6 pounds and 6 inches.

2. The center for perceiving various types of visual configurations is usually located in the brain's:
    a. right hemisphere.
    b. left hemisphere.
    c. right or left hemisphere.
    d. corpus callosum.

3. Which of the following best describes brain growth during childhood?
    a. It proceeds at a slow, steady, linear rate.
    b. The left hemisphere develops more rapidly than the right.
    c. The right hemisphere develops more rapidly than the left.
    d. It is nonlinear.

4. The most prevalent disease or condition of young children in developed nations is:
    a. obesity.
    b. tooth decay.
    c. measles.
    d. muscular dystrophy.

5. Seeing her toddler reach for a brightly glowing burner on the stove, Sheila grabs his hand and says, "No, that's very hot." Sheila's behavior is an example of:
    a. primary prevention.
    b. secondary prevention.
    c. tertiary prevention.
    d. none of the above.

6. When parents or caregivers do not provide adequate food, shelter, attention, or supervision, it is referred to as:
   a. abuse.
   b. neglect.
   c. endangering.
   d. maltreatment.

7. Which of the following is true of a developed nation in which many ethnic groups live together?
   a. Ethnic variations in height and weight disappear.
   b. Ethnic variations in stature persist, but are substantially smaller.
   c. Children of African descent tend to be tallest, followed by Europeans, Asians, and Latinos.
   d. Cultural patterns exert a stronger-than-normal impact on growth patterns.

8. Which of the following is an example of perseveration?
   a. 2-year-old Jason sings the same song over and over
   b. 3-year-old Kwame falls down when attempting to kick a soccer ball
   c. 4-year-old Kara pours water very slowly from a pitcher into a glass
   d. None of the above is an example.

9. Which of the following is an example of a fine motor skill?
   a. kicking a ball
   b. running
   c. drawing with a pencil
   d. jumping

10. Children who have been maltreated often:
    a. regard other children and adults as hostile and exploitative.
    b. are less friendly and more aggressive.
    c. are more isolated than other children.
    d. are all of the above.

11. The left half of the brain contains areas dedicated to all of the following *except*:
    a. language.
    b. logic.
    c. analysis.
    d. creative impulses.

12. Most gross motor skills can be learned by healthy children by about age:
    a. 2.   c. 5.
    b. 3.   d. 7.

13. Two of the most important factors that affect height during the play years are:
    a. socioeconomic status and health care.
    b. gender and health care.
    c. heredity and nutrition.
    d. heredity and activity level.

14. (Changing Policy) Over the past two decades, the accidental death rate for American children between the ages of 1 and 5 has:
    a. decreased, largely as a result of new safety laws.
    b. decreased, largely because parents are more knowledgeable about safety practices.
    c. increased.
    d. remained unchanged.

15. During the play years, children's appetites seem _____ they were in the first two years of life.
    a. larger than
    b. smaller than
    c. about the same as
    d. erratic, sometimes smaller and sometimes larger than

Matching Items

Match each term or concept with its corresponding description or definition.

Terms or Concepts

_____ **1.** corpus callosum
_____ **2.** gross motor skills
_____ **3.** fine motor skills
_____ **4.** kinship care
_____ **5.** foster care
_____ **6.** injury control
_____ **7.** right hemisphere
_____ **8.** left hemisphere
_____ **9.** child abuse
_____ **10.** child neglect
_____ **11.** primary prevention
_____ **12.** secondary prevention
_____ **13.** tertiary prevention

Descriptions or Definitions

a. brain area that is primarily responsible for processing language

b. brain area that is primarily responsible for recognizing visual shapes

c. legal placement of a child in the care of someone other than his or her biological parents

d. a form of care in which a relative of a maltreated child takes over from the biological parents

e. procedures to prevent unwanted events or circumstances from ever occurring

f. running and jumping

g. actions that are deliberately harmful to a child's well-being

h. actions for averting harm in the immediate situation

i. painting a picture or tying shoelaces

j. failure to appropriately meet a child's basic needs

k. an approach emphasizing accident prevention

l. actions aimed at reducing the harm that has occurred

m. band of nerve fibers connecting the right and left hemispheres of the brain

Thinking Critically About Chapter 8

Answer these questions the day before an exam as a final check on your understanding of the chapter's terms and concepts.

1. An editorial in the local paper claims that there is no reason children younger than 6 cannot be taught basic literacy skills. You write to the editor, noting that:

    a. she has an accurate grasp of developmental processes.

    b. before age 6, brain myelination and development are too immature to enable children to form links between spoken and written language.

    c. although the right hemisphere is relatively mature at age 6, the left is not.

    d. although this may be true for girls, boys (who are slower to mature neurologically) would struggle.

2. Two-year-old Carrie is hyperactive, often confused between fantasy and reality, and jumps at any sudden noise. Her pediatrician suspects that she is suffering from:

    a. shaken baby syndrome.

    b. failure to thrive.

    c. post-traumatic stress disorder.

    d. child neglect.

3. Following an automobile accident, Amira developed severe problems with her speech. Her doctor believes that the accident injured the _____ of her brain.

    a. left side

    b. right side

    c. communication pathways

    d. corpus callosum

4. Two-year-old Ali is quite clumsy, falls down frequently, and often bumps into stationary objects. Ali most likely:
   a. has a neuromuscular disorder.
   b. has an underdeveloped right hemisphere of the brain.
   c. is suffering from an iron deficiency.
   d. is a normal 2-year-old whose gross motor skills will improve dramatically during the preschool years.

5. Climbing a fence is an example of a:
   a. fine motor skill.
   b. gross motor skill.
   c. circular reaction.
   d. launching event.

6. To prevent accidental death in childhood, some experts urge forethought and planning for safety and measures to limit the damage of such accidents as do occur. This approach is called:
   a. protective analysis.
   b. safety education.
   c. injury control.
   d. childproofing.

7. After his daughter scraped her knee, Ben gently cleansed the wound and bandaged it. Ben's behavior is an example of:
   a. primary prevention.
   b. secondary prevention.
   c. tertiary prevention.
   d. none of the above.

8. Which of the following activities would probably be the most difficult for a 5-year-old child?
   a. climbing a ladder
   b. catching a ball
   c. throwing a ball
   d. pouring juice from a pitcher without spilling it

9. Of the following children, the child with the greatest risk of accidental injury is:
   a. 6-year-old Brandon, whose family lives below the poverty line.
   b. 6-year-old Stacey, whose family lives below the poverty line.
   c. 3-year-old Daniel, who comes from an affluent family.
   d. 3-year-old Bonita, who comes from an affluent family.

10. Most child maltreatment:
    a. does not involve serious physical abuse.
    b. involves a rare outburst from the perpetrator.
    c. involves a mentally ill perpetrator.
    d. can be predicted from the victim's personality characteristics.

11. A mayoral candidate is calling for sweeping policy changes to help ensure the well-being of children by promoting home ownership, high-quality community centers, and more stable neighborhoods. If these measures are effective in reducing child maltreatment, they would be classified as:
    a. primary prevention.
    b. secondary prevention.
    c. tertiary prevention.
    d. differential response.

12. A factor that would figure very little into the development of fine motor skills, such as drawing and writing, is:
    a. strength.
    b. muscular control.
    c. judgment.
    d. short, fat fingers.

13. Jason is a three-year-old child, whose hyperactivity and hypervigilance may be symptoms of:
    a. post-traumatic stress disorder.
    b. an immature corpus callosum.
    c. an immature prefrontal cortex.
    d. normal development.

14. Which aspect of brain development during the play years contributes *most* to enhancing communication among the brain's various specialized areas?
    a. increasing brain weight
    b. proliferation of dendrite networks
    c. myelination
    d. increasing specialization of brain areas

15. Three-year-old Kyle's parents are concerned because Kyle, who generally seems healthy, doesn't seem to have the hefty appetite he had as an infant. Should they be worried?
    a. Yes, because appetite normally increases throughout the preschool years.
    b. Yes, because appetite remains as good during the preschool years as it was earlier.
    c. No, because caloric need is less during the preschool years than during infancy.
    d. There is not enough information to determine whether Kyle is developing normally.

Key Terms

Using your own words, write a brief definition or explanation of each of the following terms on a separate piece of paper.

1. myelination
2. corpus callosum
3. lateralization

4. prefrontal cortex

5. perseveration

6. injury control/harm reduction

7. primary prevention

8. secondary prevention

9. tertiary prevention

10. child maltreatment

11. child abuse

12. child neglect

13. failure to thrive

14. post-traumatic stress disorder

15. reported maltreatment

16. substantiated maltreatment

17. shaken baby syndrome

18. foster care

19. kinship care

ANSWERS
CHAPTER REVIEW

1. 2; 6; 3 inches (7 centimeters); 41/2 pounds (2 kilograms); 46 pounds (21 kilograms); 46 inches (117 centimeters); percentiles; norms

2. broad

3. African; Europeans; Asians; Latinos; cultural; boys

4. genes; health; nutrition

5. nutrition

6. less; fewer

7. iron; zinc; calcium

8. sweetened cereals and drinks

9. dendrites; 75; 90; 100

10. communication; myelination; experience; fast; complex; memory; reflection

11. corpus callosum; myelinates; both sides of the brain and body

12. are not; birth; lateralization; right; before; lateralization

13. language; adults; children

14. right; logic; analysis; language; left; emotional; creative

15. is not; clumsy, wobbly, and slow

16. prefrontal cortex; mid-adolescence

17. impulsiveness; perseveration

18. is not; do not improve

19. cognition, peer relationships; emotional control; classroom learning; immaturity; asymmetry

20. gross motor; practice; brain maturation

21. other children

22. fine motor; muscular; judgment; myelination

23. artistic expression; perception; cognition

24. accidents; more

25. 40

26. injury control; harm reduction; are

27. primary prevention; secondary prevention; tertiary prevention

28. income; poorest; disease; accidents

29. decreased

30. physical; are not

31. maltreatment; abuse; neglect

32. failure to thrive; weight; hypervigilance; post-traumatic stress disorder; medical; educational

33. reported maltreatment; substantiated maltreatment; 3-to-1

34. have

35. brain; shaken baby syndrome; blood vessels; neural connections

36. memory; logical thinking; right

37. primary prevention; secondary prevention; tertiary prevention

Maltreated children tend to regard other people as hostile and exploitative, and hence are less friendly, more aggressive, and more isolated than other children. As adolescents and adults they often use drugs or alcohol, choose unsupportive relationships, become victims or aggressors, sabotage their own careers, eat too much or too little, and generally engage in self-destructive behavior.

38. foster care

39. increased

40. kinship care; adoption

PROGRESS TEST 1

Multiple-Choice Questions

1. c. is the answer. (p. 198)

    a. Serious malnutrition is much more likely to occur in infancy or in adolescence than in early childhood.

b. Although an important health problem, eating too much candy or other sweets is not as serious a problem as this.

d. Since growth is slower during the preschool years, children need fewer calories per pound during this period.

2. **b.** is the answer. (p. 200)

a. & d. The right brain is the location of areas associated with generalized emotional and creative impulses.

c. The corpus callosum helps integrate the functioning of the two halves of the brain; it does not contain areas specialized for particular skills.

3. **a.** is the answer. (p. 213)

b. This is an example of secondary prevention.

c. & d. These are examples of primary prevention.

4. **d.** is the answer. Accident rates have *decreased* during this time period. (p. 207)

5. **b.** is the answer. (pp. 198–199)

6. **c.** is the answer. (p. 203)

7. **d.** is the answer. (pp. 199, 201)

8. **a.** is the answer. (p. 205)

9. **a.** is the answer. (p. 201)

10. **c.** is the answer. (p. 198)

11. **c.** is the answer. (p. 201)

a. The corpus callosum is the band of fibers that link the two halves of the brain.

b. The myelin sheath is the fatty insulation that surrounds some neurons in the brain.

d. The temporal lobes of the brain contain the primary centers for hearing.

12. **b.** is the answer. Children with *lower* SES have *higher* accident rates. (p. 206)

13. **b.** is the answer. (p. 200)

a. The corpus callosum is not directly involved in memory.

c. Myelination of the central nervous system is important to the mastery of *fine* motor skills.

14. **a.** is the answer. (p. 199)

b. The corpus callosum begins to function long before the play years.

c. & d. Neither fine nor gross motor skills have fully matured by age 2.

15. **d.** is the answer. (p. 202)

True or False Items

1. T (p. 197)

2. F   During childhood, the brain develops faster than any other part of the body. (p. 199)

3. T (p. 200)

4. T (p. 198)

5. T (p. 202)

6. F Fine motor skills are more difficult for preschoolers to master than are gross motor skills. (p. 203)

7. F   Most serious accidents involve someone's lack of forethought. (pp. 205–206)

8. T (p. 214)

9. T (p. 209)

10. F   Although myelination is not essential for basic communication between neurons, it is essential for fast and complex communication (p. 199)

11. T (p. 200)

PROGRESS TEST 2

Multiple-Choice Questions

1. **c.** is the answer. (p. 197)

2. **a.** is the answer. (p. 201)

b. & c. The left hemisphere of the brain contains areas associated with language development.

d. The corpus callosum does not contain areas for specific behaviors.

3. **d.** is the answer. (p. 202)

b. & c. The left and right hemispheres develop at similar rates.

4. **b.** is the answer. (p. 199)

5. **b.** is the answer. (p. 206)

6. **b.** is the answer. (p. 208)

a. Abuse is deliberate, harsh injury to the body.

c. Endangerment was not discussed.

d. Maltreatment is too broad a term.

7. **c.** is the answer. (p. 197)

8. **a.** is the answer. (p. 201)

b. Kicking a ball is a gross motor skill.

c. Pouring is a fine motor skill.

9. **c.** is the answer. (p. 203)

a., b., & d. These are gross motor skills.

10. **d.** is the answer. (pp. 212–213)

11. **d.** is the answer. Brain areas that control generalized creative and emotional impulses are found in the right hemisphere. (p. 201)

12. **c.** is the answer. (p. 203)

13. **c.** is the answer. (p. 198)

14. **a.** is the answer. (p. 207)

   b. Although safety education is important, the decrease in accident rate is largely the result of new safety laws.

15. **b.** is the answer. (p. 198)

Matching Items

1. m (p. 200)   6. k (p. 205)   11. e (p. 206)
2. f (p. 203)   7. b (p. 200)   12. h (p. 206)
3. i (p. 203)   8. a (p. 200)   13. l (p. 206)
4. d (p. 214)   9. g (p. 208)
5. c (p. 213)   10. j (p. 208)

THINKING CRITICALLY ABOUT CHAPTER 8

1. **b.** is the answer. (p. 202)

2. **c.** is the answer. (p. 209)

   a. Shaken baby syndrome is a consequence of maltreatment associated with memory impairment and delays in logical thinking.

   b. Failure to thrive is associated with little or no weight gain, despite apparent good health.

   d. Child neglect simply refers to failure to meet a child's basic needs. Carrie's specific symptoms may be caused by neglect or maltreatment, but they are most directly signs of PTSD.

3. **a.** is the answer. In most people, the left hemisphere of the brain contains centers for language, including speech. (p. 200)

4. **d.** is the answer. (p. 203)

5. **b.** is the answer. (p. 203)

   a. Fine motor skills involve small body movements, such as the hand movements used in painting.

   c. & d. These events were not discussed in this chapter.

6. **c.** is the answer. (p. 205)

7. **c.** is the answer. (p. 206)

8. **d.** is the answer. (p. 203)

   a., b., & c. Preschoolers find these gross motor skills easier to perform than fine motor skills such as that described in d.

9. **a.** The strongest risk factor in accidental injuries is low SES. (p. 206)

   b. & d. Boys, as a group, suffer more injuries than girls do.

10. **a.** is the answer. (p. 209)

11. **a.** is the answer. (p. 213)

b. Had the candidate called for measures to spot the early warning signs of maltreatment, this answer would be true.

c. Had the candidate called for jailing those who maltreat children or providing greater counseling and health care for victims, this answer would be true.

d. Differential response is not discussed in the chapter; however, it refers to separate reporting procedures for high- and low-risk families.

12. **a.** is the answer. Strength is a more important factor in the development of gross motor skills. (p. 203)

13. **a.** is the answer. (p. 209)

14. **b.** is the answer. (p. 199)

15. **c.** is the answer. (p. 198)

KEY TERMS

1. **Myelination** is the insulating process that speeds up the transmission of nerve impulses. (p. 199)

2. The **corpus callosum** is a band of nerve fibers that connects the right and left hemispheres of the brain. (p. 200)

3. **Lateralization** refers to the differentiation of the two sides of the brain so that each serves specific, specialized functions. (p. 201)

4. The so-called executive area of the brain, the **prefrontal cortex** specializes in planning, selecting, and coordinating thoughts. (p. 201)

5. **Perseveration** is the tendency to stick to thoughts or actions, even after they have become useless or inappropriate. In young children, perseveration is a normal product of immature brain functions. (p. 201)

   Memory Aid: To persevere is to continue, or persist, at something.

6. **Injury control** (or **harm reduction**) is the practice of limiting the extent of injuries by anticipating, controlling, and preventing dangerous activities. (p. 205)

7. **Primary prevention** refers to actions that change overall background conditions to prevent some unwanted event or circumstance. (p. 206)

8. **Secondary prevention** involves actions that avert harm in the immediate situation. (p. 206)

9. **Tertiary prevention** involves actions taken after an adverse event occurs, aimed at reducing the harm or preventing disability. (p. 206)

10. **Child maltreatment** is intentional harm to, or avoidable endangerment of, anyone under age 18. (p. 208)

11. **Child abuse** refers to deliberate actions that are harmful to a child's physical, emotional, or sexual well-being. (p. 208)

12. **Child neglect** refers to failure to appropriately meet a child's basic physical, educational, or emotional needs. (p. 208)

13. A sign of possible child neglect, **failure to thrive** occurs when an otherwise healthy child gains little or no weight. (p. 209)

14. **Post-traumatic stress disorder (PTSD)** is a syndrome triggered by exposure to an extreme traumatic stressor. In maltreated children, symptoms of PTSD include hyperactivity and hypervigilance, sleeplessness, and confusion between fantasy and reality. (p. 209)

15. Child maltreatment that has been officially reported to the police or other authorities is called **reported maltreatment**. (p. 209)

16. Child maltreatment that has been officially reported to authorities, investigated, and verified is called **substantiated maltreatment**. (p. 209)

17. A serious condition caused by sharply and quickly shaking an infant to stop his or her crying, **shaken baby syndrome** is associated with severe brain damage that results from internal hemorrhaging and broken neural connections. (p. 212)

18. **Foster care** is a legally sanctioned, publicly supported arrangement in which children are removed from their biological parents and temporarily given to another adult to nurture. (p. 213)

19. **Kinship care** is a form of foster care in which a relative of a maltreated child becomes the child's legal caregiver. (p. 214)

Chapter Nine

The Play Years: Cognitive Development

Chapter Overview

In countless everyday instances, as well as in the findings of numerous research studies, young children reveal themselves to be remarkably thoughtful, insightful, and perceptive thinkers whose grasp of the causes of everyday events, memory of the past, and mastery of language are sometimes astonishing. Chapter 9 begins by comparing Piaget's and Vygotsky's views of cognitive development at this age. According to Piaget, young children's thought is prelogical: Between the ages of 2 and 6, they are unable to perform many logical operations and are limited by irreversible, centered, and static thinking. Lev Vygotsky, a contemporary of Piaget's, saw learning as a social activity more than as a matter of individual discovery. Vygotsky focused on the child's "zone of proximal development" and the relationship between language and thought.

The first section next focuses on what preschoolers can do, including their emerging abilities to theorize about the world. This leads into a section on language development during the play years. Although young children demonstrate rapid improvement in vocabulary and grammar, they have difficulty with abstractions, metaphorical speech, and certain rules of grammar. A discussion of whether bilingualism in young children is useful concludes the section on language.

The chapter ends with a discussion of preschool education, including a description of "quality" preschool programs and an evaluation of their impact on children.

NOTE: Answer guidelines for all Chapter 9 questions begin on page 136.

Guided Study

The text chapter should be studied one section at a time. Before you read, preview each section by skimming it, noting headings and boldface items. Then read the appropriate section objectives from the following outline. Keep these objectives in mind and, as you read the chapter section, search for the information that will enable you to meet each objective. Once you have finished a section, write out answers for its objectives.

How Young Children Think: Piaget and Vygotsky (pp. 217–225)

1. Describe and discuss the major characteristics of preoperational thought, according to Piaget.

2. Discuss Vygotsky's views on cognitive development, focusing on the concept of guided participation.

3. Explain the significance of the zone of proximal development and scaffolding in promoting cognitive growth.

4. Describe Vygotsky's view of the role of language in cognitive growth.

5. Explain the typical young child's theory of mind, noting how it is affected by cultural context.

Language (pp. 225–230)

6. (text and In Person) Describe the development of vocabulary in children, and explain the role of fast mapping in this process.

7. Describe the development of grammar during the play years, noting limitations in the young child's language abilities.

8. Discuss the advantages and disadvantages of bilingualism at a young age.

Early-Childhood Education (pp. 230–234)

9. Describe variations in early-childhood education programs.

10. Identify the characteristics of a high-quality preschool program, and briefly discuss the benefits of preschool education.

Chapter Review

When you have finished reading the chapter, work through the material that follows to review it. Complete the sentences and answer the questions. As you proceed, evaluate your performance for each section by consulting the answers beginning on page 136. Do not continue with the next section until you understand each answer. If you need to, review or reread the appropriate section in the textbook before continuing.

How Young Children Think: Piaget and Vygotsky (pp. 217–225)

1. For many years, researchers maintained that young children's thinking abilities were sorely limited by their _____ .

2. Piaget referred to cognitive development between the ages of 2 and 6 as _____ thought.

3. Young children's tendency to think about one aspect of a situation at a time is called _____ . One particular form of this characteristic is children's tendency to contemplate the world exclusively from their personal perspective, which is referred to as _____ . They also tend to focus on

_____ to the exclusion of other attributes of objects and people.

4. Preschoolers' understanding of the world tends to be _____ (static/dynamic), which means that they tend to think of their world as _____ . A closely related characteristic is _____—the inability to recognize that reversing a process will restore the original conditions from which the process began.

5. The idea that amount is unaffected by changes in appearance is called _____ . In the case of _____ _____ _____ , preschoolers who are shown pairs of checkers in two even rows and who then observe one row being spaced out will say that the spaced-out row has more checkers.

6. The term _____-_____ highlights the idea that children attempt to construct theories to explain everything they see and hear. The idea that children are "apprentices in thinking" emphasizes that children's intellectual growth is stimulated by their _____ _____ in _____ experiences of their environment. The critical element in this process is that the mentor and the child _____ to accomplish a task.

7. Much of the research from the sociocultural perspective on the young child's emerging cognition is inspired by the Russian psychologist _____ . According to this perspective, an adult can most effectively help a child solve a problem by offering _____ , _____ successes, maintaining _____ , providing _____ , and helping the child to recognize that together they are progressing toward accomplishing their goal.

8. Unlike Piaget, this psychologist believed that cognitive growth is a _____ _____ more than a matter of individual discovery.

9. Vygotsky suggested that for each developing individual there is a _____ _____ _____ _____ , a range of skills that the person can exercise with assistance but is not yet able to perform independently.

10. How and when new skills are developed depends, in part, on the willingness of tutors to _____ the child's participation in learning encounters.

11. Vygotsky believed that language is essential to the advancement of thinking in two crucial ways. The first is through the internal dialogue in which a person talks to himself or herself, called _____ _____ . In preschoolers, this dialogue is likely to be _____ (expressed silently/uttered aloud).

12. According to Vygotsky, another way language advances thinking is as the _____ of the social interaction.

13. As a result of their experiences with others, young children acquire a _____ _____ _____ that reflects their developing concepts about human mental processes.

Describe the theory of mind of children between the ages of 3 and 6.

14. Most 3-year-olds _____ (have/do not have) difficulty realizing that a belief can be false.

15. Research studies reveal that theory-of-mind development depends as much on general _____ ability as it does on

_____ _____ . A third

helpful factor is having at least one

_____ .

Finally, _____ may be a factor.

Language (pp. 225–230)

16. The skills a child needs in order to learn to read
are called _____ _____ .
Two aspects of development that make ages 2 to
6 the prime time for learning language are
_____ and _____ in
the language areas of the brain.

17. Although early childhood does not appear to be a
_____ period for language develop-
ment, it does seem to be a _____
period for the learning of vocabulary, grammar,
and pronunciation.

18. During the preschool years, a dramatic increase
in language occurs, with _____
increasing exponentially.

19. Through the process called _____
_____ preschoolers often learn
words after only one or two hearings. A closely
related process is _____
_____ , by which children are able
to apply newly learned words to other objects in
the same category.

20. Abstract nouns and metaphors are
_____ (more/no more) difficult for
preschoolers to understand.

21. Because preschool children tend to think in
absolute terms, they have difficulty with words
that express _____ , as well as
words expressing relativities of
_____ and _____ .

22. The structures, techniques, and rules that a language uses to communicate meaning define its
_____ . By age _____ ,
children typically demonstrate extensive understanding of this aspect of language.

23. Preschoolers' tendency to apply rules of grammar
when they should not is called
_____ .

Give several examples of this tendency.

24. Most developmentalists agree that bilingualism
_____ (is/is not necessarily) an
asset to children in today's world.

25. Children who speak two languages by age 5 often
are less _____ in their understand-
ing of language and more advanced in their
_____ _____
_____ . Advocates of monolingual-
ism point out that bilingual proficiency comes at
the expense of _____
_____ in the dominant language,
slowing down the development of
_____ _____ .

26. Some immigrant parents are saddened when
their children make a _____
_____ and become more fluent in
their new language than that of their home culture. The best solution is for children to become
_____ _____ , who are
fluent in both languages. This is easiest for
children when their parents _____
_____ .

Early-Childhood Education (pp. 230–234)

27. A century ago, _____
_____ opened the first structured
nursery schools for poor children in Rome. Many
new programs use an educational model inspired
by _____ that allows children to
_____ .

Other, often _____ (more/less)
structured programs, stress _____ .

28. The new early-childhood curriculum called

_____ _____ encour-

ages children to master skills not usually seen

until about age _____ .

29. Early-childhood education _____

(has/has not) always been deemed important in

most cultures. Today, developmentalists

_____ (agree/disagree) about the

value of national programs for quality early edu-

cation.

30. In 1965, _____ _____

_____ was inaugurated to give low-

income children some form of compensatory edu-

cation during the preschool years. Longitudinal

research found that graduates of similar but more

intensive, well-evaluated programs scored

_____ (higher/no higher) on

achievement tests and were more likely to attend

college and less likely to go to jail.

List several characteristics of high-quality early childhood education.

Progress Test 1

Multiple-Choice Questions

Circle your answers to the following questions and
check them with the answers on page 137. If your
answer is incorrect, read the explanation for why it is
incorrect and then consult the appropriate pages of
the text (in parentheses following the correct answer).

1. Piaget believed that children are in the preoperational stage from ages:
   a. 6 months to 1 year.   **c.** 2 to 6 years.
   b. 1 to 3 years.   **d.** 5 to 11 years.

2. Which of the following is *not* a characteristic of
preoperational thinking?
   a. focus on appearance
   b. static reasoning
   c. abstract thinking
   d. centration

3. Which of the following provides evidence that
early childhood is a sensitive period, rather than
a critical period, for language learning?
   a. People can and do master their native language after early childhood.
   b. Vocabulary, grammar, and pronunciation are
acquired especially easily during early childhood.
   c. Neurological characteristics of the young
child's developing brain facilitate language
acquisition.
   d. a. and b.
   e. a., b., and c.

4. Emergent literacy refers to the:
   a. skills needed to learn to read.
   b. "teachability" of pre-K children.
   c. best time for learning a second or third language.
   d. learning experiences provided to children by
skilled tutors.

5. Reggio Emilia is:
   a. the educator who first opened nursery schools
for poor children in Rome.
   b. the early-childhood curriculum that allows
children to discover ideas at their own pace.
   c. a new form of early-childhood education that
encourages children to master skills not usually seen until age 7 or so.
   d. the Canadian system for promoting bilingualism in young children.

6. The vocabulary of preschool children consists primarily of:
   a. metaphors.
   b. self-created words.
   c. abstract nouns.
   d. verbs and concrete nouns.

7. Preschoolers sometimes apply the rules of grammar even when they shouldn't. This tendency is
called:
   a. overregularization.   **c.** practical usage.
   b. literal language.   **d.** single-mindedness.

8. The Russian psychologist Vygotsky emphasized that:
   a. language helps children form ideas.
   b. children form concepts first, then find words to express them.
   c. language and other cognitive developments are unrelated at this stage.
   d. preschoolers learn language only for egocentric purposes.

9. Private speech can be described as:
   a. a way of formulating ideas to oneself.
   b. fantasy.
   c. an early learning difficulty.
   d. the beginnings of deception.

10. The child who has not yet grasped the principle of conservation is likely to:
    a. insist that a tall, narrow glass contains more liquid than a short, wide glass, even though both glasses actually contain the same amount.
    b. be incapable of egocentric thought.
    c. be unable to reverse an event.
    d. do all of the above.

11. In later life, High/Scope graduates showed:
    a. better report cards, but more behavioral problems.
    b. significantly higher IQ scores.
    c. higher scores on math and reading achievement tests.
    d. alienation from their original neighborhoods and families.

12. The best preschool programs are generally those that provide the most:
    a. behavioral control.
    b. positive social interactions among children and adults.
    c. instruction in conservation and other logical principles.
    d. demonstration of toys by professionals.

13. Many newer preschool programs that are inspired by Piaget stress _____ , in contrast to alternative programs that stress _____ .
    a. academics; readiness
    b. readiness; academics
    c. child development; readiness
    d. academics; child development

14. Preschoolers can succeed at tests of conservation when:
    a. they are allowed to work cooperatively with other children.

    b. the test is presented as a competition.
    c. they are informed that they are being observed by their parents.
    d. the test is presented in a simple, nonverbal, and gamelike way.

15. Through the process called fast mapping, children:
    a. immediately assimilate new words by connecting them through their assumed meaning to categories of words they have already mastered.
    b. acquire the concept of conservation at an earlier age than Piaget believed.
    c. are able to move beyond egocentric thinking.
    d. become skilled in the practical use of language.

True or False Items

Write *T (true) or F (false)* on the line in front of each statement.

_____ 1. Early childhood is a prime learning period for every child.

_____ 2. In conservation problems, many preschoolers are unable to understand the transformation because they focus exclusively on appearances.

_____ 3. Preschoolers use private speech more selectively than older children.

_____ 4. Children typically develop a theory of mind at about age 7.

_____ 5. Preoperational children tend to focus on one aspect of a situation to the exclusion of all others.

_____ 6. Piaget focused on what children cannot do rather than what they can do.

_____ 7. With the beginning of preoperational thought, most preschoolers can understand abstract words.

_____ 8. A preschooler who says "You comed up and hurted me" is demonstrating a lack of understanding of English grammar.

_____ 9. Successful preschool programs generally have a low adult–child ratio.

_____ 10. Vygotsky believed that cognitive growth is largely a social activity.

_____ 11. *Theory-theory* refers to the tendency of young children to see the world as an unchanging reflection of their current construction of reality.

Progress Test 2

Progress Test 2 should be completed during a final chapter review. Answer the following questions after you thoroughly understand the correct answers for the Chapter Review and Progress Test 1.

Multiple-Choice Questions

1. Children who speak two languages by age 5:
   a. are less egocentric in their understanding of language.
   b. are more advanced in their theory of mind.
   c. have somewhat slower vocabulary development in one or both languages.
   d. are characterized by all of the above.

2. Piaget believed that preoperational children fail conservation of liquid tests because of their tendency to:
   a. focus on appearance.
   b. fast map.
   c. overregularize.
   d. do all of the above.

3. A preschooler who focuses his or her attention on only one feature of a situation is demonstrating a characteristic of preoperational thought called:
   a. centration.   c. reversibility.
   b. overregularization.   d. egocentrism.

4. One characteristic of preoperational thought is:
   a. the ability to categorize objects.
   b. the ability to count in multiples of 5.
   c. the inability to perform logical operations.
   d. difficulty adjusting to changes in routine.

5. The zone of proximal development represents the:
   a. skills or knowledge that are within the potential of the learner but are not yet mastered.
   b. influence of a child's peers on cognitive development.
   c. explosive period of language development during the play years.
   d. normal variations in children's language proficiency.

6. According to Vygotsky, language advances thinking through private speech, and by:
   a. helping children to privately review what they know.
   b. helping children explain events to themselves.
   c. serving as a mediator of the social interaction that is a vital part of learning.
   d. facilitating the process of fast mapping.

7. Irreversibility refers to the:
   a. inability to understand that other people view the world from a different perspective than one's own.
   b. inability to think about more than one idea at a time.
   c. failure to understand that changing the arrangement of a group of objects doesn't change their number.
   d. failure to understand that undoing a process will restore the original conditions.

8. According to Piaget:
   a. it is impossible for preoperational children to grasp the concept of conservation, no matter how carefully it is explained.
   b. preschoolers fail to solve conservation problems because they center their attention on the transformation that has occurred and ignore the changed appearances of the objects.
   c. with special training, even preoperational children are able to grasp some aspects of conservation.
   d. preschoolers fail to solve conservation problems because they have no theory of mind.

9. Scaffolding of a child's cognitive skills can be provided by:
   a. a mentor.
   b. the objects or experiences of a culture.
   c. the child's past learning.
   d. all of the above.

10. Which theorist would be most likely to agree with the statement, "Learning is a social activity more than it is a matter of individual discovery"?
    a. Piaget   c. both a. and b.
    b. Vygotsky   d. neither a. nor b.

11. Children first demonstrate some understanding of grammar:
    a. as soon as the first words are produced.
    b. once they begin to use language for practical purposes.
    c. through the process called fast mapping.
    d. in their earliest sentences.

12. Balanced bilingualism is easiest for children to attain when:
    a. the parents themselves speak two languages.
    b. the second language is not taught until the child is fluent in the first.
    c. fast mapping is avoided.
    d. overregularization is discouraged.

13. Most 5-year-olds have difficulty understanding metaphors because:
    a. they have not yet begun to develop grammar.
    b. the literal nature of the fast-mapping process allows only one meaning per word.
    c. of their limited vocabulary.
    d. of their tendency to overregularize.

14. Overregularization indicates that a child:
    a. is clearly applying rules of grammar.
    b. persists in egocentric thinking.
    c. has not yet mastered the principle of conservation.
    d. does not yet have a theory of mind.

15. Regarding the value of preschool education, most developmentalists believe that:
    a. most disadvantaged children will not benefit from an early preschool education.
    b. most disadvantaged children will benefit from an early preschool education.
    c. the early benefits of preschool education are likely to disappear by grade 3.
    d. the relatively small benefits of antipoverty measures such as Head Start do not justify their huge costs.

Matching Items

Match each term or concept with its corresponding description or definition.

Terms or Concepts

_____ 1. emergent literacy
_____ 2. scaffold
_____ 3. theory of mind
_____ 4. zone of proximal development
_____ 5. overregularization
_____ 6. fast mapping
_____ 7. irreversibility
_____ 8. centration
_____ 9. conservation
_____ 10. private speech
_____ 11. guided participation
_____ 12. static reasoning

Descriptions or Definitions

a. the idea that amount is unaffected by changes in shape or placement
b. the tendency to see the world as an unchanging place
c. the cognitive distance between a child's actual and potential levels of development
d. the tendency to think about one aspect of a situation at a time
e. the process whereby the child learns through social interaction with a "tutor"
f. our understanding of mental processes in ourselves and others
g. the process by which words are learned after only one hearing
h. an inappropriate application of rules of grammar
i. the internal use of language to form ideas
j. the inability to understand that original conditions are restored by the undoing of some process
k. to structure a child's participation in learning encounters
l. the skills needed to learn to read.

Thinking Critically About Chapter 9

Answer these questions the day before an exam as a final check on your understanding of the chapter's terms and concepts.

1. An experimenter first shows a child two rows of checkers that each have the same number of checkers. Then, with the child watching, the experimenter elongates one row and asks the child if each of the two rows still has an equal number of checkers. This experiment tests the child's understanding of:
   a. reversibility.
   b. conservation of matter.
   c. conservation of number.
   d. centration.

2. A preschooler believes that a "party" is the one and only attribute of a birthday. She says that Daddy doesn't have a birthday because he never has a party. This thinking demonstrates the tendency Piaget called:
   a. egocentrism.   c. conservation of events.
   b. centration.   d. mental representation.

3. A child who understands that 6 + 3 = 9 means that 9 − 6 = 3 has had to master the concept of:
   a. reversibility.   c. conservation.
   b. number.   d. egocentrism.

4. A 4-year-old tells the teacher that a clown should not be allowed to visit the class because "Pat is 'fraid of clowns." The 4-year-old thus shows that he can anticipate how another will feel. This is evidence of the beginnings of:
   a. egocentrism.
   b. deception.
   c. a theory of mind.
   d. conservation.

5. Asked "Where do dreams come from?," a 5-year-old child is likely to answer:
   a. "from God."
   b. "from the sky."
   c. "from my pillow."
   d. "from inside my head."

6. A nursery school teacher is given the job of selecting holiday entertainment for a group of preschool children. If the teacher agrees with the ideas of Vygotsky, she is most likely to select:
   a. a simple TV show that every child can understand.
   b. a hands-on experience that requires little adult supervision.
   c. brief, action-oriented play activities that the children and teachers will perform together.
   d. holiday puzzles for children to work on individually.

7. Which of the following terms does *not* belong with the others?
   a. focus on appearances
   b. static reasoning
   c. reversibility
   d. centration

8. That a child produces sentences that follow such rules of word order as "the initiator of an action precedes the verb, the receiver of an action follows it" demonstrates a knowledge of:
   a. grammar.   c. pragmatics.
   b. semantics.   d. phrase structure.

9. The 2-year-old child who says, "We goed to the store," is making a grammatical:
   a. centration.   c. extension.
   b. overregularization.   d. fast map.

10. An experimenter who makes two balls of clay of equal amount, then rolls one into a long, skinny rope and asks the child if the amounts are still the same, is testing the child's understanding of:
    a. conservation.   c. perspective-taking.
    b. reversibility.   d. centration.

11. Dr. Jones, who believes that children's language growth greatly contributes to their cognitive growth, evidently is a proponent of the ideas of:
    a. Piaget.   c. Flavell.
    b. Chomsky.   d. Vygotsky.

12. Comparing the views of Piaget with those of Vygotsky, active learning is to guided participation as egocentrism is to:
    a. apprenticeship.   c. scaffold.
    b. structure.   d. fast mapping.

13. In describing the limited logical reasoning of preschoolers, a developmentalist is *least* likely to emphasize:
    a. irreversibility.   c. its action-bound nature.
    b. centration.   d. its static nature.

14. A preschooler fails to put together a difficult puzzle on her own, so her mother encourages her to try again, this time guiding her by asking questions such as, "For this space do we need a big piece or a little piece?" With Mom's help, the child successfully completes the puzzle. Lev Vygotsky would attribute the child's success to:
    a. additional practice with the puzzle pieces.
    b. imitation of her mother's behavior.
    c. the social interaction with her mother that restructured the task to make its solution more attainable.
    d. modeling and reinforcement.

15. Mark is answering an essay question that asks him to "discuss the positions of major developmental theorists regarding the relationship between language and cognitive development." To help organize his answer, Mark jots down a reminder that _____ contended that language is essential to the advancement of thinking, as private speech, and as a _____ of social interactions.
    a. Piaget; mediator   c. Piaget; theory
    b. Vygotsky; mediator   d. Vygotsky; theory

Key Terms

Using your own words, write a brief definition or explanation of each of the following terms on a separate piece of paper.

1. egocentrism
2. preoperational thought
3. centration
4. focus on appearance
5. static reasoning
6. irreversibility
7. conservation
8. theory-theory
9. apprentice in thinking
10. guided participation
11. zone of proximal development
12. scaffold
13. private speech
14. social mediation
15. theory of mind
16. emergent literacy
17. fast mapping
18. overregularization

ANSWERS
CHAPTER REVIEW

1. perspective (or egocentrism)
2. preoperational
3. centration; ego-centration or egocentrism; appearances
4. static; unchanging; irreversibility
5. conservation; conservation of number
6. theory-theory; guided participation; social; interact
7. Lev Vygotsky; assistance; praising; enthusiasm; instruction
8. social activity
9. zone of proximal development
10. scaffold
11. private speech; uttered aloud
12. mediator
13. theory of mind

Between the ages of 3 and 6, young children come to realize that mental phenomena may not reflect reality and that individuals can believe various things and, therefore, can be deliberately deceived or fooled.

14. have
15. language; brain maturation; brother or sister; culture
16. emergent literacy; maturation; myelination
17. critical; sensitive
18. vocabulary
19. fast mapping; logical extension
20. more
21. comparisons; time; place
22. grammar; 3
23. overregularization

Many preschoolers overapply the rule of adding "s" to form the plural, as well as the rule of adding "ed" to form the past tense. Thus, preschoolers are likely to say "foots" and "snows" and that someone "broked" a toy.

24. is
25. egocentric; theories of mind; vocabulary development; emergent literacy
26. language shift; balanced bilinguals; speak two languages themselves
27. Maria Montessori; Piaget; discover ideas at their own pace; more; readiness (or academics)

28. Reggio Emilia; 7

29. has not; agree

30. Project Head Start; higher

High-quality preschools are characterized by (a) a low adult–child ratio, (b) a trained staff (or educated parents) who are unlikely to leave the program, (c) positive social interactions among children and adults, (d) adequate space and equipment, and (e) safety.

PROGRESS TEST 1

Multiple-Choice Questions

1. **c.** is the answer. (p. 218)

2. **c.** is the answer. Preoperational children have great difficulty understanding abstract concepts. (p. 218)

3. **e.** is the answer. (p. 225)

4. **a.** is the answer. (p. 225)

5. **c.** is the answer. (p. 231)

   a. This describes Maria Montessori.

   b. This refers to Piaget's approach.

   d. The program originated in Italy.

6. **d.** is the answer. (pp. 227–228)

   a. & c. Preschoolers generally have great difficulty understanding, and therefore using, metaphors and abstract nouns.

   b. Other than the grammatical errors of overregularization, the text does not indicate that preschoolers use a significant number of self-created words.

7. **a.** is the answer. (p. 228)

   b. & d. These terms are not identified in the text and do not apply to the use of grammar.

   c. Practical usage, which also is not discussed in the text, refers to communication between one person and another in terms of the overall context in which language is used.

8. **a.** is the answer. (p. 222)

   b. This expresses the views of Piaget.

   c. Because he believed that language facilitates thinking, Vygotsky obviously felt that language and other cognitive developments are intimately related.

   d. Vygotsky did not hold this view.

9. **a.** is the answer. (p. 222)

10. **a.** is the answer. (p. 219)

b., c., & d. Failure to conserve is the result of thinking that is centered on appearances. Egocentrism and irreversibility are also examples of centered thinking.

11. **c.** is the answer. (pp. 232–233)

    b. This is not discussed in the text.

    a. & d. There was no indication of greater behavioral problems or alienation in graduates of this program.

12. **b.** is the answer. (p. 224)

13. **c.** is the answer. (p. 231)

14. **d.** is the answer. (pp. 219–220)

15. **a.** is the answer. (p. 226)

True or False Items

1. T (p. 217)

2. T (p. 219)

3. F In fact, just the opposite is true. (p. 222)

4. F Children develop a theory of mind between the ages of 3 and 6. (p. 223)

5. T (p. 218)

6. T (p. 218)

7. F Preschoolers have difficulty understanding abstract words; their vocabulary consists mainly of concrete nouns and verbs. (p. 227)

8. F In adding "ed" to form a past tense, the child has indicated an understanding of the grammatical rule for making past tenses in English, even though the construction in these two cases is incorrect. (p. 228)

9. T (p. 234)

10. T (p. 220)

11. F This describes static reasoning; theory-theory is the idea that children attempt to construct a theory to explain all their experiences. (p. 220)

PROGRESS TEST 2

Multiple-Choice Questions

1. **d.** is the answer. (p. 229)

2. **a.** is the answer. (p. 219)

   b. & c. Fast mapping and overregularization are characteristics of language development during the play years; they have nothing to do with reasoning about volume.

3. **a.** is the answer. (p. 218)

b. Overregularization is the child's tendency to apply grammatical rules even when he or she shouldn't.

c. Reversibility is the concept that reversing an operation, such as addition, will restore the original conditions.

d. This term is used to refer to the young child's belief that people think as he or she does.

4. **c.** is the answer. This is why the stage is called *pre*operational. (p. 218)

5. **a.** is the answer. (p. 221)

6. **c.** is the answer. (p. 222)

   a. & b. These are both advantages of private speech.

   d. Fast mapping is the process by which new words are acquired, often after only one hearing.

7. **d.** is the answer. (p. 218)

   a. This describes egocentrism.

   b. This is the opposite of centration.

   c. This defines conservation of number.

8. **a.** is the answer. (p. 219)

   b. According to Piaget, preschoolers fail to solve conservation problems because they focus on the *appearance* of objects and ignore the transformation that has occurred.

   d. Piaget did not relate conservation to a theory of mind.

9. **d.** is the answer. (p. 221)

10. **b.** is the answer. (p. 220)

    a. Piaget believed that learning is a matter of individual discovery.

11. **d.** is the answer. Preschoolers almost always put subject before verb in their two-word sentences. (p. 228)

12. **a.** is the answer. (pp. 230)

    b. Although there are many different approaches to promoting bilingualism, the text does not suggest that children should master one language before being exposed to another.

    c. & d. Fast mapping and overregularization are normal aspects of language development that stimulate the development of vocabulary and grammar.

13. **b.** is the answer. (p. 227)

    a. By the time children are 3 years old, their grammar is quite impressive.

    c. On the contrary, vocabulary develops so rapidly that, by age 5, children seem to be able to understand and use almost any term they hear.

d. This tendency to make language more logical by overapplying certain grammatical rules has nothing to do with understanding the *meaning* of metaphors.

14. **a.** is the answer. (p. 228)

    b., c., & d. Overregularization is a *linguistic* phenomenon rather than a characteristic type of thinking (b. and d.), or a logical principle (c.).

15. **b.** is the answer. (p. 232)

Matching Items

1. l (p. 225)	**5.** h (p. 228)	**9.** a (p. 219)
2. k (p. 221)	**6.** g (p. 226)	**10.** i (p. 222)
3. f (p. 223)	**7.** j (p. 218)	**11.** e (p. 221)
4. c (p. 221)	**8.** d (p. 218)	**12.** b (p. 218)

THINKING CRITICALLY ABOUT CHAPTER 9

1. **c.** is the answer. (p. 219)

   a. A test of reversibility would ask a child to perform an operation, such as adding 4 to 3, and then reverse the process (subtract 3 from 7) to determine whether the child understood that the original condition (the number 4) was restored.

   b. A test of conservation of matter would transform the appearance of an object, such as a ball of clay, to determine whether the child understood that the object remained the same.

   d. A test of centration would involve the child's ability to see various aspects of a situation.

2. **b.** is the answer. (p. 218)

   a. Egocentrism is thinking that is self-centered.

   c. This is not a concept in Piaget's theory.

   d. Mental representation is an example of symbolic thought.

3. **a.** is the answer. (p. 218)

4. **c.** is the answer. (p. 223)

   a. Egocentrism is self-centered thinking.

   b. Although deception provides evidence of a theory of mind, the child in this example is not deceiving anyone.

   d. Conservation is the understanding that the amount of a substance is unchanged by changes in its shape or placement.

5. **d.** is the answer. (p. 223)

   a., b., & c. These answers are typical of younger children, who have not yet developed a theory of mind.

6. **c.** is the answer. In Vygotsky's view, learning is a social activity more than a matter of individual discovery. Thus, social interaction that provides motivation and focuses attention facilitates learning. (pp. 220–221)

a., b., & d. These situations either provide no opportunity for social interaction (b. & d.) or do not challenge the children (a.).

7. **c.** is the answer. (p. 218)

a., b., & d. These are all characteristics of preoperational thinking.

8. **a.** is the answer. (p. 228)

b. & d. The text does not discuss these aspects of language.

c. Pragmatics, which is not mentioned in the text, refers to the practical use of language in varying social contexts.

9. **b.** is the answer. (p. 228)

10. **a.** is the answer. (p. 219)

11. **d.** is the answer. (p. 222)

a. Piaget believed that cognitive growth precedes language development.

b. & c. Chomsky focused on the *acquisition* of language, and Flavell emphasizes cognition.

12. **a.** is the answer. Piaget emphasized the preschooler's egocentric tendency to perceive everything from his or her own perspective; Vygotsky emphasized the preschooler's tendency to look to others for insight and guidance. (pp. 218, 221)

13. **c.** is the answer. This is typical of cognition during the first two years, when infants think exclusively with their senses and motor skills. (p. 218)

14. **c.** is the answer. (p. 221)

15. **b.** is the answer. (p. 222)

KEY TERMS

1. **Egocentrism** is Piaget's term for a type of centration in which the preoperational child views the world exclusively from his or her own perspective. (p. 217)

2. According to Piaget, thinking between ages 2 and 6 is characterized by **preoperational thought,** meaning that children cannot yet perform logical operations; that is, they cannot use logical principles. (p. 218)

Memory aid: Operations are mental transformations involving the manipulation of ideas and symbols. *Pre*operational children, who lack the ability to perform transformations, are "before" this developmental milestone.

3. **Centration** is the tendency of preoperational children to focus only on a single aspect of a situation or object. (p. 218)

4. **Focus on appearance** refers to the preoperational child's tendency to focus only on physical attributes and ignore all others. (p. 218)

5. Preoperational thinking is characterized by **static reasoning,** in which the young child sees the world as unchanging. (p. 218)

6. **Irreversibility** is the characteristic of preoperational thought in which the young child fails to recognize that a process can be reversed to restore the original conditions of a situation. (p. 218)

7. **Conservation** is the understanding that the amount or quantity of a substance or object is unaffected by changes in its appearance. (p. 219)

8. **Theory-theory** is Gopnik's term for the tendency of young children to attempt to construct theories to explain everything they experience. (p. 220)

9. According to Vygotsky, a young child is an **apprentice in thinking,** whose intellectual growth is stimulated and directed by more skilled members of society. (p. 221)

10. According to Vygotsky, **guided participation** is the process by which young children learn to think by having social experiences and by exploring their universe. As guides, parents, teachers, and older children offer assistance with challenging tasks, model problem-solving approaches, provide explicit instructions as needed, and support the child's interest and motivation. (p. 221)

11. According to Vygotsky, for each individual there is a **zone of proximal development (ZPD),** which represents the skills that are within the potential of the learner but cannot be performed independently. (p. 221)

12. Tutors who **scaffold** structure children's learning experiences in order to foster their emerging capabilities. (p. 221)

13. **Private speech** is Vygotsky's term for the internal dialogue in which a person talks to himself or herself. Private speech, which often is uttered

aloud, helps preschoolers to think, review what they know, and decide what to do. (p. 222)

14. In Vygotsky's theory, **social mediation** is a function of speech by which a person's cognitive skills are refined and extended. (p. 222)

15. A **theory of mind** is an understanding of human mental processes, that is, of one's own or another's emotions, beliefs, intentions, motives, and thoughts. (p. 223)

16. **Emergent literacy** refers to the skills needed to learn to read. (p. 225)

17. **Fast mapping** is the not very precise process by which children rapidly learn new words by quickly connecting them to words and categories that are already understood. (p. 226)

18. **Overregularization** occurs when children apply rules of grammar when they should not. It is seen in English, for example, when children add "s" to form the plural even in irregular cases that form the plural in a different way. (p. 228)

Chapter Ten

The Play Years: Psychosocial Development

Chapter Overview

Chapter 10 explores the ways in which young children begin to relate to others in an ever-widening social environment. The chapter begins where social understanding begins, with emotional development and the emergence of the sense of self. With their increasing social awareness, children become more concerned with how others evaluate them and better able to regulate their emotions. This section also explores the origins of helpful, prosocial behaviors in young children, as well as antisocial behaviors such as the different forms of aggressive behavior. The child's social skills reflect many influences, including learning from playmates through various types of play.

The next section discusses Baumrind's parenting patterns and their effects on the developing child. The usefulness of the different forms of punishment is also explored.

The chapter concludes with a description of children's emerging awareness of male–female differences and gender identity. Five major theories of gender-role development are considered.

NOTE: Answer guidelines for all Chapter 10 questions begin on page 152.

Guided Study

The text chapter should be studied one section at a time. Before you read, preview each section by skimming it, noting headings and boldface items. Then read the appropriate section objectives from the following outline. Keep these objectives in mind and, as you read the chapter section, search for the information that will enable you to meet each objective. Once you have finished a section, write out answers for its objectives.

Emotional Development (pp. 237–245)

1. Explain the relationship between Erik Erikson's third stage and the development of the self-concept.

2. Discuss the development during early childhood of emotional regulation, focusing on how it is determined by both nature and nurture.

3. Explain the views of Daniel Goleman regarding emotional development in young children.

4. Differentiate four types of aggression during the play years, and explain why certain types of aggression are more troubling to developmentalists.

5. Discuss the nature and significance of rough-and-tumble and sociodramatic play during the play years.

Parenting Patterns (pp. 246–252)

6. Compare and contrast three classic patterns of parenting and their effect on children.

7. Discuss the pros and cons of punishment, and describe the most effective method for disciplining a child.

8. Discuss how watching television and playing video games contribute to the development of aggression and other antisocial behaviors.

Boy or Girl: So What? (pp. 253–259)

9. Describe the developmental progression of gender awareness in young children.

10. Summarize five theories of gender-role development during the play years, noting important contributions of each.

Chapter Review

When you have finished reading the chapter, work through the material that follows to review it. Complete the sentences and answer the questions. As you proceed, evaluate your performance for each section by consulting the answers on page 152. Do not continue with the next section until you understand each answer. If you need to, review or reread the appropriate section in the textbook before continuing.

Emotional Development (pp. 237–245)

1. Between 3 and 6 years of age, according to Erikson, children are in the stage of

   _____ _____

   _____ . Unlike the earlier stage of

   _____ _____

   _____ , children in this stage want to begin *and* _____ something. Erikson also believed that during this stage children begin to feel _____ when their efforts result in failure or criticism.

2. Psychologists emphasize the importance of children's developing a positive _____ and feelings of pride that enable concentration and _____ and

   _____ .

3. The ability to direct or modify one's feelings is called _____ _____ . This ability begins with the control of _____ . Children who have _____ problems and lash out at other people or things are said to be _____ (overcontrolled/undercontrolled). Children who have _____ problems tend to be inhibited, fearful, and withdrawn.

4. Genetic influences _____ (are/are not) a source of variation in emotional regulation in young children. One research study found that fearful children had greater activity in the _____ _____ _____ of their brains, while those who were less withdrawn had greater activity in their _____ _____ _____ .

5. Repeated exposure to extreme stress can kill _____ and make some young children physiologically unable to regulate their emotions. Extreme stress can also affect the release of stress hormones such as _____ . One study found _____ (higher-than-normal/lower-than-normal) levels of this hormone in abused children.

Give several examples of early stress that can inhibit young children's emotional regulation.

6. Another set of influences on emotional regulation is the child's early and current _____ _____ .

7. According to _____ , the ability to direct emotions is crucial to the development of _____ _____ .

8. The ability to truly understand the emotions of another, called _____ , often leads to sharing, cooperating, and other examples of _____ _____ . In contrast, dislike for others, or _____ , may lead to actions that are destructive or deliberately hurtful. Such actions are called _____ _____ .

9. The most antisocial behavior of all is active _____ .

10. Developmentalists distinguish four types of physical aggression: _____ , used to obtain or retain an object or privilege; _____ , used in angry retaliation against an intentional or accidental act committed by a peer; _____ , which takes the form of insults or social rejection; and _____ , used in an unprovoked attack on a peer.

11. (Table 10.1) The form of aggression that is most likely to increase from age 2 to 6 is _____ _____ . Of greater concern are _____ _____ , because it can indicate a lack of _____ _____ , and _____ _____ , which is most worrisome overall.

12. Emotions are ultimately expressed in behavior related to _____ , who are other people of about the same _____ and _____ as the child.

13. Play is both _____ and _____ by culture, gender, and age.

14. The type of physical play that mimics aggression is called _____ - _____ - _____ play. A distinctive feature of this form of play, which _____ (occurs only in some cultures/is universal), is the positive facial expression that characterizes the "_____ _____ ." Age differences are evident, because this type of play relies

on the child's _____

_____ . Gender differences

_____ (are/are not) evident in rough-and-tumble play.

15. In _____ play, children act out various roles and themes in stories of their own creation. _____ (Girls/Boys) tend to engage in this type of play more often than do _____ (girls/boys).

Parenting Patterns (pp. 246–252)

16. A significant influence on early psychosocial growth is the style of _____ that characterizes a child's family life.

17. The early research on parenting styles, which was conducted by _____ , found that parents varied in their _____ toward offspring, in their strategies for _____ , in how well they _____ , and in their expectations for _____ .

18. Parents who adopt the _____ style demand unquestioning obedience from their children. In this style of parenting, nurturance tends to be _____ (low/high), maturity demands are _____ (low/high), and parent–child communication tends to be _____ (low/high).

19. Parents who adopt the _____ style make few demands on their children and are lax in discipline. Such parents _____ (are/are not very) nurturant, communicate _____ (well/poorly), and make _____ (few/extensive) maturity demands.

20. Parents who adopt the _____ style set limits and enforce rules but also listen to their children. Such parents make _____ (high/low) maturity demands, communicate _____ (well/poorly), and _____ (are/are not) nurturant. Two other styles of parenting that have been identified are _____ parenting, in which parents don't seem to care at all about their children, and

_____ parenting, in which parents give in to a child's every whim.

21. Follow-up studies indicate that children raised by _____ parents are likely to be obedient but unhappy and those raised by _____ parents are likely to lack self-control. Those raised by _____ parents are more likely to be successful, happy with themselves, and generous with others; these advantages _____ (grow stronger/weaken) over time.

22. An important factor in the effectiveness of parenting style is the child's _____ . In addition, _____ and _____ influence the child's perception of the quality of parenting. The crucial factors in how children perceive their parents are _____ _____ , _____ , and _____ for the child.

23. Culture _____ (exerts/does not exert) a strong influence on disciplinary techniques. Japanese mothers tend to use _____ as disciplinary techniques more often than do North American mothers, who are more likely to encourage _____ expressions of all sorts in their children. A disciplinary technique in which a child is required to stop all activity and sit quietly for a few minutes is the _____-_____ . This technique is widely used in _____ _____ .

(Table 10.3) State four specific recommendations for the use of punishment that are derived from developmental research findings.

a. _____

b. _____

c. _____

d. _____

24. Physical punishment of children is against the law for parents and teachers in _____ . In contrast, in some _____ nations, all parents are expected to physically punish their children.

25. Throughout the world, most parents _____ (believe/do not believe) that spanking is acceptable at times. Although spanking _____ (is/is not) effective, it may teach children to be more _____ .

26. Six major organizations concerned with the well-being of children urge parents to

_____

in order to avoid exposing their children to

_____ _____ . Those who advocate the opposite viewpoint contend that the media are merely reflecting _____ .

27. In comparison to broadcast television programs, video games are more _____ , _____ , and _____ .

28. Longitudinal research demonstrates that children who watched educational programs as young children became teenagers who had

_____ . This finding was especially true for _____ (boys/girls). Teenagers who, as children who watched violent television programs, had _____ , especially if they were _____ (boys/girls).

29. Developmentalists agree that video games and violent television programs perpetuate _____ , _____ , and _____ stereotypes; depict _____ solutions to problems with no expression of _____ ; and encourage _____ emotions rather than thoughtful _____ .

Boy or Girl: So What? (pp. 253–259)

30. Social scientists distinguish between biological, or _____ , differences between males and females, and cultural, or _____ , differences in the _____ and behaviors of males and females.

31. True sex differences are _____ (more/less) apparent in childhood than in adulthood; _____ differentiation seems more significant to children than to adults.

32. By age _____ , children can consistently apply gender labels and have a rudimentary understanding of the permanence of their own gender. By age _____ , children are convinced that certain toys and roles are appropriate for one gender but not the other. Awareness that sex is a fixed biological characteristic does not become solid until about age

_____ .

33. Freud called the period from age 3 to 6 the _____ _____ . According to his view, boys in this stage develop sexual feelings about their _____ and become jealous of their _____ . Freud called this phenomenon the _____ _____ .

34. In Freud's theory, preschool boys resolve their guilty feelings defensively through _____ with their father. Boys also develop, again in self-defense, a powerful conscience called the _____ .

35. According to Freud, during the phallic stage little girls may experience the _____ _____ , in which they want to get rid of their mother and become intimate with their father. Alternatively, they may become jealous of boys because they have a penis; this emotion Freud called _____ _____ .

36. According to behaviorism, preschool children develop gender-role ideas by being _____ for behaviors deemed appropriate for their sex and _____ for behaviors deemed inappropriate.

37. Behaviorists also maintain that children learn gender-appropriate behavior not only through direct reinforcement but also by _____ .

38. Cognitive theorists focus on children's _____ of male–female differences.

39. Gender education varies by region, socioeconomic status, and historical period, according to the _____ theory. Gender distinctions are emphasized in many _____ cultures.

This theory points out that children can maintain a balance of male and female characteristics, or _____ , only if their culture promotes that idea.

40. According to _____ theory, gender attitudes and roles are the result of interaction between _____ and _____ _____ .

41. The idea that is supported by recent research is that some gender differences are _____ based because of differences between male and female _____ .

42. These differences probably result from the differing _____ _____ that influence brain development. However, the theory maintains that the manifestations of biological origins are shaped, enhanced, or halted by _____ _____ . One example of such a factor is that prehistorically, female brains apparently favored _____ , which may have created a genetically inclined tendency for girls to _____ earlier than boys.

Progress Test 1

Multiple-Choice Questions

Circle your answers to the following questions and check them with the answers beginning on page 152. If your answer is incorrect, read the explanation for why it is incorrect and then consult the appropriate pages of the text (in parentheses following the correct answer).

1. Preschool children have a clear (but not necessarily accurate) concept of self. Typically, the preschooler believes that she or he:
   a. owns all objects in sight.
   b. is great at almost everything.
   c. is much less competent than peers and older children.
   d. is more powerful than her or his parents.

2. According to Freud, the third stage of psychosexual development, during which the penis is the focus of psychological concern and pleasure, is the:
   a. oral stage.
   b. anal stage.
   c. phallic stage.
   d. latency period.

3. Because it helps children rehearse social roles, work out fears and fantasies, and learn cooperation, an important form of social play is:
   a. sociodramatic play.
   b. mastery play.
   c. rough-and-tumble play.
   d. sensorimotor play.

4. The three *basic* patterns of parenting described by Diana Baumrind are:
   a. hostile, loving, and harsh.
   b. authoritarian, permissive, and authoritative.
   c. positive, negative, and punishing.
   d. indulgent, neglecting, and traditional.

5. Authoritative parents are receptive and loving, but they also normally:
   a. set limits and enforce rules.
   b. have difficulty communicating.
   c. withhold praise and affection.
   d. encourage aggressive behavior.

6. Children who watch a lot of violent television or play violent video games:
   a. are more likely to be violent.
   b. do less reading.
   c. tend to have lower grades in school.
   d. have all of the above characteristics.

7. (Table 10.1) Between 2 and 6 years of age, the form of aggression that is most likely to increase is:
   a. reactive   c. relational
   b. instrumental   d. bullying

8. During the play years, a child's self-concept is defined largely by his or her:
   a. expanding range of skills and competencies.
   b. physical appearance.
   c. gender.
   d. relationship with family members.

9. Behaviorists emphasize the importance of _____ in the development of the preschool child.
   a. identification   c. initiative
   b. praise and blame   d. a theory of mind

10. Children apply gender labels and have definite ideas about how boys and girls behave as early as age:
    a. 2.   c. 5.
    b. 4.   d. 7.

11. Psychologist Daniel Goleman believes that emotional regulation is especially crucial to the preschooler's developing:
    a. a sense of self.
    b. social awareness.
    c. emotional intelligence.
    d. a sense of gender.

12. Six-year-old Leonardo has superior verbal ability rivaling that of most girls his age. Dr. Laurent believes this is due to the fact that although his sex is predisposed to slower language development, Leonardo's upbringing in a linguistically rich home enhanced his biological capabilities. Dr. Laurent is evidently a proponent of:
    a. cognitive theory.
    b. psychoanalytic theory.
    c. sociocultural theory.
    d. epigenetic theory.

13. Three-year-old Jake, who lashes out at the family pet in anger, is displaying signs of _____ problems, which suggests that he is emotionally _____ .
    a. internalizing; overcontrolled
    b. internalizing; undercontrolled
    c. externalizing; overcontrolled
    d. externalizing; undercontrolled

14. Compared to Japanese mothers, North American mothers are more likely to:
    a. use reasoning to control their preschoolers' social behavior.
    b. use expressions of disappointment to control their preschoolers' social behavior.
    c. encourage emotional expressions of all sorts in their preschoolers.
    d. do all of the above.

15. When her friend hurts her feelings, Maya shouts that she is a "mean old stinker!" Maya's behavior is an example of:
    a. instrumental aggression.
    b. reactive aggression.
    c. bullying aggression.
    d. relational aggression.

True or False Items

Write *T (true) or F (false)* on the line in front of each statement.

_____ 1. According to Diana Baumrind, only authoritarian parents make maturity demands on their children.

_____ 2. Children of authoritative parents tend to be successful, happy with themselves, and generous with others.

_____ 3. True sex differences are more apparent in childhood than in adulthood.

_____ 4. Spanking is associated with higher rates of aggression toward peers.

_____ 5. Many gender differences are genetically based.

_____ 6. Children can be truly androgynous only if their culture promotes such ideas and practices.

_____ 7. Developmentalists do not agree about how children acquire gender roles.

_____ 8. By age 4, most children have definite ideas about what constitutes appropriate masculine and feminine roles.

_____ 9. Identification was defined by Freud as a defense mechanism in which people identify with others who may be stronger and more powerful than they.

_____ 10. Sociodramatic play allows children free expression of their emotions.

Progress Test 2

Progress Test 2 should be completed during a final chapter review. Answer the following questions after you thoroughly understand the correct answers for the Chapter Review and Progress Test 1.

Multiple-Choice Questions

1. Children of permissive parents are *most* likely to lack:
    a. social skills.
    b. self-control.
    c. initiative and guilt.
    d. care and concern.

2. Children learn how to manage conflict through the use of humor most readily from their interaction with:
    a. their mothers.
    b. their fathers.
    c. friends.
    d. others of the same sex.

3. The initial advantages of parenting style:
    a. do not persist past middle childhood.
    b. remain apparent through adolescence.
    c. are likely to be even stronger over time.
    d. have an unpredictable impact later in children's lives.

4. When they are given a choice of playmates, 2- to 5-year-old children:
   a. play with children of their own sex.
   b. play equally with girls and boys.
   c. segregate by gender in cultures characterized by traditional gender roles.
   d. prefer to play alone.

5. Which of the following best summarizes the current view of developmentalists regarding gender differences?
   a. Developmentalists disagree on the proportion of gender differences that are biological in origin.
   b. Most gender differences are biological in origin.
   c. Nearly all gender differences are cultural in origin.
   d. There is no consensus among developmentalists regarding the origin of gender differences.

6. According to Freud, a young boy's jealousy of his father's relationship with his mother, and the guilt feelings that result, are part of the:
   a. Electra complex.
   b. Oedipus complex.
   c. phallic complex.
   d. penis envy complex.

7. The style of parenting in which the parents make few demands on children, the discipline is lax, and the parents are nurturant and accepting is:
   a. authoritarian.
   b. authoritative.
   c. permissive.
   d. traditional.

8. Cooperating with a playmate is to _____ as insulting a playmate is to _____ .
   a. antisocial behavior; prosocial behavior
   b. prosocial behavior; antisocial behavior
   c. emotional regulation; antisocial behavior
   d. prosocial behavior; emotional regulation

9. Antipathy refers to a person's:
   a. understanding of the emotions of another person.
   b. self-understanding.
   c. feelings of anger or dislike toward another person.
   d. tendency to internalize emotions or inhibit their expression.

10. Which of the following theories advocates the development of gender identification as a means of avoiding guilt over feelings for the opposite-sex parent?
    a. behaviorism
    b. sociocultural
    c. psychoanalytic
    d. social learning

11. A parent who wishes to use a time-out to discipline her son for behaving aggressively on the playground would be advised to:
    a. have the child sit quietly indoors for a few minutes.
    b. tell her son that he will be punished later at home.
    c. tell the child that he will not be allowed to play outdoors for the rest of the week.
    d. choose a different disciplinary technique since time-outs are ineffective.

12. The preschooler's readiness to learn new tasks and play activities reflects his or her:
    a. emerging competency and self-awareness.
    b. theory of mind.
    c. relationship with parents.
    d. growing identification with others.

13. Emotional regulation is in part related to maturation of a specific part of the brain in the:
    a. prefrontal cortex.
    b. parietal cortex.
    c. temporal lobe.
    d. occipital lobe.

14. In which style of parenting is the parents' word law and misbehavior strictly punished?
    a. permissive
    b. authoritative
    c. authoritarian
    d. traditional

15. Erikson noted that preschoolers eagerly begin many new activities but are vulnerable to criticism and feelings of failure; they experience the crisis of:
    a. identity versus role confusion.
    b. initiative versus guilt.
    c. basic trust versus mistrust.
    d. efficacy versus helplessness.

Matching Items

Match each term or concept with its corresponding description or definition.

Terms or Concepts

_____ **1.** rough-and-tumble play
_____ **2.** androgyny
_____ **3.** sociodramatic play
_____ **4.** prosocial behavior
_____ **5.** antisocial behavior
_____ **6.** Electra complex
_____ **7.** Oedipus complex
_____ **8.** authoritative
_____ **9.** authoritarian
_____ **10.** identification
_____ **11.** instrumental aggression

Descriptions or Definitions

a. forceful behavior whose purpose is to obtain an object desired by another
b. Freudian theory that every daughter secretly wishes to replace her mother
c. parenting style associated with high maturity demands and low parent–child communication
d. an action performed for the benefit of another person without the expectation of reward
e. Freudian theory that every son secretly wishes to replace his father
f. parenting style associated with high maturity demands and high parent–child communication
g. two children wrestle without serious hostility
h. an action that is intended to harm someone else
i. two children act out roles in a story of their own creation
j. a defense mechanism through which children cope with their feelings of guilt during the phallic stage
k. a balance of traditional male and female characteristics in an individual

Thinking Critically About Chapter 10

Answer these questions the day before an exam as a final check on your understanding of the chapter's terms and concepts.

1. Bonita eventually copes with the fear and anger she feels over her hatred of her mother and love of her father by:
   a. identifying with her mother.
   b. copying her brother's behavior.
   c. adopting her father's moral code.
   d. competing with her brother for her father's attention.

2. A little girl who says she wants her mother to go on vacation so that she can marry her father is voicing a fantasy consistent with the _____ described by Freud.
   a. Oedipus complex
   b. Electra complex
   c. theory of mind
   d. crisis of initiative versus guilt

3. According to Erikson, before the preschool years children are incapable of feeling guilt because:
   a. guilt depends on a sense of self, which is not sufficiently established in preschoolers.
   b. they do not yet understand that they are male or female for life.
   c. this emotion is unlikely to have been reinforced at such an early age.
   d. guilt is associated with the resolution of the Oedipus complex, which occurs later in life.

4. Parents who are strict and aloof are *most* likely to make their children:
   a. cooperative and trusting.
   b. obedient but unhappy.
   c. violent.
   d. withdrawn and anxious.

5. When 4-year-old Seema grabs for Vincenzo's Beanie Baby, Vincenzo slaps her hand away, displaying an example of:
   a. bullying aggression.
   b. reactive aggression.
   c. instrumental aggression.
   d. relational aggression.

6. The belief that almost all sexual patterns are learned rather than inborn would find its strongest adherents among:
   a. cognitive theorists.
   b. behaviorists.
   c. psychoanalytic theorists.
   d. epigenetic theorists.

7. In explaining the origins of gender distinctions, Dr. Christie notes that every society teaches its children its values and attitudes regarding preferred behavior for men and women. Dr. Christie is evidently a proponent of:
   a. behaviorism.
   b. sociocultural theory.
   c. epigenetic theory.
   d. psychoanalytic theory.

8. Three-year-old Ali, who is fearful and withdrawn, is displaying signs of _____ problems, which suggests that he is emotionally _____ .
   a. internalizing; overcontrolled
   b. internalizing; undercontrolled
   c. externalizing; overcontrolled
   d. externalizing; undercontrolled

9. Summarizing her report on neurological aspects of emotional regulation, Alycia notes that young children who have internalizing problems tend to have greater activity in the:
   a. right temporal lobe
   b. left temporal lobe
   c. right prefrontal cortex
   d. left prefrontal cortex

10. Concerning children's concept of gender, which of the following statements is true?
    a. By age 3, children have a rudimentary understanding that sex distinctions are lifelong.
    b. Children as young as 1 year have a clear understanding of the physical differences between girls and boys and can consistently apply gender labels.
    c. Not until age 5 or 6 do children show a clear preference for gender-typed toys.
    d. All of the above are true.

11. Which of the following is *not* a feature of parenting used by Baumrind to differentiate authoritarian, permissive, and authoritative parents?
    a. maturity demands for the child's conduct
    b. efforts to control the child's actions
    c. nurturance
    d. adherence to stereotypic gender roles

12. Seeking to discipline her 3-year-old son for snatching a playmate's toy, Cassandra gently says, "How would you feel if Juwan grabbed your car?" Developmentalists would probably say that Cassandra's approach:
    a. is too permissive and would therefore be ineffective in the long run.
    b. would probably be more effective with a girl.
    c. will be effective in increasing prosocial behavior because it promotes empathy.
    d. will backfire and threaten her son's self-confidence.

13. Five-year-old Curtis, who is above average in height and weight, often picks on children who are smaller than he is. Curtis' behavior is an example of:
    a. bullying aggression.
    b. reactive aggression.
    c. instrumental aggression.
    d. relational aggression.

14. Which of the following is true regarding the effects of spanking?
    a. Spanking seems to reduce reactive aggression.
    b. When administered appropriately, spanking promotes psychosocial development.
    c. Spanking is associated with increased aggression toward peers.
    d. None of the above is true.

15. Aldo and Jack are wrestling and hitting each other. Although this rough-and-tumble play mimics negative, aggressive behavior, it serves a useful purpose, which is to:
    a. rehearse social roles.
    b. develop interactive skills.
    c. improve fine motor skills.
    d. do both b. and c.

Key Terms

Writing Definitions

Using your own words, write a brief definition or explanation of each of the following terms on a separate piece of paper.

1. initiative versus guilt
2. self-concept
3. emotional regulation
4. externalizing problems
5. internalizing problems
6. emotional intelligence
7. empathy

8. antipathy

9. prosocial

10. antisocial

11. instrumental aggression

12. reactive aggression

13. relational aggression

14. bullying aggression

15. peers

16. rough-and-tumble play

17. sociodramatic play

18. authoritarian parenting

19. permissive parenting

20. authoritative parenting

21. time-out

22. sex differences

23. gender differences

24. phallic stage

25. Oedipus complex

26. identification

27. superego

28. Electra complex

29. androgyny

Cross-Check

After you have written the definitions of the key terms in this chapter, you should complete the crossword puzzle to ensure that you can reverse the process—recognize the term, given the definition.

ACROSS

1. Physical play that often mimics aggression but involves no intent to harm.

3. A behavior, such as cooperating or sharing, performed to benefit another person without the expectation of a reward.

8. In psychoanalytic theory, the self-critical and judgmental part of personality that internalizes the moral standards set by parents and society.

12. Behavior that takes the form of insults or social rejection is called _____ aggression.

14. Act intended to obtain or retain an object desired by another is called _____ aggression.

15. Style of parenting in which parents make few demands on their children yet are nurturant and accepting and communicate well with their children.

DOWN

2. Cultural differences in the roles and behaviors of males and females.

4. Defense mechanism through which a person takes on the role and attitudes of a person more powerful than himself or herself.

5. Ability to manage and modify one's feelings, particularly feelings of fear, frustration, and anger.

6. In Freud's phallic stage of psychosexual development, a boy's sexual attraction toward the mother and resentment of the father.

7. Style of child-rearing in which the parents show little affection or nurturance for their children, maturity demands are high, and parent–child communication is low.

9. In Freud's phallic stage of psychosexual development, a girl's sexual attraction toward the father and resentment of the mother.

10. Style of parenting in which the parents set limits and enforce rules but do so more democratically than do authoritarian parents.
11. Form of aggression involving an unprovoked attack on another child.
13. Aggressive behavior that is an angry retaliation for some intentional or incidental act by another person.

ANSWERS
CHAPTER REVIEW

1. initiative versus guilt; autonomy versus shame; complete; guilt
2. self-concept; persistence; a willingness to try new experiences
3. emotional regulation; impulses; externalizing; undercontrolled; internalizing
4. are; right prefrontal cortex; left prefrontal cortex
5. neurons; cortisol; lower-than-normal

Prenatal examples of early stress that can inhibit emotional regulation include pregnant women who experience stress, suffer illness, or are heavy drug users. Postnatal examples include chronic infant malnourishment, injury, or fear.

6. care experiences
7. Daniel Goleman; emotional intelligence
8. empathy; prosocial behaviors; antipathy; antisocial behavior
9. aggression
10. instrumental; reactive; relational; bullying
11. instrumental aggression; reactive aggression; emotional regulation; bullying aggression
12. peers; age; status
13. universal; variable
14. rough-and-tumble; is universal; play face; social experience; are
15. sociodramatic; Girls; boys
16. parenting
17. Diana Baumrind; nurturance; discipline; communicate; maturity
18. authoritarian; low; high; low
19. permissive; are; well; few
20. authoritative; high; well; are; neglectful; indulgent
21. authoritarian; permissive; authoritative; grow stronger
22. temperament; community; cultural differences; parental warmth; support; concern

23. exerts; reasoning; emotional; time-out; North America
   a. Remember theory of mind.
   b. Remember emerging self-concept.
   c. Remember the language explosion and fast mapping.
   d. Remember that young children are not yet logical.
24. Sweden; Caribbean
25. believe; is; aggressive
26. turn off the TV; video violence; reality
27. violent, sexist, racist
28. higher grades; boys; lower grades; girls
29. sexist, ageist, and racist stereotypes; violent; empathy; quick, reactive; regulation
30. sex; gender; roles
31. less; gender
32. 2; 4; 8
33. phallic stage; mothers; fathers; Oedipus complex
34. identification; superego
35. Electra complex; penis envy
36. reinforced; punished
37. modeling
38. understanding
39. sociocultural; traditional; androgyny
40. epigenetic; genes; early experience
41. biologically; brains
42. sex hormones; environmental factors; language; speak

PROGRESS TEST 1

Multiple-Choice Questions

1. **b.** is the answer. (p. 237)
2. **c.** is the answer. (p. 254)

   a. & b. In Freud's theory, the oral and anal stages are associated with infant and early childhood development, respectively.

   d. In Freud's theory, the latency period is associated with development during the school years.
3. **a.** is the answer. (pp. 244–245)

   b. & d. These two types of play are not discussed in this chapter. Mastery play is play that helps children develop new physical and intellectual skills. Sensorimotor play captures the pleasures of using the senses and motor skills.

c. Rough-and-tumble play is physical play that mimics aggression.

4. **b.** is the answer. (pp. 246–247)

   d. Traditional is a variation of the basic styles uncovered by later research. Indulgent and neglecting are abusive styles and clearly harmful, unlike the styles initially identified by Baumrind.

5. **a.** is the answer. (p. 247)

   b. & c. Authoritative parents communicate very well and are quite affectionate.

   d. This is not typical of authoritative parents.

6. **d.** is the answer. (pp. 251–252)

7. **b.** is the answer. (p. 243)

8. **a.** is the answer. (pp. 237–238)

9. **b.** is the answer. (p. 256)

   a. This is the focus of Freud's phallic stage.

   c. This is the focus of Erikson's psychosocial theory.

   d. This is the focus of cognitive theorists.

10. **a.** is the answer. (p. 253)

11. **c.** is the answer. (p. 241)

12. **d.** is the answer. In accounting for Leonardo's verbal ability, Dr. Laurent alludes to both genetic and environmental factors, a giveaway for epigenetic theory. (p. 258)

    a., b., & c. These theories do not address biological or genetic influences on development.

13. **d.** is the answer. (p. 239)

    a. & b. Children who display internalizing problems are withdrawn and bottle up their emotions.

    c. Jake is displaying an inability to control his negative emotions.

14. **c.** is the answer. (pp. 248–249)

    a. & b. These strategies are more typical of Japanese mothers.

15. **d.** is the answer. (p. 243)

True or False Items

1. F All parents make some maturity demands on their children; maturity demands are high in both the authoritarian and authoritative parenting styles. (pp. 246–247)

2. T (p. 247)

3. F Just the opposite is true. (p. 253)

4. T (p. 250)

5. T (p. 258)

6. T (p. 258)

7. T (pp. 254–258)

8. T (p. 253)

9. T (p. 254)

10. F The reverse is true; it provides a way for children to learn emotional regulation. (p. 245)

PROGRESS TEST 2

Multiple-Choice Questions

1. **b.** is the answer. (p. 247)

2. **c.** is the answer. (p. 244)

   a. & b. Parents, especially mothers, are more understanding and self-sacrificing than playmates and so less able to teach this lesson.

   d. The text does not indicate that same-sex friends are more important in learning these than friends of the other sex.

3. **c.** is the answer. (p. 247)

4. **a.** is the answer. (p. 253)

   c. & d. The preference for same-sex playmates is universal.

5. **a.** is the answer. (p. 254)

6. **b.** is the answer. (p. 254)

   a. & d. These are Freud's versions of phallic-stage development in little girls.

   c. There is no such thing as the "phallic complex."

7. **c.** is the answer. (p. 247)

   a. & b. Both authoritarian and authoritative parents make high demands on their children.

   d. This is not one of the three parenting styles. Traditional parents could be any one of these types.

8. **b.** is the answer. (pp. 241, 242)

9. **c..** is the answer. (p. 241)

   a. This describes empathy.

   b. This describes self-concept.

   d. This describes an internalizing problem.

10. **c.** is the answer. (p. 254)

    a. & d. Behaviorism, which includes social learning theory, emphasizes that children learn about gender by rewards and punishments and by observing others.

    b. Sociocultural theory focuses on the impact of the environment on gender identification.

11. **a.** is the answer. (p. 249)

    b. & c. Time-outs involve removing a child from a situation in which misbehavior has occurred.

Moreover, these threats of future punishment would likely be less effective because of the delay between the behavior and the consequence.

d. Although developmentalists stress the need to prevent misdeeds instead of punishing them and warn that time-outs may have unintended consequences, they nevertheless can be an effective form of discipline.

12. **a.** is the answer. (pp. 237–238)

b. This viewpoint is associated only with cognitive theory.

c. Although parent–child relationships are important to social development, they do not determine readiness.

d. Identification is a Freudian defense mechanism.

13. **a.** is the answer. (p. 239)

14. **c.** is the answer. (p. 246)

15. **b.** is the answer. (p. 237)

a. & c. According to Erikson, these are the crises of adolescence and infancy, respectively.

d. This is not a crisis described by Erikson.

Matching Items

1. g (p. 244)   5. h (p. 242)   9. c (p. 246)
2. k (p. 257)   6. b (p. 254)   10. j (p. 254)
3. i (p. 244)   7. e (p. 254)   11. a (p. 243)
4. d (p. 241)   8. f (p. 247)

THINKING CRITICALLY ABOUT CHAPTER 10

1. **a.** is the answer. (pp. 254–255)

2. **b.** is the answer. (p. 254)

a. According to Freud, the Oedipus complex refers to the male's sexual feelings toward his mother and resentment toward his father.

c. & d. These are concepts introduced by cognitive theorists and Erik Erikson, respectively.

3. **a.** is the answer. (pp. 237–238)

b. Erikson did not equate gender constancy with the emergence of guilt.

c. & d. These reflect the viewpoints of learning theory and Freud, respectively.

4. **b.** is the answer. (p. 247)

5. **c.** is the answer. The purpose of Vincenzo's action is clearly to retain the Beanie Baby, rather than to retaliate (b) or bully Seema (a). (p. 243)

d. Relational aggression takes the form of a verbal insult.

6. **b.** is the answer. (p. 256)

7. **b.** is the answer. (p. 257)

8. **a.** is the answer. (p. 239)

9. **c.** is the answer. (p. 239)

a. & b. The temporal lobes are involved in speech and hearing rather than emotional regulation.

d. Children who have externalizing problems tend to have greater activity in this area.

10. **a.** is the answer. (p. 253)

b. Not until about age 2 can children consistently apply gender labels.

c. By age 2, children prefer gender-typed toys.

11. **d.** is the answer. (p. 246)

12. **c.** is the answer. (p. 241)

13. **a.** is the answer. (p. 243)

14. **c.** is the answer. (p. 250)

15. **b.** is the answer. (p. 244)

KEY TERMS

Writing Definitions

1. According to Erikson, the crisis of the preschool years is **initiative versus guilt**. In this crisis, young children eagerly take on new tasks and play activities and feel guilty when their efforts result in failure or criticism. (p. 237)

2. **Self-concept** refers to people's understanding of who they are. (p. 237)

3. **Emotional regulation** is the ability to direct or modify one's feelings, particularly feelings of fear, frustration, and anger. (p. 238)

4. Young children who have **externalizing problems** tend to experience emotions outside themselves and lash out at other people or things. (p. 239)

5. Children who have **internalizing problems** tend to be fearful and withdrawn as a consequence of their tendencies to keep their emotions bottled up inside themselves. (p. 239)

6. **Emotional intelligence** is Goleman's term for a person's understanding of how to interpret and express emotions. (p. 241)

7. **Empathy** is a person's true understanding of the emotions of another person. (p. 241)

8. **Antipathy** is a person's feelings of anger, distrust, dislike, or even hatred toward another person. (p. 241)

9. **Prosocial** behavior is an action, such as cooperating or sharing, that is performed to benefit another person without the expectation of reward. (p. 241)

10. **Antisocial** behavior is an action, such as hitting or insulting, that is deliberately hurtful or destructive. (p. 242)

11. **Instrumental aggression** is forceful behavior whose purpose is to obtain or retain an object or privilege that is also desired by another. (p. 243)

12. **Reactive aggression** is forceful behavior that is an angry retaliation for some intentional or accidental act by another person. (p. 243)

    Memory aid: Instrumental aggression is behavior that is *instrumental* in allowing a child to retain a favorite toy. **Reactive aggression** is a *reaction* to another child's behavior.

13. Forceful behavior that takes the form of verbal insults or social rejection is called **relational aggression**. (p. 243)

14. An unprovoked physical or verbal attack on another person is an example of **bullying aggression**. (p. 243)

15. **Peers** are people of about the same age and status as oneself. (p. 243)

16. **Rough-and-tumble play** is physical play that often mimics aggression but involves no intent to harm. (p. 244)

17. In **sociodramatic play**, children act out roles and themes in stories of their own creation, allowing them to examine personal concerns in a non-threatening manner. (p. 244)

18. **Authoritarian parenting** is Baumrind's term for a style of child rearing in which the parents show little affection or nurturance for their children; maturity demands are high and parent–child communication is low. (p. 246)

    Memory aid: Someone who is an **authoritarian** demands unquestioning obedience and acts in a dictatorial way.

19. **Permissive parenting** is Baumrind's term for a style of child rearing in which the parents make few demands on their children, yet are nurturant and accepting and communicate well with their children. (p. 247)

20. **Authoritative parenting** is Baumrind's term for a style of child rearing in which the parents set limits and enforce rules but are willing to listen to the child's ideas and to make compromises. (p. 247)

Memory aid: **Authoritative parents** act as *authorities* do on a subject—by discussing and explaining why certain family rules are in place.

21. A **time-out** is a form of discipline in which a child is required to stop all activity and sit quietly for a few minutes. (p. 249)

22. **Sex differences** are biological differences between females and males. (p. 253)

23. **Gender differences** are cultural differences in the roles and behavior of males and females. (p. 253)

24. In psychoanalytic theory, the **phallic stage** is the third stage of psychosexual development, in which the penis becomes the focus of psychological concerns and physiological pleasure. (p. 254)

25. According to Freud, boys in the phallic stage of psychosexual development develop a collection of feelings, known as the **Oedipus complex**, that center on sexual attraction to the mother and resentment of the father. (p. 254)

26. In Freud's theory, **identification** is the defense mechanism through which a person symbolically takes on the role and attitudes of a person more powerful than himself or herself. (p. 254)

27. In psychoanalytic theory, the **superego** is the self-critical and judgmental part of personality that internalizes the moral standards set by parents and society. (p. 254)

28. According to Freud, girls in the phallic stage may develop a collection of feelings, known as the **Electra complex**, that center on sexual attraction to the father and resentment of the mother. (p. 254)

29. **Androgyny** is a balance of traditionally female and male psychological characteristics in a person. (p. 257)

Cross-Check

ACROSS	DOWN
1. rough-and-tumble	2. gender difference
3. prosocial	4. identification
8. superego	5. emotional regulation
12. relational	6. Oedipus complex
14. instrumental	7. authoritarian
15. permissive	9. Electra complex
	10. authoritative
	11. bullying
	13. reactive

Chapter Eleven

The School Years: Biosocial Development

Chapter Overview

This chapter introduces middle childhood, the years from 7 to 11. Changes in physical size and shape are described, and the problem of obesity is addressed. The discussion then turns to the continuing development of motor and intellectual skills during the school years, culminating in an evaluation of intelligence testing. A final section examines the experiences of children with special needs, such as autistic children, those diagnosed as having an attention-deficit disorder, and those with learning disabilities. The causes of and treatments for these problems are discussed, with emphasis placed on insights arising from the new developmental psychopathology perspective. This perspective makes it clear that the manifestations of any special childhood problem will change as the child grows older and that treatment must often focus on all three domains of development.

NOTE: Answer guidelines for all Chapter 11 questions begin on page 167.

Guided Study

The text chapter should be studied one section at a time. Before you read, preview each section by skimming it, noting headings and boldface items. Then read the appropriate section objectives from the following outline. Keep these objectives in mind and, as you read the chapter section, search for the information that will enable you to meet each objective. Once you have finished a section, write out answers for its objectives.

A Healthy Time (pp. 267–271)

1. Describe normal physical growth and development during middle childhood, and account for the usual variations among children.

2. Discuss the problems of obese children in middle childhood.

3. Discuss the physical and psychological impact of chronic illness, especially asthma, during middle childhood.

Brain Development (pp. 271–276)

4. Discuss the role of brain maturation in motor and cognitive development during middle childhood.

5. Describe motor-skill development during the school years, focusing on variations due to culture, practice, and genetics.

6. Explain how achievement and aptitude tests are used in evaluating individual differences in cognitive growth, and discuss why use of such tests is controversial.

7. Describe Sternberg's and Gardner's theories of multiple intelligences, and explain the significance of these theories.

Children with Special Needs (pp. 276–286)

8. Explain the new developmental psychopathology perspective, and discuss its value in treating children with special needs.

9. Identify the symptoms of autism, and describe its most effective treatment.

10. Describe the symptoms and possible causes of ADD (attention-deficit disorder) and AD/HD (attention-deficit/hyperactivity disorder).

11. Discuss the characteristics of learning disabilities.

12. Discuss the types of treatment available for children with attention-deficit disorders.

13. Describe techniques that have been tried in efforts to educate children with special needs.

Chapter Review

When you have finished reading the chapter, work through the material that follows to review it. Complete the sentences and answer the questions. As you proceed, evaluate your performance for each section by consulting the answers on page 167. Do not continue with the next section until you understand each answer. If you need to, review or reread the appropriate section in the textbook before continuing.

1. The biggest influence on development from age 7 to 11 is the changing _____ context.

A Healthy Time (pp. 267–271)

2. Compared with biosocial development during other periods of the life span, biosocial development during this time, known as _____ _____ , is _____ (relatively smooth/often fraught with problems). For example, disease and death during these years are _____ (more common/rarer) than during any other period.

3. Children grow _____ (faster/more slowly) during middle childhood than they did earlier or than they will in adolescence. The typical child gains about _____ pounds and at least _____ inches per year.

Describe several other features of physical development during the school years.

4. Variations in growth during middle childhood are caused by differences in _____ , _____ and _____ .

5. Children are said to be overweight when their body weights are _____ (what percent?) above ideal weight for their age and height and obese when when their body weights are _____ (what percent?) above their ideal weights. Experts estimate that nearly _____ (what proportion?) of North American children are obese.

6. Childhood obesity, which is _____ (increasing/decreasing) in the United States, is hazardous to children's health because it reduces _____ and increases _____ _____ , both of which are associated with serious health problems in middle adulthood. Obese children who do not lose weight in adolescence are more likely to experience _____ and _____ health problems, especially _____ . Too much pressure, however, may contribute to the development of an _____ disorder, such as _____ or _____ .

7. Adopted children are more often overweight when their _____ (adoptive/biological) parents are obese. However, _____ factors are the main reasons for the recent increase in childhood obesity. The most significant of these is lack of _____ .

8. Compared to the past, middle childhood is now a healthier time _____ (in every nation of the world/only in developed nations).

9. During middle childhood, children are _____ (more/less) aware of one another's, or their own, physical imperfections.

10. A chronic inflammatory disorder of the airways is called _____ . This disorder is _____ (more common/less common) today than in the past.

11. The causes or triggers of asthma include

_____ , _____ , and

exposure to _____ such as pet hair.

12. The use of injections, inhalers, and pills to treat asthma is an example of _____ prevention. Less than _____ (how many?) asthmatic children in the United States benefit from this type of treatment. The best approach to treating childhood diseases is _____ _____ , which in the case of asthma includes proper _____ of homes and schools, decreased _____ , eradication of cockroaches, and safe outdoor

_____ _____ .

Brain Development (pp. 271–276)

13. The brain reaches adult size at about age _____ . Advances in brain development during middle childhood enable the control over _____ _____ , _____ , _____ , and

_____ .

Ongoing maturation of the _____ _____ allows children to analyze the _____ of their behaviors before engaging in them.

14. Two other advances in brain function at this time include the ability to _____ _____ , called _____ _____ , and the _____ of thoughts and actions that are repeated in sequence.

15. The length of time it takes a person to respond to a particular stimulus is called _____ _____ .

16. Other important abilities that continue to develop during the school years are _____ – _____ _____ , balance, and judgment of _____ .

17. Motor habits that rely on coordinating both sides of the body improve because the _____ _____ between the brain's hemispheres continues to mature. Animal research

also demonstrates that brain development is stimulated through _____ . In addition, _____ play may help boys overcome their genetic tendencies toward _____ and _____ _____ because it helps with regulation and coordination in the _____ _____ of the brain.

18. Along with brain maturation, _____ , _____ , and _____ are important factors in the development of motor skills. Approximately _____ percent of all children have a motor coordination disability serious enough to interfere with school achievement.

19. The potential to learn a particular skill or body of knowledge is a person's _____ . The most commonly used tests of this type are _____ _____ . In the original version of the most commonly used test of this type, a person's score was calculated as a _____ (the child's _____ _____ divided by the child's _____ _____ and multiplied by 100 to determine his or her _____).

20. Tests that are designed to measure what a child has learned are called _____ tests. Tests that are designed to measure learning potential are called _____ tests.

21. Two highly regarded IQ tests are the

_____ _____

_____ _____

_____ and the

_____ - _____ .

22. IQ tests are quite reliable in predicting _____ achievement.

23. IQ testing is controversial in part because no test can measure _____ without also measuring _____ or without reflecting the _____ . Another reason is that a child's intellectual potential _____ (changes/does not change) over time.

24. Robert Sternberg believes that there are three distinct types of intelligence:_____ , _____ , and _____ . Similarly, Howard Gardner describes _____ (how many?) distinct intelligences.

Children with Special Needs (pp. 276–286)

25. Among the conditions that give rise to "special needs" are _____ _____ .

26. Down syndrome and other conditions that give rise to "special needs" begin with a _____ anomaly.

27. The process of formally identifying a child with special needs usual begins with a teacher _____ , which may ultimately lead to agreement on an _____ _____ _____ for the child.

28. The field of study that is concerned with childhood psychological disorders is _____ _____ . This perspective has provided several lessons that apply to all children. Three of these are that _____ is normal; disability _____ (changes/does not change) over time; and adolescence and adulthood may be _____ .

29. This perspective also has made diagnosticians much more aware of the _____ _____ of childhood problems. This awareness is reflected in the official diagnostic guide of the American Psychiatric Association, which is the _____ _____ .

30. The most severe disturbance of early childhood is _____ , which is used to describe children who are _____ . Autism is an example of a _____ _____ _____ .

31. Autism is more common in _____ (boys/girls).

32. Children who have autistic symptoms that are less severe than those in the classic syndrome are sometimes diagnosed with _____ _____ , also called _____-_____ _____ .

33. In early childhood autism, severe deficiencies appear in three areas: _____ ability, _____ _____ , and _____ _____ .

34. Some autistic children engage in a type of speech called _____ , in which they repeat, word for word, things they have heard.

35. The unusual play patterns of autistic children are characterized by repetitive _____ or _____ play.

36. As children with pervasive developmental disorders grow older their strongest cognitive skills tend to be in the area of _____ reasoning, and their weakest, in the area of _____ cognition.

37. A disability that manifests itself in a difficulty in concentrating for more than a few moments is called _____-_____ _____ . The most common type of this disorder, which includes a need to be active, often accompanied by excitability and impulsivity, is called _____-_____/ _____ _____ . Children suffering from this disorder can be _____ , _____ , and _____ . The crucial problem in these conditions seems to be a neurological difficulty in paying _____ .

38. Researchers have identified several factors that may contribute to AD/HD. These include _____ _____ , prenatal damage from _____ , and postnatal damage, such as from _____ _____ .

39. Children who have difficulty in school that _____ (is/is not) attributable to an overall intellectual slowness, a physical handicap, or a severely stressful situation are said to have a _____ _____ . The crucial factor is a _____ _____ between expected learning and actual accomplishment.

40. A disability in reading is called _____ . Other specific academic subjects that may show a learning disability are _____ , _____ , and _____ .

41. In childhood, the most effective forms of treatment for AD/HD are _____ , _____ therapy, and changes in the _____ .

42. Certain drugs that stimulate adults, such as _____ and _____ , have a reverse effect on many hyperactive children.

43. In response to a 1975 act requiring that children with special needs be taught in the _____ _____ _____ , the strategy of not separating special-needs children into special classes, called _____ , emerged. More recently, some schools have developed a _____ _____ , in which such children spend part of each day with a teaching specialist. In the most recent approach, called _____ , learning-disabled children receive targeted help within the setting of a regular classroom.

Progress Test 1

Multiple-Choice Questions

Circle your answers to the following questions and check them with the answers beginning on page 167. If your answer is incorrect, read the explanation for why it is incorrect and then consult the appropriate pages of the text (in parentheses following the correct answer).

1. As children move into middle childhood:
   a. the rate of accidental death increases.
   b. sexual urges intensify.
   c. the rate of weight gain increases.
   d. biological growth slows and steadies.

2. Ongoing maturation of which brain area contributes most to left–right coordination?
   a. corpus callosum
   b. prefrontal cortex
   c. brainstem
   d. temporal lobe

3. A factor that is *not* primary in the development of motor skills during middle childhood is:
   a. practice.   c. brain maturation.
   b. gender.   d. heredity.

4. Dyslexia is a learning disability that affects the ability to:
   a. do math.   c. write.
   b. read.   d. speak.

5. The developmental psychopathology perspective is characterized by its:
   a. contextual approach.
   b. emphasis on the unchanging nature of developmental disorders.
   c. emphasis on the cognitive domain of development.
   d. concern with all of the above.

6. The time—usually measured in fractions of a second—it takes for a person to respond to a particular stimulus is called:
   a. the interstimulus interval.
   b. reaction time.
   c. the stimulus-response interval.
   d. response latency.

7. The underlying problem in attention-deficit/ hyperactivity disorder appears to be:
   a. low overall intelligence.
   b. a neurological difficulty in paying attention.
   c. a learning disability in a specific academic skill.
   d. the existence of a conduct disorder.

8. Most of the variation in children's growth can be attributed to:
   a. gender.
   b. nutrition.
   c. genes.
   d. the interaction of the above factors.

9. Autistic children generally have severe deficiencies in all but which of the following?
   a. social skills
   b. imaginative play
   c. echolalia
   d. communication ability

10. Although asthma has genetic origins, several environmental factors contribute to its onset, including:
   a. urbanization.
   b. airtight windows.
   c. dogs and cats living inside the house.
   d. all of the above.

11. Psychoactive drugs are most effective in treating attention-deficit/hyperactivity disorder when they are administered:
   a. before the diagnosis becomes certain.
   b. for several years after the basic problem has abated.
   c. as part of the labeling process.
   d. with psychological therapy and changes at home and at school.

12. Tests that measure a child's potential to learn a new subject are called _____ tests.
   a. aptitude
   b. achievement
   c. vocational
   d. intelligence

13. In the earliest aptitude tests, a child's score was calculated by dividing the child's _____ age by his or her _____ age to find the _____ quotient.
   a. mental; chronological; intelligence
   b. chronological; mental; intelligence
   c. intelligence; chronological; mental
   d. intelligence; mental; chronological

14. Today, approximately _____ of North American children are obese.
   a. one-eighth
   b. one-fourth
   c. one-third
   d. one-half

15. Ongoing maturation of which brain area enables schoolchildren to more effectively analyze the potential consequences of their actions?
   a. corpus callosum
   b. prefrontal cortex
   c. brainstem
   d. temporal lobe

True or False Items

Write *T (true) or F (false)* on the line in front of each statement.

_____ 1. Variations in children's growth are usually caused by diet rather than heredity.

_____ 2. Childhood obesity increases the risk for serious health problems in adulthood.

_____ 3. Genes and hereditary differences in taste preferences are the most important factors in promoting childhood obesity.

_____ 4. The quick reaction time that is crucial in some sports can be readily achieved with practice.

_____ 5. Despite the efforts of teachers and parents, most children with learning disabilities can expect their disabilities to persist and even worsen as they enter adulthood.

_____ 6. Autism is more common in boys than girls.

_____ 7. The intellectual performance of autistic children is poor in all areas.

_____ 8. Stressful living conditions are an important consideration in diagnosing a learning disability.

_____ 9. Mainstreaming is the most effective educational method for children with special needs.

_____ 10. The drugs sometimes given to children to reduce hyperactive behaviors have a reverse effect on adults.

Progress Test 2

Progress Test 2 should be completed during a final chapter review. Answer the following questions after you thoroughly understand the correct answers for the Chapter Review and Progress Test 1.

Multiple-Choice Questions

1. During the years from 7 to 11, the average child:
   a. becomes slimmer.
   b. gains about 12 pounds a year.
   c. has decreased lung capacity.
   d. is more likely to become obese than at any other period in the life span.

2. Among the factors that are known to contribute to obesity are body type, quantity and types of food eaten, and:
   a. metabolism.
   b. activity level.
   c. taste preferences.
   d. all of the above.

3. A specific learning disability that becomes apparent when a child experiences unusual difficulty in learning to read is:
   a. dyslexia.
   b. dyscalcula.
   c. AD/HD.
   d. ADD.

4. Problems in learning to write, read, and do math are collectively referred to as:
   a. learning disabilities.
   b. attention-deficit/hyperactivity disorder.
   c. hyperactivity.
   d. dyscalcula.

5. Aptitude and achievement testing are controversial in part because:
   a. most tests are unreliable with respect to the individual scores they yield.
   b. a child's intellectual potential often changes over time.
   c. they often fail to identify serious learning problems.
   d. of all of the above reasons.

6. The most effective form of help for children with AD/HD is:
   a. medication.
   b. psychological therapy.
   c. environmental change.
   d. a combination of some or all of the above.

7. A key factor in reaction time is:
   a. whether the child is male or female.
   b. brain maturation.
   c. whether the stimulus to be reacted to is an auditory or visual one.
   d. all of the above.

8. The first noticeable symptom of autism is usually:
   a. the lack of spoken language.
   b. abnormal social responsiveness.
   c. both a. and b.
   d. unpredictable.

9. Which of the following is true of children with a diagnosed learning disability?
   a. They are, in most cases, average in intelligence.
   b. They often have a specific physical handicap, such as hearing loss.
   c. They often lack basic educational experiences.
   d. All of the above are true.

10. Which of the following is a key factor in the automization of children's thoughts and actions?
    a. the continuing myelination of neurons
    b. diet
    c. activity level
    d. All of the above are key factors.

11. Which approach to education may best meet the needs of learning-disabled children in terms of both skill remediation and social interaction with other children?
    a. mainstreaming
    b. special education
    c. inclusion
    d. resource rooms

12. Asperger syndrome is a disorder in which:
    a. body weight fluctuates dramatically over short periods of time.
    b. verbal skills seem normal, but social perceptions and skills are abnormal.
    c. an autistic child is extremely aggressive.
    d. a child of normal intelligence has difficulty mastering a specific cognitive skill.

13. Which of the following is *not* a contributing factor in most cases of AD/HD?
    a. genetic inheritance
    b. dietary sugar and caffeine
    c. prenatal damage
    d. postnatal damage

14. Tests that measure what a child has already learned are called _____ tests.
    a. aptitude
    b. vocational
    c. achievement
    d. intelligence

15. Which of the following is *not* a type of intelligence identified in Robert Sternberg's theory?
    a. academic
    b. practical
    c. achievement
    d. creative

Matching Items

Match each term or concept with its corresponding description or definition.

Terms or Concepts

_____ **1.** dyslexia
_____ **2.** automatization
_____ **3.** Asperger syndrome
_____ **4.** attention-deficit/hyperactivity disorder
_____ **5.** asthma
_____ **6.** echolalia
_____ **7.** autism
_____ **8.** developmental psychopathology
_____ **9.** DSM-IV-R
_____ **10.** learning disability
_____ **11.** mainstreaming

Descriptions or Definitions

a. set of symptoms in which a child has impaired social skills despite having normal speech and intelligence
b. speech that repeats, word for word, what has just been heard
c. the diagnostic guide of the American Psychiatric Association
d. process by which thoughts and actions become routine and no longer require much thought
e. system in which learning-disabled children are taught in general education classrooms
f. disorder characterized by self-absorption
g. chronic inflammation of the airways
h. behavior problem involving difficulty in concentrating, as well as excitability and impulsivity
i. applies insights from studies of normal development to the study of childhood disorders
j. an unexpected difficulty with one or more academic skills
k. difficulty in reading

Thinking Critically About Chapter 11

Answer these questions the day before an exam as a final check on your understanding of the chapter's terms and concepts.

1. According to developmentalists, the best game for a typical group of 8-year-olds would be:
   a. football or baseball.
   b. basketball.
   c. one in which reaction time is not crucial.
   d. a game involving one-on-one competition.

2. Dr. Rutter, who believes that knowledge about normal development can be applied to the study and treatment of psychological disorders, evidently is working from which of the following perspectives?
   a. clinical psychology
   b. developmental psychopathology
   c. behaviorism
   d. psychoanalysis

3. Nine-year-old Jack has difficulty concentrating on his classwork for more than a few moments, repeatedly asks his teacher irrelevant questions, and is constantly disrupting the class with loud noises. If his difficulties persist, Jack is likely to be diagnosed as suffering from:
   a. dyslexia.
   b. Asperger syndrome.
   c. autism.
   d. attention-deficit/hyperactivity disorder.

4. Angela was born in 1984. In 1992, she scored 125 on an intelligence test. Using the original formula, what was Angela's mental age when she took the test?
   a. 6   **c.** 10
   b. 8   **d.** 12

5. Ten-year-old Clarence is quick-tempered, easily frustrated, and is often disruptive in the classroom. Clarence may be suffering from:
   a. dyslexia.
   b. Asperger syndrome.
   c. attention-deficit disorder.
   d. attention-deficit/hyperactivity disorder.

6. Because 11-year-old Wayne is obese, he runs a greater risk of developing:
   a. heart problems.
   b. diabetes.
   c. psychological problems.
   d. all of the above.

7. Of the following individuals, who is likely to have the fastest reaction time?
   a. a 7-year-old
   b. a 9-year-old
   c. an 11-year-old
   d. an adult

8. Harold weighs about 20 pounds more than his friend Jay. During school recess, Jay can usually be found playing soccer with his classmates, while Harold sits on the sidelines by himself. Harold's rejection is likely due to his:
   a. being physically different.
   b. being dyslexic.
   c. intimidation of his schoolmates.
   d. being hyperactive.

9. In determining whether an 8-year-old has a learning disability, a teacher looks primarily for:
   a. exceptional performance in a subject area.
   b. the exclusion of other explanations.
   c. a family history of the learning disability.
   d. both a. and b.

10. Although 9-year-old Carl has severely impaired social skills, his intelligence and speech are normal. Carl is evidently displaying symptoms of:
    a. autism.
    b. ADD.
    c. AD/HD.
    d. Asperger syndrome.

11. If you were to ask an autistic child with echolalia, "what's your name?" the child would probably respond by saying:
    a. nothing.
    b. "what's your name?"
    c. "your name what's?"
    d. something that was unintelligible.

12. Jennifer has been diagnosed as having a pervasive developmental disorder. As she grows older, it is likely that her strongest cognitive skills will be in the area of _____ and her weakest in the area of _____ .
    a. social cognition; abstract reasoning
    b. abstract reasoning; social cognition
    c. creativity; practical intelligence
    d. practical intelligence; academic intelligence

13. Danny has been diagnosed as having attention-deficit/hyperactivity disorder. Every day his parents make sure that he takes the proper dose of Ritalin. His parents should:
    a. continue this behavior until Danny is an adult.
    b. try different medications when Danny seems to be reverting to his normal overactive behavior.
    c. make sure that Danny also has psychotherapy.
    d. not worry about Danny's condition; he will outgrow it.

14. Concluding her presentation on "Asthma During Middle Childhood," Amanda mentions each of the following *except* that:
    a. asthma is much more common today than 20 years ago.
    b. genetic vulnerability is rarely a factor in a child's susceptibility to developing asthma.
    c. the incidence of asthma continues to increase.
    d. carpeted floors, airtight windows, and less outdoor play increase the risk of asthma attacks.

15. Howard Gardner and Robert Sternberg would probably be most critical of traditional aptitude and achievement tests because they:
    a. inadvertently reflect certain nonacademic competencies.
    b. do not reflect knowledge of cultural ideas.
    c. measure only a limited set of abilities.
    d. underestimate the intellectual potential of disadvantaged children.

Key Terms

Using your own words, write a brief definition or explanation of each of the following terms on a separate piece of paper.

1. middle childhood
2. overweight
3. obesity
4. asthma
5. automatization
6. reaction time
7. aptitude
8. IQ test
9. achievement test
10. Wechsler Intelligence Scale for Children (WISC)
11. child with special needs
12. individual education plan (IEP)

13. developmental psychopathology

14. DSM-IV

15. pervasive developmental disorders

16. autism

17. Asperger syndrome

18. attention-deficit disorder (ADD)

19. AD/HD (attention-deficit hyperactivity disorder)

20. learning disability

21. dyslexia

22. mainstreaming

23. least restrictive environment (LRE)

24. resource room

25. inclusion

ANSWERS

CHAPTER REVIEW

1. social

2. middle childhood; relatively smooth; rarer

3. more slowly; 5 to 7; 2

During the school years, children generally become slimmer, muscles become stronger, and lung capacity increases.

4. genes; gender; nutrition

5. 20; 30; one-third

6. increasing; exercise; blood pressure; physical; psychological; depression; eating; bulimia; anorexia nervosa

7. biological; environmental; exercise

8. in every nation of the world

9. more

10. asthma; more common

11. genes; infections; allergens

12. tertiary; half; primary prevention; ventilation; pollution; play spaces

13. 7; emotional outbursts; perseveration, inattention, the insistence on routines; prefrontal cortex; consequences

14. pay special heed to one source of information among many; selective attention; automatization

15. reaction time

16. hand–eye coordination; movement

17. corpus callosum; play; rough-and-tumble; hyperactivity; learning disabilities; frontal lobes

18. culture, practice, heredity; 6

19. aptitude; IQ tests; quotient; mental age; chronological age; IQ

20. achievement; aptitude

21. Wechsler Intelligence Scale for Children (WISC); Stanford-Binet

22. school

23. aptitude; achievement; culture; changes

24. academic; creative; practical; eight

25. aggression, anxiety, autism, conduct disorder, depression, developmental delay, learning disability, Down syndrome, attachment disorder, attention-deficit disorder, bipolar disorder, and Asperger syndrome

26. biological

27. referral; individual education plan (IEP)

28. developmental psychopathology; abnormality; changes; better or worse

29. social context; *Diagnostic and Statistical Manual of Mental Disorders* (DSM-IV-R)

30. autism; self-absorbed; pervasive developmental disorder

31. boys

32. Asperger syndrome; high-functioning autism

33. communication; social skills; imaginative play

34. echolalia

35. movements; compulsive

36. abstract; social

37. attention-deficit disorder; attention deficit/hyperactivity disorder; inattentive; impulsive; overactive; attention

38. genetic vulnerability; teratogens; lead poisoning

39. is not; learning disability; measured discrepancy

40. dyslexia; math; spelling; handwriting

41. medication; psychological; family and school environment

42. amphetamines; methylphenidate (Ritalin)

43. least restrictive environment (LRE); mainstreaming; resource room; inclusion

PROGRESS TEST 1

Multiple-Choice Questions

1. **d.** is the answer. (p. 267)

2. **a.** is the answer. (p. 271)

3. **b.** Gender is not mentioned as a factor in the development of motor skills. (p. 273)

4. **b.** is the answer. (p. 282)

    a. Though not defined in the text, this is called dyscalcula.

c. & d. The text does not give labels for learning disabilities in writing or speaking.

5. **a.** is the answer. (p. 277)

b. & c. Because of its contextual approach, developmental psychopathology emphasizes *all* domains of development. Also, it points out that behaviors change over time.

6. **b.** is the answer. (p. 273)

7. **b.** is the answer. (p. 282)

8. **d.** is the answer. (p. 268)

9. **c.** is the answer. Echolalia *is* a type of communication difficulty, a characteristic form of speech of many autistic children. (pp. 280–281)

10. **d.** is the answer. (p. 270)

11. **d.** is the answer. (p. 284)

12. **a.** is the answer. (p. 274)

b. Achievement tests measure what has already been learned.

c. Vocational tests, which, as their name implies, measure what a person has learned about a particular trade, are achievement tests.

d. Intelligence tests measure general aptitude, rather than aptitude for a specific subject.

13. **a.** is the answer. (p. 274)

14. **c.** is the answer. (p. 268)

15. **b.** is the answer. (p. 272)

a. Maturation of the corpus callosum contributes to left–right coordination.

c. & d. These brain areas, which were not discussed in this chapter, play important roles in regulating sleep–waking cycles (brainstem) and hearing and language abilities (temporal lobe).

True or False Items

1. F Variations in children's growth are caused by heredity and gender as well as nutrition. (p. 268)

2. T (p. 268)

3. F Environmental factors are more important in promoting obesity during middle childhood. (p. 268)

4. F Reaction time depends on brain maturation and is not readily affected by practice. (p. 273)

5. F Due to the interplay of maturation, treatment, and contextual change, the behaviors associated with any problem can change. (pp. 278–279)

6. T (p. 280)

7. F Autistic children show isolated areas of remarkable skill. (p. 281)

8. F Stressful living conditions must be excluded before diagnosing a learning disability. (p. 282)

9. F Mainstreaming did not meet all children's educational needs. (p. 284)

10. T (p. 283)

PROGRESS TEST 2

Multiple-Choice Questions

1. **a.** is the answer. (p. 268)

b. & c. During this period children gain about 5 pounds per year and experience increased lung capacity.

d. Although childhood obesity is a common problem, the text does not indicate that a person is more likely to become obese at this age than at any other.

2. **d.** is the answer. (p. 268)

3. **a.** is the answer. (p. 282)

b. Although not discussed in the text, this learning disability involves math rather than reading.

c. & d. These disorders do not manifest themselves in a particular academic skill but instead appear in psychological processes that affect learning in general.

4. **a.** is the answer. (p. 282)

b. & c. AD/HD is a disorder that usually does not manifest itself in specific subject areas. Hyperactivity is a facet of this disorder.

d. Dyslexia is a learning disability in reading only.

5. **b.** is the answer. (p. 275)

6. **d.** is the answer. (p. 283)

7. **b.** is the answer. (p. 273)

8. **c.** is the answer. (p. 280)

9. **a.** is the answer. (p. 282)

10. **a.** is the answer. (p. 272)

11. **c.** is the answer. (p. 284)

a. Many general education teachers are unable to cope with the special needs of some children.

b. & d. These approaches undermined the social integration of children with special needs.

12. **b.** is the answer. (p. 280)

13. **b.** is the answer. (p. 282)

14. **c.** is the answer. (p. 274)

15. **c.** is the answer. (p. 275)

Matching Items

1. k (p. 282)   5. g (p. 270)   9. c (p. 279)
2. d (p. 272)   6. b (p. 281)   10. j (p. 282)
3. a (p. 280)   7. f (p. 280)   11. e (p. 284)
4. h (p. 281)   8. i (p. 277)

THINKING CRITICALLY ABOUT CHAPTER 11

1. **c.** is the answer. (p. 273)

    a. & b. Each of these games involves skills that are hardest for schoolchildren to master.

    d. Because one-on-one sports are likely to accentuate individual differences in ability, they may be especially discouraging to some children.

2. **b.** is the answer. (p. 277)

3. **d.** is the answer. (p. 281)

    a. Jack's difficulty is in concentrating, not in reading (dyslexia).

    b. & c. Autism is characterized by a lack of communication skills; Asperger syndrome is a milder form of autism.

4. **c.** is the answer. At the time she took the test, Angela's chronological age was 8. Knowing that her IQ was 125, we can solve the equation to yield a mental age value of 10. (p. 274)

5. **d.** is the answer. (p. 281)

6. **d.** is the answer. (p. 268)

7. **d.** is the answer. (p. 273)

8. **a.** is the answer. (p. 268)

    b., c., & d. Obese children are no more likely to be dyslexic, physically intimidating, or hyperactive than other children.

9. **d.** is the answer. (p. 282)

10. **d.** is the answer. (p. 280)

11. **b.** is the answer. (p. 281)

12. **b.** is the answer. (p. 281)

13. **c.** is the answer. Medication alone cannot ameliorate all the problems of AD/HD. (p. 283)

14. **b.** is the answer. Genes typically *do* play a role in a child's susceptibility to asthma. (p. 270)

15. **c.** is the answer. Both Sternberg and Gardner believe that there are multiple intelligences rather than the narrowly defined abilities measured by traditional aptitude and achievement tests. (p. 275)

    a., b., & d. Although these criticisms are certainly valid, they are not specifically associated with Sternberg or Gardner.

KEY TERMS

1. **Middle childhood** is the period from age 7 to 11. (p. 267)

2. A person whose body weight is 20–29 percent above that considered ideal for the person's age and height is designated as **overweight.** (p. 268)

3. **Obesity** is a body weight that is 30 percent or more above the weight that is considered ideal for the person's age and height. (p. 268)

4. **Asthma** is a disorder in which the airways are chronically inflamed. (p. 270)

5. **Automatization** is the process by which thoughts and actions that are repeated often enough to become routine no longer require much conscious thought. (p. 272)

6. **Reaction time** is the length of time it takes a person to respond to a particular stimulus. (p. 273)

7. **Aptitude** is the potential to learn a particular skill or body of knowledge. (p. 274)

8. **IQ tests** are aptitude tests, which were originally designed to yield a measure of intelligence and calculated as mental age divided by chronological age, multiplied by 100. (p. 274)

9. **Achievement tests** are tests that measure what a child has already learned in a particular academic subject or subjects. (p. 274)

10. The **Wechsler Intelligence Scale for Children (WISC)** is a widely used IQ test for school-age children that assesses vocabulary, general knowledge, memory, and spatial comprehension. (p. 274)

11. A **child with special needs** is one who, because of physical or mental disability, requires extra help in order to learn. (p. 277)

12. An **individual education plan (IEP)** is a legal document that specifies a set of educational goals for a child with special needs. (p. 277)

13. **Developmental psychopathology** is a field that applies the insights from studies of normal development to the study and treatment of childhood disorders, and vice versa. (p. 277)

14. The fourth edition of the *Diagnostic and Statistical Manual of Mental Disorders* **(DSM-IV-R),** developed by the American Psychiatric Association, is the leading means of diagnosing mental disorders. (p. 279)

15. **Pervasive developmental disorders,** such as autism, are disorders that affect numerous aspects of the psychological growth of a child under age 3. (p. 279)

16. **Autism** is a severe disturbance of early childhood characterized by an inability to communicate with others in an ordinary way, by extreme self-absorption, and by an inability to learn normal speech. (p. 280)

17. **Asperger syndrome** is a disorder in which a person has near normal speech and intelligence but severely impaired social interaction; also called *high-functioning autism.* (p. 280)

18. **ADD (attention-deficit disorder)** is a condition in which a child has great difficulty concentrating but is not impulsive or overactive. (p. 281)

19. **AD/HD (attention-deficit/hyperactivity disorder)** is a behavior problem in which the individual has great difficulty concentrating and is often inattentive, impulsive, and overactive. (p. 281)

20. A **learning disability** is a difficulty in a particular cognitive skill that is not attributable to overall intellectual slowness, a physical handicap, or a severely stressful living condition. (p. 282)

21. **Dyslexia** is a learning disability in reading. (p. 282)

22. **Mainstreaming** is an educational approach in which children with special needs are included in regular classrooms. (p. 284)

23. A **least restrictive environment (LRE)** is a legally required school setting that offers special-needs children as much freedom as possible to benefit from the instruction available to other children, often in a mainstreamed classroom. (p. 284)

24. A **resource room** is a classroom equipped with special material, in which children with special needs spend part of their day working with a trained specialist in order to learn basic skills. (p. 284)

25. **Inclusion** is an educational approach in which children with special needs receive individualized instruction within a regular classroom setting. (p. 284)

Chapter Twelve

Chapter Overview

Chapter 12 examines the development of cognitive abilities in children from ages 7 to 11. The first section discusses the views of Piaget and Vygotsky regarding the child's cognitive development, which involves a growing ability to use logic and reasoning (as emphasized by Piaget) and to benefit from social interactions with skilled mentors (as emphasized by Vygotsky).). Because the school years are also a time of expanding moral reasoning, this section also examines Kohlberg's stage theory of moral development as well as current evaluations of his theory.

The second section focuses on changes in the child's processing speed and capacity, control processes, knowledge base, and metacognition. It also looks at language development during middle childhood. During this time, children develop a more analytic understanding of words and show a marked improvement in their language skills.

The last section covers educational and environmental conditions that are conducive to learning by schoolchildren, including how reading, math, and science are best taught, and fluency in a second language.

NOTE: Answer guidelines for all Chapter 12 questions begin on page 182.

Guided Study

The text chapter should be studied one section at a time. Before you read, preview each section by skimming it, noting headings and boldface items. Then read the appropriate section objectives from the following outline. Keep these objectives in mind and, as you read the chapter section, search for the information that will enable you to meet each objective. Once you have finished a section, write out answers for its objectives.

Building on Piaget and Vygotsky (pp. 289–295)

1. Identify and discuss the logical operations of concrete operational thought, and give examples of how these operations are demonstrated by schoolchildren.

2. Discuss Vygotsky's views regarding the influence of the sociocultural context on learning during middle childhood.

3. Outline Kohlberg's stage theory of moral development.

7. Discuss advances in the control processes, especially selective attention and metacognition, during middle childhood.

4. Identify and evaluate several criticisms of Kohlberg's theory, and discuss sociocultural effects on moral development.

Language (pp. 367–372)

8. Describe the development of language during the school years, noting changing abilities in vocabulary and pragmatics.

Information Processing (pp. 296–301)

5. Describe the components of the information-processing system, noting how they interact.

Teaching and Learning (pp. 301–310)

9. Differentiate several approaches to teaching reading and math, and discuss evidence regarding the effectiveness of these methods.

6. Explain how processing speed increases in middle childhood as the result of advances in automatization and a larger knowledge base.

10. Identify several conditions that foster the learning of a second language, and describe the best approaches to bilingual education.

11. (text and Thinking Like a Scientist) Discuss the concept of a hidden curriculum and the merits of smaller class size.

Chapter Review

When you have finished reading the chapter, work through the material that follows to review it. Complete the sentences and answer the questions. As you proceed, evaluate your performance for each section by consulting the answers beginning on page 182. Do not continue with the next section until you understand each answer. If you need to, review or reread the appropriate section in the textbook before continuing.

Building on Piaget and Vygotsky (pp. 289–295)

1. According to Piaget, between ages 7 and 11, children are in the stage of _____ _____ _____ . Unlike Piaget, Vygotsky regarded instruction by _____ as crucial to cognitive development.

2. The concept that objects can be organized into categories according to some common property is _____ .

3. The logical principle that certain characteristics of an object remain the same even when other characteristics change is _____ . The idea that a transformation process can be reversed to

restore the original condition is _____ . The logical principle that two things can change in opposite ways to balance each other out is _____ .

4. Cross-cultural studies of classification and other logical processes demonstrate that these principles _____ (apply/do not apply) throughout the world.

5. Contemporary developmentalists believe that Piaget underestimated the influence of _____ , _____ , and _____ on cognitive development. In doing so, he also underestimated the _____ in development from one child to another.

6. The theorist who has extensively studied moral development by presenting subjects with stories that pose ethical dilemmas is _____ . According to his theory, the three levels of moral reasoning are _____ , _____ , and _____ .

7. (Table 12.1) In preconventional reasoning, emphasis is on getting _____ and avoiding _____ . "Might makes right" describes stage _____ (1/2), whereas "look out for number one" describes stage _____ (1/2).

8. (Table 12.1) In conventional reasoning, emphasis is on _____ _____ , such as being a dutiful citizen, in stage _____ (3/4), or winning approval from others, in stage _____ (3/4).

9. (Table 12.1) In postconventional reasoning, emphasis is on _____ _____ , such as _____ _____ (stage 5) and _____ _____ _____ (stage 6).

10. During middle childhood, children's moral reasoning generally falls at the _____ and _____ levels.

11. One criticism of Kohlberg's theory is that the later stages reflect values associated with _____ intellectual values . Another is that Kohlberg ignored the moral development of _____ .

12. It is now well established that different cultures _____ (have/do not have) distinctive morals and values.

13. Carol Gilligan believes that females develop a _____ _____ _____ , based on concern for the well-being of others, more than a _____ _____ _____ , based on depersonalized standards of right and wrong.

Information Processing (pp. 296–301)

14. The idea that the advances in thinking that accompany middle childhood occur because of basic changes in how children take in, store, and process data is central to the _____-_____ theory.

15. Incoming stimulus information is held for a split second in the _____ _____ , after which most of it is lost.

16. Meaningful material is transferred into _____ _____ , which is sometimes called _____-_____ _____ . This part of memory handles mental activity that is _____ .

17. The part of memory that stores information for days, months, or years is _____-_____ _____ . Crucial in this component of the system is not only storage of the material but also its _____ .

18. Children in the school years are better learners and problem solvers than younger children are, because they have faster _____ , and they have a larger _____ _____ .

19. One reason for the cognitive advances of middle childhood is _____ maturation, especially the _____ of nerve pathways and the development of the _____ _____ .

20. Processing capacity also becomes more efficient through _____ , as familiar mental activities become routine.

21. Memory ability improves during middle childhood in part because of the child's expanded _____ _____ .

22. The knowledge base also depends on _____ and _____ .

23. The mechanisms of the information-processing system that regulate the analysis and flow of information are the _____ _____ .

24. The ability to use _____ _____—to screen out distractors and concentrate on relevant information—improves steadily during the school years and beyond.

25. The ability to evaluate a cognitive task to determine what to do—and to monitor one's performance—is called _____ . This ability becomes evident by age _____ .

26. The practical application of linguistic knowledge is called the _____ of language.

27. During middle childhood, some children learn as many as _____ new words a day. Unlike the vocabulary explosion of the play years, this language growth is distinguished by _____ , _____ , and the ability to make connections between one bit of knowledge and another and later vocabulary performance in school.

28. Schoolchildren's love of words is evident in their _____ , secret _____ , and _____ that they tell.

Teaching and Learning (pp. 301–311)

29. There _____ (is/is not) universal agreement on how best to educate schoolchildren. Internationally and historically, there has been agreement that schools should teach _____ , _____ , and _____ .

30. Some researchers distinguish among the _____ curriculum, which refers to the content endorsed by _____ _____ ; the _____ curriculum, which refers to what is actually offered; and the _____ curriculum, that the students actually learn.

31. (text and Thinking Like a Scientist) Every culture creates its own _____ _____ , the unofficial priorities that influence every aspect of school learning. Two aspects of this curriculum are the _____ , and the number of _____ . The evidence supporting the popular assumption that smaller class size results in better learning is _____ (strong/weak).

32. Two distinct approaches to teaching reading are the _____ approach, in which children learn the sounds of letters first, and the _____-_____ approach, in which children are encouraged to develop all their language skills at the same time. Most developmentalists believe that _____(both approaches/neither approach/only the phonics approach/only the whole-language approach) make(s) sense.

33. The lower the family income, the less developed a child's _____ and _____ . This indicates that language development and reading attainment _____ (correlate/do not correlate) with _____ status. The crucial factor in this relationship is the child's actual _____ to language.

34. The best predictor of school achievement and overall intelligence is _____ _____ .

35. Worldwide, literacy has _____ (increased/decreased/not changed) over the past 50 years.

36. Many nations have decided that _____ and _____are the key areas of the curriculum, perhaps because advances in these areas seem to be connected to a nation's _____development.

37. In the United States, math was traditionally taught through _____ _____ . A more recent approach replaces this type of learning by emphasizing _____ _____ , estimating and _____ .

38. Cross-cultural research reveals that North American teachers present math at a lower level with more _____ but less _____ to other learning. In contrast, teachers in Japan work more _____ to build children's knowledge.

39. The gap between rich and poor families in their access to computers has been called the _____ . Students who never use computers score _____ (much lower/much higher/almost the same) in math and science as students who often use computers.

40. Most of the world's children _____ (learn/do not learn) a second language. The best time to learn a second language by listening and talking is during _____ , and the best time to teach a second language is during _____ _____ .

41. The approach to bilingual education in which the child's instruction occurs entirely in the second language is called _____ _____ . In _____ _____ programs, the child is taught first in his or her native language, until the second language is taught as a "foreign" language.

42. (Table 12.4) In ESL, or _____ _____ programs, children must master the basics of English before joining regular classes with other children. In contrast, _____ _____ requires that teachers instruct children in both their native language as well as in English.

43. Immersion programs were successful in _____ , when English-speaking children were initially placed in French-only classrooms. Immersion tends to fail if the child feels _____ , _____ , or _____ _____ .

44. The crucial difference between success and failure in second-language learning rests with _____ _____ , who indicate to the children whether learning a second language is really valued. When both languages are valued, _____ _____ is likely to occur. When second-language learning fails and neither language is learned well, a child is said to be _____ .

Progress Test 1

Multiple-Choice Questions

Circle your answers to the following questions and check them with the answers on page 183. If your answer is incorrect, read the explanation for why it is incorrect and then consult the appropriate pages of the text (in parentheses following the correct answer).

1. According to Piaget, the stage of cognitive development in which a person understands specific logical ideas and can apply them to concrete problems is called:
   a. preoperational thought.
   b. operational thought.
   c. concrete operational thought.
   d. formal operational thought.

2. Which of the following is the *most* direct reason that thinking speed continues to increase throughout adolescence?
   a. the increasing myelination of neural axons
   b. the continuing development of the frontal cortex
   c. learning from experience
   d. neurological maturation

3. The idea that an object that has been transformed in some way can be restored to its original form by undoing the process is:
   a. identity.   c. reciprocity.
   b. reversibility.   d. automatization.

4. Information-processing theorists contend that major advances in cognitive development occur during the school years because:
   a. the child's mind becomes more like a computer as he or she matures.
   b. children become better able to process and analyze information.
   c. most mental activities become automatic by the time a child is about 13 years old.
   d. the major improvements in reasoning that occur during the school years involve increased long-term memory capacity.

5. The ability to filter out distractions and concentrate on relevant details is called:
   a. metacognition.
   b. information processing.
   c. selective attention.
   d. decentering.

6. Concrete operational thought is Piaget's term for the school-age child's ability to:
   a. reason logically about things and events he or she perceives.
   b. think about thinking.
   c. understand that certain characteristics of an object remain the same when other characteristics are changed.
   d. understand that moral principles may supercede the standards of society.

7. The term for the ability to monitor one's cognitive performance—to think about thinking—is:
   a. pragmatics.
   b. information processing.
   c. selective attention.
   d. metacognition.

8. Long-term memory is _____ permanent and _____ limited than working memory.
   a. more; less
   b. less; more
   c. more; more
   d. less; less

9. In making moral choices, according to Gilligan, females are more likely than males to:
   a. score at a higher level in Kohlberg's system.
   b. emphasize the needs of others.
   c. judge right and wrong in absolute terms.
   d. formulate abstract principles.

10. Compared to more advantaged children, children from low-income families show deficits in their development of:
   a. vocabulary.
   b. grammar.
   c. sentence length.
   d. all the above.

11. The best predictor of a child's achievement in school is:
   a. the school achievement of the child's parents.
   b. vocabulary size.
   c. the child's socioeconomic status.
   d. class size.

12. Which of the following is *not* an approach used successfully in the United States to avoid the shock of complete immersion in the teaching of English?
   a. reverse immersion
   b. English as a second language
   c. bilingual education
   d. total immersion

13. The idea that two things can change in opposite directions, yet balance each other out is:
   a. identity.
   b. reversibility.
   c. reciprocity.
   d. automatization.

14. Between 9 and 11 years of age, children are most likely to demonstrate moral reasoning at which of Kohlberg's stages?
   a. preconventional
   b. conventional
   c. postconventional
   d. It is impossible to predict based only on a child's age.

15. Of the following, which was not identified as an important factor in the difference between success and failure in second-language learning?
   a. the age of the child
   b. the attitudes of the parents
   c. community values regarding second language learning
   d. the difficulty of the language

True or False Items

Write T (*true*) or F (*false*) on the line in front of each statement.

_____ 1. A major objection to Piaget's theory is that he underestimated the influence of context, instruction, and culture.

_____ 2. Learning a second language is increasingly necessary because of globalization.

_____ 3. During middle childhood, children are passionately concerned with issues of right and wrong.

_____ 4. As a group, Japanese and Korean children outscore children in the United States and Canada in math and science.

_____ 5. The process of telling a joke involves remembering the right words and their sequence, a skill usually not mastered before middle childhood.

_____ 6. Children who use computers frequently score much higher in math and science than do students who rarely use computers.

_____ 7. The best time to learn a second language by listening and talking is during middle childhood.

_____ 8. Most information that comes into the sensory memory is lost or discarded.

_____ 9. Information-processing theorists believe that advances in the thinking of school-age children occur primarily because of changes in long-term memory.

_____ 10. New standards of math education in many nations emphasize problem-solving skills rather than simple memorization of formulas.

Progress Test 2

Progress Test 2 should be completed during a final chapter review. Answer the following questions after you thoroughly understand the correct answers for the Chapter Review and Progress Test 1.

Multiple-Choice Questions

1. According to Piaget, 8- and 9-year-olds can reason only about concrete things in their lives. "Concrete" means:
   a. logical.
   b. abstract.
   c. tangible or specific.
   d. mathematical or classifiable.

2. Research regarding Piaget's theory has found that:
   a. cognitive development seems to be considerably less affected by sociocultural factors than Piaget's descriptions imply.
   b. the movement to a new level of thinking is much more erratic than Piaget predicted.
   c. there is no dramatic shift in the thinking of children when they reach the age of 5.
   d. all of the above are true.

3. The increase in processing speed that occurs during middle childhood is partly the result of:
   a. ongoing myelination of axons.
   b. neurological development in the limbic system.
   c. the streamlining of the knowledge base.
   d. all of the above.

4. When psychologists look at the ability of children to receive, store, and organize information, they are examining cognitive development from a view based on:
   a. the observations of Piaget.
   b. information processing.
   c. behaviorism.
   d. the idea that the key to thinking is the sensory register.

5. Kohlberg's stage theory of moral development is based on his research on a group of boys and on:
   a. psychoanalytic ideas.
   b. Piaget's theory of cognitive development.
   c. Carol Gilligan's research on moral dilemmas.
   d. questionnaires distributed to a nationwide sample of high school seniors.

6. The logical operations of concrete operational thought are particularly important to an understanding of the elementary-school subject(s) of:
   a. spelling.
   b. reading.
   c. math and science.
   d. social studies.

7. Although older school-age children are generally at the conventional level of moral reasoning, *when* they reach a particular level depends on:
   a. the specific context and the child's opportunity to discuss moral issues.
   b. the level of moral reasoning reached by their parents.
   c. how strongly their peers influence their thinking.
   d. whether they are male or female.

8. Which of the following Piagetian ideas is *not* widely accepted by developmentalists today?
   a. The thinking of school-age children is characterized by a more comprehensive logic than that of preschoolers.
   b. Children are active learners.
   c. How children think is as important as what they know.
   d. Context, instruction, and culture are less important in a child's developing cognitive ability than his or her active exploration and hypothesis testing.

9. Processing capacity refers to:
   a. the ability to selectively attend to more than one thought.
   b. the amount of information that a person is able to hold in working memory.
   c. the size of the child's knowledge base.
   d. all of the above.

10. The retention of new information is called:
    a. retrieval.
    b. storage.
    c. automatization.
    d. metacognition.

11. According to Kohlberg, a person who is a dutiful citizen and obeys the laws set down by society would be at which level of moral reasoning?
    a. preconventional stage one
    b. preconventional stage two
    c. conventional
    d. postconventional

12. Which aspect of the information-processing system assumes an executive role in regulating the analysis and transfer of information?
    a. sensory register
    b. working memory
    c. long-term memory
    d. control processes

13. An example of schoolchildren's growth in meta-cognition is their understanding that:
    a. transformed objects can be returned to their original state.
    b. rehearsal is a good strategy for memorizing, but outlining is better for understanding.
    c. objects may belong to more than one class.
    d. they can use different language styles in different situations.

14. Which of the following most accurately states the relative merits of the phonics approach and the whole-language approach to teaching reading?
    a. The phonics approach is more effective.
    b. The whole-language approach is the more effective approach.

    c. Both approaches have merit.
    d. Both approaches have been discarded in favor of newer, more interactive methods of instruction.

15. Ideally, children should be fluent in a second language by what age?
    a. 8
    b. 9
    c. 11
    d. 15

Matching Items
Match each term or concept with its corresponding description or definition.

Terms or Concepts

_____ 1. automatization
_____ 2. reversibility
_____ 3. conventional
_____ 4. identity
_____ 5. information processing
_____ 6. selective attention
_____ 7. retrieval
_____ 8. storage
_____ 9. metacognition
_____ 10. total immersion
_____ 11. postconventional
_____ 12. preconventional

Descriptions or Definitions

a. the ability to screen out distractions and concentrate on relevant information
b. the idea that a transformation process can be undone to restore the original conditions
c. the idea that certain characteristics of an object remain the same even when other characteristics change
d. developmental perspective that conceives of cognitive development as the result of changes in the processing and analysis of information
e. moral reasoning in which the individual focuses on his or her own welfare
f. moral reasoning in which the individual follows principles that supersede the standards of society
g. an educational technique in which instruction occurs entirely in the second language
h. accessing previously learned information
i. holding information in memory
j. moral reasoning in which the individual considers social standards and laws to be primary
k. process by which familiar mental activities become routine
l. the ability to evaluate a cognitive task and to monitor one's performance on it

Thinking Critically About Chapter 12

Answer these questions the day before an exam as a final check on your understanding of the chapter's terms and concepts.

1. Of the following statements made by children, which best exemplifies the logical principle of identity?
   a. "You can't leave first base until the ball is hit!"
   b. "See how the jello springs back into shape after I poke my finger into it?"
   c. "I know it's still a banana, even though it's mashed down in my sandwich."
   d. "You're my friend, so I don't have to use polite speech like I do with adults."

2. Which of the following statements is the clearest indication that the child has grasped the principle of reversibility?
   a. "See, the lemonade is the same in both our glasses; even though your glass is taller than mine, it's narrower."
   b. "Even though your dog looks funny, I know it's still a dog."
   c. "I have one sister and no brothers. My parents have two children."
   d. "I don't cheat because I don't want to be punished."

3. After moving to a new country, a child's parents are struck by the greater tendency of math teachers in their new homeland to work collaboratively and to emphasize social interaction in the learning process. To which country have these parents probably moved?
   a. the United States   c. Japan
   b. Germany   d. Australia

4. Dr. Larsen believes that the cognitive advances of middle childhood occur because of basic changes in children's thinking speed, knowledge base, and memory retrieval skills. Dr. Larsen evidently is working from the _____ perspective.
   a. Piagetian
   b. Vygotskian
   c. information-processing
   d. psychoanalytic

5. Some researchers believe that cognitive processing speed and capacity increase during middle childhood because of:
   a. the myelination of nerve pathways.
   b. the maturation of the frontal cortex.
   c. better use of cognitive resources.
   d. all of the above.

6. Mei-Chin is able to sort her Legos into groups according to size. Clearly, she has an understanding of the principle of:
   a. classification.   c. reversibility.
   b. identity.   d. reciprocity.

7. For a 10-year-old, some mental activities have become so familiar or routine as to require little mental work. This development is called:
   a. selective attention.   c. metacognition.
   b. identity.   d. automatization.

8. Lana is 4 years old and her brother Roger is 7. The fact that Roger remembers what their mother just told them about playing in the street while Lana is more interested in the children playing across the street is due to improvements in Roger's:
   a. selective attention.   c. control processes.
   b. automatization.   d. long-term memory.

9. Which of the following statements is the best example of Kohlberg's concept of stage 1 preconventional moral reasoning?
   a. "Might makes right."
   b. "Law and order."
   c. "Nice boys do what is expected of them."
   d. "Look out for number one."

10. According to Carol Gilligan, a girl responding to the hypothetical question of whether an impoverished child should steal food to feed her starving dog is most likely to:
    a. respond according to a depersonalized standard of right and wrong.
    b. hesitate to take a definitive position based on the abstract moral premise of "right and wrong.""
    c. immediately respond that the child was justified in stealing the food.
    d. respond unpredictably, based on her own personal experiences.

11. Four-year-old Tasha, who is learning to read by sounding out the letters of words, evidently is being taught using which approach?
    a. phonics
    b. whole-word
    c. total immersion
    d. reverse immersion

12. The study of street children in Brazil revealed that:
    a. many never attended school.
    b. many scored poorly on standardized math tests.
    c. many were quite adept at using math practically to sell fruit, candy, and other products to earn their living.
    d. all of the above were true.

13. During the school board meeting a knowledgeable parent proclaimed that the board's position on achievement testing and class size was an example of the district's "hidden curriculum." The parent was referring to the:
    a. unofficial and unstated educational priorities of the school district.
    b. Political agendas of individual members of the school board.
    c. Legal mandates for testing and class size established by the state board of education.
    d. None of the above.

14. Critics of Kohlberg's theory of moral development argue that it:
    a. places too much emphasis on sociocultural factors.
    b. places too much emphasis on traditional, religious beliefs.
    c. is biased toward liberal, Western intellectual values.
    d. can't be tested.

15. Andy understands that a ball of clay that is flattened and rolled into a rope hasn't changed in size. Andy's awareness demonstrates an understanding of the logical principle of:
    a. classification.   c. reversibility.
    b. identity.   d. reciprocity.

Key Terms
Writing Definitions

Using your own words, write a brief definition or explanation of each of the following terms on a separate piece of paper.

1. concrete operational thought
2. classification
3. identity
4. reversibility
5. reciprocity
6. preconventional moral reasoning
7. conventional moral reasoning
8. postconventional moral reasoning
9. morality of care
10. morality of justice
11. sensory memory
12. working memory
13. long-term memory
14. knowledge base
15. control processes
16. selective attention
17. metacognition
18. hidden curriculum
19. phonics approach
20. whole-language approach
21. total immersion

Cross-Check

After you have written the definitions of the key terms in this chapter, you should complete the crossword puzzle to ensure that you can reverse the process—recognize the term, given the definition.

ACROSS

3. Processes that regulate the analysis and flow of information in memory.
7. According to Gilligan, men develop a morality of _____ .
9. The part of memory that stores unlimited amounts of information for days, months, or years.
10. English as a second language.
11. Psychologist who developed an influential theory of cognitive development.
12. According to the theorist in 11 across, cognitive development occurs in _____ .
14. One of Kohlberg's harshest critics.
16. According to Piaget, the type of cognitive operations that occur during middle childhood.
17. Moral reasoning in which the individual considers social standards and laws to be primary.

DOWN

1. The body of knowledge that has been learned about a particular area.
2. The part of memory that handles current, conscious mental activity.
3. According to Gilligan, females develop a morality of _____ .
4. The ability to evaluate a cognitive task in order to determine what to do.
5. Process by which familiar mental activities become routine.
6. Ongoing neural process that speeds up neural processing.
8. An approach to teaching a second language in which the teacher instructs the children in school subjects using their native language as well as the second language.
13. Neurological development in the _____ cortex during middle childhood helps speed neural processing.
15. The main characteristic of concrete operational thinking is the ability to use _____ .

ANSWERS

CHAPTER REVIEW

1. concrete operational thought; others (or peers, schools, and teachers)
2. classification
3. identity; reversibility; reciprocity
4. apply
5. context; instruction; culture; variability
6. Kohlberg; preconventional; conventional; postconventional
7. rewards; punishments; 1; 2
8. social rules; 4; 3
9. moral principles; social contracts; universal ethical principles
10. preconventional; conventional
11. Western; women
12. have
13. morality of care; morality of justice
14. information-processing
15. sensory memory (register)
16. working memory; short-term memory; conscious

17. long-term memory; retrieval
18. processing speed; processing capacity
19. neurological; myelination; frontal cortex
20. automatization
21. knowledge base
22. opportunity; motivation
23. control processes
24. selective attention
25. metacognition; 8 or 9
26. pragmatics
27. 20; logic; memory
28. poems; languages; jokes
29. is not; reading; writing; arithmetic
30. intended; political and educational leaders; implemented; attained
31. hidden curriculum; length of the school day and year; students per teacher; weak
32. phonics; whole-language; both approaches
33. vocabulary; grammar; correlate; socioeconomic; exposure
34. vocabulary size
35. increased
36. math; science; economic
37. rote learning; concepts; problem solving; probability
38. definitions; connection; collaboratively
39. digital divide; almost the same
40. learn; early childhood; middle childhood
41. total immersion; reverse immersion
42. English as a second language; bilingual education
43. Canada; shy; stupid; socially isolated
44. the attitudes of parents, teachers, and the community; additive bilingualism; semilingual

PROGRESS TEST 1

Multiple-Choice Questions

1. **c.** is the answer. (p. 289)

    a. Preoperational thought is "pre-logical" thinking.

    b. There is no such stage in Piaget's theory.

    d. Formal operational thought extends logical reasoning to abstract problems.

2. **c.** is the answer. (p. 297)

    a., b., & d. Although myelination and the development of the frontal cortex, which are both examples of neurological maturation, partly account for increasing speed of processing, learning is a more direct cause.

3. **b.** is the answer. (p. 291)

    a. This is the concept that certain characteristics of an object remain the same even when other characteristics change.

c. This is the concept that two things can change in opposite directions to balance each other out.

d. This is the process by which familiar mental activities become routine and automatic.

4. **b.** is the answer. (p. 296)

    a. Information-processing theorists use the mind–computer metaphor at every age.

    c. Although increasing automatization is an important aspect of development, the information-processing perspective does not suggest that most mental activities become automatic by age 13.

    d. Most of the important changes in reasoning that occur during the school years are due to the improved processing capacity of the person's *working memory*.

5. **c.** is the answer. (p. 298)

    a. This is the ability to evaluate a cognitive task and to monitor one's performance on it.

    b. Information processing is a perspective on cognitive development that focuses on how the mind analyzes, stores, retrieves, and reasons about information.

    d. Decentering, which refers to the school-age child's ability to consider more than one aspect of a problem simultaneously, is not discussed in this chapter.

6. **a.** is the answer. (p. 289)

    b. This refers to metacognition.

    c. This refers to Piaget's concept of identity.

    d. This is characteristic of Kohlberg's postconventional moral reasoning.

7. **d.** is the answer. (p. 299)

    a. Pragmatics refers to the practical use of language to communicate with others.

    b. The information-processing perspective views the mind as being like a computer.

    c. This is the ability to screen out distractions in order to focus on important information.

8. **a.** is the answer. (p. 296)
9. **b.** is the answer. (pp. 294–295)
10. **d.** is the answer. (p. 304)
11. **b.** is the answer. (p. 305)
12. **a.** is the answer. (p. 309)
13. **c.** is the answer. (p. 291)
14. **b.** is the answer. (p. 293)
15. **d.** is the answer. (p. 309)

True or False Items

1. T (p. 292)

2. T (p. 308)

3. T (p. 293)

4. T (p. 306)

5. T (p. 300)

6. F   Students who never use computers score almost as high as students who often use computers. (p. 308)

7. F   The best time to learn a second language by listening and talking is during *early* childhood. (p. 308)

8. T   (p. 296)

9. F   They believe that the changes are due to basic changes in control processes. (p. 298)

10. T (p. 306)

PROGRESS TEST 2

Multiple-Choice Questions

1. **c.** is the answer. (p. 289)

2. **b.** is the answer. (p. 292)

3. **a.** is the answer. (p. 297)

    b. Neurological development in the frontal cortex facilitates processing speed during middle childhood.   The limbic system, which was not discussed in this chapter, is concerned with emotions.

    c. Processing speed is facilitated by *growth*, rather than streamlining, of the knowledge base.

4. **b.** is the answer. (p. 296)

5. **b.** is the answer. (p. 292)

6. **c.** is the answer. (p. 291)

7. **a.** is the answer. (p. 294)

    b., c., & d. Although these may be factors, they don't necessarily determine the child's level of moral reasoning.

8. **d.** is the answer. (p. 292)

9. **b.** is the answer. (p. 297)

10. **b.** is the answer. (p. 296)

    a. This is the *accessing* of already learned information.

    c. Automatization is the process by which well-learned activities become routine and automatic.

    d. This is the ability to evaluate a task and to monitor one's performance on it.

11. **c.** is the answer. (p. 293)

12. **d.** is the answer. (p. 298)

    a. The sensory register stores incoming information for a split second.

    b. Working memory is the part of memory that handles current, conscious mental activity.

    c. Long-term memory stores information for days, months, or years.

13. **b.** is the answer. (p. 299)

14. **c.** is the answer. (pp. 303–304)

15. **c.** is the answer. (p. 308)

Matching Items

1. k (p. 297)   5. d (p. 296)   9. l (p. 299)
2. b (p. 291)   6. a (p. 298)   10. g (p. 309)
3. j (p. 293)   7. h (pp. 296–297)   11. f (p. 293)
4. c (p. 290)   8. i (p. 296)   12. e (p. 293)

THINKING CRITICALLY ABOUT CHAPTER 12

1. **c.** is the answer. (p. 291)

    a., b., & d. Identity is the logical principle that certain characteristics of an object (such as the shape of a banana) remain the same even when other characteristics change.

2. **a.** is the answer. (p. 291)

    b., c., & d. Reversibility is the logical principle that something that has been changed (such as the height of lemonade poured from one glass into another) can be returned to its original shape by reversing the process of change (pouring the liquid back into the other glass).

3. **c.** is the answer. (p. 308)

4. **c.** is the answer. (p. 296)

    a. This perspective emphasizes the logical, active nature of thinking during middle childhood.

    b. This perspective emphasizes the importance of social interaction in learning.

    d. This perspective does not address the development of cognitive skills.

5. **d.** is the answer. (p. 297)

6. **a.** is the answer. (p. 290)

7. **d.** is the answer. (p. 297)

    a. Selective attention is the ability to focus on important information and screen out distractions.

    b. Identity is the logical principle that certain characteristics of an object remain the same even when other characteristics change.

c. Metacognition is the ability to evaluate a task and to monitor one's performance on it.

8. **c.** is the answer. (p. 298)

a. Selective attention *is* a control process, but c. is more specific and thus more correct.

b. Automatization refers to the tendency of well-rehearsed mental activities to become routine and automatic.

d. Long-term memory is the part of memory that stores information for days, months, or years.

9. **a.** is the answer. (p. 293)

b. & c. These exemplify conventional moral reasoning.

d. This exemplifies stage two preconventional moral reasoning.

10. **b.** is the answer. Gilligan contends that females' morality of care makes them reluctant to judge right and wrong in absolute terms because they are socialized to be nurturant and caring. (p. 294)

11. **a.** is the answer. (p. 303)

b. This approach encourages children to develop all their language skills at the same time.

c. & d. These are approaches to bilingual instruction, not reading instruction.

12. **d.** is the answer. (p. 292)

13. **a.** is the answer. (p. 302)

14. **c.** is the answer. (p. 294)

15. **d.** is the answer. (p. 291)

KEY TERMS

Writing Definitions

1. During Piaget's stage of **concrete operational thought,** lasting from ages 7 to 11, children can think logically about concrete events and objects but are not able to reason abstractly. (p. 289)

2. **Classification** is the process of organizing things into groups according to some common property. (p. 290)

3. In Piaget's theory, **identity** is the logical principle that certain characteristics of an object remain the same even when other characteristics change. (p. 290)

4. **Reversibility** is the logical principle that a transformation process can be reversed to restore the original conditions. (p. 291)

5. **Reciprocity** is the logical principle that two things can change in opposite ways in order to balance each other out. (p. 291)

6. Kohlberg's first level of moral reasoning, **preconventional moral reasoning**, emphasizes obedience to authority in order to avoid punishment (stage 1) and being nice to other people so they will be nice to you (stage 2). (p. 293)

7. Kohlberg's second level of moral reasoning, **conventional moral reasoning**, emphasizes winning the approval of others (stage 3) and obeying the laws set down by those in power (stage 4). (p. 293)

8. Kohlberg's third level, **postconventional moral reasoning**, emphasizes the social and contractual nature of moral principles (stage 5) and the existence of universal ethical principles (stage 6). (p. 293)

9. According to Carol Gilligan, compared with boys and men, girls and women are more likely to develop a **morality of care** that is based on nurturance, compassion, and being nonjudgmental. (p. 294)

10. According to Carol Gilligan, compared with girls and women, boys and men are more likely to develop a **morality of justice** based on depersonalized and absolute standards of right and wrong. (p. 294)

11. **Sensory memory** is the first component of the information-processing system that stores incoming stimuli for a split second, after which it is passed into working memory, or discarded as unimportant. (p. 296)

12. **Working memory** is the component of the information-processing system that handles current, conscious mental activity; also called short-term memory. (p. 296)

13. **Long-term memory** is the component of the information-processing system that stores unlimited amounts of information for days, months, or years. (p. 296)

14. The **knowledge base** is a broad body of knowledge in a particular subject area that has been learned and on which additional learning can be based. (p. 297)

15. **Control processes** (such as selective attention and metacognition) regulate the analysis and flow of information within the information-processing system. (p. 298)

16. **Selective attention** is the ability to screen out distractions and concentrate on relevant information. (p. 298)

17. **Metacognition** is the ability to evaluate a cognitive task to determine what to do and to monitor one's performance on that task. (p. 299)

18. The **hidden curriculum** is the unofficial, unstated, or implicit rules and priorities that influence the academic curriculum and every other aspect of school learning. (p. 302)

19. The **phonics approach** is a method of teaching reading by having children learn the sounds of letters before they begin to learn words. (p. 303)

20. The **whole-language approach** is a method of teaching reading by encouraging children to develop all their language skills simultaneously. (p. 303)

21. **Total immersion** is an approach to bilingual education in which the child's instruction occurs entirely in the new language. (p. 309)

Cross-Check

ACROSS

3. control
7. justice
9. long-term
10. ESL
11. Piaget
12. stages
14. Gilligan
16. concrete
17. conventional

DOWN

1. knowledge base
2. working
3. care
4. metacognition
5. automization
6. myelination
8. bilingual
13. frontal
15. logic

Chapter Thirteen

The School Years: Psychosocial Development

Chapter Overview

This chapter brings to a close the unit on the school years. We have seen that from ages 7 to 11, the child becomes stronger and more competent, mastering the biosocial and cognitive abilities that are important in his or her culture. Psychosocial accomplishments are equally impressive.

The first section of the chapter begins by exploring the growing social competence of children, as described by Freud and Erikson and behaviorist, cognitive, sociocultural, and epigenetic theorists. The section continues with a discussion of the growth of social cognition and self-understanding.

Children's interaction with peers and others in their ever-widening social world is the subject of the next section. Although the peer group often is a supportive, positive influence on children, some children are rejected by their peers or become the victims of bullying.

The next section explores the problems and challenges often experienced by school-age children in our society, including the experience living in single-parent, stepparent, and blended families. The chapter closes with a discussion of the ways in which children cope with stressful situations.

NOTE: Answer guidelines for all Chapter 13 questions begin on page 197.

Guided Study

The text chapter should be studied one section at a time. Before you read, preview each section by skimming it, noting headings and boldface items. Then read the appropriate section objectives from the following outline. Keep these objectives in mind and, as you read the chapter section, search for the information that will enable you to meet each objective. Once you have finished a section, write out answers for its objectives.

The Child's Emotions and Concerns (pp. 313–316)

1. Identify the themes or emphases of different theoretical views of the psychosocial development of school-age children.

2. Describe the development of self-understanding during middle childhood and its implications for children's self-esteem.

The Peer Group (pp. 317–323)

3. Discuss the importance of peer groups to the development of school-age children.

4. Discuss how friendship circles change during the school years.

5. Discuss the plight of two types of rejected children.

6. (text and Thinking Like a Scientist) Discuss the special problems of bullies and their victims, and describe possible ways of helping such children.

Families and Children (pp. 323–330)

7. Identify the essential ways in which functional families nurture school-age children.

8. Differentiate ten basic family structures.

9. Discuss family factors that affect the child's development.

10. Discuss the impact of blended families and other family structures on the psychosocial development of the school-age child.

Coping with Problems (pp. 330–335)

11. Discuss the concept of resilience, and identify the variables that influence the impact of stresses on schoolchildren.

12. Discuss several factors that seem especially important in helping children to cope with stress.

Chapter Review

When you have finished reading the chapter, work through the material that follows to review it. Complete the sentences and answer the questions. As you proceed, evaluate your performance for each section by consulting the answers beginning on page 197. Do not continue with the next section until you understand each answer. If you need to, review or reread the appropriate section in the textbook before continuing.

The Child's Emotions and Concerns (pp. 313–316)

1. Freud describes middle childhood as the period of _____ , when emotional drives are _____ , psychosexual needs are _____ , and unconscious conflicts are _____ .

2. According to Erikson, the crisis of middle childhood is _____ _____ _____ .

3. Developmentalists influenced by behaviorism are more concerned with children's _____ of new cognitive abilities; those influenced by the cognitive perspective focus on _____ . One offshoot of the grand theories, _____ _____ theory, stresses the combination of _____ and _____ that allows children to understand themselves and to be effective and competent. In addition to comparing children from different parts of the world, _____ theory examines various _____ within one nation. Epigenetic theory notes that not only are schoolchildren _____ driven to master the skills they will need in adulthood, but girls and boys have different visions and _____ _____ for adulthood.

4. As their self-understanding sharpens, children gradually become _____ (more/less) self-critical, and their self-esteem _____ (rises/dips). One reason is that they more often evaluate themselves through _____ _____ .

5. One example of how culture influences social comparison is the tendency of many social groups to teach children not to be too _____ . Research demonstrates that academic and social competence are fostered more by _____ evaluation of achievement than by artificially high _____ .

The Peer Group (pp. 317–323)

6. A peer group is defined as _____ _____ . Difficulties with peers _____ (place/do not place) children at risk for developing psychological problems.

7. During middle childhood, children care _____ (more/less) about the opinions of their peers than they did when they were younger. They also become _____ (more/less) dependent on each other and must learn to _____ , _____ , _____ , and defend themselves.

8. Having a personal friend is _____ (more/less) important to children than acceptance by the peer group.

9. Friendships during middle childhood become more _____ and _____ . As a result, older children _____ (change/do not change) friends as often and find it _____ (easier/harder) to make new friends.

10. Middle schoolers tend to choose best friends whose _____ , _____ , and _____ are similar to their own.

11. Children who are not really rejected but not picked as friends are _____ . Children who are actively rejected tend to be either _____ - _____ or _____ - _____ .

Give an example of the immaturity of rejected children.

12. Bullying is defined as _____ efforts to inflict harm through _____ , _____ , or _____ attacks. A key aspect in the definition of bullying is that harmful attacks are _____ .

13. Contrary to the public perception, in middle childhood bullies usually _____ (have/do not have) friends who admire them.

14. Victims of bullying are often _____ -rejected children. Less often, _____ -rejected children become _____ - _____ . Bullies and their victims _____ (are/are not) usually of the same gender.

15. Boys who are bullies are often above average in _____ , whereas girls who are bullies are often above average in _____ _____ . Boys who are bullies typically use _____ aggression, whereas girls use _____ aggression. Bullying may also be _____ , and obvious, or _____ .

16. Culture _____ (is/is not) a major factor in the incidence of bullying. For instance, a child's _____ status and behavior change from year to year and from place to place. For another, changes in the extent and type of bullying are common in the _____ grades.

Describe the effects of bullying on children.

17. Bullying is _____ (fairly easy/difficult) to change. The origins of bullying and other kinds of _____ behavior may lie in _____ _____ that are present at birth and then strengthened by _____ _____ , poor _____ _____ , and other deficits.

18. (Thinking Like a Scientist) An effective intervention in controlling bullying is to change the _____ _____ within the school so that bully–victim cycles are not allowed to persist.

Families and Children (pp. 323–330)

19. There is an ongoing debate between those who believe that _____ and _____ are more important influences on children's psychosocial development and those who believe that a child's _____ are much more powerful. Even so, all researchers agree that both _____ and _____ are important.

20. Research demonstrates that _____ (shared/nonshared) influences on most traits are far greater than _____ (shared/nonshared) influences.

21. Family function refers to how well the family _____ _____ .

22. A functional family nurtures school-age children by meeting their basic _____ , encouraging _____ , fostering the development of _____ , nurturing peer _____ , and providing _____ and _____ .

23. (text and Table 13.2) Family structure is defined as the _____ _____ .

Identify each of the following family structures:

a. _____ A family that includes three or more biologically related generations, including parents and children.

b. _____ A family that consists of the father, the mother, and their biological children.

c. _____ A family that consists of one parent with his or her biological children.

d. _____ A family consisting of two parents, at least one with biological children from another union.

e. _____ A family that consists of children living in their grandparents' home, either with our without their parents.

f. _____ A family that consists of one or more nonbiological children whom adults have legally taken to raise as their own.

g. _____ A family that consists of one or more orphaned, neglected, abused, or delinquent children who are temporarily cared for by an adult to whom they are not biologically related.

h. _____ A family that consists of a parent, his or her biological children, and his or her spouse, who is not biologically related to the children.

i. _____ A family that consists of one or two grandparents and their grandchildren.

j. _____ A family that consists of a homosexual couple and the biological or adopted children of one or both partners.

24. Longitudinal research studies demonstrate that children can thrive _____ (only in certain family structures/in almost any family structure).

Give several reasons for the benefits of the nuclear family structure.

25. When researchers control for differences in wealth, education, health, and hostility, the developmental differences between children raised in different family structures _____ (persist/disappear).

26. Children in every type of family structure grow up very well and sometimes run into trouble. Thus, family _____ seems more critical than family _____ .

27. Family income _____ (correlates/does not correlate) with optimal child development. A second factor that has a crucial impact on children is the _____ that characterizes family interaction. This latter factor explains why _____ families are problematic for many children.

28. Single parents tend to be _____ (older/younger) than married parents.

29. Parents who use harsh discipline are usually categorized as _____ . In the United States, however, many _____-, _____-, and _____- American families use harsh discipline yet are also warm and accepting of their children. An important factor in the impact of this pattern on children is how _____ or _____ the family is.

Coping with Problems (pp. 330–335)

30. Some children are better able to adapt within the context of adversity, that is, they seem to be more _____ . This trait is a _____ process that represents a _____ adaptation to stress.

31. The impact of a given stress on a child (such as divorce) depends on three factors:

a. _____

b. _____

c. _____

32. The importance of daily _____ explains why _____ is so difficult for children. An important factor in the impact of a given stressor is the child's _____ . One study found that children's coping depended more on their _____ of events than on the nature of the events themselves.

33. Another element that helps children deal with problems is the _____ _____ they receive.

34. During middle childhood, there are typically _____ (fewer/more) sources of social support. This can be obtained from grandparents or siblings, for example, or from _____ and _____ . In addition, _____ can also be psychologically protective for children in difficult circumstances.

Progress Test 1

Multiple-Choice Questions

Circle your answers to the following questions and check them with the answers on page 198. If your answer is incorrect, read the explanation for why it is incorrect and then consult the appropriate pages of the text (in parentheses following the correct answer).

1. Because it highlights how school-age children advance in learning, cognition, and culture, _____ theory is particularly relevant to middle childhood.
   a. Freud's psychoanalytic
   b. Erikson's psychosocial
   c. sociocultural
   d. social cognitive

2. A common thread running through the five major developmental theories is that cultures throughout history have selected ages 7 to 11 as the time for:
   a. a period of latency.
   b. the emergence of a theory of mind.
   c. more independence and responsibility.
   d. intellectual curiosity.

3. The best strategy for helping children who are at risk of developing serious psychological problems because of multiple stresses would be to:
   a. obtain assistance from a psychiatrist.
   b. increase the child's competencies or social supports.
   c. change the household situation.
   d. reduce the peer group's influence.

4. In explaining psychosocial development during the school years, Professor Wilson stresses the combination of maturation and experience that allows children to understand themselves and to be effective and competent. Professor Wilson is evidently working from the perspective of:
   a. behaviorism.
   b. Erik Erikson's theory of development.
   c. social cognitive theory.
   d. psychodynamic theory.

5. Girls who are bullies are often above average in _____ , whereas boys who are bullies are often above average in _____ .
   a. size; verbal assertiveness
   b. verbal assertiveness; size
   c. intelligence; aggressiveness
   d. aggressiveness; intelligence

6. As rejected children get older, their:
   a. problems often get worse.
   b. problems usually decrease.
   c. friendship circles typically become smaller.
   d. their peer group becomes less important to their self-esteem.

7. Compared with average or popular children, rejected children tend to be:
   a. brighter and more competitive.
   b. affluent and "stuck-up."
   c. economically disadvantaged.
   d. socially immature.

8. Compared to middle school boys, middle school girls are more likely to emphasize _____ in their friendship networks.
   a. fewer but closer friends
   b. friendships with members of the opposite sex
   c. similar interests and values
   d. friendships with others who are not the same age or sex

9. Artificially high self-esteem in schoolchildren:
   a. fosters academic competence.
   b. fosters social competence.
   c. fosters both academic and social competence.
   d. is less beneficial in fostering academic and social competence than a more objective evaluation of achievement.

10. Older schoolchildren tend to be _____ vulnerable to the stresses of life than children who are just beginning middle childhood because they _____ .
   a. more; tend to overpersonalize their problems
   b. less; have developed better coping skills
   c. more; are more likely to compare their well-being with that of their peers
   d. less; are less egocentric

11. Bully-victims are typically children who would be categorized as:
   a. aggressive-rejected.
   b. withdrawn-rejected.
   c. isolated-rejected.
   d. immature-rejected.

12. Bullying during middle childhood:
   a. occurs only in certain cultures.
   b. is more common in rural schools than in urban schools.
   c. seems to be universal.
   d. is rarely a major problem, since other children usually intervene to prevent it from getting out of hand.

13. During the school years, children become _____ selective about their friends, and their friendship groups become _____ .
   a. less; larger   c. more; larger
   b. less; smaller   d. more; smaller

14. Which of the following was *not* identified as a pivotal issue in determining whether divorce or some other problem will adversely affect a child during the school years?
   a. how many other stresses the child is already experiencing
   b. how the child interprets the stress
   c. how much the stress affects the child's daily life
   d. the specific structure of the child's family

15. Erikson's crisis of the school years is that of:
   a. industry versus inferiority.
   b. acceptance versus rejection.
   c. initiative versus guilt.
   d. male versus female.

True or False Items

Write T (*true*) or F (*false*) on the line in front of each statement.

_____ 1. As they evaluate themselves according to increasingly complex self-theories, school-age children typically experience a rise in self-esteem.

_____ 2. During middle childhood, acceptance by the peer group is valued more than having a close friend.

_____ 3. Children from low-income homes often have lower self-esteem.

_____ 4. Bullies and their victims are usually of the same gender.

_____ 5. Children who are labeled "resilient" demonstrate an ability to adapt positively in all situations.

_____ 6. The quality of family interaction seems to be a more powerful predictor of children's development than the actual structure of the family.

_____ 7. Withdrawn-rejected and aggressive-rejected children both have problems regulating their emotions.

_____ 8. Most cultures recognize the school years as the time to give children more independence and responsibility.

_____ 9. Most aggressive-rejected children clearly interpret other people's words and behavior.

_____ 10. School-age children are less able than younger children to cope with chronic stresses.

_____ 11. Children's ability to cope with stress may depend as much on their appraisal of events as on the objective nature of the events themselves.

_____ 12. Friendship circles become wider as children grow older.

Progress Test 2

Progress Test 2 should be completed during a final chapter review. Answer the following questions after you thoroughly understand the correct answers for the Chapter Review and Progress Test 1.

Multiple-Choice Questions

1. Children who are categorized as _____ are particularly vulnerable to bullying.
   a. aggressive-rejected
   b. passive-aggressive
   c. withdrawn-rejected
   d. passive-rejected

2. Environmental influences on children's traits that result from contact with different teachers and peer groups are classified as:
   a. shared influences.
   b. nonshared influences.
   c. epigenetic influences.
   d. nuclear influences.

3. Compared to parents in other family structures, parents in a nuclear family tend to be:
   a. wealthier.
   b. better educated.
   c. healthier.
   d. all of the above.

4. Approximately half of all school-age children live in:
   a. one-parent families.
   b. blended families.
   c. extended families.
   d. nuclear families.

5. Typically, children in middle childhood experience a decrease in self-esteem as a result of:
   a. a wavering self-theory.
   b. increased awareness of personal shortcomings and failures.
   c. rejection by peers.
   d. difficulties with members of the opposite sex.

6. A 10-year-old's sense of self-esteem is most strongly influenced by his or her:
   a. peers.   c. mother.
   b. siblings.   d. father.

7. Which of the following most accurately describes how friendships change during the school years?
   a. Friendships become more casual and less intense.
   b. Older children demand less of their friends.
   c. Older children change friends more often.
   d. Close friendships increasingly involve members of the same sex, ethnicity, and socioeconomic status.

8. Which of the following is an accurate statement about school-age bullies?
   a. They are socially perceptive but not empathic.
   b. They usually have a few admiring friends.
   c. They are adept at being aggressive.
   d. All of the above are accurate statements.

9. (Thinking Like a Scientist) The most effective intervention to prevent bullying in the school is to:
   a. change the social climate through community-wide and classroom education.
   b. target one victimized child at a time.
   c. target each bully as an individual.
   d. focus on improving the academic skills of all children in the school.

10. Which of the following most accurately describes the relationship between family income and child development?
   a. Adequate family income allows children to own whatever possessions help them to feel accepted.

   b. Because parents need not argue about money, household wealth provides harmony and stability.
   c. the basic family functions are enhanced by adequate family income.
   d. Family income is not correlated with child development.

11. Two factors that most often help the child cope well with multiple stresses are social support and:
   a. social comparison.
   b. religious faith.
   c. remedial education.
   d. referral to mental health professionals.

12. An 8-year-old child who measures her achievements by comparing them to those of her friends is engaging in social:
   a. cognition.   c. reinforcement.
   b. comparison.   d. modeling.

13. Family _____ is more crucial to children's well-being than family _____ is.
   a. structure; SES
   b. SES; stability
   c. stability; SES
   d. function; structure

14. According to Freud, the period between ages 7 and 11 when a child's sexual drives are relatively quiet is the:
   a. phallic stage.
   b. genital stage.
   c. period of latency.
   d. period of industry versus inferiority.

15. Children who are forced to cope with one serious ongoing stress (for example, poverty or large family size) are:
   a. more likely to develop serious psychiatric problems.
   b. no more likely to develop problems.
   c. more likely to develop intense, destructive friendships.
   d. less likely to be accepted by their peer group.

Matching Items

Match each term or concept with its corresponding description or definition.

Terms or Concepts

_____ 1. behaviorism
_____ 2. nuclear family
_____ 3. social comparison
_____ 4. cognitive theory
_____ 5. foster family
_____ 6. aggressive-rejected
_____ 7. withdrawn-rejected
_____ 8. sociocultural theory
_____ 9. epigenetic theory
_____ 10. blended family
_____ 11. extended family

Descriptions or Definitions

a. focused on the acquisition of new skills
b. adults living with their children from previous marriages as well as their own biological children
c. a father, a mother, and the biological children they have together
d. focused on the development of social awareness
e. children who are disliked because of their confrontational nature
f. evaluating one's abilities by measuring them against those of other children
g. three or more generations of biologically related individuals living together
h. children who are disliked because of timid, anxious behavior
i. views middle schoolers' independence as the result of a species need
j. a family in which one or more children are temporarily cared for by an adult individual or couple to whom they are not biologically related
k. focused on the development of self-understanding

Thinking Critically About Chapter 13

Answer these questions the day before an exam as a final check on your understanding of the chapter's terms and concepts.

1. As an advocate of the epigenetic perspective, Dr. Wayans is most likely to explain a 10-year-old boy's interest in auto racing as the result of:
   a. the repression of psychosexual needs.
   b. the acquisition of new skills.
   c. greater self-understanding.
   d. the child's use of his father as a role model.

2. Dr. Ferris believes that skill mastery is particularly important because children develop views of themselves as either competent or incompetent in skills valued by their culture. Dr. Ferris is evidently working from the perspective of:
   a. behaviorism.
   b. social learning theory.
   c. Erik Erikson's theory of development.
   d. Freud's theory of development.

3. The Australian saying that "tall poppies" are cut down underscores the fact that:
   a. older children often ignore their parents and teachers.
   b. culture influences standards of social comparison.
   c. middle childhood is a time of emotional latency.
   d. personal friendships become even more important in middle childhood.

4. Ten-year-old Ramón, who is disliked by many of his peers because of his antagonistic, confrontational nature, would probably be labeled as:
   a. a bully-victim.
   b. withdrawn-rejected.
   c. aggressive-rejected.
   d. resilient.

5. In explaining why some ethnic minority children in the United States become happy and successful despite the fact that their parent(s) use(s) harsh discipline, a developmentalist would point out that:
   a. such parents also tend to be warm and accepting of their children.
   b. immigrant and African-American communities tend not to isolate single mothers.
   c. these children often are raised in communities in which many people help in child rearing.
   d. all of the above are true.

6. Sandra's family consists of her biological mother, her stepfather, and his two daughters from a previous marriage. Sandra's family would be classified as:
   a. nuclear.
   b. stepparent.
   c. blended.
   d. extended.

7. In discussing friendship, 9-year-old children, in contrast to younger children, will:
   a. deny that friends are important.
   b. state that they prefer same-sex playmates.
   c. stress the importance of loyalty and similar interests.
   d. be less choosy about who they call a friend.

8. Children who have serious difficulties in peer relationships during elementary school:
   a. are at a greater risk of having emotional problems later in life.
   b. usually overcome their difficulties in a year or two.
   c. later are more likely to form an intense friendship with one person than children who did not have difficulties earlier on.
   d. do both b. and c.

9. Concluding her presentation on resilient children, Brenda notes that:
   a. children who are truly resilient, are resilient in all situations.
   b. resilience is merely the absence of pathology.
   c. resilience is a stable trait that becomes apparent very early in life.
   d. resilience is a dynamic process that represents a positive adaptation to significant adversity or stress.

10. Of the following children, who is likely to have the lowest overall self-esteem?
    a. Karen, age 5   c. Carl, age 9
    b. David, age 7   d. Cindy, age 10

11. Ten-year-old Benjamin is less optimistic and self-confident than his 5-year-old sister. This may be explained in part by the tendency of older children to:
    a. evaluate their abilities by comparing them with their own competencies a year or two earlier.
    b. evaluate their competencies by comparing them with those of others.
    c. be less realistic about their own abilities.
    d. do both b. and c.

12. Kyle and Jessica are as different as two siblings can be, despite growing up in the same nuclear family structure. In explaining these differences, a developmentalist is likely to point to:
    a. shared environmental influences.
    b. nonshared environmental influences.
    c. genetic differences and shared environmental influences.
    d. genetic differences and nonshared environmental influences.

13. Of the following children, who is most likely to become a bully?
    a. Karen, who is taller than average
    b. David, who is above average in verbal assertiveness
    c. Carl, who is insecure and lonely
    d. Cindy, who was insecurely attached

14. I am an 8-year-old who frequently is bullied at school. If I am like most victims of bullies, I am probably:
    a. obese.
    b. unattractive.
    c. a child who speaks with an accent.
    d. anxious and insecure.

15. Of the following children, who is most likely to have one, and only one, "best friend"?
    a. 10-year-old Juan
    b. 7-year-old Marcy
    c. 10-year-old Christina
    d. 7-year-old Andrew

Key Terms

Using your own words, write a brief definition or explanation of each of the following terms on a separate piece of paper.

1. latency
2. industry versus inferiority
3. social cognitive theory
4. social comparison
5. peer group
6. aggressive-rejected children
7. withdrawn-rejected children
8. bullying
9. bully-victim
10. family function
11. family structure
12. nuclear family
13. stepparent family
14. blended family
15. adoptive family
16. one-parent family
17. grandparent family
18. extended family
19. grandparents alone
20. homosexual family
21. foster family

ANSWERS

CHAPTER REVIEW

1. latency; quieter; repressed; submerged
2. industry versus inferiority
3. acquisition; self-understanding; social cognitive; maturation; experience; sociocultural; subcultures; genetically; role models
4. more; dips; social comparison
5. outstanding; objective; self-esteem
6. a group of individuals of similar age and social status who play, work, or learn together; place
7. more; more; negotiate, compromise, share
8. more
9. intense; intimate; do not change; harder
10. interests; values; backgrounds
11. neglected; aggressive-rejected; withdrawn-rejected

Rejected children often misinterpret social situations—considering a compliment to be sarcastic, for example.

12. systematic; physical, verbal, social; repeated
13. have
14. withdrawn; aggressive; bully-victims; are
15. size; verbal assertiveness; physical; relational; direct; indirect
16. is; social; transitional

Bullied children are anxious, depressed, and underachieving and have lower self-esteem and painful memories.

17. difficult; antisocial; brain abnormalities; insecure attachment; emotional regulation
18. social climate
19. genes; peers; parents; nature; nurture
20. nonshared; shared
21. works to meet the needs of its members
22. needs; learning; self-esteem; friendships; harmony; stability
23. genetic and legal relationships among the members of a family
    a. extended family
    b. nuclear family
    c. one-parent family
    d. blended family
    e. grandparent family
    f. adoptive family
    g. foster family
    h. stepparent family
    i. grandparents alone
    j. homosexual family
24. in almost any family structure

Parents in a nuclear family tend to be wealthier, better educated, psychologically and physically healthier, more willing to compromise, and less hostile than other parents.

25. disappear
26. function; structure
27. correlates; warmth or conflict; blended
28. younger
29. authoritarian; Asian; African; Mexican; isolated; supported
30. resilient; dynamic; positive
31. a. how many other stresses the child is experiencing

b. how the stress affects the child's daily life

c. how the child interprets the stress

32. routines; homelessness; attitude; appraisal

33. social support

34. more; peers; pets; religion

PROGRESS TEST 1

Multiple-Choice Questions

1. **d.** is the answer. (p. 314)

   a. Freud described middle childhood as a period of emotional latency.

   b. Erikson emphasized children's efforts to develop feelings of competency.

   c. Sociocultural theory emphasizes the impact of the children's cultures and subcultures on their development.

2. **b.** is the answer. (pp. 314–315)

3. **b.** is the answer. (pp. 314–315)

4. **c.** is the answer. (p. 314)

5. **b.** is the answer. (p. 320)

6. **a.** is the answer. (p. 319)

7. **d.** is the answer. (p. 319)

8. **a.** is the answer. (p. 318)

   b. & c. Both boys and girls form same-sex groups, and both choose friends with similar interests and values.

9. **d.** is the answer. (p. 316)

10. **b.** is the answer. (p. 334)

11. **a.** is the answer. (p. 320)

    b. Withdrawn-rejected children are frequently the victims of bullies, but rarely become bullies themselves.

    c. & d. There are no such categories.

12. **c.** is the answer. (p. 321)

    d. In fact, children rarely intervene, unless a best friend is involved.

13. **d.** is the answer. (p. 318)

14. **d.** is the answer. (p. 331)

15. **a.** is the answer. (p. 313)

True or False Items

1. F   In fact, just the opposite is true. (p. 316)

2. F   In fact, just the opposite is true. (p. 317)

3. T (p. 328)

4. T (p. 320)

5. F   A given child is not resilient in all situations. (p. 330)

6. T (p. 328)

7. T (p. 319)

8. T (pp. 314–315)

9. F   Just the opposite is true: They tend to misinterpret other people's words and behavior. (p. 319)

10. F   Because of the coping strategies that many school-age children develop, they are better able than younger children to cope with stress. (p. 330)

11. T (p. 332)

12. F   Friendship circles become narrower because friendships become more selective and exclusive. (p. 318)

PROGRESS TEST 2

Multiple-Choice Questions

1. **c.** is the answer. (p. 320)

   a. These are usually bullies.

   b. & d. These are not subcategories of rejected children.

2. **b.** is the answer. (p. 324)

   a. Shared influences are those that occur because children are raised by the same parents in the same home.

   c. & d. There are no such influences.

3. **d.** is the answer. (p. 327)

4. **d.** is the answer. (p. 326)

5. **b.** is the answer. (pp. 315–316)

   a. This tends to promote, rather than reduce, self-esteem.

   c. Only 10 percent of schoolchildren experience this.

   d. This issue becomes more important during adolescence.

6. **a.** is the answer. (p. 316)

7. **d.** is the answer. (p. 318)

   a., b., & c. In fact, just the opposite is true of friendship during the school years.

8. **d.** is the answer. (p. 320)

9. **a.** is the answer. (p. 322)

10. **c.** is the answer. (p. 328)

11. **b.** is the answer. (p. 334)

12. **b.** is the answer. (p. 316)

13. **d.** is the answer. (p. 328)

14. **c.** is the answer. (p. 313)

15. b. is the answer. (pp. 331–332)

c. & d. The text did not discuss how stress influences friendship or peer acceptance.

Matching Items

1. a (p. 314)	**5.** j (p. 327)	**9.** i (p. 314)
2. c (p. 327)	**6.** e (p. 319)	**10.** b (p. 327)
3. f (p. 316)	**7.** h (p. 319)	**11.** g (p. 327)
4. k (p. 314)	**8.** d (p. 314)	

THINKING CRITICALLY ABOUT CHAPTER 13

1. d. is the answer. (p. 314)

a. This describes an advocate of Freud's theory of development.

b. This is the viewpoint of a behaviorist.

c. This is the viewpoint of a cognitive theorist.

2. c. is the answer. The question describes what is, for Erikson, the crisis of middle childhood: industry versus inferiority. (p. 313)

3. b. is the answer. (p. 316)

4. c. is the answer. (p. 319)

5. d. is the answer. (p. 329)

6. c. is the answer. (p. 327)

a. A nuclear family consists of a husband and wife and their biological offspring.

b. Although Sandra does live with a stepparent, because she also lives with the biological children from his previous marriage, her family would be classified as blended.

d. An extended family includes children living with one or more of their biological parents, one or more grandparents, and often other relatives as well.

7. c. is the answer. (p. 318)

8. a. is the answer. (p. 319)

9. d. is the answer. (p. 330)

10. d. is the answer. Self-esteem decreases throughout middle childhood. (p. 316)

11. b. is the answer. (p. 316)

a. & c. These are more typical of preschoolers than school-age children.

12. d. is the answer. (pp. 324–325)

13. d. is the answer. (p. 321)

a. & b. It is taller-than-average *boys* and verbally assertive *girls* who are more likely to bully others.

c. This is a common myth.

14. d. is the answer. (p. 320)

a., b., & c. Contrary to popular belief, victims are no more likely to be fat or homely or to speak with an accent than nonvictims are.

15. c. is the answer. (p. 318)

a. & d. The trend toward fewer but closer friends is more apparent among girls.

b. At the end of middle childhood, children become more choosy and have fewer friends.

KEY TERMS

1. In Freud's theory, middle childhood is a period of **latency,** during which emotional drives are quieter, psychosexual needs are repressed, and unconscious conflicts are submerged. (p. 313)

2. According to Erikson, the crisis of middle childhood is that of **industry versus inferiority**, in which children try to master many skills and develop views of themselves as either competent or incompetent and inferior. (p. 313)

3. **Social cognitive theory** stresses the importance of maturation and experience in stimulating learning, cognition, and cultural advances in children. (p. 314)

4. **Social comparison** is the tendency to assess one's abilities, achievements, social status, and other attributes by measuring them against those of others, especially those of one's peers. (p. 316)

5. A **peer group** is a group of individuals of roughly the same age and social status who play, work, or learn together. (p. 317)

6. The peer group shuns **aggressive-rejected children** because they are overly confrontational. (p. 319)

7. **Withdrawn-rejected children** are shunned by the peer group because of their withdrawn, anxious behavior. (p. 319)

8. **Bullying** is the repeated, systematic effort to inflict harm on a child through physical, verbal, or social attacks. (p. 320)

9. A **bully-victim** is a bully who has also been a victim of bullying. (p. 320)

10. **Family function** refers to the ways families work to foster the development of children by meeting their physical needs, encouraging them to learn, and providing harmony and stability. (p. 325)

11. **Family structure** refers to the legal and genetic relationships among the members of a particular family. (p. 326)

12. A **nuclear family** consists of two parents and their mutual biological offspring. (p. 327)

13. A **stepparent family** consists of one parent, his or her biological children, and his or her spouse, who is not biologically related to the children. (p. 327)

14. A **blended family** consists of two parents, at least one with biological children from another union, and any children the adults have together. (p. 327)

15. An **adoptive family** consists of one or more non-biological children whom adults have legally taken as their own. (p. 327)

16. A **one-parent family** consists of one parent and his or her (biological) children. (p. 327)

17. A **grandparent family** consists of children living in their grandparents' home, either with or without their parents. (p. 327)

18. An **extended family** consists of three or more generations of biologically related individuals. (p. 327)

19. A **grandparents alone** family consists of one or two grandparents acting as surrogate parents for children whose biological parents are unable to live with their children. (p. 327)

20. A **homosexual family** consists of a homosexual couple and their biological or adopted children. (p. 327)

21. A **foster family** consists of one or more orphaned, neglected, abused, or delinquent children who are temporarily being cared for by an unrelated adult. (p. 327)

Chapter Fourteen

Adolescence: Biosocial Development

Chapter Overview

Between the ages of 10 and 20, young people cross the great divide between childhood and adulthood. This crossing encompasses all three domains of development—biosocial, cognitive, and psychosocial. Chapter 14 focuses on the dramatic changes that occur in the biosocial domain, beginning with puberty and the growth spurt. The biosocial metamorphosis of the adolescent is discussed in detail, with emphasis on factors that affect the age of puberty and sexual maturation.

Although adolescence is, in many ways, a healthy time of life, the text addresses three health hazards that too often affect adolescence: poor nutrition, sexual misbehavior and sexual abuse, and the use of alcohol, tobacco, and other drugs.

NOTE: Answer guidelines for all Chapter 14 questions begin on page 212.

Guided Study

The text chapter should be studied one section at a time. Before you read, preview each section by skimming it, noting headings and boldface items. Then read the appropriate section objectives from the following outline. Keep these objectives in mind and, as you read the chapter section, search for the information that will enable you to meet each objective. Once you have finished a section, write out answers for its objectives.

Puberty Begins (pp. 341–350)

1. Outline the biological events of puberty.

2. Discuss the emotional and psychological impact of pubertal hormones.

3. Identify several factors that influence the onset of puberty.

4. Describe the growth spurt in both the male and the female adolescent, focusing on changes in body weight and height.

5. Describe the changes in the body's internal organs that accompany the growth spurt.

6. Discuss the development of the primary sex characteristics in males and females during puberty.

7. Discuss the development of the secondary sex characteristics in males and females during puberty.

Hazards to Health (pp. 350–360)

8. Discuss the nutritional needs and problems of adolescents.

9. Discuss the potential problems associated with premature sexual activity.

10. Discuss sexual abuse, noting its prevalence and consequences for development.

11. (text and Changing Policy) Discuss drug use and abuse among adolescents today, including its prevalence, its significance for development, and the best methods of prevention.

Chapter Review

When you have finished reading the chapter, work through the material that follows to review it. Complete the sentences and answer the questions. As you proceed, evaluate your performance for each section by consulting the answers beginning on page 212. Do not continue with the next section until you understand each answer. If you need to, review or reread the appropriate section in the textbook before continuing.

Puberty Begins (pp. 341–350)

1. The period of rapid physical growth and sexual maturation that ends childhood and brings the young person to adult size, shape, and sexual potential is called _____ . The physical changes of puberty typically are complete _____ (how long?) after puberty begins. Although puberty begins at various ages, the _____ is almost always the same.

   List, in order, the major physical changes of puberty in

   Girls: _____

   _____

   Boys: _____

   _____

2. Puberty begins when a hormonal signal from the _____ triggers hormone production in the _____ _____ , which in turn triggers increased hormone production by the _____ _____ and by the _____ , which include

the _____ in males and the
_____ in females. This route, called
the _____ _____ , also
triggers the development of the
_____ and _____ sex-
ual characteristics.

3. The hormone _____ causes the
gonads to dramatically increase their production
of sex hormones, especially _____
in girls and _____ in boys.

4. The increase in the hormone _____
is dramatic in boys and slight in girls, whereas
the increase in the hormone _____
is marked in girls and slight in boys. Conflict,
moodiness, and sexual urges _____
(usually do/do not usually) increase during adolescence. This is due in part to the increasingly
high levels of hormones such as
_____ . During puberty, hormonal
levels have their greatest emotional impact
_____ (directly/indirectly), via the
_____
_____
of _____
_____ .

5. The age of puberty is _____(highly
variable/quite consistent from child to child).

6. Normal children begin to notice pubertal changes
between the ages of _____ and
_____ .

7. The average American girl experiences her first
menstrual period, called _____ ,
between ages _____ and
_____ , with age _____
the average.

8. Genes are an important factor in the timing of
menarche, as demonstrated by the fact that
_____ and _____
reach menarche at very similar ages.

9. Stocky individuals tend to experience puberty
_____ (earlier/later) than
those with taller, thinner builds.

10. Menarche seems to be related to the accumulation
of a certain amount of body _____ .

11. For both sexes, fat is limited by chronic
_____ , which therefore delays
puberty by several years.

12. Another influence on the age of puberty is
_____ .

13. Research from many nations suggests that family
stress may _____ (accelerate/
delay) the onset of puberty.

14. Stress may cause production of the hormones that
cause _____ . Support for this
hypothesis comes from a study showing that
early puberty was associated with
_____ and
_____ .

15. An evolutionary explanation of the stress-puberty
hypothesis is that ancestral females growing up
in stressful environments may have increased
their _____ _____ by
accelerating physical maturation.

16. For girls, _____
(early/late) maturation may be especially troublesome.

Describe several common problems and developmental hazards experienced by early-maturing girls.

17. For boys, _____
(early/late) maturation is usually more difficult.

Describe several characteristics and/or problems of
late-maturing boys.

18. A major _____ spurt occurs in late childhood and early adolescence, during which growth proceeds from the _____ (core/extremities) to the _____ (core/extremities).At the same time, children begin to _____ (gain/lose) weight at a relatively rapid rate.

19. The change in weight that typically occurs between 10 and 12 years of age is due primarily to the accumulation of body _____ .

20. The amount of weight gain an individual experiences depends on several factors, including _____ , _____ , _____ , and _____ .

21. During the growth spurt, a greater percentage of fat is retained by _____ (males/females), who naturally have a higher proportion of body fat in adulthood.

22. About a year after the height and weight changes occur, a period of _____ increase occurs, causing the pudginess and clumsiness of an earlier age to disappear. In boys, this increase is particularly notable in the _____ body.

23. Internal organs also grow during puberty. The _____ increase in size and capacity, the _____ doubles in size, heart rate _____ (increases/decreases), and blood volume _____ (increases/decreases). These changes increase the adolescent's physical _____ .

24. During puberty, one organ system, the _____ system, decreases in size, making teenagers _____ (more/less) susceptible to respiratory ailments.

Explain why the physical demands placed on a teenager, as in athletic training, should not be the same as those for a young adult of similar height and weight.

25. The hormones of puberty also affect the _____ rhythm, causing changes in when the teenager needs the most sleep. In addition, hormones cause many relatively minor physical changes that can have significant emotional impact. These include increased activity in _____ , _____ , and _____ glands.

26. Changes in _____

_____ _____ involve the sex organs that are directly involved in reproduction. By the end of puberty, reproduction _____ (is/is still not) possible.

Describe the major changes in primary sex characteristics that occur in both sexes during puberty.

27. In girls, the event that is usually taken to indicate sexual maturity is _____ . In boys, the indicator of reproductive potential is the first ejaculation of seminal fluid containing sperm, which is called _____ . In both sexes, full reproductive maturity occurs _____ (at this time/several years later).

28. Sexual features other than those associated with reproduction are referred to as _____

_____ _____ .

Describe the major pubertal changes in the secondary sex characteristics of both sexes.

29. Two secondary sex characteristics that are mistakenly considered signs of womanhood and manliness, respectively, are _____ _____ and

_____ .

Hazards to Health (pp. 350–360)

30. The minor illnesses of childhood, including _____ , _____ , _____ , and _____ _____ , are _____ (less common/more common) during adolescence. The diseases of adulthood are _____ (common/rare). Death rates caused by _____ and _____ increase markedly from ages 10 to 25.

31. Due to rapid physical growth, the adolescent needs a higher daily intake of _____ , _____ , and _____ . Specifically, the typical adolescent needs about 50 percent more of the minerals _____ , _____ , and _____ during the growth spurt. Inadequate consumption of _____ is particularly troubling because it is a good source of the _____ needed for bone growth.

32. Most teenagers eat _____ (few/most) meals at home. As a result, they are likely to consume too much _____ , _____ , and _____ .

33. Because of menstruation, adolescent females need additional _____ in their diets and are more likely to suffer _____-_____ _____ than any other subgroup of the population.

34. Adolescents' mental conception of, and attitude toward, their physical appearance is referred to as their _____ _____ . Most girls think they look too _____ , and many boys think they look too _____ . These distorted perceptions

may lead to the life-threatening diseases _____ and _____ . _____ in girls; for boys, they can lead to _____ _____ .

35. Because puberty occurs _____ (earlier/later) than it used to and marriage occurs _____ (earlier/later), one-fourth of all adolescents are sexually active by age _____ , and about one-half are active _____ .

36. Sexually active teenagers have higher rates of _____ _____ _____ such as _____ , _____ _____ , _____ , and _____ .

37. Risk of exposure to HIV increases if a person:

   a. _____

   b. _____

   c. _____

38. A second developmental risk for sexually active adolescent girls is _____ . If this happens within a year or two of menarche, girls are at increased risk of many complications, including _____ _____ . Teenage motherhood slows _____ achievement and restricts _____ growth. Babies of young teenagers have a higher risk of _____ and _____ complications, including _____ and _____ _____ .

39. Any activity in which an adult uses an unconsenting person for his or her own sexual stimulation or pleasure is considered _____ _____ . When such activity involves a young person, whether or not genital contact is involved, it is called _____ _____ _____ .

40. The damage done by sexual abuse depends on many factors, including how often it is _____ , how much it distorts _____-_____ , if it is _____ , or if it impairs the child's relationships with _____ .

41. Sexual victimization often begins in _____ and typically is committed by _____ . Overt sexual abuse typically begins at _____ .

42. An estimated _____ percent of child molesters are _____ _____ _____ .

43. Adolescent problems, such as pregnancy, drug abuse, and suicide often are tied to past _____ _____ .

44. Drug _____ always harms physical and psychological development, whether or not the drug becomes _____ . Drug _____ may or may not be harmful, depending on the reasons for, and the effects of, that use.

45. Tobacco, alcohol, and marijuana may act as _____ _____ , opening the door not only to regular use of multiple drugs but also to other destructive behaviors, such as risky _____ , school _____ , and _____ .

46. By decreasing food consumption and the absorption of nutrients, tobacco can limit the adolescent _____ _____ .

47. Because alcohol loosens _____ and impairs _____ , even moderate use can be destructive in adolescence. Alcohol also impairs _____ and _____ by damaging the brain's _____ and _____ .

48. Marijuana _____ (slows/accelerates) thinking processes, particularly those related to _____ and _____ reasoning.

49. About _____ (how many?) high school seniors admit to using at least one drug in the last month, with _____ being the most common.

50. Whether a particular teenager uses drugs, and what drugs he or she uses, depends largely on his or her _____ , the _____ , and the national _____ .

51. (Changing Policy) Students who participate in Project D.A.R.E. are _____ (more/no more) likely to abstain from drugs over the high school years than those who do not.

52. (Changing Policy) Three factors that protect against drug use are

    a. _____

    b. _____

    c. _____

Progress Test 1

Multiple-Choice Questions

Circle your answers to the following questions and check them with the answers beginning on page 213. If your answer is incorrect, read the explanation for why it is incorrect and then consult the appropriate pages of the text (in parentheses following the correct answer).

1. Which of the following most accurately describes the sequence of pubertal development in girls?
   a. breasts and pubic hair; growth spurt in which fat is deposited on hips and buttocks; first menstrual period; ovulation
   b. growth spurt; breasts and pubic hair; first menstrual period; ovulation
   c. first menstrual period; breasts and pubic hair; growth spurt; ovulation
   d. breasts and pubic hair; growth spurt; ovulation; first menstrual period

2. Although both sexes grow rapidly during adolescence, boys typically gain more than girls in their:
   a. muscle strength.
   b. body fat.
   c. internal organ growth.
   d. lymphoid system.

3. For girls, the first readily observable sign of the onset of puberty is:
   a. the onset of breast growth.
   b. the appearance of facial, body, and pubic hair.
   c. a change in the shape of the eyes.
   d. a lengthening of the torso.

4. More than any other group in the population, adolescent girls are likely to have:
   a. asthma.
   b. acne.
   c. iron-deficiency anemia.
   d. testosterone deficiency.

5. The HPA axis is the:
   a. route followed by many hormones to regulate stress, growth, sleep, and appetite.
   b. pair of sex glands in humans.
   c. cascade of sex hormones in females and males.
   d. area of the brain that regulates the pituitary gland.

6. For males, the secondary sex characteristic that usually occurs last is:
   a. breast enlargement.
   b. the appearance of facial hair.
   c. growth of the testes.
   d. the appearance of pubic hair.

7. For girls, the specific event that is taken to indicate fertility is _____ ; for boys, it is _____ .
   a. the growth of breast buds; voice deepening
   b. menarche; spermarche
   c. anovulation; the testosterone surge
   d. the growth spurt; pubic hair

8. The most significant hormonal changes of puberty include an increase of _____ in _____ and an increase of _____ in _____ .
   a. progesterone; boys; estrogen; girls
   b. estrogen; boys; testosterone; girls
   c. progesterone; girls; estrogen; boys
   d. estrogen; girls; testosterone; boys

9. In general, most adolescents are:
   a. overweight.
   b. satisfied with their appearance.
   c. dissatisfied with their appearance.
   d. unaffected by cultural attitudes about beauty.

10. Estrogen is to ovaries as:
    a. testosterone is to adrenals
    b. testosterone is to testes.
    c. GnRH is to ovaries.
    d. GnRH is to testicles.

11. The damage caused by sexual abuse depends on all of the following factors *except*:
    a. repeated incidence.
    b. the gender of the perpetrator.
    c. distorted adult–child relationships.
    d. impairment of the child's ability to relate to peers.

12. Early physical growth and sexual maturation:
    a. tend to be equally difficult for girls and boys.
    b. tend to be more difficult for boys than for girls.
    c. tend to be more difficult for girls than for boys.
    d. are easier for both girls and boys than late maturation.

13. Pubertal changes in growth and maturation typically are complete how long after puberty begins?
    a. one year
    b. two years
    c. three or four years
    d. The variation is too great to generalize.

14. The hypothalamus/pituitary/adrenal axis triggers:
    a. puberty.
    b. the growth spurt.
    c. the development of sexual characteristics.
    d. all of the above.

15. Due to differences in _____ , in earlier times puberty occurred _____ than it does today.
    a. social attitudes; later
    b. social attitudes; earlier
    c. nutrition; later
    d. nutrition; earlier

True or False Items

Write T (*true*) or F (*false*) on the line in front of each statement.

_____ 1. More calories are necessary during adolescence than at any other period during the life span.

_____ 2. During puberty, hormones have their greatest impact indirectly, rather than directly.

_____ 3. The first indicator of reproductive potential in males is menarche.

_____ 4. Lung capacity, heart size, and total volume of blood increase significantly during adolescence.

_____ 5. Puberty generally begins sometime between ages 8 and 14.

_____ 6. The minor illnesses of childhood become less common in adolescence.

_____ 7. Each culture and age cohort has its own patterns of drug use and abuse during adolescence.

_____ 8. Childhood habits of overeating and underexercising usually lessen during adolescence.

_____ 9. Early-maturing girls tend to have lower self-esteem.

_____ 10. Both the sequence and timing of pubertal events vary greatly from one young person to another.

Progress Test 2

Progress Test 2 should be completed during a final chapter review. Answer the following questions after you thoroughly understand the correct answers for the Chapter Review and Progress Test 1.

Multiple-Choice Questions

1. Which of the following is the correct sequence of pubertal events in boys?
   a. growth spurt, pubic hair, facial hair, first ejaculation, lowering of voice
   b. pubic hair, first ejaculation, growth spurt; lowering of voice, facial hair
   c. lowering of voice, pubic hair, growth spurt, facial hair, first ejaculation
   d. growth spurt, facial hair, lowering of voice, pubic hair, first ejaculation

2. Which of the following statements about adolescent physical development is *not* true?
   a. Hands and feet generally lengthen before arms and legs.
   b. Facial features usually grow before the head itself reaches adult size and shape.
   c. Oil, sweat, and odor glands become more active.
   d. The lymphoid system increases slightly in size, and the heart increases by nearly half.

3. In puberty, a hormone that increases markedly in girls (and only somewhat in boys) is:
   a. estrogen.   c. androgen.
   b. testosterone.   d. menarche.

4. Nutritional deficiencies in adolescence are frequently the result of:
   a. eating red meat.
   b. poor eating habits.
   c. anovulatory menstruation.
   d. excessive exercise.

5. In females, puberty is typically marked by a(n):
   a. significant widening of the shoulders.
   b. significant widening of the hips.
   c. enlargement of the torso and upper chest.
   d. decrease in the size of the eyes and nose.

6. Nonreproductive sexual characteristics, such as the deepening of the voice and the development of breasts, are called:
   a. gender-typed traits.
   b. primary sex characteristics.
   c. secondary sex characteristics.
   d. pubertal prototypes.

7. Puberty is initiated when hormones are released from the _____ , then from the _____ gland, and then from the adrenal glands and the _____ .
   a. hypothalamus; pituitary; gonads
   b. pituitary; gonads; hypothalamus
   c. gonads; pituitary; hypothalamus
   d. pituitary; hypothalamus; gonads

8. By age 17, what percent of adolescent of adolescents have had intercourse?
   a. 25 percent
   b. 50 percent
   c. 90 percent
   d. The percentage is different in girls and boys.

9. Alcohol impairs memory and self-control by damaging the:
   a. hippocampus and prefrontal cortex.
   b. pituitary gland.
   c. hypothalamus.
   d. gonads.

10. Statistically speaking, to predict the age at which a girl first has sexual intercourse, it would be *most* useful to know her:
    a. socioeconomic level.
    b. race or ethnic group.
    c. religion.
    d. age at menarche.

11. Use of gateway drugs is:
    a. more typical of affluent teenagers who are experiencing an identity crisis.
    b. both a cause and a symptom of adolescent problems.
    c. less likely to result in alcohol-abuse problems later on.
    d. less helpful to teens trying to resist later peer pressure leading to long-term addiction.

12. Compounding the problem of sexual abuse of boys, abused boys:
    a. feel shame at the idea of being weak.
    b. have fewer sources of emotional support.
    c. are more likely to be abused by fathers.
    d. have all of the above problems.

13. Puberty is *most accurately* defined as the period:
    a. of rapid physical growth that occurs during adolescence.
    b. during which sexual maturation is attained.
    c. of rapid physical growth and sexual maturation that ends childhood.
    d. during which adolescents establish identities separate from their parents.

14. Which of the following does *not* typically occur during puberty?
    a. The lungs increase in size and capacity.
    b. The heart's size and rate of beating increase.
    c. Blood volume increases.
    d. The lymphoid system decreases in size.

15. Teenagers' susceptibility to respiratory ailments typically _____ during adolescence, due to a(n) _____ in the size of the lymphoid system.
    a. increases; increase
    b. increases; decrease
    c. decreases; increase
    d. decreases; decrease

Matching Items

Match each term or concept with its corresponding description or definition.

Terms or Concepts

_____ 1. puberty
_____ 2. GnRH
_____ 3. testosterone
_____ 4. estrogen
_____ 5. growth spurt
_____ 6. primary sex characteristics
_____ 7. menarche
_____ 8. spermarche
_____ 9. secondary sex characteristics
_____ 10. body image

Descriptions or Definitions

a. onset of menstruation
b. period of rapid physical growth and sexual maturation that ends childhood
c. hormone that increases dramatically in boys during puberty
d. hormone that causes the gonads to increase their production of sex hormones
e. hormone that increases dramatically in girls during puberty
f. first sign is increased bone length
g. attitude toward one's physical appearance
h. physical characteristics not involved in reproduction
i. the sex organs involved in reproduction
j. first ejaculation containing sperm

Thinking Critically About Chapter 14

Answer these questions the day before an exam as a final check on your understanding of the chapter's terms and concepts.

1. Concluding her talk on adolescent alcohol use and brain damage, Maya notes that:
   a. studies have shown only that alcohol use is correlated with damage to the prefrontal cortex.
   b. thus far, studies have shown only that alcohol use is correlated with damage to the hippocampus.
   c. animal research studies demonstrate that alcohol does not merely correlate with brain abnormalities; it causes them.
   d. alcohol use causes brain abnormalities only in teens who are genetically vulnerable.

2. I am the hormone that causes the gonads to dramatically increase their production of sex hormones. Who am I?
   a. GnRH
   b. cortisol
   c. estrogen
   d. testosterone

3. Twelve-year-old Kwan is worried because his twin sister has suddenly grown taller and more physically mature than he. His parents should:
   a. reassure him that the average boy is about two years behind the average girl in the timing of puberty.
   b. tell him that within a year or less he will grow taller than his sister.
   c. tell him that one member of each fraternal twin pair is always shorter.
   d. encourage him to exercise more to accelerate the onset of his growth spurt.

4. Calvin, the class braggart, boasts that because his beard has begun to grow, he is more virile than his male classmates. Jacob informs him that:
   a. the tendency to grow facial and body hair has nothing to do with virility.
   b. beard growth is determined by heredity.
   c. girls also develop some facial hair and more noticeable hair on their arms and legs, so it is clearly not a sign of masculinity.
   d. all of the above are true.

5. The most likely source of status for a late-maturing, middle-SES boy would be:
   a. academic achievement or vocational goal.
   b. physical build.
   c. athletic prowess.
   d. success with the opposite sex.

6. Which of the following students is likely to be the most popular in a sixth-grade class?
   a. Vicki, the most sexually mature girl in the class
   b. Sandra, the tallest girl in the class
   c. Brad, who is at the top of the class scholastically
   d. Dan, the tallest boy in the class

7. Regarding the effects of early and late maturation on boys and girls, which of the following is *not* true?
   a. Early maturation is usually easier for boys to manage than it is for girls.
   b. Late maturation is usually easier for girls to manage than it is for boys.
   c. Late-maturing girls may be drawn into involvement with older boys.
   d. Late-maturing boys may not "catch up" physically, or in terms of their self-images, for many years.

8. Teenagers whose parents are divorced and those who live in cities often experience puberty _____ than other teens, perhaps as a result of _____ .
   a. earlier; greater stress
   b. later; greater stress
   c. earlier; poor nutrition
   d. later; poor nutrition

9. Twenty-four-year-old Connie, who has a distorted view of sexuality, has gone from one abusive relationship with a man to another. It is likely that Connie:
   a. has been abusing drugs all her life.
   b. was sexually abused as a child.
   c. will eventually become a normal, nurturing mother.
   d. had attention-deficit disorder as a child.

10. When developmentalists say that hormones have an indirect effect on adolescent moods and emotions, they mean that:
   a. hormones directly affect appetite and nutrition, which dramatically influence emotionality.
   b. the variation in emotionality from teen to teen is too great to state that there is a direct impact.
   c. it is the social responses of others to hormonally triggered changes in appearance that trigger adolescent moods.
   d. all of the above occur.

11. Regarding gender patterns of drug use, which of the following is *not* true?
    a. The United States is almost the only nation in which adolescent girls are as likely as adolescent boys to smoke.
    b. In the United States, most teen girls who smoke are of European extraction.
    c. In most Asian and African countries, few women smoke.
    d. In the United States, smoking among teen girls has decreased dramatically over the past five years.

12. Of the following teenagers, those most likely to be distressed about their physical development are:
    a. late-maturing girls.
    b. late-maturing boys.
    c. early-maturing boys.
    d. girls or boys who masturbate.

13. Thirteen-year-old Kristin seems apathetic and lazy to her parents. You tell them:
    a. that Kristin is showing signs of chronic depression.
    b. that Kristin may be experiencing psychosocial difficulties.
    c. that Kristin has a poor attitude and needs more discipline.
    d. to have Kristin's iron level checked.

14. I am a hormone that rises steadily during puberty in both males and females. What am I?
    a. estrogen   c. GnRH
    b. testosterone   d. menarche

15. Eleven-year-old Linda, who has just begun to experience the first signs of puberty, laments, "When will the agony of puberty be over?" You tell her that the major events of puberty typically end about _____ after the first visible signs appear.
    a. 6 years   c. 2 years
    b. 3 or 4 years   d. 1 year

Key Terms

Writing Definitions

Using your own words, write a brief definition or explanation of each of the following terms on a separate piece of paper.

1. adolescence
2. puberty
3. hypothalamus
4. pituitary gland
5. adrenal glands
6. HPA axis
7. gonads
8. estrogen
9. testosterone
10. menarche
11. spermarche
12. growth spurt
13. primary sex characteristics
14. secondary sex characteristics
15. sexually transmitted infections (STIs)
16. sexual abuse
17. child sexual abuse
18. drug use
19. drug abuse
20. drug addiction
21. gateway drugs

Cross-Check

After you have written the definitions of the key terms in this chapter, you should complete the crossword puzzle to ensure that you can reverse the process—recognize the term, given the definition.

ACROSS

1. Glands near the kidneys that are stimulated by the pituitary at the beginning of puberty.
7. The first ejaculation of seminal fluid containing sperm.
12. The first menstrual period.
15. The ovaries in girls and the testes or testicles in boys.
17. Gland that stimulates the adrenal glands and the sex glands in response to a signal from the hypothalamus.
18. Event, which begins with an increase in bone length and includes rapid weight gain and organ growth, that is one of the many observable signs of puberty.
19. Ingestion of a drug, regardless of the amount or affect of ingestion.

DOWN

1. The period of biological, cognitive, and psychosocial transition from childhood to adulthood.
2. Organ system, which includes the tonsils and adenoids, that decreases in size at adolescence.
3. Area of the brain that sends the hormonal signal that triggers the biological events of puberty.
4. Widely abused gateway drug that loosens inhibitions and impairs judgment.
5. Dependence on a drug or a behavior in order to feel physically or psychologically at ease.
6. Drugs—usually tobacco, alcohol, and marijuana—whose use increases the risk that a person will later use harder drugs.
8. Ingestion of a drug to the extent that it impairs the user's well-being.
9. Body characteristics that are not directly involved in reproduction but that signify sexual development.
10. Main sex hormone in males.
11. Gateway drug that decreases food consumption, the absorption of nutrients, and fertility.
13. Main sex hormone in females.
14. Period of rapid physical growth and sexual maturation that ends childhood and brings the young person to adult size.
16. Sex organs that are directly involved in reproduction.

ANSWERS

CHAPTER REVIEW

1. puberty; three or four years; sequence

Girls: onset of breast growth, initial pubic hair, peak growth spurt, widening of the hips, first menstrual period, completion of pubic-hair growth, and final breast development

Boys: growth of the testes, initial pubic hair, growth of the penis, first ejaculation, peak growth spurt, voice deepening, beard development, and completion of pubic-hair growth

2. hypothalamus; pituitary gland; adrenal glands; gonads (sex glands); testes; ovaries; HPA axis; primary; secondary
3. GnRH (gonadotropin-releasing hormone); estrogen; testosterone
4. testosterone; estrogen; usually do; testosterone; indirectly; visible signs; sexual maturation
5. highly variable
6. 8; 14
7. menarche; 9; 15; 12

8. mothers; daughters
9. earlier
10. fat
11. malnutrition
12. stress
13. accelerate
14. puberty; conflicted relationships within the family; an unrelated man living in the home
15. reproductive success
16. early

Early-maturing girls may be teased about their big feet or developing breasts. Those who date early may begin "adult" activities at an earlier age, may be pressured by their dates to be sexually active, and may suffer a decrease in self-esteem.

17. late

Late-maturing boys who are short and skinny and who are not athletic are likely to be shunned by girls. They tend to be academically successful. However, the timing of puberty is not so crucial for boys as for girls.

18. growth; extremities; core; gain
19. fat
20. sex; heredity; diet; exercise
21. females
22. muscle; upper
23. lungs; heart; decreases; increases; endurance
24. lymphoid; less

The fact that the more visible spurts of weight and height precede the less visible ones of the muscles and organs means that athletic training and weight lifting should match the young person's size of a year or so earlier.

25. circadian; oil; sweat; odor
26. primary sex characteristics; is

Girls: growth of ovaries and uterus and thickening of the vaginal lining

Boys: growth of testes and lengthening of penis; also scrotum enlarges and becomes pendulous

27. menarche; spermarche; several years later
28. secondary sex characteristics

Males grow taller than females and become wider at the shoulders than at the hips. Females take on more fat all over and become wider at the hips, and their breasts begin to develop. About 65 percent of boys experience some temporary breast enlargement. As the lungs and larynx grow, the adolescent's voice (especially in boys) becomes lower. Head and body

hair become coarser and darker in both sexes. Facial hair (especially in boys) begins to grow.

29. breast development; facial and body hair
30. flu; colds; earaches; childhood diseases; less common; rare; violence; injury
31. calories; vitamins; minerals; calcium; iron; zinc; milk; calcium
32. few; salt; sugar; fat
33. iron; iron-deficiency anemia
34. body image; fat; weak; anorexia; bulimia nervosa; drug use
35. earlier; later; 14; before they graduate from high school
36. sexually transmitted infections; gonorrhea; genital herpes; syphilis; chlamydia
37. a. is already infected with other STIs
    b. has more than one sexual partner within a year
    c. does not use condoms during intercourse
38. pregnancy; spontaneous abortion, high blood pressure, stillbirth, cesarean section, and a low-birthweight baby; educational; personal; prenatal; birth; low birthweight; brain damage
39. sexual abuse; child sexual abuse
40. repeated; adult–child relationships; coercive; peers
41. childhood; fathers or stepfathers; puberty
42. 30 to 50 percent; adolescent boys who had been abused themselves
43. sexual abuse
44. abuse; addictive; use
45. gateway drugs; sex; failure; violence
46. growth rate
47. inhibitions; judgment; memory; self-control; hippocampus; prefrontal cortex
48. slows; memory; abstract
49. half; alcohol
50. peers; community; culture
51. no more
52. a. active, problem-solving style of coping
    b. competence and well-being
    c. cognitive maturity

PROGRESS TEST 1

Multiple-Choice Questions

1. a. is the answer. (p. 341)

2. **a.** is the answer. (p. 347)

   b. Girls gain more body fat than boys do.

   c. & d. The text does not indicate that these are different for boys and girls.

3. **a.** is the answer. (p. 341)

4. **c.** is the answer. This is because each menstrual period depletes some iron from the body. (p. 351)

5. **a.** is the answer. (p. 342)

   b. This describes the gonads.

   c. These include estrogen and testosterone.

   d. This is the hypothalamus.

6. **b.** is the answer. (p. 341)

7. **b.** is the answer. (p. 345)

8. **d.** is the answer. (p. 342)

9. **c.** is the answer. (p. 351)

   a. Although some adolescents become overweight, many diet and lose weight in an effort to attain a desired body image.

   d. On the contrary, cultural attitudes about beauty are an extremely influential factor in the formation of a teenager's body image.

10. **b.** is the answer. (p. 342)

11. **b.** is the answer. (p. 354)

12. **c.** is the answer. (p. 346)

13. **c.** is the answer. (p. 341)

14. **d.** is the answer. (p. 342)

15. **c.** is the answer. (p. 345)

True or False Items

1. T (p. 350)

2. T (p. 343)

3. F   The first indicator of reproductive potential in males is ejaculation of seminal fluid containing sperm (spermarche). Menarche (the first menstrual period) is the first indication of reproductive potential in females. (p. 345)

4. T (p. 347)

5. T (p. 344)

6. T (p. 350)

7. T (pp. 356–357)

8. F These habits generally *worsen* during adolescence. (pp. 350–351)

9. T (p. 346)

10. F   Although there is great variation in the timing of pubertal events, the sequence is very similar for all young people. (p. 344)

PROGRESS TEST 2

Multiple-Choice Questions

1. **b.** is the answer. (pp. 341)

2. **d.** is the answer. During adolescence, the lymphoid system *decreases* in size and the heart *doubles* in size. (p. 347)

3. **a.** is the answer. (pp. 342–343)

   b. Testosterone increases markedly in boys.

   c. Androgen is another name for testosterone.

   d. Menarche is the first menstrual period.

4. **b.** is the answer. (pp. 350–351)

5. **b.** is the answer. (p. 347)

   a. The shoulders of males tend to widen during puberty.

   c. The torso typically lengthens during puberty.

   d. The eyes and nose *increase* in size during puberty.

6. **c.** is the answer. (p. 349)

   a. Although not a term used in the textbook, a gender-typed trait is one that is typical of one sex but not of the other.

   b. Primary sex characteristics are those involving the reproductive organs.

   d. This is not a term used by developmental psychologists.

7. **a.** is the answer. (p. 342)

8. **b.** is the answer. (p. 352)

9. **a.** is the answer. (p. 356)

10. **d.** is the answer. (p. 346)

11. **b.** is the answer. (p. 355)

12. **a.** is the answer. (p. 354)

    b. This was not discussed in the text.

    c. This is true of girls.

13. **c.** is the answer. (p. 341)

14. **b.** is the answer. Although the size of the heart increases during puberty, heart rate *decreases*. (p. 347)

15. **d.** is the answer. (p. 347)

Matching Items

1. b (p. 341)   5. f (p. 346)   9. h (p. 349)
2. d (p. 342)   6. i (p. 348)   10. g (p. 351)
3. c (p. 342)   7. a (p. 345)
4. e (p. 342)   8. j (p. 345)

THINKING CRITICALLY ABOUT CHAPTER 14

1. **c.** is the answer. (p. 356)

2. **a.** is the answer. (p. 342)

3. **a.** is the answer. (p. 344)

   b. It usually takes longer than one year for a pre-pubescent male to catch up with a female who has begun puberty.

   c. This is not true.

   d. The text does not suggest that exercise has an effect on the timing of the growth spurt.

4. **d.** is the answer. (p. 349)

5. **a.** is the answer. (p. 346)

   b., c., & d. These are more typically sources of status for early-maturing boys.

6. **d.** is the answer. (p. 346)

   a. & b. Early-maturing girls are often teased and criticized by their friends.

   c. During adolescence, physical stature is typically a more prized attribute among peers than is scholastic achievement.

7. **c.** is the answer. It is *early*-maturing girls who are often drawn into involvement with older boys. (p. 346)

8. **a.** is the answer. (p. 345)

9. **b.** is the answer. (pp. 354–355)

10. **c.** is the answer. (pp. 343–344)

11. **d.** is the answer. (p. 359)

12. **b.** is the answer. (p. 346)

   a. Late maturation is typically more difficult for boys than for girls.

   c. Early maturation is generally a positive experience for boys.

   d. Adolescent masturbation is no longer the source of guilt or shame that it once was.

13. **d.** Kristin's symptoms are typical of iron-deficiency anemia, which is more common in teenage girls than in any other age group. (p. 351)

14. **c.** is the answer. (p. 342)

   a. Only in girls do estrogen levels rise markedly during puberty.

   b. Only in boys do testosterone levels rise markedly during puberty.

   d. Menarche is the first menstrual period.

15. **b.** is the answer. (p. 341)

KEY TERMS

1. **Adolescence** is the period of biological, cognitive, and psychosocial transition from childhood to adulthood. (p. 341)

2. **Puberty** is the period of rapid physical growth and sexual maturation that ends childhood and brings the young person to adult size, shape, and sexual potential. (p. 341)

3. The **hypothalamus** is the part of the brain that regulates eating, drinking, body temperature, and the production of hormones via the pituitary gland. (p. 342)

4. The **pituitary gland,** in response to a biochemical signal from the hypothalamus, produces hormones that regulate growth and control other glands. (p. 342)

5. The **adrenal glands** secrete epinephrine and norepinephrine, hormones that prepare the body to deal with emergencies or stress. (p. 342)

6. The **HPA axis** (hypothalamus/pituitary/adrenal axis) is the route followed by many hormones to trigger puberty and to regulate stress, growth, and other bodily changes. (p. 342)

7. The **gonads** are the pair of sex glands in humans—the ovaries in females and the testes or testicles in males. (p. 342)

8. **Estrogen** is a sex hormone that is secreted in greater amounts by females than by males. (p. 342)

9. **Testosterone** is a sex hormone that is secreted more by males than by females. (p. 342)

10. **Menarche,** which refers to the first menstrual period, is the specific event that is taken to indicate fertility in adolescent girls. (p. 345)

11. **Spermarche,** which refers to the first ejaculation of sperm, is the specific event that is taken to indicate fertility in adolescent boys. (p. 345)

12. The **growth spurt,** which is a period of relatively sudden and rapid physical growth of every part of the body, is one of the many observable signs of puberty. (p. 346)

13. During puberty, changes in the **primary sex characteristics** involve those sex organs that are directly involved in reproduction. (p. 348)

14. During puberty, changes in the **secondary sex characteristics** involve parts of the body that are not directly involved in reproduction but that signify sexual development. (p. 349)

15. **Sexually transmitted infections (STIs)** such as syphilis, gonorrhea, herpes, and AIDS, are those that are spread by sexual contact. (p. 352)

16. **Sexual abuse** is the use of an unconsenting person for one's own sexual pleasure. (p. 354)

17. **Child sexual abuse** is any activity in which an adult uses a child for his or her own sexual stimulation or pleasure—even if the use does not involve physical contact. (p. 354)

18. **Drug use** is the ingestion of a drug, regardless of the amount or effect of ingestion. (p. 355)

19. **Drug abuse** is the ingestion of a drug to the extent that it impairs the user's biological or psychological well-being. (p. 355)

20. **Drug addiction** is a person's dependence on a drug or a behavior in order to feel physically or psychologically at ease. (p. 355)

21. **Gateway drugs** are drugs—usually tobacco, alcohol, and marijuana—whose use increases the risk that a person will later use harder drugs. (p. 355)

Cross-Check

ACROSS

1. adrenal
7. spermarche
12. menarche
15. gonads
17. pituitary
18. growth spurt
19. drug use

DOWN

1. adolescence
2. lymphoid
3. hypothalamus
4. alcohol
5. drug addiction
6. gateway drugs
8. drug abuse
9. secondary
10. testosterone
11. tobacco
13. estrogen
14. puberty
16. primary

Chapter Fifteen

Adolescence: Cognitive Development

Chapter Overview

Chapter 15 begins by describing the cognitive advances of adolescence. With the attainment of formal operational thought, the developing person becomes able to think in an adult way, that is, to be logical, to think in terms of possibilities, to reason scientifically and abstractly.

Even those who reach the stage of formal operational thought spend much of their time thinking at less advanced levels. The discussion of adolescent egocentrism supports this generalization in showing that adolescents have difficulty thinking rationally about themselves and their immediate experiences. Adolescent egocentrism makes them see themselves as psychologically unique and more socially significant than they really are.

The second section explores the adolescent decision-making process in relation to school, jobs, sex, and risk taking in general. The discussion relates choices made by adolescents to their cognitive abilities and typical shortcomings. As adolescents enter secondary school, their grades often suffer and their level of participation decreases. The rigid behavioral demands and intensified competition of most secondary schools do not, unfortunately, provide a supportive learning environment for adolescents.

NOTE: Answer guidelines for all Chapter 15 questions begin on page 225.

Guided Study

The text chapter should be studied one section at a time. Before you read, preview each section by skimming it, noting headings and boldface items. Then read the appropriate section objectives from the following outline. Keep these objectives in mind and, as you read the chapter section, search for the information that will enable you to meet each objective. Once

you have finished a section, write out answers for its objectives.

Intellectual Advances (pp. 363–372)

1. Describe advances in thinking during adolescence.

2. Describe evidence of formal operational thinking during adolescence, and provide examples of adolescents' emerging ability to reason deductively and inductively.

3. Discuss the increasing importance of intuitive thinking in adolescence, particularly as manifested in adolescent egocentrism.

4. Explain adolescents' use of illogical, intuitive thought even when they are capable of logical thought.

Adolescent Decision Making (pp. 372–382)

5. Briefly discuss why the typical adolescent should not make major life decisions.

6. Evaluate the typical secondary school's ability to meet the cognitive needs of the typical adolescent.

7. Discuss whether part-time employment is advisable for adolescents.

8. Discuss sex education and global trends in teen pregnancies and births.

9. Discuss the influence of education, national trends, and culture on adolescent risk taking.

Chapter Review

When you have finished reading the chapter, work through the material that follows to review it. Complete the sentences and answer the questions. As you proceed, evaluate your performance for each section by consulting the answers beginning on page 225. Do not continue with the next section until you understand each answer. If you need to, review or reread the appropriate section in the textbook before continuing.

Intellectual Advances (pp. 363–372)

1. Adolescent thinking advances in three ways: basic _____ _____ continue to develop, _____ emerges, and _____ thinking becomes quicker and more compelling. The basic skills of thinking, learning, and remembering that advance during the school-age years _____ (continue to progress/ stabilize) during adolescence.

2. Advances in _____ _____ improve concentration, while a growing _____

_____ and memory skills allow teens to connect new ideas to old ones, and strengthened _____ help them become better students. Brain maturation _____ (is complete/continues).

3. Reaction time _____ (improves/slows) as a result of ongoing _____ , and the brain's _____ _____ becomes more densely packed. This latter development results in significant advances in the _____ _____ of the brain.

4. Improvements in language include a better understanding of the nuances of _____ and _____ choice, which makes _____-_____ more sophisticated.

5. Piaget's term for the fourth stage of cognitive development is _____ _____ thought. Other theorists may explain adolescent advances differently, but virtually all theorists agree that adolescent thought _____ (is/is not) qualitatively different from children's thought.

6. (Thinking Like a Scientist) Piaget devised a number of famous tasks involving _____ principles to study how children of various ages reasoned hypothetically and deductively.

(Thinking Like a Scientist) Briefly describe how children reason differently about the "balance beam" problem at ages 7, 10, and 13.

7. The kind of thinking in which adolescents consider unproven possibilities that are logical but not necessarily real is called _____-_____ thinking.

8. During adolescence, they become more capable of _____ reasoning—that is, they can begin with a general _____ or _____ and draw logical _____ from it. This type of reasoning is a hallmark of formal operational thought.

9. They also make great strides in _____ (inductive/deductive) reasoning.

10. In addition to advances in the formal, logical, _____-_____ thinking described by Piaget, adolescents advance in their _____ cognition.

11. Theorists refer to hypothetical-deductive reasoning as _____ thought. The second mode of thinking, which begins with a prior _____ , is called _____ . The brain pathways that enable these two types of thinking are variously called _____ _____ .

12. The adolescent's belief that he or she is uniquely significant and that the social world revolves around him or her is a psychological phenomenon called _____ _____ .

13. An adolescent's tendency to feel that he or she is somehow immune to the consequences of dangerous or illegal behavior is expressed in the _____ _____ .

14. An adolescent's tendency to imagine that her or his own life is unique, heroic, or even legendary, and that she or he is destined for great accomplishments, is expressed in the _____ _____ .

15. Adolescents, who believe that they are under constant scrutiny from nearly everyone, create for themselves an _____ _____ .

16. Although intuitive thinking generally is
_____ and _____ , it is
also often _____ .

17. Together, the _____ thinking that is
used in school and the _____ think-
ing used in one's personal life create a type of
_____ _____ .

Adolescent Decision Making (pp. 372–382)

18. Adults try to protect teenagers from poor judgment for three reasons:

    a. _____

    _____

    b. _____

    _____

    c. _____

    _____

Cite several benefits of graduating from high school.

19. Instead of there being a good fit between adolescents' needs and the schools, there is often a
_____ _____ .

20. Compared to elementary schools, most secondary
schools feature _____
_____ , rigid _____
_____ , and _____
_____ that do not meet adolescents'
needs.

21. Internationally, education systems vary in
_____ , _____ , and
average _____ _____ .

22. In general, teenagers in the United States work
_____ (more/less) and learn
_____ (more/less) than teenagers
elsewhere. Attitudes regarding after-school jobs
_____ (vary/do not vary) from
country to country.

23. In some nations, such as _____ ,
almost no adolescent is employed or even does
significant chores at home. In many
_____ countries, many older adoles-
cents have jobs as part of their school curriculum.
Most parents in the United States
_____ (approve/do not approve) of
youth employment.

24. Perhaps because many of today's jobs for adolescents are not _____ , research finds
that when adolescents are employed more than
_____ hours a week, their grades
suffer.

25. The teen birth rate is _____
(increasing/decreasing) since the 1980s. In the
United States, this trend has occurred in
_____ (every/most) ethnic and age
group, but most dramatically among
_____-_____ . At the
same time, condom use has _____
(increased/decreased).

26. Sexual activity among adolescents _____
(is/is not) more diverse than it was 10 years ago.

27. Most secondary schools _____ (pro-
vide/do not provide) sex education.

Progress Test 1

Multiple-Choice Questions

Circle your answers to the following questions and
check them with the answers beginning on page 226.
If your answer is incorrect, read the explanation for
why it is incorrect and then consult the appropriate
pages of the text (in parentheses following the correct
answer).

1. Many psychologists consider the distinguishing
feature of adolescent thought to be the ability to
think in terms of:
    a. moral issues.
    b. concrete operations.
    c. possibility, not just reality.
    d. logical principles.

2. Piaget's last stage of cognitive development is:
    a. formal operational thought.
    b. concrete operational thought.
    c. universal ethical principles.
    d. symbolic thought.

3. Advances in metacognition deepen adolescents' abilities in:
   a. studying.
   b. the invincibility fable.
   c. the personal fable.
   d. adolescent egocentrism.

4. The adolescent who takes risks and feels immune to the laws of mortality is showing evidence of the:
   a. invincibility fable.   c. imaginary audience.
   b. personal fable.   d. death instinct.

5. Imaginary audiences, invincibility fables, and personal fables are expressions of adolescent:
   a. morality.   c. decision making.
   b. thinking games.   d. egocentrism.

6. The typical adolescent is:
   a. tough-minded.
   b. indifferent to public opinion.
   c. self-absorbed and hypersensitive to criticism.
   d. all of the above.

7. When adolescents enter secondary school, many:
   a. experience a drop in their academic performance.
   b. are less motivated than they were in elementary school.
   c. are less conscientious than they were in elementary school.
   d. experience all of the above.

8. During adolescence, which area of the brain becomes more densely packed and efficient, enabling adolescents to analyze possibilities and to pursue goals more effectively?
   a. hypothalamus
   b. brain stem
   c. adrenal glands
   d. prefrontal cortex

9. Thinking that begins with a general premise and then draws logical conclusions from it is called:
   a. inductive reasoning.
   b. deductive reasoning.
   c. intuitive thinking.
   d. hypothetical reasoning.

10. Serious reflection on important issues is a wrenching process for many adolescents because of their newfound ability to reason:
    a. inductively.   c. hypothetically.
    b. deductively.   d. symbolically.

11. Hypothetical-deductive thinking is to heuristic thinking as:
    a. rational analysis is to intuitive thought.
    b. intuitive thought is to rational analysis.
    c. experiential thinking is to intuitive reasoning.
    d. intuitive thinking is to analytical reasoning.

12. Many adolescents seem to believe that *their* love-making will not lead to pregnancy. This belief is an expression of the:
    a. personal fable.   c. imaginary audience.
    b. invincibility fable.   d. "game of thinking."

13. A parent in which of the following countries is *least* likely to approve of her daughter's request to take a part-time job after school?
    a. the United States   c. Great Britain
    b. Germany   d. Japan

14. Sex education classes today tend to:
    a. focus on practice with emotional expression and social interaction.
    b. be based on scare tactics designed to discourage sexual activity.
    c. be more dependent upon bringing the parents and other authoritative caregivers into the education process.
    d. have changed in all of the above ways.

15. To estimate the risk of a behavior, such as unprotected sexual intercourse, it is most important that the adolescent be able to think clearly about:
    a. universal ethical principles.
    b. personal beliefs and self-interest.
    c. future consequences.
    d. peer pressure.

True or False Items

Write T (*true*) or F (*false*) on the line in front of each statement.

_____ 1. High school graduates live longer, are richer, and more likely to stay out of jail than those who do not graduate.

_____ 2. Adolescents are generally better able than 8-year-old to recognize the validity of arguments that clash with their own beliefs.

_____ 3. Adolescents are typically very sensitive to criticism.

_____ 4. Most adolescents who engage in risky behavior are unaware of the consequences of their actions.

_____ 5. Adolescents often create an imaginary audience as they envision how others will react to their appearance and behavior.

_____ 6. Myelination of brain neurons is completed by the beginning of adolescence.

_____ 7. The teen birth rate continues to rise throughout the world.

_____ 8. Inductive reasoning is a hallmark of formal operational thought.

_____ 9. Adults are generally wiser than adolescents in calculating the risks and benefits of a decision.

_____ 10. Few adolescents can, or should, decide their future careers.

Progress Test 2

Progress Test 2 should be completed during a final chapter review. Answer the following questions after you thoroughly understand the correct answers for the Chapter Review and Progress Test 1.

Multiple-Choice Questions

1. Adolescents who fall prey to the invincibility fable may be more likely to:
   a. engage in risky behaviors.
   b. suffer from depression.
   c. have low self-esteem.
   d. drop out of school.

2. Thinking that extrapolates from a specific experience to form a general premise is called:
   a. inductive reasoning.
   b. deductive reasoning.
   c. intuitive thinking.
   d. hypothetical reasoning.

3. The underlying reason for the improved cognitive skills of adolescents is:
   a. the more challenging curriculum of middle school and high school.
   b. brain maturation.
   c. the increased demands they make of themselves.
   d. the fact that brain myelination is completed by the beginning of puberty.

4. When young people overestimate their significance to others, they are displaying:
   a. concrete operational thought.
   b. adolescent egocentrism.
   c. a lack of cognitive growth.
   d. immoral development.

5. The personal fable refers to adolescents imagining that:
   a. they are immune to the dangers of risky behaviors.
   b. they are always being scrutinized by others.
   c. their own lives are unique, heroic, or even legendary.
   d. the world revolves around their actions.

6. The typical secondary school environment:
   a. has more rigid behavioral demands than the average elementary school.
   b. does not meet the cognitive needs of the typical adolescent.
   c. emphasizes competition.
   d. is described by all of the above.

7. As compared to elementary schools, most secondary schools exhibit all of the following *except*:
   a. a more flexible approach to education.
   b. intensified competition.
   c. inappropriate academic standards.
   d. less individualized attention.

8. Teenagers need protection from poor judgment because:
   a. they are particularly likely to overrate the joys of the moment.
   b. adolescent choices can be long-lasting.
   c. the younger a person is, the more serious are the consequences of risk taking.
   d. of all the above reasons.

9. Research has shown that adolescents who work at after-school jobs more than 20 hours per week:
   a. are more likely to use drugs as adults.
   b. have lower grades.
   c. are more likely to engage in unprotected sex.
   d. have all of the above characteristics.

10. Analytic thinking is to _____ thinking as emotional force is to _____ thinking.
    a. intuitive; egocentric
    b. egocentric; intuitive
    c. formal; intuitive
    d. intuitive; formal

11. One of the hallmarks of formal operational thought is:
    a. egocentrism.   c. symbolic thinking.
    b. deductive reasoning. d. all of the above.

12. Analytic thinking and experiential thinking:
    a. both use the same neural pathways in the brain.
    b. are really the same type of information processing.
    c. both improve during adolescence.
    d. are characterized by all of the above.

13. The ongoing myelination of brain neurons during adolescence:
    a. makes teens especially self-focused.
    b. allows teens to grasp and connect ideas much faster than younger children can.
    c. contributes to adolescent egocentrism.
    d. is most focused in brain areas related to visual processing.

14. Evidence that revised sex education programs are working comes from the fact that _____ is (are) declining.
    a. the birth rate among teenagers
    b. the percentage of sexually active teenagers
    c. the use of condoms among teenagers
    d. all of the above

15. To avoid a volatile mismatch, a school should:
    a. focus on cooperative rather than competitive learning.
    b. base grading on individual test performance.
    c. establish the same goals for every student.
    d. vary its settings and approach according to children's developmental stages and cognition.

Matching Items

Match each term or concept with its corresponding description or definition.

Terms or Concepts

_____ 1. invincibility fable
_____ 2. imaginary audience
_____ 3. sexually active
_____ 4. hypothetical thought
_____ 5. deductive reasoning
_____ 6. inductive reasoning
_____ 7. formal operational thought
_____ 8. personal fable
_____ 9. volatile mismatch
_____ 10. adolescent egocentrism

Descriptions or Definitions

a. the tendency of adolescents to focus on themselves to the exclusion of others
b. adolescents feel immune to the consequences of dangerous behavior
c. adolescents feel destined for fame and fortune
d. the idea held by many adolescents that others are intensely interested in them, especially in their appearance and behavior
e. defined by a more diverse set of behaviors today than in the past
f. reasoning about propositions that may or may not reflect reality
g. the last stage of cognitive development, according to Piaget
h. thinking that moves from premise to conclusion
i. thinking that moves from a specific experience to a general premise
j. a clash between a teenager's needs and the structure and functioning of his or her school

Thinking Critically About Chapter 15

Answer these questions the day before an exam as a final check on your understanding of the chapter's terms and concepts.

1. Summarizing her presentation on the volatile mismatch between the needs of adolescents and the traditional structure of their schools, Megan notes that:
   a. most secondary schools feature intensified competition.
   b. most schools in the United States are still focused on the needs of the elite.
   c. the academic standards of most schools do not reflect adolescents' needs.
   d. all of the above are true.

2. An experimenter hides a ball in her hand and says, "Either the ball in my hand is red or it is not red." Most preadolescent children say:
   a. the statement is true.
   b. the statement is false.
   c. they cannot tell if the statement is true or false.
   d. they do not understand what the experimenter means.

3. Fourteen-year-old Monica is very idealistic and often develops crushes on people she doesn't even know. This reflects her newly developed cognitive ability to:
   a. deal simultaneously with two sides of an issue.
   b. take another person's viewpoint.
   c. imagine possible worlds and people.
   d. see herself as others see her.

4. Which of the following is the *best* example of a personal fable?
   a. Adriana imagines that she is destined for a life of fame and fortune.
   b. Ben makes up stories about his experiences to impress his friends.
   c. Kalil questions his religious beliefs when they seem to offer little help for a problem he faces.
   d. Julio believes that every girl he meets is attracted to him.

5. Which of the following is the *best* example of the adolescent's ability to think hypothetically?
   a. Twelve-year-old Stanley feels that people are always watching him.
   b. Fourteen-year-old Mindy engages in many risky behaviors, reasoning that "nothing bad will happen to me."
   c. Fifteen-year-old Philip feels that no one understands his problems.
   d. Thirteen-year-old Josh delights in finding logical flaws in virtually everything his teachers and parents say.

6. Frustrated because of the dating curfew her parents have set, Melinda exclaims, "You just don't know how it feels to be in love!" Melinda's thinking demonstrates:
   a. the invincibility fable.
   b. the personal fable.
   c. the imaginary audience.
   d. adolescent egocentrism.

7. Compared to her 13-year-old brother, 17-year-old Yolanda is likely to:
   a. be more critical about herself.
   b. be more egocentric.
   c. have less confidence in her abilities.
   d. be more capable of reasoning hypothetically.

8. Nathan's fear that his friends will ridicule him because of a pimple that has appeared on his nose reflects a preoccupation with:
   a. his personal fable.
   b. the invincibility fable.
   c. an imaginary audience.
   d. preconventional reasoning.

9. Thirteen-year-old Malcolm, who lately is very sensitive to the criticism of others, feels significantly less motivated and capable than when he was in elementary school. Malcolm is probably:
   a. experiencing a sense of vulnerability that is common in adolescents.
   b. a lower-track student.
   c. a student in a school that emphasizes cooperation.
   d. all of the above.

10. The reasoning behind the conclusion, "if it waddles like a duck and quacks like a duck, then it must be a duck," is called:
    a. experiential thinking.
    b. heuristic thinking.
    c. inductive reasoning.
    d. deductive reasoning.

11. Seventy-year-old Artemis can't understand why his daughter doesn't want her teenage son to work after school. "In my day," he says, "we learned responsibility and a useful trade by working throughout high school." You wisely point out that:
    a. most after-school jobs for teens today are not very meaningful.
    b. after-school employment tends to have a more negative impact on boys than girls.
    c. attitudes are changing; today, most American parents see adolescent employment as a waste of time.
    d. teens in most European countries almost never work after school.

12. Who is the *least* likely to display mature decision making?
    a. Brenda, an outgoing 17-year-old art student
    b. Fifteen-year-old Kenny, who has few adults in whom he confides
    c. Monique, a well-educated 15-year-old
    d. Damon, an 18-year-old high school graduate who lives alone

13. After hearing that an unusually aggressive child has been in full-time day care since he was 1 year old, 16-year-old Keenan concludes that non-parental care leads to behavior problems. Keenan's conclusion is an example of:
    a. inductive reasoning.
    b. deductive reasoning.
    c. hypothetical thinking.
    d. adolescent egocentrism.

14. At a recent meeting of the middle school parents association, Mr. Bush spoke against a proposed sex education unit. He argued that if teenagers know too much about sex and contraception, they will be encouraged to experiment. Is he correct?
    a. Yes, teaching adolescents about contraception encourages them to have sexual intercourse.
    b. Yes, teaching adolescents about contraception encourages them to have sexual intercourse and eventually increases its frequency.
    c. Yes, teaching adolescents about contraception encourages them to have sexual intercourse, increases its frequency, and increases the number of sexual partners.
    d. No, teaching adolescents about contraception does not increase their sexual activity.

15. Dr. Malone, who wants to improve the effectiveness of her adolescent sex-education class, would be well advised to:
    a. focus on the biological facts of reproduction and disease, because teenage misinformation is largely responsible for the high rates of unwanted pregnancy and STIs.
    b. personalize the instruction, in order to make the possible consequences of sexual activity more immediate to students.
    c. teach boys and girls in separate classes, so that discussion can be more frank and open.
    d. use all of the above strategies.

Key Terms

Using your own words, write a brief definition or explanation of each of the following terms on a separate piece of paper.

1. formal operational thought
2. hypothetical thought
3. deductive reasoning
4. inductive reasoning
5. adolescent egocentrism
6. invincibility fable
7. personal fable
8. imaginary audience
9. volatile mismatch
10. sexually active

ANSWERS
CHAPTER REVIEW

1. cognitive skills; logic; intuitive; continue to progress
2. selective attention; knowledge base; metacognition; continues
3. improves; myelination; prefrontal cortex; executive functions
4. grammar; vocabulary; code-switching
5. formal operational; is
6. scientific

Preschoolers have no understanding of how to solve the problem. By age 7, children understand balancing the weights but don't know that distance from the center is also a factor. By age 10, they understand the concepts but are unable to coordinate them. By ages 13 or 14, they are able to solve the problem.

7. hypothetical-deductive

8. deductive; premise; theory; conclusions

9. inductive

10. hypothetical-deductive; intuitive

11. analytic; belief or assumption; intuitive (or heuristic or experiential); conscious/unconscious, explicit/implicit; factual/creative

12. adolescent egocentrism

13. invincibility fable

14. personal fable

15. imaginary audience

16. quick; emotional; wrong

17. analytic; experiential; cognitive economy

18. a. The consequences of risk taking are more serious the younger a person is

    b. Adolescent choices are long-lasting

    c. Adolescents overrate the joys of the moment and ignore future costs

High school graduates stay healthier, live longer, are richer, and are more likely to marry, vote, stay out of jail, and buy homes than their less educated contemporaries.

19. volatile mismatch

20. intensified competition; behavioral demands; academic standards

21. expectations; curriculum; class size

22. more; less; vary

23. Japan; European; approve

24. meaningful; 20

25. decreasing; every; African-Americans; increased

26. is

27. provide

PROGRESS TEST 1

Multiple-Choice Questions

1. **c.** is the answer. (p. 366)

   a. Although moral reasoning becomes much deeper during adolescence, it is not limited to this stage of development.

   b. & d. Concrete operational thought, which *is* logical, is the distinguishing feature of childhood thinking.

2. **a.** is the answer. (p. 364)

   b. In Piaget's theory, this stage precedes formal operational thought.

   c. & d. These are not stages in Piaget's theory.

3. **a.** is the answer. (p. 363)

   b., c., & d. These are examples of limited reasoning ability during adolescence.

4. **a.** is the answer. (p. 368)

   b. This refers to adolescents' tendency to imagine their own lives as unique, heroic, or even legendary.

   c. This refers to adolescents' tendency to fantasize about how others will react to their appearance and behavior.

   d. This is a concept in Freud's theory.

5. **d.** is the answer. These thought processes are manifestations of adolescents' tendency to see themselves as being much more central and important to the social scene than they really are. (p. 368)

6. **c.** is the answer. (p. 363)

7. **d.** is the answer. (p. 375)

8. **d.** is the answer. (p. 364)

   a., b., & c. These "lower" brain centers and endocrine glands, which are not involved in conscious reasoning, control hunger and thirst (hypothalamus); sleep and arousal (brainstem); and the production of stress hormones (adrenal glands).

9. **b.** is the answer. (p. 366)

   a. Inductive reasoning moves from specific facts to a general conclusion.

   c. By its very nature, intuitive thinking does not move logically either from a general conclusion to specific facts or from specific facts to a general conclusion.

   d. Hypothetical reasoning involves thinking about possibilities rather than facts.

10. **c.** is the answer. (p. 366)

11. **a.** is the answer. (p. 367)

    c. Heuristic thinking is both experiential *and* intuitive.

12. **b.** is the answer. (p. 368)

    a. This refers to adolescents' tendency to imagine their own lives as unique, heroic, or even mythical.

    c. This refers to adolescents' tendency to fantasize about how others will react to their appearance and behavior.

d. This is the adolescent ability to suspend knowledge of reality in order to think playfully about possibilities.

13. **d.** is the answer. Japanese adolescents almost never work after school. (p. 376)

    a. American parents generally approve of adolescent employment.

    b. & c. Jobs are an important part of the school curriculum in many European countries.

14. **a.** is the answer. (pp. 378–379)

    b. Scare tactics were often a central feature of earlier sex education classes.

    c. Generally speaking, parents are not effective sex educators.

15. **c.** is the answer. (pp. 372–373)

True or False Items

1. T (p. 373)
2. T (p. 367)
3. T (p. 363)
4. F Adolescents are aware of the fact, but they fail to think through the possible consequences. (p. 372)
5. T (p. 368)
6. F Myelination continues through adolescence. (p. 363)
7. F The teen birth rate worldwide has dropped since the 1980s. (p. 377)
8. F Deductive reasoning is a hallmark of formal operational thought. (p. 366)
9. F In fact, the worse outcomes of decision making are far more common after age 20. (p. 372)
10. T (p. 376)

PROGRESS TEST 2

Multiple-Choice Questions

1. **a.** is the answer. (p. 368)

   b., c., & d. The invincibility fable leads some teens to believe that they are immune to the dangers of risky behaviors; it is not necessarily linked to depression, low self-esteem, or the likelihood that an individual will drop out of school.

2. **a.** is the answer. (p. 366)

   b. Deductive reasoning begins with a general premise and then draws logical conclusions from it.

c. By its very nature, intuitive thinking does not move logically either from a general conclusion to specific facts or from specific facts to a general conclusion.

d. Hypothetical reasoning involves thinking about possibilities rather than facts.

3. **b.** is the answer. (p. 363)

   a. & c. Although these may or may not be true, the *underlying* reason for improved cognitive skills is the ongoing maturation of the brain.

   d. Myelination of brain neurons continues during adolescence.

4. **b.** is the answer. (p. 368)
5. **c.** is the answer. (p. 368)

   a. This describes the invincibility fable.

   b. This describes the imaginary audience.

   d. This describes adolescent egocentrism in general.

6. **d.** is the answer. (p. 374)
7. **a.** is the answer. (p. 374)
8. **d.** is the answer. (p. 372)
9. **d.** is the answer. (p. 377)
10. **c.** is the answer. (p. 367)
11. **b.** is the answer. (p. 366)
12. **c.** is the answer. (p. 366)
13. **b.** is the answer. (p. 363)
14. **a.** is the answer. (p. 377)

    b. & c. These are on the rise.

15. **d.** is the answer. (pp. 373, 376)

Matching Items

1. b (pp. 368)
2. d (p. 368)
3. e (p. 378)
4. f (p. 366)
5. h (p. 366)
6. i (p. 366)
7. g (p. 364)
8. c (p. 368)
9. j (p. 373)
10. a (p. 368)

THINKING CRITICALLY ABOUT CHAPTER 15

1. **d.** is the answer. (p. 374)
2. **c.** is the answer. Although this statement is logically verifiable, preadolescents who lack formal operational thought cannot prove or disprove it. (p. 364)
3. **c.** is the answer. (p. 366)
4. **a.** is the answer. (p. 368)

   b. & d. These behaviors are more indicative of a preoccupation with the imaginary audience.

c. Kalil's questioning attitude is a normal adolescent tendency that helps foster moral reasoning.

5. **d.** is the answer. (p. 366)

   a. This is an example of the imaginary audience.

   b. This is an example of the invincibility fable.

   c. This is an example of adolescent egocentrism.

6. **d.** is the answer. (p. 368)

7. **d.** is the answer. (p. 366)

8. **c.** is the answer. (p. 368)

   a. In this fable, adolescents see themselves destined for fame and fortune.

   b. In this fable, young people feel that they are somehow immune to the consequences of common dangers.

   d. This is a stage of moral reasoning in Kohlberg's theory, as discussed in Chapter 12.

9. **a.** is the answer. (p. 376)

10. **c.** is the answer. (p. 366)

    a. & b. Experiential (or heuristic) thinking, is more intuitive and less logical.

    d. Deductive thinking moves from from a general conclusion to specific principles; this example moves from particulars to a general conclusion.

11. **a.** is the answer. (p. 377)

    b. There is no evidence of a gender difference in the impact of employment on adolescents.

    c. & d. In fact, just the opposite are true.

12. **b.** is the answer. Mature decision making is least likely to be displayed by adolescents who are under age 16, who have less education, and who have few adults to talk with. (p. 373)

13. **a.** is the answer. (p. 366)

    b. Keenan is reasoning from the specific to the general, rather than vice versa.

    c. Keenan is thinking about an actual observation, rather than a hypothetical possibility.

    d. Keenan's reasoning is focused outside himself, rather than being self-centered.

14. **d.** is the answer. (p. 379)

15. **b.** is the answer. (pp. 378–379)

KEY TERMS

1. In Piaget's theory, the last stage of cognitive development, which arises from a combination of maturation and experience, is called **formal operational thought.** A hallmark of formal operational thinking is the capacity for hypothetical, logical, and abstract thought. (p. 364)

2. **Hypothetical thought** involves reasoning about propositions and possibilities that may or may not reflect reality. (p. 366)

3. **Deductive reasoning** is thinking that moves from the general to the specific, or from a premise to a logical conclusion. (p. 366)

4. **Inductive reasoning** is thinking that moves from one or more specific experiences or facts to a general conclusion. (p. 366)

5. **Adolescent egocentrism** refers to the tendency of adolescents to see themselves as much more socially significant than they actually are. (p. 368)

6. Adolescents who experience the **invincibility fable** feel that they are immune to the dangers of risky behaviors. (p. 368)

7. Another example of adolescent egocentrism is the **personal fable,** through which adolescents imagine their own lives as unique, heroic, or even legendary. (p. 368)

8. Adolescents often create an **imaginary audience** for themselves, as they assume that others are as intensely interested in them as they themselves are. (p. 368)

9. When teenagers' individual needs do not match the size, routine, and structure of their schools, a **volatile mismatch** may occur. (p. 373)

10. Traditionally, **sexually active** teenagers were those who have had intercourse. (p. 378)

Chapter Sixteen

Adolescence: Psychosocial Development

Chapter Overview

Chapter 16 focuses on the adolescent's psychosocial development, particularly the formation of identity, which is required for the attainment of adult status and maturity. Depression, self-destruction, and suicide—the most perplexing problems of adolescence—are then explored. The special problems posed by adolescent lawbreaking are discussed, and suggestions for alleviating or treating these problems are given. The final section examines the influences of family and friends on adolescent psychosocial development, including the development of romantic relationships. The chapter concludes with the message that although no other period of life is characterized by so many changes in the three domains of development, for most young people the teenage years are happy ones. Furthermore, serious problems in adolescence do not necessarily lead to lifelong problems.

NOTE: Answer guidelines for all Chapter 16 questions begin on page 239.

Guided Study

The text chapter should be studied one section at a time. Before you read, preview each section by skimming it, noting headings and boldface items. Then read the appropriate section objectives from the following outline. Keep these objectives in mind and, as you read the chapter section, search for the information that will enable you to meet each objective. Once you have finished a section, write out answers for its objectives.

The Self and Identity (pp. 385–391)

1. Describe the development of identity during adolescence.

2. Describe the four major identity statuses, and give an example of each.

3. Discuss the problems encountered in the formation of gender and ethnic identities, and describe cultural effects on identity formation.

Sadness and Anger (pp. 391–397)

4. Discuss adolescent suicide, noting contributing factors and gender, ethnic, and national variations.

5. Discuss delinquency among adolescents today, noting its incidence and prevalence, significance for later development, and best approaches for prevention or treatment.

Family and Friends (pp. 397–406)

6. Discuss parental influence on identity formation, including the effect of parent–adolescent conflict and other aspects of family functioning.

7. Discuss the constructive functions of peer relationships and close friendships during adolescence and the unique challenges faced by immigrants.

8. Discuss the development of male–female relationships during adolescence, including the challenges faced by gay and lesbian adolescents.

Conclusion (pp. 406–407)

9. Discuss the theme of this text as demonstrated by adolescent development.

Chapter Review

When you have finished reading the chapter, work through the material that follows to review it. Complete the sentences and answer the questions. As you proceed, evaluate your performance for each section by consulting the answers beginning on page 239. Do not continue with the next section until you understand each answer. If you need to, review or reread the appropriate section in the textbook before continuing.

The Self and Identity (pp. 385–391)

1. The momentous changes that occur during the teen years challenge adolescents to find their own _____ . In this process, many adolescents experience _____ _____ , or various fantasies about what their futures might be if one or another course of action is followed.

2. Adolescents may take on a _____ _____ ; that is, they act in ways they know to be contrary to their true nature. Three variations on this identity status are the _____ _____ _____ , the _____ _____ _____ ,

and the _____ _____

_____ .

3. According to Erikson, the challenge of adolescence is _____ _____

_____ _____ .

4. The ultimate goal of adolescence is to establish a new identity that involves both repudiation and assimilation of childhood values; this is called

_____ _____ .

5. The young person who prematurely accepts earlier roles and parental values without exploring alternatives or truly forging a unique identity is experiencing identity _____ .

6. An adolescent who adopts an identity that is the opposite of the one he or she is expected to adopt has taken on a _____

_____ .

7. The young person who has few commitments to goals or values and is apathetic about defining his or her identity is experiencing

_____ _____ .

8. A time-out period during which a young person experiments with different identities, postponing important choices, is called an identity

_____ . An obvious institutional example of this in the United States is attending

_____ .

9. The psychologist who developed a set of questions to measure identity statuses is

_____ _____ .

Generally speaking, developmentalists are more interested in ongoing identity _____ than in _____ .

10. People _____ (can/generally cannot) achieve identity in one domain and still be searching for their identity in another. Identity is formed both from _____ , as when a person recognizes his or her true nature, and from _____ , in response to _____ forces.

11. A person's identification as either male or female is called _____ _____ .

This includes accepting all the _____ and _____ that society assigns to that biological category.

12. Gender identity and _____ identity are often connected because male and female roles are defined differently by different _____ .

13. In general, ethnic identity becomes more important when adolescents see their background as

_____ .

Today, about _____ percent of all teenagers are not of European descent.

Sadness and Anger (pp. 391–397)

14. Psychologists categorize emotional problems in two ways: _____ problems, which are directed inward and include

_____ ;

and _____ problems, which include _____ .
Both types of problems _____ (increase gradually/increase suddenly/decrease gradually/decrease suddenly) at adolescence.

15. Cross-sequential research studies show that, from ages 6 to 18, people generally feel _____ (more/less) competent each year in most areas of their lives.

16. Clinical depression _____ (increases/decreases) at puberty, especially among _____ (males/females).

17. Thinking about committing suicide, called _____ _____ , is _____ (common/relatively rare) among high school students.

18. Adolescents under age 20 are _____ (more/less) likely to kill themselves than adults are.

19. Most suicide attempts in adolescence _____ (do/do not) result in death. A deliberate act of self-destruction that does not result in death is called a _____ .

20. List five factors that affect whether thinking about suicide leads to a self-destructive act or to death.

    a. _____

    b. _____

    c. _____

    d. _____

    e. _____

21. The rate of suicide is higher for adolescent _____ (males/females). The rate of parasuicide is higher for _____ (males/females).

22. Around the world, cultural differences in the rates of suicidal ideation and completion _____ (are/are not) apparent.

23. When a town or school sentimentalizes the "tragic end" of a teen suicide, the publicity can trigger

    _____ _____ .

(Table 16.3) Briefly describe ethnic differences in suicide rates in the United States.

Breaking the Law (pp. 512–516)

24. Psychologists influenced by the _____ perspective believe that adolescent rebellion and defiance are normal, particularly for adolescent _____ (boys/girls).

25. Arrests are far more likely to occur during the _____ _____ of life than during any other time period. Although statistics indicate that the _____ (incidence/prevalence) of arrests is highest among this age group, they do not reveal how widespread, or _____ , lawbreaking is among this age group.

26. If all acts of "juvenile delinquency" are included, the prevalence of adolescent crime is _____ (less/greater) than official records report.

Briefly describe data on gender and ethnic differences in adolescent arrests.

27. The victims of crime tend to be _____ (teenagers/adults).

28. Experts find it useful to distinguish _____-_____ offenders, whose criminal activity stops by age 21, from _____-_____-_____ offenders, who become career criminals.

29. Developmentalists have found that it _____ (is/is not) currently possible to distinguish children who actually will become career criminals.

30. Adolescents who later become career criminals are among the first of their cohort to

    _____ .

    They also are among the least involved in _____ activities and tend to be _____ in preschool and elementary school. At an even earlier age, they show signs of _____ _____ , such as being slow in _____ development, being _____ , or having poor _____ control.

31. For most delinquents, residential incarceration in a prison or reform school usually _____ (is/is not) the best solution.

Family and Friends (pp. 397–406)

32. People who focus on differences between the younger and older generations speak of a _____ _____ . An exception occurs when the parents grow up in a very different _____ .

33. The idea that family members in different developmental stages have a natural tendency to see the family in different ways is called the

_____ _____ .

34. Parent–adolescent conflict is most common in _____ (early/late) adolescence and is particularly notable with _____ (mothers/fathers) and their _____ (early/late)-maturing _____ (sons/daughters). This conflict often involves _____ , which refers to repeated, petty arguments about daily habits.

35. Among Chinese-, Korean-, and Mexican-American teens, conflict tends to arise in _____ (early/late) adolescence, possibly because these cultures encourage _____ in their children and emphasize family _____ .

36. Four other elements of family functioning that have been heavily researched include

_____ , _____ , _____ , and _____ .

37. In terms of family control, a powerful deterrent to delinquency, risky sex, and drug abuse is

_____ _____ .

Too much interference, however, may contribute to adolescent _____ . Particularly harmful to teens are threats to withdraw love and support, or _____

_____ .

38. The largely constructive role of peers runs counter to the notion of _____

_____ . Social pressure to conform _____ (falls/rises) dramatically in early adolescence, until about age _____ , when it begins to _____ (fall/rise).

39. Adolescents whose parents are immigrants comprise a(n) _____ (increasing/decreasing) proportion of all teenagers in almost every nation of the world.

Briefly outline the four-stage progression of heterosexual involvement.

40. Cultural patterns _____ (affect/do not affect) the _____ and _____ of these stages, but the basic _____ seems to be based on _____ factors.

41. For gay and lesbian adolescents, added complications usually _____ (slow down/speed up) romantic attachments. In cultures that are _____ , many young men and women with homosexual or lesbian feelings may _____ their feelings or try to _____ or _____ them.

42. Most parents _____ (overestimate/underestimate) the significance of romantic relationships during adolescence.

Conclusion (pp. 406–407)

43. For most young people, the teenage years overall are _____ (happy/unhappy) ones.

44. Adolescents who have one serious problem _____ (often have/do not usually have) others.

45. In most cases, adolescent problems stem from earlier developmental events such as

_____ .

Progress Test 1

Multiple-Choice Questions

Circle your answers to the following questions and check them with the answers on page 240. If your answer is incorrect, read the explanation for why it is incorrect and then consult the appropriate pages of the text (in parentheses following the correct answer).

1. According to Erikson, the primary task of adolescence is that of establishing:
   a. basic trust.
   b. an identity.
   c. intimacy.
   d. integrity.

2. According to developmentalists who study identity formation, foreclosure involves:
   a. accepting an identity prematurely, without exploration.
   b. taking time off from school, work, and other commitments.
   c. opposing parental values.
   d. failing to commit oneself to a vocational goal.

3. When adolescents adopt an identity that is the opposite of the one they are expected to adopt, they are considered to be taking on a:
   a. foreclosed identity.
   b. diffused identity.
   c. negative identity.
   d. reverse identity.

4. The main sources of emotional support for most young people who are establishing independence from their parents are:
   a. older adolescents of the opposite sex.
   b. older siblings.
   c. teachers.
   d. peer groups.

5. For members of minority ethnic groups, identity achievement may be particularly complicated because:
   a. their cultural ideal clashes with the Western emphasis on adolescent self-determination.
   b. peers, themselves torn by similar conflicts, can be very critical.
   c. parents and other relatives tend to emphasize ethnicity and expect teens to honor their roots.
   d. of all of the above reasons.

6. In a crime-ridden neighborhood, parents can protect their adolescents by keeping close watch over activities, friends, and so on. This practice is called:
   a. generational stake.
   b. foreclosure.
   c. peer screening.
   d. parental monitoring.

7. Conflict between adolescent girls and their mothers is most likely to involve:
   a. bickering over hair, neatness, and other daily habits.
   b. political, religious, and moral issues.
   c. peer relationships and friendships.
   d. relationships with boys.

8. If there is a "generation gap," it is likely to occur in _____ adolescence and to center on issues of _____ .
   a. early; morality
   b. late; self-discipline
   c. early; self-control
   d. late; politics

9. Which of the following best describes how identity is formed?
   a. It is almost always formed "from without" as social forces push a teenager to adopt a particular identity.
   b. Identity is a process of discovery.
   c. For most teens, identity is blindly accepted, as parents, culture, and other sociocultural factors create their impact.
   d. Identity is constructed from within, when a person recognizes his or her true nature, or from without, in response to social forces.

10. Fifteen-year-old Cindy, who has strong self-esteem and is trying out a new, artistic identity "just to see how it feels," is apparently exploring:
    a. an acceptable false self.
    b. a pleasing false self.
    c. an experimental false self.
    d. none of the above.

11. If the vast majority of cases of a certain crime are committed by a small number of repeat offenders, this would indicate that the crime's:
    a. incidence is less than its prevalence.
    b. incidence is greater than its prevalence.
    c. incidence and prevalence are about equal.
    d. incidence and prevalence are impossible to calculate.

12. Thirteen-year-old Adam, who never has doubted his faith, identifies himself as an orthodox member of a particular religious group. A developmentalist would probably say that Adam's religious identity is:
    a. achieved.
    b. foreclosed.
    c. in moratorium.
    d. oppositional in nature.

13. The early signs of life-course-persistent offenders include all of the following *except*:
   a. signs of brain damage early in life.
   b. antisocial school behavior.
   c. delayed sexual intimacy.
   d. use of alcohol and tobacco at an early age.

14. Regarding gender differences in self-destructive acts, the rate of parasuicide is _____ and the rate of suicide is _____ .
   a. higher in males; higher in females
   b. higher in females; higher in males
   c. the same in males and females; higher in males
   d. the same in males and females; higher in females

15. Conflict between parents and adolescent offspring is:
   a. most likely to involve fathers and their early-maturing offspring.
   b. more frequent in single-parent homes.
   c. more likely between early-maturing daughters and their mothers.
   d. likely in all of the above situations.

True or False Items

Write T (*true*) or F (*false*) on the line in front of each statement.

_____ **1.** A person can achieve identity in one domain but still be searching in another.

_____ **2.** Most adolescents have political views and educational values that are markedly different from those of their parents.

_____ **3.** Peer pressure is inherently destructive to the adolescent seeking an identity.

_____ **4.** For most adolescents, group socializing and dating precede the establishment of true intimacy with one member of the opposite sex.

_____ **5.** Worldwide, arrests are more likely to occur during the second decade of life than at any other time.

_____ **6.** Most adolescent self-destructive acts are a response to an immediate and specific psychological blow.

_____ **7.** The majority of adolescents report that they have at some time engaged in law-breaking that might have led to arrest.

_____ **8.** In finding themselves, teens try to find an identity that is stable, consistent, and mature.

_____ **9.** From ages 6 to 18, children feel more competent, on average, each year in most areas of their lives.

_____ **10.** Increased accessibility of guns is a factor in the increased rate of youth suicide in the United States.

Progress Test 2

Progress Test 2 should be completed during a final chapter review. Answer the following questions after you thoroughly understand the correct answers for the Chapter Review and Progress Test 1.

Multiple-Choice Questions

1. In one international study, adolescents were asked to "name one concern or problem that causes you to feel worried or pressured." Which of the following categories was not one of those most often mentioned?
   a. material desires
   b. school
   c. interpersonal relationships
   d. sexuality

2. Adolescents who adopt an acceptable false self:
   a. report greater self-understanding than those whose false self arises from a wish to impress others.
   b. report higher self-esteem than those whose false self arises from a wish to "see how it feels."
   c. tend to feel depressed and hopeless.
   d. have all of the above characteristics.

3. Parent–teen conflict among Chinese-, Korean-, and Mexican-American families often surfaces late in adolescence because these cultures:
   a. emphasize family closeness.
   b. value authoritarian parenting.
   c. encourage autonomy in children.
   d. do all of the above.

4. If the various cases of a certain crime are committed by many different offenders, this would indicate that the crime's:
   a. incidence is less than its prevalence.
   b. incidence is greater than its prevalence.
   c. incidence and prevalence are about equal.
   d. incidence and prevalence are impossible to calculate.

5. Thinking about committing suicide is called:
   a. cluster suicide.
   b. parasuicide.
   c. suicidal ideation.
   d. fratracide.

6. Which of the following was *not* noted in the text regarding peer relationships among gay and lesbian adolescents?
   a. Romantic attachments are usually slower to develop.
   b. In homophobic cultures, many gay teens try to conceal their homosexual feelings by becoming heterosexually involved.
   c. Many girls who will later identify themselves as lesbians are oblivious to these sexual urges as teens.
   d. In many cases, a lesbian girl's best friend is a boy, who is more at ease with her sexuality than another girl might be.

7. The adolescent experiencing identity diffusion is typically:
   a. very apathetic.
   b. experimenting with alternative identities without trying to settle on any one.
   c. willing to accept parental values wholesale, without exploring alternatives.
   d. one who rebels against all forms of authority.

8. Cross-sequential studies of individuals from ages 6 to 18 show that:
   a. children feel less competent each year in most areas of their lives.
   b. the general emotional trend in adolescence is more downward than upward.
   c. self-esteem generally begins to decrease at about age 12.
   d. all of the above are true.

9. Crime statistics show that during adolescence:
   a. males and females are equally likely to be arrested.
   b. males are more likely to be arrested than females.
   c. females are more likely to be arrested than males.
   d. males commit more crimes than females but are less likely to be arrested.

10. Which of the following is the most common problem behavior among adolescents?
    a. pregnancy
    b. daily use of illegal drugs
    c. minor lawbreaking
    d. attempts at suicide

11. A time-out period during which a young person experiments with different identities, postponing important choices, is called a(n):
    a. identity foreclosure. c. identity diffusion.
    b. negative identity.   d. identity moratorium.

12. When adolescents' political, religious, educational, and vocational opinions are compared with their parents', the so-called generation gap is:
    a. much smaller than when the younger and older generations are compared overall.
    b. much wider than when the younger and older generations are compared overall.
    c. wider between parents and sons than between parents and daughters.
    d. wider between parents and daughters than between parents and sons.

13. Which of the following is *not* true regarding the rate of clinical depression among adolescents?
    a. At puberty the rate more than doubles.
    b. It affects a higher proportion of teenage boys than girls.
    c. Genetic vulnerability is a predictor of teenage depression.
    d. The adolescent's school setting is a factor.

14. Parent–teen conflict tends to center on issues related to:
    a. politics and religion.
    b. education.
    c. vacations.
    d. daily details, such as musical tastes.

15. According to a review of studies from various nations, suicidal ideation is:
    a. not as common among high school students as is popularly believed.
    b. more common among males than females.
    c. more common among females than among males.
    d. so common among high school students that it might be considered normal.

Matching Items

Match each term or concept with its corresponding description or definition.

Terms or Concepts

_____ **1.** identity
_____ **2.** identity achievement
_____ **3.** foreclosure
_____ **4.** negative identity
_____ **5.** identity diffusion
_____ **6.** identity moratorium
_____ **7.** generation gap
_____ **8.** generational stake
_____ **9.** parental monitoring
_____ **10.** parasuicide
_____ **11.** cluster suicide

Descriptions or Definitions

a. premature identity formation
b. a group of suicides that occur in the same community, school, or time period
c. the adolescent has few commitments to goals or values
d. differences between the younger and older generations
e. self-destructive act that does not result in death
f. awareness of where children are and what they are doing
g. an individual's self-definition
h. a time-out period during which adolescents experiment with alternative identities
i. the adolescent establishes his or her own goals and values
j. family members in different developmental stages see the family in different ways
k. an identity opposite of the one an adolescent is expected to adopt

Thinking Critically About Chapter 16

Answer these questions the day before an exam as a final check on your understanding of the chapter's terms and concepts.

1. From childhood, Sharon thought she wanted to follow in her mother's footsteps and be a homemaker. Now, at age 40 with a home and family, she admits to herself that what she really wanted to be was a medical researcher. Erik Erikson would probably say that Sharon:
   a. adopted a negative identity when she was a child.
   b. experienced identity foreclosure at an early age.
   c. never progressed beyond the obvious identity diffusion she experienced as a child.
   d. took a moratorium from identity formation.

2. Fifteen-year-old David is rebelling against his devoutly religious parents by taking drugs, stealing, and engaging in other antisocial behaviors. Evidently, David has:
   a. foreclosed on his identity.
   b. declared an identity moratorium.
   c. adopted a negative identity.
   d. experienced identity diffusion.

3. Summarizing her presentation on suicide, Britney notes that worldwide:
   a. parasuicide is higher for females but completed suicide is higher for males.
   b. Parasuicide is higher for males but completed suicide is higher for females.
   c. Parasuicide and completed suicide are equally prevalent in females and males.
   d. The prevalence of parasuicide and completed suicide varies too greatly from country to country to generalize.

4. In 1957, 6-year-old Raisel and her parents emigrated from Mexico to the United States. Because her parents hold to the values and customs of their native land, Raisel is likely to have:
   a. an easier time achieving her own unique identity.
   b. a more difficult time forging her identity.
   c. a greater span of time in which to forge her own identity.
   d. a shorter span of time in which to forge her identity.

5. An adolescent exaggerates the importance of differences in her values and those of her parents. Her parents see these differences as smaller and less important. This phenomenon is called the:
   a. generation gap.
   b. generational stake.
   c. family enigma.
   d. parental imperative.

6. In our society, the most obvious examples of institutionalized moratoria on identity formation are:
   a. the Boy Scouts and the Girl Scouts.
   b. college and the military.
   c. marriage and divorce.
   d. bar mitzvahs and baptisms.

7. First-time parents Norma and Norman are worried that, during adolescence, their healthy parental influence will be undone as their children are encouraged by peers to become sexually promiscuous, drug-addicted, or delinquent. Their wise neighbor, who is a developmental psychologist, tells them that:
   a. during adolescence, peers are generally more likely to complement the influence of parents than they are to pull their friends in the opposite direction.
   b. research suggests that peers provide a negative influence in every major task of adolescence.
   c. only through authoritarian parenting can parents give children the skills they need to resist peer pressure.
   d. unless their children show early signs of learning difficulties or antisocial behavior, parental monitoring is unnecessary.

8. Which of the following statements would a 13-year-old girl be most likely to make?
   a. "Boys are a sort of disease."
   b. "Boys are stupid although important to us."
   c. "Boys hate you if you're ugly and brainy."
   d. "Boys are a pleasant change from girls."

9. Who of the following is most likely to manifest an internalizing problem?
   a. Joe, who is 10 years old and hates school
   b. Karen, who is 8 and lives with her grandparents
   c. Christina, who is 15 and has a history of emotional problems
   d. Gary, who is 16 and is part of a very angry peer group

10. Rosaria is an adolescent in an immigrant family. In response to the conflict between the peer-group emphasis on adolescent freedom and the values of her family's culture, Rosaria is most likely to:
    a. rebel against her family, possibly leaving home.
    b. join a delinquent group.
    c. give in to parental control.
    d. ask to live with her grandparents.

11. Statistically, the person least likely to commit a crime is a(n):
    a. African-American or Hispanic adolescent.
    b. middle-class white male.
    c. white adolescent of any socioeconomic background.
    d. Asian-American.

12. Ray was among the first of his friends to have sex, drink alcohol, and smoke cigarettes. These attributes, together with his having been hyperactive and having poor emotional control, would suggest that Ray is at high risk of:
    a. becoming an adolescent-limited offender.
    b. becoming a life-course-persistent offender.
    c. developing an antisocial personality.
    d. foreclosing his identity prematurely.

13. Carl is a typical 16-year-old adolescent who has no special problems. It is likely that Carl has:
    a. contemplated suicide.
    b. engaged in some minor illegal act.
    c. struggled with "who he is."
    d. done all of the above.

14. Statistically, who of the following is most likely to commit suicide?
    a. Micah, an African-American female
    b. Yan, an Asian-American male
    c. James, a American Indian male
    d. Alison, a European-American female

15. Coming home from work, Malcolm hears a radio announcement warning parents to be alert for possible cluster suicide signs in their teenage children. What might have precipitated such an announcement?
    a. government statistics that suicide is on the rise in the 1990s
    b. the highly publicized suicide of a teen from a school in his town
    c. the recent crash of an airliner, killing all on board
    d. any of the above

Key Terms

Using your own words, write a brief definition or explanation of each of the following terms on a separate piece of paper.

1. identity
2. possible selves
3. false self
4. identity versus role confusion
5. identity achievement
6. foreclosure
7. negative identity
8. identity diffusion
9. identity moratorium
10. gender identity
11. internalizing problems
12. externalizing problems
13. suicidal ideation
14. parasuicide
15. cluster suicide
16. incidence
17. prevalence
18. adolescent-limited offender
19. life-course-persistent offender
20. generation gap
21. generational stake
22. bickering
23. parental monitoring
24. peer pressure

ANSWERS
CHAPTER REVIEW

1. identity; possible selves
2. false self; acceptable false self; pleasing false self; experimental false self
3. identity versus role confusion
4. identity achievement
5. foreclosure
6. negative identity
7. identity diffusion
8. moratorium; college
9. James Marcia; processes; statuses
10. can; within; without; social
11. gender identity; roles; behaviors

12. ethnic; cultures
13. more; negative; foreclose; different from that of others; 40
14. internalizing; depression, eating disorders, self-mutilation, overuse of sedative drugs, clinical depression, and suicide; externalizing; injuring others, destroying property, and defying authority; increase suddenly
15. less
16. increases; females
17. suicidal ideation; common
18. less
19. do not; parasuicide
20. a. the availability of lethal methods
    b. the extent of parental supervision
    c. the use of alcohol and other drugs
    d. gender
    e. the attitudes about suicide held by the adolescent's culture
21. males; females
22. are
23. cluster suicides

American Indian and Alaskan Native males have the highest rates, followed by European-American males, Hispanic-American and African-American males, American Indian females, Asian-American males, and so on.

24. psychoanalytic; boys
25. second decade; incidence; prevalent
26. greater

Adolescent males are three times as likely to be arrested as females, and African-American youth are three times as likely to be arrested as European-Americans, who are three times as likely to be arrested as Asian-Americans. However, confidential self-reports find much smaller gender and ethnic differences.

27. teenagers
28. adolescent-limited; life-course-persistent
29. is
30. have sex and use gateway drugs; school; antisocial; brain damage; language; hyperactive; emotional
31. is not
32. generation gap; place
33. generational stake
34. early; mothers; early; daughters; bickering
35. late; dependency; closeness

36. communication; support; connectedness; control

37. parental monitoring; depression; psychological control

38. peer pressure; rises; 14; fall

39. increasing

The progression begins with groups of same-sex friends. Next, a loose, public association of a girl's group and a boy's group forms. Then, a smaller, heterosexual group forms from the more advanced members of the larger association. Finally, more intimate heterosexual couples peel off.

40. affect; timing; manifestation; sequence; biological

41. slow down; homophobic; deny; change; conceal

42. underestimate

43. happy

44. often have

45. genetic vulnerability, prenatal injury, family disruptions and discord, learning difficulties, lack of emotional regulation in elementary school, inadequate community intervention

PROGRESS TEST 1

Multiple-Choice Questions

1. **b.** is the answer. (p. 385)

   a. According to Erikson, this is the crisis of infancy.

   c. & d. In Erikson's theory, these crises occur later in life.

2. **a.** is the answer. (p. 387)

   b. This describes an identity moratorium.

   c. This describes a negative identity.

   d. This describes identity diffusion.

3. **c.** is the answer. (p. 388)

4. **d.** is the answer. (p. 401)

5. **d.** is the answer. (p. 390)

6. **d.** is the answer. (p. 399)

   a. The generational stake refers to differences in how family members from different generations view the family.

   b. Foreclosure refers to the premature establishment of identity.

   c. Peer screening is an aspect of parental monitoring, but it was not specifically discussed in the text.

7. **a.** is the answer. (p. 398)

8. **c.** is the answer. (pp. 397–398)

9. **d.** is the answer. (p. 389)

10. **c.** is the answer. (p. 386)

    a. & b. Teenagers who try out these false selves tend to feel either worthless and depressed (acceptable false self) or experience the psychological consequences of living an identity just to impress or please others (pleasing false self).

11. **b.** is the answer. Incidence is how often a particular circumstance (such as lawbreaking) occurs; prevalence is how widespread the circumstance is. A crime that is committed by only a few repeat offenders is not very prevalent in the population. (p. 395)

12. **b.** is the answer. Foreclosed members of a religious group have, like Adam, never really doubted. (pp. 388–389)

    a. Because there is no evidence that Adam has asked the "hard questions" regarding his religious beliefs, a developmentalist would probably say that his religious identity is not achieved.

    c. Adam clearly does have a religious identity.

    d. There is no evidence that Adam's religious identity was formed in opposition to expectations.

13. **c.** is the answer. Most life-course-persistent offenders are among the earliest of their cohort to have sex. (p. 396)

14. **b.** is the answer. (p. 394)

15. **c.** is the answer. (p. 398)

    a. In fact, parent–child conflict is more likely to involve mothers and their early-maturing offspring.

    b. The text did not compare the rate of conflict in two-parent and single-parent homes.

True or False Items

1. T (p. 389)

2. F   Parent–teen conflicts center on day-to-day details, not on politics or moral issues. (p. 398)

3. F   Just the opposite is true. (p. 401)

4. T (p. 403)

5. T (p. 395)

6. F   Most self-destructive acts stem from many earlier developmental events. (p. 406)

7. T (p. 396)

8. T (p. 388)

9. F   Just the opposite is true. (p. 391)

10. T (p. 394)

PROGRESS TEST 2

Multiple-Choice Questions

1. **d.** is the answer. (p. 387, Figure 16.1)

2. **c.** is the answer. (p. 386)

3. **a.** is the answer. For this reason, autonomy in their offspring tends to be delayed. (p. 398)

4. **c.** is the answer. (p. 395)

   a. This answer would have been correct if the question had stated, "If the majority of cases of a crime are committed by a small number of repeat offenders."

   b. Because it is simply the total number of cases of an event or circumstance (such as a crime), incidence cannot be less than prevalence.

5. **c.** is the answer. (p. 393)

6. **d.** is the answer. In fact, lesbian adolescents find it easier to establish strong friendships with same-sex heterosexual peers than homosexual teenage boys do. (pp. 404–405)

7. **a.** is the answer. (p. 388)

   b. This describes an adolescent undergoing an identity moratorium.

   c. This describes identity foreclosure.

   d. This describes an adolescent who is adopting a negative identity.

8. **d.** is the answer. (pp. 391–392)

9. **b.** is the answer. (p. 396)

10. **c.** is the answer. (p. 396)

11. **d.** is the answer. (p. 388)

    a. Identity foreclosure occurs when the adolescent prematurely adopts an identity, without fully exploring alternatives.

    b. Adolescents who adopt an identity that is opposite to the one they are expected to develop have taken on a negative identity.

    c. Identity diffusion occurs when the adolescent is apathetic and has few commitments to goals or values.

12. **a.** is the answer. (p. 397)

    c. & d. The text does not suggest that the size of the generation gap varies with the offspring's sex.

13. **b.** is the answer. (p. 392)

14. **d.** is the answer. (p. 398)

    a., b., & c. In fact, on these issues parents and teenagers tend to show substantial *agreement*.

15. **d.** is the answer. (p. 393)

Matching Items

1. g (p. 385)
2. i (p. 387)
3. a (p. 387)
4. k (p. 388)
5. c (p. 388)
6. h (p. 388)
7. d (p. 397)
8. j (p. 398)
9. f (p. 399)
10. e (p. 393)
11. b (p. 395)

THINKING CRITICALLY ABOUT CHAPTER 16

1. **b.** is the answer. Apparently, Sharon never explored alternatives or truly forged a unique personal identity. (p. 387)

   a. Individuals who rebel by adopting an identity that is the opposite of the one they are expected to adopt have taken on a negative identity.

   c. Individuals who experience identity diffusion have few commitments to goals or values. This was not Sharon's problem.

   d. Had she taken a moratorium on identity formation, Sharon would have experimented with alternative identities and perhaps would have chosen that of a medical researcher.

2. **c.** is the answer. (p. 388)

3. **a.** is the answer. (p. 394)

4. **b.** is the answer. Ethnic adolescents struggle with finding the right balance between transcending their background and becoming immersed in it. (p. 390)

   c. & d. The text does not suggest that the amount of time adolescents have to forge their identities varies from one ethnic group to another or has changed over historical time.

5. **b.** is the answer. (p. 398)

   a. The generation gap refers to actual differences in attitudes and values between the younger and older generations. This example is concerned with how large these differences are perceived to be.

   c. & d. These terms are not used in the text in discussing family conflict.

6. **b.** is the answer. (p. 388)

7. **a.** is the answer. (p. 401)

   b. In fact, just the opposite is true.

   c. Developmentalists recommend authoritative, rather than authoritarian, parenting.

   d. Parental monitoring is important for all adolescents.

8. **b.** is the answer. (p. 403)

9. **c.** is the answer. (p. 391)

   a., b., & d. Both internalizing and externalizing problems increase markedly at adolescence (not

a. or b.), and externalizing problems are more common among boys (not a. or d.).

10. **c.** is the answer. Adolescent girls in immigrant families are most likely to live docilely at home until an early marriage. (p. 402)

   a. & b. Boys are most likely to do these things.

   d. This may be the parents' response to problems with their children.

11. **d.** is the answer. (p. 396)

12. **b.** is the answer. (p. 396)

13. **d.** is the answer. (pp. 385, 393, 396)

14. **c.** is the answer. (p. 394)

15. **b.** is the answer. (p. 395)

   a., c., & d. Cluster suicides occur when the suicide of a local teen leads others to attempt suicide.

KEY TERMS

1. **Identity,** as used by Erikson, refers to a person's self-definition as a unique individual in terms of roles, attitudes, beliefs, and aspirations. (p. 385).

2. Many adolescents try out **possible selves,** or variations on who they are, who they might like to become, and who they fear becoming. (pp. 385–386)

3. Some adolescents display a **false self,** acting in ways that are contrary to who they really are in order to be accepted (the acceptable false self), to impress or please others (the pleasing false self), or "just to see how it feels" (the experimental false self). (p. 386)

4. Erikson's term for the psychosocial crisis of adolescence, **identity versus role confusion,** refers to adolescents' need to combine their self-understanding and social roles into a coherent identity. (p. 387)

5. In Erikson's theory, **identity achievement** occurs when adolescents attain their new identity by establishing their own goals and values and abandoning some of those set by their parents and culture and accepting others. (p. 387)

6. In **foreclosure,** according to Erikson, the adolescent forms an identity prematurely, accepting parents' or society's roles and values wholesale, without truly forging a unique personal identity. (p. 387)

7. Adolescents who take on a **negative identity,** according to Erikson, adopt an identity that is the opposite of the one they are expected to adopt. (p. 388)

8. Adolescents who experience **identity diffusion,** according to Erikson, have few commitments to goals or values and are often apathetic about trying to find an identity. (p. 388)

9. According to Erikson, in the process of finding a mature identity, many young people seem to declare an **identity moratorium,** a kind of time-out during which they experiment with alternative identities without trying to settle on any one. (p. 388)

10. **Gender identity** is a person's self-identification of being female or male, including the roles and behaviors that society assigns to that sex. (p. 389)

11. **Internalizing problems** are emotional problems that are manifested inward, when troubled individuals inflict harm on themselves, for example, through eating disorders, self-mutilation, and drug abuse. (p. 391)

12. **Externalizing problems** are emotional problems that are manifested outward, when people "act out," injuring others, destroying property, and defying authority. (p. 391)

13. **Suicidal ideation** refers to thinking about committing suicide, usually with some serious emotional and intellectual or cognitive overtones. (p. 393)

14. **Parasuicide** is a deliberate act of self-destruction that does not result in death. (p. 393)

15. A **cluster suicide** refers to a series of suicides or suicide attempts that are precipitated by one initial suicide and that occur in the same community, school, or time period. (p. 395)

16. **Incidence** is how often a particular circumstance (such as lawbreaking) occurs. (p. 395)

17. **Prevalence** is how widespread within a population a particular behavior or circumstance is. (p. 395)

18. **Adolescent-limited offenders** are juvenile delinquents whose criminal activity stops by age 21. (p. 396)

19. **Life-course-persistent offenders** are adolescent lawbreakers who later become career criminals. (p. 396)

20. The **generation gap** refers to the alleged distance between generations in values, behaviors, and knowledge. (p. 397)

21. The **generational stake** refers to the need of each family member, because of that person's different developmental stage, to see family interactions in a certain way. (p. 398)

22. **Bickering** refers to the repeated, petty arguing that typically occurs in early adolescence about common, daily life activities. (p. 398)

23. **Parental monitoring** is parental watchfulness about where one's child is, what he or she is doing, and with whom. (p. 399)

24. **Peer pressure** refers to the social pressure to conform with one's friends in behavior, dress, and attitude. It may be positive or negative in its effects. (p. 401)

Chapter Seventeen

Early Adulthood: Biosocial Development

Chapter Overview

In this chapter we encounter the developing person in the prime of life. Early adulthood is the best time for hard physical labor—because strength is at a peak—and for reproduction—because overall health is good and fertility is high. However, with the attainment of full maturity, a new aspect of physical development comes into play—that is, decline. Chapter 17 takes a look at how people perceive changes that occur as the body ages as well as how decisions they make regarding lifestyle affect the course of their overall development.

The chapter begins with a description of the growth, strength, and health of the individual during adulthood, as well as both visible age-related changes, such as wrinkling, and less obvious changes, such as declines in the efficiency of the body's systems. Sexual-reproductive health, a matter of great concern to young adults, is also discussed, with particular attention paid to trends in sexual responsiveness during adulthood and fertility problems that may develop. The second section looks at several emotional problems that are more prevalent during young adulthood than at any other period of the life span: destructive dieting, eating disorders, drug abuse and addiction, psychopathology, and violence.

NOTE: Answer guidelines for all Chapter 17 questions begin on page 256.

Guided Study

The text chapter should be studied one section at a time. Before you read, preview each section by skimming it, noting headings and boldface items. Then read the appropriate section objectives from the following outline. Keep these objectives in mind and, as you read the chapter section, search for the information that will enable you to meet each objective. Once you have finished a section, write out answers for its objectives.

Growth, Strength, and Health (pp. 413–422)

1. Describe the changes in growth, strength, and overall health that occur during early adulthood.

2. Describe age-related changes in physical appearance that become noticeable by the late 20s.

3. Describe gender differences in senescence and possible reasons for their existence.

4. Discuss changes in the efficiency of various body functions, focusing on the significance of these changes for the individual.

5. Identify age-related trends in the sexual responsiveness of both men and women during the decades from 20 to 40.

6. Describe the main causes of infertility in men and women, and list several techniques used to treat this problem, noting some of the issues raised by the techniques.

Emotional Problems in Early Adulthood?
(pp. 423–432)

7. Identify the potentially harmful effects of repeated dieting.

8. Describe the typical victims of anorexia nervosa and bulimia nervosa, and discuss possible explanations for these disorders.

9. Discuss the causes and consequences of drug abuse during early adulthood.

10. Discuss the nature and causes of major depression and schizophrenia.

11. Discuss gender differences in violence.

Chapter Review

When you have finished reading the chapter, work through the material that follows to review it. Complete the sentences and answer the questions. As you proceed, evaluate your performance for each section by consulting the answers beginning on page 256. Do not continue with the next section until you understand each answer. If you need to, review or reread the appropriate section in the textbook before continuing.

1. The beginning of young adulthood is the best time for _____

_____

_____

(three categories) .

Growth, Strength, and Health (pp. 413–422)

2. Girls usually reach their maximum height by age
_____ , and boys by age
_____ .

3. Growth in _____ and increases in
_____ continue into the 20s.

4. Physical strength reaches a peak at about age
_____ and then decreases.

5. Medical attention in early adulthood is more
often necessitated by _____
than by illness.

6. Of the fatal diseases, _____ is the
leading killer of adults under age 75, with fewer
than 1 in 10,000 being adults between
_____ and _____
years of age. However, young adulthood is the
most dangerous time for _____
death.

7. When overall growth stops, _____ ,
or age-related gradual physical decline, begins.
The rate of this decline is influenced by
_____ , the _____ ,
and _____ _____ .

8. The earliest signs of aging include wrinkles,
caused by loss of _____ in facial
skin, and the first _____
_____ , caused by a loss of pigment-
producing cells in the head.

9. Lung efficiency, as measured by
_____ _____ ,
decreases about _____ percent per
decade beginning in the 20s.

10. The kidneys begin to lose their efficiency at about
age _____ , declining about
_____ percent per decade.

11. Notable decline occurs in the ability of the eye's
_____ to focus on
_____ (near/far) objects. At about
age _____ this decline reaches the
point where it is labeled _____ , and
reading glasses are needed. Age-related hearing

loss, or _____ , generally becomes
apparent at about age _____ .

12. Aging occurs more quickly among people who
are _____ , low _____
_____ , and from
_____ _____ .

13. Females generally _____ (are
healthier/are not healthier) than men. Compared
to men, females have better _____ in
early adulthood, fewer _____
_____ in middle age, and live on
average _____ years (how many?)
longer than men.

14. Two ways in which females are at a health disadvantage compared to males are
_____ and _____-
_____ problems.

15. The imbalance in elderly women and men is due
to the fact that more _____
(younger/older) _____
(males/females) die.

16. Three types of explanations have been proposed
for why there is an imbalance of elderly women
and elderly men. One _____ explanation is based on the evolutionary need for
females to _____ . Another,
_____ explanation suggests that the
difference is due to the fact that men take more
_____ than women. A third,
_____ explanation, suggests that
women are more likely to engage in
_____ , _____ ,
_____ , and _____
activities—all of which are protective of health

17. Many of the body's functions serve to maintain
_____ ; that is, they keep physiological functioning in a state of balance. Many of
these mechanisms are regulated by the
_____ , which is often referred to as
the brain's _____ gland.

18. For body weight, there is a homeostatic _____ _____ that is affected by _____ , _____ , _____ , _____ , and _____ . The older a person is, the _____ (less time/longer) it takes for these adjustments to occur. This makes it more difficult for older bodies to adapt to, and recover from _____ .

19. For most of us, our bodies, if adequately maintained, are capable of functioning quite well until we are at least age _____ . The declines of aging primarily affect our _____ , which is defined as _____ .

20. The muscles of the body _____ (do/do not) have the equivalent of an organ reserve.

21. The average maximum heart rate _____ (declines/remains stable/increases) with age. Resting heart rate _____ (declines/remains stable/increases) with age.

Briefly explain why most of the age-related biological changes that occur during the first decades of adulthood are of little consequence to the individual.

22. Age-related biological changes are particularly noticeable in professional _____ and serious weekend players.

23. Performance in sports that demand vigorous _____ motor skills peaks _____ (earlier/later) than those that demand _____ motor skills. An important factor in the impact of aging on athletic performance, however, is the individual's _____ .

24. Male and female bodies _____ (do/do not) follow a similar sequence of sexual activation at every age.

25. The sequence of sexual activation begins with _____ , followed by _____ _____ , release through _____ , followed by _____ and _____ .

26. During the early years of manhood, sexual excitement, which includes _____ _____ and _____ _____ , can occur very quickly and frequently. As men grow older, they often need stimulation that is more _____ or _____ to initiate sexual excitement.

27. Age-related trends in sexual responsiveness _____ (are/are not) as clear-cut for women. As they mature from adolescence toward middle adulthood, women become more likely to experience _____ .

State four possible reasons for this age-related trend in women.

28. In the United States in 2000, 85 percent of newborns had a mother younger than _____ and a father younger than _____ .

29. Between _____ and _____ percent of all married couples experience infertility, which is defined as _____ _____ .

30. The most common fertility problems in men lie in abnormalities in the _____ , _____ , or _____ of sperm.

List several factors that can alter normal sperm development.

31. The most common fertility problem in women is difficulty with _____ . This may result from anything that impairs a woman's normal bodily functioning, including being _____ or _____ .

32. Most women find that ovulation becomes _____ (more/less) regular as middle age approaches. Older women take _____ (longer/less time) to conceive, and they are more likely to give birth to _____ when they do.

33. The other common fertility problem for women is blocked _____ _____ , often caused by _____ _____ _____ that was not treated promptly.

34. Most physicians recommend that women begin their childbearing before age _____ and would-be fathers before age _____ .

35. Many infertility problems can also be overcome by modern medical techniques, such as _____ to open blocked genital ducts or fallopian tubes, or the use of _____ to stimulate ovulation. Another possibility is _____ _____ _____ , in which ova are fertilized outside the ovaries. This technique is successful about _____ percent of the time. Techniques such as this are called _____ _____ _____ , and are generally most effective with couples under age _____ .

Emotional Problems in Early Adulthood (pp. 423–432)

36. Although young adults are generally healthy, they are more likely than older adults to use _____ and to suffer from _____ . Two problems that are more common in females are _____ and _____ . A problem that is more common among young adult males is _____ .

37. To measure whether a person is too fat or too thin, clinicians calculate his or her _____ _____ , defined as the ratio of _____ (in kilograms) divided by _____ (in meters squared).

38. The subset of the population that is most likely to connect self-concept to body image is women of _____ ancestry.

39. One survey of North American dieters reported that the average woman during early adulthood would like to weigh _____ pounds less, and the average man about _____ pounds more.

40. Dieting may also trigger physiological changes that lead to an eating disorder such as _____ _____ , an affliction characterized by _____ .

41. Anorexia nervosa is diagnosed on the basis of four symptoms:

    a. _____

    b. _____

    c. _____

    d. _____

42. Anorexia is a disease of the _____ context that was rare before _____ .

43. The other major eating disorder is _____ _____ , which is _____ (more/less) common disorder and involves successive bouts of binge eating followed by purging through vomiting or massive doses of laxatives.

44. Binge-purge eating can cause a wide range of health problems, including damage to the _____ _____ and _____ _____ from the strain of electrolyte imbalance. A group that is at particular risk for eating disorders is _____ _____ .

Briefly summarize how each of the major theories of development views eating disorders.

Psychoanalytic theory

Behaviorism

Cognitive theory

Sociocultural theory

Epigenetic theory

45. Drug abuse is defined as using a drug in a manner that is _____ .

46. When the absence of a drug in a person's system causes physiological or psychological craving, _____ is apparent.

47. Women use drugs _____ (less often than/as often as/more often than) men do. Internationally, _____-_____ countries have the highest rates of drug use.

48. State four reasons for the high rate of drug use and abuse in the first years of adulthood.

   a. _____
   b. _____
   c. _____
   d. _____

49. Drug use generally _____ (increases/ decreases) during young adulthood, in part due to _____ norms. Other factors that discourage drug use are _____ .

50. Compared to others their age, young adult drug users are more likely to _____ _____ .

51. Major depression is more common among _____ (women/men). People who have more activity in the _____ _____ cortex of the brain, or in the emotional hotspot of the _____ , are more vulnerable to depression.

52. Three neurotransmitters that are involved in depression are _____ , _____ , and _____ .

53. The disorder characterized by bizarre thoughts, delusions, and hallucinations is _____ , which is usually caused by _____ .

54. Worldwide, young men are far more likely than women to die a _____ _____ . One reason for this difference may be the fact that higher levels of the hormone _____ correlate with angry reactions to events. Another reason has to do with the way in in which males are _____ .

55. Some experts believe that aggression is the result of an "explosive combination" of high _____ and dashed

_____ . A blow to the individual's _____ is more likely to result in violence when the individual is under the influence of _____ ; when there is a _____ present; and when the individual lacks _____ .

Progress Test 1

Multiple-Choice Questions

Circle your answers to the following questions and check them with the answers on page 257. If your answer is incorrect, read the explanation for why it is incorrect and then consult the appropriate pages of the text (in parentheses following the correct answer).

1. Senescence refers to:
   a. a loss of efficiency in the body's regulatory systems.
   b. age-related gradual physical decline.
   c. decreased physical strength.
   d. vulnerability to disease.

2. When do noticeable increases in height stop?
   a. at about the same age in men and women
   b. at an earlier age in women than in men
   c. at an earlier age in men than in women
   d. There is such diversity in physiological development that it is impossible to generalize regarding this issue.

3. A difference between men and women during early adulthood is that men have:
   a. a higher percentage of body fat.
   b. lower metabolism.
   c. proportionately more muscle.
   d. greater organ reserve.

4. The majority of young adults rate their own health as:
   a. very good or excellent.
   b. average or fair.
   c. poor.
   d. worse than it was during adolescence.

5. The automatic adjustment of the body's systems to keep physiological functions in a state of equilibrium, even during heavy exertion, is called:
   a. organ reserve.   c. stress.
   b. homeostasis.   d. muscle capacity.

6. Which of the following temperamental characteristics was *not* identified as being typical of drug abusers?
   a. attraction to excitement
   b. intolerance of frustration
   c. extroversion
   d. vulnerability to depression

7. As men grow older:
   a. they often need more direct stimulation to initiate sexual excitement.
   b. a longer time elapses between the beginning of sexual excitement and full erection.
   c. a longer time elapses between orgasm and the end of the refractory period.
   d. all of the above occur.

8. It is estimated that infertility affects:
   a. at least half of all married couples in which the woman is in her early 30s.
   b. men more than women.
   c. about one-third of all married couples.
   d. about 15 percent of all married couples.

9. The decrease in physical strength that occurs during the decade of the 30s:
   a. occurs more rapidly in the arm and upper torso than in the legs.
   b. occurs more rapidly in the back and leg muscles than in the arm.
   c. occurs at the same rate throughout the body.
   d. varies from individual to individual.

10. Body mass index is calculated as:
    a. height divided by weight.
    b. weight divided by height squared.
    c. the percentage of total weight that is fat.
    d. the percentage of total weight that is muscle.

11. In vitro fertilization is a solution for infertility that is caused by:
    a. sperm motility problems.
    b. low sperm count.
    c. low sperm count or ovulatory problems.
    d. PID.

12. A 50-year-old woman can expect to retain what percentage of her strength at age 20?
    a. 25   c. 75
    b. 50   d. 90

13. According to epigenetic theory, eating disorders such as anorexia nervosa are more common in young women who are genetically susceptible to:

    a. depression.   **c.** obesity.

    b. alcohol abuse.   **d.** suicide.

14. Major depression is likely to be diagnosed when individual displays:

    a. a loss of interest or pleasure in activities lasting two weeks or more.

    b. social withdrawal accompanied by self-destructive behaviors.

    c. disorganized emotions and thoughts.

    d. delusions.

15. Which of the following was *not* suggested as a reason for the high rate of drug use and abuse in the first years of adulthood?

    a. Young adults often have friends who use drugs.

    b. Young adults are trying to imitate their parents' behavior.

    c. Young adults may use drugs as a way of relieving job or educational stress.

    d. Young adults often fear social rejection.

True or False Items

Write T (*true*) or F (*false*) on the line in front of each statement.

_____ **1.** Conditioned older athletes can perform much better than unconditioned younger persons.

_____ **2.** Few adults actually use all the muscle capacity that they could develop during young adulthood.

_____ **3.** The older a person is, the longer it takes for his or her blood glucose level to return to normal after heavy exertion.

_____ **4.** Age-related trends in sexual responsiveness are similar for men and women.

_____ **5.** African-Americans use drugs more often during early adulthood than do whites or Hispanics.

_____ **6.** Compared with a woman in her 20s, a 40-year-old woman is more likely to have cycles with no ovulation and cycles in which several ova are released.

_____ **7.** Most physicians recommend that women who want to have children begin childbearing by age 35.

_____ **8.** Women of European descent are at particular risk for eating disorders.

_____ **9.** A healthy BMI is somewhere between 19 and 25.

_____ **10.** Heredity is rarely a factor in causing schizophrenia.

Progress Test 2

Progress Test 2 should be completed during a final chapter review. Answer the following questions after you thoroughly understand the correct answers for the Chapter Review and Progress Test 1.

Multiple-Choice Questions

1. The early 20s are the peak years for:

    a. hard physical work.

    b. problem-free reproduction.

    c. athletic performance.

    d. all of the above.

2. Of the fatal diseases, _____ is the leading cause of death in young adults.

    a. heart disease   **c.** diabetes

    b. cancer   **d.** multiple sclerosis

3. The first sign of aging that is likely to be noticed by a man around age 30 is:

    a. reduced organ reserve.

    b. diminishing physical strength.

    c. failure of homeostatic mechanisms during heavy exertion.

    d. graying or thinning of the hair.

4. The efficiency of the lungs:

    a. remains stable throughout the 20s.

    b. begins to decline during the 20s.

    c. begins to decline during the 30s.

    d. declines significantly at about age 30.

5. Normally, the average resting heart rate for both men and women:

    a. declines noticeably during the 30s.

    b. declines much faster than does the average maximum heart rate.

    c. reaches a peak at about age 30.

    d. remains stable until late adulthood.

6. As they mature from adolescence through early adulthood, women become more likely to experience orgasm during love-making in part because:

    a. the woman's responses occur earlier because of increased experience.

    b. with experience, both partners are more likely to focus on aspects of love-making that intensify the woman's sexual responses.

    c. they are less concerned about becoming pregnant.

    d. of all of the above reasons.

7. The most common fertility problem in men lies in:
   a. the low number of their sperm.
   b. the sperm's poor motility.
   c. pelvic inflammatory disease.
   d. both a. and b.

8. PID refers to:
   a. a drug taken to stimulate ovulation.
   b. a sexually transmitted disease.
   c. pelvic inflammatory disease.
   d. fertilization outside the uterus.

9. A technique that involves fertilization of the ovum outside the uterus is referred to as:
   a. varicoceles.
   b. artificial insemination.
   c. in vitro fertilization.
   d. surrogate fertilization.

10. People who are vulnerable to depression have greater activity in which area of the brain?
    a. pituitary gland
    b. right prefrontal cortex
    c. temporal lobe
    d. cerebellum

11. The typical bulimic patient is a:
    a. college-age woman.
    b. woman who starves herself to the point of emaciation.
    c. woman in her late 40s.
    d. woman who suffers from life-threatening obesity.

12. Which of the following was *not* identified as a cause of schizophrenia?
    a. genes
    b. severe early trauma
    c. anoxia at birth
    d. low birthweight

13. Relative to all other age groups, young adult males are at increased risk for virtually every kind of:
    a. eating disorder.
    b. violence.
    c. acute disease.
    d. chronic disease.

14. Drug abuse, except when it involves cigarette smoking, often eases:
    a. during adolescence.
    b. in the early 20s.
    c. before age 30.
    d. during late adulthood.

15. Researchers have found that athletic performance peaks earliest in sports that require:
    a. fine motor skills.
    b. vigorous gross motor skills.
    c. greater flexibility than physical strength.
    d. extensive conditioning before peak performance is achieved.

Matching Items

Match each definition or description with its corresponding term.

Terms

_____ **1.** senescence
_____ **2.** homeostasis
_____ **3.** organ reserve
_____ **4.** infertility
_____ **5.** motility
_____ **6.** pelvic inflammatory disease (PID)
_____ **7.** body mass index
_____ **8.** in vitro fertilization (IVF)
_____ **9.** anorexia nervosa
_____ **10.** bulimia nervosa

Definitions or Descriptions

a. fertilization of ova outside the body
b. a condition characterizing about 15 percent of all married couples
c. often caused by sexually transmitted diseases
d. extra capacity for responding to stressful events
e. a state of physiological equilibrium
f. an affliction characterized by binge-purge eating
g. age-related decline
h. the ratio of a person's weight divided by his or her height
i. an affliction characterized by self-starvation
j. with age, declines in male sperm

Thinking Critically About Chapter 17

Answer these questions the day before an exam as a final check on your understanding of the chapter's terms and concepts.

1. Your instructor asks you to summarize, in one sentence, the extent and cause of biosocial decline during early adulthood. You wisely respond:

   a. "Any difficulties experienced by young adults in biosocial development are usually related to factors other than aging per se."
   b. "Significant declines in all aspects of physical well-being become apparent by the mid 20s."
   c. "With the attainment of full maturity, development is released from the constraints of heredity."
   d. "The first signs of aging are usually not apparent until middle adulthood."

2. When we are hot, we perspire in order to give off body heat. This is an example of the way our body functions maintain:

   a. senescence.   **c.** endometriosis.
   b. homeostasis.   **d.** motility.

3. Due to a decline in organ reserve, 28-year-old Brenda:

   a. has a higher resting heart rate than she did when she was younger.
   b. needs longer to recover from strenuous exercise than she did when she was younger.
   c. has a higher maximum heart rate than her younger sister.
   d. has all of the above.

4. Summarizing the results of cross-sectional research, the lecturer states that "Women's sexual responses are heightened by age." The most likely explanation for the lecturer's statement is that:

   a. in women, sexual sensitivity increases with age.
   b. with age, men's responses slow down, allowing women more time to experience orgasm.
   c. the sample is unrepresentative of the population.
   d. cross-sectional research tends to exaggerate age differences.

5. If Benny is like most men, as he grows older, he will require:

   a. less direct stimulation to become sexually excited.
   b. a shorter refractory period following each orgasm.
   c. a longer time between erection and ejaculation.
   d. all of the above.

6. Corretta and Vernon Castle have been trying to conceive a baby for more than a year. Because they are both in their 40s, their physician suspects that:

   a. Vernon is infertile.
   b. Corretta is infertile.
   c. neither Vernon nor Corretta is infertile.
   d. Vernon and Corretta are equally likely to be infertile.

7. Which of the following has been proposed as an explanation of why older women outnumber older men?

   a. Because of the evolutionary need to reproduce and care for young children, women are protected until their child-bearing years are over.

   b. Because men are taught to be tough, they take more risks and avoid precautions.

   c. Women are more likely to engage in marriage, family life, friendship, and help-seeking.

   d. Each of these has been proposed as an explanation of why older women outnumber older men.

8. Sheila dieted for several weeks until she lost ten pounds. Upon returning to a normal diet, she is horrified to find that she has gained some of the weight back. It is likely that Sheila's weight gain was caused by:

   a. overconsumption of high-fat foods.

   b. too little exercise in her daily routine.

   c. her homeostatic mechanism returning to her natural set point.

   d. a low body set point.

9. Of the following, who is most likely to suffer from anorexia nervosa?

   a. Bill, a 23-year-old professional football player

   b. Florence, a 30-year-old account executive

   c. Lynn, a 20-year-old college student

   d. Carl, a professional dancer

10. Twenty-year-old Gwynn, who is nine pounds heavier than the national average for her height and build, should probably:

    a. go on a crash diet, since every additional pound of fat is hazardous to her health.

    b. gradually reduce her weight to slightly below the national average.

    c. realize that because of her high body set point she will be unable to have children.

    d. not worry, since this is probably a healthy weight for her body.

11. As a psychoanalyst, Dr. Mendoza is most likely to believe that eating disorders are caused by:

    a. the reinforcing effects of fasting, bingeing, and purging.

    b. low self-esteem and depression, which act as a stimulus for destructive patterns of eating.

    c. unresolved conflicts with parents.

    d. the desire of working women to project a strong, self-controlled image.

12. Michael, who is in his mid-20s, is most likely to seek medical attention for:

    a. a common cold.

    b. a sports- or drug-related injury.

    c. a life-threatening chronic illness.

    d. infertility.

13. Dr. Ramirez suspects Jennifer may be suffering from anorexia because her BMI is:

    a. lower than 18.

    b. lower than 25.

    c. higher than 25.

    d. higher than 30.

14. Lucretia, who has a body mass index of 24, has been trying unsuccessfully to lose ten pounds. It is likely that her difficulty is due to the fact that:

    a. she has a glandular disorder.

    b. she suffers from bulimia nervosa.

    c. her natural weight set point is higher than she would like.

    d. her obesity is accompanied by a very low metabolic rate.

15. Nathan has a powerful attraction to excitement, a low tolerance for frustration, and a vulnerability to depression. He also may be vulnerable to:

    a. alcoholism.

    b. cocaine abuse.

    c. most psychoactive drugs.

    d. none of the above.

Key Terms

Using your own words, write a brief definition or explanation of each of the following terms on a separate piece of paper.

1. senescence

2. homeostasis

3. set point

4. organ reserve

5. infertility

6. pelvic inflammatory disease (PID)

7. in vitro fertilization (IVF)

8. assisted reproductive technology (ART))

9. body-mass index (BMI)

10. anorexia nervosa

11. bulimia nervosa

12. drug addiction

ANSWERS

CHAPTER REVIEW

1. hard physical work, problem-free reproduction, peak athletic performance

2. 16; 18

3. muscle; fat

4. 30

5. injuries

6. cancer; 20; 34; violent

7. senescence; genes; environment; personal choices

8. elasticity; gray hairs

9. vital capacity; 5

10. 30; 4

11. lens; near; 60; presbyopia; presbycusis; 60

12. male; socioeconomic status; ethnic minorities

13. are healthier; health habits; fatal diseases; five

14. undernourishment; reproductive-system

15. younger; males

16. biological; reproduce and care for young children; cognitive; risks; psychosocial; marriage; family life; friendship; help-seeking

17. homeostasis; pituitary; master

18. set point; genes; diet; age; hormones; exercise; longer; physical stress

19. 70; organ reserve; the extra capacity that each organ has for responding to unusually stressful events or conditions that demand intense or prolonged effort

20. do

21. declines; remains stable

The declines of aging primarily affect our organ reserve. In the course of normal daily life, adults seldom have to call upon this capacity, so the deficits in organ reserve generally go unnoticed.

22. athletes

23. gross; earlier; fine; lifestyle

24. do

25. arousal; peak excitement; orgasm; refraction; recovery

26. faster heartbeat; penile erection; direct (or explicit); prolonged

27. are not; orgasm

Four reasons are:

  a. The slowing of the man's responses lengthens the sex act, providing the more prolonged stimulation that many women need to reach orgasm.

  b. With experience, both partners may be more likely to recognize and focus on those aspects of love-making that intensify the woman's sexual responses.

  c. The culture may teach women that sex is violent and that they should say no to it. It may take years for women to acknowledge and appreciate their sexuality.

  d. According to the ethological perspective, age-related increases in sexual passions among women are the result of the reduced likelihood of reproduction.

28. 35; 45

29. 2; 30; being unable to conceive a child after a year or more of intercourse without contraception

30. number; shape; motility

Anything that impairs normal body functioning, such as illness with a high fever; medical therapy involving radiation or prescription drugs; exposure to environmental toxins; unusual stress; or drug abuse, alcoholism, or cigarette smoking can affect the number, shape, and motility of the sperm.

31. ovulation; underweight; obese

32. less; longer; twins

33. fallopian tubes; pelvic inflammatory disease (PID)

34. 30; 40

35. surgery; drugs; in vitro fertilization (IVF); 30; assisted reproductive technology (ART); 35

36. drugs; psychopathologies; dieting; eating disorders; violence

37. body mass index (BMI); weight; height

38. European

39. eight; five

40. anorexia nervosa; self-starvation

41. a. refusal to maintain body weight at least 85 percent of normal for age

  b. an intense fear of gaining weight

  c. disturbed body perception

  d. lack of menstruation

42. social; 1950

43. bulimia nervosa; more

44. gastrointestinal system; cardiac arrest; college women

According to psychoanalytic theory, women with eating disorders have a conflict with their mothers, who provided their first nourishment. According to behaviorism, disordered eating may set up a stimulus–response chain in which self-starvation relieves emotional stress and tension. Cognitive theory suggests that as women enter the workplace they try to project a strong, self-controlled, "masculine" image. Sociocultural explanations focus on the contemporary cultural pressures to be model-like in appearance. Epigenetic theory suggests that because self-starvation may cause menstruation to cease and sexual hormones to decrease, girls who are genetically susceptible to depression or addiction may resort to this self-destructive behavior to relieve the pressures to marry and reproduce.

45. harmful to physical, cognitive, or psychosocial well-being

46. drug addiction

47. less often than; English-speaking

48. **a.** For some young adults, drug abuse is a way of striving for independence from parents and helps them escape the life stresses that cluster during the 20s.

    b. Genes that predispose to drug use include attraction to excitement and vulnerability to depression—traits that increase in adolescence and young adulthood.

    c. The group activities of young adults, including large parties, concerts, and sports events, often promote drug use.

    d. Young adults are the group least likely to be regularly exposed to religious faith and practice.

49. decreases; social; medical advice, marriage, and religious involvement

50. avoid, fail, or drop out of college; lose or quit jobs; be employed below their potential; be involved in transitory, uncommitted sexual relationships; die violently; and experience serious psychological difficulties

51. women; right prefrontal; amygdala

52. dopamine; norepinephrine; serotonin

53. schizophrenia; genes

54. violent death; testosterone; socialized

55. self-esteem; expectations; self-concept; alcohol; weapon; self-restraint

PROGRESS TEST 1

Multiple-Choice Questions

1. **b.** is the answer. (p. 414)

    a., c., & d. Each of these is a specific example of the more general process of senescence.

2. **b.** is the answer. (p. 413)

3. **c.** is the answer. (p. 413)

    a. & b. These are true of women.

    d. Men and women do not differ in this characteristic.

4. **a.** is the answer. (p. 414)

5. **b.** is the answer. (p. 417)

    a. This is the extra capacity that each organ of the body has for responding to unusually stressful events or conditions that demand intense or prolonged effort.

    c. Stress, which is not defined in this chapter, refers to events or situations that tax the body's resources.

    d. This simply refers to a muscle's potential for work.

6. **c.** is the answer. (p. 428)

7. **d.** is the answer. (p. 420)

8. **d.** is the answer. (p. 421)

    b. Until middle age, infertility is equally likely in women and men.

9. **b.** is the answer. (p. 413)

10. **b.** is the answer. (p. 423)

11. **c.** is the answer. (p. 422)

12. **d.** is the answer. (p. 418)

13. **a.** is the answer. Depression and low self-esteem often serve as stimulus triggers for fasting, bingeing, and purging, which may temporarily relieve these states of emotional distress. (p. 427)

14. **a.** is the answer. (p. 430)

    c. & d. These are possible symptoms of schizophrenia.

    b. This combination of behaviors is not indicative of any particular form of psychopathology.

15. **b.** is the answer. In fact, just the opposite is true. Young adults may use drugs to express independence from their parents. (p. 428)

True or False Items

1. T (p. 419)

2. T (p. 418)

3. T (p. 418)

4. F Age seems to affect men and women differently with respect to sexual responsiveness—with men becoming less responsive and women, more responsive. (p. 420)

5. F Just the opposite is true. (p. 428)

6. T (p. 421)

7. F Physicians recommend that women begin childbearing by age 30. (p. 421)

8. T (p. 423)

9. T (p. 424)

10. F Genes are a major cause of schizophrenia. (p. 431)

PROGRESS TEST 2

Multiple-Choice Questions

1. **d.** is the answer. (p. 413)

2. **b.** is the answer. (p. 414)

3. **d.** is the answer. (p. 414)

   a., b., & c. These often remain unnoticed until middle age.

4. **b.** is the answer. (p. 414)

5. **d.** is the answer. (p. 419)

6. **b.** is the answer. (p. 420)

7. **d.** is the answer. (p. 421)

   c. This is a common fertility problem in women.

8. **c.** is the answer. (p. 421)

   b. Sexually transmitted diseases can cause PID.

   d. This describes in vitro fertilization.

9. **c.** is the answer. (p. 421)

   a. These are varicose veins in the testes and partially blocked genital ducts.

   b. In this technique, sperm collected from a male donor are artificially inserted into the uterus.

   d. In this technique, fertilization occurs outside the uterus but it involves another woman who carries the fetus.

10. **b.** is the answer. (p. 430)

    a. The pituitary is the master gland of the brain that is involved in regulating growth.

    c. The temporal lobe is involved in hearing and speech.

    d. The cerebellum plays an important role in regulating body position and balance.

11. **a.** is the answer. (p. 426)

    b. This describes a woman suffering from anorexia nervosa.

    c. Eating disorders are much more common in younger women.

    d. Most women with bulimia nervosa are usually close to normal in weight.

12. **d.** is the answer. (p. 431)

13. **b.** is the answer. (p. 431)

    a. Eating disorders are more common in women than men.

    c. & d. Disease is relatively rare at this age.

14. **c.** is the answer. (p. 427)

15. **b.** is the answer. (p. 419)

Matching Items

1. g (p. 414) 5. j (p. 421) 8. a (p. 422)
2. e (p. 417) 6. c (p. 421) 9. i (p. 424)
3. d (p. 418) 7. h (p. 423) 10. f (p. 426)
4. b (p. 421)

THINKING CRITICALLY ABOUT CHAPTER 17

1. **a.** is the answer. (p. 413)

   b. Physical declines during the 20s are usually of little consequence.

   c. This is not true nor does it address the instructor's request.

   d. The first signs of aging become apparent at an earlier age.

2. **b.** is the answer. (p. 417)

   a. This is age-related gradual physical decline.

   c. This is a common fertility problem for women.

   d. This refers to the swimming ability of sperm.

3. **b.** is the answer. (p. 419)

   a. Resting heart rate remains stable throughout adulthood.

   c. Maximum heart rate declines with age.

4. **b.** is the answer. (p. 420)

5. **c.** is the answer. (p. 420)

6. **d.** is the answer. Infertility becomes increasingly common with advancing age. (p. 421)

7. **d.** is the answer. (p. 417)

8. **c.** is the answer. (p. 417)

9. **c.** is the answer. (p. 424)

   a. & d. Eating disorders are more common in women than men.

   b. Eating disorders are more common in younger women.

10. **d.** is the answer. (pp. 423–424)

11. **c.** is the answer. (p. 427)

    a. & b. These explanations would more likely be offered by those who emphasize behaviorism or cognitive theory.

    d. This is a sociocultural explanation of eating disorders.

12. **b.** is the answer. (p. 413)

13. **a.** is the answer. (p. 424)

    b. This is a healthy BMI.

    c., & d. These BMIs are associated with being overweight.

14. **c.** is the answer. (p. 423)

    a. & d. There is no evidence that Lucretia has a glandular disorder or is obese. In fact, a BMI of 24 is well within the normal weight range.

    b. There is no evidence that Lucretia is bingeing and purging.

15. **c.** is the answer. (p. 428)

    a. & b. Although these are also correct, they are both psychoactive drugs, making c. the best answer.

KEY TERMS

1. **Senescence** is age-related gradual physical decline throughout the body. (p. 414)

2. **Homeostasis** refers to the process by which body functions are automatically adjusted to keep our physiological functioning in a state of balance. (p. 417)

3. **Set point** is the specific body weight that a person's homeostatic processes strive to maintain. (p. 417)

4. **Organ reserve** is the extra capacity of each body organ for responding to unusually stressful events or conditions that demand intense or prolonged effort. (p. 418)

5. A couple is said to experience **infertility** if they have been unable to conceive a child after a year or more of intercourse without contraception. (p. 421)

6. **Pelvic inflammatory disease (PID)** is a common fertility problem for women, in which pelvic infections lead to blocked fallopian tubes. (p. 421)

7. **In vitro fertilization (IVF)** is a technique in which ova are surgically removed from the ovaries and fertilized by sperm in the laboratory. (p. 422)

8. **Assisted reproductive technology (ART)** refers to the various medical interventions that can help infertile couples have children. (p. 422)

9. The **body mass index (BMI)** is the ratio of a person's weight in kilograms divided by his or her height in meters squared. (p. 423)

10. **Anorexia nervosa** is an affliction characterized by self-starvation that is most common in high-achieving college-age women. (p. 424)

11. **Bulimia nervosa** is an eating disorder that involves compulsive binge eating followed by purging through vomiting or taking massive doses of laxatives. (p. 426)

12. **Drug addiction** is evident in a person when the absence of a drug in his or her body produces the drive to ingest more of the drug. (p. 427)

Chapter Eighteen

Early Adulthood: Cognitive Development

Chapter Overview

During the course of adulthood, there are many shifts in cognitive development—in the speed and efficiency with which we process information, in the focus and depth of our cognitive processes, perhaps in the quality, or wisdom, of our thinking. Developmental psychologists use three different approaches in explaining these shifts, with each approach providing insights into the nature of adult cognition. This chapter takes a postformal approach, describing age-related changes in an attempt to uncover patterns.

The chapter begins by describing how adult thinking differs from adolescent thinking. The experiences and challenges of adulthood result in a new, postformal thought, evidenced by practical, flexible, and dialectical thinking—the dynamic, in-the-world cognitive style that adults typically use to solve the problems of daily life.

The second section explores how the events of early adulthood can affect moral development. Of particular interest are Fowler's six stages in the development of faith.

The third section examines the effect of the college experience on cognitive growth; findings here indicate that years of education correlate with virtually every measure of cognition as thinking becomes progressively more flexible and tolerant.

NOTE: Answer guidelines for all Chapter 18 questions begin on page 270.

Guided Study

The text chapter should be studied one section at a time. Before you read, preview each section by skimming it, noting headings and boldface items. Then read the appropriate section objectives from the following outline. Keep these objectives in mind and, as you read the chapter section, search for the information that will enable you to meet each objective. Once

you have finished a section, write out answers for its objectives.

1. Describe three approaches to the study of adult cognition.

Postformal Thought (pp. 436–445)

2. Identify the main characteristics of postformal thought, and describe how it differs from formal operational thought.

3. (text and Thinking Like a Scientist) Describe the contexts and effects of stereotype threat, and discuss findings of research studies aimed at reducing stereotype threat.

4. Define dialectical thought, and give examples of its usefulness.

5. Discuss the effects of culture on cognition.

Adult Moral Reasoning (pp. 445–449)

6. Explain Carol Gilligan's view of how moral reasoning changes during adulthood.

7. Explain how the Defining Issues Test helps relate moral development to other aspects of adult cognition and life satisfaction.

8. Briefly describe the six stages of faith outlined by James Fowler.

Cognitive Growth and Higher Education (pp. 449–456)

9. Discuss the relationship between cognitive growth and higher education.

10. Compare college students today with their counterparts of a decade or two ago.

Chapter Review

When you have finished reading the chapter, work through the material that follows to review it. Complete the sentences and answer the questions. As you proceed, evaluate your performance for each section by consulting the answers on page 270. Do not continue with the next section until you understand each answer. If you need to, review or reread the appropriate section in the textbook before continuing.

1. Unlike the relatively "straightforward" cognitive growth of earlier ages, cognitive development during adulthood is _____ and _____ . Developmentalists have used three approaches to explain this development: the _____ approach, the _____ approach, and the _____-_____ approach.

Postformal Thought (pp. 436–445)

2. Compared to adolescent thinking, adult thinking is more _____ , _____ , and _____ .

3. Reasoning that is adapted to the subjective real-life contexts to which it is applied is called _____ _____ . It is

characterized by problem _____ rather than problem _____ .

4. Developmentalists distinguish between _____ thinking, which arises from the _____ experiences and _____ of an individual, and _____ thinking, which follows abstract _____ . The latter kind of thinking is _____ (more/less) adaptive for schoolchildren, adolescents, and young adults than for mature adults.

5. The difference between adolescent and young adult reasoning is particularly apparent for reasoning involving _____ questions.

6. In contrast to adolescent _____- _____ regarding personal experiences, adults are more likely to demonstrate _____ _____ when suggesting solutions to real-life problems.

7. When the mere possibility of being negatively stereotyped arouses emotions that disrupt cognition, _____ _____ has occurred. This is especially common during _____ , when _____ and/or _____ _____ is being developed. Strong identification with a group to which one belongs, even when that group is discriminated against, is healthier than _____ or

_____ .

8. (Thinking Like a Scientist) Stereotype threat can make _____ and _____ doubt their academic ability. As a result they may become _____ in academic contexts and _____ with intellectual achievement.

9. (Thinking Like a Scientist) Adults today _____ (have/do not have) fewer sexist and racial stereotypes than they did in the past. Research studies have shown that intellectual performance among students increases if they _____ the concept that intelligence is plastic and can be changed.

10. Some theorists consider _____ _____ the most advanced form of cognition. This thinking recognizes that every idea, or _____ , implies an opposing idea, or _____ ; these are then forged into a(n) _____ of the two. This type of thinking fosters a worldview that recognizes that most of life's important questions _____ (have/do not have) single, unchangeable, correct answers.

11. Some researchers believe that some _____ encourage flexible, dialectical reasoning more than others. According to this view, ancient _____ philosophy has led Europeans to use _____ _____ , whereas and _____ have led Asians to think more _____ .

12. Although all adults _____ (think/ do not think) in a postformal manner, life experiences _____ (can/cannot) move a person's thinking past the formal operational stage.

Adult Moral Reasoning (pp. 445–449)

13. According to James Rest, one catalyst for propelling young adults from a lower moral stage to a higher one is _____ .

14. Other researchers maintain that in order to be capable of "truly ethical" reasoning, a person must have experienced sustained responsibility for _____ .

15. Carol Gilligan believes that in matters of moral reasoning _____ (males/ females) tend to be more concerned with the question of rights and justice, whereas _____ (males/females) are more concerned with personal relationships. Other moral issues that contemporary adults are likely to confront arise from increasing _____ and _____ . They also arise from television, popular music, and the _____ .

16. The current approach to research on moral reasoning is based on a series of questions about moral reasoning called the _____ _____ _____ . In general, scores on this test increase with _____ and with each year of _____ .

17. The theorist who has outlined six stages in the development of faith is _____ .

18. In the space below, identify and briefly describe each stage in the development of faith.

    Stage One: _____
    _____

    Stage Two: _____
    _____

    Stage Three: _____
    _____

    Stage Four: _____
    _____

    Stage Five: _____
    _____

    Stage Six: _____
    _____

19. Although Fowler's stage theory of faith _____ (is/is not) totally accepted, the idea that religion plays an important role in human development _____ (is/is not).

Cognitive Growth and Higher Education
(pp. 449–456)

20. Years of education _____ (are/are not) strongly correlated with most measures of adult cognition.

Briefly outline the year-by-year progression in how the thinking of college students becomes more flexible and tolerant.

21. William Perry found that the thinking of students, over the course of their college careers, progressed through _____ levels of complexity.

22. Research has shown that the more years of higher education a person has, the deeper and more _____ that person's reasoning is likely to become.

23. Worldwide, the number of students who receive higher education _____ (has increased/ has not increased) since the first half of the twentieth century.

24. Collegiate populations have become _____ (more/less) diverse in recent years. The values and _____ of students are also _____ (the same/ different). The structure of higher education also _____ (has changed/remains the same).

25. Some developmentalists believe that a college education today is a _____ (more powerful/less powerful) force in producing cognitive growth than it might have been. Among the factors that may explain why are _____ effects, _____ effects, and _____ rates.

26. One cohort difference is that most of today's college students _____ (work/do not work) during their college years. Selection effects refer to the possibility that advanced cognition doesn't result directly from a college education but from factors that _____ with college attendance. Only about _____ (how many?) of the students who enroll in college actually graduate.

27. (In Person) Young full-time students living on campus are _____ (more/less) likely to accept cheating than are students who commute. Many students have a _____ (broader/more limited) definition of cheating than professors. For example, many students seem unaware of the rules defining _____ .

28. (In Person) Dr. Berger's analysis of cheating behavior led her to suspect that students may have a different _____ _____ that encourages cheating in order to cope with institutions that penalize those who are _____ _____ and those who are educationally _____ .

Progress Test 1

Multiple-Choice Questions

Circle your answers to the following questions and check them with the answers beginning on page 270. If your answer is incorrect, read the explanation for why it is incorrect and then consult the appropriate pages of the text (in parentheses following the correct answer).

1. Differences in the reasoning maturity of adolescents and young adults are most likely to be apparent when:
    a. low-SES and high-SES groups are compared.
    b. ethnic-minority adolescents and adults are compared.
    c. ethnic-majority adolescents and adults are compared.
    d. emotionally charged issues are involved.

2. Which of the following is *not* one of the major approaches to the study of adult cognition described in the text?
    a. the information-processing approach
    b. the postformal approach
    c. the systems approach
    d. the psychometric approach

3. Compared to adolescent thinking, adult thinking tends to be:
    a. more flexible.   c. more dialectical.
    b. more practical.   d. all of the above.

4. A hallmark of mature adult thought is the:
    a. ability to engage in dialectical thinking.
    b. reconciliation of both objective and subjective approaches to real-life problems.
    c. adoption of conjunctive faith.
    d. all of the above.

5. According to James Fowler, the experience of college often is a springboard to:
    a. intuitive-projective faith
    b. mythic-literal faith
    c. individual-reflective faith
    d. synthetic-conventional faith

6. Which approach to adult cognitive development focuses on life-span changes in the efficiency of encoding, storage, and retrieval?
    a. postformal
    b. information-processing
    c. psychometric
    d. dialectical

7. Postformal thinking is most useful for solving _____ problems.
    a. science   c. everyday
    b. mathematics   d. abstract, logical

8. The term for the kind of thinking that involves the consideration of both poles of an idea and their reconciliation, or synthesis, in a new idea is:
    a. subjective thinking.
    b. postformal thought.
    c. adaptive reasoning.
    d. dialectical thinking.

9. Thesis is to antithesis as _____ is to _____ .
    a. a new idea; an opposing idea
    b. abstract; concrete
    c. concrete; abstract
    d. provisional; absolute

10. Which of the following adjectives best describe(s) cognitive development during adulthood?
    a. multidirectional and multicontextual
    b. linear
    c. steady
    d. tumultuous

11. Which of the following most accurately describes postformal thought?
    a. subjective thinking that arises from the personal experiences and perceptions of the individual
    b. objective reasoning that follows abstract, impersonal logic
    c. a form of logic that combines subjectivity and objectivity
    d. thinking that is rigid, inflexible, and fails to recognize the existence of other potentially valid views

12. The Defining Issues Test is a:
    a. standardized test that measures postformal thinking.
    b. projective test that assesses dialectical reasoning.
    c. series of questions about moral dilemmas.
    d. test that assesses the impact of life events on cognitive growth.

13. According to Carol Gilligan:
    a. in matters of moral reasoning, females tend to be more concerned with the question of rights and justice.
    b. in matters of moral reasoning, males tend to put human needs above principles of justice.
    c. moral reasoning advances during adulthood in response to the more complex moral dilemmas that life poses.
    d. all of the above are true.

14. Which of the following was not identified as a factor in why college education is a less powerful force in producing cognitive growth?
    a. selection effects   c. grade inflation
    b. dropout rates   d. cohort effects

15. Research has revealed that a typical outcome of college education is that students become:
    a. very liberal politically.
    b. less committed to any particular ideology.
    c. more committed to a particular ideology.
    d. less open-minded.

True or False Items

Write T (*true*) or F (*false*) on the line in front of each statement.

_____ 1. Only about half of all students who enroll in college eventually graduate.

_____ 2. Adult cognitive growth is more straightforward than that of childhood and adolescence.

_____ 3. Objective, logical thinking is "adaptive" for the school-age child and adolescent who is in Piaget's formal operational stage.

_____ 4. Because they recognize the changing and subjective nature of beliefs and values, dialectical thinkers avoid making personal or intellectual commitments.

_____ 5. Certain kinds of experiences during adulthood—especially those that entail assuming responsibility for others—can propel an individual from one level of moral reasoning to another.

_____ 6. In recent years, the number of college students has risen dramatically, both in residential and in nonresidential colleges.

_____ 7. Postformal thought is less absolute and less abstract than formal thought.

_____ 8. Mythic-literal faith, like other "lower" stages in the development of faith, is not generally found past adolescence.

_____ 9. (Thinking Like a Scientist) Students who internalize that intelligence is plastic are less likely to experience stereotype threat.

_____ 10. The college student of today is more likely to live at home and attend school on a part-time basis than were the students of the previous generation.

Progress Test 2

Progress Test 2 should be completed during a final chapter review. Answer the following questions after you thoroughly understand the correct answers for the Chapter Review and Progress Test 1.

Multiple-Choice Questions

1. Which approach to adult cognitive development emphasizes the analysis of components of intelligence?
   a. postformal   c. information-processing
   b. psychometric   d. all of the above

2. Which approach to adult cognitive development "picks up where Piaget left off"?
   a. psychometric
   b. information-processing
   c. postformal
   d. dialectical

3. As adult thinking becomes more focused on occupational and interpersonal demands, it also becomes less inclined toward:
   a. single-mindedness.
   b. dialectical thought.
   c. adaptive thought.
   d. all of the above.

4. The result of dialectical thinking is a view that:
   a. one's self is an unchanging constant.
   b. few of life's important questions have single, correct answers.
   c. "everything is relative."
   d. all of the above are true.

5. The existence of a fifth, postformal stage of cognitive development during adulthood:
   a. is recognized by most developmentalists.
   b. has very little empirical support.
   c. remains controversial among developmental researchers.
   d. is widely accepted in women, but not in men.

6. Formal operational thinking is most useful for solving problems that:
   a. involve logical relationships or theoretical possibilities.
   b. require integrative skills.
   c. involve the synthesis of diverse issues.
   d. require seeing perspectives other than one's own.

7. College seems to make people more accepting of other people's attitudes because it:
   a. boosts self-esteem.
   b. promotes recognition of many perspectives.
   c. promotes extroversion.
   d. does all of the above.

8. The goal of dialectical thinking is forging a(n) _____ from opposing poles of an idea.
   a. thesis   c. synthesis
   b. antithesis   d. hypothesis

9. Formal operational thinking is to postformal thinking as _____ is to _____.
   a. psychometric; information-processing
   b. adolescence; adulthood
   c. thesis; antithesis
   d. self-esteem; extroversion

10. Carol Gilligan suggests that during adulthood:
    a. men and women come to recognize the limitations of basing moral reasoning solely on principles of justice.
    b. men and women come to recognize the limitations of basing moral reasoning solely on individual needs.
    c. men and women develop a more reflective, less absolute moral awareness.
    d. all of the above are true.

11. According to James Fowler, individual-reflective faith is marked by:
    a. a willingness to accept contradictions.
    b. a burning need to enunciate universal values.
    c. a literal, wholehearted belief in myths and symbols.
    d. the beginnings of independent questioning of teachers and other figures of authority.

12. (Thinking Like a Scientist) Research studies have shown that college students who cheat :
    a. are more likely to believe that the purpose of school is to get good grades rather than to learn.

    b. have a much broader definition of cheating than professors do.
    c. usually have the same value system as their professors regarding academic dishonesty.
    d. are more likely to break social and legal rules throughout their lives.

13. According to James Fowler, the simplest stage of faith is the stage of:
    a. universalizing faith.
    b. intuitive-projective faith.
    c. mythic-literal faith.
    d. conventional faith.

14. Many of the problems of adult life are characterized by ambiguity, partial truths, and extenuating circumstances, and therefore are often best solved using _____ thinking.
    a. formal   c. postformal
    b. reintegrative   d. executive

15. Research has shown that one effect of college on students is:
    a. a switch from conservative to liberal ideas.
    b. a greater recognition of political, social, and religious views that differ from their own.
    c. movement from synthetic-conventional faith to individual-reflective faith.
    d. a greater ability to make commitments.

Thinking Critically About Chapter 18

Answer these questions the day before an exam as a final check on your understanding of the chapter's terms and concepts.

1. Concluding her comparison of postformal thinking with Piaget's cognitive stages, Lynn notes that:
   a. postformal thinking is characterized by "problem finding."
   b. formal operational thinking is characterized by "problem solving."
   c. intuitive, postformal thinking is used when logical reasoning is too cumbersome.
   d. all of the above are true.

2. Carol Gilligan's research suggests that the individual who is most likely to allow the context of personal relationships to wholly determine moral decisions is a:
   a. 20-year-old man.
   b. 20-year-old woman.
   c. 40-year-old woman.
   d. 50-year-old person of either sex.

3. Research suggests that a college sophomore or junior is most likely to have reached a phase in which he or she:
   a. believes that there are clear and perfect truths to be discovered.
   b. questions personal and social values, and even the idea of truth itself.
   c. rejects opposing ideas in the interest of finding one right answer.
   d. accepts a simplistic either/or dualism.

4. (Table 18.3) In his scheme of cognitive and ethical development, Perry describes a position in which the college student says, "I see I'm going to have to make my own decisions in an uncertain world with no one to tell me I'm Right." This position marks the culmination of a phase of:
   a. either/or dualism.
   b. modified dualism.
   c. relativism.
   d. commitments in relativism.

5. Which of the following is an example of responding to a stereotype threat?
   a. Because Jessie's older sister teases her for not being as good as she is at math, Jessie protects her self-concept by devaluing math.
   b. Feeling angered that others may think him less capable because of his ethnicity, Liam becomes flustered when trying to solve a problem in front of the class.
   c. Dave writes a scathing criticism of an obviously racist comment made by a local politician.
   d. As an elderly adult, Kathy takes pride in displaying her quick wit and intelligence to others.

6. Dr. Polaski studies how thinking during adulthood builds on the earlier formal thinking skills of adolescence. Evidently, Dr. Polaski follows the _____ approach to the study of development.
   a. postformal   c. cognitive
   b. psychometric   d. information-processing

7. Jack's uncle believes strongly in God but recognizes that other, equally moral people do not. The openness of his faith places him in which of Fowler's stages?
   a. universalizing faith
   b. conjunctive faith
   c. individual-reflective faith
   d. mythic-literal faith

8. When she was younger, May-Ling believed that "Honesty is always the best policy." She now realizes that although honesty is desirable, it is not *always* the best policy. May-Ling's current thinking is an example of _____ thought.
   a. formal   c. mythic-literal
   b. dialectical   d. conjunctive

9. Who would be the most likely to agree with the statement, "To be truly ethical a person must have the experience of sustained responsibility for the welfare of others"?
   a. Labouvie-Vief   c. Piaget
   b. Kohlberg   d. Fowler

10. Spike is in his third year at a private, religious liberal arts college, while his brother Lee is in his third year at a public, secular community college. In terms of their cognitive growth, what is the most likely outcome?
    a. Spike will more rapidly develop complex critical thinking skills.
    b. Lee will develop greater self-confidence in his abilities since he is studying from the secure base of his home and family.
    c. All other things being equal, Spike and Lee will develop quite similarly.
    d. It is impossible to predict.

11. In concluding her presentation on "The College Student of Today," Coretta states that:
    a. "The number of students in higher education has increased significantly in virtually every country worldwide."
    b. "There are more low-income and ethnic-minority students today than ever before."
    c. There are more women and minority instructors than ever before.
    d. all of the above are true.

12. (Thinking Like a Scientist) Research demonstrates that all but which of the following are effective in reducing stereotype threat among college students?
    a. creating educational environments among students who have gender in common.
    b. creating educational environments among students who have race in common.
    c. interventions that help students internalize the concept that intelligence can change.
    d. educational programs that sensitize men ethnic majority students to the impact of gender and ethnic stereotypes on other students.

13. In concluding his paper on postformal thinking, Stanley notes that:
    a. postformal thinking is not the same kind of universal, age-related stage that Piaget described for earlier cognitive growth.

b. very few adults attain this highest stage of reasoning.

c. most everyday problems require sensitivity to subjective feelings and therefore do not foster postformal thinking.

d. all of the above are true.

14. Which of the following would be most helpful to know about a person in predicting that individual's level of cognitive development?

    a. age

    b. educational background

    c. household income

    d. Cognitive development is unpredictable from any of these factors.

15. In Fowler's theory, at the highest stages of faith development, people incorporate a powerful vision of compassion for others into their lives. This stage is called:

    a. conjunctive faith.

    b. individual-reflective faith.

c. synthetic-conventional faith.

d. universalizing faith.

Key Terms

Writing Definitions

Using your own words, write a brief definition or explanation of each of the following terms on a separate piece of paper.

1. postformal thought

2. subjective thought

3. objective thought

4. stereotype threat

5. dialectical thought

6. thesis

7. antithesis

8. synthesis

9. Defining Issues Test

Cross Check

After you have written the definitions of the key terms in this chapter, you should complete the crossword puzzle to ensure that you can reverse the process—recognize the term, given the definition.

ACROSS

1. Stage of faith in which a person has a powerful vision of compassion, justice, and love that applies to all people.

7. The final stage of dialectical thinking.

8. A proposition or statement of belief.

13. Theorist who believes that as their life experiences expand, both males and females broaden their moral perspectives.

15. Type of thinking that arises from the personal experiences and perceptions of an individual.

16. Moral reasoning theorist who developed the DIT.

DOWN

2. Faith that is magical, illogical, imaginative, and filled with fantasy.

3. Thinking that involves consideration of both poles of an idea simultaneously.

4. Theorist who delineated six stages of faith.

5. Thinking that is suited to solving real-world problems and is less abstract, less absolute, and more integrative and synthetic than formal thought.

6. Test of moral reasoning that consists of a series of questions about moral dilemmas.

9. Approach to adult cognition that analyzes components of intelligence such as those measured by IQ tests.
10. Second stage of dialectical thinking.
11. Thinking that follows abstract, impersonal logic.
12. During early adulthood, the experience that deepens thinking and leads people to become more tolerant of views that differ from their own.
14. Theorist who described the progressive changes in thinking during the college years.

ANSWERS
CHAPTER REVIEW

1. multidirectional; multicontextual; postformal; psychometric; information-processing
2. practical; flexible; dialectical
3. postformal thought; finding; solving
4. subjective; personal; perceptions; objective; logic; more
5. emotional
6. single-mindedness; cognitive flexibility (or flexible problem solving)
7. stereotype threat; adolescence; ethnic identity; gender identity; disidentification; counteridentification
8. women; minorities; anxious; disidentify
9. have; internalize
10. dialectical thought; thesis; antithesis; synthesis; do not have
11. cultures; Greek; analytic logic; Confucianism and Taoism; dialectically
12. do not think; can
13. college
14. the welfare of others
15. males; females; globalization; immigration; Internet
16. Defining Issues Test; age; education
17. James Fowler
18. Intuitive-projective faith is magical, illogical, filled with fantasy, and typical of children ages 3 to 7.

    Mythic-literal faith, which is typical of middle childhood, is characterized by taking the myths and stories of religion literally.

    Synthetic-conventional faith is a nonintellectual acceptance of cultural or religious values in the context of interpersonal relationships.

    Individual-reflective faith is characterized by intellectual detachment from the values of culture and the approval of significant others.

    Conjunctive faith incorporates both powerful unconscious ideas and rational, conscious values.

Universalizing faith is characterized by a powerful vision of universal compassion, justice, and love that leads people to put their own personal welfare aside in an effort to serve these values.

19. is not; is
20. are

First-year students often believe that there are clear and perfect truths to be found. This phase is followed by a wholesale questioning of values. Finally, after considering opposite ideas, students become committed to certain values, at the same time realizing the need to remain open-minded.

21. nine
22. dialectical
23. has increased
24. more; attitudes; different; has changed
25. less powerful; cohort; selection; dropout
26. work; correlate; half
27. more; more limited; plagiarism
28. value system; culturally different; underprepared

PROGRESS TEST 1

Multiple-Choice Questions

1. **d.** is the answer. (p. 437)

    a., b., & c. Socioeconomic status and ethnicity do not predict reasoning maturity.
2. **c.** is the answer. (p. 435)
3. **d.** is the answer (p. 436)
4. **b.** is the answer. (p. 437)
5. **c.** is the answer. (p. 448)
6. **b.** is the answer. (p. 435)

    a. This approach emphasizes the emergence of a new stage of thinking that builds on the skills of formal operational thinking.

    c. This approach analyzes the measurable components of intelligence.

    d. This is a type of thinking rather than an approach to the study of cognitive development.
7. **c.** is the answer. (p. 436)

    a., b., & d. Because of its more analytical nature, formal thinking is most useful for solving these types of problems.
8. **d.** is the answer. (p. 443)

    a. Thinking that is subjective relies on personal reflection rather than objective observation.

    b. Although dialectical thinking *is* characteristic of postformal thought, this question refers specifically to dialectical thinking.

    c. Adaptive reasoning, which also is characteristic of postformal thought, goes beyond mere logic in solving problems to also explore real-life complexities and contextual circumstances.

9. **a.** is the answer (p. 443)

10. **a.** is the answer. (p. 435)

   b. & c. Comparatively speaking, linear and steady are *more* descriptive of childhood and adolescent cognitive development.

11. **b.** is the answer. (p. 436)

12. **d.** is the answer. (p. 447)

13. **c.** is the answer. (p. 447)

   a. In Gilligan's theory, this is more true of males than females.

   b. In Gilligan's theory, this is more true of females than males.

14. **c.** is the answer. (p. 455)

15. **c.** is the answer. Although they become more committed, they realize they need to remain open-minded. (p. 451)

True or False Items

1. T   Most people today attend college primarily to secure better jobs. (p. 456)

2. F   Adult cognitive growth is multidirectional. (p. 435)

3. T (p. 437)

4. F   Dialectical thinkers recognize the need to make commitments to values even though these values will change over time. (p. 443)

5. T (p. 446)

6. F   There are more nonresidential students. (p. 452)

7. T (p. 436)

8. F   Many adults remain in the "lower" stages of faith, which, like "higher" stages, allow for attaining strength and wholeness. (pp. 448)

9. T (p. 442)

10. T (p. 452)

PROGRESS TEST 2

Multiple-Choice Questions

1. **b.** is the answer. (p. 435)

   a. This approach emphasizes the possible emergence in adulthood of new stages of thinking that build on the skills of earlier stages.

   c. This approach studies the encoding, storage, and retrieval of information throughout life.

2. **c.** is the answer. (p. 435)

3. **a.** is the answer. (p. 439)

   b. & c. During adulthood, thinking typically becomes more dialectical and adaptive.

4. **b.** is the answer. (p. 443)

   a. & c. On the contrary, a dialectic view recognizes the limitations of extreme relativism and that one's self evolves continuously.

5. **c.** is the answer. (p. 436)

6. **a.** is the answer. (p. 437)

   b., c., & d. Postformal thought is most useful for solving problems such as these.

7. **b.** is the answer. (p. 451)

   a. & c. The impact of college on self-esteem and extroversion were not discussed. Moreover, it is unclear how such an impact would make a person more accepting of others.

8. **c.** is the answer. (p. 443)

   a. A thesis is a new idea.

   b. An antithesis is an idea that opposes a particular thesis.

   d. Hypotheses, which are testable predictions about behavior, are not an aspect of dialectical thinking.

9. **b.** is the answer. (p. 436)

10. **d.** is the answer. (p. 447)

11. **d.** is the answer. (p. 448)

   a. This describes conjunctive faith.

   b. This describes universalizing faith.

   c. This describes mythic-literal faith.

12. **a.** is the answer. (p. 454)

   b. In fact, students who cheat generally have a more limited definition of cheating than their professors do.

   c. The text suggests that students who cheat may have a different value system that encourages cooperation in order to cope with institutions that penalize students who are culturally different or educationally underprepared.

   d. The text does not suggest that students who cheat become lifelong rule breakers.

13. **b.** is the answer. (p. 448)

14. **c.** is the answer. (p. 436)

   a. Formal thinking is best suited to solving problems that require logic and analytical thinking.

   b. & d. These terms are not discussed in the text.

15. **b.** is the answer. (p. 451)

   a. The text does not discuss stability or change in students' political views.

   c. This is James Fowler's stage theory of the development of faith.

   d. This is true but not part of Perry's theory.

THINKING CRITICALLY ABOUT CHAPTER 18

1. **d.** is the answer. (p. 436)

2. **b.** is the answer. (p. 447)

   a. According to Gilligan, males tend to be more concerned with human rights and justice than with human needs and personal relationships, which are more the concern of females.

   c. & d. These answers are incorrect because, according to Gilligan, as people mature and their experience of life expands, they begin to realize that moral reasoning based chiefly on justice principles or on individual needs is inadequate to resolve real-life moral dilemmas.

3. **b.** is the answer. (pp. 450–451)

   a. First-year college students are more likely to believe this is so.

   c. & d. Over the course of their college careers, students become *less* likely to do either of these.

4. **c.** is the answer. (p. 451)

5. **b.** is the answer. (pp. 439–441)

6. **a.** is the answer. (p. 435)

   b. This approach analyzes components of intelligence such as those measured by IQ tests.

   c. Each of these approaches is cognitive in nature.

   d. This approach studies the encoding, storage, and retrieval of information throughout life.

7. **b.** is the answer. (p. 448)

8. **b.** is the answer. May-Ling has formed a synthesis between the thesis that honesty is the best policy and its antithesis. (p. 443)

   a. This is an example of postformal rather than formal thinking.

   c. & d. These are stages in the development of faith as proposed by James Fowler.

9. **b.** is the answer. (p. 446)

   a. & c. Neither Labouvie-Vief nor Piaget focuses on ethics in their theories.

   d. Fowler's theory, which identifies stages in the development of faith, does not emphasize this experience.

10. **c.** is the answer. (p. 451)

11. **d.** is the answer. (p. 452)

12. **d.** is the answer. (p. 442)

13. **a.** is the answer. (p. 436)

    b. Because postformal thinking is typical of adult thought, this is untrue.

    c. It is exactly this sort of problem that *fosters* postformal thinking.

14. **c.** is the answer. (p. 450)

15. **d.** is the answer. (p. 448)

KEY TERMS

Writing Definitions

1. Proposed by some developmentalists as a fifth stage of cognitive development, **postformal thought** is suited to solving real-world problems and is more practical, more flexible, and more dialectical than adolescent thought. (p. 436)

2. **Subjective thought** is thinking that arises from our personal experiences and perceptions. (p. 437)

3. **Objective thought** is thinking that follows abstract, impersonal logic. (p. 437)

4. **Stereotype threat** is the possibility that one's behavior may be misused to confirm another person's prejudiced attitude. (p. 439)

5. **Dialectical thought** is thinking that involves considering both poles of an idea (thesis and antithesis) simultaneously and then forging them into a synthesis. (p. 443)

6. The first stage of dialectical thinking, a **thesis** is a proposition or statement of belief. (p. 443)

7. A statement that contradicts the thesis, an **antithesis** is the second stage of dialectical thinking. (p. 443)

8. The final stage of dialectical thinking, the **synthesis** reconciles thesis and antithesis into a new more comprehensive level of truth (p. 443)

9. The **Defining Issues Test (DIT)** is a series of questions developed by James Rest about moral dilemmas used to research moral reasoning. (p. 447)

Cross-Check

ACROSS	DOWN
1. universalizing	2. intuitive-projective
7. synthesis	3. dialectical
8. thesis	4. Fowler
13. Gilligan	5. postformal
15. subjective	6. Defining Issues
16. Rest	9. psychometric
	10. antithesis
	11. objective
	12. college
	14. Perry

Chapter Nineteen

Early Adulthood: Psychosocial Development

Chapter Overview

Biologically mature and no longer bound by parental authority, the young adult typically is now free to choose a particular path of development. Today, the options are incredibly varied. Not surprisingly, then, the hallmark of psychosocial development during early adulthood is diversity. Nevertheless, developmentalists have identified several themes or patterns that help us understand the course of development between the ages of 20 and 40.

The chapter begins with a discussion of the two basic psychosocial needs of adulthood, love and work. No matter what terminology is used, these two needs are recognized by almost all developmentalists.

The next section addresses the need for intimacy in adulthood, focusing on the development of friendship, love, and marriage. The impact of divorce on families is discussed.

The final section of the chapter is concerned with generativity, or the motivation to achieve during adulthood, highlighting the importance of work and parenthood and addressing the special challenges facing stepparents, adoptive parents, and foster parents.

NOTE: Answer guidelines for all Chapter 19 questions begin on page 284.

Guided Study

The text chapter should be studied one section at a time. Before you read, preview each section by skimming it, noting headings and boldface items. Then read the appropriate section objectives from the following outline. Keep these objectives in mind and, as you read the chapter section, search for the information that will enable you to meet each objective. Once you have finished a section, write out answers for its objectives.

Theories of Adulthood (pp. 459–464)

1. Identify the two basic tasks, or crises, of adulthood, and explain how the viewpoint of most developmentalists regarding adult stages has shifted.

2. Explain how the social clock influences the timing of important events during early adulthood.

Intimacy (pp. 464–476)

3. Review the developmental course of friendship during adulthood, noting factors that promote friendship and gender differences in friendship patterns.

4. Identify Sternberg's three components of love, and discuss the pattern by which they develop in relationships.

5. Discuss the impact of cohabitation on relationships, and identify three factors that influence marital success.

6. Discuss the impact of the social context on divorce, the reasons for today's rising divorce rate, and the usual impact of divorce on families.

7. Describe the different forms of spouse abuse.

Generativity (pp. 528–539)

8. Discuss the importance of work to the individual and whether the traditional stages of the career cycle are pertinent to today's workers.

9. Discuss gender and ethnic diversity in the workplace.

10. Focusing on broad themes, describe the stages of the family life cycle, noting the rewards and challenges of each stage, and discuss the effects of multiple roles on family members.

11. Discuss the special challenges facing stepparents, adoptive parents, and foster parents.

Chapter Review

When you have finished reading the chapter, work through the material that follows to review it. Complete the sentences and answer the questions. As you proceed, evaluate your performance for each section by consulting the answers beginning on page 284. Do not continue with the next section until you understand each answer. If you need to, review or reread the appropriate section in the textbook before continuing.

Theories of Adulthood (pp. 459–464)

1. Developmentalists generally agree that two psychosocial needs must be met during adulthood. These are _____

_____

_____ .

2. According to Freud, the healthy adult was one who could _____ and

_____ .

3. According to Maslow, the need for

_____ and _____ was

followed by a need for _____ and

_____ .

4. In Erikson's theory, the identity crisis of adolescence is followed in early adulthood by the crisis

of _____ _____

_____ , and then later by the crisis

of _____ _____

_____ .

5. Today, most social scientists regard adult lives as

less _____ and _____

than stage models suggest.

Briefly describe what was in the 1950s the most common pattern of development during the early and
middle 20s.

6. Although most developmentalists

_____ (take/do not take) a strict

stage view of adulthood, they do recognize that

development is influenced by the

_____ _____ ,

which is defined as _____

_____ .

7. A prime influence on the social clock is

_____ _____ . The

lower a person's SES, the _____

(younger/older) the age at which he or she is

expected to leave school, begin work, marry, have

children, and so forth.

8. The influence of SES is particularly apparent with

regard to the age at which _____

(men/women) are expected to

_____ and finish _____ .

9. Women from low-SES backgrounds may feel

pressure to marry by age _____ ,

and most stop childbearing by age _____ ,

whereas wealthy women may not feel pressure to

marry until age _____ or to stop

childbearing until age _____ .

Intimacy (pp. 464–476)

10. Two main sources of intimacy in early adulthood

are _____ _____

and _____ _____ .

11. As a buffer against stress, as guides to self-awareness, and as a source of positive feelings,

_____ are particularly important.

Briefly state why this is so.

12. Young adulthood is the prime time to solidify

friendships and make new ones for two reasons:

a. _____

_____

b. _____

_____

13. Four factors that promote friendship by serving

as _____ _____

_____ are

a. _____

b. _____

c. _____

d. _____

14. When it comes to our close confidants, most of us

have two or three basic _____ , and

everyone who has those traits is _____

from consideration.

15. (In Person) Gender differences in friendship

_____ (are/are not) especially

apparent during adulthood. In general, men's

friendships are based on _____

_____ and _____ ,

whereas friendships between women tend to be

more _____ and _____ .

Briefly contrast the types of conversations men and women are likely to have with their friends.

16. Research has shown that _____ (women/men) are more likely to reveal their weaknesses to friends, whereas when _____ (women/men) do so, they expect practical advice rather than sympathy.

17. The typical _____ (female/male) friendship pattern seems to be better in terms of meeting intimacy needs.

18. Robert Sternberg has argued that love has three distinct components—_____ , _____ , and _____ — that often occur in a _____ _____ .

19. Sternberg believes that the relative absence or presence of these components gives rise to _____ (how many?) different forms of love.

20. Relationships grow because _____ _____ intensifies, leading to the gradual establishment and strengthening of _____ .

21. When commitment is added to passion and intimacy, the result is _____ love.

22. With time, _____ tends to fade and _____ tends to stabilize, even as _____ develops.

23. Arranged marriages are _____ (rare today/still common in many nations).

24. Increasingly common among young adults in many countries is the living pattern called _____ , in which two unrelated adults of the opposite sex live together in a committed sexual relationship.

25. Cohabitation _____ (does/does not) seem to benefit the participants. Cohabitants tend

to be less _____ , less _____ , and less satisfied with their _____ _____ than married people. Research also demonstrates that cohabitation increases _____ .

26. In the United States today, the proportion of adults who are unmarried is _____ (higher/lower) than in the previous 100 years; only _____ percent of brides are virgins; nearly _____ percent of all first births are to unmarried mothers; and the divorce rate is _____ percent of the marriage rate.

27. Adults in many developed nations spend about _____ of the years between 20 and 40 single.

28. Compared to those who are single, married people are _____ , _____ , and _____ .

29. The younger marriage partners are when they first wed, the _____ (more/ less) likely their marriage is to succeed. According to Erikson, this may be because intimacy is hard to establish until _____ is secure.

30. Marriage between people who are similar in age, SES, ethnicity, and the like, called _____ , is _____ (more/less) likely to succeed than marriage that is outside the group, called _____ . Similarity in leisure interests and _____ preferences, called _____ _____ , is particularly important to marital success.

31. A third factor affecting marriage is _____ _____ , the extent to which the partners perceive equality in the relationship. According to _____ theory, marriage is an arrangement in which each person contributes something useful to the other.

32. An estimated _____ percent of all adults in the United States spend part of adulthood in gay or lesbian partnerships. Homosexual couples _____ (have/do not have)

the same relationship problems as heterosexual couples.

33. In the United States, almost one out of every _____ first marriages ends in divorce. This rate _____ (varies/does not vary significantly) from country to country. Worldwide, divorce has _____ (increased/decreased/remained stable) over most of the past 50 years but has _____ recently.

34. Many developmentalists believe that spouses today expect _____ (more/less) from each other than spouses in the past did.

35. Most people find the initial impact of divorce to be quite _____ (negative/positive) and adjustment to divorce _____ (more/less) difficult than they expected.

State three reasons why this is so.

36. Another adjustment problem is that the ex-spouses' _____ _____ usually shrinks in the first year after divorce.

37. Newly divorced people are more prone to _____ _____ _____ .

    In most cases, such effects _____ (do/do not) eventually dissipate with time.

38. Compared to others, single divorced adults are _____ (most/least) likely to be very happy with their lives.

Identify several factors that contribute to spouse abuse.

39. One form of spouse abuse, _____ , _____ , entails outbursts of fighting, with both partners sometimes becoming involved.

40. The second type of abuse, _____ _____ , occurs when one partner, almost always the _____ , uses a range of methods to punish and degrade the other. This form of abuse leads to the _____-_____ syndrome and _____ (becomes/does not usually become) more extreme with time.

Generativity (pp. 476–485)

41. The motivation to _____ is one of the strongest of human motives. The observable expression of this motive _____ (varies/does not vary) with culture, personality, gender, and cohort.

42. Even more important to workers than their paycheck is the opportunity that work provides to satisfy _____ needs by allowing them to:

    a. _____ _____ .

    b. _____ _____ .

    c. _____ _____ .

    d. _____ _____ .

43. Today, the employment scene is very different than it was before. One reason for this is the shift in developing nations from an economy based on _____ to one based on _____ , and in developed nations from an economy based on _____ to one based on _____ and _____ .

44. Among the fastest-growing occupations in the United States are _____ _____ _____ .

45. In many of today's jobs, although the skills are quite _____ , they may be obsolete tomorrow. This means that people in their 20s should seek educational and vocational settings that foster a variety of general abilities such as _____ .

46. Another reason for the variability in the job cycle is that workers today are more _____ . For example, in developed nations nearly _____ (how much?) the civilian labor force is female. _____ diversity in the work place is also much greater today than in the past.

47. In the happiest couples, _____ (one/neither/both) spouse(s) work(s) either very long hours or very few hours.

48. Many women and members of ethnic minorities continue to experience difficulty in breaking through the _____ _____ , an invisible barrier to career advancement.

State two implications of these trends for young adults just starting out in the work world.

49. Women who are simultaneously wife, mother, and employee_____ (inevitably/do not necessarily) experience the stress of multiple obligations called _____ _____ .

In fact, among families where both spouses work _____ _____ is more prevalent as two people share obligations.

50. Generally speaking, adults who balance marital, parental, and vocational roles _____ (are/are not) happier and more successful than those who function in only one or two of them.

51. Today, family _____—coordinating housework, child care, work schedules, and so on—typically requires a level of planning and mutual agreement that was unnecessary in earlier generations.

52. Following a divorce, the financial burden of child rearing usually falls more heavily on the _____parent, who is most often the _____.

53. Proportionately, about _____ of all North American adults will become stepparents, adoptive parents, or foster parents at some point in their lives.

54. Strong bonds between parent and child are particularly hard to create when a child has already formed _____ to other caregivers.

55. Because they are legally connected to their children for life, _____ (adoptive/ step/foster) parents have an advantage in establishing bonds with their children.

56. Stepchildren, foster children, and adoptive children tend to leave home _____ . (at the same age as/earlier than/later than) children living with one or both biological parents.

Progress Test 1

Multiple-Choice Questions

Circle your answers to the following questions and check them with the answers on page 285. If your answer is incorrect, read the explanation for why it is incorrect and then consult the appropriate pages of the text (in parentheses following the correct answer).

1. According to Erik Erikson, the first basic task of adulthood is to establish:
   a. a residence apart from parents.
   b. intimacy with others.
   c. generativity through work or parenthood.
   d. a career commitment.

2. Most social scientists who study adulthood emphasize that:

   a. intimacy and generativity take various forms throughout adulthood.
   b. adult lives are less orderly and predictable than stage models suggest.
   c. each culture has a somewhat different social clock.
   d. all of the above are true.

3. Which of the following was *not* identified as a gateway to attraction?

   a. physical attractiveness
   b. frequent exposure
   c. similarity of attitudes
   d. apparent availability

4. The social circles of ex-spouses usually _____ in the first year following a divorce.

   a. shrink
   b. grow larger
   c. become more fluid
   d. become less fluid

5. In the United States and other Western countries, the lower a person's socioeconomic status:

   a. the younger the age at which the social clock is "set" for many life events.
   b. the older the age at which the social clock is "set" for many life events.
   c. the more variable are the settings for the social clock.
   d. the less likely it is that divorce will occur.

6. According to Erikson, the failure to achieve intimacy during early adulthood is most likely to result in:

   a. generativity.   c. role diffusion.
   b. stagnation.   d. isolation.

7. Friendships are important for young adults because:

   a. friendship ties are voluntary.
   b. compared to earlier cohorts, they are less likely to be caring for older relatives.
   c. they are likely to postpone marriage.
   d. of all the above reasons.

8. Beginning with the lower-level needs, what is the correct order in Maslow's hierarchy?

   a. self-fulfillment, psychological, basic
   b. psychological, basic, self-fulfillment
   c. basic, psychological, self-fulfillment
   d. basic, self-fulfillment, psychological

9. According to Robert Sternberg, consummate love emerges:

   a. as a direct response to passion.
   b. as a direct response to physical intimacy.
   c. when commitment is added to passion and intimacy.
   d. during the early years of parenthood.

10. An arrangement in which two unrelated, unmarried adults of the opposite sex live together is called:

    a. cross-sex friendship.
    b. a passive-congenial pattern.
    c. cohabitation.
    d. affiliation.

11. Differences in religious customs or rituals are *most* likely to arise in a:

    a. homogamous couple.
    b. heterogamous couple.
    c. cohabiting couple.
    d. very young married couple.

12. Who formulated the concept that major life transitions occur at approximately ages 20, 30, and 40, based on his study of a small group of men in the 1960s?

    a. Erik Erikson
    b. Daniel Levinson
    c. Abraham Maslow
    d. Robert Sternberg

13. Homogamy is to heterogamy as:

    a. marriage outside the group is to marriage within the group.
    b. marriage within the group is to marriage outside the group.
    c. companionate love is to passionate love.
    d. passionate love is to companionate love.

14. Adults who successfully combine the roles of spouse, parent, and employee tend to report:

    a. less overall happiness than other adults.
    b. more overall happiness than other adults.
    c. regrets over parental roles.
    d. problems in career advancement.

15. Compared to adolescents who live with their biological parents, stepchildren, foster children, and adoptive children:

    a. leave home at an older age.
    b. leave home at a younger age.
    c. have fewer developmental problems.
    d. have the same developmental problems.

True or False Items

Write T (*true*) or F (*false*) on the line in front of each statement.

_____ 1. According to Erikson, the adult experiences a crisis of intimacy versus isolation and, after that, a crisis of generativity versus stagnation.

_____ 2. A prime influence on the cultural clock-setting is socioeconomic status.

_____ 3. According to Sternberg, early in a relationship, companionate love is at its highest.

_____ 4. The younger the bride and groom, the more likely their marriage is to succeed.

_____ 5. Cohabitation solves all the problems that might arise after marriage.

_____ 6. Most successful couples learn to compromise.

_____ 7. Most divorced fathers manage to fulfill the emotional and financial needs of their children after divorce, even if they do not have custody.

_____ 8. Because of the complexity of the high-tech work world, most young adults can expect to remain at the same job throughout their careers.

_____ 9. Abuse is common among unmarried couples living together, whether heterosexual, gay, or lesbian.

_____ 10. Many stepchildren are fiercely loyal to the absent parent.

Progress Test 2

Progress Test 2 should be completed during a final chapter review. Answer the following questions after you thoroughly understand the correct answers for the Chapter Review and Progress Test 1.

Multiple-Choice Questions

1. Erikson theorizes that if generativity is not attained, the adult is most likely to experience:
   a. lack of advancement in his or her career.
   b. infertility or childlessness.
   c. feelings of emptiness and stagnation.
   d. feelings of profound aloneness or isolation.

2. The key difference between common couple violence and intimate terrorism is:
   a. the presence of mental illness in the violent partner in intimate terrorism.
   b. the violent control of one partner by the other in intimate terrorism.
   c. the presence of children in intimate terrorism.
   d. the cyclical nature of common couple violence.

3. Kwame and Kendra both enjoy dancing, going to the movies, and working out. Developmentalists would say their marriage is characterized by:
   a. heterogamy.
   b. homogamy.
   c. social homogamy.
   d. b and c.

4. The prime effect of the social clock is to make an individual aware of:
   a. his or her socioeconomic status.
   b. the diversity of psychosocial paths during early adulthood.
   c. the means of fulfilling affiliation and achievement needs.
   d. the "right" or "best" time for assuming adult roles.

5. Today, the economy of developed nations is shifting from a focus on _____ to a focus on _____ .
   a. industry; information
   b. service; information
   c. agriculture; industry
   d. labor; agriculture

6. Which of the following is not true today regarding marriage?
   a. The proportion of adults who are unmarried is higher than at any time in the past century.
   b. The rate of first marriages in young adulthood is the highest in 50 years.
   c. Nearly one-half of all first births are to single mothers.
   d. The divorce rate is 49 percent of the marriage rate.

7. (In Person) Whereas men's friendships tend to be based on _____ , friendships between women tend to be based on _____ .
   a. shared confidences; shared interests
   b. cooperation; competition
   c. shared interests; shared confidences
   d. finding support for personal problems; discussion of practical issues

8. (Research Report) According to Robert Sternberg, the three dimensions of love are:
   a. passion, intimacy, and consummate love.
   b. physical intimacy, emotional intimacy, and consummate love.
   c. passion, commitment, and consummate love.
   d. passion, intimacy, and commitment.

9. Research on cohabitation in the United States suggests that:
   a. relatively few young adults ever live with an unrelated partner of the other sex.
   b. adults who are divorced or widowed sometimes cohabit.
   c. adults who cohabit tend to be happier and healthier than married people are.
   d. marriages preceded by cohabitation are less durable.

10. A homogamous marriage is best defined as a marriage between:
    a. people who are physically similar to each other.
    b. people of similar social backgrounds.
    c. people of dissimilar socioeconomic backgrounds.
    d. two caring people of the same sex.

11. The text suggests that the main reason for the rising divorce rate is that today's couples experience:
    a. greater rigidity of sex roles in marriage.
    b. higher expectations about marriage and the marriage partner.
    c. deterioration in their overall communication skills.
    d. increased incidence of drug- and alcohol-related abuse.

12. Today's work force:
    a. is more diverse than in previous years.
    b. should not expect to remain in one career for their entire working lives.
    c. must exhibit a greater sensitivity to cultural differences.
    d. is characterized by all of the above.

13. Over the years of adulthood, people who balance marital, parental, and vocational loads:
    a. inevitably suffer from the stress of role overload.
    b. are far more likely to divorce.
    c. generally are happier than those who function in only one or two of these roles.
    d. Both a. and b.

14. Stepparents, adoptive parents, and foster parents:
    a. experience rewards that go beyond the immediate household.
    b. have basically the same parenting problems as biological parents.
    c. tend to have fewer problems as parents because they typically begin parenthood when the children are older.
    d. typically develop equally secure attachments to their children as do biological parents.

15. Depending on the amount of stress they are under, women who simultaneously serve as mother, wife, and employee may experience:
    a. marital equity.
    b. a glass ceiling.
    c. role overload.
    d. social homogamy.

Matching Items

Match each definition or description with its corresponding term.

Terms

_____ **1.** social clock
_____ **2.** cohabitation
_____ **3.** intimate terrorism
_____ **4.** heterogamy
_____ **5.** marital equity
_____ **6.** social exchange theory
_____ **7.** social homogamy
_____ **8.** glass ceiling
_____ **9.** homogamy
_____ **10.** common couple violence

Definitions or Descriptions

a. abusive relationship that leads to battered-wife syndrome
b. an invisible barrier to career advancement
c. the similarity with which a couple regard leisure interests and role preferences
d. a marriage between people with dissimilar interests and backgrounds
e. the culturally set timetable at which key life events are deemed appropriate
f. predicts success in marriages in which each partner contributes something useful to the other
g. arrangement in which two unrelated adults of the opposite sex live together
h. the extent to which partners perceive equality in their relationship
i. a marriage between people with similar interests and backgrounds
j. abusive relationship that tends to improve with time

Thinking Critically About Chapter 19

Answer these questions the day before an exam as a final check on your understanding of the chapter's terms and concepts.

1. Summarizing his presentation on the attempts of American developmentalists to subdivide the periods of adulthood, Seth notes that:
   a. changes in life structure are predictable throughout adulthood.
   b. adulthood is more definable than at any time in recent history.
   c. both a and b are true.
   d. most developmentalists agree that matching particular ages with particular stages of development is a limited approach.

2. Marie notes that her parents have been married for 25 years even though each seems somewhat unfulfilled in terms of their relationship. Her friends had a similar relationship and divorced after five years. Given the research on divorce, how might Marie explain the differences?
   a. "My parents are just much more patient with and understanding of each other."
   b. "Couples today expect more of each other."
   c. "My parents feel that they must stay together for financial reasons."
   d. "I can't understand what keeps my parents together."

3. JoniJill and Randy did not anticipate the problems they encountered after their divorce. This is most likely because:
   a. they did not focus on the needs that had been met during their marriage.
   b. emotional entanglements lingered after the divorce.
   c. the conflict engendered by the divorce led to anger and bitterness.
   d. of both a. and b.

4. In order to determine ways to lower the high rate of divorce, Dr. Wilson is conducting research on marital satisfaction and the factors that contribute to it. Which of the following would he consider to be important factors?
   a. homogamy
   b. social homogamy
   c. marital equity
   d. All of the above contribute to marital satisfaction.

5. Rwanda and Rodney have been dating for about a month. Their relationship is most likely characterized by:
   a. strong feelings of commitment.
   b. consummate love.
   c. physical intimacy and feelings of closeness.
   d. all of the above.

6. I am 25 years old. It is most likely that I:
   a. am married.
   b. am divorced.
   c. have never been married.
   d. am divorced and remarried.

7. If asked to explain the high failure rate of marriages between young adults, Erik Erikson would most likely say that:
   a. achievement goals are often more important than intimacy in early adulthood.
   b. intimacy is difficult to establish until identity is formed.
   c. divorce has almost become an expected stage in development.
   d. today's cohort of young adults has higher expectations of marriage than did previous cohorts.

8. Of the following people, who is *least* likely to report being "very happy" with his or her present life?
   a. Drew, who has never married
   b. Leah, who became a widow five years ago
   c. Malcolm, who has been married ten years
   d. Sharice, a single, divorced adult

9. Which of the following employer initiatives would be most likely to increase employee job satisfaction?
   a. offering higher wages
   b. offering improved worker benefits
   c. the opportunity to develop personal skills
   d. All of the above have about the same impact on employee satisfaction.

10. Which of the following would be the *worst* advice for a young adult entering the job market today?
    a. Seek education that fosters a variety of general abilities and human relations skills.
    b. Expect that educational requirements for work will shift every few years.
    c. To avoid diluting your skills, concentrate your education on preparing for one specific job.
    d. Be flexible and willing to adjust to the varied pacing and timing of today's jobs.

11. Of the following people, who is the most likely to encounter a glass ceiling in his or her career?
    a. Ben, a middle-aged white social worker
    b. Simone, an African American engineer
    c. Don, an Asian American attorney
    d. Paul, a white banker in his mid-20s

12. As compared to biological parents, which of the following is most likely to be true of stepparents, adoptive parents, and foster parents?
    a. They are rarely able to win the love of the child away from the biological parents.
    b. They are more humble, less self-absorbed, and more aware of the problems facing children.
    c. They tend to favor their own children over adopted, foster, or stepchildren.
    d. They keep their children at home much longer than do biological parents.

13. Arthur and Mabel have been married for 5 years. According to Sternberg, if their relationship is a satisfying one, which of the following best describes their relationship?
    a. They are strongly committed to each other.
    b. They are passionately in love.
    c. They are in the throes of establishing intimacy.
    d. They are beginning to wonder why the passion has left their relationship.

14. Your brother, who became a stepparent when he married, complains that he can't seem to develop a strong bond with his 9-year-old stepchild. You tell him:
    a. strong bonds between parent and child are particularly hard to create once a child is old enough to have formed attachments to other caregivers.
    b. the child is simply immature emotionally and will, with time, warm up considerably.
    c. most stepparents find that they eventually develop a deeper, more satisfying relationship with stepchildren than they had ever imagined.
    d. he should encourage the child to think of him as the child's biological father.

15. Your sister, who is about to marry, seeks your advice on what makes a happy marriage. You should mention that all but which one of the following factors contribute to marital happiness?
    a. cohabitation before marriage
    b. the degree to which a couple is homogamous or heterogamous
    c. the degree of marital equity
    d. whether identity needs have been met before marriage

Key Terms

Using your own words, write a brief definition or explanation of each of the following terms on a separate piece of paper.

1. intimacy versus isolation
2. generativity versus stagnation
3. social clock
4. gateways to attraction
5. cohabitation
6. homogamy
7. heterogamy
8. social homogamy
9. social exchange theory
10. common couple violence
11. intimate terrorism
12. glass ceiling
13. role overload
14. role buffering

ANSWERS

CHAPTER REVIEW

1. affiliation and achievement (affection and instrumentality or interdependence and independence or communion and agency)
2. love; work
3. love; belonging; success; esteem
4. intimacy versus isolation; generativity versus stagnation
5. orderly; predictable

In the 1950s, men in their early 20s would finish their education, choose their occupation, marry, buy a house, and have children. Women would marry and have children.

6. do not take; social clock; the culturally set timetable that establishes when various events and endeavors are appropriate
7. socioeconomic status; younger
8. women; marry; childbearing
9. 18; 30; 30; 40
10. close friendship; romantic partnership
11. friends

Friends choose each other, often for the very qualities that make them good sources of emotional support. They are also a source of self-esteem.

12. a. Most young adults try to postpone the overriding commitments of marriage and having children.
    b. Because today's elderly are healthier, few young adults must provide care for aging parents.
13. gateways to attraction
    a. physical attractiveness
    b. apparent availability
    b. absence of "exclusion criteria"
    b. frequent exposure
14. filters; excluded
15. are; shared activities; interests; intimate; emotional

Women talk more often about their intimate concerns and delve deeper into personal and family issues; men typically talk about external matters such as sports, politics, or work.

16. women; men
17. female
18. passion; intimacy; commitment; developmental progression
19. seven
20. personal intimacy; commitment
21. consummate
22. passion; intimacy; commitment
23. still common in many nations
24. cohabitation
25. does not; happy; healthy; financial status; stress
26. higher; 10; 50; 49
27. half
28. happier; healthier; richer
29. less; identity
30. homogamy; more; heterogamy; role; social homogamy
31. marital equity; social exchange
32. 2 to 5 percent; have
33. two; varies; increased; stabilized
34. more
35. negative; more

First, until the divorce, ex-spouses often are unaware of things that were going well. Second, even after divorce, emotional dependence between the former partners often is strong. Third, other people behave unpredictably and badly, creating new problems instead of providing needed social support.

36. social circle

37. loneliness, disequilibrium, promiscuous sexual behavior, and erratic patterns of eating, sleeping, working, and drug and alcohol use; do

38. least

Many factors contribute to spouse abuse, including social pressures that create stress, cultural values that condone violence, personality pathologies, and drug and alcohol addiction.

39. common couple violence

40. intimate terrorism; husband; battered-wife; becomes

41. achieve; varies

42. generativity

    a. develop and use their personal skills

    b. express their creative energy

    c. aid and advise coworkers

    d. contribute to the community

43. agriculture; industry; industry; information; service

44. those related to computers; others include physical or occupational therapist, human service worker, home health aide, medical assistant, fitness trainer, and special education teacher

45. specific; decision making, memory, cooperation, and problem solving

46. diverse; half; Ethnic

47. neither

48. glass ceiling

First, success at work today depends more than ever on the same human relations skills needed in successful friendships and marriages. Second, to be successful today workers must be able to adapt to the varied work environment.

49. do not necessarily; role overload; role buffering

50. are

51. logistics

52. custodial; mother

53. one-third

54. attachments

55. adoptive

56. earlier than

PROGRESS TEST 1

Multiple-Choice Questions

1. **b.** is the answer. (p. 460)

2. **d.** is the answer. (p. 462)

3. **c.** is the answer. (p. 465)

4. **a.** is the answer. (p. 474)

    c. & d. The fluidity of social circles following divorce was not discussed.

5. **a.** is the answer. (p. 463)

    d. Low SES is actually a risk factor for divorce.

6. **d.** is the answer. (p. 460)

    a. Generativity is a characteristic of the crisis following the intimacy crisis.

    b. Stagnation occurs when generativity needs are not met.

    c. Erikson's theory does not address this issue.

7. **d.** is the answer. (p. 465)

8. **c.** is the answer. (p. 460)

9. **c.** is the answer. (p. 468)

    d. Sternberg's theory is not concerned with the stages of parenthood.

10. **c.** is the answer. (p. 469)

11. **b.** is the answer. (p. 470)

    a. By definition, homogamous couples share values, background, and the like.

    c. & d. These may or may not be true, depending on the extent to which such a couple is homogamous.

12. **b.** is the answer. (pp. 461–462)

13. **b.** is the answer. (p. 470)

14. **b.** is the answer. (p. 481)

    c. Most parents report that they are pleased that they have had children.

15. **b.** is the answer. (p. 484)

    c. & d. The text does not discuss variations in the incidence of developmental problems in the various family structures.

True or False Items

1. T (p. 460)

2. T (p. 463)

3. F This comes only with time. (p. 467)

4. F Just the reverse is true. (p. 470)

5. F Cohabitation does *not* solve the problems of marriage. (p. 469)

6. T (p. 471)

7. F   Most divorced fathers gradually lose the intimate bonds formed through daily and nightly interactions. (p. 483)

8. F   Most young adults should learn basic skills so that they have the flexibility to move into different jobs. (p. 478)

9. T (p. 475)

10. T (p. 483)

PROGRESS TEST 2

Multiple-Choice Questions

1. **c.** is the answer. (p. 460)

a. Lack of career advancement may prevent generativity.

b. Erikson's theory does not address these issues.

d. Such feelings are related to the need for intimacy rather than generativity.

2. **b.** is the answer. (p. 475)

3. **c.** is the answer. (pp. 470–471)

4. **d.** is the answer. (p. 462)

5. **a.** is the answer. (p. 477)

b. Today, the economies of developed nations focus on *both* service and information.

c. This describes the shift in the economies of poor, undeveloped nations.

6. **b.** is the answer. The rate of first marriages in young adulthood is the *lowest* in 50 years. (p. 470)

7. **c.** is the answer. (p. 465)

8. **d.** is the answer. (p. 467)

a., b., & c. According to Sternberg, consummate love emerges when commitment is added to passion and intimacy.

9. **b.** is the answer. (p. 469)

a. Slightly more than half of all women aged 25 to 40 in the United States cohabit before their first marriage.

c. In fact, a large study of adults found that cohabitants were much *less* happy and healthy than married people were.

d. No such finding was reported in the text.

10. **b.** is the answer. (p. 470)

a. & d. These characteristics do not pertain to homogamy.

c. This describes a heterogamous marriage.

11. **b.** is the answer. (p. 473)

12. **d.** is the answer. (pp. 477–479)

13. **c.** is the answer. (p. 481)

14. **a.** is the answer. (p. 484)

d. Without the emotional pull of both early contact and genetic connections, close attachments may be difficult to establish.

15. **c.** is the answer. However, role overload may not always be experienced by women serving multiple functions. (p. 481)

a. Just the opposite may be true. She may feel that she is shouldering the burden of responsibility.

b. & d. These may be true but they have nothing to do with her feeling overloaded.

Matching Items

1. e (p. 462)	**5.** h (p. 471)	**9.** i (p. 470)
2. g (p. 469)	**6.** f (p. 471)	**10.** j (p. 475)
3. a (p. 475)	**7.** c (p. 471)	
4. d (p. 470)	**8.** b (p. 479)	

THINKING CRITICALLY ABOUT CHAPTER 19

1. **d.** is the answer. (pp. 461–462)

2. **b.** is the answer. (p. 473)

3. **d.** is the answer. (p. 474)

4. **d.** is the answer. The most successful relationships are between people of similar backgrounds and similar interests. The partners' perceptions of marital equity are also important. (pp. 470–471)

5. **c.** is the answer. (p. 467)

a. & b. These feelings emerge more gradually in relationships.

6. **c.** is the answer. (p. 470)

7. **b.** is the answer. (p. 470)

a. In Erikson's theory, the crisis of intimacy *precedes* the need to be productive through work.

c. & d. Although these items are true, Erikson's theory does not address these issues.

8. **d.** is the answer. (p. 474)

9. **c.** is the answer. (p. 476)

10. **c.** is the answer. (p. 478)

a., b., & d. These would all be good pieces of advice for new workers today.

11. **b.** is the answer. (p. 479)

a., c., & d. Women and members of minority groups are more likely to encounter glass ceilings in their careers.

12. **b.** is the answer. (p. 484)

13. **a.** is the answer. (p. 468)

14. **a.** is the answer. (p. 483)

   b. Many stepchildren remain fiercely loyal to the absent parent.

   c. Most stepparents actually have unrealistically high expectations of the relationship they will establish with their stepchildren.

   d. Doing so would only confuse the child and, quite possibly, cause resentment and further alienation.

15. **a.** is the answer. Cohabitation before marriage does *not* strengthen the relationship. (p. 469)

KEY TERMS

1. According to Erik Erikson, the first crisis of adulthood is **intimacy versus isolation**, which involves the need to share one's personal life with someone else or risk profound loneliness and isolation. (p. 460)

2. In Erikson's theory, the second crisis of adulthood is **generativity versus stagnation**, which involves the need to be productive in some meaningful way, usually through work or parenthood. (p. 460)

3. The **social clock** represents the culturally set timetable that establishes when various events and behaviors in life are appropriate and called for. (p. 462)

4. **Gateways to attraction** refer to the various qualities, such as physical attractiveness, availability, and frequent exposure, that contribute to the formation of friendships and intimate relationships. (p. 465)

5. Increasingly common among young adults in all industrialized countries is the living pattern called **cohabitation**, in which two unrelated adults of the opposite sex live together in a committed sexual relationship. (p. 469)

6. **Homogamy** refers to marriage between people who are similar in attitudes, socioeconomic status, interests, ethnicity, religion, and the like. (p. 470)

7. **Heterogamy** refers to marriage between people who are dissimilar in attitudes, interests, SES, religion, ethnic background, and goals. (p. 470)

8. **Social homogamy** is defined as similarity in leisure interests and role preferences. (p. 471)

9. According to social **exchange theory,** social behavior is aimed at maximizing the benefits of a behavior and minimizing the costs. (p. 471)

10. **Common couple violence** is a form of abuse in which one or both partners in a couple engage in outbursts of verbal and physical attack. (p. 475)

11. **Intimate terrorism** is the form of spouse abuse in which the husband uses violent methods of accelerating intensity to isolate, degrade, and punish the wife. (p. 475)

12. A **glass ceiling** is an invisible barrier to career advancement that is most often encountered by women and minority workers. (p. 479)

13. **Role overload** refers to the stress of multiple obligations that may occur for an adult who is simultaneously a spouse, a parent, and an employee. (p. 481)

14. **Role buffering** is a situation in a family where both spouses are employed in which one role that a parent plays reduces the disappointments that may occur in other roles. (p. 481)

Chapter Twenty

Middle Adulthood: Biosocial Development

Chapter Overview

This chapter deals with biosocial development during the years from 40 to 60. The first section describes changes in appearance and in the functioning of the sense organs and vital body systems, noting the potential impact of these changes. This section also discusses the changes in the sexual-reproductive system that occur during middle adulthood. The next section discusses the latest ways in which variations in health are measured to reflect quality of living as well as traditional measures of illness and death rates. The third section discusses the health habits of middle-aged adults, focusing on smoking, drinking, gaining weight, and exercise. The chapter concludes with an exploration of variations in health related to ethnicity, pointing out that, overall, middle-aged persons are healthier today than in earlier cohorts.

NOTE: Answer guidelines for all Chapter 20 questions begin on page 299.

Guided Study

The text chapter should be studied one section at a time. Before you read, preview each section by skimming it, noting headings and boldface items. Then read the appropriate section objectives from the following outline. Keep these objectives in mind and, as you read the chapter section, search for the information that will enable you to meet each objective. Once you have finished a section, write out answers for its objectives.

Primary and Secondary Aging (pp. 491–498)

1. Identify the typical physical changes of middle adulthood and discuss their impact.

2. Describe how the functioning of the sense organs and vital body systems change during middle adulthood.

3. Identify the typical changes that occur in the sexual-reproductive system during middle adulthood.

Measuring Health (pp. 498–502)

4. Differentiate four measures of health.

5. Explain the concepts of quality-adjusted life years and disability-adjusted life years.

Chapter Review

When you have finished reading the chapter, work through the material that follows to review it. Complete the sentences and answer the questions. As you proceed, evaluate your performance for each section by consulting the answers beginning on page 299. Do not continue with the next section until you understand each answer. If you need to, review or reread the appropriate section in the textbook before continuing.

Health Habits Through the Years (pp. 502–508)

6. Describe the relationship between health and certain lifestyle factors—smoking, alcohol use, gaining weight, and exercise.

Primary and Secondary Aging (pp. 491–498)

1. Age-related changes that are inevitable consequences of aging are called _____ _____ , while those that are the consequence of unhealthy behaviors are called

   _____ _____ .

2. Secondary aging includes many _____ and _____ conditions, most of which _____ (can be slowed or reversed/cannot be altered) by a change in behavior or by medical interventions.

3. Some of the normal changes in appearance that occur during middle adulthood include

   _____

   _____

   _____

Ethnic Variations in Health (pp. 509–516)

7. Explain how variations in health are related to ethnicity.

4. Between ages 35 and 65, the lens of the eye becomes _____ _____ and the cornea becomes _____ .

5. As part of _____ aging, the rate of hearing loss is faster in _____ (women/men).

6. With normal aging, the ability to hear differences in _____ _____ declines faster than the ability to understand

   _____ .

8. Discuss possible reasons for ethnic variations in health.

7. Some losses in hearing during middle adulthood are the result of _____ and some are the consequence of _____ .

8. Speech-related hearing losses are first apparent for _____-(high/low) frequency sounds.

9. Systemic declines in the efficiency and the organ reserve of the _____ , _____ , and _____ _____ make middle-aged people _____ (more/less) vulnerable to chronic disease. Declines are also evident in the _____ system, resulting in an increased risk of _____ diseases such as _____ _____ and _____ .

10. Thanks to better _____ _____ and _____ _____ , the overall death rate before age _____ has declined dramatically throughout the _____ (entire/ developed) world. This is especially true for the two leading causes of death in this age group: _____ _____ and _____ . The overall health of middle-aged adults _____ (varies/does not vary) significantly from one nation to another.

11. At an average age of _____ , a woman reaches _____ , as ovulation and menstruation stop and the production of the hormones _____ , _____ , and _____ drops considerably.

12. All the various biological changes that extend from three years before to three years after cessation of the menstrual cycle are referred to as the _____ . The first symptom is typically shorter _____ , _____ followed by variations in the timing of her _____ . Symptoms such as hot flashes and flushes and cold sweats are caused by _____ _____ , that is, a temporary disruption in the body mechanisms that maintain body temperature.

13. Two other serious changes caused by reduced levels of _____ are loss of bone _____ , which can lead to the thin and brittle bones that accompany _____ , and an increase of arterial fat deposits that can set the stage for _____ _____ _____ .

14. The psychic consequences of menopause are _____ (variable/not variable). European and North American cultures' perceptions of this aspect of menopause _____ (have/have not) changed over time.

15. Over the past two or three decades, many women used _____ _____ _____ to reduce perimenopausal symptoms.

16. Long-term use of HRT beyond menopause has been shown to increase the risk of _____ and has no proven effects on _____ .

17. Physiologically, men _____ (do/do not) experience anything like menopause. Although the average levels of testosterone decline gradually, if at all, with age, they can dip if a man becomes _____ _____ or unusually worried.

Measuring Health (pp. 498–502)

18. Perhaps the most solid indicator of health of given age groups is the rate of _____ , or death. This rate is often _____ -adjusted to take into account the higher death rate among the very old. By this measure, the country with the lowest rate is _____ , and the country with the highest rate is _____ .

19. A more comprehensive measure of health is _____ , defined as _____ of all kinds.

20. To truly portray quality of life, we need to measure _____ , which refers to a person's inability to perform basic activities, and

_____ , which refers to how healthy and energetic a person feels.

21. In terms of quality of life, _____ is probably the most important measure of health.

22. The concept of _____-_____ _____ indicates how many years of full vitality are lost as a result of a particular disease or disability. The reciprocal of this statistic is known as _____-_____ _____ .

23. The total reduction in vitality that is caused by a disease-induced disability in a given population is called the _____ _____ _____ .

Health Habits Through the Years (pp. 502–508)

24. Health improvements that are undertaken early add more _____ than do treatments begun after an illness has been recognized.

25. For most conditions and diseases, it is a person's _____ _____ over the years that have the greatest influence on delaying and preventing physiological decline.

26. Cigarette-smoking is a known risk factor for most serious diseases, including _____ _____ .

27. All smoking diseases are _____- and _____-sensitive. Although smoking rates have dropped in North America, rates in most _____ nations and in _____ and _____ _____ nations have not. These statistics highlight the importance of _____ _____ in smoking.

28. Some studies find that adults who drink moderately may live longer, possibly because alcohol increases the blood's supply of _____-_____ , a protein that helps reduce

the amount of _____-_____ _____ in the body. Another possible explanation of the relationship between moderate drinking and longevity is that moderate drinking may reduce _____ and aid_____ . However, even moderate alcohol consumption poses a heath risk if it is associated with _____ or _____ .

List some of the health hazards of excessive alcohol use.

29. Overweight, defined as _____ , is present in _____ (what percent?) of middle-aged residents of the United States. Obesity, defined as _____ , is a risk factor for _____ , _____ , and _____ , and a contributing factor for _____ , the most common disability for older adults.

30. Throughout much of the world, the percentage of people who are overweight or obese is _____ (less than/greater than/about the same as) that of previous generations.

31. Some experts believe that people of African, _____ , or _____-_____ ethnicity are _____ (harmed/unharmed) by a BMI of 25–30. Experts _____ (agree/do not agree) that a BMI over 30 is always harmful.

32. Between ages 20 and 50, a person's metabolism _____ (slows/increases) by about a third, which means that middle-aged people need to eat _____ (more/less) simply to maintain their weight.

33. Current explanations for the trends in overweight and obesity focus on _____ factors, on _____ , and on _____ .

34. The best way to lose weight is to _____ . People who are active _____ (do/do not) have lower rates of serious illness and death than inactive people. An additional advantage is enhanced _____ functioning due to improved circulation to the _____ .

List some of the health benefits of regular exercise.

Ethnic Variations in Health (pp. 509–516)

35. Individuals who are relatively well-educated, financially secure, and living in or near cities tend to live _____ (shorter/longer) lives and have _____ (more/ fewer) chronic illnesses or disabilities.

36. The reasons for regional differences in the health of Americans include variations in

_____

_____ .

37. Between the ages of 45 and 54, the chance of dying is twice as high for_____ , and only half as high for _____ , as it is for European Americans. In between are the mortality rates for _____ _____ and _____- _____ . Self-reported health status, morbidity, and disability _____ (do/do not) follow the same ethnic patterns as does mortality.

38. In all minority groups, the illness and death rates among recent immigrants are _____ (higher/lower) than among long-time U.S. residents.

State several possible explanations for this difference.

39. In examining ethnic differences in health, developmentalists recognize that there _____ (are/are not) ethnic differences in genetic risks for certain illnesses.

40. The U.S. health care system works less well for people who are _____ _____ and for those who are _____ . Members of these groups are less likely than others to have _____ _____ or to seek _____ _____ . Another reason is that doctors, like all people, are subject to _____ , which influences the treatments they recommend for patients who are members of ethnic minority groups. A third reason is that the members of ethnic minorities are less likely to seek _____ care.

41. Compared to people in rich nations, those in poor nations _____ (experience/do not experience) higher rates of disease, injury, and death. Conditions such as lung and breast cancer, which once were more common among the rich than the poor, have been called _____ _____ .

42. Socioeconomic status may help explain why the health of immigrants is generally _____ (better/worse) than that of native-born members of the same ethnic group. Immigrants often were raised in families with relatively _____ (high/low) SES.

43. Among the health hazards that accompany the social context of poverty is more _____ , more _____ , and more _____ _____ of every kind.

44. Among African-American adult males, those of higher SES have _____ (higher/lower) rates of hypertension, likely caused by greater _____

_____ .

Progress Test 1

Multiple-Choice Questions

Circle your answers to the following questions and check them with the answers on page 300. If your answer is incorrect, read the explanation for why it is incorrect and then consult the appropriate pages of the text (in parentheses following the correct answer).

1. During the years from 40 to 60, the average adult:
   a. becomes proportionally slimmer.
   b. gains about 5 pounds per year.
   c. gains about 1 pound per year.
   d. is more likely to have pockets of fat settle on various parts of the body.

2. (Thinking Like a Scientist) Regarding health, the "tragedy of the commons" refers to the tendency of people to:
   a. seek their own immediate pleasure even when doing so harms the well-being of society.
   b. avoid confronting medical symptoms that might signify serious illness.
   c. passively accept medical treatment and fail to assume responsibility for their own health habits.
   d. do all of the above.

3. Age-related deficits in speech-related hearing are most noticeable for:
   a. high-frequency sounds.
   b. low-frequency sounds.
   c. mid-range-frequency sounds.
   d. rapid conversation.

4. Primary aging refers to age-related changes that are:
   a. the consequence of unhealthy behaviors.
   b. caused by society's failure to eliminate unhealthy conditions.
   c. inevitable.
   d. reversible if health habits improve.

5. Which of the following is an example of a secondary age-related loss?:
   a. Genes on the sex chromosomes cause men's hearing to decline twice as fast as women's.

   b. Between the ages of 35 and 65, the lens of the eye becomes less elastic.
   c. As we grow older, the corneas of our eyes become flatter.
   d. Adults who have spent years working on loud machines develop specific hearing deficits.

6. At midlife, individuals who _____ tend to live longer and have fewer chronic illnesses or disabilities.
   a. are relatively well educated
   b. are financially secure
   c. live in or near cities
   d. are or do all of the above

7. The term that refers to diseases of all kinds is:
   a. mortality.   **c.** disability.
   b. morbidity.   **d.** vitality.

8. On average, women reach menopause at age:
   a. 39.   **c.** 46.
   b. 42.   **d.** 51.

9. In explaining ethnic variations in health and illness during middle age, _____ factors are more important than_____ factors.
   a. genetic; social and psychological
   b. social and psychological; genetic
   c. intrinsic; cultural
   d. cultural; extrinsic

10. The reduction in estrogen production during and after menopause increases the risk of:
   a. osteoporosis.
   b. coronary heart disease.
   c. both a. and b.
   d. none of the above.

11. Mortality is usually expressed as:
   a. the number of deaths each year per 1,000 individuals in a particular population.
   b. the total number of deaths per year in a given population.
   c. the average age of death among the members of a given population.
   d. the percentage of people of a given age who are still living.

12. The concept that indicates how many years of full physical, intellectual, and social health are lost to a particular physical disease or disability is:
   a. vitality.
   b. disability.
   c. morbidity.
   d. quality-adjusted life years.

13. The total reduction in vitality that is caused by a specific condition is called the:
   a. DALY.
   b. QALY.
   c. burden of disease.
   d. morbidity rate.

14. Which of the following is true of all smoking diseases?
   a. They are a natural result of smoking for ten years or more, whether or not the person eventually quit.
   b. They are related to dosage of nicotine taken in and to length of time the person has smoked.
   c. They are all incurable.
   d. They are all based on the psychological addiction to tobacco.

15. The first symptom of the climacteric is usually:
   a. shorter menstrual cycles.
   b. a drop in the production of progesterone.
   c. increased variation in the timing of ovulation.
   d. weight gain.

True or False Items

Write T (*true*) or F (*false*) on the line in front of each statement.

_____ 1. The mortality rate of middle-aged European Americans is higher than that of middle-aged African Americans.

_____ 2. During middle age, back muscles, connecting tissues, and bones lose strength.

_____ 3. Approximately half of all middle-aged Americans are obese.

_____ 4. Moderate users of alcohol are more likely than teetotalers to have heart attacks.

_____ 5. Those who exercise regularly have lower rates of serious illness than do sedentary people.

_____ 6. Middle-aged adults are less likely to improve their health habits than are members of any other age group.

_____ 7. During middle adulthood, sexual responses slow down, particularly in men.

_____ 8. The climacteric refers specifically to the psychological changes that accompany menopause.

_____ 9. Despite popular reference to it, there is no "male menopause."

_____ 10. A woman's culture, expectations, and attitude, more than biology, determine her psychological reaction to menopause.

Progress Test 2

Progress Test 2 should be completed during a final chapter review. Answer the following questions after you thoroughly understand the correct answers for the Chapter Review and Progress Test 1.

Multiple-Choice Questions

1. For most people, the normal changes in appearance that occur during middle age have the greatest impact on their:
   a. physical strength.   c. cardiovascular reserve.
   b. flexibility.   d. self-image.

2. Of the following, which is the most costly to society?
   a. disability   c. mortality
   b. morbidity   d. acute illness

3. The two leading cases of death during middle age are:
   a. accidents and cancer.
   b. accidents and heart disease.
   c. cancer and heart disease.
   d. different for men and women.

4. People are more vulnerable to disease during middle adulthood because:
   a. they exercise beyond their capacity.
   b. they tend to have poorer health habits.
   c. their vital body systems decline in efficiency.
   d. of all of the above reasons.

5. Overall, the death rate of people between ages 40 and 60 is about _____ what it was fifty years ago.
   a. one-and-a-half times   c. one-third
   b. twice   d. one-half

6. Menopause is caused by a sharp decrease in the production of:
   a. estrogen.
   b. progesterone.
   c. testosterone.
   d. all of the above.

7. To be a true index of health, morbidity rates must be refined in terms of which of the following health measure(s)?
   a. mortality rate
   b. disability and mortality rates
   c. vitality
   d. disability and vitality

8. The term "male menopause" was probably coined to refer to:
   a. the sudden dip in testosterone that sometimes occurs in men who have been sexually inactive.
   b. age-related declines in fertility among men.
   c. men suffering from erectile dysfunction.
   d. age-related declines in testosterone levels in middle-aged men.

9. Which of the following is *not* true regarding hormone replacement therapy (HRT)?
   a. Long-term use (10 years or more) increases the risk of heart disease, stroke, and breast cancer.
   b. HRT reduces hot flashes and decreases the risk of osteoporosis.
   c. HRT has no proven effects on senility.
   d. For most women, the benefits of HRT outweigh the risks.

10. Compared to European-American women, African-American women have _____ rates of diagnosed breast cancer and are _____ likely to die once they are diagnosed.
    a. lower; more
    b. lower; less
    c. higher; more
    d. higher; less

11. Which of the following was *not* suggested as an explanation for variations in health among recent immigrants and long-time U.S. residents?
    a. Hardier individuals tend to emigrate.
    b. Immigrants who are more assimilated tend to have healthier lifestyles.
    c. Recent immigrants tend to be more optimistic.
    d. Recent immigrants have stronger family support.

12. Which of the following is *not* true regarding alcohol consumption?
    a. Alcohol decreases the blood's supply of high-density lipoprotein.
    b. Alcohol dependence is more common in middle adulthood.
    c. Alcohol is a major cause of injury and disease worldwide.
    d. Alcohol abuse is the main cause of cirrhosis of the liver.

13. The highest rates of overweight and obesity are found during:
    a. adolescence.
    b. early adulthood.
    c. middle adulthood.
    d. late adulthood.

14. Which of the following is true of sexual expressiveness in middle age?
    a. Menopause impairs a woman's sexual relationship.
    b. Men's frequency of ejaculation increases until approximately age 55.
    c. Signs of arousal in a woman are as obvious as they were at age 20.
    d. The levels of sex hormones gradually diminish and responses slow down.

15. A BMI over 30:
    a. is less harmful among people of African-, Latino, or Asian-American ethnicity.
    b. is less harmful among European-Americans.
    c. is less harmful to women than men.
    d. is always harmful.

Matching Items

Match each definition or description with its corresponding term.

Terms

_____ 1. mortality
_____ 2. morbidity
_____ 3. vitality
_____ 4. disease of affluence
_____ 5. menopause
_____ 6. climacteric
_____ 7. burden of disease
_____ 8. HRT
_____ 9. osteoporosis
_____ 10. disability
_____ 11. quality-adjusted life years

Definitions or Descriptions

a. disease of all kinds
b. a measure that combines indicators of premature death and disability
c. lung cancer or breast cancer
d. often prescribed to treat the symptoms of menopause
e. a condition of thin and brittle bones
f. death; as a measure of health, it usually refers to the number of deaths each year per thousand individuals
g. the cessation of ovulation and menstruation
h. more important to quality of life than any other measure of health
i. the various biological and psychological changes that precede menopause
j. the inability to perform normal activities
k. concept that indicates how many years of full vitality are lost to a particular disease

Thinking Critically About Chapter 20

Answer these questions the day before an exam as a final check on your understanding of the chapter's terms and concepts.

1. Worldwide, the leading cause of disability-adjusted life years is:
   a. HIV/AIDS.
   b. heart disease.
   c. lower respiratory tract infections.
   d. malnutrition.

2. Mr. Johnson has experienced more frequent colds and bouts of flu since he became 45 years old. His increased susceptibility to illness is likely due to:
   a. a reduction in the effectiveness of his immune system.
   b. an increase in immune-system activity to compensate for other age-related declines.
   c. a decrease in the level of testosterone circulating in his bloodstream.
   d. an increase in the level of testosterone circulating in his bloodstream.

3. Fifty-five-year-old Dewey is concerned because sexual stimulation seems to take longer and needs to be more direct than earlier. As a friend, you should tell him:
   a. "You should see a therapist. It is not normal."
   b. "See a doctor if your 'sexual prowess' doesn't improve soon. You may have some underlying physical problem."
   c. "Don't worry. This is normal for middle-aged men."
   d. "You're too old to have sex, so just give it up."

4. The mortality rates of the following ethnic groups, in order from highest to lowest, are:
   a. Asian-Americans; African-Americans; European-Americans.
   b. African-Americans; Asian-Americans; European-Americans.
   c. African-Americans; European-Americans; Asian-Americans.
   d. European-Americans; African-Americans; Asian-Americans.

5. Which of the following would entail the greatest loss of QALYs?

   a. a 70-year-old man dies in an automobile accident.

   b. a 20-year-old woman is permanently disabled and unable to work following an automobile accident.

   c. a 50-year-old man is forced to switch jobs after a skiing accident.

   d. It is impossible to determine from the information given.

6. Of the following individuals, who is least likely to seek preventive care?

   a. Rita, a middle-aged European-American.

   b. Michael, who is 55 and Asian-American.

   c. Mariogla, who is 30 and Hispanic-American.

   d. Martin, age 60 and African-American

7. Forty-five-year-old Val is the same weight she has been since college and continues to eat the same types and amounts of food she has always eaten. In order to maintain her weight through middle age, Val should:

   a. continue to eat the same amounts and types of foods.

   b. reduce her caloric intake.

   c. eat more foods high in LDL.

   d. reduce her intake of foods high in HDL.

8. Kirk wants to move to the part of the world that has the longest average life expectancy. You tell him to buy a ticket to:

   a. Germany.   c. France.

   b. Canada.   d. Japan.

9. Which of the following measures would likely yield the greatest return in quality-adjusted life years?

   a. a program of widespread immunization

   b. an education campaign that promotes self-examination for breast tumors

   c. mandatory screening for genetic disorders in newborns

   d. risk-factor screening for Alzheimer's disease

10. Lung cancer is no longer considered a disease of affluence because:

    a. today, educated people are less likely to smoke.

    b. lung cancer deaths are higher today among the poor.

    c. even poor people today can afford to buy cigarettes.

    d. of all the above reasons.

11. Fifty-year-old Beth has a college degree and a good job and lives near Seattle, Washington. Compared to her sister, who dropped out of high school and is struggling to survive on a dairy farm in rural Wisconsin, Beth is most likely to:

    a. live longer.

    b. have fewer chronic illnesses.

    c. have fewer disabilities.

    d. do or have all of the above.

12. Morbidity is to mortality as _____ is to _____ .

    a. disease; death

    b. death; disease

    c. inability to perform normal daily activities; disease

    d. disease; subjective feeling of being healthy

13. Your middle-aged father is more likely to suffer from rheumatoid arthritis than you are because:

    a. rheumatoid arthritis is an autoimmune disease.

    b. with age, the immune system is more likely to attack the body itself.

    c. the immune system begins to decline during middle age.

    d. of both a. & b.

    e. of a., b., & c.

14. Jack, who is approaching middle age, wants to know which health habits have the greatest influence on physical well-being. You point to:

    a. smoking.   c. exercise.

    b. overeating.   d. all of the above.

15. Compared to his identical twin brother, 48-year-old Andy has lower blood pressure, better circulation, a lower ratio of body fat to body weight, and higher HDL in his blood. The most probable explanation for these differences is that Andy:

    a. doesn't smoke.

    b. eats a high-fiber diet.

    c. engages in regular exercise.

    d. does all of the above.

Key Terms

Using your own words, write a brief definition or explanation of each of the following terms on a separate piece of paper.

1. primary aging

2. secondary aging

3. menopause

4. osteoporosis

5. hormone replacement therapy (HRT)

6. mortality

7. morbidity

8. disability

9. vitality

10. QALYs (quality-adjusted life years)

11. disability-adjusted life years (DALYs)

12. burden of disease

13. diseases of affluence

ANSWERS
CHAPTER REVIEW

1. primary aging; secondary aging

2. diseases; chronic; can be slowed or reversed

3. hair turns gray and thins; skin becomes drier and more wrinkled; middle-age spread occurs; pockets of fat settle on the upper arms, buttocks, and eyelids; back muscles, connecting tissues, and bones lose strength, causing some individuals to become shorter; many become noticeably overweight

4. less elastic; flatter

5. primary; men

6. pure tones; conversation

7. genes (or primary aging); ear damage (or secondary aging)

8. high

9. lungs; heart; digestive system; more; immune; autoimmune; rheumatoid arthritis; lupus

10. medical practices; health practices;70; developed; heart disease; cancer; varies

11. 51; menopause; estrogen; progesterone; testosterone

12. climacteric (or perimenopause); menstrual cycles; period; vasomotor instability

13. estrogen; calcium; osteoporosis; coronary heart disease

14. variable; have

15. hormone replacement therapy (HRT)

16. heart disease, stroke, and breast cancer; senility

17. do not; sexually inactive

18. mortality; age; Japan; Sierra Leone

19. morbidity; disease

20. disability; vitality

21. vitality

22. quality-adjusted life years (QALYs); disability-adjusted life years (DALYs)

23. burden of disease

24. QALYs

25. health habits

26. cancer of the lung, bladder, kidney, mouth, and stomach, heart disease, stroke, pneumonia, and emphysema

27. dose-; duration-; European; Asian; Latin American; social norms

28. HDL (high-density lipoprotein); LDL(low-density lipoprotein); tension; digestion; cigarette smoking; overeating

Heavy drinking is the main cause of cirrhosis of the liver; it also stresses the heart and stomach, destroys brain cells, hastens calcium loss, decreases fertility, and is a risk factor for many forms of cancer.

29. a BMI of 25 or higher; 65 percent; a BMI of 30 or higher; heart disease; diabetes; stroke; arthritis

30. greater than

31. Latino, Asian-American; unharmed; agree

32. slows; less

33. environmental; evolution; genes

34. exercise more; do; cognitive; brain

Regular aerobic exercise increases heart and lung capacity, lowers blood pressure, increases HDL in the blood, and enhances cognitive functioning. It also sometimes helps reduce depression and hostility.

35. longer; fewer

36. the quality of the environment and health care, as well as genetic, dietary, religious, socioeconomic, medical, and cultural patterns

37. African-Americans; Asian-Americans; Native Americans; Hispanic-Americans; do

38. lower

One reason is that people who emigrate tend to be hardier. Another is health habits, which tend to be healthier in those less assimilated, particularly with regard to alcohol use, exercise, and diet. Recent immigrants also tend to be more optimistic and have stronger family communication and support.

39. are

40. ethnic minorities; poor; health insurance; medical care; bias; preventive

41. experience; diseases of affluence

42. better; high

43. pollution; crowding; health hazards
44. higher; work stress

PROGRESS TEST 1

Multiple-Choice Questions

1. **d.** is the answer. (p. 492)
   b. & c. Weight gain varies substantially from person to person.

2. **a.** is the answer. (p. 508)

3. **a.** is the answer. (p. 492)

4. **c.** is the answer. (p. 491)

5. **d.** is the answer. (p. 491)
   a., b., & c. Each of these is an example of a primary, age-related loss.

6. **d.** is the answer. (p. 509)

7. **b.** is the answer. (p. 498)
   a. This is the overall death rate.
   c. This refers to a person's inability to perform normal activities of daily living.
   d. This refers to how physically, intellectually, and socially healthy an individual feels.

8. **d.** is the answer. (p. 495)

9. **b.** is the answer. (p. 511)
   c. & d. Genes and culture are intrinsic and extrinsic factors, respectively.

10. **c.** is the answer. (p. 495)

11. **a.** is the answer. (p. 498)

12. **d.** is the answer. (p. 499)
    a. Vitality is a measure of how healthy and energetic a person feels.
    b. Disability measures only the inability to perform basic activities.
    c. Morbidity refers only to the rate of disease.

13. **c.** is the answer. (p. 501)
    a. DALYs are measures of the impact that disability has on quality of life.
    b. QALYs indicate how many years of an individual's vitality are lost due to a particular disease or disability.
    d. Morbidity refers to the rate of diseases of all kinds in a given population.

14. **b.** is the answer. (p. 503)

15. **a.** is the answer. (p. 495)

True or False Items

1. F The death rate for African-Americans is twice that of European-Americans. (p. 510)
2. T (p. 492)
3. F Approximately two of every three are overweight, and 30 percent are obese. (p. 505)
4. F Moderate use of alcohol is associated with reduced risk of heart attacks. (p. 504)
5. T (p. 507)
6. F Middle-aged adults are much more likely to improve their health habits than younger adults. (p. 502)
7. T (p. 495)
8. F The climacteric refers to both the physiological and the psychological changes that accompany menopause. (p. 495)
9. T (p. 497)
10. T (p. 496)

PROGRESS TEST 2

Multiple-Choice Questions

1. **d.** is the answer. (p. 492)
   a., b., & c. For the most part, the normal physical changes of middle adulthood have no significant health consequences.

2. **a.** is the answer. When a person is disabled, society not only loses an active contributor but may also need to provide special care. (pp. 498–499)

3. **c.** is the answer. (p. 494)
   d. The leading causes of death are the same for women and men.

4. **c.** is the answer. (p. 493)
   a. If anything, people exercise under their capacity.
   b. In fact, the middle-aged often have better health habits.

5. **d.** is the answer. (p. 494)

6. **d.** is the answer. (p. 495)

7. **d.** is the answer. (pp. 498–499)

8. **a.** is the answer. (p. 497)
   b. Most men continue to produce sperm throughout adulthood and are, therefore, theoretically fertile indefinitely.
   c. This disorder was not discussed.

d For men, there is no sudden drop in hormone levels during middle adulthood.

9. **d.** is the answer. (p. 496)

10. **a.** is the answer. (p. 514)

11. **b.** is the answer. Recent immigrants, who are less assimilated, tend to have healthier lifestyles. (p. 511)

12. **a.** is the answer. Alcohol increases the blood's supply of HDL, which is one possible reason that adults who drink in moderation may live longer than "teetotalers." (p. 504)

13. **c.** is the answer. (p. 505)

14. **d.** is the answer. (p. 495)

15. **d.** is the answer. (p. 506)

Matching Items

1. f (p. 498)   5. g (p. 495)   9. e (p. 495)
2. a (p. 498)   6. i (p. 495)   10. j (p. 498)
3. h (p. 499)   7. b (p. 501)   11. k (p. 499)
4. c (p. 513)   8. d (p. 496)

THINKING CRITICALLY ABOUT CHAPTER 20

1. **c.** is the answer. See Table 20.3. (p. 501)

2. **a.** is the answer. Although declines in the immune system begin in adolescence, they are not evident until middle adulthood, when recovery from all types of illness takes longer. (p. 493)

3. **c.** is the answer. (p. 497)

4. **c.** is the answer. (p. 510)

5. **b.** is the answer. Being permanently disabled and unable to work, the 20-year-old woman clearly has lost more years of vitality than either an elderly man, who statistically would be expected to die soon anyway (a.), or a middle-aged man who is simply forced to change jobs following an accident (c.). (p. 499)

6. **d.** is the answer. Men, especially members of ethnic minorities, rarely see doctors. (p. 513)

7. **b.** is the answer. (p. 506)

   a. As Val ages, her metabolism will slow down, so she should reduce her caloric intake.

   c. & d. Just the opposite is true. She should decrease her intake of foods high in LDL and increase her intake of foods high in HDL.

8. **d.** is the answer. (p. 498)

9. **a.** is the answer. (p. 500)

10. **d.** is the answer. (p. 513)

11. **d.** is the answer. People who are relatively well-educated, financially secure, and live in or near cities tend to receive all of these benefits. (p. 509)

12. **a.** is the answer. (p. 498)

   b. This answer would be correct if the statement were "Mortality is to morbidity."

   c. This answer would be correct if the statement were "Disability is to morbidity."

   d. This answer would be correct if the statement were "Morbidity is to vitality.."

13. **d.** is the answer. (p. 494)

   c. & e. The immune system actually begins to decline during adolescence.

14. **d.** is the answer. (p. 502)

15. **c.** is the answer. (p. 507)

   a. & b. Although both of these behaviors promote health, only regular aerobic exercise produces all the health benefits that Andy is experiencing.

KEY TERMS

1. **Primary aging** refers to changes that are inevitable as people grow older. (p. 491)

2. **Secondary aging** refers to changes that are caused by a person's unhealthy habits or societal conditions. (p. 491)

3. At **menopause,** which usually occurs around age 51, ovulation and menstruation stop and the production of the hormones estrogen, progesterone, and testosterone drops. (p. 495)

4. **Osteoporosis** is a condition of porous and brittle bones, caused by a loss of calcium, leading to increased fractures and frailty in old age for which women who are thin, Caucasian, and postmenopausal are at increased risk. (p. 495)

5. **Hormone replacement therapy (HRT)** is intended to help relieve menopausal symptoms, especially in women who experience an abrupt drop in hormone level because their ovaries are surgically removed. (p. 496)

6. **Mortality** means death. As a measure of health, it usually refers to the number of deaths each year per thousand members of a given population. (p. 498)

7. **Morbidity** means disease. As a measure of health, it refers to the rate of diseases of all kinds in a given population, which can be sudden and severe (acute) or extend over a long time period (chronic). (p. 498)

8. **Disability** refers to a person's inability to perform normal activities of daily life. (p. 498)

9. **Vitality** refers to how healthy and energetic—physically, intellectually, and socially—an individual actually feels. (p. 499)

10. **Quality-adjusted life years (QALYs)** is the concept that indicates how many years of full vitality an individual loses due to a particular disease or disability. (p. 499)

11. **Disability-adjusted life years (DALYs)** are the reciprocal of QALYs and a measure of the impact that disability has on quality of life. (p. 500)

12. **Burden of disease** refers to the total loss in vitality in a population that is caused by a particular disease or disability. (p. 501)

13. A **disease of affluence,** such as lung cancer or breast cancer, is one that is—or once was—more common among wealthier people and nations than in poorer ones. (p. 513)

Chapter Twenty-One

Middle Adulthood: Cognitive Development

Chapter Overview

The way psychologists conceptualize intelligence has changed considerably in recent years. Chapter 21 begins by examining the contemporary view of intelligence, which emphasizes it's multidimensional nature. Most experts now believe that there are several distinct intelligences rather than a single general entity.

The chapter then examines the multidirectional nature of intelligence, noting that some abilities (such as short-term memory) decline with age, while others (such as vocabulary) generally increase. This section includes a discussion of the debate over whether cognitive abilities inevitably decline during adulthood, or may possibly remain stable or even increase.

The next section focuses on the tendency of adults to select certain aspects of their lives to focus on as they age. In doing so, they optimize development in those areas and compensate for declines in others. Each person's cognitive development occurs in a unique context influenced by variations in genes, life experiences, and cohort effects.

A final section discusses the cognitive expertise that often comes with experience, pointing out the ways in which expert thinking differs from that of the novice. Expert thinking is more specialized, flexible, and intuitive and is guided by more and better problem-solving strategies.

The chapter concludes with a discussion of stress and ways of coping with stress. Although stress is everywhere, for humans, cognitive appraisal of a stressful even is critical in determining whether or not that event becomes a stressor.

NOTE: Answer guidelines for all Chapter 21 questions begin on page 312.

Guided Study

The text chapter should be studied one section at a time. Before you read, preview each section by skimming it, noting headings and boldface items. Then read the appropriate section objectives from the following outline. Keep these objectives in mind and, as you read the chapter section, search for the information that will enable you to meet each objective. Once you have finished a section, write out answers for its objectives.

What Is Intelligence? (pp. 519–530)

1. Briefly trace the history of the controversy regarding adult intelligence, including the findings of cross-sectional and longitudinal research and how cross-sequential research compensates for their shortcomings.

2. Distinguish between fluid and crystallized intelligence, and explain how each is affected by age.

3. Differentiate the three fundamental forms of intelligence described by Robert Sternberg, and discuss how each tends to vary over the life span.

4. Outline Howard Gardner's theory of intelligence, noting the impact of genes, culture, and aging on the various dimensions of intelligence.

Selective Gains and Losses (pp. 530–540)

5. Explain the concept of selective optimization with compensation.

6. Describe how the cognitive processes of experts differ from those of novices.

7. Discuss the impact of stressors on development during middle adulthood and differentiate two forms of coping.

Chapter Review

When you have finished reading the chapter, work through the material that follows to review it. Complete the sentences and answer the questions. As you proceed, evaluate your performance for each section by consulting the answers on page 312. Do not continue with the next section until you understand each answer. If you need to, review or reread the appropriate section in the textbook before continuing.

What Is Intelligence? (pp. 519–530)

1. Historically, psychologists have thought of intelligence as _____ (a single entity/several distinct abilities).

2. A leading theoretician, _____, argued that there is such a thing as general intelligence, which he called _____.

3. For the first half of the twentieth century, psychologists were convinced that intelligence peaks during _____ and then gradually declines.

4. During the 1950s, Nancy Bayley and Melita Oden found that on several tests of concept mastery, the scores of gifted individuals _____ (increased/decreased/remained unchanged) between ages 20 and 50.

5. Follow-up research by Bayley demonstrated a general _____ (increase/decrease) in intellectual functioning from childhood through young adulthood. This developmental trend was true on _____, _____, and _____, key subtests on _____ _____ _____.

6. Bayley's study is an example of a _____ (cross-sectional/longitudinal) research design. Earlier studies relied on _____ (cross-sectional/longitudinal) research designs.

Briefly explain why cross-sectional research can sometimes yield a misleading picture of adult development.

7. Throughout the world, studies have shown a general trend toward _____ (increasing/decreasing) average IQ over successive generations. This trend is called the _____ _____ , and because of it, IQ tests are _____ every 15 years or so.

8. Cite three reasons that longitudinal findings may be misleading.

   a. _____

   b. _____

   c. _____

9. One of the first researchers to recognize the problems of cross-sectional and longitudinal studies of intelligence was _____ .

10. Schaie developed a new research technique combining cross-sectional and longitudinal approaches, called _____-_____ research.

Briefly explain this type of research design.

11. Using this design, Schaie found that on five _____ _____ _____ , most people improved throughout most of adulthood. The results of this research are known collectively as the _____ _____ _____ .

12. In the 1960s, researchers _____ and _____ differentiated two aspects of intelligence, which they called _____ and _____ intelligence.

13. As its name implies, _____ intelligence is flexible reasoning used to draw inferences and understand relations between concepts. This type of intelligence is also made up of basic mental abilities, including _____ _____ , _____ _____ , and

_____ _____ _____ .

14. The accumulation of facts, information, and knowledge that comes with education and experience with a particular culture is referred to as _____ intelligence.

15. During adulthood, _____ intelligence declines markedly, along with related abilities such as _____ _____ and _____-_____ _____ . However, if a person's intelligence is simply measured by one _____ score, this decline is temporarily disguised by a(n) _____ (increase/decrease) in _____ intelligence.

16. The theorist who has proposed that intelligence is composed of three fundamental aspects is _____ . The _____ aspect consists of the mental processes that foster academic proficiency by making efficient learning, remembering, and thinking possible. This type of thinking is particularly valued at

_____ (what stage of life?).

17. The _____ aspect enables the person to be flexible and innovative when dealing with new situations. This type of thinking is always _____ rather than _____ , meaning that such thinkers frequently find _____ solutions to problems rather than relying on the one that has always been considered correct.

18. The _____ aspect concerns the ability to adapt to the contextual demands of a given situation. This type of thinking is particularly useful for managing the conflicting personalities in a _____ or _____ .

19. Practical intelligence _____ (is/is not) related to traditional intelligence as measured by IQ tests.

20. Schaie's research on adult changes in intelligence reveals an increase in cognitive abilities from age _____ until the late _____ , except for

_____ ,

which begins to shift slightly downward by age
_____ .

21. The researcher who believes that there are eight distinct intelligences is _____ .
Evidence from brain-damaged people _____ (supports/does not support) the multidimensional view of intelligence.

22. The value placed on different dimensions of intellectual ability _____ (varies/ does not vary) from culture to culture _____ (and/but not) from one stage of life to another.

Selective Gains and Losses (p. 530–540)

23. Researchers such as Paul and Margaret Baltes have found that people devise alternative strategies to compensate for age-related declines in ability. They call this _____ _____ _____ _____ .

24. Some developmentalists believe that as we age, we develop specialized competencies, or _____ , in activities that are important to us.

25. There are several differences between experts and novices. First, novices tend to rely more on _____ (formal/informal) procedures and rules to guide them, whereas experts rely more on their _____ and the immediate _____ to guide them. This makes the actions of experts more _____ and less _____ .

26. Second, many elements of expert performance become _____ , almost instinctive, which enables experts to process information more quickly and efficiently.

27. A third difference is that experts have more and better _____ for accomplishing a particular task.

28. A final difference is that experts are more _____ .

29. In developing their abilities, experts point to the importance of _____ , usually at least _____ (how long?) before their full potential is achieved. This highlights the importance of _____ in the development of expertise.

30. Research studies indicate that the benefits of expertise are quite _____ (general/specific) and that practice and specialization _____ (can/cannot) always overcome the effects of age.

31. Researchers distinguish stress, which is everywhere, from _____ , which are circumstances or events that damage a person's physical or psychological well-being. These circumstances contribute to a variety of adverse health conditions, including _____ _____ .

32. For humans, _____ _____ of an event is critical in determining whether or not that event becomes a stressor.

33. In _____-_____ coping, people try to cope with stress by tackling the problem directly. In _____-_____ coping, people cope with stress by trying to change their emotions. Generally speaking, _____ (younger/older) adults are more likely to attack a problem and _____ (younger/ older) adults to accept it.

34. Many psychologists consider _____-_____ coping to be the most effective in the long run.

Progress Test 1

Multiple-Choice Questions

Circle your answers to the following questions and check them with the answers beginning on page 312. If your answer is incorrect, read the explanation for why it is incorrect and then consult the appropriate pages of the text (in parentheses following the correct answer).

Multiple-Choice Questions

1. Most of the evidence for an age-related decline in intelligence came from:
   a. cross-sectional research.
   b. longitudinal research.
   c. cross-sequential research.
   d. random sampling.

2. The major flaw in cross-sectional research is the virtual impossibility of:
   a. selecting subjects who are similar in every aspect except age.
   b. tracking all subjects over a number of years.
   c. finding volunteers with high IQs.
   d. testing concept mastery.

3. Because of the limitations of other research methods, K. Warner Schaie developed a new research design based on:
   a. observer-participant methods.
   b. in-depth questionnaires.
   c. personal interviews.
   d. both cross-sectional and longitudinal methods.

4. Why don't traditional intelligence tests reveal age-related declines in processing speed and short-term memory during adulthood?
   a. They measure only fluid intelligence.
   b. They measure only crystallized intelligence.
   c. They separate verbal and nonverbal IQ scores, obscuring these declines.
   d. They yield a single IQ score, allowing adulthood increases in crystallized intelligence to mask these declines.

5. Which of the following is most likely to *decrease* with age?
   a. vocabulary
   b. accumulated facts
   c. speed of thinking
   d. practical intelligence

6. The basic mental abilities that go into learning and understanding any subject have been classified as:
   a. crystallized intelligence.
   b. plastic intelligence.
   c. fluid intelligence.
   d. rote memory.

7. Some psychologists contend that intelligence consists of fluid intelligence, which _____ during adulthood, and crystallized intelligence, which _____ .
   a. remains stable; declines
   b. declines; remains stable
   c. increases; declines
   d. declines; increases

8. Charles Spearman argued for the existence of a single general intelligence factor, which he referred to as:
   a. *g*.
   b. practical intelligence.
   c. analytic intelligence.
   d. creative intelligence.

9. The Flynn effect refers to:
   a. the trend toward increasing average IQ.
   b. age-related declines in fluid intelligence.
   c. ethnic differences in average IQ scores.
   d. the impact of practice on expertise.

10. The shift from conscious, deliberate processing of information to a more unconscious, effortless performance requires:
    a. automatic responding.
    b. subliminal execution.
    c. plasticity.
    d. encoding.

11. Concerning expertise, which of the following is true?
    a. In performing tasks, experts tend to be more set in their ways, preferring to use strategies that have worked in the past.
    b. The reasoning of experts is usually more formal, disciplined, and stereotypic than that of the novice.
    c. In performing tasks, experts tend to be more flexible and to enjoy experimentation more than novices do.
    d. Experts often have difficulty adjusting to situations that are exceptions to the rule.

12. In general, problem-focused coping is to emotion-focused coping as:
    a. men are to women.
    b. women are to men.
    c. older adults are to younger adults.
    d. younger adults are to older adults.

13. Which of the following describes the results of Nancy Bayley's follow-up study of members of the Berkeley study?
    a. Most subjects reached a plateau in intellectual functioning at age 21.
    b. The typical person at age 36 improved on two of ten subtests of adult intelligence scales: picture completion and arithmetic.
    c. The typical person at age 36 was still improving on the most important subtests of the intelligence scale.
    d. No conclusions could be reached because the sample of subjects was not representative.

14. Which of the following is *not* one of the general conclusions of research about intellectual changes during adulthood?
    a. In general, most intellectual abilities increase or remain stable throughout early and middle adulthood until the 60s.
    b. Cohort differences have a powerful influence on intellectual differences in adulthood.
    c. Intellectual functioning is affected by educational background.
    d. Intelligence becomes less specialized with increasing age.

15. The psychologist who has proposed that intelligence is composed of analytic, creative, and practical aspects is:
    a. Charles Spearman.   c. Robert Sternberg.
    b. Howard Gardner.   d. K. Warner Schaie.

True or False Items

Write T (*true*) or F (*false*) on the line in front of each statement.

_____ 1. Age impairs processing speed and short-term memory.
_____ 2. A person's IQ is unaffected by years of schooling.
_____ 3. To date, cross-sectional research has shown a gradual increase in intellectual ability.
_____ 4. Longitudinal research usually shows that intelligence in most abilities increases throughout early and middle adulthood.
_____ 5. By age 60, most people decline in even the most basic cognitive abilities.
_____ 6. IQ scores have shown a steady upward drift over most of the twentieth century.
_____ 7. All people reach an intellectual peak in adolescence.
_____ 8. Historically, most psychologists have considered intelligence to be comprised of several distinct abilities.
_____ 9. Today, most researchers studying cognitive abilities believe that intelligence is multidimensional.
_____ 10. Compared to novices, experts tend to be more intuitive and less stereotyped in their work performance.

Progress Test 2

Progress Test 2 should be completed during a final chapter review. Answer the following questions after you thoroughly understand the correct answers for the Chapter Review and Progress Test 1.

Multiple-Choice Questions

1. The debate over the status of adult intelligence focuses on the question of its inevitable decline and on:
    a. pharmacological deterrents to that decline.
    b. the accompanying decline in moral reasoning.
    c. its possible continuing growth.
    d. the validity of longitudinal versus personal-observation research.

2. Which of the following generational differences emerged in Schaie's studies of intelligence?
    a. Recent cohorts of young adults were better at math than those who were young in previous decades.
    b. Recent cohorts of young adults were better at reasoning ability, but worse at math, than those who were young in previous decades.
    c. Recent cohorts of young adults were better at all intellectual abilities than those who were young in previous decades.
    d. Recent cohorts of young adults were worse at all intellectual abilities than those who were young in previous decades.

3. The accumulation of facts that comes about with education and experience has been classified as:
   a. crystallized intelligence.
   b. plastic intelligence.
   c. fluid intelligence.
   d. rote memory.

4. According to the text, the current view of intelligence recognizes all of the following characteristics *except*:
   a. multidimensionality.
   b. plasticity.
   c. interindividual variation.
   d. *g*.

5. Thinking that is more intuitive, flexible, specialized, and automatic is characteristic of:
   a. fluid intelligence.
   b. crystallized intelligence.
   c. expertise.
   d. plasticity.

6. The _____ nature of intelligence was attested to by Howard Gardner, who proposed the existence of eight different intelligences.
   a. multidirectional   c. plastic
   b. multidimensional   d. practical

7. For people, a critical factor in determining whether a situation or event becomes a stressor is:
   a. the person's age.
   b. the person's gender.
   c. the person's ethnicity.
   d. cognitive appraisal.

8. At the present stage of research in adult cognition, which of the following statements has the most research support?
   a. Intellectual abilities inevitably decline from adolescence onward.
   b. Each person's cognitive development occurs in a unique context influenced by variations in genes, life experiences, and cohort effects.
   c. Some 90 percent of adults tested in cross-sectional studies show no decline in intellectual abilities until age 40.
   d. Intelligence becomes crystallized for most adults between ages 32 and 41.

9. Research on expertise indicates that during adulthood, intelligence:
   a. increases in most primary mental abilities.
   b. increases in specific areas of interest to the person.
   c. increases only in those areas associated with the individual's career.
   d. shows a uniform decline in all areas.

10. Research indicates that during adulthood declines occur in:
    a. crystallized intelligence.
    b. fluid intelligence.
    c. both crystallized and fluid intelligence.
    d. neither crystallized nor fluid intelligence.

11. Fluid intelligence is based on all of the following *except*:
    a. short-term memory.   c. speed of thinking.
    b. abstract thinking.   d. general knowledge.

12. In recent years, researchers are more likely than before to consider intelligence as:
    a. a single entity.
    b. primarily determined by heredity.
    c. entirely the product of learning.
    d. made up of several abilities.

13. One of the drawbacks of longitudinal studies of intelligence is that:
    a. they are especially prone to the distortion of cohort effects.
    b. people who are retested may show improved performance as a result of practice.
    c. the biases of the experimenter are more likely to distort the results than is true of other research methods.
    d. all of the above are true.

14. To a developmentalist, an *expert* is a person who:
    a. is extraordinarily gifted at a particular task.
    b. is significantly better at a task than people who have not put time and effort into performing that task.
    c. scores at the ninetieth percentile or better on a test of achievement.
    d. is none of the above.

15. One reason for the variety in patterns in adult intelligence is that during adulthood:

    a. intelligence is fairly stable in some areas.

    b. intelligence increases in some areas.

    c. intelligence decreases in some areas.

    d. people develop specialized competencies in activities that are personally meaningful.

Matching Items

Match each definition or description with its corresponding term.

Terms

_____ **1.** fluid intelligence

_____ **2.** crystallized intelligence

_____ **3.** analytic intelligence

_____ **4.** selective optimization with compensation

_____ **5.** expert

_____ **6.** creative intelligence

_____ **7.** practical intelligence

_____ **8.** expertise

_____ **9.** problem-focused

_____ **10.** emotion-focused

Definitions or Descriptions

a. intellectual skills used in everyday problem solving

b. someone who is notably more skilled and knowledgeable about a topic than the average person is.

c. all the mental abilities that foster academic proficiency

d. specialized competence

e. flexible reasoning used to draw inferences

f. the capacity for flexible and innovative thinking

g. the tendency of adults to optimize certain aspects of their lives in order to offset declines in other areas.

h. the accumulation of facts, information, and knowledge

i. coping that attacks a problem directly

j. coping that focuses on changing how one feels about a situation

Thinking Critically About Chapter 21

Answer these questions the day before an exam as a final check on your understanding of the chapter's terms and concepts.

1. In identifying the multiple aspects of intelligence, Gardner explains that:

    a. intelligence appears in three fundamental forms.

    b. a general intelligence can be inferred from these various abilities.

    c. each intelligence has its own neurological network in a particular section of the brain.

    d. fluid intelligence declines with age, while crystallized intelligence increases.

2. In Sternberg's theory, which aspect of intelligence is most similar to the abilities comprising fluid intelligence?

    a. analytic

    b. creative

    c. practical

    d. None of the above is part of Sternberg's theory.

3. Concerning the acquisition of fluid and crystallized intelligence, most experts agree that:

    a. both fluid and crystallized intelligence are primarily determined by heredity.

    b. both fluid and crystallized intelligence are primarily acquired through learning.

    c. fluid intelligence is primarily genetic, whereas crystallized intelligence is primarily learned.

    d. the nature-nurture distinction is invalid.

4. Professor Iglesias is a psychometrician. This means that she specializes in the:
   a. study of intelligence.
   b. study of cognitive development.
   c. measurement of psychological characteristics, especially intelligence.
   d. measurement of age-related psychopathologies.

5. Compared to novice chess players, chess experts most likely:
   a. have superior long-term memory.
   b. have superior short-term memory.
   c. are very disciplined in their play, sticking closely to formal rules for responding to certain moves their opponents might make.
   d. are quite flexible in their play, relying on their years of practice and accumulated experience.

6. A psychologist has found that the mathematical ability of adults born in the 1920s is significantly different from that of those born in the 1950s. She suspects that this difference is a reflection of the different educational emphases of the two historical periods. This is an example of:
   a. longitudinal research.   c. a cohort effect.
   b. sequential research.   d. all of the above.

7. Sharetta knows more about her field of specialization now at age 45 than she did at age 35. This increase is most likely due to:
   a. an increase in crystallized intelligence.
   b. an increase in fluid intelligence.
   c. increases in both fluid and crystallized intelligence.
   d. a cohort difference.

8. A contemporary developmental psychologist is most likely to *disagree* with the statement that:
   a. many people show increases in intelligence during middle adulthood.
   b. for many behaviors, the responses of older adults are slower than those of younger adults.
   c. intelligence peaks during adolescence and declines thereafter.
   d. intelligence is multidimensional and multidirectional.

9. Regarding their accuracy in measuring adult intellectual decline, cross-sectional research is to longitudinal research as _____ is to _____ .
   a. underestimate; overestimate
   b. overestimate; underestimate
   c. accurate; inaccurate
   d. inaccurate; accurate

10. Dr. Hatfield wants to analyze the possible effects of retesting, cohort differences, and aging on adult changes in intelligence. Which research method should she use?
    a. cross-sectional   c. cross-sequential
    b. longitudinal   d. case study

11. Joseph has remained associated with interesting and creative people throughout his life. In contrast, James has become increasingly isolated as he has aged. Given these lifestyle differences, which aspect of intelligence will be most affected in Joseph and James?
    a. fluid intelligence
    b. crystallized intelligence
    c. overall IQ
    d. It is impossible to predict how their intelligence will be affected.

12. When Merle retired from teaching, he had great difficulty adjusting to the changes in his lifestyle. Robert Sternberg would probably say that Merle was somewhat lacking in which aspect of his intelligence?
    a. analytic   c. practical
    b. creative   d. plasticity

13. Cherie, who is upset after learning that a less-experienced coworker received the promotion she had been expecting, schedules a meeting with her boss to discuss her concerns. Cherie's strategy for coping with this stressor is an example of:
    a. problem-focused coping.
    b. emotion-focused coping.
    c. reaction formation.
    d. displacement.

14. Compared to her 20-year-old daughter, 40-year-old Lynda is likely to perform better on measures of what type of intelligence?
    a. fluid
    b. practical
    c. analytic
    d. none of the above

15. After a rude driver cuts into Kwame's lane and nearly causes an accident, Kwame attempts to control his initial feelings of anger by reasoning that the driver may not have seen his car or perhaps was dealing with an emergency. Kwame's style of coping with this potential stressor is best described as:

   a. active.
   b. passive.
   c. emotion-focused.
   d. problem-focused.

Key Terms

Using your own words, write a brief definition or explanation of each of the following terms on a separate piece of paper.

1. general intelligence (g)
2. Flynn effect
3. fluid intelligence
4. crystallized intelligence
5. analytic intelligence
6. creative intelligence
7. practical intelligence
8. selective optimization with compensation
9. expertise
10. expert

ANSWERS

CHAPTER REVIEW

1. a single entity
2. Charles Spearman; g
3. adolescence
4. increased
5. increase; vocabulary; comprehension; information; adult intelligence scales
6. longitudinal; cross-sectional

Cross-sectional research may be misleading because each age group has its own unique history of life experiences and because in each generation academic intelligence increases as a result of improved education.

7. increasing, Flynn effect; renormed
8. a. People who are retested several times may improve their performance simply as a result of practice.

   b. Because people may drop out of lengthy longitudinal studies, the remaining subjects may be a self-selected sample.
   c. Longitudinal research takes a long time.
9. Schaie
10. cross-sequential

In this approach, each time the original group of subjects is retested a new group is added and tested at each age interval.

11. primary mental abilities; Seattle Longitudinal Study
12. Cattell; Horn; fluid; crystallized
13. fluid; inductive reasoning; abstract thinking; speed of thinking
14. crystallized
15. fluid; processing speed; short-term memory; IQ; increase; crystallized
16. Robert Sternberg; analytic; the beginning of adulthood
17. creative; divergent; convergent; unusual
18. practical; family; organization
19. is not
20. 20; 50s; number ability; 40
21. Howard Gardner; supports
22. varies; and
23. selective optimization with compensation
24. expertise
25. formal; accumulated experience; context; intuitive; stereotypic
26. automatic
27. strategies
28. flexible (or creative)
29. practice; 10 years; motivation
30. specific; cannot
31. stressors; heart attacks, strokes, overeating, alcohol abuse, severe depression, anger
32. cognitive appraisal
33. problem-focused coping; emotion-focused coping; younger; older
34. problem-focused

PROGRESS TEST 1

Multiple-Choice Questions

1. a. is the answer. (p. 520)

b. Although results from this type of research may also be misleading, longitudinal studies often demonstrate age-related *increases* in intelligence.

c. Cross-sequential research is the technique devised by K. Warner Schaie that combines the strengths of the cross-sectional and longitudinal methods.

d. Random sampling refers to the selection of subjects for a research study.

2. **a.** is the answer. (p. 520)

   b. This is a problem in longitudinal research.

   c. & d. Neither of these is particularly troublesome in cross-sectional research.

3. **d.** is the answer. (p. 522)

   a., b., & c. Cross-sequential research as described in this chapter is based on *objective* intelligence testing.

4. **d.** is the answer. (p. 524)

   a. & b. Traditional IQ tests measure both fluid and crystallized intelligence.

5. **c.** is the answer. (p. 524)

   a., b., & d. These often increase with age.

6. **c.** is the answer. (p. 523)

   a. Crystallized intelligence is the accumulation of facts and knowledge that comes with education and experience.

   b. Although intelligence is characterized by plasticity, "plastic intelligence" is not discussed as a specific type of intelligence.

   d. Rote memory is memory that is based on the conscious repetition of to-be-remembered information.

7. **d.** is the answer. (pp. 523–524)

8. **a.** is the answer. (p. 519)

   b. Practical intelligence refers to the intellectual skills used in everyday problem solving and is identified in Sternberg's theory.

   c. & d. These are two other aspects of intelligence identified in Sternberg's theory.

9. **a.** is the answer. (p. 521)

10. **a.** is the answer. (p. 533)

    b. This was not discussed in the chapter.

    c. Plasticity refers to the flexible nature of intelligence.

    d. Encoding refers to the placing of information into memory.

11. **c.** is the answer. (p. 534)

    a., b., & d. These are more typical of *novices* than experts.

12. **d.** is the answer. Younger adults are more likely to attack a problem; older adults are more likely to accept it, coping by changing their feelings about it. (p. 538)

    a. & b. Women and men do not differ in their tendencies toward emotion- or problem-focused coping.

13. **c.** is the answer. (p. 520)

    b. The text does not indicate that they improved on those tests.

    d. No such criticism was made of Bayley's study.

14. **d.** is the answer. In fact, intelligence often becomes *more specialized* with age. (p. 531)

15. **c.** is the answer. (p. 525)

    a. Charles Spearman proposed the existence of an underlying general intelligence, which he called *g*.

    b. Howard Gardner proposed that intelligence consists of eight autonomous abilities.

    d. K. Warner Schaie was one of the first researchers to recognize the potentially distorting cohort effects on cross-sectional research.

True or False Items

1. T (p. 524)

2. F   Intellectual functioning as measured by IQ tests is powerfully influenced by years of schooling. (p. 529)

3. F   Cross-sectional research shows a decline in intellectual ability. (p. 520)

4. T (pp. 520–521)

5. F   Many adults show intellectual improvement over most of adulthood, with no decline, even by age 60. (p. 522)

6. T (p. 521)

7. F   Psychologists now agree that intelligence does *not* peak in adolescence and decline thereafter. (p. 520)

8. F   Historically, psychologists have conceived of intelligence as a single entity. (p. 519)

9. T (pp. 525–528)

10. T (p. 532)

PROGRESS TEST 2

Multiple-Choice Questions

1. **c.** is the answer. (p. 520)

2. **b.** is the answer. (pp. 526–527)

3. **a.** is the answer. (p. 524)

b. Although intelligence is characterized by plasticity, "plastic intelligence" is not discussed as a specific type of intelligence.

c. Fluid intelligence consists of the basic abilities that go into the understanding of any subject.

d. Rote memory is based on the conscious repetition of to-be-remembered information.

4. **d.** is the answer. This is Charles Spearman's term for his idea of a general intelligence, in which intelligence is a single entity. (p. 519)

a. Multidirectionality simply means that abilities follow different trajectories with age, as explained throughout the chapter.

c. Interindividual variation is a way of saying that each person is unique.

5. **c.** is the answer. (pp. 532–534)

6. **a.** is the answer. (p. 528)

b. Multidimensional refers to the idea that intelligence or any characteristic involves many aspects.

7. **d.** is the answer. (p. 537)

a., b., & c. Research suggests that, for humans, cognitive appraisal of events is critical in determining whether they become stressors. Age, gender and ethnicity were not discussed as important variables in whether or not events are appraised as stressful

8. **b.** is the answer. (p. 531)

a. There is agreement that intelligence does *not* peak during adolescence.

c. Cross-sectional research usually provides evidence of *declining* ability throughout adulthood.

d. Crystallized intelligence refers to the accumulation of knowledge with experience; intelligence does not "crystallize" at any specific age.

9. **b.** is the answer. (p. 536)

10. **b.** is the answer. (p. 524)

a., c., & d. Crystallized intelligence typically *increases* during adulthood.

11. **d.** is the answer. This is an aspect of crystallized intelligence. (p. 524)

12. **d.** is the answer. (pp. 525–528)

a. Contemporary researchers emphasize the different aspects of intelligence.

b. & c. Contemporary researchers see intelligence as the product of both heredity and learning.

13. **b.** is the answer. (pp. 521–522)

a. This is a drawback of cross-sectional research.

c. Longitudinal studies are no more sensitive to experimenter bias than other research methods.

14. **b.** is the answer. (p. 532)

15. **d.** is the answer. (p. 531)

Matching Items

1. e (p. 523)   5. b (p. 532)   9. i (p. 538)
2. h (p. 524)   6. f (p. 525)   10. j (p. 538)
3. c (p. 525)   7. a (p. 525)
4. g (p. 530)   8. d (p. 530)

THINKING CRITICALLY ABOUT CHAPTER 21

1. **c.** is the answer. (p. 528)
   a. This is Sternberg's theory.
   b. This refers to Spearman's view of a *g* factor.
   d. While this is true, it is not part of Gardner's theory.

2. **a.** is the answer. This aspect consists of mental processes fostering academic proficiency by making efficient learning, remembering, and thinking possible. (p. 525)
   b. This aspect enables the person to accommodate successfully to changes in the environment.
   c. This aspect concerns the extent to which intellectual functions are applied to situations that are familiar or novel in a person's history.

3. **d.** is the answer. This is so in part because the acquisition of crystallized intelligence is affected by the quality of fluid intelligence. (p. 524)

4. **c.** is the answer. (p. 519)

5. **d.** is the answer. (p. 534)
   a. & b. The text does not suggest that experts have special memory abilities.
   c. This describes the performance of novice rather than experts.

6. **c.** is the answer. (p. 527)
   a. & b. From the information given, it is impossible to determine which research method the psychologist used.

7. **a.** is the answer. (p. 524)
   b. & c. According to the research, fluid intelligence declines markedly during adulthood.
   d. Cohort effects refer to generational differences in life experiences.

8. **c.** is the answer. (p. 520)

9. **b.** is the answer. (p. 520)
   c. & d. Both cross-sectional and longitudinal research are potentially misleading.

10. **c.** is the answer. (p. 522)

   a. & b. Schaie developed the cross-sequential research method to overcome the drawbacks of the cross-sectional and longitudinal methods, which were susceptible to cohort and retesting effects, respectively.

   d. A case study focuses on a single subject and therefore could provide no information on cohort effects.

11. **b.** is the answer. Because the maintenance of crystallized intelligence depends partly on how it is used, the consequences of remaining socially involved or of being socially isolated become increasingly apparent in adulthood. (p. 531)

12. **b.** is the answer. Creative intelligence enables the person to accommodate successfully to changes in the environment, such as those accompanying retirement. (p. 525)

   a. This aspect of intelligence consists of mental processes that foster efficient learning, remembering, and thinking.

   c. This aspect of intelligence concerns the extent to which intellectual functions are applied to situations that are familiar or novel in a person's history.

   d. Plasticity refers to the flexible nature of intelligence; it is not an aspect of Sternberg's theory.

13. **a.** is the answer. (p. 538)

   b. In this style of coping, people try to change their emotions.

   c. & d. these are examples of psychological defenses.

14. **b.** is the answer. (p. 525)

15. **c.** is the answer. (p. 538)

   a. & b. These forms of coping were not described in the textbook.

   d. In problem-focused coping, people try to solve their problems by attacking them in some way. Problem-focused coping would probably have been counterproductive (and dangerous) in this situation.

KEY TERMS

1. **General intelligence (g)** is the idea that intelligence is one basic trait, underlying all cognitive abilities, according to Spearman. (p. 519)

2. The **Flynn effect** refers to the trend toward increasing average IQ over successive generations. (p. 521)

3. **Fluid intelligence** is made up of those basic mental abilities—inductive reasoning, abstract thinking, short-term memory, speed of thinking, and the like—required for understanding any subject matter. (p. 523)

4. **Crystallized intelligence** is the accumulation of facts, information, and knowledge that comes with education and experience within a particular culture. (p. 524)

5. In Robert Sternberg's theory, **analytic intelligence** includes all the mental processes that foster academic proficiency by making efficient learning, remembering, and thinking possible. (p. 525)

6. In Sternberg's theory, **creative intelligence** involves the capacity for flexible and innovating thinking. (p. 525)

7. According to Sternberg, **practical intelligence** involves the capacity to adapt one's behavior to the demands of the situation. This type of intelligence includes the intellectual skills used in everyday problem solving. (p. 525)

8. **Selective optimization with compensation** describes the tendency of adults to select certain aspects of their lives to focus on, and optimize, in order to compensate for declines in other areas. (p. 530)

9. A hallmark of adulthood is the development of **expertise**, or specialized competencies, in activities that are personally meaningful to the individual. (p. 530)

10. According to developmentalists, an **expert** is someone who is notably more skilled and knowledgeable about a specific intellectual topic or practical ability than the average person is. (p. 532)

Chapter Twenty-Two

Middle Adulthood: Psychosocial Development

Chapter Overview

Chapter 22 is concerned with midlife, commonly believed to be a time of crisis and transition, when self-doubt, reevaluation of career goals, changes in family responsibilities, and a growing awareness of one's mortality lead to turmoil. The chapter first examines the question of whether there is stability of personality throughout adulthood, identifying five basic clusters of personality traits that remain fairly stable throughout adulthood. One personality trend that does occur during middle age, as gender roles become less rigid, is the tendency of both sexes to take on characteristics typically reserved for the opposite sex. The section also shows that although middle adulthood may have its share of pressures and stress, a crisis is not inevitable.

The second section explores changes in the marital relationship and relationships with relatives in middle adulthood. It also depicts the changing dynamics between middle-aged adults and their adult children and aging parents, describing the various demands of the younger and older generations.

The final section of the chapter examines the evolution of work in the individual's life during middle adulthood. As many women and men begin to balance their work lives with parenthood and other concerns, many engage in a scaling back of their effort in the workplace.

NOTE: Answer guidelines for all Chapter 22 questions begin on page 328.

Guided Study

The text chapter should be studied one section at a time. Before you read, preview each section by skimming it, noting headings and boldface items. Then read the appropriate section objectives from the following outline. Keep these objectives in mind and, as you read the chapter section, search for the informa-

tion that will enable you to meet each objective. Once you have finished a section, write out answers for its objectives.

Personality Throughout Adulthood (pp. 543–549)

1. Describe the Big Five clusters of personality traits, and discuss reasons for their relative stability during adulthood.

2. Explain the concept of an ecological niche, noting how it interacts with personality.

3. Explain the tendency toward gender role convergence during middle age, and discuss problems with the concept of the midlife crisis.

Family Relationships in Midlife (pp. 549–564)

4. Discuss how and why marital relationships tend to change during middle adulthood.

5. Discuss the impact of divorce and remarriage during middle adulthood, including reasons for the high divorce rate among the remarried, and describe the dilemma faced by middle-aged women in the "marriage market."

6. Characterize the relationship between middle-aged adults, their siblings, and the older and younger generations.

7. Differentiate three patterns of grandparent–grandchild relationships, and discuss historical trends in their prevalence.

8. Discuss the reasons for and value of grandparents becoming surrogate parents.

9. Discuss whether middle-aged adults are accurately described as the "sandwich generation."

Work in Middle Adulthood (pp. 564–569)

10. Describe how the balance among work, family, and self often shifts during middle adulthood.

Chapter Review

When you have finished reading the chapter, work through the material that follows to review it. Complete the sentences and answer the questions. As you proceed, evaluate your performance for each section by consulting the answers beginning on page 328. Do not continue with the next section until you understand each answer. If you need to, review or reread the appropriate section in the textbook before continuing.

Personality Throughout Adulthood (pp. 543–549)

1. The major source of developmental continuity during adulthood is the stability of

_____ .

2. List and briefly describe the Big Five personality factors.

a. _____

_____

b. _____

_____

c. _____

_____

d. _____

_____

e. _____

_____

3. Whether a person ranks high or low in each of the Big Five is determined by the interacting influences of _____ , _____ , early-_____ _____ , and the experiences and choices made at a younger age. By age _____ , the Big Five usually become quite stable. This stability results in large part from the fact that by this age most people have settled into an _____ _____ .

4. Certain traits such as _____ toward others and _____ about oneself are influenced by friends and jobs and thus may change if the _____ changes.

5. Of the Big Five traits, _____ and _____ tend to increase slightly with age, while _____ and _____ tend to decrease. The most stable trait seems to be _____ .

6. The cumulative experiences of living a life often lead to greater _____ with age.

7. During middle age, gender roles _____ (loosen/become more rigid). Some researchers even believe that there is a _____ _____ of personality traits. There may even be a _____ _____ , as women become more _____ , while men become more able to openly express _____ or _____ .

8. One reason for gender-role shifts during middle age is that reduced levels of _____ _____ may free men and women to express previously suppressed traits. However, it is also possible that these biological changes are caused by _____ _____ .

9. The psychoanalyst who believed that everyone has both a masculine and feminine side is _____ . According to this theory, middle-aged adults begin to explore the _____ _____ of their personality.

10. Longitudinal research suggests a _____ explanation for gender convergence in personality. The current cohort of middle-aged adults is _____ (more/less) marked in their convergence of sex roles because sex roles today are _____ (more/less) sharply defined than in the past.

11. The notion of a midlife crisis _____ (is/is not) accepted by most developmentalists as an inevitable event during middle age.

Family Relationships in Midlife (pp. 549–564)

12. Being the "generation in the middle," middle-aged adults are the _____ _____ of their families.

13. The group of people with whom we form relationships that guide us through life constitutes our _____ _____ .

14. For the majority of middle-aged adults, their most intimate relationship is with their _____ . For some, however, intimacy is achieved through _____ with a partner.

15. The belief that adults frequently experience role overload at midlife _____ (is/is not) borne out by research studies.

16. Throughout adulthood, the family relationship most closely linked to personal happiness, health, and companionship is _____ .

17. After the first decade or so, marital happiness tends to gradually _____ (increase/decrease). Spouse abuse is more common among _____ (younger/middle-aged) spouses than among _____ (younger/middle-aged) spouses.

List several possible reasons for this finding.

18. Divorce in middle adulthood is typically _____ (more/less) difficult than divorce in early adulthood.

19. Most divorced people remarry, on average, within _____ years of being divorced.

State several of the benefits that remarriage may bring to middle-aged adults.

20. Second marriages end in divorce _____ (more/less) often than first marriages.

21. Middle-aged _____ (women/men) are disadvantaged when it comes to finding a marriage partner for two reasons:

    a. _____

    b. _____

22. American families today are _____ . (more/less) likely to consist of several generations living under the same roof. The role of family dynamics at midlife is sometimes ignored because the word _____ is often confused with _____ , the latter defined as _____

    _____ .

23. Because of their role in maintaining the links between the generations, middle-aged adults become the _____ . This role tends to be filled most often by _____ (women/men).

24. The relationship between most middle-aged adults and their parents tends to _____ (improve/worsen) with time. One reason is that, as adult children mature, they develop a more _____ view of the relationship as a whole.

Briefly explain why this is especially true *today*.

25. Three generations of a family living under one roof is more common among _____ - and _____ - Americans.

26. Whether or not middle-aged adults and their parents live together depends mostly on _____ , which is the belief that

    _____ .

27. The "hourglass effect" describes the relationships between _____ , who often become _____ (closer/more distant) in the second half of life than they were in young adulthood.

28. Most middle-aged adults _____ (maintain/do not maintain) close relationships with their children.

29. In the United States, nearly _____ (what proportion?) of all middle-aged parents have at least one child still living with them. This is most likely to happen when the parents are

    _____

    and the children are _____

    _____ .

30. More than two-thirds of Americans become a _____ during middle adulthood. Most react quite _____ (positively/negatively) to the occurrence of this event.

31. The grandparent–grandchild bond tends to be closer if the grandchild is relatively _____ , if the parent is the _____ , and if the grandparent is _____ .

32. Grandparent–grandchild relationships take one of three forms: _____ , _____ , or _____ . A century ago, most American grandparents adopted a _____ role. The _____ pattern, which was prevalent among grandparents for most of the twentieth century, is rare today among those who

    _____ .

33. Most contemporary grandparents seek the _____ role as they strive for the love and respect of their grandchildren while maintaining their own _____ .

34. Among native-born Americans, the involved pattern of grandparenting is found most often in _____ families.

State several reasons that this is so.

35. Grandparents who take over the work of raising their children's children are referred to as _____ _____ . This role is more common when parents are _____

_____ .

36. Grandparents are most likely to provide surrogate care for children who need

_____ _____ , such as infants who are _____-

_____ or school-age boys who are _____ . If the relationship is the result of a legal decision that the parents were _____ or _____ , it becomes _____ _____ .

37. More than one in _____ (how many?) grandparents witnesses the divorce of an adult child. As a result, the parents of the _____ ex-spouse are often shut out of their grandchildren's lives.

38. It was once popularly believed that the demands placed on middle-aged adults by the younger and older generations were so burdensome that this group was referred to as the

_____ .

Generally speaking, this belief _____ (has been/has not been) supported by research.

Work in Middle Adulthood (pp. 564–569)

39. As people age, the _____ (intrinsic/extrinsic) rewards associated with working tend to become more important than the _____ (intrinsic/extrinsic) rewards.

40. Job security usually _____ (increases/decreases) during middle adulthood.

41. The popular belief that men are more concerned with their work than their family life _____ (is/is not) supported by research.

42. Both men and women report that being a good _____ , a loving _____ , and a loyal _____ are more important than being a good _____ .

43. During _____ adulthood, the combined demands of the workplace and the individual's own aspirations for promotion often create _____ .

44. In general, adults are physically and psychologically healthier if they have _____ (one primary role/multiple roles).

45. During the _____ stage of marriage, women and men with children often engage in a _____ _____ of their employment effort in order to combine work and _____ .

Briefly describe three different scaling-back strategies.

46. Mandatory retirement is _____ (legal/illegal) in most jobs and in most nations. Workers who retire before age _____ tend to be poorer and sicker than their employed age-mates.

47. (Changing Policy) Average salary and average household income are highest in

_____ _____ .

48. (Changing Policy) Current fears about the retirement costs of the _____-

_____ generation have _____ (reduced/increased) the income of young adults, who pay proportionally _____ (less/more) Social Security than older workers. As a backlash, some have called for _____ _____

in the form of equal contributions from each generation.

Progress Test 1

Multiple-Choice Questions

Circle your answers to the following questions and check them with the answers beginning on page 329. If your answer is incorrect, read the explanation for why it is incorrect and then consult the appropriate pages of the text (in parentheses following the correct answer).

1. The most important factor in how a person adjusts to middle age is his or her:
   a. gender.
   b. developmental history.
   c. age.
   d. race.

2. The Big Five personality factors are:
   a. emotional stability, openness, introversion, sociability, locus of control.
   b. neuroticism, extroversion, openness, emotional stability, sensitivity.
   c. extroversion, agreeableness, conscientiousness, neuroticism, openness.
   d. neuroticism, gregariousness, extroversion, impulsiveness, openness.

3. Concerning the prevalence of midlife crises, which of the following statements has the greatest empirical support?
   a. Virtually all men, and most women, experience a midlife crisis.
   b. Virtually all men, and about 50 percent of women, experience a midlife crisis.
   c. Women are more likely to experience a midlife crisis than are men.
   d. Few contemporary developmentalists believe that the midlife crisis is a common experience.

4. Middle-age shifts in personality often reflect:
   a. increased agreeableness, conscientiousness, and generativity.
   b. rebellion against earlier life choices.
   c. the tightening of gender roles.
   d. all of the above.

5. During middle age, gender roles tend to:
   a. become more distinct.
   b. reflect patterns established during early adulthood.

   c. converge.
   d. be unpredictable.

6. Regarding the concept of the "sandwich generation," most developmentalists agree that:
   a. middle-aged adults often are burdened by being pressed on one side by adult children and on the other by aging parents.
   b. women are more likely than men to feel "sandwiched.'
   c. men are more likely than women to feel "sandwiched."
   d. this concept is largely a myth.

7. Which of the following statements best describes the relationship of most middle-aged adults to their aging parents?
   a. The relationship tends to improve with time.
   b. During middle adulthood, the relationship tends to deteriorate.
   c. For women, but not men, the relationship tends to improve with time.
   d. The relationship usually remains as good or as bad as it was in the past.

8. In families, middle-aged adults tend to function as the _____ , celebrating family achievements, keeping the family together, and staying in touch with distant relatives.
   a. sandwich generation
   b. nuclear bond
   c. intergenerational gatekeepers
   d. kinkeepers

9. Which of the following is not one of the basic forms of grandparent–grandchild relationships?
   a. autonomous   c. companionate
   b. involved   d. remote

10. During middle adulthood, scaling back refers to the tendency of both men and women to:
    a. limit their involvement in activities that take away from their careers.
    b. deliberately put less than full effort into their work.
    c. pull away from their spouses as they reevaluate their life's accomplishments.
    d. explore the "shadow sides" of their personalities.

11. Most grandparents today strive to establish a(n) _____ relationship with their grandchildren.
    a. autonomous   c. companionate
    b. involved   d. remote

12. Concerning the degree of stability of personality traits, which of the following statements has the greatest research support?
    a. There is little evidence that personality traits remain stable during adulthood.
    b. In women, but less so in men, there is notable continuity in many personality characteristics.
    c. In men, but less so in women, there is notable continuity in many personality characteristics.
    d. In both men and women, there is notable continuity in many personality characteristics.

13. People who exhibit the personality dimension of _____ tend to be outgoing, active, and assertive.
    a. extroversion   c. conscientiousness
    b. agreeableness   d. neuroticism

14. According to Jung's theory of personality:
    a. as men and women get older, gender roles become more distinct.
    b. to some extent, everyone has both a masculine and a feminine side to his or her character.
    c. the recent blurring of gender roles is making adjustment to midlife more difficult for both men and women.
    d. gender roles are most distinct during childhood.

15. Which of the following personality traits was *not* identified in the text as tending to remain stable throughout adulthood?
    a. neuroticism   c. openness
    b. introversion   d. conscientiousness

True or False Items

Write T (*true*) or F (*false*) on the line in front of each statement.

_____ 1. At least 75 percent of American men experience a significant midlife crisis between ages 38 and 43.

_____ 2. Better than age as a predictor of whether a midlife crisis will occur is an individual's developmental history.

_____ 3. By age 30, an individual's basic personality traits become stable.

_____ 4. The current cohort of middle-aged adults is notable for the marked convergence of their sex roles.

_____ 5. In the United States in most cases, several generations live together.

_____ 6. Today's parents are less likely to maintain close relationships with their adult children.

_____ 7. After the first 10 years, marital happiness is more likely to increase than to decrease.

_____ 8. Typically, money and services flow from young adults to middle-aged parents.

_____ 9. As adults mature, personality tends to improve.

_____ 10. There is no evidence that the stability of personality traits is influenced by heredity.

Progress Test 2

Progress Test 2 should be completed during a final chapter review. Answer the following questions after you thoroughly understand the correct answers for the Chapter Review and Progress Test 1.

Multiple-Choice Questions

1. An individual's "social convoy" is most likely to be made up of:
   a. older relatives.
   b. younger relatives.
   c. people of the same gender.
   d. members of the same generation.

2. Which of the following would be a good example of an ecological niche?
   a. an extrovert marries an introvert
   b. a conscientious person cohabits with someone who is disorganized
   c. a sculptor marries a canvas artist
   d. a workaholic marries a homebody

3. Which of the following factors play a role in whether grandparents will become surrogate parents?
   a. Both parents are full-time college students.
   b. The child is a rebellious school-age boy.
   c. One parent is busy establishing a career and the other does not want to assume the burden of raising a child.
   d. The parents are too old to care for a child.

4. Which of the following explains why, among native-born Americans, involved grandparenting is most common in minority families?
   a. lack of trust that the majority culture will transmit values, beliefs, language, and customs
   b. inability to afford high-priced, quality day care
   c. the availability of grandparents, who often are not well positioned in the labor market
   d. Each of the above is a reason involved grandparenting is most common in minority families.

5. Whether a person ranks high or low in each of the Big Five personality factors is determined by:
   a. heredity.
   b. temperament.
   c. his or her lifestyle.
   d. the interaction of genes, culture, and early experiences.

6. Regarding the strength of the contemporary family bond, most developmentalists believe that:
   a. family links are considerably weaker in the typical contemporary American family than in earlier decades.
   b. family links are considerably weaker in the typical contemporary American family than in other cultures.
   c. both a. and b. are true.
   d. despite the fact that families do not usually live together, family links are not weaker today.

7. Which of the following statements best describes the relationship of most middle-aged adults to their adult children?
   a. The relationship tends to improve with time.
   b. During middle adulthood, the relationship tends to deteriorate.
   c. For women, but not men, the relationship tends to improve with time.
   d. The relationship usually remains as good or as bad as it was in the past.

8. Which of the following statements explains why couples are particularly likely to report an increase in marital satisfaction during middle adulthood?
   a. Marital satisfaction is closely tied to financial security, which tends to improve during middle adulthood.

b. The successful launching of children is a source of great pride and happiness.
   c. There often is improvement in marital equity during this period.
   d. For all of the above reasons, couples are likely to report improvement in their marriages during middle adulthood.

9. Middle-aged men and women may feel freer to express previously suppressed traits because of:
   a. reduced levels of sex hormones.
   b. less restrictive cultural roles.
   c. historical trends in gender roles.
   d. all of the above reasons.

10. Which of the following is not true concerning marriage during middle adulthood?
   a. Divorce at this time is more difficult than divorce in early adulthood.
   b. Most middle-aged divorced adults remarry within five years.
   c. Remarriages break up more often than first marriages.
   d. Remarried people report higher average levels of happiness than people in first marriages.

11. Which of the following was not cited as a factor in the great diversity of grandparent–grandchild relationships today?
   a. ethnic traditions
   b. the health of the older generation
   c. the developmental stage of the grandchild
   d. the developmental stage of the grandparent

12. Which of the following personality traits tends to remain stable throughout adulthood?
   a. agreeableness   c. openness
   b. neuroticism   d. all of the above

13. The trend toward relatively uninvolved grandparenting in middle age:
   a. provides more independence for each generation.
   b. diminishes the sense of generational continuity.
   c. is particularly unfortunate in immigrant groups, in which grandparents traditionally are responsible for passing on values, traditions, and customs.
   d. does all of the above.

14. Of the following, which is a biological explanation offered in the text for the tendency of both men and women to move toward more similar gender roles during middle age?
    a. Sex hormones decline during this period.
    b. Life experiences lead to a loosening of traditional gender roles.
    c. Both sexes have a "shadow side" to their personality that emerges at midlife.
    d. The physical changes of this time, including decreased functioning of most vital systems, lead to a reassessment of the purpose of life.

15. Concerning developmental changes in personality traits, the text notes that:
    a. there are no significant changes in personality as people move through middle adulthood.
    b. because women are more likely than men to experience an abrupt transition in their roles, their personalities are more likely to change.
    c. experience often leads to greater generativity.
    d. b. and c. are true.

Matching Items

Match each definition or description with its corresponding term.

Terms

_____ 1. companionate
_____ 2. kinkeepers
_____ 3. sandwich generation
_____ 4. surrogate parents
_____ 5. remote
_____ 6. extroversion
_____ 7. agreeableness
_____ 8. conscientiousness
_____ 9. neuroticism
_____ 10. social convoy
_____ 11. involved
_____ 12. ecological niche
_____ 13. familism
_____ 14. openness

Definitions or Descriptions

a. tendency to be outgoing
b. grandparent-grandchild relationship sought by most grandparents today
c. tendency to be imaginative
d. type of grandparenting common a century ago
e. tendency to be organized
f. those who focus more on the family
g. tendency to be helpful
h. type of grandparenting common throughout most of the twentieth century
i. those pressured by the needs of the older and younger generations
j. tendency to be moody
k. role grandparents may be called on to play when parents are poor, young, or newly divorced
l. the belief that family members should remain close and supportive of one another
m. a chosen lifestyle and context
n. "a protective layer of social relations"

Thinking Critically About Chapter 22

Answer these questions the day before an exam as a final check on your understanding of the chapter's terms and concepts.

1. Forty-five-year-old Ken, who has been single-mindedly climbing the career ladder, now feels that he has no more opportunity for advancement and that he has neglected his family and made many wrong decisions in charting his life's course. Ken's feelings are probably signs of:
   a. normal development during middle age.
   b. an unsuccessful passage through early adulthood.
   c. neuroticism.
   d. his being in the sandwich generation.

2. For her class presentation, Christine plans to discuss the Big Five personality factors. Which of the following is *not* a factor that Christine will discuss?
   a. extroversion   c. independence
   b. openness   d. agreeableness

3. It has long been assumed that, for biological reasons, I will inevitably experience a midlife crisis. I am:
   a. a middle-aged man.
   b. a middle-aged woman.
   c. either a middle-age man or a middle-aged woman.
   d. neither a. nor b.

4. Ben and Karen, both 35 years old, have been married 10 years and have two small children. Since the couple is still in the "establishment" stage of their marriage, it is likely that:
   a. one spouse will work full time while the other works part time.
   b. both will work full-time, one at a higher-paying job and one at a lower-paying "career."
   c. they will take turns, with one working full speed while the other does most of the housework and child care.
   d. They will follow any one of the above "scaling back" strategies.

5. Compared to when they were younger, middle-aged Sarah is likely to become more _____ , while middle-aged Donald becomes more _____ .
   a. introverted; extroverted
   b. assertive; emotionally expressive

   c. disappointed with life; satisfied with life
   d. extroverted; introverted

6. The parents of Rebecca and her middle-aged twin, Josh, have become frail and unable to care for themselves. It is likely that:
   a. Rebecca and Josh will play equal roles as caregivers for their parents.
   b. Rebecca will play a larger role in caring for their parents.
   c. Josh will play a larger role in caring for their parents.
   d. If Rebecca and Josh are well educated, their parents will be placed in a professional caregiving facility.

7. During middle adulthood a person's overall happiness:
   a. tends to decrease.
   b. strongly correlates with his or her marital happiness.
   c. tends to increase.
   d. is most strongly related to his or her career satisfaction.

8. Ben and Nancy have been married for 10 years. Although they are very happy, Nancy worries that with time this happiness will decrease. Research would suggest that Nancy's fear:
   a. may or may not be reasonable, depending on whether she and her husband are experiencing a midlife crisis.
   b. is reasonable, since marital discord is most common in couples who have been married 10 years or more.
   c. is unfounded, since after the first 10 years or so, the longer a couple has been married, the happier they tend to be.
   d. is probably a sign of neuroticism.

9. Of the following, the best example of a "cohort bridge" is:
   a. 25-year-old Karen, who is caring for her frail grandfather.
   b. 50-year-old Jack, who describes his relationship with his granddaughter as "autonomous."
   c. 45-year-old Danielle, who is explaining her daughter's taste in music to her own mother.
   d. 60-year-old Leonard, who sends money each month to his daughter and son-in-law.

10. Fifty-year-old Kenneth remarried this year following his divorce three years ago. It is likely that Kenneth will:

   a. become healthier.
   b. become more social.
   c. have improved relationships with his children.
   d. experience all of the above.
   e. experience none of the above.

11. Both of Brenda's marriages ended in divorce. Which of the following was *not* suggested in the text as a reason remarriages break up more often than first marriages?

   a. Some people are temperamentally prone to divorce.
   b. The more times a person has been married, the more likely it is that a current marriage will end in divorce.
   c. People generally feel less commitment in second marriages.
   d. For some people, divorce is less troublesome than having to accept a mate as he or she is.

12. Lilly enjoys her grandchildren on her own terms, visiting when she chooses and not interfering with their upbringing. Lilly's grandparenting style would best be described as:

   a. remote.   c. companionate.
   b. involved.   d. autonomous.

13. After a painful phone call with her unhappy middle-aged mother, your college roommate confides her fear that she will not be able to handle the burdens of children, career, and caring for her aging parents. Your response is that:

   a. she's right to worry, since middle-aged women who juggle these roles simultaneously almost always feel unfairly overburdened.
   b. her mother's unhappiness is a warning sign that she herself may be genetically prone toward developing a midlife crisis.
   c. Both a. and b. are true.
   d. If these roles are important to her, if her relationships are satisfying, and if the time demands are not overwhelming, filling these roles is likely to be a source of satisfaction.

14. All his life, Bill has been a worrier, often suffering from bouts of anxiety and depression. Which personality cluster best describes these traits?

   a. neuroticism   c. openness
   b. extroversion   d. conscientiousness

15. Jan and her sister Sue have experienced similar frequent changes in careers, residences, and spouses. Jan has found these upheavals much less stressful than Sue and so is probably characterized by which of the following personality traits?

   a. agreeableness   c. openness
   b. conscientiousness d. extroversion

Key Terms

Writing Definitions

Using your own words, write a brief definition or explanation of each of the following terms on a separate piece of paper.

1. Big Five
2. ecological niche
3. gender convergence
4. gender crossover
5. midlife crisis
6. social convoy
7. kinkeeper
8. familism
9. remote grandparents
10. involved grandparents
11. companionate grandparents
12. surrogate parents
13. sandwich generation

Cross Check

After you have written the definitions of the key terms in this chapter, you should complete the crossword puzzle to ensure that you can reverse the process—recognize the term, given the definition.

ACROSS

3. The belief that family members should be close and supportive of one another.
6. Clusters of personality traits that remain quite stable throughout adulthood.
9. Grandparents who enjoy involvement with their grandchildren on their own terms while maintaining their autonomy and living separately.
11. Because they are often squeezed by the needs of the younger and older generations, middle-aged adults are often referred to as the _____ generation.
12. The years between ages 40 and 65.
13. Distant grandparents who are honored, respected, and obeyed by the younger generations.
14. Grandparents who live in or nearby their grandchildren's household and who are actively involved in their day-to-day lives.
15. The extent to which a person is anxious, moody, and self-punishing.

DOWN

1. A person who celebrates family achievements, gathers the family together, and keeps in touch with family members who have moved away.
2. A period of unusual anxiety and radical reexamination that is widely associated with middle age.
4. Tendency of many middle-aged workers to begin to balance their work lives with other concerns.
5. The extent to which a person is outgoing , assertive, and active.
7. The lifestyle and social context into which adults settle that are compatible with their individual personality needs and interests.
8. The extent to which a person is organized, deliberate, and conforming.
10. The extent to which a person is kind, helpful, and easy-going.

ANSWERS

CHAPTER REVIEW

1. personality
2. a. extroversion: outgoing, assertive
   b. agreeableness: kind, helpful
   c. conscientiousness: organized, conforming
   d. neuroticism: anxious, moody
   e. openness: imaginative, curious
3. genes; culture; childhood experiences; 30; do; ecological niche
4. warmth; confidence; context
5. agreeableness; conscientiousness; openness; neuroticism; extroversion
6. generativity
7. loosen; gender convergence; gender crossover; assertive; tenderness; sadness
8. sex hormones; life changes
9. Carl Jung; shadow side
10. historical; less; less
11. is not
12. cohort bridges

13. social convoy

14. spouse; cohabitation

15. is not

16. marriage

17. increase; younger; middle-aged

Families at this stage typically have greater financial security and have met the goal of raising a family. In addition, disputes over equity in domestic work and other issues of parenting generally subside. A third reason is that many couples have more time for each other.

18. more

19. five

Divorced women typically become financially more secure, and divorced men typically become healthier and more social once they have a new partner. For men, bonds with a new wife's custodial children or a new baby replace strained relationships with children from the previous marriage.

20. more

21. women

   a. Middle-aged men tend to marry younger women.

   b. Men die at younger ages.

22. less; family; household; people who eat and sleep together in the same dwelling

23. kinkeepers; women

24. improve; balanced

Most of today's elderly are healthy, active, and independent, giving them and their grown children a measure of freedom and privacy that enhances the relationship between them.

25. Hispanic; Asian

26. familism; family members should be close and supportive of one another

27. siblings; closer

28. maintain

29. half; in good health; financially needed, perhaps because they are unemployed or single parents

30. grandparent; positively

31. young; first sibling to have children; neither too young nor too old

32. remote; involved; companionate; remote; involved; were born in the United States

33. companionate; independence (autonomy)

34. minority

Many immigrant and minority families:

• do not trust the majority culture to transmit their cultural values, language, and customs.

• have grandparents who are not well positioned in the labor market, and can afford to be caregivers

• have parents who are poor, and therefore forced to rely on free care provided by grandparents

35. surrogate parents; poor, young, unemployed, drug- or alcohol-addicted, single, or newly divorced

36. intensive involvement; drug-affected; rebellious; abusive; neglectful; kinship care

37. three; noncustodial

38. sandwich generation, has not been

39. intrinsic; extrinsic

40. increases

41. is not

42. parent; spouse; friend; worker

43. early; workaholics

44. multiple roles

45. establishment; scaling back; parenthood

One spouse may choose to work part time. Or, both partners may work full time, one at a "job" to earn money and the other at a lower-paying "career." In another scaling-back strategy, the partners take turns pursuing work and domestic and child care.

46. illegal; 60

47. middle adulthood

48. baby-boom; reduced; more; generational equity

PROGRESS TEST 1

Multiple-Choice Questions

1. **b.** is the answer. (p. 548)

2. **c.** is the answer. (p. 544)

3. **d.** is the answer. (p. 548)

   a. & b. Recent studies have shown that the prevalence of the midlife crisis has been greatly exaggerated.

   c. The text does not suggest a gender difference in terms of the midlife crisis.

4. **a.** is the answer. (p. 545)

   b. This answer reflects the notion of a midlife crisis—a much rarer event than is popularly believed.

   c. Gender roles tend to loosen in middle adulthood.

5. **c.** is the answer. (p. 546)

a. Gender roles become *less* distinct during middle adulthood.

b. Gender roles often are most distinct during early adulthood, after which they tend to loosen.

d. Although there *is* diversity from individual to individual, gender-role shifts during middle adulthood are nevertheless predictable.

6. **d.** is the answer. (p. 562)

b. & c. Women are no more likely than men to feel burdened by the younger and older generations.

7. **a.** is the answer. (p. 554)

c. The relationship improves for both men and women.

d. Because most of today's elderly are healthy, active, and independent, this gives them and their grown children a measure of freedom and privacy that enhances the relationship between them.

8. **d.** is the answer. (p. 553)

a. This was a term used to describe middle-aged women and men, who are pressured by the needs of both the younger and older generations.

b. & c. These terms are not used in the text.

9. **a.** is the answer. (p. 558)

10. **b.** is the answer. (p. 566)

11. **c.** is the answer. (p. 558)

a. This is not one of the basic patterns of grandparenting.

b. This pattern was common for most of the twentieth century.

d. This pattern was common a century ago.

12. **d.** is the answer. (p. 545)

13. **a.** is the answer. (p. 544)

b. This is the tendency to be kind and helpful.

c. This is the tendency to be organized, deliberate, and conforming.

d. This is the tendency to be anxious, moody, and self-punishing.

14. **b.** is the answer. (p. 547)

a. Jung's theory states just the opposite.

c. If anything, the loosening of gender roles would make adjustment easier.

d. According to Jung, gender roles are most distinct during adolescence and early adulthood, when pressures to attract the other sex and the "parental imperative" are highest.

15. **b.** is the answer. (p. 545)

True or False Items

1. F   Studies have found that crises at midlife are not inevitable. (p. 548)

2. T (p. 548)

3. T (p. 545)

4. F   In fact, the current cohort is *less* marked in their convergence of sex roles because male and female roles are already less sharply defined than before. (p. 547)

5. F   This is no longer true in the United States. (p. 553)

6. F   Just the opposite is true. (p. 556)

7. T (p. 550)

8. F   Everything flows in the opposite direction. (p. 557)

9. T (p. 545)

10. F The stability of personality is at least partly attributable to heredity. (p. 544)

PROGRESS TEST 2

Multiple-Choice Questions

1. **d.** is the answer. (p. 549)

2. **c.** is the answer. (p. 544)

3. **b.** is the answer. Grandparents are most likely to act as surrogate parents if the parents are poor, young, unemployed, drug- or alcohol-addicted, single or newly divorced, or if the child needs intensive involvement or is rebellious (as in b.). (p. 560)

4. **d.** is the answer. (p. 559)

5. **d.** is the answer. (p. 544)

6. **d.** is the answer. (p. 553)

7. **a.** is the answer. (p. 556)

c. The relationship improves for both men and women.

d. It generally improves, especially if the children have emerged from adolescence successfully. Because most of today's elderly are healthy, active, and independent, this gives them and their grown children a measure of freedom and privacy that enhances the relationship between them.

8. **d.** is the answer. (p. 550)

9. **d.** is the answer. (pp. 546–547)

10. **d.** is the answer. (p. 552)

11. **b.** is the answer. (p. 558)

12. **d.** is the answer. (p. 545)

13. **d.** is the answer. (pp. 558–559)

14. **a.** is the answer. (p. 546)

  b. This explanation is *not* biological.

  c. This explanation, offered by Carl Jung, is also *not* biological.

  d. This explanation, although part biological, was not offered in the text.

15. **c.** is the answer. (p. 546)

Matching Items

1. b (p. 558)   6. a (p. 544)   11. h (p. 558)
2. f (p. 553)   7. g (p. 544)   12. m (p. 544)
3. i (p. 562)   8. e (p. 544)   13. l (p. 554)
4. k (p. 560)   9. j (p. 544)   14. c (p. 544)
5. d (p. 558)   10. n (p. 549)

THINKING CRITICALLY ABOUT CHAPTER 22

1. **a.** is the answer. (p. 548)

  b. & c. Ken's feelings are common in middle-aged male workers, and not necessarily indicative of neuroticism.

  d. The sandwich generation refers to middle-aged adults being squeezed by the needs of the younger and older generations.

2. **c.** is the answer. (p. 544)

3. **d.** is the answer. Researchers have found no evidence that a midlife crisis is inevitable in middle adulthood. (p. 548)

4. **a.** is the answer. (p. 566)

5. **b.** is the answer. This is an example of the convergence of gender roles during middle adulthood. (p. 546)

  a. & d. Extroversion is a relatively *stable* personality trait. Moreover, there is no gender difference in the developmental trajectory of this trait.

  c. There is no gender difference in life satisfaction at any age.

6. **b.** is the answer. Because women tend to be kinkeepers, Rebecca is likely to play a larger role than her brother. (p. 554)

  d. The relationship of education to care of frail parents is not discussed in the text.

7. **b.** is the answer. (p. 550)

8. **c.** is the answer. (p. 550)

  a. Marital satisfaction can be an important buffer against midlife stress.

  d. There is no reason to believe Nancy's concern is abnormal, or neurotic.

9. **c.** is the answer. Only in this example is a member of one generation drawing together, or bridging, members of the younger and older generations. (p. 549)

10. **d.** is the answer. (p. 551)

11. **c.** is the answer. (pp. 551–552)

12. **c.** is the answer. (p. 558)

  a. Remote grandparents are more distant from their grandchildren than Lilly is.

  b. Involved grandparents are more active than Lilly in the day-to-day life of their grandchildren.

  d. This is not one of the basic patterns of grandparenting.

13. **d.** is the answer. (p. 565)

14. **a.** is the answer. (p. 544)

  b. This is the tendency to be outgoing.

  c. This is the tendency to be imaginative and curious.

  d. This is the tendency to be organized, deliberate, and conforming.

15. **c.** is the answer. Openness to new experiences might make these life experiences less threatening. (p. 544)

KEY TERMS

Writing Definitions

1. The **Big Five** are clusters of personality traits that remain quite stable throughout adulthood. (p. 544)

2. **Ecological niche** refers to the lifestyle and social context adults settle into that are compatible with their individual personality needs and interests. (p. 544)

3. **Gender convergence** is the tendency of the sexes to become more similar as women and men age. (p. 546)

4. **Gender crossover** is the idea that each sex takes on the other sex's roles and traits in later life. (p. 546)

5. A one-popular myth, the **midlife crisis** is a period of unusual anxiety, radical reexamination, and sudden transformation that is widely associated with middle age but has more to do with developmental history than with chronological age. (p. 548)

6. A **social convoy** is a group of people of the same generation who guide, encourage, and socialize each other as they move through life. (p. 549)

7. Because women tend to focus more on family than men do, they are the **kinkeepers,** the people who celebrate family achievements, gather the family together, and keep in touch with family members who have moved away. (p. 553)

8. **Familism** is the idea that family members should support each other because family unity is more important than individual freedom and success. (p. 554)

9. **Remote grandparents** are distant but esteemed elders, who are honored, respected, and obeyed by the younger generations. (p. 558)

10. **Involved grandparents** live in or nearby the grandchildren's household and are actively involved in their day-to-day lives. (p. 558)

11. **Companionate grandparents** enjoy involvement with grandchildren on their own terms while maintaining their autonomy and living separately. (p. 558)

12. Grandparents who take over the work, cost, and worry of raising their grandchildren due to their children's extreme social problems are called **surrogate parents**. (p. 560)

13. Middle-aged adults were once commonly referred to as the **sandwich generation** because of the false belief that they are often squeezed by the needs of the younger and older generations. (p. 562)

Cross-Check

ACROSS

3. familism
6. Big Five
9. companionate
11. sandwich
12. middle age
13. remote
14. involved
15. neuroticism

DOWN

1. kinkeeper
2. midlife crisis
4. scaling back
5. extroversion
7. ecological niche
8. conscientiousness
10. agreeableness

Chapter Twenty-Three

Late Adulthood: Biosocial Development

Chapter Overview

Chapter 23 covers biosocial development during late adulthood, discussing the myths and reality of this final stage of the life span. In a society such as ours, which glorifies youth, there is a tendency to exaggerate the physical decline brought on by aging. In fact, the changes that occur during the later years are largely a continuation of those that began earlier in adulthood, and the vast majority of the elderly consider themselves to be in good health.

Nonetheless, the aging process is characterized by various changes in appearance, by an increased incidence of impaired vision and hearing, and by declines in the major body systems. These are all changes to which the individual must adjust. In addition, the incidence of life-threatening diseases becomes more common with every decade.

Several theories have been advanced to explain the aging process. The most useful of these focus on our genetic makeup and cellular malfunctions, which includes declining immune function. However, environment and lifestyle factors also play a role, as is apparent from studies of those who live a long life.

NOTE: Answer guidelines for all Chapter 23 questions begin on page 345.

Guided Study

The text chapter should be studied one section at a time. Before you read, preview each section by skimming it, noting headings and boldface items. Then read the appropriate section objectives from the following outline. Keep these objectives in mind and, as you read the chapter section, search for the information that will enable you to meet each objective. Once you have finished a section, write out answers for its objectives.

Prejudice and Predictions (pp. 576–582)

1. Define ageism, and identify two reasons for changing views about old age.

2. Describe ongoing changes in the age distribution of the American population.

3. Distinguish among three categories of the aged, and explain the current state of the dependency ratio.

Primary Aging in Late Adulthood (pp. 583–592)

4. Differentiate between primary and secondary aging, and list several characteristic effects of aging on the individual's appearance, noting how the aged see themselves.

5. Describe age-related problems in vision and hearing.

6. Discuss the adjustments older adults may have to make in various areas of life in order to maintain optimal functioning.

7. Describe age-related changes in the body's major organ systems and explain the concept of compression of morbidity.

Theories of Aging (pp. 593–599)

8. Outline the wear-and-tear and genetic aging theories of aging.

9. Explain senescence from an epigenetic theory perspective.

10. Discuss the cellular aging theory, and explain what the Hayflick limit is and how it supports the idea of a genetic clock.

11. Explain how the immune system functions, and describe age-related changes in its functioning.

The Centenarians (pp. 599–602)

12. Identify lifestyle characteristics associated with the healthy, long-lived adult.

Chapter Review

When you have finished reading the chapter, work through the material that follows to review it. Complete the sentences and answer the questions. As you proceed, evaluate your performance for each section by consulting the answers on page 345. Do not continue with the next section until you understand each answer. If you need to, review or reread the appropriate section in the textbook before continuing.

Prejudice and Prediction (pp. 576–582)

1. The prejudice that people tend to feel about older people is called _____ .

2. The cultural bias that labels older people as infirm and ill _____ (is/is not) weakening.

3. The multidisciplinary study of aging is called _____ . The traditional medical specialty devoted to aging is _____ . Most doctors in this field see patients who are _____ , which leads them to consider aging as an _____ .

4. In the past, when populations were sorted according to age, the resulting picture was a(n) _____ , with the youngest and _____ (smallest/ largest) group at the bottom and the oldest and _____ (smallest/largest) group at the top.

List two reasons for this picture.

a. _____
   _____

b. _____
   _____

5. Today, because of _____ _____ and increased _____ , the shape of the population is becoming closer to a(n) _____ .

6. The fastest-growing segment of the population is people age _____ and older.

7. The shape of the demographic pyramid _____ (varies/is the same) throughout the world. _____ .

8. The ratio of self-sufficient, productive adults to dependent children and elderly adults is called the _____ _____ . Because of the declining _____ rate and the small size of the cohort just entering _____ _____ , this ratio is _____ (lower/higher) than it has been for a century.

9. There is an inverse ratio between birth rates and _____ . Most people over age 65 _____ (are/are not) "dependent. "

10. Approximately _____ percent of the elderly live in nursing homes.

11. Older adults who are healthy, relatively well off financially, and integrated into the lives of their families and society are classified as _____-_____ .

12. Older adults who suffer physical, mental, or social deficits are classified as _____-_____ . The _____-_____ are dependent on others for almost everything; they are _____ (the majority/a small minority) of those over age 65. Age _____ (is/is not) an accurate predictor of dependency. For this reason, some gerontologists prefer to use the terms _____ aging, _____ aging, and _____ aging.

13. Researchers have been able to extend the life of some animal species by reducing their _____ .

14. Vitamin and mineral needs _____ (increase/decrease) with age. However, calorie requirements _____ (increase/decrease) by about _____ percent from those of early and middle adulthood. During late adulthood, a diet that is _____ and healthy is even more important than earlier.

Primary Aging in Late Adulthood (pp. 583–592)

15. Developmentalists distinguish between the irreversible changes that occur with time, called _____ _____ , and _____ _____ , which refers to changes caused by particular _____ or _____ . This latter category of age-related changes _____ (is/is not) inevitable with the passage of time.

16. An increasingly important factor in late adulthood is _____ .

17. As people age, the skin becomes _____ , _____ , and _____ (more/less) elastic, which produces wrinkling and makes blood vessels and pockets of fat more visible. Dark patches of skin known as "_____ _____" also become visible. Many men experience the genetic condition called _____ _____ _____ .

18. Most older people are _____ than they were in early adulthood, because their _____ have settled closer together.

19. With age, body fat tends to collect more in the _____ and _____ than in the arms, legs, and upper face.

20. Body weight is often _____ (higher/lower) in late adulthood, particularly in _____ (men/women), who have more _____ and less body _____ than the other sex.

21. The leading cause of death from injury after age 60 are _____ . How well a person is able to move his or her _____ _____ is one of the best predictors of vitality in old age.

22. For many of the healthy elderly, the most troubling part of aging is _____ _____ .

23. More than _____ percent of those older than 80 have one of the three major eye diseases of the elderly. The first of these, _____ , involves a thickening of the _____ of the eye. The second, _____ , involves the _____ of the eyeball because of a buildup of _____ within the eye. The disease _____ _____ _____ involves deterioration of the _____ .

24. The leading cause of legal blindness among the elderly is _____ _____ _____ .

25. Age-related hearing loss, or _____ , affects about _____ percent of those aged 65 and older. Some elderly persons experience a buzzing or ringing in the ears called _____ . The hard-of-hearing are often mistakenly thought to be _____ or _____ _____ , and are more subject to _____ and _____ .

26. Many people function well with sensory impairment, for three reasons: _____ , _____ _____ , and _____ .

27. Sometimes younger adults automatically lapse into _____ when they talk to older adults.

Describe this form of speech.

28. During late adulthood, all the major body systems become _____ and less _____ . As a result, serious diseases such as _____ _____ _____ , _____ , _____ _____ _____ _____ , and most forms of _____ are much more common in late adulthood.

29. Whether a person becomes ill also depends than on past _____ _____ and current _____ .

30. Older people take _____ (less/more) time to recover from illnesses and are _____ (less/more) likely to die of them.

31. A frequent sleep complaint among older adults is _____ , which is often treated by prescription _____ drugs.

Explain why this medical intervention may be particularly harmful in late adulthood.

32. Frequent waking during the night becomes more common during late adulthood because the decrease in the brain's _____ _____ with advancing age means sleep is not as deep and _____ are not as long.

33. Many gerontologists now recommend _____ rather than pharmacological solutions to treat insomnia in the elderly.

34. A goal of many researchers is a limiting of the time any person spends ill, that is, a(n) _____ _____ _____ .

Theories of Aging (pp. 593–599)

35. The oldest theory of aging is the _____-_____-_____ theory, which compares the human body to a(n) _____ . Overall, this analogy _____ (is a good one/doesn't hold up).

State three facts that support the wear-and-tear theory.

36. Some theorists believe that, rather than being a mistake, aging is incorporated into the _____ plans of all species.

37. The oldest age to which members of a species can live, called the _____ _____ , which in humans is approximately _____ years, is quite different from _____ _____ ,which is defined as _____ _____ .

38. Life expectancy varies according to _____ , _____ , and _____ factors that affect frequency of _____ in childhood, adolescence, or middle age. In the United States today, average life expectancy at birth was about _____ for men and _____ for women.

39. In ancient times, average life expectancy was only about _____ years, due to the fact that _____ .
In 1900, in developed nations, the average life expectancy was about age _____ .
This increase was due largely to better

   _____ _____ measures, including _____ ,

   _____ , and _____ .

Briefly state one possible explanation for primary aging according to epigenetic theory.

40. The leading causes of death in early adulthood are _____ (genetic/nongenetic) events. Among the genetic diseases that evolutionary process would have no reason to select against are _____

   _____ .

41. Another theory of aging suggests that some occurrence in the _____ themselves, such as the accumulation of accidents that occur during _____ , causes aging. According to this theory, toxic environmental agents and the normal process of _____ repair result in _____ that damage the instructions for creating new cells.

42. Another aspect of the cellular theory of aging is that metabolic processes can cause electrons to separate from their atoms, resulting in atoms called _____ that scramble DNA molecules or produce errors in cell maintenance and repair.

43. Free radical damage may be slowed by certain _____ that nullify the effects of free radicals. These include vitamins

   _____ , _____ ,

and _____ , and the mineral

_____ .

44. When human cells are allowed to replicate outside the body, the cells stop replicating at a certain point, referred to as the _____

   _____ . Cells from people with diseases characterized by accelerated aging replicate _____ (more/fewer) times before dying.

45. According to this theory, DNA acts as a genetic _____ , switching on genes that promote aging at a genetically predetermined age. Support for this theory comes from several diseases that involve premature signs of aging and early death, including _____

   _____ and the rare disease

   _____ .

46. The "attack" cells of the immune system include the _____ from the bone marrow, which create _____ that attack invading _____ and

   _____ , and the _____

from the _____ gland, which produce substances that attack any kind of infected cells.

47. Over the course of adulthood the power, production, and efficiency of T and B cells

   _____ (increases/decreases/remains constant).

48. Additional support for the immune theory of aging comes from research on AIDS, or

   _____ _____

   _____ _____ , which is

caused by _____ , or

   _____ _____

   _____ .

49. Individuals with stronger immune systems tend to live _____ (longer/shorter) lives than their contemporaries. This has led some researchers to conclude that the _____ of the immune system is *the* cause of aging.

50. Females tend to have _____ (weaker/stronger) immune systems than males, as well as _____ (smaller/ larger) thymus glands. However, as a result, women are more vulnerable to _____ diseases such as rheumatoid arthritis.

The Centenarians (pp. 599–602)

51. The places famous for long-lived people are in _____ , _____ regions where pollution is minimized. Furthermore, in these places, tradition ensures that the elderly are _____ and play an important social role. Because of the absence of _____ _____ , some researchers believe the people in these regions are lying about their true age.

List four characteristics shared by long-lived people in these regions.

a. _____

b. _____

c. _____

d. _____

Progress Test 1

Multiple-Choice Questions

Circle your answers to the following questions and check them with the answers on page 346. If your answer is incorrect, read the explanation for why it is incorrect and then consult the appropriate pages of the text (in parentheses following the correct answer).

1. Ageism is:
  a. the study of aging and the aged.
  b. prejudice or discrimination against older people.
  c. the genetic disease that causes children to age prematurely.
  d. the view of aging that the body and its parts deteriorate with use.

2. The U.S. demographic pyramid is becoming a square because of:
  a. increasing birth rates and life spans.
  b. decreasing birth rates and life spans.
  c. decreasing birth rates and increasing life spans.
  d. rapid population growth.

3. Primary aging refers to the:
  a. changes that are caused by illness.
  b. changes that can be reversed or prevented.
  c. irreversible changes that occur with time.
  d. changes that are caused by poor health habits.

4. Geriatrics is the:
  a. medical specialty devoted to aging.
  b. study of secondary aging.
  c. multidisciplinary study of old age.
  d. study of optimal aging.

5. Which disease involves the hardening of the eyeball due to the buildup of fluid?
  a. cataracts
  b. glaucoma
  c. senile macular degeneration
  d. myopia

6. As a result of the slowdown and loss of efficiency in the body's major systems, which of the following is more common in late adulthood?
  a. coronary heart disease
  b. strokes
  c. most forms of cancer
  d. All of the above are equally common.

7. A direct result of damage to cellular DNA is:
  a. errors in the reproduction of cells.
  b. an increase in the formation of free radicals.
  c. decreased efficiency of the immune system.
  d. the occurrence of a disease called progeria.

8. Which theory explains aging as due in part to mutations in the cell structure?
  a. wear and tear
  b. immune system deficiency
  c. cellular accidents
  d. genetic clock

9. According to the cellular aging theory of a genetic clock, aging:
  a. is actually directed by the genes.
  b. occurs as a result of damage to the genes.
  c. occurs as a result of hormonal abnormalities.
  d. can be reversed through environmental changes.

10. Laboratory research on the reproduction of cells cultured from humans and animals has found that:
    a. cell division cannot occur outside the organism.
    b. the number of cell divisions was the same regardless of the species of the donor.
    c. the number of cell divisions was different depending on the age of the donor.
    d. under the ideal conditions of the laboratory, cell division can continue indefinitely.

11. Presbycusis refers to age-related:
    a. hearing losses.
    b. decreases in ability of the eyes to focus on distant objects.
    c. changes in metabolism.
    d. changes in brain activity during sleep.

12. Highly unstable atoms that have unpaired electrons and cause damage to other molecules in body cells are called:
    a. B cells.   c. free radicals.
    b. T cells.   d. both a. and b.

13. In triggering our first maturational changes and then the aging process, our genetic makeup is in effect acting as a(n):
    a. immune system.
    b. secondary ager.
    c. demographic pyramid.
    d. genetic clock.

14. Age-related changes in the immune system include all of the following *except*:
    a. shrinkage of the thymus gland.
    b. loss of T cells.
    c. reduced efficiency in repairing damage from B cells.
    d. reduced efficiency of antibodies.

15. Women are more likely than men to:
    a. have stronger immune systems.
    b. have smaller thymus glands.
    c. be immune to autoimmune diseases such as rheumatoid arthritis.
    d. have all of the above traits.

True or False Items

Write T (*true*) or F (*false*) on the line in front of each statement.

_____ 1. The dependency ratio is higher than it has been for a century.

_____ 2. People with stronger immune systems tend to live longer than their contemporaries.

_____ 3. Because of demographic changes, the majority of America's elderly population is now predominantly old-old rather than young-old.

_____ 4. Gerontologists focus on distinguishing aging in terms of the quality of aging, that is, in terms of young-old versus old-old.

_____ 5. Although the production of T cells declines with age, the efficiency of the immune system is not affected.

_____ 6. The immune system helps to control the effects of cellular damage.

_____ 7. A decline in the number of free radicals may accelerate the aging process.

_____ 8. Although average life expectancy is increasing, maximum life span has remained unchanged.

_____ 9. Although older people are more susceptible to disease, they tend to recover faster from most illnesses.

_____ 10. The importance of lifestyle factors in contributing to longevity is underscored by studies of the long-lived.

Progress Test 2

Progress Test 2 should be completed during a final chapter review. Answer the following questions after you thoroughly understand the correct answers for the Chapter Review and Progress Test 1.

Multiple-Choice Questions

1. People tend to view late adulthood more negatively than is actually the case because:
   a. they are afraid of their own impending death.
   b. of the tendency to categorize and judge people on the basis of a single characteristic.
   c. of actual experiences with older people.
   d. they were taught to do so from an early age by their parents.

2. An important demographic change in America is that:
   a. ageism is beginning to diminish.
   b. population growth has virtually ceased.
   c. the median age is falling.
   d. the number of older people in the population is increasing.

3. Changes in appearance during late adulthood include all of the following *except* a:
   a. slight reduction in height.
   b. significant increase in weight.
   c. redistribution of body fat.
   d. marked wrinkling of the skin.

4. Heart disease and cancer are:
   a. caused by aging.
   b. genetic diseases.
   c. examples of secondary aging.
   d. all of the above.

5. As a result of the _____ birth rate, the population dependency ratio is _____ than it was at the turn of the twentieth century.
   a. increasing; higher
   b. increasing; lower
   c. decreasing; higher
   d. decreasing; lower

6. Regarding the body's self-healing processes, which of the following is not true?
   a. The hormone estrogen may offer women some protection against heart disease.
   b. Given a healthy lifestyle, cellular errors accumulate slowly, causing little harm.
   c. Aging makes cellular repair mechanisms less efficient.
   d. Women who postpone childbirth have less efficient cellular repair mechanisms.

7. In ancient times, the average life expectancy was only about 20 years primarily because:
   a. so many babies died.
   b. there were few effective treatments for serious illnesses.
   c. accidents and warfare took scores of lives in most parts of the world.
   d. people did not understand the importance of a healthy diet to longevity.

8. The oldest age to which a human can live is ultimately limited by:
   a. cellular accidents.
   b. the maximum life span.
   c. the average life expectancy.
   d. the Hayflick limit.

9. The disease called progeria, in which aging occurs prematurely in children, provides support for explanations of aging that focus on:
   a. wear and tear.
   b. cellular accidents.
   c. cross-linkage.
   d. a genetic clock.

10. Senile macular degeneration is:
    a. the leading cause of deafness among the elderly.
    b. an eye disease in which the retina deteriorates.
    c. experienced as a ringing or rhythmic buzzing in the ears.
    d. experienced by one-third of those older than 74.

11. In studies of three regions of the world known for the longevity of their inhabitants, the long-lived showed all of the following characteristics *except*:
    a. their diets were moderate.
    b. they were spared from doing any kind of work.
    c. they interacted frequently with family members, friends, and neighbors.
    d. they engaged in some form of exercise on a daily basis.

12. In defending itself against internal and external invaders, the immune system relies on two kinds of "attack" cells: _____, manufactured in the bone marrow, and _____, manufactured by the thymus gland.
    a. B cells; T cells
    b. T cells; B cells
    c. free radicals; T cells
    d. B cells; free radicals

13. The view of aging that the body and its parts deteriorate with use and with accumulated exposure to environmental stresses is known as the _____ theory.
    a. programmed senescence
    b. genetic clock
    c. cellular accidents
    d. wear-and-tear

14. Worldwide, the fastest-growing age group are those:
    a. under 5 years of age.
    b. between 20 and 30 years of age.
    c. between 60 and 70 years of age.
    d. over age 100.

15. In humans, average life expectancy varies according to all of the following *except*:
    a. historical factors.
    b. ethnic factors.
    c. cultural factors.
    d. socioeconomic factors.

Matching Items

Match each term or concept with its corresponding description or definition.

Terms or Concepts

_____ 1. young-old
_____ 2. old-old
_____ 3. glaucoma
_____ 4. cataracts
_____ 5. B cells
_____ 6. T cells
_____ 7. compression of morbidity
_____ 8. oxygen free radicals
_____ 9. Hayflick limit
_____ 10. primary aging
_____ 11. secondary aging

Descriptions or Definitions

a. the universal changes that occur as we grow older
b. limiting the time a person is ill
c. the number of times a cell replicates before dying
d. unstable atoms with unpaired electrons that damage cells
e. attack infected cells and strengthen other aspects of the immune system's functioning
f. the majority of the elderly
g. thickening of the lens of the eye
h. the minority of the elderly
i. create antibodies that attack bacteria and viruses
j. age-related changes that are caused by health habits, genes, and other conditions
k. hardening of the eyeball due to the buildup of fluid

Thinking Critically About Chapter 23

Answer these questions the day before an exam as a final check on your understanding of the chapter's terms and concepts.

1. Which of the following is *most* likely to be a result of ageism?
   a. the participation of the elderly in community activities
   b. laws requiring workers to retire by a certain age
   c. an increase in multigenerational families
   d. greater interest in the study of gerontology

2. Loretta majored in psychology at the local university. Because she wanted to serve her community, she applied to a local agency to study the effects of aging on the elderly. Loretta is a:
   a. developmental psychologist.
   b. behaviorist.
   c. gerontologist.
   d. demographer.

3. An 85-year-old man enjoys good health and actively participates in family and community activities. This person is best described as being:
   a. ageist.   c. old-old.
   b. young-old.   d. a gerontologist.

4. Concluding her presentation on demographic trends in the United States, Marisa states that, "By the year 2030:
   a. there will be more people aged 60 and older than below age 30."
   b. there will be more people aged 30 to 59 than below age 30."
   c. there will be more people below age 30 than above age 60."
   d. the American population will be divided roughly into thirds—one-third below age 30, one-third aged 30 to 59, and one-third aged 60 and older."

5. Renne has to spend time at a nursing facility because of a broken kneecap. Although the facility contains a large dining room for residents, she prefers to eat alone in her room. The *most* likely reason for this is:
   a. her failed hearing.
   b. that she has digestive problems and does not want anyone to know.
   c. she does not want to be with other old people.
   d. all of the above.

6. Professor Wilson believes that primary aging occurs because there is no reason for "mother nature" to waste resources on adults who are no longer able to produce the next generation. Professor Wilson is evidently a proponent of:
   a. wear-and-tear theory.
   b. cellular aging theory.
   c. epigenetic theory.
   d. free radical theory.

7. In summarizing research evidence concerning the causes of aging, you should state that:
   a. "Errors in cellular duplication cannot explain primary aging."
   b. "Impairments of the immune system are closely involved in aging."
   c. "Aging is simply a mistake; species are not genetically programmed to die."
   d. a., b., and c. are equally accurate.

8. A flu that younger adults readily recover from can prove fatal to older adults. The main reason for this is that older adults:
   a. are often reluctant to consult doctors.
   b. have a greater genetic predisposition to the flu.
   c. have diminished immunity.
   d. are often weakened by inadequate nutrition.

9. The wear-and-tear theory might be best suited to explain:
   a. the overall process of aging.
   b. the wrinkling of the skin that is characteristic of older adults.
   c. the arm and shoulder problems of a veteran baseball pitcher.
   d. the process of cell replacement by which minor cuts are healed.

10. With regard to nutrition, most elderly should probably be advised to:
    a. take large doses of vitamins and, especially, antioxidants.
    b. eat foods that are high in calories.
    c. consume a varied and healthy diet.
    d. eat large meals but eat less often.

11. I am a cell that is produced in the bone marrow that creates antibodies to destroy bacteria and viruses. Who am I?
    a. B cell
    b. T cell
    c. thymus cell
    d. free radical

12. Extrapolating from the results of research studies of human and animal health and longevity, Shelly suggests that human life could potentially be extended by:
    a. careful diet.
    b. social respect.
    c. regular exercise.
    d. all of the above.

13. Mary and Charlie are both 50. As they advance through adulthood, it is likely that:
    a. Charlie will be healthier than Mary.
    b. until late adulthood, Charlie is more likely to suffer a serious disease.
    c. Mary's immune responses will be weaker.
    d. all of the above are true.

14. Because age is not an accurate predictor of dependency, some gerontologists prefer to use the term _____ to refer to the *young-old*, and the term _____ to refer to the *oldest-old*.
    a. optimal aging; usual aging
    b. usual aging; impaired aging
    c. impaired aging; optimal aging
    d. optimal aging; impaired aging

15. In concluding her presentation on human longevity, Katrina states that:
    a. current average life expectancy is about twice what it was at the turn of the century.
    b. current maximum life span is about twice what it was at the turn of the century.
    c. both average life expectancy and maximum life span have increased since the turn of the century.
    d. although maximum life span has not increased, average life expectancy has, because infants are less likely to die.

Key Terms

Writing Definitions

Using your own words, write a brief definition or explanation of each of the following terms on a separate piece of paper.

1. ageism
2. gerontology
3. geriatrics
4. dependency ratio
5. young-old
6. old-old
7. oldest-old

8. primary aging
9. secondary aging
10. cataracts
11. glaucoma
12. senile macular degeneration
13. elderspeak
14. compression of morbidity
15. wear-and-tear theory

16. maximum life span
17. average life expectancy
18. oxygen free radicals
19. antioxidants
20. Hayflick limit
21. genetic clock
22. B cells
23. T cells

Cross Check

After you have written the definitions of the key terms in this chapter, you should complete the crossword puzzle to ensure that you can reverse the process—recognize the term, given the definition.

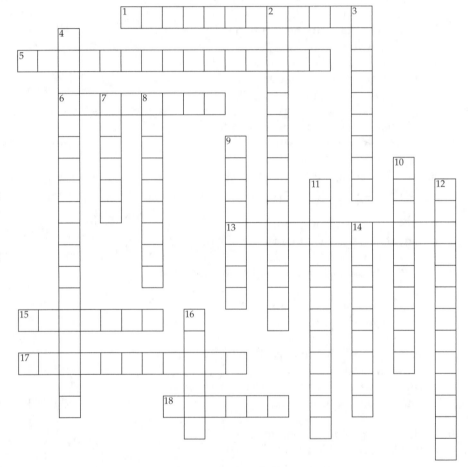

ACROSS

1. Compounds such as vitamins A, E, and C that nullify the effects of oxygen free radicals.
5. Maximum number of years that a particular species is genetically programmed to live.
6. Eye disease that can destroy vision, caused by the hardening of the eyeball due to the buildup of fluid.
13. The study of old age.
15. The universal and irreversible physical changes that occur as people get older is referred to as _____ aging.
17. Theory of aging that the parts of the human body deteriorate with use as well as due to accumulated exposure to pollution and radiation, toxic foods, drugs, disease, and various other stresses.
18. Older people who suffer physical, mental, or social deficits in later life.

DOWN

2. Ratio of self-sufficient, productive adults to children and the elderly.
3. The changes that occur with age that are caused by health habits, genes, and other influences that vary from person to person are referred to as _____ aging.
4. Highly unstable atoms with unpaired electrons that are capable of reacting with other molecules in the cell, tearing them apart and possibly accelerating aging.
7. Prejudice against older people.
8. Common eye disease involving the thickening of the lens that, left untreated, can distort vision.

9. Elderly people who are healthy and vigorous.
10. The study of populations and social statistics associated with these populations.
11. Theory of aging that the regulatory mechanism in the cells' DNA controls cellular processes and "times" aging and the moment of death.
12. Maximum number of times that cells cultured from humans and animals divide before dying.
14. Elderly adults who are dependent on others for almost everything.
16. Immune system cells that are manufactured in the bone marrow and create antibodies that attack specific invading bacteria and viruses.

ANSWERS

CHAPTER REVIEW

1. ageism

2. is

3. gerontology; geriatrics; ill; illness

4. pyramid; largest; smallest
   a. Each generation of young adults gave birth to more than enough children to replace themselves.
   b. A sizable number of each cohort died before advancing to the next higher section of the pyramid.

5. fewer births; survival; square

6. 100

7. varies

8. dependency ratio; birth; late adulthood; higher

9. longevity; are not

10. 5

11. young-old

12. old-old; oldest-old; a small minority; is not; optimal; usual; impaired

13. diet

14. increase; decrease; 10; varied

15. primary aging; secondary aging; conditions; illnesses; is not

16. how people cope with primary aging

17. dryer; thinner; less; age spots; male pattern baldness

18. shorter; vertebrae

19. torso; lower face

20. lower; men; muscle; fat

21. falls; lower body

22. isolation from other people

23. 40; cataracts; lens; glaucoma; hardening; fluid; senile macular degeneration; retina

24. senile macular degeneration

25. presbycusis; 40; tinnitis; retarded; mentally ill; depression; demoralization

26. technology; specialist care; determination

27. elderspeak

Like babytalk, elderspeak uses simple and short sentences, exaggerated emphasis, slower talk, higher pitch, and repetition.

28. slower; efficient; coronary heart disease, strokes, chronic obstructive pulmonary disease; cancer

29. health habits; exercise

30. more; more

31. insomnia; narcotic

Prescription doses are often too strong for an older person, causing confusion, depression, or impaired cognition.

32. electrical activity; dreams

33. cognitive

34. compression of morbidity

35. wear-and-tear; machine; doesn't hold up

Women who have never been pregnant tend to live longer than other women. People who are overweight tend to sicken and die at younger ages. One breakthrough of modern medical technology is replacement of worn-out body parts.

36. genetic

37. maximum life span; 120; average life expectancy; the number of years the average newborn of a particular species is likely to live

38. historical; cultural; socioeconomic; death; 74; 80

39. 20; so many babies died; 50; public health; sanitation, immunizations, and antibiotics

One explanation is that since reproduction is essential for the survival of our species, it was genetically important for deaths to occur either very early in life or after childbearing and child rearing.

40. nongenetic; Parkinson's disease, Huntington's disease, Alzheimer's disease, type II diabetes, coronary heart disease, and osteoporosis

41. cells; cell reproduction; DNA; mutations

42. oxygen free radicals

43. antioxidants; A; C; E; selenium

44. Hayflick limit; fewer

45. clock; Down syndrome; progeria

46. B cells; antibodies; bacteria; viruses; T cells; thymus

47. decreases

48. acquired immune deficiency syndrome; HIV; human immunodeficiency virus

49. longer; decline

50. stronger; larger; autoimmune

51. rural; mountainous; respected; verifiable birth or marriage records
   a. Diet is moderate, consisting mostly of fresh vegetables.
   b. Work continues throughout life.
   c. Families and community are important.
   d. Exercise and relaxation are part of the daily routine.

PROGRESS TEST 1

Multiple-Choice Questions

1. **b.** is the answer. (p. 577)

   a. This is gerontology.

   c. This is progeria.

   d. This is the wear-and-tear theory.

2. **c.** is the answer. (p. 579)

3. **c.** is the answer. (p. 583)

   a., b., & d. These are examples of secondary aging.

4. **a.** is the answer. (p. 577)

5. **b.** is the answer. (p. 585)

   a. Cataracts are caused by a thickening of the lens.

   c. This disease involves deterioration of the retina.

   d. Myopia, which was not discussed in this chapter, is nearsightedness.

6. **d.** is the answer. (p. 589)

7. **a.** is the answer. (p. 596)

   b. In fact, free radicals damage DNA, rather than vice versa.

   c. The immune system compensates for, but is not directly affected by, damage to cellular DNA.

   d. This genetic disease occurs too infrequently to be considered a *direct* result of damage to cellular DNA.

8. **c.** is the answer. (pp. 596)

9. **a.** is the answer. (p. 597)

   b. & c. According to the genetic clock theory, time, rather than genetic damage or hormonal abnormalities, regulates the aging process.

   d. The genetic clock theory makes no provision for environmental alteration of the genetic mechanisms of aging.

10. **c.** is the answer. (p. 597)

11. **a.** is the answer. (p. 586)

12. **c.** is the answer. (p. 596)

    a. & b. These are the "attack" cells of the immune system.

13. **d.** is the answer. (p. 597)

    a. This is the body's system for defending itself against bacteria and other "invaders."

    b. Secondary aging is caused not only by genes but also by health habits and other influences.

    c. This is a metaphor for the distribution of age

groups, with the largest and youngest group at the bottom, and the smallest and oldest group at the top.

14. **c.** is the answer. B cells create antibodies that *repair* rather than damage cells. (p. 597)

15. **a.** is the answer. (p. 598)

    b. & c. Women have *larger* thymus glands than men. They are also *more* susceptible to autoimmune diseases.

True or False Items

1. F The ratio is lower than it has ever been, with fewer people who are dependent on others for care. (p. 579)

2. T (p. 598)

3. F Although our population is aging, the terms *old-old* and *young-old* refer to degree of physical and social well-being, not to age. (p. 580)

4. T (p. 580)

5. F The declining production of T cells contributes to diminished immunity. (p. 598)

6. T (p. 597)

7. F Inasmuch as free radicals damage DNA and other molecules, it is their *presence* that may contribute to aging. (p. 596)

8. T (p. 594)

9. F Older people tend to recover more slowly from illnesses than younger people do. (p. 590)

10. T (p. 601)

PROGRESS TEST 2

Multiple-Choice Questions

1. **b.** is the answer. (p. 577)

2. **d.** is the answer. (pp. 578–579)

   a. Ageism is prejudice, not a demographic change.

   b. Although birth rates have fallen, population growth has not ceased.

   c. Actually, with the "squaring of the pyramid," the median age is rising.

3. **b.** is the answer. Weight often decreases during late adulthood. (pp. 583–584)

4. **c.** is the answer. (p. 583)

   a. & b. Over time, the interaction of accumulating risk factors with age-related weakening of the heart and relevant genetic weaknesses makes the elderly increasingly vulnerable to heart disease.

5. c. is the answer. (p. 579)

6. d. is the answer. The text does not discuss the impact of age of childbearing on a woman's cell repair mechanisms. However, it does note that women who have never been pregnant may *extend* life. (p. 593)

7. a. is the answer. (p. 595)

b. Serious illnesses are more likely among older adults.

c. & d. Although both of these may be true, neither is the primary reason for an average life expectancy of only 20 years.

8. b. is the answer. (p. 594)

a. This is a theory of aging.

c. This statistic refers to the number of years the average newborn of a particular species is likely to live.

d. This is the number of times a cultured cell replicates before dying.

9. d. is the answer. (p. 597)

a. & b. Progeria is a genetic disease; it is not caused by the wearing out of the body or by cellular mutations.

c. This explanation for aging was not discussed.

10. b. is the answer. (p. 586)

a. Senile macular degeneration is an *eye* disease.

c. This describes tinnitis.

d. Senile macular degeneration affects one in six of those older than 80.

11. b. is the answer. In fact, just the opposite is true. (pp. 600–601)

12. a. is the answer. (pp. 597–598)

13. d. is the answer. (p. 593)

a. & b. According to these theories, aging is genetically predetermined.

c. This theory attributes aging and disease to the accumulation of cellular errors.

14. d. is the answer. (p. 578)

15. b. is the answer. (p. 594)

Matching Items

1. f (p. 580)	**5.** i (p. 597)	**9.** c (p. 597)
2. h (p. 580)	**6.** e (p. 598)	**10.** a (p. 583)
3. k (p. 585)	**7.** b (p. 591)	**11.** j (p. 583)
4. g (p. 585)	**8.** d (p. 596)	

THINKING CRITICALLY ABOUT CHAPTER 23

1. b. is the answer. (p. 577)

2. c. is the answer. (p. 577)

a. Although Loretta is probably a developmental psychologist, that category is too broad to be correct.

b. Behaviorism describes her approach to studying, not what she is studying.

d. Demographics is the study of populations.

3. b. is the answer. (p. 580)

a. An ageist is a person who is prejudiced against the elderly.

c. People who are "old-old" have social, physical, and mental problems that hamper their successful aging.

d. A gerontologist is a person who studies aging.

4. d. is the answer. (p. 579)

5. a. is the answer. Most older adults suffer from hearing loss, and this often makes them more likely to want to remain socially isolated. (p. 586)

b. & c. There is no indication that she has digestive problems or that she does not want to associate with other older people.

6. c. is the answer. (p. 595)

7. b. is the answer. (pp. 597–598)

a. Errors in cellular duplication *do*, in part, explain primary aging.

c. For each species there *does* seem to be a genetically programmed maximum life span.

8. c. is the answer. (p. 590)

a. In fact, older adults are more likely to consult doctors.

b. There is no evidence that this is true.

d. Most older adults are adequately nourished.

9. c. is the answer. In this example, excessive use of the muscles of the arm and shoulder has contributed to their "wearing out." (p. 593)

10. c. is the answer. (p. 581)

a. Large doses of vitamins can be harmful.

b. Older adults need fewer calories to maintain body weight.

d. This is an unhealthy dietary regimen.

11. a. is the answer. (p. 597)

b. T cells are manufactured in the thymus gland.

c. There is no such thing.

d. Free radicals are unstable atoms that may accelerate aging.

12. d. is the answer. (p. 599)

13. b. is the answer. (p. 598)

a. At that age, women tend to be healthier than men.

c. Throughout life, women generally have *stronger* immune systems than men do.

14. d. is the answer. (p. 581)

15. d. is the answer. (p. 594)

a. Current average life expectancy is twenty-eight years more than it was at the turn of the century.

b. & c. Maximum life span has not changed since the turn of the century.

KEY TERMS

1. Ageism is prejudice against older people. (p. 577)

2. Gerontology is the study of old age. (p. 577)

3. Geriatrics is the medical specialty devoted to aging. (p. 577)

4. The **dependency ratio** is the ratio of self-sufficient, productive adults to children and elderly adults. (p. 579)

5. Most of America's elderly can be classified as **young-old,** meaning that they are "healthy and vigorous, relatively well-off financially, well integrated into the lives of their families and communities, and politically active." (p. 580)

6. Older people who are classified as **old-old** are those who suffer severe physical, mental, or social problems in later life. (p. 580)

7. Elderly adults who are classified as **oldest-old** are dependent on others for almost everything. (p. 580)

8. Primary aging refers to the universal and irreversible physical changes that occur as people get older. (p. 583)

9. Secondary aging refers to changes that are more common as people age but are caused by health habits, genes, and other influences that vary from person to person. (p. 583)

10. Cataracts are a common eye disease involving the thickening of the lens of the eye that, left untreated, can distort vision. (p. 585)

11. Glaucoma is an eye disease that can destroy vision; it is caused by the hardening of the eyeball due to the buildup of fluid. (p. 585)

12. The leading cause of legal blindness in the elderly, **senile macular degeneration** involves deterioration of the retina. (p. 586)

13. Elderspeak is a babyish way of speaking to older adults, using simple sentences, a slower rate, higher pitch, and repetition. (p. 588)

14. Researchers who are interested in improving the health of the elderly focus on a **compression of morbidity,** that is, a limiting of the time any person spends ill. (p. 591)

15. According to the **wear-and-tear theory** of aging, the parts of the human body deteriorate with use as well as with accumulated exposure to pollution and radiation, toxic foods, drugs, disease, and various other stresses. (p. 593)

16. The **maximum life span** is the maximum number of years that a particular species is genetically programmed to live. For humans, the maximum life span is approximately 120 years. (p. 594)

17. Average life expectancy is the number of years the average newborn of a particular species is likely to live. (p. 594)

18. Oxygen free radicals are highly unstable atoms with unpaired electrons that are capable of reacting with other molecules in the cell, tearing them apart and possibly accelerating aging. (p. 596)

19. Antioxidants are compounds such as vitamins A, E, and C that nullify the effects of oxygen free radicals. (p. 596)

20. The **Hayflick limit** is the maximum number of times that cells cultured from humans and animals divide before dying. (p. 597)

21. According to one theory of aging, our genetic makeup acts, in effect, as a **genetic clock,** triggering hormonal changes, regulating cellular reproduction and repair, and "timing" aging and the moment of death. (p. 597)

22. B cells are immune system cells that are manufactured in the bone marrow and create antibodies that attack specific invading bacteria and viruses. (p. 597)

Memory aid: The *B* cells come from the *b*one marrow and attack *b*acteria.

23. T cells are immune system cells that are manufactured in the thymus and produce substances that attack infected cells of the body. (p. 597)

Cross-Check

ACROSS	DOWN
1. antioxidants	2. dependency ratio
5. maximum life span	3. secondary
6. glaucoma	4. oxygen free radicals
13. gerontology	7. ageism
15. primary	8. cataracts
17. wear-and-tear	9. young-old
18. old-old	10. demography
	11. genetic clock
	12. Hayflick limit
	14. oldest-old
	16. B cells

Chapter Twenty-Four

Late Adulthood: Cognitive Development

Chapter Overview

This chapter describes the changes in cognitive functioning associated with late adulthood. The first section reviews the parts of the information-processing system, providing experimental evidence that suggests declines in both the control processes and the retrieval strategies of older adults.

The second section describes neurological and other reasons for this decline. Nonetheless, real-life conditions provide older adults with ample opportunity to compensate for the pattern of decline observed in the laboratory. It appears that, for most people, cognitive functioning in daily life remains essentially unimpaired.

The main reason for reduced cognitive functioning during late adulthood is dementia, the subject of the third section. This pathological loss of intellectual ability can be caused by a variety of diseases and circumstances; risk factors, treatment, and prognosis differ accordingly.

The final section of the chapter makes it clear that cognitive changes during late adulthood are by no means restricted to declines in intellectual functioning. For many individuals, late adulthood is a time of great aesthetic, creative, philosophical, and spiritual growth.

NOTE: Answer guidelines for all Chapter 24 questions begin on page 360.

Guided Study

The text chapter should be studied one section at a time. Before you read, preview each section by skimming it, noting headings and boldface items. Then read the appropriate section objectives from the following outline. Keep these objectives in mind and, as you read the chapter section, search for the information that will enable you to meet each objective. Once you have finished a section, write out answers for its objectives.

Changes in Information Processing (pp. 605–611)

1. Summarize the laboratory findings regarding changes in the sensitivity of the sensory register and the capacity of working memory during late adulthood.

2. Summarize the laboratory findings regarding changes in the older adult's ability to access the knowledge base and to use control processes efficiently.

3. Distinguish between explicit and implicit memory, and discuss resistance as a reason for declining control.

Reasons for Age-Related Change (pp. 611–617)

4. Suggest several reasons, other than the aging process itself, that might contribute to age-related declines in cognitive functioning.

5. (text and Thinking Like a Scientist) Explain how noninvasive neuroimaging techniques have changed neuroscientists' understanding of how the brain works, and describe age-related changes in the brain.

6. Discuss secondary aging as a cause of cognitive decline.

7. Characterize and explain discrepancies between how the elderly perform on memory and problem-solving tasks in the laboratory, on the one hand, and in daily life, on the other.

Dementia (pp. 618–625)

8. Identify the two most common forms of dementia, and discuss the differences between them.

9. Identify and describe other organic causes of dementia as well as causes of reversible dementia.

New Cognitive Development in Later Life (pp. 625–630)

10. (text and In Person) Discuss the claims of developmentalists regarding the possibility of positive cognitive development during late adulthood, and cite several areas of life in which such development may occur.

Chapter Review

When you have finished reading the chapter, work through the material that follows to review it. Complete the sentences and answer the questions. As you proceed, evaluate your performance for each section by consulting the answers beginning on page 360. Do not continue with the next section until you understand each answer. If you need to, review or reread the appropriate section in the textbook before continuing.

Changes in Information Processing (pp. 605–611)

1. In Schaie's longitudinal study, beginning at about age _____ , older adults began to show significant declines on the five "primary mental abilities": _____
_____ , _____
_____ , _____
_____ , _____
_____ , and _____
_____ .

2. Researchers agree, however, that there are significant _____ (differences/similarities) in intellectual ability in later life.

3. The _____ _____ stores incoming sensory information for a split second after it is received. Research suggests that age _____ (has no impact on/causes small declines in) the sensitivity and power of the sensory register.

4. Age-related changes in the sensory register _____ (can/cannot) easily be compensated for.

5. In order for sensory information to be registered, it must cross the _____ _____ . Due to sensory-system declines, some older people _____ (can/cannot) register certain information.

6. One study found that _____ accounted for nearly one-third of the variance in cognitive scores for older adults.

7. Some experts believe that the simplest way to predict how much an older person has aged intellectually may be to measure _____ , _____ , or _____ .

8. Once information is perceived, it must be placed in _____ _____ .

9. Of all the aspects of information processing, _____ _____ is the component that shows the most substantial declines with age.

10. Working memory has two interrelated functions: to temporarily _____ information and then to _____ it.

11. Older adults are particularly likely to experience difficulty when they are asked to remember several items of information while _____ them in complex ways. This is especially true if the new information is mixed with material that is _____ .

12. The difficulty older adults have in multitasking is called the _____-_____ .

13. The _____ _____ consists of the storehouse of information held in _____-_____ memory. This storehouse is far from perfect, because

_____ _____ and _____ _____ allow most material to be forgotten, never reaching this part of memory. And those memories that do are still subject to _____ .

14. Long-term memory for _____ remains unimpaired over the decades, and may even increase at least until age _____ . Also unimpaired are specific areas of _____ . Events that are _____ in nature and based on _____ rather than factual details are also remembered better.

15. A common memory error is _____ _____ , not remembering who or what was the source of a specific piece of information.

16. One way of investigating long-term memory and aging has been to make _____-_____ comparisons of people's memories of public events or facts. Another has been to probe memory of _____ learning.

17. Overall, how much of their knowledge base is available to older adults seems to depend less on _____ _____ and more on _____ _____ .

18. Research on memory reveals that the particulars of the _____ _____ are crucial in how well elderly people perform.

19. The _____ _____ of the information-processing system function in an executive role and include _____ mechanisms, _____ strategies, _____ _____ , and _____ _____ .

20. Older adults are more likely to rely on prior _____ , general _____ , and _____ _____ .

Use of _____ strategies also worsens with age.

21. A significant part of the explanation for memory difficulties in the aged may be inadequate _____ _____ .

22. Memory takes two forms: _____ memory is "automatic" memory involving _____ , _____ responses, _____ procedures, and the _____ . This type of memory is _____ (more/less) vulnerable to age-related deficits than is _____ memory. This latter type of memory involves _____ , _____ , _____ , and the like, most of which was _____ (consciously/unconsciously) learned.

23. As people get older, differences in implicit and explicit memory might be reflected in their remembering how to _____ a particular task but not being as able to _____ its actions.

24. Some decline in control processes may also be the result of _____ , or refusing to change familiar strategies, rather than a direct result of aging.

Reasons for Age-Related Changes (pp. 611–617)

25. Declines in cognitive functioning may be caused by _____ _____ , _____ _____ , or _____ .

26. Neural-cell loss probably _____ (is/is not) the main factor behind age-related declines in cognitive functioning.

27. One universal change is a _____ in brain processes This can be traced to reduced production of _____ , including _____ , _____ , _____ , and _____ . It is also due to reductions in the volume of _____ _____ , the speed of the _____ ,

and the pace of activation of various parts of the cortex.

28. According to some experts, the slowing of brain processes means that thinking becomes _____ , _____ , and _____ with advancing age. Using memory tricks and reminders, however, older adults often are able to _____ for slower processing and _____ .

29. (Thinking Like a Scientist) Two noninvasive neuroimaging techniques that allow researchers to see the dynamic workings of the brain are _____ and _____ scans. These techniques involve neuroimaging that is _____ , that is, in living brains.

30. (Thinking Like a Scientist) Neuroscience has demonstrated that the brain has _____ (one or two/many) language areas. Imaging studies have also shown that _____ and _____ can be formed in adulthood, that intellectual ability _____ (correlates/does not correlate) with brain size, that attention-deficit disorder may be caused by an immature _____ _____ , and that people use their brains differently as they age.

31. (Thinking Like a Scientist) Older brains sometimes show more brain activity, perhaps because their brains compensate for intellectual slowdown by _____ . Another possible explanation is that the brain "_____ " and no longer uses a different region for each function.

32. The overall slowdown of cognitive abilities that often occurs in the days or months before death is called _____ _____ .

33. Declines in cognitive functioning may also be associated with systemic conditions that affect the brain and other organs such as _____ , _____ , _____ , and

Several factors contribute to these diseases, including _____

_____ .

34. Declines in cognitive functioning may also be associated with ageism, including disparaging _____ .

35. Older adults may _____ (overestimate/underestimate) their memory skills when they were younger; consequently, they tend to _____ (overestimate/underestimate) their current memory losses. As a result of this misperception, older adults may lose _____ in their memory.

36. The impact of ageist stereotypes on cognitive functioning is revealed in a study in which the memory gap between old and young _____ (deaf/hearing) _____ (Chinese/American) students was twice as great as that for _____ (deaf/hearing) _____ (Chinese/American) students and five times as great as that for _____ .

37. Laboratory tests of memory may put older persons at a disadvantage because they generally use _____ material, which reduces motivation in older adults.

38. Most older adults _____ (do/do not) consider memory problems a significant handicap in daily life.

Dementia (pp. 618–625)

39. Although pathological loss of intellectual ability in elderly people is often referred to as _____ , a more precise term for this loss is _____ , which is defined as _____ .

40. Traditionally, when dementia occurred before age _____ , it was called _____ _____ ; when it occurred after this age, it was called

_____ _____ . This age-based distinction is arbitrary, however, because the same _____ may occur at any age.

41. Dementia, which can be caused by more than 70 diseases and circumstances, is characterized by _____ _____ and _____ . Dementia lasts a long time; that is, it is _____ .

42. The most common form of dementia is

_____ _____ . This disorder is characterized by abnormalities in the _____ _____ , called _____ and _____ , that destroy normal brain functioning.

43. Plaques are formed _____ (inside/outside) the brain cells from a protein called _____ ; tangles are masses of protein found _____ (inside/outside) the cells. Plaques and tangles usually begin in the _____ of the brain.

44. Physiologically, the brain damage that accompanies this disease _____ (does/does not) vary with the age of the victim.

45. With age, Alzheimer's disease becomes _____ (more/no more/less) common, affecting about one in every _____ adults over age 65 and about 1 in every _____ over age 85.

46. About _____ (what proportion?) of the population inherits the gene _____ , which increases the risk of Alzheimer's disease. The protective _____ allele of the same gene may dissipate the _____ that cause the formation of plaques.

47. When Alzheimer's disease appears in _____ (middle/late) adulthood, which is quite _____ (common/rare), it usually progresses _____ (less/more) quickly, reaching the last phase within _____ years. In

such cases, the disease is caused by one of several _____ abnormalities.

48. The first stage of Alzheimer's disease is marked by _____ about recent events. Most people _____ (recognize/do not recognize) that they have a memory problem during this stage, which is often indistinguishable from the normal decline in _____ memory.

49. In the second stage, there are noticeable deficits in the person's _____ and _____-_____ . Changes in _____ are common in this stage. The third stage begins when memory loss becomes dangerous and _____ because the person can no longer manage _____ _____ _____ . People in the fourth stage require _____-_____ _____ . In the fifth stage, people no longer_____ and do not respond with any action or emotion at all. In general, death comes _____ (how many years?) after stage one.

50. The second major type of dementia is _____ _____ . This condition occurs because a temporary obstruction of the _____ _____ , called a(n) _____ , prevents a sufficient supply of blood from reaching the brain. This causes destruction of brain tissue, commonly called a(n) _____ .

51. The underlying cause of VaD or MID is systemic _____ , which is common in people who have problems with their _____ systems, including those with _____ _____ , _____ , tingling or _____ in their extremities, and _____ . Measures to improve circulation, such as _____ , or to control hypertension and diabetes through _____ and _____ , can help to prevent or control the progress of VaD.

52. Unlike the person with Alzheimer's disease, the person with VaD shows a _____ (gradual/sudden) drop in intellectual functioning. The prognosis for a person with VaD is generally quite _____ (good/poor).

53. Another category of dementias, called _____ _____ , originates in brain areas that do not directly involve thinking and memory. These dementias, which cause a progressive loss of _____ control, include _____ disease, _____ disease, and _____ _____ .

54. The best known of these dementias is _____ _____ , which produces muscle tremors or rigidity. This disease is related to the degeneration of neurons that produce the neurotransmitter _____ .

55. Many AIDS and syphilis patients develop a brain _____ that causes dementia.

56. Chronic alcoholism can lead to _____ syndrome, the chief symptom of which is severely impaired _____-_____ _____ .

57. Oftentimes, the elderly are thought to be suffering from brain disease when, in fact, their symptoms are a sign of _____ dementia caused by some other factor such as _____ , _____ , _____ , _____ , _____ , _____ , or other _____ _____ .

58. The most common cause of reversible dementia is _____ . Symptoms of dementia can result from drug _____ that occur when a person is taking several different medications. This problem is made worse by the fact that many of the drugs prescribed to older adults can, by themselves, slow down _____ _____ .

59. In general, psychological illnesses such as schizophrenia are _____ (more/less) com-

mon in the elderly than in younger adults. Approximately _____ percent of the elderly who are diagnosed as demented are actually experiencing psychological illness.

60. At some time during their later years, _____ (many/a small percentage of) older adults experience symptoms of depression. Generally speaking, depression _____ (is/is not) very treatable in late adulthood.

61. One consequence of untreated depression among the elderly is that the rate of _____ is higher for those over age _____ than for any other group.

New Cognitive Development in Later Life
(pp. 625–630)

62. According to Erik Erikson, older adults are more interested in _____

_____ than younger adults and, as the "social witnesses" to life, are more aware of the _____ of the generations.

63. According to Abraham Maslow, older adults are more likely to achieve _____ .

64. Many people become more appreciative of _____ and _____ _____ as they get older.

65. Many people also become more _____ and _____ than when they were younger.

66. One form of this attempt to put life into perspective is called the _____ _____ , in which the older person connects his or her own life with the future.

67. One of the most positive attributes commonly associated with older people is _____ , which Baltes defines as expert knowledge in the _____ _____ of life.

Progress Test 1
Multiple-Choice Questions

Circle your answers to the following questions and check them with the answers beginning on page 361. If your answer is incorrect, read the explanation for why it is incorrect and then consult the appropriate pages of the text (in parentheses following the correct answer).

1. The information-processing component that is concerned with the temporary storage of incoming sensory information is:
   a. working memory.   c. the knowledge base.
   b. long-term memory.   d. the sensory register.

2. (Thinking Like a Scientist) Neuroimaging studies have demonstrated each of the following *except*
   a. the human brain has dozens of areas that are activated when language is used.
   b. intellectual ability does not correlate with brain size.
   c. people use their brains differently as they age.
   d. most people, most of the time, only use about 10 percent of their brain capacity.

3. The two basic functions of working memory are:
   a. storage that enables conscious use and processing of information.
   b. temporary storage and processing of sensory stimuli.
   c. automatic memories and retrieval of learned memories.
   d. permanent storage and retrieval of information.

4. Memory for skills is called:
   a. explicit memory.   c. episodic memory.
   b. declarative memory.   d. implicit memory.

5. Strategies to retain and retrieve information in the knowledge base are part of which basic component of information processing?
   a. sensory register   c. control processes
   b. working memory   d. explicit memory

6. The plaques and tangles that accompany Alzheimer's disease usually begin in the:
   a. temporal lobe.
   b. frontal lobe.
   c. hippocampus.
   d. cerebral cortex.

7. Secondary aging factors that may explain some declines in cognitive functioning include:
   a. fewer opportunities for learning in old age.
   b. disparaging self-perceptions of cognitive abilities.
   c. difficulty with traditional methods of measuring cognitive functioning.
   d. all of the above.

8. When using working memory, older adults have particular difficulty:
   a. holding several items of information in memory while analyzing them in complex ways.
   b. picking up faint sounds.
   c. processing blurry images.
   d. recalling the meaning of rarely used vocabulary.

9. The most common cause of reversible dementia is:
   a. a temporary obstruction of the blood vessels.
   b. genetic mutation.
   c. overmedication.
   d. depression.

10. Dementia refers to:
   a. pathological loss of intellectual functioning.
   b. the increasing forgetfulness that sometimes accompanies the aging process.
   c. abnormal behavior associated with mental illness and with advanced stages of alcoholism.
   d. a genetic disorder that doesn't become overtly manifested until late adulthood.

11. Which of the following diseases does *not* belong with the others?
   a. Huntington's disease
   b. Parkinson's disease
   c. multiple sclerosis
   d. multi-infarct dementia

12. Alzheimer's disease is characterized by:
   a. a proliferation of plaques and tangles in the cerebral cortex.
   b. a destruction of brain tissue as a result of strokes.
   c. rigidity and tremor of the muscles.
   d. an excess of fluid pressing on the brain.

13. Multi-infarct dementia and Alzheimer's disease differ in their progression in that:
   a. multi-infarct dementia never progresses beyond the first stage.

   b. multi-infarct dementia is marked by sudden drops and temporary improvements, whereas decline in Alzheimer's disease is steady.
   c. multi-infarct dementia leads to rapid deterioration and death, whereas Alzheimer's disease may progress over a period of years.
   d. the progression of Alzheimer's disease may be halted or slowed, whereas the progression of multi-infarct dementia is irreversible.

14. Medication has been associated with symptoms of dementia in the elderly for all of the following reasons *except*:
   a. standard drug dosages are often too strong for the elderly.
   b. the elderly tend to become psychologically dependent upon drugs.
   c. drugs sometimes have the side effect of slowing mental processes.
   d. the intermixing of drugs can sometimes have detrimental effects on cognitive functioning.

15. The primary purpose of the life review is to:
   a. enhance one's spirituality.
   b. produce an autobiography.
   c. give advice to younger generations.
   d. put one's life into perspective.

True or False Items

Write T (*true*) or F (*false*) on the line in front of each statement.

_____ 1. As long as their vision and hearing remain unimpaired, older adults are no less efficient than younger adults at inputting information.

_____ 2. Changes in the sensory register are a major contributor to declines in information processing.

_____ 3. Cultural attitudes are unrelated to impaired thinking in the elderly.

_____ 4. A majority of the elderly feel frustrated and hampered by memory loss in their daily lives.

_____ 5. In studies of problem solving in real-life contexts, the scores of older adults were better than those of younger adults.

_____ 6. The majority of cases of dementia are organically caused.

_____ 7. Alzheimer's disease is partly genetic.

_____ 8. When brain cells die, existing cells may take over their functions.

_____ 9. Late adulthood is often associated with a narrowing of interests and an exclusive focus on the self.

_____ 10. According to Maslow, self-actualization is actually more likely to be reached during late adulthood.

Progress Test 2

Progress Test 2 should be completed during a final chapter review. Answer the following questions after you thoroughly understand the correct answers for the Chapter Review and Progress Test 1.

Multiple-Choice Questions

1. Research suggests that aging results in:
   a. increased sensitivity of the sensory register.
   b. a significant decrease in the sensitivity of the sensory register that cannot usually be compensated for.
   c. a small decrease in the sensory register's sensitivity that can usually be compensated for.
   d. no noticeable changes in the sensory register.

2. Which of the following most accurately characterizes age-related changes in working memory?
   a. The ability to screen out distractions and inhibit irrelevant thoughts declines.
   b. Storage capacity declines while processing efficiency remains stable.
   c. Storage capacity remains stable while processing efficiency declines.
   d. Both storage capacity and processing efficiency remain stable.

3. Information remembered for years or decades is stored in:
   a. sensory register.   c. long-term memory.
   b. working memory.   d. short-term memory.

4. Conscious memory for words, data, and concepts is called _____ memory.
   a. sensory
   b. implicit
   c. explicit
   d. knowledge base

5. In general, with increasing age the control processes used to remember new information:
   a. become more efficient.
   b. become more complex.
   c. become more intertwined.
   d. become simpler and less efficient.

6. Which type of memory is most vulnerable to age-related deficits?
   a. sensory register
   b. implicit memory
   c. explicit memory
   d. knowledge base

7. Regarding the role of genes in Alzheimer's disease, which of the following is _not_ true?
   a. Some people inherit a gene that increases their risk of developing the disease.
   b. Some people inherit a gene that lowers their risk of developing the disease.
   c. Most people inherit either the protective or the destructive gene.
   d. Alzheimer's disease is a multifaceted disease that involves multiple genetic and environmental factors.

8. One study tested memory in different age groups by requiring younger and older adults to remember to make telephone calls at a certain time. It was found that:
   a. older adults did worse than younger adults because their memories were not as good.
   b. older adults did better than younger adults because they were able to trust their memories.
   c. older adults did better than younger adults because they didn't trust their memories and therefore used various reminders.
   d. older adults did worse than younger adults because they were less accustomed to having to do things at a certain time.

9. Laboratory studies of memory in late adulthood often fail to take into account the effects of:
   a. the knowledge base of older adults.
   b. the testing process itself.
   c. the explicit memory that is central to the functioning of older adults.
   d. the ability of older adults to rely on their long-term memories.

10. Dementia:
    a. is more likely to occur among the aged.
    b. has no relationship to age.
    c. cannot occur before the age of 60.
    d. is an inevitable occurrence during late adulthood.

11. The most common form of dementia is:
    a. Alzheimer's disease.
    b. multi-infarct dementia.
    c. Parkinson's disease.
    d. alcoholism and depression.

12. Organic causes of dementia include all of the following *except*:

    a. Parkinson's disease.   **c.** brain tumors.

    b. multiple sclerosis.   **d.** leukemia.

13. The psychological illness most likely to be misdiagnosed as dementia is:

    a. schizophrenia.   **c.** personality disorder.

    b. depression.   **d.** phobic disorders.

14. On balance, it can be concluded that positive cognitive development during late adulthood:

    a. occurs only for a small minority of individuals.

    b. leads to thought processes that are more appropriate to the final stage of life.

    c. makes older adults far less pragmatic than younger adults.

    d. is impossible in view of increasing deficits in cognitive functioning.

15. A key factor underlying the older adult's cognitive developments in the realms of aesthetics, philosophy, and spiritualism may be:

    a. the realization that one's life is drawing to a close.

    b. the despair associated with a sense of isolation from the community.

    c. the need to leave one's mark on history.

    d. a growing indifference to the outside world.

Matching Items

Match each definition or description with its corresponding term.

Terms

    1. sensory register

    2. working memory

    3. knowledge base

    4. control processes

    5. subcortical dementias

    6. dementia

    7. Alzheimer's disease

    8. multi-infarct dementia (MID)

    9. Parkinson's disease

    10. source amnesia

    11. life review

Definitions or Descriptions

    a. the inability to remember the origins of a specific piece of information

    b. temporarily stores information for conscious processing

    c. strategies for retaining and retrieving information

    d. severely impaired thinking, memory, or problem-solving ability

    e. stores incoming sensory information for a split second

    f. caused by a temporary obstruction of the blood vessels

    g. stores information for several minutes to several decades

    h. caused by a degeneration of neurons that produce dopamine

    i. putting one's life into perspective

    j. characterized by plaques and tangles in the cerebral cortex

    k. brain disorders that do not directly involve thinking and memory

Thinking Critically About Chapter 24

Answer these questions the day before an exam as a final check on your understanding of the chapter's terms and concepts.

1. Leland's parents are in their 70s, and he wants to do something to ensure that their cognitive abilities remain sharp for years to come. As a friend, what would you encourage Leland to suggest that his parents do?
   a. They should take long walks several times a week.
   b. They should spend time reading and doing crossword puzzles.
   c. They should go to a neurologist for regular checkups.
   d. They should do a. and b.

2. Summarizing her presentation on aging and cognitive decline, Martina states that many researchers believe that the simplest way to predict how much an older person has aged intellectually is to measure his or her:
   a. reaction time.
   b. cerebral blood volume.
   c. vision, hearing, or smell.
   d. working memory capacity.

3. Although 75-year-old Sharonda remembers a relative once telling her that her ancestors were royalty in their native country, she can't recall which relative it was. Like many older adults, Sharonda is evidently displaying signs of:
   a. multi-infarct dementia.
   b. Alzheimer's disease.
   c. subcortical dementia.
   d. source amnesia.

4. Depression among the elderly is a serious problem because:
   a. rates of depression are far higher for the elderly than for younger adults.
   b. in late adulthood depression becomes extremely difficult to treat.
   c. depression in the elderly often goes untreated, contributing to a higher rate of suicide than for any other age group.
   d. organic forms of dementia cause depression.

5. Because she has trouble screening out distractions and inhibiting irrelevant thoughts, 70-year-old Lena is likely to:
   a. have suffered a mini-stroke.
   b. be at increased risk of developing dementia.
   c. experience typical age-related declines in her working memory.
   d. have some type of reversible dementia.

6. Developmentalists believe that older people's tendency to reminisce:
   a. represents an unhealthy preoccupation with the self and the past.
   b. is an underlying cause of age segregation.
   c. is a necessary and healthy process.
   d. is a result of a heightened aesthetic sense.

7. A patient has the following symptoms: blurred vision, slurred speech, and mental confusion. The patient is probably suffering from:
   a. Alzheimer's disease.
   b. vascular dementia
   c. Huntington's disease.
   d. Parkinson's disease.

8. Because of deficits in the sensory register, older people may tend to:
   a. forget the names of people and places.
   b. be distracted by irrelevant stimuli.
   c. miss details in a dimly lit room.
   d. reminisce at length about the past.

9. Holding material in your mind for a minute or two requires which type of memory?
   a. short-term memory   c. long-term memory
   b. explicit memory   d. sensory register

10. Marisa's presentation on "Reversing the Age-Related Slowdown in Thinking" includes all of the following points *except*:
    a. regular exercise.
    b. avoiding the use of anti-inflammatory drugs.
    c. cognitive stimulation.
    d. consumption of antioxidants.

11. Which type of material would 72-year-old Jessica probably have the greatest difficulty remembering?
    a. the dates of birth of family members
    b. a short series of numbers she has just heard
    c. the first house she lived in
    d. technical terms from her field of expertise prior to retirement

12. Sixty-five-year-old Lena is becoming more reflective and philosophical as she grows older. A developmental psychologist would probably say that Lena:
    a. had unhappy experiences as a younger adult.
    b. is demonstrating a normal, age-related tendency.
    c. will probably become introverted and reclusive as she gets older.
    d. feels that her life has been a failure.

13. Concerning the public's fear of Alzheimer's disease, which of the following is true?
    a. A serious loss of memory, such as that occurring in people with Alzheimer's disease, can be expected by most people once they reach their 60s.
    b. From 65 to 85, the incidence of Alzheimer's disease rises from 1 in 100 to 1 in 5.
    c. Alzheimer's disease is much more common today than it was 50 years ago.
    d. Alzheimer's disease is less common today than it was 50 years ago.

14. At the present stage of research into cognitive development during late adulthood, which of the following statements has the greatest support?
    a. There is uniform decline in all stages of memory during late adulthood.
    b. Long-term memory shows the greatest decline with age.
    c. Working memory shows the greatest decline with age.
    d. The decline in memory may be the result of the failure to use effective encoding and retrieval strategies.

15. Lately, Wayne's father, who is 73, harps on the fact that he forgets small things such as where he put the house keys and has trouble eating and sleeping. The family doctor diagnoses Wayne's father as:
    a. being in the early stages of Alzheimer's disease.
    b. being in the later stages of Alzheimer's disease.
    c. suffering from senile dementia.
    d. possibly suffering from depression.

Key Terms

1. control processes
2. explicit memory
3. implicit memory
4. terminal decline
5. dementia
6. Alzheimer's disease
7. vascular dementia (VaD)/multi-infarct dementia (MID)
8. subcortical dementias
9. Parkinson's disease
10. life review
11. wisdom

ANSWERS
CHAPTER REVIEW

1. 60; verbal meaning; spatial orientation; inductive reasoning; number ability; word fluency
2. differences
3. sensory memory (or register); causes small declines in
4. can
5. sensory threshold; cannot
6. sensory impairment
7. vision; hearing; smell
8. working memory
9. working memory
10. store; process
11. analyzing; distracting
12. dual-task deficit
13. knowledge base; long-term; selective attention; selective memory; alteration
14. vocabulary; 80; expertise; happy; emotions
15. source amnesia
16. cross-sectional; high school
17. how long ago information was learned; how well it was learned
18. testing process
19. control processes; storage; retrieval; selective attention; logical analysis
20. knowledge; principles; rules of thumb; retrieval
21. control processes

22. implicit; habits; emotional; routine; senses; less; explicit; words; data; concepts; consciously

23. perform; describe

24. resistance

25. primary aging; secondary aging; ageism

26. is not

27. slowdown; neurotransmitters; dopamine; glutamate; acetylcholine; serotonin; neural fluid; cerebral blood flow

28. slower; simpler; shallower; compensate; sensory deficits

29. PET; fMRI; in vivo

30. many; neurons; dendrites; does not correlate; prefrontal cortex

31. recruiting extra brain areas; dedifferentiates

32. terminal decline

33. hypertension; diabetes; arteriosclerosis; and diseases affecting the lungs; poor eating habits, smoking, and lack of exercise

34. stereotypes

35. overestimate; overestimate; confidence

36. hearing; American; deaf; American; Chinese

37. meaningless

38. do not

38. senility; dementia; severely impaired judgment, memory, or problem-solving ability

40. 60; presenile dementia; senile dementia (or senile psychosis); symptoms

41. mental confusion; forgetfulness; chronic

42. Alzheimer's disease; cerebral cortex; plaques; tangles

43. outside; B-amyloid; inside; hippocampus

44. does not

45. more; 100; 5

46. one-fifth; apoE4; apoE2; proteins

47. middle; rare; more; three to five; genetic

48. absentmindedness; recognize; explicit

49. concentration; short-term memory; personality; debilitating; basic daily needs; full-time care; talk; 10 to 15

50. vascular dementia or multi-infarct dementia; blood vessels; infarct; stroke (or ministroke)

51. arteriosclerosis; circulatory; heart disease, hypertension, numbness, diabetes; regular exercise; diet; drugs

52. sudden; poor

53. subcortical dementias; motor; Parkinson's; Huntington's; multiple sclerosis

54. Parkinson's disease; dopamine

55. infection

56. Korsakoff's; short-term memory

57. reversible; medication; inadequate nutrition; alcohol abuse; depression; mental illness

58. overmedication; interactions; mental processes

59. less; 10

60. many; is

61. suicide; 60

62. arts, children, and the whole of human experience; interdependence

63. self-actualization

64. nature; aesthetic experiences

65. reflective; philosophical

66. life review

67. wisdom; fundamental pragmatics

PROGRESS TEST 1

Multiple-Choice Questions

1. **d.** is the answer. (p. 606)

   a. Working memory deals with mental, rather than sensory, activity.

   b. & c. Long-term memory, which contains the knowledge base, includes information that is stored for several minutes to several years.

2. **d.** is the answer. (pp. 611–612)

3. **a.** is the answer. (p. 607)

   b. These are the functions of the sensory register.

   c. This refers to long-term memory's processing of implicit and explicit memories, respectively.

   d. This is the function of long-term memory.

4. **d.** is the answer. (p. 610)

   a. & b. Explicit memory is memory of facts and experiences, which is why it is often called declarative memory.

   c. This type of memory, which is a type of explicit memory, was not discussed.

5. **c.** is the answer. (p. 609)

6. **c.** is the answer. (p. 618)

7. **d.** is the answer. (pp. 614–615)

8. **a.** is the answer. (p. 607)

   b. & c. These may be true, but they involve sensory memory rather than working memory.

   d. Memory for vocabulary, which generally is very good throughout adulthood, involves long-term memory.

9. **c.** is the answer. (p. 622)

10. **a.** is the answer. (p. 618)

11. **d.** is the answer. Each of the other answers is an example of subcortical dementia. (p. 621)

12. **a.** is the answer. (p. 618)

    b. This describes multi-infarct dementia.

    c. This describes Parkinson's disease.

    d. This was not given in the text as a cause of dementia.

13. **b.** is the answer. (p. 621)

    a. Because multiple infarcts typically occur, the disease *is* progressive in nature.

    c. The text does not suggest that MID necessarily leads to quick death.

    d. At present, Alzheimer's disease is untreatable.

14. **b.** is the answer. (pp. 622–623)

15. **d.** is the answer. (p. 626)

True or False Items

1. F The slowing of perceptual processes and decreases in attention associated with aging are also likely to affect efficiency of input. (pp. 607–608)

2. F If they do in fact occur, changes in the sensory register are too insignificant to seriously affect information processing. (p. 606)

3. F In fact, cultural attitudes can lead to impaired thinking in the elderly. (p. 616)

4. F Most older adults perceive some memory loss but do not feel that it affects their daily functioning. (p. 616)

5. T (p. 617)

6. T (pp. 618–622)

7. T (p. 619)

8. T (p. 613)

9. F Interests often broaden during late adulthood, and there is by no means exclusive focus on the self. (pp. 625–626)

10. T (p. 625)

PROGRESS TEST 2

Multiple-Choice Questions

1. **c.** is the answer. (p. 606)

2. **a.** is the answer. (p. 607)

3. **c.** is the answer. (p. 607)

    a. The sensory register stores information for a split second.

    b. Working memory stores information briefly.

    d. Short-term memory is another name for working memory.

4. **c.** is the answer. (p. 610)

    a. Sensory memory, or the sensory register, stores incoming sensory information for only a split second.

    b. This is unconscious, automatic memory for skills.

    c. Explicit memory *is* only one part of the knowledge base. Another part—implicit memory—is unconscious memory for skills.

5. **d.** is the answer. (p. 609)

6. **c.** is the answer. (p. 610)

    a. & b. Age-related deficits in these types of memory are minimal.

    d. Although explicit memory *is* part of the knowledge base, another part—implicit memory—shows minimal age-related deficits.

7. **c.** is the answer. Only one-fifth of all people inherit the destructive gene. The text does not indicate that everyone else inherits the protective gene. (p. 619)

8. **c.** is the answer. (p. 617)

9. **b.** is the answer. Laboratory experiments test explicit memory, not implicit memory. (p. 616)

10. **a.** is the answer. Although age is not the key factor, it is true that dementia is more likely to occur in older adults. (p. 618)

11. **a.** is the answer. (p. 618)

    b. MID is responsible for about 15 percent of all dementia.

    c. & d. Compared to Alzheimer's disease, which accounts for about 70 percent of all dementia, these account for a much lower percentage.

12. **d.** is the answer. (p. 618)

13. **b.** is the answer. (p. 623)

    a. & c. These psychological illnesses are less common in the elderly than in younger adults, *and* less common than depression among the elderly.

    d. This disorder was not discussed in association with dementia.

14. **b.** is the answer. (pp. 625–627)

    a. & d. Positive cognitive development is *typical* of older adults.

    c. Pragmatism is one characteristic of wisdom, an attribute commonly associated with older people.

15. **a.** is the answer. (p. 626)

    b. & c. Although these may be true of some older adults, they are not necessarily a *key* factor in cognitive development during late adulthood.

d. In fact, older adults are typically *more* concerned with the whole of human experience.

Matching Items

1. e (p. 606)   5. k (p. 622)   9. h (p. 622)
2. b (p. 607)   6. d (p. 618)   10. a (p. 608)
3. g (p. 607)   7. j (p. 618)   11. i (p. 626)
4. c (p. 609)   8. f (p. 621)

THINKING CRITICALLY ABOUT CHAPTER 24

1. **d.** is the answer. While c. might be something they should do, the most important things are for them to get exercise and maintain activities that promote cognitive stimulation. (p. 614)

2. **c.** is the answer. (p. 606)

3. **d.** is the answer. (p. 608)

   a., b., & c. Sharonda's inability to recall the source of this information is a common form of forgetfulness among older adults; it is not necessarily a sign of dementia.

4. **c.** is the answer. (p. 624)

   a. In general, psychological illnesses are less common in the elderly than in younger adults.

   b. Depression is quite treatable at any age.

   d. Symptoms of *depression* are often mistaken as signs of *dementia*.

5. **c.** is the answer. (p. 607)

   a., b., & d. Lena's symptoms are not indicative of any type of dementia.

6. **c.** is the answer. (p. 627)

   d. This would lead to a greater appreciation of nature and art, but not necessarily to a tendency to reminisce.

7. **b.** is the answer. (p. 621)

8. **c.** is the answer. (p. 606)

   a. & d. The sensory register is concerned with noticing sensory events rather than with memory.

   b. Age-related deficits in the sensory register are most likely for ambiguous or weak stimuli.

9. **a.** is the answer. (p. 607)

   b. Explicit memory involves words, data, concepts, and the like. It is *a part of* long-term memory.

   c. Long-term memory includes information remembered for years or decades.

   d. The sensory register stores information for a split second.

10. **b.** is the answer. In fact, *use* of anti-inflammatory drugs may help sustain cognitive functioning in old age. (p. 614)

11. **b.** is the answer. Older individuals are particularly likely to experience difficulty holding new information in mind, particularly when it is essentially meaningless. (p. 616)

    a., c., & d. These are examples of long-term memory, which declines very little with age.

12. **b.** is the answer. (p. 626)

13. **b.** is the answer. (p. 619)

    c. & d. The text does not indicate the existence of cohort effects in the incidence of Alzheimer's disease.

14. **d.** is the answer. (p. 609)

    a. Some aspects of information processing, such as long-term memory, show less decline with age than others, such as working memory.

    b. & c. The text does not indicate that one particular subcomponent of memory shows the *greatest* decline.

15. **d.** is the answer. (p. 623)

    a., b., & c. The symptoms Wayne's father is experiencing are those of depression, which is often misdiagnosed as dementia in the elderly.

KEY TERMS

1. Memory **control processes,** which include strategies for retaining information, retrieval strategies for reaccessing information, selective attention, and rules or strategies that aid problem solving, tend to become simpler and less efficient with age. (p. 609)

2. **Explicit memory** is memory of consciously learned words, data, and concepts. This type of memory is more vulnerable to age-related decline than implicit memory. (p. 610)

3. **Implicit memory** is unconscious or automatic memory involving habits, emotional responses, routine procedures, and the senses. (p. 610)

4. **Terminal decline** is the overall slowdown of cognitive abilities that often occurs in the days or months before death. (p. 614)

5. **Dementia** is severely impaired judgment, memory, or problem-solving ability that is irreversible and caused by organic brain damage or disease. (p. 618)

6. **Alzheimer's disease (AD),** a progressive disorder that is the most common form of dementia, is characterized by plaques and tangles in the cerebral cortex that destroy normal brain functioning. (p. 618)

7. **Vascular dementia (VaD)/Multi-infarct dementia (MID),** which accounts for about 15 percent of all dementia, occurs because an infarct, or temporary obstruction of the blood vessels (often called a stroke), prevents a sufficient supply of blood from reaching an area of the brain. It is characterized by sporadic and progressive loss of brain functioning. (p. 621)

8. **Subcortical dementias** such as Parkinson's disease, Huntington's disease, and multiple sclerosis cause a progressive loss of motor control, which initially does not directly involve thinking or memory. (p. 622)

9. **Parkinson's disease,** which produces dementia as well as muscle rigidity or tremors, is related to the degeneration of neurons that produce dopamine. (p. 622)

10. In the **life review,** an older person attempts to put his or her life into perspective by recalling and recounting various aspects of life to members of the younger generations. (p. 626)

11. As used in this context, **wisdom** refers to expert knowledge in the fundamental pragmatics of life. (p. 628)

Chapter Twenty-Five

Late Adulthood: Psychosocial Development

Chapter Overview

There is great variation in development after age 65. Certain psychosocial changes are common during this stage of the life span —retirement, the death of a spouse, and failing health —yet people respond to these experiences in vastly different ways.

Individual experiences may help to explain the fact that theories of psychosocial aging, discussed in the first section of the chapter, are often diametrically opposed. The second section of the chapter focuses on the challenges to generativity that accompany late adulthood, such as finding new sources of achievement once derived from work. In the third section, the importance of marriage, friends, neighbors, and family in providing social support is discussed, as are the different experiences of married and single older adults. The final section focuses on the frail elderly— the minority of older adults, often poor and/or ill, who require extensive care.

NOTE: Answer guidelines for all Chapter 25 questions begin on page 376.

Guided Study

The text chapter should be studied one section at a time. Before you read, preview each section by skimming it, noting headings and boldface items. Then read the appropriate section objectives from the following outline. Keep these objectives in mind and, as you read the chapter section, search for the information that will enable you to meet each objective. Once you have finished a section, write out answers for its objectives.

Theories of Late Adulthood (pp. 634–644)

1. Explain the central premises of self-theories of psychosocial development during late adulthood.

2. Discuss Erikson's stage of integrity versus despair and the process of achieving integrity in old age.

3. Identify and describe the stratification theories of psychosocial development during late adulthood.

4. Discuss dynamic theories of late adulthood.

Keeping Active (pp. 644–649)

5. Discuss several sources of achievement for retired people during late adulthood.

6. Discuss the issue of generational equity in relation to the political activism of the elderly.

The Social Convoy (pp. 649–656)

7. Describe the components of the social convoy, and explain this convoy's increasing importance during late adulthood.

8. Discuss how, and why, marriage relationships tend to change as people grow old.

9. Discuss the impact of being old and single (never-married, divorced, or widowed) on both women and men.

10. Discuss friendships among older people.

11. Discuss the relationship between the generations as it exists today, and identify several reasons for the current pattern of detachment.

The Frail Elderly (pp. 656–665)

12. Describe the frail elderly, and explain why their number is growing.

13. (text and Changing Policy) Identify and discuss four factors that may protect the elderly from frailty.

14. Discuss alternative care arrangements for the frail elderly, identifying some of the potential advantages and disadvantages of each.

15. Describe the typical case of elder abuse.

Chapter Review

When you have finished reading the chapter, work through the material that follows to review it. Complete the sentences and answer the questions. As you proceed, evaluate your performance for each section by consulting the answers beginning on page 376. Do not continue with the next section until you understand each answer. If you need to, review or reread the appropriate section in the textbook before continuing.

Theories of Late Adulthood (pp. 634–644)

1. Theories of psychosocial development in late adulthood include _____ theories, _____ theories, and _____ theories.

2. _____ theories emphasize the active part that individuals play in their own psychosocial development. As one such theorist, _____ , described it, people attempt to _____ .

3. The most comprehensive theory is that of _____ , who called life's final crisis _____ versus _____ .

4. Another version of self theory suggests that the search for _____ is lifelong. This idea originates in Erikson's crisis of _____ versus _____ .

5. Partly as a result of changes in _____ , _____ , and _____ , maintaining identity during late adulthood is particularly challenging. In the strategy _____ _____ , new experiences are incorporated unchanged. This strategy involves _____ reality in order to maintain self-esteem.

6. The opposite strategy is _____ _____ , in which people adapt to

new experiences by changing their self-concept. This process can be painful, since it may cause people to doubt their _____ and _____ , leading to what Erikson called _____ .

7. Paul Baltes emphasizes _____ _____ _____ _____ , which is the idea that individuals set their own _____ , assess their own _____ , and then figure out how to accomplish what they want to achieve despite the _____ and _____ of later life.

8. People who have a strong sense of _____ believe that they can master any situation life presents, including aging. Research studies demonstrate that there is a negative correlation between this belief and feelings of _____ , _____ , and _____ . Studies also reveal that women tend to feel more effective at _____ _____ ; men tend to feel more effective at _____ _____ .

9. Self theories have recently received strong support from research in the field of _____ _____ , which has shown that various life events seem to be at least as much affected by _____ as by life circumstances. Studies of twins have found that genetic influences often _____ (weaken/become more apparent) later in life. Behavioral geneticists _____ (often/sometimes/never) claim that any aspect of the self is entirely genetic.

10. Theorists who emphasize _____ maintain that _____ forces limit individual _____ and direct life at every stage. One form of this theory focuses on _____ _____ , reflecting how industrialized nations segregate the oldest generation.

11. According to _____ theory, in old age the individual and society mutually withdraw from each other. This theory is _____ (controversial among/ almost universally accepted by) gerontologists.

12. The opposite idea is expressed in _____ theory, which holds that older adults remain socially active. According to this theory, if older adults do disengage, they do so _____ (willingly/unwillingly).

13. The dominant view is that the more _____ the elderly play, the greater their _____ _____ and the longer their lives.

14. The most recent view of age stratification is that disengagement theory and activity theory are too _____ . According to this view, older adults become more _____ in their social contacts.

15. Two other categories of stratification that are especially important in late adulthood are _____ and _____ . Another stratification theory, which draws attention to the values underlying the gender divisions promoted by society, is _____ theory. According to this theory, _____ policies and _____ values make later life particularly burdensome for women.

16. Currently in the United States, women make up nearly _____ (what proportion?) of the population over age 65 and 70 percent of the elderly who are _____ .

17. According to the _____ _____ theory, race is a _____ _____ , and racism and racial discrimination shape the experiences and attitudes of both racial _____ and racial _____ .

18. Some theorists believe that stratification theory unfairly stigmatizes _____ and _____ groups. They point out that compared to European-Americans, elderly _____ - and _____ -

Americans are more often nurtured by _____ families. As a result of this _____ , fewer are put in nursing homes. Similarly, elderly women are less likely than elderly men to be _____ and _____ because they tend to be _____ and _____ .

19. An important concept in age stratification theory is that _____ shifts often change the meaning of gender and ethnicity.

20. To better understand stratification theory, a _____ perspective is needed. In many nations, age stratification is not apparent, and how people are treated depends more on factors such as their _____ , _____ _____ , and _____ _____ _____ .

21. According to _____ theory, each person's life is an active, changing, self-propelled process occurring within ever-changing _____ contexts.

22. According to _____ theory, people experience the changes of late adulthood in much the same way they did earlier in life. Thus, the so-called _____ _____ personality traits are maintained throughout old age.

23. The dynamic viewpoint stresses that the entire _____ _____ works toward _____ , even as elements of _____ _____ change.

24. Self theories echo _____ theories in the importance they place on childhood _____ and _____ . Social stratification theories apply many concepts from _____ theory. And the stress on dynamic change is an extension of _____ theory.

Keeping Active (pp. 644–649)

25. Many of the elderly use the time they once spent earning a living to pursue _____ interests.

26. The eagerness of the elderly to pursue educational interests is exemplified by the rapid growth of

_____ , a program in which older people live on college campuses and take special classes.

27. Compared to younger adults, older adults are _____ (more/less) likely to feel a strong obligation to serve their community.

28. About 40 percent of the elderly in the United States are involved in structured _____ , often through _____ , _____ , or _____ .

29. Many elderly people also provide regular _____ _____ to an elderly relative or _____ _____ , also usually for relatives.

30. Religious faith _____ (increases/ remains stable/decreases) as people. Religious institutions are particularly important to older Americans who feel _____ _____ .

31. By many measures, the elderly are more _____ active than any other age group. Compared to younger people, the elderly are more likely to _____ _____ . Although the political activism of the older generation causes some younger adults to voice concerns regarding _____ _____ , the idea that the elderly are narrowly focused on their self-interest is unfair.

32. The major United States organization affecting the elderly is the _____ .

33. Many older adults stay busy by maintaining their _____ and _____ . This reflects the desire of most elderly people to _____ (relocate when they retire/age in place). One result of this is that many of the elderly live _____ .

34. Rather than moving, many elderly people prefer to remain in the neighborhoods in which they raised their children, thus creating _____ _____ retirement communities.

The Social Convoy (pp. 649–656)

35. The phrase _____ _____ highlights the fact that the life course is traveled in the company of others.

36. Elderly Americans who are married tend to be _____ , _____ , and _____ than those who never married or who are divorced or widowed.

37. The best predictor of the nature of a marriage in its later stages is _____ _____ .

Give two possible reasons that marriages may improve with time.

38. Poor health generally has a _____ (major/minor) impact on the marital relationship.

39. There are four times as many _____ (widows/widowers) as _____ (widows/widowers), due to choices that were made during _____ _____ .

40. The death of a mate usually means not only the loss of a close friend and lover but also a lower _____ , less _____ , a(n) _____ social circle, and disrupted _____ _____ .

41. In general, living without a spouse is somewhat easier for _____ (widows/ widowers).

State several reasons for this being so.

42. A study of loneliness found that adults without partners _____ (were/were not) lonelier than adults with partners and that divorced or widowed adults _____ (were/were not) lonelier than never-married adults. The loneliest of all were _____ _____ . The least lonely were _____ .

43. Only about _____ percent of those currently over age 65 in the United States have never married.

44. Older people's satisfaction with life is more strongly correlated to contact with _____ than to contact with younger members of their own family.

45. Compared to men, women tend to have _____ (larger/smaller) social circles, including _____ and a close _____ (male/female) friend who is not related.

46. Because more people are living longer, more older people are part of _____ families than at any time in history. Sometimes, this takes the form of a _____ family, in which there are more _____ than in the past but with only a few members in each generation.

47. Today, when one generation needs help, assistance typically flows from the _____ (younger/older) generation to their _____ (parents/children) instead of vice versa.

48. While intergenerational relationships are clearly important to both generations, they also are likely to include _____ and _____ . The _____– _____ relationship is an example of this.

The Frail Elderly (pp. 656–665)

49. Elderly people who are physically infirm, very ill, or cognitively impaired are called the _____ _____ .

50. The crucial sign of frailty is an inability to perform the _____ _____ , which comprise five tasks: _____ , _____ , _____ , _____ , and _____ _____ .

51. Actions that require some intellectual competence and forethought are classified as _____ _____ . These include such things as _____ _____ .

52. The number of frail elderly is _____ (increasing/decreasing). One reason for this trend is that _____ _____ . A second reason is that medical care now _____ _____ . A third is that health care emphasizes _____ _____ more than _____ _____ . The result has been an increasing _____ (morbidity/ mortality) rate, even as _____ (morbidity/mortality) rates fall. A final reason is that adequate nutrition, safe housing, and other preventive measures often don't reach those who _____ _____ .

53. One of the best defenses against frailty is an active drive for _____ and _____ . These measures are better predictors of future frailty than is _____ or _____ . The dynamic perspective also reminds us that some people enter late adulthood with protective _____ in place. These include _____ .

54. (Changing Policy) Many elderly persons never become frail because of four protective factors: _____ , _____ _____ , _____ _____ , and _____ _____ .

55. In caring for the frail elderly, cultures such as that of _____ (which country?) stress the obligation of children to their parents, rather than of the elderly caring for each another, as in the _____ _____ .

State three reasons that caregivers may feel unfairly burdened and resentful.

a. _____
   _____

b. _____
   _____

c. _____
   _____

56. An especially helpful form of caregiver support is _____ , in which a professional caregiver takes over to give the family caregiver a break.

57. The frail elderly are particularly vulnerable to _____ _____ . Most cases of elder maltreatment _____ (involve/do not involve) family members.

58. Many older Americans and their relatives feel that _____ _____ should be avoided at all costs.

Progress Test 1

Multiple-Choice Questions

Circle your answers to the following questions and check them with the answers beginning on page 377. If your answer is incorrect, read the explanation for why it is incorrect and then consult the appropriate pages of the text (in parentheses following the correct answer).

1. According to disengagement theory, during late adulthood people tend to:
   a. become less role-centered and more passive.
   b. have regrets about how they have lived their lives.
   c. become involved in a range of new activities.
   d. exaggerate lifelong personality traits.

2. (Changing Policy) Regarding generational equity, which of the following is implicit in a life-span perspective?
   a. The current distribution of benefits is particularly imbalanced for racial minorities.

   b. The outlay of public funds for health care is weighted toward preventive medicine in childhood and adolescence.
   c. As a group, the elderly are wealthier than any other age group.
   d. Each age and cohort has its own particular and legitimate economic needs that other generations might fail to appreciate.

3. Elderhostel is:
   a. a special type of nursing home in which the patients are given control over their activities.
   b. a theory of psychosocial development advocating that the elderly can help each other.
   c. an agency that allows older people of the opposite sex to live together unencumbered by marriage vows.
   d. a program in which older people live on college campuses and take special classes.

4. Longitudinal studies of monozygotic and dizygotic twins have found evidence that:
   a. genetic influences weaken as life experiences accumulate.
   b. strongly supports disengagement theory.
   c. some traits seem even more apparent in late adulthood than earlier.
   d. all of the above are true.

5. A former pilot, Eileen has always been proud of her 20/20 vision. Although to the younger members of her family it is obvious that her vision is beginning to fail, Eileen denies that she is having any difficulty and claims that she could still fly an airplane if she wanted to. An identity theorist would probably say that Eileen's distortion of reality is an example of:
   a. identity assimilation.
   b. identity accommodation.
   c. selective optimization.
   d. disengagement.

6. Because women tend to be caregivers, they are:
   a. more likely than men to be depressed.
   b. more likely than men to be lonely.
   c. more likely than men to be depressed and lonely.
   d. less likely than men to be lonely or depressed.

7. The idea that individuals set their own goals, assess their abilities, and figure out how to accomplish what they want to achieve during late adulthood is referred to as:
   a. disengagement.
   b. selective optimization with compensation.
   c. dynamic development.
   d. age stratification.

8. After retirement, the elderly are likely to:
   a. pursue educational interests.
   b. become politically involved.
   c. do volunteer work because they feel a particular commitment to their community.
   d. do any of the above.

9. Which of the following theories does *not* belong with the others?
   a. disengagement theory
   b. feminist theory
   c. critical race theory
   d. continuity theory

10. Which of the following is most true of the relationship between the generations today?
    a. Because parents and children often live at a distance from each other, they are not close.
    b. Older adults prefer not to interfere in their children's lives.
    c. Younger adults are eager to live their own lives and do not want to care for their parents.
    d. The generations tend to see and help each other frequently.

11. On average, older widows:
    a. live about 10 years after their husband dies.
    b. almost always seek another husband.
    c. find it more difficult than widowers to live without a spouse.
    d. experience all of the above.

12. In general, during late adulthood the *fewest* problems are experienced by individuals who:
    a. are married.
    b. have always been single.
    c. have long been divorced.
    d. are widowed.

13. Which of the following is true of adjustment to the death of a spouse?
    a. It is easier for men in all respects.
    b. It is initially easier for men but over the long term it is easier for women.
    c. It is emotionally easier for women but financially easier for men.

d. It is determined primarily by individual personality traits, and therefore shows very few sex differences.

14. According to dynamic theories:
    a. self-integrity is maintained throughout life.
    b. adults make choices and interpret reality in such a way as to express themselves as fully as possible.
    c. people organize themselves according to their particular characteristics and circumstances.
    d. each person's life is largely a self-propelled process, occurring within ever-changing social contexts.

15. Which of the following most accurately expresses the most recent view of developmentalists regarding stratification by age?
    a. Aging makes a person's social sphere increasingly narrow.
    b. Disengagement is always the result of ageism.
    c. Most older adults become more selective in their social contacts.
    d. Older adults need even more social activity to be happy than they did earlier in life.

True or False Items

Write T (*true*) or F (*false*) on the line in front of each statement.

_____ 1. Behavioral geneticists claim that all aspects of the self are entirely genetic.

_____ 2. As one of the most disruptive experiences in the life span, widowhood tends to have similar effects on men and women.

_____ 3. Theories that stress dynamic change are an extension of behavioral genetics.

_____ 4. Religious faith increases with age.

_____ 5. Older adults do not understand the social concerns of younger age groups.

_____ 6. Most developmentalists support the central premise of disengagement theory.

_____ 7. About 40 percent of the elderly are involved in structured volunteer work.

_____ 8. Most older people suffer significantly from a lack of close friendships.

_____ 9. Nearly one in two older adults makes a long-distance move after retirement.

_____ 10. Loneliness during late adulthood is greater for individuals who were never married than for any other group.

Progress Test 2

Progress Test 2 should be completed during a final chapter review. Answer the following questions after you thoroughly understand the correct answers for the Chapter Review and Progress Test 1.

Multiple-Choice Questions

1. Critics of disengagement theory point out that:
   a. older people want to substitute new involvements for the roles they lose with retirement.
   b. disengagement usually is not voluntary on the part of the individual.
   c. disengagement often leads to greater life satisfaction for older adults.
   d. disengagement is more common at earlier stages in the life cycle.

2. A beanpole family is one that consists of:
   a. fewer generations with fewer members than in the past.
   b. fewer generations with more members than in the past.
   c. more generations than in the past but with only a few members in each generation.
   d. more generations with more members than in the past.

3. According to continuity theory, during late adulthood people:
   a. become less role-centered.
   b. become more passive.
   c. become involved in a range of new activities.
   d. cope with challenges in much the same way they did earlier in life.

4. Developmentalists who believe that stratification theory unfairly stigmatizes women and minority groups point out that:
   a. European-Americans are more likely than African-Americans to be placed in nursing homes.
   b. elderly women are less likely than men to be lonely and depressed.
   c. multigenerational families and churches often nurture Hispanic-Americans.
   d. all of the above are true.

5. Following retirement, most elderly people:
   a. relocate to sunny climate.
   b. spend less time on housework and unnecessary chores.

   c. prefer to age in place.
   d. move in with their children.

6. (Changing Policy) Protective factors that act as buffers for the elderly include:
   a. personality and social setting.
   b. financial resources and age.
   c. attitude and social network.
   d. none of the above.

7. The major United States organization affecting the elderly is:
   a. Elderhostel.
   b. the AARP.
   c. Foster Grandparents.
   d. Service Corps of Retired Executives.

8. Developmentalists fear that because younger African-Americans are less dependent on family and church, they may experience greater social isolation in late adulthood than did earlier generations. If this does in fact occur, it would most directly:
   a. provide support for disengagement theory.
   b. be an example of how a cohort shift can change the meaning of ethnicity.
   c. illustrate the process of selective optimization with compensation.
   d. support activity theory.

9. Which of the following would *not* be included as an instrumental activity of daily life?
   a. grocery shopping   c. making phone calls
   b. paying bills   d. taking a walk

10. One of the most important factors contributing to life satisfaction for older adults appears to be:
    a. contact with friends.
    b. contact with younger family members.
    c. the number of new experiences to which they are exposed.
    d. continuity in the daily routine.

11. Research studies of loneliness among elderly adults have reported each of the following results *except*:
    a. elderly women tend to be lonelier than men.
    b. adults without partners were lonelier than adults with partners.
    c. divorced adults were lonelier than never-married adults.
    d. widowed adults were lonelier than never-married adults.

12. In general, the longer a couple has been married, the more likely they are to:
    a. be happier with each other.
    b. have frequent, minor disagreements.
    c. feel the relationship is not equitable.
    d. do all of the above.

13. Which of the following is *not* true regarding long-term marriages?
    a. Married elders tend to be healthier than those who never married.
    b. Absolute levels of conflict and emotional intensity drop over time.
    c. Marriages generally change for the better in late adulthood.
    d. Marriages improve in late adulthood, unless one spouse becomes seriously ill.

14. Which of the following is *not* a major factor contributing to an increase in the number of frail elderly?
    a. an increase in average life expectancy
    b. a research focus on acute, rather than chronic, illnesses
    c. inadequate expenditures on social services
    d. a lack of facilities in many areas to care for the elderly

15. According to Erikson, achieving integrity during late adulthood above all involves:
    a. the ability to perceive one's own life as worthwhile.
    b. being open to new influences and experiences.
    c. treating other people with respect.
    d. developing a consistent and yet varied daily routine.

Matching Items

Match each definition or description with its corresponding term.

Terms

_____ 1. disengagement theory
_____ 2. self theories
_____ 3. continuity theory
_____ 4. generational equity
_____ 5. activity theory
_____ 6. stratification theories
_____ 7. activities of daily life (ADLs)
_____ 8. instrumental activities of daily life (IADLs)
_____ 9. dynamic theories
_____ 10. Elderhostel

Definitions or Descriptions

a. theories such as Erik Erikson's that emphasize self-actualization
b. an educational program for the elderly
c. eating, bathing, toileting, walking, and dressing
d. theory that a person's life is an active, largely self-propelled process that occurs within ever-changing social contexts.
e. theory that people become less role-centered as they age
f. actions that require intellectual competence and forethought
g. equal contributions from, and fair benefits for, each age cohort
h. theories such as feminist theory and critical race theory that focus on the limitations on life choices created by social forces
i. theory that elderly people become socially withdrawn only involuntarily
j. theory that each person copes with late adulthood in the same way he or she did earlier in life

Thinking Critically About Chapter 25

Answer these questions the day before an exam as a final check on your understanding of the chapter's terms and concepts.

1. Which of the following statements *most* accurately describes psychosocial development in late adulthood?
   a. Many leading gerontologists believe that people become more alike as they get older.
   b. Older adults generally fit into one of two distinct personality types.
   c. Many gerontologists believe that the diversity of personalities and patterns is especially pronounced among the elderly.
   d. Few changes in psychosocial development occur after middle adulthood.

2. An advocate of which of the following theories would be most likely to agree with the statement, "Because of their more passive style of interaction, older people are less likely to be chosen for new roles"?
   a. disengagement   c. self
   b. continuity   d. dynamic

3. An advocate for feminist theory would point out that:
   a. since most social structures and economic policies have been established by men, women's needs are devalued.
   b. women in the United States make up the majority of the elderly and the elderly poor.
   c. many elderly women are expected to care for frail relatives even if it strains their own health.
   d. all of the above are true.

4. Professor Martin states that "membership in certain groups can place the elderly at risk for a number of dangers." Professor Martin evidently is an advocate of which theory of psychosocial development?
   a. self theories   c. dynamic
   b. social stratification d. continuity

5. When they retire, most older adults:
   a. immediately feel more satisfied with their new way of life.
   b. engage in a variety of social activities.
   c. have serious, long-term difficulties adjusting to retirement.
   d. disengage from other roles and activities as well.

6. The one *most* likely to agree with the statement, "Older adults have an obligation to help others and serve the community," is:
   a. a middle-aged adult.   c. an older man.
   b. an older woman.   d. an older adult.

7. An elderly man with dementia is most likely to be cared for by his spouse in _____ and by his children in _____ .
   a. Korea; the United States
   b. the United States; Korea
   c. Japan; Sweden
   d. Sweden; Japan

8. (Research Report) Research indicates that the primary perpetrators of elder abuse are:
   a. professional caregivers.
   b. mean-spirited strangers.
   c. another relative.
   d. middle-aged children.

9. Which of the following best describes the relationship between the elderly and younger generations?
   a. If children move, the elderly will also move in order to continue to be near them.
   b. The elderly enjoy social contact with the younger generation and particularly enjoy having long visits from their grandchildren.
   c. Assistance typically flows from the older generation to their children.
   d. The relationship between mothers and daughters improves with age, with conflict decreasing substantially.

10. Of the following older adults, who is most likely to be involved in a large network of intimate friendships?
    a. William, a 65-year-old who never married
    b. Darrel, a 60-year-old widower
    c. Florence, a 63-year-old widow
    d. Kay, a 66-year-old married woman

11. Following a heated disagreement over family responsibilities, Sidney's grandson stormed away shouting "Why should I listen to you?" Afterward, Sidney is filled with despair and feels that all his years of work to build a strong family were wasted. An identity theorist would probably say that Sidney is demonstrating:
    a. identity assimilation.
    b. identity accommodation.
    c. selective optimization.
    d. a healthy identity that is firm but flexible.

12. Claudine is the primary caregiver for her elderly parents. The amount of stress she feels in this role depends above all on:
    a. how frail her parents are.
    b. her subjective interpretation of the support she receives from others.
    c. her relationship to her parents prior to their becoming frail.
    d. her overall financial situation.

13. Wilma's elderly mother needs help in taking care of the instrumental activities of daily life. Such activities would include which of the following?
    a. bathing
    b. eating
    c. paying bills
    d. all of the above

14. In concluding her presentation on the frail elderly, Janet notes that "the number of frail elderly is currently _____ than the number who are active, financially stable, and capable; however, the frail elderly are _____ in absolute number."
    a. greater; decreasing
    b. less; increasing
    c. greater; increasing
    d. less; decreasing

15. Jack, who is 73, looks back on his life with a sense of pride and contentment; Eleanor feels unhappy with her life and that it is "too late to start over." In Erikson's terminology, Jack is experiencing _____ , while Eleanor is experiencing _____ .
    a. generativity; stagnation
    b. identity; emptiness
    c. integrity; despair
    d. completion; termination

Key Terms

Using your own words, write a brief definition or explanation of each of the following terms on a separate piece of paper.

1. self theories
2. integrity versus despair
3. stratification theories
4. disengagement theory
5. activity theory
6. dynamic theories
7. continuity theory
8. Elderhostel
9. social convoy
10. frail elderly
11. activities of daily life (ADLs)
12. instrumental activities of daily life (IADLs)
13. respite care

ANSWERS
CHAPTER REVIEW

1. self; stratification; dynamic
2. Self; Abraham Maslow; self-actualize
3. Erik Erikson; integrity; despair
4. identity; identity; role confusion
5. appearance; health; employment; identity assimilation; distorting
6. identity accommodation; values; beliefs; despair
7. selective optimization with compensation; goals; abilities; limitations; declines
8. self-efficacy; fear, loneliness, distress; selecting and maintaining friendships and at deepening their spiritual lives; managing money and getting things done
9. behavioral genetics; genes; become more apparent; never
10. stratification; social; choice; age stratification
11. disengagement; controversial among
12. activity; unwillingly
13. roles; life satisfaction
14. extreme; selective
15. gender; ethnicity; feminist; social; cultural
16. 60; poor
17. critical race; social construct; minorities; majorities
18. women; minority; African; Hispanic; multigenerational; familism; lonely; depressed; caregivers; kinkeepers
19. cohort
20. multicultural; personality; family connections; ability to work
21. dynamic; social
22. continuity; Big Five
23. social system; continuity; individual lives
24. psychoanalytic; self-concept; identity; sociocultural; epigenetic
25. educational

26. Elderhostel

27. more

28. volunteering; churches; hospitals; schools

29. personal care; child care

30. increases; alienated from society

31. politically; vote in elections and lobby for their interests; generational equity

32. AARP (formerly the American Association of Retired Persons)

33. home; yard; age in place; alone

34. naturally occurring

35. social convoy

36. healthier; wealthier; happier

37. its nature early on

One reason may be traced to the effects of their children, who were a prime source of conflict when they were younger but are now a source of pleasure. Another is that all the shared contextual factors tend to change both partners in similar ways, bringing them closer together in personality, perspectives, and values.

38. minor

39. widows; widowers; young adulthood

40. income; status; broken; daily routines

41. widows

One reason is that elderly women often expect to outlive their husbands and have anticipated this event. Another is that in most communities widows can get help from support groups. A third is that many elderly men were dependent on their wives to perform the basic tasks of daily living.

42. were; were; men currently without a partner who had lost two or more wives through death or divorce within the past few years; wives still in their first marriage

43. 4

44. friends

45. larger; relatives; female

46. multigenerational; beanpole; generations

47. older; children

48. tension; conflict; mother–daughter

49. frail elderly

50. activities of daily life (ADLs); eating; bathing; toileting; dressing; transferring from a bed to a chair

51. instrumental activities of daily life (IADLs); shopping, paying bills, driving a car, taking medications, and keeping appointments

52. increasing; more people are reaching old age; prolongs life; death postponement; life enhancement; morbidity; mortality; need them the most

53. autonomy; control; income; health; buffers; family members and friends, past education and continued educational opportunity, pensions, good health habits

54. attitude; social network; physical setting; financial resources

55. Korea; United States

a. If one relative is doing the caregiving, other family members tend to feel relief rather than an obligation to help.

b. Care receivers and caregivers often disagree about the nature and extent of care that is needed.

c. Services designed for caregivers are difficult to obtain from social agencies.

56. respite care

57. elder abuse; involve

58. nursing homes

PROGRESS TEST 1

Multiple-Choice Questions

1. **a.** is the answer. (p. 638)

   b. This answer depicts a person struggling with Erikson's crisis of integrity versus despair.

   c. This answer describes activity theory.

   d. Disengagement theory does not address this issue.

2. **d.** is the answer. (pp. 647–648)

   a. Some people believe this, but it is not advocated by life-span developmentalists.

   b. Just the opposite is true.

   c. Although some of the elderly are among the richest, most are in the middle-income bracket.

3. **d.** is the answer. (p. 645)

4. **c.** is the answer. (p. 637)

   a. Such studies have found that genetic influences do not weaken with age.

   b. This research provides support for self theories rather than disengagement theory.

5. **a.** is the answer. (p. 636)

   b. Accommodating people adapt to new experiences (such as failing vision) by changing their self-concept.

   c. People who selectively optimize are more realistic in assessing their abilities than Eileen evidently is.

d. There is no sign that Eileen is disengaging, or withdrawing from her social relationships.

6. **d.** is the answer. (p. 640)

7. **b.** is the answer. (p. 636)

a. This is the idea that the elderly withdraw from society as they get older.

c. This is the theory that each person's life is a self-propelled process occurring within ever-changing social contexts.

d. According to this theory, the oldest generation is segregated from the rest of society.

8. **d.** is the answer. Contrary to earlier views that retirement was not a happy time, researchers now know that the elderly are generally happy and productive, spending their time in various activities. (pp. 645–647)

9. **d.** is the answer. Each of the other theories can be categorized as a stratification theory. (p. 643)

10. **d.** is the answer. (pp. 654–655)

11. **a.** is the answer. (p. 651)

b. & c. In fact, just the opposite is true.

12. **a.** is the answer. (p. 649)

13. **c.** is the answer. (p. 652)

14. **d.** is the answer. (p. 643)

a. This expresses continuity theory.

b. This expresses self theory.

c. This expresses stratification theory.

15. **c.** is the answer. (p. 639)

a. This is the central idea behind disengagement theory.

b. & d. These ideas are expressions of activity theory.

True or False Items

1. F They claim only a third to a half of the variation in characteristics is genetic. (p. 638)

2. F Women tend to be more prepared and have more friends to sympathize with them. Men, who tend to depend on their wives for basic needs and emotional support, find it hard to turn to others for help. (pp. 651–652)

3. T (p. 643)

4. T (p. 646)

5. F In fact, older adults are willing to vote against the interests of their own group if a greater good is at stake. (pp. 647–648)

6. F In fact, disengagement theory has *few* serious defenders. (p. 638)

7. T (p. 646)

8. F Most older adults have at least one close friend and, as compared with younger adults, are less likely to feel a need for more friendships. (pp. 652–653)

9. F A minority of older adults moves to another state. (p. 648)

10. F If anything, loneliness tends to be less in never-married older adults. (p. 652)

PROGRESS TEST 2

Multiple-Choice Questions

1. **a.** is the answer. (p. 638)

b. If disengagement were *not* voluntary, this would not be a choice of the elderly.

c. & d. Neither of these answers is true, nor a criticism of disengagement theory.

2. **c.** is the answer. (p. 654)

3. **d.** is the answer. (p. 643)

a. & b. These answers describe disengagement theory.

c. This answer pertains to activity theory.

4. **d.** is the answer. (p. 641)

5. **c.** is the answer. (p. 648)

6. **c.** is the answer. (p. 660)

7. **b.** is the answer. (p. 647)

a. Elderhostel is an educational program for older adults.

c. & d. These service organizations affect a much smaller percentage of the elderly.

8. **b.** is the answer. (p. 643)

a. & d. This finding does not bear directly on either theory of late adulthood.

c. Selective optimization is an example of *successful* coping with the losses of late adulthood, which would seem to run counter to feelings of social isolation.

9. **d.** is the answer. (p. 656)

10. **a.** is the answer. (p. 653)

b., c., & d. The importance of these factors varies from one older adult to another.

11. **a.** is the answer. (p. 652)

12. **a.** is the answer. (p. 649)

b. & c. The longer a couple has been married, the *less* likely they are to have frequent disagreements or feel that the relationship is not equitable.

13. **d.** is the answer. Generally, older spouses accept each other's frailties and tend to each other's needs with feeling of affection. (p. 650)

14. **c.** is the answer. Many nations spend substantial money on services for the elderly. (p. 657)

    a. As more people reach old age, the absolute numbers of frail individuals will increase.

    b. Such research neglects the study of diseases that are nonfatal, yet disabling.

    d. Services are relatively scarce in rural areas, where a large number of elderly people reside.

15. **a.** is the answer. (p. 634)

Matching Items

1. e (p. 638)	**5.** i (p. 638)	**8.** f (p. 656)
2. a (p. 634)	**6.** h (p. 638)	**9.** d (p. 643)
3. j (p. 643)	**7.** c (p. 656)	**10.** b (p. 645)
4. g (p. 648)		

THINKING CRITICALLY ABOUT CHAPTER 25

1. **c.** is the answer. (p. 633)

2. **a.** is the answer. (p. 638)

    b. Continuity theory, a type of dynamic theory, maintains that older adults cope with aging in much the same ways as when they were younger.

    c. Self theories emphasize the quest for self-actualization.

    d. Dynamic theories emphasize that life is a self-propelled, ever-changing process within an ever-changing social context.

3. **d.** is the answer. (p. 640)

4. **b.** is the answer. "Groups" are the social "strata" that this theory focuses on. (p. 638)

    a. & c. These theories emphasize the efforts of the individual to reach his or her full potential (self theories) by interpreting experiences in the face of ever-changing social contexts (dynamic theories, of which continuity theory is one [d.]).

5. **b.** is the answer. (p. 644)

    a. Although the text does not say this specifically, the discussion of the many activities engaged in by elderly people suggests a strong level of satisfaction.

d. There is much evidence that *conflicts* with disengagement theory.

6. **d.** is the answer. (pp. 645–646)

    a. Middle-aged adults tend to be more focused on individual and family needs.

    b. & c. The text does not suggest that there is a gender difference in older adults' sense of obligation to serve others.

7. **b.** is the answer. (p. 661)

    c. & d. The text does not compare care for the frail elderly in these countries.

8. **d.** is the answer. (p. 663)

9. **c.** is the answer. (p. 665)

    a. Even if children move, their parents prefer to stay in their homes.

    b. Although the elderly enjoy social contact with the younger generations, they prefer shorter visits.

    d. Tension and conflict continues throughout life in mother–daughter relationships.

10. **c.** is the answer. (p. 652)

    a. & b. At every age, women have larger social circles and more intimate relationships with their friends than men.

    d. Widows tend to be more involved in friendship networks than married women.

11. **b.** is the answer. (p. 636)

    a. People who assimilate are *unlikely* to doubt their values or beliefs.

    c. Selective optimization, which has no direct bearing on Sidney's response, refers to adults who structure their lives so that they can do what they want despite the physical and cognitive losses of late adulthood.

    d. On the contrary, Sidney's self-doubt is an unhealthy sign of crumbling too easily in the face of this circumstance.

12. **b.** is the answer. (p. 662)

13. **c.** is the answer. (p. 656)

    a. & b. These are examples of "activities of daily life."

14. **b.** is the answer. (pp. 656–657)

15. **c.** is the answer. (p. 634)

    a. This is not the crisis of late adulthood in Erikson's theory.

    b. & d. These are not crises in Erikson's theory.

KEY TERMS

1. **Self theories** such as Erik Erikson's theory focus on how adults make choices, confront problems, and interpret reality in such a way as to express themselves as fully as possible. (p. 634)

2. The final stage of development, according to Erik Erikson, is **integrity versus despair,** in which older adults seek to integrate the unique experiences with their vision of community. (p. 634)

3. **Stratification theories** emphasize that social forces limit individual choices and affect the ability to function. (p. 638)

4. According to **disengagement theory,** aging results in role relinquishment, social withdrawal, and passivity. (p. 638)

5. **Activity theory** is the view that older people remain active in a variety of social spheres and become withdrawn only unwillingly. (p. 638)

6. According to **dynamic theories,** each person's life is an active, ever-changing, largely self-propelled process that occurs within ever-changing social contexts. (p. 643)

7. According to the **continuity theory** of aging, each person copes with late adulthood in much the same way that he or she coped with earlier periods of life. (p. 643)

8. **Elderhostel** is a program in which adults aged 55 and older live on college campuses and take special classes. (p. 645)

9. The **social convoy** is the network of people with whom we establish meaningful relationships as we travel through life. (p. 649)

10. The **frail elderly** are the minority of adults over age 65 who are physically infirm, very ill, or cognitively impaired. (p. 656)

11. In determining frailty, gerontologists often refer to the **activities of daily life (ADLs),** which comprise five tasks: eating, bathing, toileting, dressing, and transferring from a bed to a chair. (p. 656)

12. The **instrumental activities of daily life (IADLs)** are actions that require some intellectual competence and forethought, such as shopping for food, paying bills, and taking medication. (p. 656)

13. **Respite care** is an arrangement in which a professional caregiver takes over to give a family caregiver a break from caring for a frail elderly person. (p. 662)

Epilogue

Death and Dying

Epilogue Overview

Death marks the close of the life span—a close individuals must come to terms with both for themselves and their loved ones. Indeed, an understanding and acceptance of death is crucial if life is to be lived to the fullest.

The first section focuses on how dying patients and their families plan for death and with the controversial issue of whether and when we should hasten the death of a loved one. The section also discusses hospice and other forms of palliative care designed to help the terminally ill patient to die "a good death."

The next section explores the reactions that death prompts, noting that perceptions of death vary markedly according to their historical and cultural context. Although the concept of an unvarying sequence of stages among the dying is not universally accepted, the pioneering work of Elisabeth Kübler-Ross was instrumental in revealing the emotional gamut of terminally ill patients and the importance of honest communication.

The final section deals with changing expressions of bereavement and how people can be aided in the process of recovery.

NOTE: Answer guidelines for all Epilogue questions begin on page 388.

Guided Study

The text Epilogue should be studied one section at a time. Before you read, preview each section by skimming it, noting headings and boldface items. Then read the appropriate section objectives from the following outline. Keep these objectives in mind and, as you read the Epilogue section, search for the information that will enable you to meet each objective. Once you have finished a section, write out answers for its objectives.

Deciding How to Die (pp. Ep-1–Ep-7)

1. Explain the concept of palliative care, focusing on the advantages and disadvantages of hospices.

2. Discuss the steps that patients, family members, and medical personnel can take to plan for a swift, pain-free, and dignified death.

3. (text and Research Report) Discuss issues surrounding euthanasia.

Preparing for Death (pp. Ep-7–Ep-12)

4. Identify Kübler-Ross's stages of dying, and discuss these stages in light of more recent research.

5. Describe some cultural variations in how death is viewed and treated.

6. Describe some religious variations in how death is viewed and treated.

Coping with Bereavement (pp. Ep-12–Ep-16)

7. Describe recent changes in the mourning process, and suggest steps that can be taken in helping someone to recover from bereavement.

Epilogue Review

When you have finished reading the Epilogue, work through the material that follows to review it. Complete the sentences and answer the questions. As you proceed, evaluate your performance for each section by consulting the answers beginning on page 388. Do not continue with the next section until you understand each answer. If you need to, review or reread the appropriate section in the textbook before continuing.

1. Customs and rituals related to dying, death, and bereavement function to bring

   _____ , _____ , and

   then _____ . Some developmentalists are concerned about the cultural loss of these rituals due to increasing _____ .

Deciding How to Die (pp. Ep-1–Ep-7)

2. Over most of human history, dying was accepted as a _____ . By the end of the twentieth century, however, death became less of an _____ event.

3. A major factor in our understanding of the psychological needs of the dying was the pioneering work of _____ .

4. In recent years, physicians have become _____ (more/less) accepting of death, especially when the _____

   _____ is gone.

5. The institution called the _____ provides care to terminally ill patients. The first modern institution of this type was opened in London by _____ .

6. Insurance companies typically will not pay for hospice care unless the person is expected to die within _____ (how many?) months.

7. Most hospices _____ (will/will not) serve children.

State several criticisms of hospice care.

8. Medical care that is designed not to treat an illness but to relieve pain and suffering is called
_____ _____ .

9. The least tolerable physical symptom of fatal illness is _____ . Physicians once worried about causing _____ if pain relievers such as _____ were given too freely, but they increasingly realize that pain destroys _____ and _____ faster than almost any infection. Pain medication for dying patients may have the _____ _____ of reducing pain while _____
_____ .

10. All competent individuals _____ (have the legal right/do not necessarily have the legal right) to control decisions related to life-prolonging treatments, including _____
_____ , in which a seriously ill person is allowed to die naturally, and
_____ _____ , in which someone intentionally acts to terminate the life of a suffering person. Usually, if a patient prefers to die naturally, the order_____ is placed on that person's hospital chart.

11. Some people make a _____
_____ to indicate what medical intervention they want if they become incapable of expressing those wishes. To avoid complications, each person should also designate a
_____ _____
_____ , someone who can make decisions for them if needed.

12. Proxies _____ (do/do not) guarantee a problem-free death. One problem is that _____ members may disagree with the proxy; another is that proxy directives may be _____ by hospital staff.

13. Active euthanasia is _____ (legal/illegal) in most parts of the world. In
_____-_____
_____ , a doctor provides the means for someone to end his or her own life. In

_____ _____ , a patient asks someone else to cause his or her death.

14. In the United States, the state of _____ has allowed physician-assisted suicide since 1998 but under very strict guidelines. Since that time, concerns that physician-assisted suicide might be used more often with minorities, the poor, and the disabled _____ (have/have not) been proven to be well-founded.

Preparing for Death (pp. Ep-7–Ep-12)

15. The study of death is called _____ .

16. Kübler-Ross's research led her to propose that the dying go through _____ (how many?) emotional stages. In order, the stages of dying are _____ , _____ , _____ , _____ , and _____ .

17. Other researchers typically _____ (have/have not) found the same five stages of dying occurring in sequence.

18. A "good death" is one that is _____ , _____ , and _____ and that occurs at _____ , surrounded by _____ . Because of modern medical techniques, a swift and peaceful death is _____ (more/less) difficult to ensure today than in the past.

19. Through the study of death we have learned that perceptions of death are _____ (variable/the same) in all cultures.

20. In most _____ traditions, elders take on an important new status through death.

21. In many _____ nations, death affirms religious faith and caring for the dying is a holy reminder of mortality.

22. Among Buddhists, disease and death are inevitable sufferings, which may bring _____ . Among _____ , helping the dying to relinquish their ties to this world and prepare for the next is considered an obligation for the immediate family.

23. Preparations for death are not emphasized in the _____ tradition because hope for _____ should never be extinguished.

24. Many _____ believe that death is the beginning of eternity in _____ or _____ ; thus, they welcome or fear it.

25. Two themes that emerge in religious and cultural variations of death practices are

    a. _____

    b. _____

Coping with Bereavement (pp. Ep-12–Ep-16)

26. The sense of loss following a death is called _____ . An individual's emotional response to this sense of loss is called _____ .

27. The ceremonies and behaviors that comprise the public response to a death are called _____ . These ceremonies are designed by _____ to channel _____ toward _____ of life.

28. A crucial factor in mourning is people's search for _____ in death. This is typically more difficult for deaths that are _____ or _____ .

29. In recent times, mourning has become more _____ , less _____ , and less _____ . Younger generations are likely to prefer _____ _____ , while older generations prefer _____ _____ . One result of these trends is that those who have lost a loved one are more likely to experience _____ _____ and _____ _____ than in the past.

30. The practice of excluding unmarried partners, ex-spouses, and other people from mourning may create "_____ _____ ."

31. List two steps that others can follow to help a bereaved person.

    a. _____

    b. _____

32. One thing that may be more harmful than helpful to a bereaved person is _____ _____ .

33. A frequent theme of those who work with the bereaved is the value of a(n) _____ _____ .

Progress Test 1

Circle your answers to the following questions and check them with the answers on page 389. If your answer is incorrect, read the explanation for why it is incorrect and then consult the appropriate pages of the text (in parentheses following the correct answer).

Multiple-Choice Questions

1. Passive euthanasia is most accurately described as:

    a. care designed to relieve pain and suffering.
    b. a situation in which treatment relieves pain while at the same time hastening death.
    c. a situation in which a person is allowed to die naturally.
    d. a situation in which someone takes action to bring about another person's death.

2. Medical advances have meant that death today is more often:

    a. far less painful for the dying individual.
    b. emotionally far less painful for the bereaved.
    c. a solitary, lengthy, and painful experience.
    d. predictable, and therefore a less traumatic experience.

3. Kübler-Ross's stages of dying are, in order:

    a. anger, denial, bargaining, depression, acceptance.
    b. depression, anger, denial, bargaining, acceptance.
    c. denial, anger, bargaining, depression, acceptance.
    d. bargaining, denial, anger, acceptance, depression.

4. Most adults hope that they will die:
  a. with little pain.
  b. with dignity.
  c. swiftly.
  d. in all of the above ways..

5. *Hospice* is best defined as:
  a. a document that indicates what kind of medical intervention a terminally ill person wants.
  b. mercifully allowing a person to die by not doing something that might extend life.
  c. an alternative to hospital care for the terminally ill.
  d. providing a person with the means to end his or her life.

6. Palliative care refers to:
  a. heroic measures to save a life.
  b. conservative medical care to treat an illness.
  c. efforts to relieve pain and suffering.
  d. allowing a terminally ill patient to die naturally.

7. A situation in which, at a patient's request, another person acts to terminate his or her life is called:
  a. involuntary euthanasia.
  b. voluntary euthanasia.
  c. a physician-assisted suicide.
  d. DNR.

8. Which of the following is a normal response in the bereavement process?
  a. experiencing powerful emotions
  b. culturally diverse emotions
  c. a lengthy period of grief
  d. All of the above are normal responses.

9. A double effect in medicine refers to a situation in which:
  a. the effects of one drug on a patient interact with those of another drug.
  b. medication relieves pain and has a secondary effect of hastening death.
  c. family members disagree with a terminally ill patient's proxy.
  d. medical personnel ignore the wishes of a terminally ill patient and his or her proxy.

10. Criticisms made against hospices include all of the following *except*:
  a. the number of patients served is limited.
  b. in some cases a life is being ended that might have been prolonged.
  c. burnout and the rapid growth of hospices might limit the number of competent hospice workers.
  d. the patient is needlessly isolated from family and friends.

True or False Items

Write T (*true*) or F (*false*) on the line in front of each statement.

_____ **1.** Hospice care is affordable to all who need it.

_____ **2.** Subsequent research has confirmed the accuracy of Kübler-Ross's findings regarding the five stages of dying.

_____ **3.** Modern life-prolonging medical technologies have tended to make dying a pain-free, dignified death more difficult and less likely to occur.

_____ **4.** Following the death of a loved one, the bereaved can best ensure their psychological health and well-being by increasing their social contacts and the number of activities in which they are involved.

_____ **5.** To help a bereaved person, one should ignore the person's depression.

_____ **6.** Researchers agree that the hospice is beneficial to the dying person and his or her family.

_____ **7.** Physician-assisted suicide and voluntary euthanasia are legal almost everywhere in the world.

_____ **8.** Hospices administer pain-killing medication but do not make use of artificial life-support systems.

_____ **9.** In the long run, the bereavement process may have a beneficial effect on the individual.

_____ **10.** There is general consensus that hospice care is a good alternative to hospital care for the dying.

Progress Test 2

Progress Test 2 should be completed during a final review of the Epilogue. Answer the following questions after you thoroughly understand the correct answers for the Epilogue Review and Progress Test 1.

Multiple-Choice Questions

1. Kübler-Ross's primary contribution was to:
   a. open the first hospice, thus initiating the hospice movement.
   b. show how the emotions of the dying occur in a series of clear-cut stages.
   c. bring attention to the psychological needs of dying people.
   d. show the correlation between people's conceptualization of death and their developmental stage.

2. In recent times, mourning has become all of the following *except*:
   a. more private.
   b. less emotional.
   c. more likely to lead to social isolation.
   d. more religious.

3. Which of the following is *not* a limitation of hospices?
   a. Most insurance plans will not pay for hospice care unless the patient has been diagnosed as terminally ill.
   b. Hospice care can be very expensive.
   c. Almost no hospices serve children.
   d. The dying typically do not receive skilled medical care.

4. A health care proxy is most accurately described as a(n):
   a document that indicates what medical intervention an individual wants if he or she becomes incapable of expressing those wishes.
   b. person chosen by another person to make medical decisions if the second person becomes unable to do so.
   c. situation in which, at a patient's request, someone else ends his or her life.
   d. indication on a patient's chart not to use heroic life-saving measures.

5. Younger generations tend to prefer _____ and older generations tend to prefer _____ .
   a. burial after a traditional funeral; burial after a traditional funeral

b. a small memorial service after cremation; a small memorial service after cremation
   c. burial after a traditional funeral; a small memorial service after cremation
   d. a small memorial service after cremation; burial after a traditional funeral

6. Research reveals that Kübler-Ross's stages of dying:
   a. occur in sequence in virtually all terminally ill patients.
   b. do not occur in hospice residents.
   c. are typical only in Western cultures.
   d. make feelings about death seem much more predictable and universal than they actually are.

7. Living wills are an attempt to:
   a. make sure that passive euthanasia will not be used in individual cases.
   b. specify the extent of medical treatment desired in the event of terminal illness.
   c. specify conditions for the use of active euthanasia.
   d. ensure that death will occur at home rather than in a hospital.

8. Many _____ welcome or fear death because they believe it is the beginning of eternity in heaven or hell.
   a. Buddhists
   b. Muslims
   c. Christians
   d. Jews

9. Ritual is to emotion as:
   a. grief is to mourning.
   b. mourning is to grief.
   c. affirmation is to loss.
   d. loss is to affirmation.

10. Healing after the death of a loved one is most difficult when:
    a. the death is a long, protracted one.
    b. the bereaved is not allowed to mourn in the way or she wishes.
    c. a period of grief has already elapsed.
    d. there are no other mourners.

Matching Items

Match each term or concept with its corresponding description or definition.

Terms or Concepts

_____ 1. DNR
_____ 2. hospice
_____ 3. living will
_____ 4. voluntary euthanasia
_____ 5. double effect
_____ 6. physician-assisted suicide
_____ 7. palliative care
_____ 8. grief
_____ 9. bereavement

Definitions or Descriptions

a. hospice treatment that relieves suffering and safeguards dignity
b. an alternative to hospital care for the terminally ill
c. hospital chart order to allow a terminally ill patient to die naturally
d. a document expressing a person's wishes for treatment should he or she become terminally ill and incapable of making such decisions
e. providing the means for a terminally ill patient to end his or her life
f. an individual's response to the loss of a loved one
g. the sense of loss following a death
h. intentionally taking an action to end the life of a terminally ill patient
i. situation in which a pain-relieving drug also hastens the death of a terminally ill patient

Thinking Critically About the Epilogue

Answer these questions the day before an exam as a final check on your understanding of the chapter's terms and concepts.

1. Among my people, elders take on an important new status through death as they join the ancestors who watch over our entire village. I am:
   a. African.   c. Hindu.
   b. Muslim.   d. Native American.

2. Among my people, family members have an obligation to help the dying to relinquish their ties to this world and prepare for the next. I am:
   a. African.   c. Hindu.
   b. Muslim.   d. Native American.

3. The terminally ill patient who is convinced his laboratory tests must be wrong is probably in which of Kübler-Ross's stages?
   a. denial
   b. anger
   c. depression
   d. bargaining

4. Dr. Aziz, who specializes in the study of death, would most likely describe himself as a(n):
   a. palliative care specialist.
   b. thanatologist.
   c. geriatric specialist.
   d. euthanist.

5. Following 30-year-old Ramón's unexpected and violent death, which of the following individuals is most likely to experience disenfranchised grief?
   a. Kent, his unmarried partner
   b. Janet, the younger sister with whom he has not been in touch for years
   c. His father, who divorced Kent's mother two years earlier
   d. His biological mother, who put Kent up for adoption when he was a baby

6. Dr. Welby writes the orders DNR (do not resuscitate) on her patient's chart. Evidently, the patient has requested:
   a. a living will.
   b. hospice care.
   c. voluntary euthanasia.
   d. an assisted suicide.

7. Seeing his terminally ill father without hope and in excruciating pain, Carl agreed to provide the means for him to end his life. This is an example of:
   a. passive euthanasia.
   b. voluntary euthanasia.
   c. an assisted suicide.
   d. an act that became legal in most countries in 1993.

8. The doctor who injects a terminally ill patient with a lethal drug is practicing:
   a. passive euthanasia.
   b. active euthanasia.
   c. an assisted suicide.
   d. an act that became legal in most countries in 1993.

9. Which of the following statements would probably be the most helpful to a grieving person?
   a. "Why don't you get out more and get back into the swing of things?"
   b. "You're tough; bear up!"
   c. "If you need someone to talk to, call me any time."
   d. "It must have been his or her time to die."

10. Dr. Robins is about to counsel her first terminally ill patient and his family. Research suggests that her most helpful strategy would be to:
    a. keep most of the facts from the patient and his family in order not to upset them.
    b. be truthful to the patient but not his family.
    c. be truthful to the family only, and swear them to secrecy.
    d. honestly inform both the patient and his family.

Key Terms
Using your own words, write a brief definition or explanation of each of the following terms on a separate piece of paper.

1. hospice
2. palliative care
3. double effect
4. passive euthanasia
5. active euthanasia
6. living will
7. health care proxy
8. physician-assisted suicide
9. voluntary euthanasia
10. thanatology
11. bereavement
12. grief
13. mourning

ANSWERS
EPILOGUE REVIEW

1. acceptance; hope; reaffirmation; globalization
2. part of life; everyday
3. Elisabeth Kübler-Ross
4. more; quality of life
5. hospice; Cecily Saunders
6. six
7. will not

The fact that hospice patients must be diagnosed as terminally ill and give up all hope of recovery severely limits the number of participants. Patients and their families must accept this diagnosis, agreeing that life or a cure is virtually impossible. Also, hospice care is expensive and therefore not available to everyone. Finally, hospices were typically designed to meet the needs of adults with terminal cancer, not for older patients with combinations of illnesses that are not necessarily fatal.

8. palliative care
9. pain; addiction; morphine; health; vitality; double effect; speeding up death
10. have the legal right; passive euthanasia; active euthanasia; DNR (do not resuscitate)
11. living will; health care proxy
12. do not; family; ignored
13. illegal; physician-assisted suicide; voluntary euthanasia
14. Oregon; have not
15. thanatology
16. five; denial; anger; bargaining; depression; acceptance
17. have not
18. swift; painless; dignified; home; friends and family; more
19. variable
20. African
21. Muslim
22. enlightenment; Hindus
23. Jewish; life
24. Christians; heaven; hell

25. **a.** Religious and spiritual concerns often reemerge at death.

    b. Returning to one's roots is common for dying people.

26. bereavement; grief

27. mourning; cultures; grief; reaffirmation

28. meaning; unexpected; violent

29. private; emotional; religious; small memorial services after cremation; burial after a traditional funeral; social isolation; physical illness

30. disenfranchised grief

31. **a.** Be aware that powerful, complicated, and culturally diverse emotions are likely.

    b. Understand that bereavement is often a lengthy process.

32. expecting certain reactions from that person

33. intimate, caring relationship

PROGRESS TEST 1

Multiple-Choice Questions

1. **c.** is the answer. (p. Ep-4)
   a. This describes palliative care.
   b. This is the "double effect" that sometimes occur with morphine and other opiate drugs.
   d. This is active euthanasia.

2. **c.** is the answer. (p. Ep-8)

3. **c.** is the answer. (p. Ep-7)

4. **d.** is the answer. (p. Ep-8)

5. **c.** is the answer. (p. Ep-2)
   a. This is a living will.
   b. & d. These are forms of euthanasia.

6. **c.** is the answer. (p. Ep-3)

7. **b.** is the answer. (p. Ep-5)
   a. There is no such thing as involuntary euthanasia.
   c. In this situation, a doctor provides the means for a *patient* to end his or her own life.
   d. DNR, or *do not resuscitate*, refers to a situation in which medical personnel allow a terminally ill person who has experienced severe pain to die naturally.

8. **d.** is the answer. (pp. Ep-12–Ep-13)

9. **b.** is the answer. (p. Ep-3)

10. **d.** is the answer. A central feature of hospices is that the dying are *not* isolated from loved ones, as they might be in a hospital. (p. Ep-2)

True or False Items

1. F Hospice care is too expensive for most. (p. Ep-3)

2. F Later research has not confirmed Kübler-Ross's findings that the emotions of an individual faced with death occur in orderly stages. (p. Ep-7)

3. T (p. Ep-8)

4. F The psychological well-being of the bereaved depends above all on their being able to openly express their grief. (p. Ep-14)

5. F A friend should listen, sympathize, and not ignore the mourner's pain. (p. Ep-15)

6. F Hospices have significant benefits, but some people are critical of them in part because they deny hope to the dying and because they are expensive. (p. Ep-3)

7. F These practices are *illegal* throughout most of the world. (p. Ep-5)

8. T (p. Ep-2)

9. T (p. Ep-16)

10. F Hospice care remains a controversial subject. (p. Ep-3)

PROGRESS TEST 2

Multiple-Choice Questions

1. **c.** is the answer. (p. Ep-2)

2. **d.** is the answer. In recent times, mourning has become less religious than formerly. (p. Ep-14)

3. **d.** is the answer. Hospices generally *do* provide patients with skilled medical care. (p. Ep-3)

4. **b.** is the answer. (p. Ep-4)
   a. This is a living will.
   c. This is voluntary euthanasia.
   d. This refers to "DNR."

5. **d.** is the answer. (p. Ep-14)

6. **d.** is the answer. (pp. Ep-7–Ep-8)
   b. & c. There is no evidence that hospice residents experience different emotional stages than others who are dying or that these stages are a product of Western culture.

7. **b.** is the answer. (p. Ep-4)

8. **c.** is the answer. (p. Ep-10)

9. **b.** is the answer. Mourning refers to the ceremonies and rituals that a religion or culture prescribes for bereaved people, and grief refers to an individual's emotional response to bereavement. (p. Ep-12)

10. b. is the answer. (p. Ep-14)

> **a. & c.** In such situations, death is expected and generally easier to bear.
>
> **d.** This issue was not discussed.

Matching Items

1. c (p. Ep-4)	**5.** i (p. Ep-3)	**9.** g (p. Ep-12)
2. b (p. Ep-2)	**6.** e (p. Ep-5)	
3. d (p. Ep-4)	**7.** a (p. Ep-3)	
4. h (p. Ep-5)	**8.** f (p. Ep-12)	

THINKING CRITICALLY ABOUT THE EPILOGUE

1. a. is the answer. (p. Ep-9)

> **b.** The text notes that in many Muslim nations, death serves to affirm religious faith.
>
> **d.** The text does not discuss the way in which Native Americans conceptualize death.

2. c. is the answer. (p. Ep-10)

3. a. is the answer. (p. Ep-7)

4. b. is the answer. (p. Ep-7)

> **a.** Palliative care is care aimed at relieving the suffering of a dying person.
>
> **c.** Such a person would study elderly people, but not necessarily those who are dying.
>
> **d.** There is no such term.

5. a. is the answer. (p. Ep-14)

> **b., c., & d.** Because each of these individuals is biologically related to Ramón, none is likely to be excluding from mourning his death.

6. b. is the answer. (p. Ep-2)

> **a.** A living will is a document expressing how a person wishes to be cared for should he or she become terminally ill.
>
> **c.** This is when a person *intentionally acts* to end another's life.
>
> **d.** In this situation, a person provides the means for another to take his or her own life.

7. b. is the answer. (p. Ep-5)

8. b. is the answer. (p. Ep-4)

9. c. is the answer. (p. Ep-14)

> **a., b., & d.** These statements discourage the bereaved person from mourning.

10. d. is the answer. (p. Ep-2)

KEY TERMS

1. A **hospice** is an institution in which terminally ill patients receive palliative care. (p. Ep-2)

2. **Palliative care,** such as that provided in a hospice, is care that relieves suffering while safeguarding the person's dignity. (p. Ep-3)

3. A **double effect** is a situation in which medication has the intended effect of relieving a dying person's pain and the secondary effect of hastening death. (p. Ep-3)

4. **Passive euthanasia** involves allowing a seriously ill person to die naturally by witholding medical interventions. (p. Ep-4)

5. **Active euthanasia** involves a person taking action to end another person's life in order to relieve suffering. (p. Ep-4)

6. A **living will** is a document that specifies what medical intervention a person wants if he or she becomes incapable of expressing those wishes. (p. Ep-4)

7. A **health care proxy** is a person chose to make medical decisions for someone else if the second person become unable to do so. (p. Ep-4)

8. A **physician-assisted suicide** is one in which a doctor provides the means for a person to end his or her life. (p. Ep-5)

9. **Voluntary euthanasia** is when at a patient's request, someone intentionally acts to terminate his or her life. (p. Ep-5)

10. **Thanatology** is the study of death. (p. Ep-7)

11. **Bereavement** is the sense of loss people feel following a death. (p. Ep-12)

12. **Grief** refers to an individual's emotional response to bereavement. (p. Ep-12)

13. **Mourning** refers to the ceremonies and rituals that a religion or culture prescribes for bereaved people. (p. Ep-12)

Appendix B

Appendix B Overview

The first section describes two ways of gathering information about development: library research and using the Internet. The second section discusses the various ways in which developmentalists ensure that their studies are valid.

NOTE: Answer guidelines for all Appendix B questions begin on page 393.

Guided Study

Appendix B should be studied one section at a time. Before you read, preview each section by skimming it, noting headings and boldface items. Then read the appropriate section objectives from the following outline. Keep these objectives in mind and, as you read the appendix section, search for the information that will enable you to meet each objective. Once you have finished a section, write out answers for its objectives.

Learning More (pp. B-1–B-4)

1. Identify several helpful resources for conducting library research on development, and state four guidelines for systematic observation.

2. Discuss the advantages and disadvantages of using the Internet to learn more about development.

Ways to Make Research More Valid (pp. B-4–B-6)

3. Describe the six techniques used by psychologists to ensure the validity of their research.

Appendix B Review

When you have finished reading Appendix B, work through the material that follows to review it. Complete the sentences and answer the questions. As you proceed, evaluate your performance for each section by consulting the answers beginning on page 393. Do not continue with the next section until you understand each answer. If you need to, review or reread the appropriate section in the textbook before continuing.

Learning More (pp. B-1–B-4)

1. Two collections of abstracts that review current articles from developmental journals are _____ and _____ .

2. Three journals that cover development in all three domains are _____ , _____ and _____ .

3. Two advantages of using the Internet to learn about development are

   a. _____

   b. _____

4. Two disadvantages of using the Internet are

   a. _____

   b. _____

Ways to Make Research More Valid (pp. B-4–B-6)

5. To make statements about people in general, called a _____ , scientists study a group of research _____ , called a _____ .

6. An important factor in selecting this group is _____ _____ ; that is, the group must be large enough to ensure that the results are not distorted by extreme cases.

7. When a sample is typical of the group under study—in gender, ethnic background, and other important variables—the sample is called a(n) _____ _____ .

8. When the person carrying out research is unaware of the purpose of the research, that person is said to be in a state of _____ .

9. Researchers use _____ _____ to define variables in terms of specific, observable behavior that can be measured precisely.

10. To test a hypothesis, researchers often compare a(n) _____ _____ , which receives some special treatment called the _____ _____ , with a(n) _____ _____ , which does not. To test the possible effects of this treatment, the two groups are compared in terms of some _____ _____ .

Progress Test

Circle your answers to the following questions and check them with the answers on page 394. If your answer is incorrect, read the explanation for why it is incorrect and then consult the appropriate pages of the text (in parentheses following the correct answer).

1. A valuable collection of abstracts that review current articles from a variety of developmental journals is:
   a. *Psycscan: Developmental Psychology.*
   b. *Child Development Abstracts and Bibliography.*
   c. *Developmental Psychology.*
   d. a. and b.
   e. a., b., & c.

2. Which of the following is *not* one of the journals that publish research on all three domains of development ?
   a. *The Developmentalist*
   b. *Developmental Psychology.*
   c. *Human Development*
   d. *Child Development*

3. Which of the following is a disadvantage of conducing Internet research?
   a. You can spend hours sifting through information that turns out to be useless.
   b. Anybody can put anything on the Internet.
   c. There is no evaluation of bias on Internet sites.
   d. Each of the above is a disadvantage of Internet research.

4. To say that the study of development is a science means that developmentalists:
   a. use many methods to make their research more objective and more valid.
   b. take steps to ensure that a few extreme cases do not distort the overall statistical picture.
   c. recognize the importance of establishing operational definitions.
   d. do all of the above.

5. The entire group of people about whom a scientist wants to learn is called the:
   a. reference group.
   b. sample.
   c. representative sample.
   d. population.

6. A researcher's conclusions after conducting a study are not valid because a few extreme cases distorted the results. In designing this study, the researcher evidently failed to pay attention to the importance of:
   a. sample size.
   b. "blindness."
   c. representativeness.
   d. all of the above.

7. Rachel made a study of students' opinions about different psychology professors. She took great care to survey equal numbers of male and female students, students who received high grades and students who received low grades, and members of various minorities. Clearly, Rachel wished to ensure that data were obtained from a:
   a. population.
   b. "blind" sample.
   c. representative sample.
   d. comparison group.

8. A person who gathers data in a state of "blindness" is one who:
   a. is unaware of the purpose of the research.
   b. is allowing his or her personal beliefs to influence the results.
   c. has failed to establish operational definitions for the variables under investigation.
   d. is basing the study on an unrepresentative sample of the population.

9. Which of the following is an example of a good operational definition of a dependent variable?
   a. walking
   b. aggression
   c. 30 minutes of daily exercise
   d. taking steps without support

10. The comparison group in an experiment:
    a. receives the treatment of interest.
    b. does not receive the treatment of interest.
    c. is always drawn from a population different from the experimental group.
    d. must be larger in size than the experimental group.

11. For a psychologist's generalizations to be valid, the sample must be representative of the population under study. The sample must also be:
    a. significant.
    b. all the same age.
    c. large enough.
    d. none of the above.

12. The particular individuals who are studied in a specific research project are called the:
    a. independent variables.
    b. dependent variables.
    c. participants.
    d. population.

Key Terms

Using your own words, write a brief definition or explanation of each of the following terms on a separate piece of paper.

1. population
2. participants
3. sample
4. sample size
5. representative sample
6. blindness
7. experimental group
8. comparison group

ANSWERS
APPENDIX B REVIEW

1. *Psycscan: Developmental Psychology; Child Development Abstracts and Bibliography*

2. *Developmental Psychology; Child Development Human Development*

3. a. Virtually everything you might want to know is on the Internet.
   b. The Internet is quick and easy to use, any time of the day or night.

4. a. There is so much information available on the Internet that it is easy to waste time.

b. Anybody can put anything on the Internet.

5. population; participants; sample
6. sample size
7. representative sample
8. blindness
9. operational definitions
10. experimental group; independent variable; comparison group; dependent variable

PROGRESS TEST

1. **d.** is the answer. (p. B-1)
2. **a.** is the answer. (pp. B-1–B-2)
3. **d.** is the answer. (pp. B-2–B-3)
4. **d.** is the answer. (pp. B-4–B-6)
5. **d.** is the answer. (p. B-4)
6. **a.** is the answer. (p. B-4)

   b. "Blindness" has no relevance here.

   c. Although it is true that a distorted sample is unrepresentative, the issue concerns the small number of extreme cases—a dead giveaway to sample size.

7. **c.** is the answer. Rachel has gone to great lengths to make sure that her student sample is typical of the entire population of students who takes psychology courses. (p. B-5)
8. **a.** is the answer. (p. B-5)
9. **d.** is the answer. (p. B-5)

   a., b., & c. Each of these definitions is too ambiguous to qualify as an operational definition.

10. **b.** is the answer. (p. B-6)

    a. This describes the experimental group.

    c. The comparison group must be similar to the experimental group (and therefore drawn from the same population).

    d. The comparison group is usually the same size as the experimental group.

11. **c.** is the answer. (p. B-4)
12. **c.** is the answer. (p. B-4)

    a. These are the factors that a researcher manipulates in an experiment.

    b. These are the outcomes that a researcher measures in an experiment.

    d. It is almost always impossible to include every member of a population in an experiment.

KEY TERMS

1. The **population** is the entire group of individuals who are of particular concern in a scientific study. (p. B-4)
2. **Participants** are the people who are studied in a research project. (p. B-4)
3. A **sample** is a subset of individuals who are drawn from a specific population. (p. B-4)
4. **Sample size** refers to the number of subjects in a specific sample. (p. B-4)
5. A **representative sample** is a group of research subjects who accurately reflect key characteristics of the population being studied. (p. B-4)
6. **Blindness** is the situation in which data gatherers and their research participants are deliberately kept unaware of the purpose of the study in order to avoid unintentionally biasing the results. (p. B-5)
7. The **experimental group** in an experiment is the group of research participants who experience the condition or treatment (independent variable) under investigation. (p. B-6)
8. The **comparison group** in an experiment is the group of research participants who are comparable to those in the experimental group in every relevant way except that they do not experience the independent variable. (p. B-6)